CROATIA

'Croatia is that rare breed, a country where tourism merges into travel, where discoveries of 'pinch-me' perfection and wonder are waiting to be made, as familiar and as exotic as ever.'

James Stewart

About the Guide

The **full-colour introduction** gives the authors' overview of the country, together with suggested **itineraries** and a regional **'where to go' map** and **feature** to help you plan your trip.

Illuminating and entertaining **cultural chapters** on local history, culture, food, wine and everyday life give you a rich flavour of the country.

Planning Your Trip starts with the basics of when to go, getting there and getting around, coupled with other useful information, including a section for disabled travellers. The **Practical A–Z** deals with all the **essential information** and **contact details** that you may need while you are away.

The **regional chapters** are arranged in a loose touring order, with plenty of public transport and driving information. The author's top **'Don't Miss'** **sights** are highlighted at the start of each chapter.

A **language and pronunciation guide**, a **glossary** of cultural terms, ideas for **further reading** and a comprehensive **index** can be found at the end of the book.

Although everything listed in this guide is **personally recommended**, our author inevitably has his own favourite places to eat and stay. Whenever you see this **Author's Choice** icon beside a listing, you will know that it is a little bit out of the ordinary.

Hotel Price Guide (*see also* p.63)

Expensive	€€€	over 1,000Kn / €137
Moderate	€€	500–1,000Kn / €68–137
Inexpensive	€	under 500Kn / €65

Restaurant Price Guide (*see also* p.69)

Expensive	€€€	over 160Kn / €23
Moderate	€€	110–160Kn / €15–23
Inexpensive	€	under 110Kn / €15

About the Author

James Stewart was born in Bangor, Northern Ireland, and has lived in Sydney and Barcelona. With the castanets hung up in London (for now), he has nursed a reluctant camper van across Europe as the author of several Cadogan guides.

2nd Edition published 2009

01 INTRODUCING CROATIA

Top: Pag lace
Above: Old Town, near Peristyle, Split, Dalmatia

A Slavic nation that looks West not East, located where north Europe meets the south and Christianity meets Islam, Croatia is all about cultural tectonics. It is a nation created where the plates of European civilization have jostled and been subducted by the flow of history. Understand that, and you are halfway to making sense of a country that is by turns familiar and exotic, a cross-breed of Central European business head, Mediterranean heart and hospitable Balkan soul, which has baffled and seduced outsiders ever since the Romans began to take holidays on the east Adriatic around 2,000 years ago.

The judders as those plates rub against one another have always rippled through Croatia, but the recent upheaval was a shock even by the standard of its own turbulent history – the implosion of Communism, a fight for survival and a traumatic birth, all within five years. With independence, Croatia has scrambled to modernize, but it has also paused to evaluate what it has. Just as it says on the adverts, Croatia is a taste of the Mediterranean as it used to be, not by accident or because a Croatian National Trust has issued edicts, but because that's the way people like it. Yes, relics of Tito's Soviet-inspired industrial pipe-dreams are dotted here and there. Yes, in August, poster places such as Dubrovnik, the Makarska Riviera or Rovinj are frantic. But take to back roads just to see where they go, or linger in one of 1,185 islands washed by the cleanest seas in the Med, and the essentially timeless spirit of Croatia is easier to grasp. Whether in lazy, mazy coastal towns where the *korzo* stroll is sacrosanct, or in the deep countryside where people and land are in perfect harmony, there's a sense of continuity and preservation of a timeless past.

Above: Roman amphitheatre, Pula, Istria
Opposite: Rovinj, Istria

For national tourism strategists, that means concrete carbuncles are out, and small hotels in pristine bays are in. Croatia is at its best when sampled straight, no mixer. It has chic resorts and chirpy fleshpots, but its soul resides in lost worlds like Lastovo and Vis, the bucolic Zagorje, or in Italianate hamlets atop Istrian hills, all places in which to discover the *fjaka* mood Dalmatians live for. It is in the scent of pines and wild herbs and hot dust as intoxicating as *rakija* spirit, in *konoba* soul-food, organic long before the term was invented, or fresh fish simply but perfectly grilled. It can be glimpsed in scenes of virile green vines and silver olives splashed by rust-red soils like passionate Fauvist canvases, or in the Impressionism of shepherds half-seen through a golden halo of dusty sunlight.

You can loaf by the pool with a thriller, of course. But if you seek it, Croatia is that rare breed, a country where tourism merges into travel, where discoveries of 'pinch-me' perfection and wonder are waiting to be made, as familiar and as exotic as ever.

Above: Sljeme cable car, near Zagreb
Below: Rovinj, Istria

Where to Go

While Croatia is rightly famed for its coastline, much of its appeal is that it is hard to pin down. You don't have to travel too far to realize that Croatia packs a lot of landscape into its small area. Nor is the diversity simply scenic – each of the regions has its own character; part due to topography, part due to history, but also because people like their local traditions. So where you go will depend on your idea of holiday heaven.

We begin the book in the easygoing capital of **Zagreb**, then move into the surrounding landscapes of **North Croatia**: the fairytale Zagorje and Turopolje, Slavonia, and southwest past Karlovac to Slunj. West is **Istria**, *terra magica* for the Romans, who left antiquities in Pula, *terra incognita* in its Tuscany-esque interior – why so few outsiders stray from coastal Rovinj or Poreč is a mystery. Between Istria and North Croatia is the **Kvarner Gulf** region, with *belle époque* resorts Opatija and Lovran, *bura*-blasted islands, the celebrated Plitvice Lakes and the stupendous gorges of Paklenica.

Heading south, into **North Dalmatia**, you come to Zadar, regional capital of an area where unspoilt vistas abound, whether the little-explored Zadar archipelago, pristine Kornati islands and burbling waterworld of Krka, or medieval Trogir. **Central Dalmatia** begins in sassy Split, an antique-modern metropolis that is the launchpad for some of the most famous islands: Brač and Hvar, plus gourmet hideaway Vis. And then south to **Dubrovnik and South Dalmatia**, for the famous former republic, and also for the yesteryear-paced Elafiti islands or Lastovo.

Chapter Divisions

Above: Veliki slap waterfall, Plitvice Lakes

Opposite, top: Cliffs off Dugi Otok, Kornati National Park
Opposite, bottom: Plitvice Lakes

Natural Wonders

At 21,850 square miles, Croatia is just a tenth the size of the UK or an eighth smaller than California. The surprise, then, is that there is such diversity of scenery behind the famous 2,000km coastline. Many of the best bits are protected within the country's eight national parks – but not all. Travel an hour inland from the beach resorts on the coast and you are among 1,700m peaks in the Velebit mountains, where brown bears outnumber people. Continental Croatia is another world again; a place of bucolic tradition and fairytale images among the hummocky hills of Zagorje or rustic villages of Lonjsko polje. These are some of the best natural sights:

- Kopački Rit, the wetland reserve acclaimed for its waterbirds, pp.122–3
- Stepping into an East European fairytale in stork villages in Lonjsko polje, pp.132–3
- Velika Paklenica gorge, mighty limestone cleft beloved by rock-climbers, pp.217–18
- Plitvice Lakes, waterfalls and lakes in the centre – touristy but essential, pp.224–6
- Striking islands like pumice stone in Kornati National Park, pp.248–9
- Skradinski buk waterfalls, Krka National Park, pp.256–7

Above: Rab Town, Rab Island

101 Dalmatians and Other Islands

Croatia's islands are the ones on which the Greeks set many of their myths – Jason and his Argonauts fled with the Golden Fleece past Cres and Lošinj, and Odysseus was held captive for seven years on Mljet. The Greeks have been coming back to the islands ever since, and for most of us no trip to Croatia is complete without the thrill of disembarking from a ferry to an unknown island. Island-hopping is one of the great joys of Croatia. It encourages you to travel footloose and change plans by whim. A lack of time is an issue faced with over a thousand islands sprayed along 2,000km of coast like a comet trail, and

Above: Hvar Town, Hvar Island

drivers in peak season may find plans disrupted by queues on popular routes. But whether you want to play in, on or under the cleanest seas in the Mediterranean, whether your idea of nightlife is banging house beats, cocktails in a stylish bar or *rakija*-sipping on a quiet harbour, Croatia has an idyll to suit you. These are some of our favourites.

- Veli Brijun, the bizarre Neverland retreat of Comrade Tito, pp.150–2
- Rab, a multi-hued medieval town, pp.210–14
- Pag, a moonscape island that hosts a Croatian Ibiza each summer, pp.219–23
- Hvar, Riviera chic in a Renaissance setting, pp.289–98
- Vis, high-end escapism in the most distant island of the Croatian Adriatic, pp.299–303
- Šipan, drop off the radar just 45 minutes from Dubrovnik, p.336
- Korčula, a gorgeous medieval port chockfull of palaces and charm, pp.346–53
- Lastovo, one of the last frontiers of Croatian tourism, pp.353–6

Above: Pag cheese

Opposite, top: Croatian wines

Opposite, centre: Cooking with a peka

Opposite, bottom: Nightlife in Zadar, Dalmatia

Tastes of Croatia

Look at a European map to understand Croatian cuisine. In the continental north it shows the no-nonsense tastes of its neighbours Austria and Hungary: filling fare such as schnitzel, strudel and *štruckli*, stodgy cheese-filled pastry parcels like oversized ravioli, while Slavonia shares Hungary's love of paprika in spicy sausage *kulen* or gulash. The coast opts instead for a classic Mediterranean seafood diet that revolves around fresh fish, typically charcoal-grilled then served with a drizzle of olive oil. It also shares the Italian taste for pasta, risotto and prosciutto ham, known as *pršut*, or sheep's cheese from Pag, *Paški sir*, similar to Parmesan and best with olives. However, one homegrown dish to sample is lamb, veal or octopus prepared *ispod peke*. This cooking method used by the Illyrians involves the dish being covered by a *peka* lid and buried in embers – slow cooking at its best. Istria is home to Italian-style cooking as well as more gourmet stars than anywhere else in the country, although the Opatija riviera and Hvar Town are worthwhile diversions for any gourmand.

TERAN
Grgić
DINGAČ
PINOT

Above: *Poklad carnival event, Lastovo*

Croatia's Living Past

Part Mitteleuropa, part Mediterranean, with a residue of Balkan soul whatever its protests to the contrary, modern Croatia stages traditional festivals that are exotic and familiar by turns. Although few events unite the nation except for Catholic high days or Carnival on Shrove Tuesday, regions – towns, even – are renowned for their events; *see* p. 53 for an at-a-glance list. Continental Croatia hosts the largest folk festivals; distinctive pastoral pageants, with spectacular embroidered costume and much use of the lute-like tamburica. Dalmatia, meanwhile, honours its timeless traditions of fishing and *kalpa*, a close-harmony song somewhere between a barber-shop quartet and a sea shanty. It also has a preference for medieval jousts or sword pageants, a relic of the Mediterranean region's battles against Ottoman Turks. Korčula Town stages a condensed version of the Moreška sword dance throughout summer. Remember, too, that right through the high season, folk dances are held in Dubrovnik twice a week by the Linđo and in Čilipi nearby on Sunday morning. Try to catch at least one of these:

- International Folklore Festival, Zagreb, late July: the nation's folk spectacular, p.94
- Đakovo Embroidery, Đakovo, late September: authentic Slavonian tradition, p.130
- Rab Knights' Tournament, Rab Town, early May and mid July: crossbow pageant, p.214
- Sinjska alka, Sinj, first Sunday in August: rollicking medieval joust, p.285
- Summer Festival, Dubrovnik, July–August: Croatia's premier cultural extravaganza, p.330
- Carnival, Lastovo, Shrove Tuesday: unique and a mite strange, just like Lastovo, p.355

Itinerary 1: Roman to Renaissance – Art and Architecture Along the Coast

Dubrovnik is Croatia's crown jewel, so brilliant and flawlessly crafted that it often outshines the culture elsewhere on this coastline. Take this itinerary as a sketch only – start midway to combine it with a stay in Dubrovnik or simply stop wherever takes your fancy. This is a coastline that is best savoured slowly.

Day 1 Begin in Istria at Poreč with the mosaics of the Basilica of Euphrasius, then drive to Rovinj, its old town a living museum in its own right. Renaissance charmer Svetvinčenat nearby offers escape from the crowds.

Day 2 South to Pula, which has both five-star antiquities, notably the world's sixth-largest amphitheatre, and first-class chefs. The best beaches in the area are on Cape Kamenjak.

Days 3–4 Take your pick from sister islands Cres and Krk; the former has the charm in Italianate Cres Town and cultural villages Osor and Lubenice, the latter is home to a Romanesque cathedral, vineyards and famous beaches. They're linked by regular ferries if you're in a hurry.

Days 5–6 It's either a long drive or a ferry ride from Valbiska, Krk, to reach Rab, whose Gothic-Renaissance timewarp in an old town and sand beaches should please everyone. If you don't mind moving fast, combine Rab with a day on Pag.

Day 7 Stop off at Nin, the birthplace of Slavic Croatia, en route to Zadar, the capital of north Dalmatia with relics of its Roman roots but whose mish-mash of architecture defies eras. Don't miss the museum of ecclesiastical art.

Day 8 A treat of church architecture today – Šibenik and its UNESCO-listed Renaissance cathedral, and Trogir, with its Romanesque reply. Peruse its galleries then simply explore the medieval old town by instinct.

Days 9–10 Croatia's second city Split is worth a visit for its metropolitan zip as much as the architecture of Diocletian's Palace, where antiquity is everyday. There are some blockbuster museums, too – the Ivan Meštrovic Gallery is a must. Then go inland to see the city's progenitor, the Roman ruins of Solin.

Days 11–12 Catch a ferry to Hvar for Hvar Town for a dose of Riviera café culture in a Renaissance setting. Stari Grad, where you land, is a quietly bohemian haunt with a Renaissance mansion, Tvrdalj, while Vrboska is worth a look for the Venetian Old Masters in its church.

Day 13 Depending on the day, catch a ferry from Stari Grad or set aside at least a half-day for ferry-hopping

Top: Basilica of Euphrasius, Poreč, Istria
Above: The Palace of Diocletian, Split

(Sucuraj–Drvenik, Ploče–Trpanj then Orebić–Korčula Town). The goal is Korčula Town, a pocket-sized Dubrovnik. Lumbarda 6km south is a mellow bolthole with beaches on the doorstep.

Day 14 Continue south: by ferry to the Pelješac peninsula, then through Croatia's premier vineyards to walled Ston for lunch. Beyond are Trsteno's Renaissance gardens and finally the queen of the Adriatic herself, Dubrovnik.

Top: Korčula Town
Bottom: Mljet Island

Itinerary 2: A Week Off the Beaten Track from Dubrovnik

A car will only slow you down on this island-hopping route – most ferries to the Elafiti islands are passenger-only. It's worth picking up timetables for the area before you begin to plan your strategy for the ferry connections.

Day 1 By ferry from Dubrovnik to Lopud: a sleepy harbour, overgrown aromatic paths to a ruined fort and sandy Šunj – a beach bar provides cocktails, just add the sunset.

Day 2 On by ferry to Šipan to ramble along footpaths off the valley Šipansko polje between Šipanska luka and Suđurađ. Reserve a table at Kod Marko, Šipanska luka for a perfect dinner.

Day 3 By boat from Suđurađ to Mljet, the greenest island in the Adriatic, which is covered in a quilt of pines. It's at its lushest around the Veliko jezero lake, protected as a national park, reached by connecting bus from Sobra to Polače.

Day 4 Back to Sobra. Depending on the day, you can either continue west from Sobra or must first return to Dubrovnik to catch a ferry to reach Korčula Town. Explore its medieval grid or rent a bicycle and go 6km south to Lumbarda for wine-tasting and Pržina beach.

Day 5 Use Korčula Town as a base from which to explore. Hire a scooter or car and traverse the Pelješac peninsula opposite – climb Sv Ilija mountain above Orebić, buy dingac and postup wines in Potomje, or laze on Divna-Trpanj beach or at small resort Žuljana. Or else stay on Korčula to find isolated bays like Pupnatska luka or head into the hills with a donkey safari organized by Kantun Tours (*see* p.352).

Days 6–7 Take a co-ordinated bus from Korčula Town to port Vela Luka to embark on a ferry to Lastovo. This barely developed island is pure Mediterranean escapism. Its joys are those of simple holidaymaking: walks, lazy lunches and swimming in Lučica, Zaklopatica and Skrivena luka.

CONTENTS

Reference

Maps and Plans

Contents

History

02

To write a history of Croatia is to become ensnared in the tangled narratives of European ambitions. This is border country, situated on the ramparts between West and East and coveted by millennia of empire-hungry nations. The Greeks, Illyrians, Romans, Venetians, Hungarians, Ottomans, French, Serbs and, of course, the Croats themselves have, at various times and with varying degrees of success, invaded, raided, been repulsed or governed, literally shaping a country whose fate has been decided in a violent tug-of-war between international rivals. And, like every conflict, it was the civilians – the Croats themselves – who seemed to suffer most. Although his habit of pandering to far-right nationalism leaves a nasty taste in the mouth, then-president Franjo Tuđman was spot-on in 1992. With formal recognition by Europe on 15 January, officially joining the Western community by which it defines itself, Croatia dared to believe it could realize 'a thousand-year-old dream of independence'.

Prehistory: The First Million Years

The oldest trace of humanoid life in this part of Europe is a sculpted pebble chisel (about one million BC) discovered in a cave near Pula. Afterwards, however, **Stone Age man** seemed blind to the allure of Croatia's coast. In the Zagorje region of continental Croatia some 130,000 years ago, '**Krapina Man**' loped around hillsides, a robust Neanderthal spin-off who had a deft hand with flint tools and a taste for bone marrow, if the finds in a cave in Krapina are any guide. It's fair to assume **Neanderthal man** colonized elsewhere, too, but if so he covered his tracks well, leaving only a couple of skeletons in a cave in nearby Varaždin which were radiocarbon-dated to *c.* 30,000 BC.

His quarrelsome successor *Homo sapiens* makes a belated debut around 4000 BC. **Neolithic man** left pottery painted with spiral motifs in the Grabac cave of the Hvar limestone uplands, and kept himself toasty before prehistoric fires in the Great Cave of Vela Luka, Korčula, an island scattered with tumuli *c.* 4000 BC. So we know people had boats, lived by agriculture in settled farming communities and held religious beliefs. In inland Istria, **Bronze Age** groups formed small fortified villages on hilltops still occupied to this day. More sophisticated still was the Copper Age culture which flourished on the banks of the Danube in east Slavonia, evidenced by the rich ceramics, notably a tubby ritual dove featured on the 20Kn note, now the prize of the Archaeological Museum in Zagreb, discovered in Vučedol, 5km from Vukovar.

Things get more interesting with the arrival of the **Illyrians** (Jliri) around 1000 BC. United by a penchant for dry-stone hilltop fortresses if not politics, they spread south in mighty tribal groups: the **Liburnians** (Liburni) of the Kvarner region, shipbuilders and sailors who traded amber from Krk with the ancient Greeks and dropped anchor in a port that became Zadar; or the **Histri**, who christened their stamping ground, Istria, and confused Roman writers (including rigorous Pliny the Elder) into thinking mythic Illyrians Jason and his Argonauts had sailed through these parts. Sea traders and shepherds the **Delmati** occupied the coast and highlands further south and put up such resistance to colonization that the Romans named the region after them.

The **Greeks** themselves are the biggest let-down in Croatia. In the 4th century BC, ships of the republic of Syracuse (Sicily) hove off Croatia's shores to establish colonies such as Issa (today's Vis), where a few ancient graves remain. They served as a springboard for mainland colonization, founding towns such as Tragurion (Trogir) and Lumbarda on Korčula. For a century or so all was well, and the Greeks introduced local Illyrians to all the little benefits of advanced civilization: refined craftsmanship, glassware, fine wines, olive oil and salt. Less enthused by colonists of his territory was King Agron, monarch of a south Illyrian nation which stretched from present-day Dalmatia to Albania. On his death around 231 BC, **Queen Teuta** ascended the throne and vowed to drive the arrivals back into the sea. The Greeks called on their natural allies the Romans for help and a pair of ambassadors came knocking at Teuta's door and traded diplomatic insults which so outraged Illyrian courtiers that they let sharp steel do the talking. A bad move, as it transpired, because in 229 BC an incensed Senate ordered the imperial army across the Adriatic for the first time.

Romans and Byzantines: 230 BC–AD 600

The well-drilled legions quickly swatted aside Teuta's rabble. **Tiberius** (later elevated to emperor) spared the queen's life in return for an annual tribute and acknowledgement of the authority of Rome, a more crushing defeat than any execution, then masterminded a little Balkan colonization of his own. Modern Croatia and Bosnia were methodically annexed as **Illyricum** (168 BC), then reorganized after AD 9 revolts into the more manageable provinces of **Dalmatia**, a coastal strip which stretched to the Sava river (in Slavonia), and **Pannonia** (modern Bosnia and north into Hungary).

Initially, the east Adriatic colonies of Illyricum lured the usual suspects: garrison commanders and legionnaires, get-rich-quick entrepreneurs hoping to coin a quick denarius. But as Roman roads brought swift retaliation and Illyrian rebellions fizzled out, communities founded on Illyrian settlements stabilized and indulged in tentative, then rampant trade. Salona (today's Solin) blossomed into the powerful capital of the east Adriatic, nearby Zadar (Jadar) was laid with the largest Forum of the Adriatic, while in Istria, a *terra magica* an easy march from Italy, Pola (Pula) received an awe-inspiring 23,000-seater amphitheatre, Roman patricians led a life of ease in *villae rusticae* and an imperial *castrum* appeared on every peninsula. But, like many an imperial power, the Romans overstretched themselves. In AD 395, they were forced to split their territory into East and West Empires, and by the early 5th century those bogeymen of Europe, the **Goths**, were hammering at the gates. Indeed, the coast, located in the Western Empire, fell briefly to Ostrogoth king Teodoric (AD 493), until **Justinian**, ruler of the Eastern Empire, came to the rescue in AD 535. But the Byzantine ruler had problems of his own and few forces to spare for Dalmatia. Slavic tribes and the **Avars**, a fierce Central Asian people whose ceaseless marauding would spark a currency crisis in Europe, rushed to fill the power vacuum, heaping more strife on a dying civilization. Within 14 years of Pope Gregory's AD 600 letter to the bishop of Salona to commiserate about raids, Salona and Epidaurum (Cavtat) lay in ruins, their refugees fleeing to offshore islands or staggering away to found Split and Dubrovnik.

The Croats Arrive: AD 600–900

Into this landscape of decay and disintegration appeared the Croats. The nitty-gritty of how, when and why remains lost in the mists of time, although scholars agree it was some time in the mid-7th century. Three centuries after the event, Byzantine emperor Constantine Porphyrogenitus took all the credit, claiming his ancestor Emperor Heraclius invited – nay, ordered – the Slavs to immigrate after the sack of Salona, a dubious tale, probably spun to woo the nation back to Byzantium.

Adding to the confusion is a disagreement about origins based on the Croats' name for themselves, **Hrvat** (hence Hrvatska for Croatia). Some academics talk of Persian roots, pointing to Greek texts about the Horavotos tribe and suggesting they picked up the Slavic tongue on their way west. Another idea is that a nomadic people under Hunnic authority mingled with Slavic tribes and chewed Hunnic into Hrvat. Whatever the truth, everyone agrees the Croats crossed the Danube, then migrated southwest across the Balkan peninsula. Clans lived in fiefdoms, each managed by a *župan* (county head) and all beholden to a regional *knez* (prince). A respected theory states that the Hrvat were the tribe which occupied the region's heartland, bordered by the river Cetina and the Velebit mountains. These were the White Croatians, it goes, distinct from the Pannonian Croats of today's Slavonia. Although it is only a theory, the separation will be heard down the centuries of our tale.

Around AD 800, the Byzantines made way for the **Franks** in all but the Zadar region of Dalmatia, a potentially tricky handover that Croat tribes managed with aplomb by accepting Christianity, a central tenet of the Carolingians espoused by the ever-zealous missionary Charlemagne. The Christian flame in Croatia had been kept alive by refugees from the devastated Roman settlements – indeed, those who fled from Salona cheekily converted the mausoleum of Emperor Diocletian into a church that matured into the cathedral of Split – but it was the Franks who preached the Word to the newcomer Croats. The baptism also won them plaudits from surrounding Christian states, their legitimacy sealed when one **Vladislav** founded a bishopric at Nin, former Roman Aenona, and announced himself Duke of Croatia and Dalmatia in 821, thereby establishing a national figurehead. Ruling from the inland fortress of Knin, his blood-line successors, kings such as **Mislav** (835–45) and **Trpimir** (845–64), pushed borders ever-outwards, repulsing Bulgarian and Arabian pretenders, while liberally dolloping their lands with churches carved with woven plaits, possibly borrowed from Celtic knotwork, possibly learned from the Illyrians.

Glory and Gloom: 900–1100

It was one of their successors that shifted the embryonic nation from bit-part player to leading actor on the region's stage. **Tomislav** (910–28) gathered to his side a mighty army – the ever-hyperbolic Porphyrogenitus raves about over 100,000 troops – to bat away Bulgarians and ambitious Hungarians, and unite Dalmatia and Pannonia. Supported by the weight of Rome, a ruler who received 'Dear beloved son Tomislav' letters from the pope declared himself *rex* and was crowned King of Croatia and Dalmatia in 925, on the battlefield itself, they say. This was a force Byzantium had to take seriously. It ceded sovereignty over remaining Dalmatian titles, Split, Trogir, Zadar and islands such as Rab and Krk, accelerating the integration of Dalmatian towns into the fledgling nation. King Tomislav, meanwhile, knuckled down to his domain, centralizing the nation's church under the authority of the Latinate bishops of Split, a smart manoeuvre which brought control of the church on to home soil without cocking a snook at the pope.

However, without a national powerbase, Croatia was exposed. Kings literally went round in circles, shifting between regal seats to maintain authority over a nation of self-governing cities. Hungary continued to press for weak spots during Tomislav's reign. Worse, Venetian doge Peter II Orseolo cast an eye across the Adriatic in 1000 and made a land-grab under the pretence of crushing Dalmatian pirates, forcing cities such as Zadar, Biograd na moru and Korčula to acknowledge him Dux Dalmatiae (Duke of Dalmatia). To weld up the cracks, **Petar Krešimir IV** (1058–75) turned to Rome, agreeing to stamp out the use of Glagolitic liturgical script (*see* **Topics**, pp.40–1) as a *quid pro quo* for evicting the Venetians, thereby regaining control of Dalmatia. He also shifted his capital from isolated Knin to the thick of the action, Biograd na moru, and portioned up his empire into thirds under the stewardship of a loyal *ban* (viceroy).

Ban of Pannonia **Dimitar Zvonimir** (1075–89) emerged victorious from the usual clash of mettle and steel that followed a king's death, because he acknowledged papal rule, slipping Pope Gregory VII a backhander purse of gold each year. Poor Zvonimir. His was an entirely pragmatic move, one par for the course in the cloak-and-dagger of medieval politics, but because he died childless and opened the door for his brother-in-law **King Ladislav of Hungary** to claim the crown, he has been cast as a national scapegoat. Indeed, later political spinners dreamed up a curse, supposedly uttered on his deathbed, that condemned the 'unfaithful Croats' to labour under foreign rule. In truth, it was his brother **Koloman** who did for them. In 1097 he rode before a Hungarian army to meet the unofficial king of Dalmatian nobles, one **Petar Svačić**, and won the day in a victory which left corpses, Petar's included, strewn all over the mountain of Gvozd, renamed Petrova Gora (Petar's Mountain). Hungarian rule was sealed in statute through the **Pacta Conventa** (1102), a deal that granted Croatia autonomy – its own borders, a ruling *ban* (viceroy) and a *sabor* (parliament) – so long as it recognized the ultimate authority of the Hungarian crown. After such a total rout, Dalmatia's dirty dozen chiefs had no choice. They signed, Koloman rode on for his coronation at Biograd na moru, and Croatia began eight centuries tied to Hungary.

Hungarian Early Years: 1100–1400

If they reconciled subjugation with the protection which came with a powerful monarch, the Dalmatians had good reason to feel cheated. The troops never arrived when Zadar sat out a 10-year siege by Venice and the Kvarner islands were raided on **King Bela III**'s (1173–96) watch. Indeed, Rab was lost. La Serenissima returned again after his death, bribing a fleet of Crusaders to sack Zadar in 1202 and make off with all the gold they could carry, an attack for which it received a severe papal wigging.

Even this was small beer compared with a **Tartar invasion** in 1242. A great Mongol horde swept west across the vast flats of Slavonia, forcing **King Bela IV** (1235–70) to put on hold his attempts to subdue a rebellious *ban* of Bosnia – permanently, as it turned out, thus forever losing land seized by Tomislav – and hot-foot it from Zagreb to the Dalmatian coast. The Mongols poured after him, forcing the court to scuttle between seaboard towns, until finally he was caught at Trogir. The Tartars called him out, and just as it seemed the game was up, the horde saddled up and rode back east – Khan Ogadai had just died. Overwhelmed with relief, King Bela IV toured the country pinning 'royal free town' medals to towns that had come to his aid.

His death in 1270 allowed Croatian aristocratic superpowers, including the Zrinskis and Frankopans, elevated for valour in skirmishes against Venice (*see* p.113), to flex their muscles, a good thing for an independent Croatia, a bad one for national interests, since in the ensuing power struggle Venice again snuck across the Adriatic to add Šibenik, Trogir then Split to its title deeds. Hungarian king **Louis of Anjou** (1342–82) briefly knocked heads together and notched up victories against Venice, but it was a false dawn. When he died with no male heir, the air thickened with dispute and murder as Croatian nobles bickered over a successor. Louis's son-in-law **Sigismund of Luxembourg** was elected, but so what? Still rankled by Hungarian ties, Dalmatian nobility swore fealty to **Ladislas of Naples** and through clever manoeuvring and powerful friends were first to get him onto the throne in Biograd na moru (1403).

Now there was only Sigismund to deal with – Sigismund, backed by the armies of Hungary and Slavonia. Ladislas needed hard cash and fast. And so, in 1409, **Venice**, after centuries of expensive wars and sieges and plunder, was handed Dalmatia on a plate, at the knock-down rate of 10,000 ducats. By 1420, the islands and seaboard from Zadar to Ploče were in its grasp, squeezed ever-tighter during a 370-year occupation until every last resource had been drained. Yes, Italian rule bequeathed architectural prizes whose swoony good looks go straight to the head; yes, it introduced the art of the Renaissance to the east Adriatic. But for Dalmatia the sell-off was a disaster, condemning it to a status as a mere vassal state. Worse still, Ladislas turned and fled.

A New Power Rising: 1400–1600

Croatia had seen off one threat from the east, albeit more by good luck than sharp steel; now it faced a more resolute power. The **Ottoman Turks** were on the march, consuming the Byzantine Empire. The fall of Constantinople in 1453 sent shockwaves of panic rippling northwest and by the late-1460s the Turks were on Croatia's doorstep as Bosnia succumbed with barely a whimper. The Frankopan dukes exhorted **King Mathias** (1458–90) to seek an alliance with Venice and were swiftly dispossessed of their prize possession, Senj, probably why they gave up Krk to Venice themselves. On 9 September 1493, a Croatian force of 8,000 foot troops and 2,000 feudal cavalry mustered to stem the Ottoman advance on Krbavsko polje, a moor 30km south of the Plitvice Lakes. It was a massacre. The 8,000 Turkish cavalry sliced through the Croat forces, wiping out much of the nation's aristocracy in a single bloody day and prising open the door to the coast. By 1500, the Ottoman flag fluttered over Makarska. A decade later a raiding party was on the banks of the Sava, just 10km from Zagreb. The Ottomans seemed unstoppable, and writers describe a nation whose mood was black with the pall of impending doom. Small wonder that in 1519 Pope Leo X gibbered about Croatia as '*Antemurale Christianitatis*' – on the ramparts of Christendom.

So far Hungary had watched nervously from the sidelines without bothering to help. In 1526, it received its come-uppance. Now under **Suleyman the Magnificent**, the Ottoman steamroller swung towards Hungary and on 21 August crossed the River Drava. King Louis II rode out to meet them but his puny force was no match for the 200,000-strong Turkish host. The **Battle of Mohács** (Bitka na Mohačkom polju) was a rout, settled, they say, in an hour, which notched up another conquest for Suleyman.

With Hungarian Louis dead and childless, Queen Maria's Austrian brother-in-law **Ferdinand I of Habsburg** was swiftly ensconced on the Bohemian throne. The aristocrats who survived the Krbavsko polje massacre had beseeched the Habsburg court for aid at Imperial Diets in the early 1520s. Now the *sabor* symbolically voted Ferdinand Habsburg as their ruler; whether their judgements were affected by the vote being cast 'before lunch and not having had any breakfast', as the Diet minutes explain, is unclear. The nobles hoped for a regional power to shore up their borders and in his debut speech Ferdinand promised extra troops. They dutifully arrived, but to no avail. The Ottomans rolled on, taking the mountain stronghold of Klis in 1537, and moving west into any area not occupied by Venice, which had negotiated a non-aggression pact based on mutual Adriatic trade. By the 1540s, they had pushed deep into Slavonia, eating up territory to Požega east and south to just below Karlovac. At the close of the 16th century, Croatia was a sliver of its former self, bordered roughly to the north by a line from the Međimurje to Rijeka, to the south from Sisak to Karlovac, and to the west by the Kvarner mainland coast. The rest was parcelled out between the Venetians (on the coast and islands), the Ottomans (inland) and the Dubrovnik Republic (*see* pp.336–9), whose sweet-tongued diplomacy let it sit out the tug-of-war pulling the nation apart.

Still the Ottomans pushed on. In desperation the Habsburgs formed a wagon-circle of border fortresses, establishing the **Military Frontier** (*Vojna Krajina*). Initially these were manned by mercenaries, then a bright spark suggested offering war refugees from Bosnia and Dalmatia, the **Vlachs** (or Morlachs as the Croats knew them), who knew a thing or two about front-line defence, freedom from feudal rule if they served as border guards. The *sabor* huffed at Orthodox refugees in its midst – worse, immigrants over which it had no dominion – but its protests counted for nought.

Regroup and Redress: 1600–1800

In truth, the Military Frontier was a sticking plaster, underfunded and ill-supplied. So the **Battle of Sisak** (Bitka kod Siska) was a surprise to everyone. In 1593, a force of 4,500 professional troops was cobbled together as the Ottoman Turks took Sisak, the back door to Zagreb 30km away, and with the ferocity of desperate men defeated a cocky Ottoman force. The Ottomans weren't invincible after all. Indeed, they never pushed deeper, and in the following decades Croatia won the day in border skirmishes, recovering land. That the Habsburgs bowed to expediency afterwards and sought peace by negotiating fixed borders infuriated a Croatian aristocracy flushed with victory. Petar Zrinski and Fran Krsto Frankopan were executed in 1671 for a plot to overthrow the feckless Habsburg crown, thereby wiping out the last Croatian feudal superpower with any clout in a court that was increasingly Hungarianized (*see* p.113).

The Ottoman wave which had reached its high-water mark nearly a century earlier broke at the **Siege of Vienna** (1683), then rolled back, **Prince Eugene of Savoy**, the most dashing of Habsburg commanders, charging across Slavonia after the retreating Turkish army to recapture every fortress along the way. By 1699, the Turks made the best of a bad job and sued for peace, renouncing all claim to Hungary and Croatia in the **Treaty of Sremski Karlovci**, and by 1718 Slavonia had been restored, fixing the border with Bosnia that exists to this day. Guarded by the Habsburgs' Military Frontier, Croat and Orthodox peasant refugees returned to normality, but land title deeds were divvied out to Hungarian and German aristocrats, little thank you gifts for assistance, increasing Habsburg control over a weak *sabor* and sparking a construction boom in Slavonia as the nobles built themselves Baroque manors and hunting lodges. The shift was consolidated in 1799 by **Empress Maria Theresa**, a closet absolutist who demoted the Sabor to an adjunct of the Royal Hungarian Chancellery, responsible only for drafting speeches and electing Hungarian assembly representatives.

Meanwhile, in Dalmatia... If Slavonia had a tale of woe, Dalmatia's was a sob story. Having opted for non-confrontation, then pushed out as the Ottoman power waned, the Venetians resumed their policy of subjugation through starvation. This was colonial exploitation at its worst. With the casual disdain of a far power, La Serenissima set bargain-basement prices for raw materials then dictated that they could only be exported to Venice. All manufactured goods had to be imported – from Venice. The plunder of forests to maintain the Venetian fleet had reduced much of the region to dust; Pag remains a moonscape to this day. By the end of the century, one shocked visitor reported a wretched people who grubbed for roots and ate grass. Even free city-republic Dubrovnik was in rags, shaken to its foundations by an earthquake in 1667.

Liberté et Révolution: 1800–The First World War

Into the devastation stepped **Napoleon Bonaparte.** In 1797, he dissolved the Venetian Republic and swapped Istria and Dalmatia for Habsburg-owned Lombardy, then retook them by force after the Habsburgs dared square up to France as the Austrian–British–Swedish Third Coalition. Back in French hands (1806) under the enlightened governance of **Marshal Marmont**, the east Adriatic seaboard coalesced as the **Illyrian Provinces**. For the first time in centuries, Dalmatia's future was looking up. The French governor abolished feudal rule, built roads and hospitals, reforested hills. He also made education compulsory and promoted the use of Croatian in schools and newspapers. It wasn't all philanthropy, of course, rather a strategy to unify the southern Slavs and so build a bulwark against current superpowers the Habsburgs and Russia.

It was also a blip. With progress undermined by a confrontational church, its religious hocus-pocus anathema to the secular ideals of the French Revolution and which resented the heavy taxes demanded to pay for reform, French rule came to a chilly end in the wastes of Russia, and the **Treaty of Vienna** (1815) put the Adriatic in Habsburg hands.

Although Napoleon failed in uniting the Slavs, he succeeded in firing Croatian national pride, igniting a sense of a shared identity between Croat and Serb to fuel the **Illyrian Movement**, a nice, neutral term which harked back to pre-Roman division. Inspired by the Serbian rebellion that shook off the Ottomans in 1830 and the faint call of *liberté, fraternité et egalité*, so-so Romantic writer **Ljudevit Gaj** (1809–72) fathered a movement for cultural revival which gripped the nation's intellectuals. By 1839 the supine *sabor* was sufficiently emboldened to call for 'Illyrian' to be taught in schools, even daring to champion the reunion of Dalmatia and Slavonia. Vienna, which had initially pandered to the rabble, got the jitters in 1843 and outlawed the word 'Illyria'. The movement mutated into the **National Party** and the **Croatian National Revival** gathered pace in politics and culture.

A new dawn seemed on the horizon in 1848. Civic riots flared in Habsburg-ruled Milan, Bavaria, even Vienna, and Hungarian monarchists agitated for separation. To dampen the growing fire of nationalism in Croatia, the Austrians bowed to public sentiment and elevated to *ban* **Josip Jelačić**, a much-eulogized garrison commander of the Military Frontier. He gambled. Pitching in for the Austrians to curry favour for Croatia as a 'Slavic Austria' free of Hungary, he marched on the Habsburgs' rebels in Budapest with 40,000 men, then to Vienna to snuff out revolution there. It was all for naught. The debt owed by Emperor Ferdinand was forfeit when he abdicated, and his son **Franz Josef I**, with his absolutist interior minister Alexander Bach, imposed an even more punitive centralized regime on Croatia. Or, as Hungarians quipped gleefuly, 'What Hungary received as a punishment, Croatia received as a reward.'

The Habsburg reshuffle which divided power as the **Dual Monarchy** of Austria-Hungary (1867) also split Croatia into independently governed states: Austria retained Dalmatia, and Hungary took everywhere else, appointing its own *ban* and creaming off 55 per cent taxes to Budapest. National unity seemed further away than ever, too, as political dissent fragmented. At the head of the National Party was **Juraj Strossmayer**, the charismatic and brilliant bishop of Đakovo, who charmed all who met him. Only a unity of Croats and Serbs in an independent state of the Austro-Hungarian empire, a Yugoslav (South Slav) nation, could ensure stability, he preached. Not so, objected **Ante Starčević**, founder of the **Croatian Party of Rights** (Hrvatska stranka prava). With a militant's suspicion of Orthodox Serbs, he called for a union of Slavonia, Dalmatia and Istria (and optimistically Slovenia) under a king of Croatia.

The Hungarian-appointed *ban* had a splendid time, dividing and ruling, and stoking conflicts by dissolving the Military Frontier (1881) to bring the Serb-dominated Bosnia-Hercegovina into Croatia. Croatian Serbs, egged on by the Orthodox Church and Starčević's inflammatory rhetoric, nurtured Serbian unity, Croats were aghast at the sudden Orthodox power in their midst. So, Hungarian blood must have chilled in 1905 when Serb politicians in Zadar, once guaranteed equal rights, backed a call by Croat Rijeka councillors for a united Dalmatia-Slavonia. A year later the two sides swept the board in elections as the Croat-Serb Coalition. The Hungarians played whispering politics in the *sabor*, but for once only served to bind the factions closer.

Yugoslavia Mark I: 1914–40

Then, on 28 June 1914, Archduke Franz Ferdinand met his assassin's bullet in Sarajevo and the world tipped into chaos. Sensing which way the wind was blowing and fearing another great postwar carve-up, a handful of Croatian politicians dug out Strossmayer's plans for **Yugoslavia**, a 'South Slav' state of Croats, Serbs and Slovenes to stand against predatory powers. The **Yugoslav Committee** declared itself in Paris in 1915, then spent 1917 sitting around a negotiation table with Serbian leaders in Corfu, discussing the fine print for an equal-rights constitutional monarchy headed by Serbia's Karađođević dynasty in Belgrade. The collapse of the Austro-Hungarian Empire rushed the **National Council of Slovenes, Croats and Serbs** into declaring independence from Vienna and Budapest in October 1918, but within a month Croatia was in chaos. Italy annexed Zadar, Rijeka and Pula as spoils of war promised by the Allies' **Treaty of London** (1915). Caught between the Kingdom of Italy and the Kingdom of Serbia, and without a card to play the National Council said a prayer and signed up for the latter on 1 December 1918.

The **Kingdom of Serbs, Croats and Slovenes** was always an unequal marriage. For a start, currency union in Serbian favour had been achieved at Croatian expense. Also 'Joe Peasant' was riled at the introduction of a Serbian monarchy, ending dreams of a people's state. And Croatia was sold down the river with the **Treaty of Rapallo** (1920), which not only formalized the Italians' land-grab, but threw in Istria and the islands of Lošinj, Cres and Lastovo. In short it was a botch-job, done in a hurry.

In 1918 **Croatian Peasant Party** (**HSS**; Hrvatska seljačka stranka) leader **Stjepan Radić** had chastised leaders for rushing to sign up to the kingdom 'like drunken geese in the fog'. Now he claimed a mandate for an independent state after Croatian elections in 1920 gave him a 55 per cent majority. Belgrade packed him off to prison instead, from which he emerged a few years later, repackaged his idea as a federal autonomy and found an unlikely ally in a former adversary, Serbian politician **Svetozar Pribičević**, to form the popular **Peasant-Democrat Coalition** (Seljačko-demokratska koalicija). Whether Belgrade ordered Montenegro deputy Puniša Račić to assassinate Radić in the parliamentary chamber was never confirmed, but the ensuing ethnic unrest allowed King Aleksander to dissolve parliament and impose a dictatorship, renamed the **Kingdom of Yugoslavia** (Kraljevine Jugoslavija) as a whitewash which hid the fact that Serbia held 90 per cent of parliamentary seats.

From Fascism to Communism: The Second World War–1989

The two factions that emerged from the débâcle approached Croatian independence from opposite directions. On one side was the **Communist Party of Yugoslavia** (Komunistička partija Jugoslavije) which despite the name agitated for separate states. On the other was the **Ustaše**. Zagreb political minion **Ante Pavelić** formed his reactionary party the day after the dissolution and learned the ropes in Mussolini's Fascist Italy, until his party's assassination of King Aleksander in Marseille in 1934 proved too embarrassing even for Il Duce.

His big break came with the outbreak of war. Yugoslavia's neutrality meant little to Hitler, and in April 1941 German troops goose-stepped into Zagreb. The then outlawed Ustaše was rebranded as the **Independent State of Croatia** (**NDH**; Nezavisna država Hrvatska) and installed as a puppet government, leaving Pavelić free to indulge dictatorial fantasies in a 'Greater Croatia', comprising most of Bosnia and western Serbia and ruled as a carbon-copy Fatherland. While Yugoslavia was portioned out between Germany and Italy, he purged Croatia of its 'enemies' by giving Orthodox Serbs and Jews a choice: Catholicism or mass murder. It is estimated that 80 per cent of the Jewish population (*c.* 45,000) and around 80–120,000 Serbs were rounded up and murdered in pogroms or death camps such as Jasenovac with a cruelty that appalled even the Nazis. The final toll killed in camps was spun by all sides for agitprop as soon as the war ended, from the postwar Communists' claim of 600,000 dead, to the 60,000 later offered by later-president Franjo Tuđman. It remains a touchy subject. Bosnian Muslims escaped the slaughter, deemed Catholics, lapsed after centuries of Ottoman rule.

Resistance by the Serbian *četniks* mutated into a vengeful slaughter of Croats, so anti-Fascist hopes transferred to Partisans of the outlawed Communist Party, whose non-ethnic creed and charismatic leader **Josip Broz Tito** (*see* box, overleaf) won popular support. The capitulation of Italy (1943) which delivered most of Dalmatia and Istria convinced Winston Churchill they were the real deal, and the British offered aid and diplomatic recognition in 1944. On 20 October 1944, Tito swept with his Red Army into Belgrade, then Zagreb on 8 May 1945. Triumph at last. And also retribution. To preserve his anti-Communist force, Pavelić ordered the NDH Domobrani (home guard) to flee north and, fearing reprisals, they needed no second bidding. They met a 150-strong British troop at Bleiburg, Austria, and offered to surrender to the Allies in return for protection from the Partisans. Packed on to trains, they rolled back south into Yugoslavia. Depending on whose propaganda you believe, 30,000–200,000 'Fascist collaborators' were massacred by the Partisans, either shot immediately or marched to death camps. Impartial statisticians put the figure at around 50,000. Pavelić himself slipped through the net, sneaking from Austria to Italy then to Argentina, and dying in Spain in 1957.

Yugoslavia buried its dead and Marshal Tito put his house in order. Dalmatia and Istria were reclaimed in statute and, with the mandate of a People's Front electoral victory, he unveiled the **Republic of Yugoslavia** on 29 November 1945, a federation of Croatia, Serbia, Slovenia, Bosnia-Hercegovina, Montenegro and Macedonia modelled on Communist Russia. Change was rapid. Out went small businesses and the estates of the aristocracy; in came workers' co-operatives and nationalized industry, especially the heavy industry with which Soviet states infested themselves to generate income. In too came Soviet bully-boy tactics – dissenters got a knock on the door at midnight and then prison to preserve a one-party state, and the once-untouchable Catholic Church reeled under the attacks, justified because it was seen as complicit in the NDH regime.

To his credit, Tito also stamped out any whiff of ethnic tub-thumping, fearful of the tears that rent the social fabric in the early 1940s. And, after renouncing Stalin (1948) for his meddling, and with his state now semi-established, he softened the USSR hard line. In the 1960s he turned again to the West, promoting trade and tourism to jump-start a level of economic growth that took everyone by surprise. But he could not paper over growing cracks. A skirmish about language caused by a semi-official Serb–Croat dictionary exploded into a spat about cultural superiority.

Josip Broz Tito (1892–1980)

No figure strides over Croatia's modern political landscape like Tito. Nor is any as intriguing. The seventh child of a peasant couple, Josip Broz was born in Kumrovec on 7 May 1892. Having failed primary school first grade, the 12-year-old worked as a locksmith then a metalworker during 1910–11, a period which ignited his passion for workers' rights. His idealism was further stoked by capture on the Russian Front (1915) as an Austro-Hungarian conscript, and upon his 1917 release, fired by the people's cause and now fluent in Russian, he took a train to Petrograd to fight alongside Lenin's Bolsheviks, then the Red Guard of the Russian Civil War.

He returned to Croatia in 1920, still plain Josip Broz, and shot up the ranks of the outlawed Communist Party of Yugoslavia (CPY) as a charismatic underground activist, his appeal only increased by stints behind bars. By 1927, the man who led a metalworkers' union in public, in private sat on the Zagreb branch committee. By 1930 Moscow had named him the deputy of the CPY central committee Politburo, then seconded him for a year to the Balkan branch of its own Comintern in the Russian capital. Perhaps inspired by the iconic names of his heroes Lenin and Stalin, from 1934 he sported the catchy *nom de guerre* 'Tito', justified in quasi-autobiography *Tito Speaks* as a homage to 18th-century writer Tito Brezovački, but better understood as a showman's touch he never lost. He returned from Moscow in 1937, first to revive a Yugoslav party weakened by Stalin's paranoid purges, then to lead it.

It was the Second World War that made him. After Yugoslav capitulation to Germany in 1941, Tito became not just a party leader, but a figurehead of Fascist resistance as the military commander of the Liberation Front. Initially, the Partisan struggle was masterminded from Belgrade – Tito did nothing to suppress a story which relates that he sat coolly at a café with his pistol as German troops hunted him down. But, as successes notched up, he pushed ever outwards. Italian capitulation in 1943 enabled him to establish renegade governments in Dalmatia and Istria, a move which won the support of the British, who had tired of a Yugoslav government in exile that was all talk. Those exiled politicans howled in protest when Tito, now a self-elevated marshal with a weakness for gold braid and big hats, emerged as the nation's leader in 1945. To the victor, the spoils.

And now things get interesting. In a Communist country, Tito could have been – perhaps should have been – a Soviet stooge. But a dictator who had already bristled at Moscow's rebuke for his independent foreign-policy decisions declared enough was enough when Stalin tried to depose him in 1948, and publically denounced a Kremlin policy of the 'unconditional subordination of small socialist countries'. Yugoslavia was kicked smartly out of the Soviet fold, which earned him brownie points – and, more importantly, dollars – from the West and gave him free rein to introduce his brand of independent socialism, with profit-sharing for workers in state-run enterprises, an ideology caught, like Yugoslavia, between East and West. Tito healed the rift with the Kremlin upon Stalin's death in 1953, and in the 1960s nurtured his image as magnanimous world statesman by cofounding the Non-Aligned Nations Movement with Nehru and Nasser.

Yet it's hard to pin down a leader who admonished his nation that 'life is not a holiday' but had a weakness for showboating with Hollywood glitterati such as Sophia Loren, Elizabeth Taylor and Richard Burton (who played his friend in the 1972 film *The Fifth Offensive*); a dictator who practised 'soft' Communism while packing off Stalinist opponents to an island gulag like Goli otok, off Rab. Behind the scenes of the flamboyant public figure who had four glamorous wives (none Croatian, incidentally, and two Serbian), who went through a string of mistresses and maintained a fleet of flashy Cadillacs and Rolls-Royces, was a leader quick to suppress dissent. And the man of the people who granted his citizens more free movement than those in any other eastern bloc country was the same one who gave the nod to the 1945 Bleiburg atrocity. That recent revelation has tarnished his reputation. Nevertheless, his name still commands the respect of many older citizens, with much rose-tinted talk of an era of plenty when there was public healthcare for all.

As history proved after his death on 4 May 1980, Tito's greatest achievement was probably to keep Yugoslavia's simmering cauldron of resentments from boiling over. Just as he quashed

dissent, the perceptive dictator stamped out all nationalism except Yugoslavian, and suppressed anything that might upset the balance of his six-republic nation, as the members of the Croatian Spring independence movement discovered. In practice, that meant a juggling act, often playing nationalities off against each other and wooing all through sheer force of personality. But, as the photos of Tito chameleon-like with world leaders suggest – here jovial with JFK, there severe with Colonel Gaddafi – perhaps being all things to all people was his greatest strength.

More serious was Croatia and Slovenia's protest that their booming economies propped up the weak southern states, a fair complaint when Belgrade creamed off 90 per cent of the profits of their collectivized enterprises. Belgrade got the cash, Dalmatia got the traffic, joked Croatians sourly. Another bone of contention was that, although Serbs comprised only 12 per cent of the Croatian population, they were the majority in officialdom: 70 per cent of the police, 40 per cent of government and nearly all the army.

Grumbles blossomed into full-blown dissent with the 1971 '**Croatian Spring**' (Hrvatsko proljeće), a protest movement of intellectuals and students led by reformers in the Communist Party of Croatia. Tito's retribution was clean and swift – to purge the party with mass 'resignations' and prison for some – and probably seemed the best cure for a wounded nation. Instead, the resentment festered, interpreted as Serbian repression or sabre-rattling by xenophobic Croats, depending on which side you were on.

Yugoslavia began to fragment almost as soon as the train bearing Comrade Tito's body rumbled from Ljubljana to Belgrade in May 1980. 'After Tito there will be Tito,' declared the Party, increasingly marginalized and ignored by everyone as inflation galloped out of control and repayments on Tito's Western loans began to bite. In 1989, Serbia stamped out calls for independence in the majority Albanian autonomous province of **Kosovo**, which gave Serb Communist Party chairman **Slobodan Milošević** an excuse to purge the state and media of enemies within – liberals and non-Serbs – then secure Montenegro. The 19th-century expansionist goal of a Greater Serbia seemed to have been revived. Milošević muttered darkly about battles to come.

Change was in the air in late 1989. The Berlin Wall fell in November; the once-solid USSR was crumbling. For Croatia it was crunch time. In spring 1990 **Franjo Tuđman**, a former general and Croatian Spring agitator at the head of the **Croatian Democratic Union** (**HDZ**; Hrvatska demokratska zajednica), won a 40 per cent vote on the back of a snide catchphrase '*Zna se*' ('It's known'), rhetoric about past national glories, and promises about secession from Yugoslavia and a reduced Serbian presence in the state and police. For the nation's 600,000 Serbs, this revived memories of the Second World War, especially when the *sabor* slipped into a new constitution a passage that Serbs were no longer a 'constituent' part of Croatia but a 'national minority'.

1990–95: The Homeland War

Against this background, the formation of the **Serbian Democratic Party** (**SDS**; Srpska demokratska stranka) in February 1990 in Knin, a drab Serbian-dominated town inland from Šibenik, was probably inevitable. And if the rhetoric of the Belgrade media had fuelled previous unrest, the new Croatian constitution poured petrol on it. By June a referendum for Serbian autonomy led to the declaration of statelet **Kninska Krajina**, fronted by erstwhile-dentist and baby-faced fanatic Milan Babić and guarded by troops of the **Yugoslav People's Army (JNA**; Jugoslavenska narodna armija) from a nearby base. Tuđman ordered two élite police helicopters to Knin. Yugoslav Air Force MiGs turned them back. Stand-off.

Slovenia was first to vote for independence from Yugoslavia in December 1990. Croatia followed suit in May 1991 and on 25 June the nations grasped the nettle and walked out of Yugoslavia. The tipping point had arrived. Fighting in **Slovenia** ended after 10 days, in part because Slovenian territorials outnumbered local JNA troops 20 to one, but largely, too, because it did not feature in Milošević's plans for a Greater Serbia. Croatia did. Throughout that spring, Belgrade-backed Knin militia, the 'Kninđas', a pun on *ninja*, had pushed Krajina's borders west to Plitvice, evicting Croatians then advancing again when Serbian JNA troops arrived, ostensibly to keep the peace but in reality to secure territory. Now, with a three-month European Commission moratorium on independence as a fig leaf, the JNA pulled out of Slovenia to concentrate on its true target. Under the conceit of protecting local Serbs (only 25 per cent of the population) from Croatian aggressors, JNA tanks rolled into the Baranja region of east Slavonia in August and besieged Vukovar in late August, evicting Croats to create the **Serbian Autonomous Province of Slavonia and Baranja**.

Tuđman took the gloves off and ordered his National Guard to surround JNA bases. In October, Yugoslav jets fired on the *sabor* in a bungled assassination attempt on Tuđman while JNA and Montenegro forces lobbed shells into Dubrovnik, and in the now-proclaimed Republic of Serbian Krajina the JNA pushed ever west, hoping to split Croatia in two at Zadar, just as it had been of old. A month later Vukovar finally fell, exhausted and shattered. Sadly, the butchery there had only just begun (*see* p.124).

Vukovar's devastation seemed to shock the world into action. As 14,000 troops of the UN Protection Force (Unprofor) patrolled conflict zones, in January 1992 the EC, under pressure from Germany and the Vatican, hailed an independent Croatia. The USA followed suit and in May Croatia was welcomed into the United Nations. All good, of course, but the UN's demilitarized zones were a stopgap that solved nothing. Indeed, the JNA was only too happy to pull back, since UN troops helped consolidate territorial gains – 26 per cent of Croatia. In Croatia, anger increased with every month of the status quo, and even impartial observers frowned at Russian troops' pally elations with Serbs in Vukovar. So, with world condemnation of Serbian actions in Bosnia ringing in his ears, Tuđman seized the moment. In January 1993 Croat troops poured over demarcation lines near Zadar, recapturing strategic areas around the Maslenica Bridge. Any sympathy he enjoyed was lost, however, by the PR disaster of atrocities in Muslim Bosnia in the spring and summer of 1993, which saw Croats branded aggressors as vicious as the Serbs.

With the **Washington Agreement** of March 1994, Bosnia went on to the back burner and thoughts turned again to home. In May, a two-day push retook Serb-held border territory in western Slavonia, then, on 4 August, a massive artillery bombardment of Knin launched **Operation Storm** (Oluja), a pincer-movement on the rebel Serb Krajina. As Serbians fled east into north Bosnia, on 5 August Croatian troops roared into Knin and unfurled the chequered Croatian flag above the town where all the trouble had begun four years previously. The war was effectively over. Around 6,600 Croats were dead, 13,700 'missing', and the nation was burdened with around 200,000 refugees.

The Aftermath: 1996–Present

The story doesn't quite end there. The **Dayton Accord** (1995) resolved the Bosnian question, while under the **Erdut Agreement**, the UN patrolled east Slavonia until it was reintegrated into Croatia in January 1998. Serbs and Croats were – are – far from reconciled, however, not helped after the war by Tuđman, an unrepentant ultra-nationalist who paid lip service to reconciliation but did almost nothing to help around 350,000 Serb refugees return to Croatia. While his jingoistic rhetoric about country, church and respect for authority was lapped up during the nation's painful birth, it was an anachronism now. Worse, his political machinations were far too close to Communist tactics of old for comfort, with the same autocratic tendency to manipulate the state-owned television to silence opposition or wield influence through bribes and threats. The NDZ also managed a cosy club for business fat cats, a new élite of untouchables who held all the wealth and power. For everyday Croats, meanwhile, life was harder than ever, the economy shattered by conflict, its all-important tourism in tatters. The international community was also disgusted with Tuđman, who spouted divisive and inflammatory tosh on Bosnia despite the Dayton deal – somehow he missed the laughable hypocrisy of demands for an autonomous statelet for Croatians – and dragged his heels on the extradition of war crimes suspects; one UN chief justice reported Croatia to the Security Council for its 'delinquency', and the UN threated sanctions in 1996 and 1999.

With Tuđman entombed beneath black granite in Zagreb's Mirogoj cemetery in December 1999, the public delivered its verdict through the ballot box that January – a centre-left coalition of the **Social Democrat Party** and **Croatian Social Liberal Party** won a sweeping 54 per cent majority to the HDZ's 24 per cent. And this despite a media blitz which saw little but HDZ propaganda on TV that Christmas. **Stipe Mesić**, Croatian prime minister as Yugoslavia imploded, bounced back, his soft diplomacy after Tuđman's hard line a good thing for a nation that was looking increasingly lonely; repudiating Tuđman's policies in Bosnia thawed frosty relations with the next-door neighbours. He was also received with smiles from the European community for arresting **General Mirko Norac** for war crimes, a national hero for many people in Croatia who was sentenced to 12 years in March 2003, and for persuading **General Rahim Ademi** to stand voluntarily before The Hague, a decision which so infuriated the nationalists that they motioned a no-confidence vote in parliament. Prime minister **Ivica Račan** survived, but was so weakened he bowed to nationalists in September 2002 and refused to hand over retired **General Janko Bobetko**, indicted for war crimes by The Hague tribunal. Health grounds were cited.

A more difficult juggling act was **General Ante Gotovina**, at home the patriotic hero who masterminded Operation Storm, in The Hague the third most-wanted man on the war crimes list. Gotovina went into hiding as soon as Ademi gave himself up, sheltered by renegade officials despite howls of protest from The Hague tribunal. Račan's apparent willingness to kowtow to The Hague had played badly at home, prompting a swing back to the HDZ, reinvented as a centre-right party, in November 2003 elections. But just like his predecessor, new prime minister **Ivo Sanader** was caught on the twin horns of public patriotism and intense diplomatic pressure from abroad.

Worse still, the issue threatened to derail entry into the **EU** – when its form plopped on to the union's doormat in February 2003, Croatia was the first country in the west Balkans to apply for membership to the federal club, a central plank of HDZ electioneering. With Gotovina still at large and America and member states making a lot of bad noise about a nation that cocked a snook at international law, accession talks scheduled for March 2005 were put on ice. This was now serious for a nation which defined itself as Western rather than Balkan. That October, Sanader passed on new information to tribunal investigators and in December 2005 Gotovina was arrested as he sat down to dinner in a Tenerife hotel, the biggest coup for The Hague since Slobodan Milošević went into the dock in 2001. Expediency perhaps, but also a shift which sees the Croatian state making the leap towards European democratic ideals.

Another milestone on the hard road to reconciliation was reached in March 2006. Milošević, the 'Butcher of the Balkans', died a few years into a war crimes trial he had stalled through political showboating, and Serbian Krajina leader Milan Babić, who fled his rebel statelet to grow mushrooms near Belgrade until testimony against Milošević led to his own indictment for war crimes, committed suicide. Croatia may have been robbed of seeing international justice done, but its image as a separate nation which had outgrown its fractious eastern neighbours was sealed as Europe looked on with distaste at images of Serbian mourning for Milošević; just a minority of die-hard nationalists, perhaps, but internationally damaging nonetheless.

With the two ghosts of its war were exocised, the trial of Gotovina began belatedly in March 2008, dredging up bad feeling as it did so – a poll after the arrest found that 60 per cent of Croats believed that Gotovina was not guilty. Perhaps more tricky was that the promised fast-track into the EU had stalled, in part due to rumbling conflicts with former Yugoslav neighbours. Slovenia, now part of the EU, threatens to veto Croatian membership unless a Communist-era dispute over land and sea borders is resolved, while relations with Bosnia have cooled due to plans for a bridge that will see the main coast road leapfrog onto the Pelješac peninsula and bypass Bosnian territory. The EU has also voiced concerned over Croatia's continuing hostility to Serbia, mafia-style corruption and attacks against journalists, particularly those who report on organized crime and corruption. Perhaps more worrying is that some founder European nations now question the concept of continued enlargement of the union. The diplomats say Croatia's seat is ready at the EU table by 2011. If so, its struggle is likely finally to be left in peace; afforded full honours, certainly, but an event which a forward-looking nation can let slip into its past. Watch this space.

Art and Architecture

03

Croatian art and architecture mirrors the nation's colonial past and most of what you see is a reflection of foreign tastes, Venetian on the coast, Austro-Hungarian in the north, just occasionally bearing the patriotic stamp of home-grown styles.

Roman and Byzantine: 1st–7th Centuries

Although the Illyrians and Greeks got there first, you're hard pressed to find their remains on the Croatian coast. But what the Romans left behind makes up for it. The ancestors of modern holiday villas, ***villae rusticae*** sprouted all along the coast for wealthy patricians, long vanished, but leaving little bits of wall and mosaic everywhere. The nation's Roman prize is Pula's 1st-century **amphitheatre**, the sixth largest in the world, whose sheer jaw-dropping scale overshadows the superbly ornamented Arch of the Sergi family or handsome Temple of Augustus. Further south, the AD 290 *castrum*-cum-villa of **Emperor Diocletian** is welded into the very architectural fabric of Split, a must-see on the European Grand Tour, still a wonder. Split is also home to an Archaeology Museum with prize finds from **Salona**, Roman capital of the east Adriatic whose ruins are 6km inland. Byzantine Emperor Justinian introduced the mystery of Byzantium in the 6th century, spawning **Christian basilicas** which retained the Roman atrium but propped their naves on columns and developed the apse. Emboldened by vanity, Bishop Euphrasius produced the 6th-century stunner in Poreč, its apse covered in a shimmering skin of golden mosaics on a par with those in Ravenna.

Into Romanesque: 8th–14th Centuries

The big break from Latinate styles comes with the arrival of the Croats in the 7th century, introducing **interwoven plait** (*pleter*) ornamentation like Celtic knots, possibly learned from the Illyrians. The first appearance of a vigorous art which was chiselled on every early medieval church portal and screen, and is enmeshed in the national psyche – later-president Franjo Tuđman used it on election posters in 1990 to tap into rising nationalism, and it still wraps around police hatbands – is on a hexagonal font from Nin's Holy Cross church, the first church the Croats ever built styled as a 9th-century Greek cross. The font, and the finest overview of early Croat art you'll find, are in the **Museum of Croatian Archaeological Monuments** in Split. At the other end of the scale of **pre-Romanesque** to Nin's tiny temple is the contemporary St Donat's in Zadar, a mighty galleried rotunda with three apses, partly built from Roman odds and ends. As the first kings established stability and the embryonic Croatia found its stride in the 12th century, its architects began to improvise with **Romanesque**. The Roman arches and apses of earlier basilicas are handled with assurance, floor plans experiment with three aisles, and façades are now decorated, typically with a sash of blind arcades. Zadar's Cathedral of St Anastasia (1285) is the high point, conceived as an architectural pick-me-up after a Venetian raid, with Krk Cathedral a close second. For the first time, the New Testament is carved into a 3-D cartoon strip for illiterates to read, dividing into 28 cells on the oak doors of Split's St Domnius Cathedral (1214). Then there is **Master Radovan**'s astounding late Romanesque portal of St Lawrence Cathedral in Trogir (1240), a medieval treasure whose head-spinning jumble of sacred, secular and good old hocus-pocus kicks plain Byzantine into the long grass for good.

Venetian Gothic and Renaissance: 15th–17th Centuries

Northern Gothic's strict dogma of ogival vaulting, angular arches and moon rocket spires to point eyes to heaven failed to touch southern hearts. **Gothic** in Croatia is of the enchanting Venetian style, imported to Istria and Dalmatia after La Serenissima's buy-out of King Ladislas in 1409, stripped-down and subtle on Split's old town hall or the Korčula Town cathedral portal. Giveaways on patricians' mansions are slender Venetian Gothic windows, which introduce the elegant lines of Byzantine and Arabic trade partners to plain lancet arches to classy effect – see the Ćipiko Palace in Trogir. Zadar-born, Venice-schooled architect **Juraj Dalmatinac** (1400–73) dabbled in Gothic, too, but gave it up to make his name as the superstar of **Renaissance**, a switch told in the 16th-century nave of his Šibenik Cathedral, the nation's UNESCO-listed star piece. More than any movement before, the Renaissance was a revolution in the head that overlaid pure classical style with the sophistication of an age giddy with the possibilities of humanism and science – to humanity, the power and the kingdom. Take the Rector's Palace in Dubrovnik, a statement of Ragusan Republic ambition, or sensitive sculptures in the St John chapel of Trogir Cathedral by Dalmatinac pupil **Nikola Firentlnac** (*c.* 1477–1505). Big names also won commissions to plan **defence walls** as the threat from Ottoman Turks grew, producing Dubrovnik's 15th-century bulwarks – Dalmatinac drew its Minčeta Tower – or the star-shaped fortress of Karlovac (1579). Although the minions suffered, the Renaissance was a fine old time for the élite, as evidenced by their **town houses**, typically with a courtyard staircase up to a galleried first floor. At the same time as philosophy elevated man to a minor god, able to craft nature to his own purpose, they also treated themselves to summer country retreats such as Trsteno, a return to *villae rusticae*, with ordered gardens as a nod to the Age of Reason, axial stone pillars for a vine-laden trellis and a bench for poetry readings.

Croatian painting took its first steps away from Byzantine icons in the 15th century, inspired by the new styles imported from Venice. Dalmatia's **Blaž Jurjev Trogiranin**, on show in his home town Trogir and Korčula Town, overlays late Gothic Italian style on Byzantine mystery to produce rich works of shimmering gilt, while the stability of Dubrovnik's golden age nurtured exquisite art by the likes of **Lovro Dobričević** (*c.* 1420– 78) and especially **Nikola Božidarević** (1460–1517), a master artist with the finest brush on the east Adriatic and the first to dabble in Italian humanism. The rustic retort to Dubrovnik's high-falutin' comes from **Vincent of Kastav**, whose rollicking frescoes in Istrian chapels, famously St Mary's in Beram (1474), are painted with a wry eye for local colour and even crack a joke or two. **Julije Klović** (1498–1578) also deserves a mention, the Michelangelo of the miniature, who painted in Rome for the Pope and Medici and tutored El Greco. His works hang in the British Museum, the Uffizi and the Louvre.

Northern Baroque: 18th Century

While the coast fizzed with activity, North Croatia was far too preoccupied with Turks to bother with buildings. That changed overnight with a peace treaty of 1699, and throughout the 1700s thickets of cranes sprouted across Slavonia to spread **northern Baroque**, imported by Jesuits and interpreted as a riposte to Ottoman architecture. Easy access to Germanic artists and architects helped, especially in

Varaždin, the nation's elegant stage-set of Habsburg Baroque drawn on a slate wiped clean by fire. Elsewhere, a garrison town replaced the minarets of Ottoman-occupied **Osijek**, **Požega** celebrated with a new main square, and **Zagreb** took in hand its upper town, laid with nobles' palaces and the charming St Catherine's Church. **Country manors** are also dotted about near the capital and in east Slavonia, erected by Hungarian and German aristocrats who were gifted estate title deeds as thank-you presents for help in Habsburg campaigns. They're almost all in private hands, so concentrate instead on the **pilgrimage churches** that celebrated victory; exuberant furniture and frescoes in Krapina's Holy Mother from Jerusalem or the sensory overload of Belec's Church of St Mary of the Snows, frescoed by the era's northern star **Ivan Ranger** (1700–53), a Pauline monk from the Tirol known for his Italiante *trompe l'œil*. Baroque also found its way south to a **Dubrovnik** shaken to its foundations by an earthquake (1667); star pieces here are the Italian Baroque Cathedral and Jesuit Church.

Into the Modern: 19th–20th Centuries

The fall of La Serenissima's bright star tipped Dalmatia from 18th-century slump into total atrophy. Not so **Zagreb**. Reinstated as the nation's capital in 1776, it received a formal lower town grid in the 1830s, onto which Germanic architects such as Austrian **Hermann Bollé** dotted the big statements required of a European capital. Most are the pompous revival buildings that were all the rage in north Europe – Bollé's monstrous neo-Gothic Cathedral or neo-Baroque pile of the Croatian National Theatre, for example. This infatuation with historicism also encouraged efforts to conserve rather than plunder the past in Dalmatia. Diocletian's Palace in Split was restored, and for the first time amateur archaeologists scraped off the top soil to uncover Roman sites such as Salona. The Viennese Secession largely passed Croatia by, represented only by the severe union of function and symmetry on the National and University Library in Zagreb, the prize piece perhaps, but not nearly so enchanting as the holiday homes of Austro-Hungarian grandees in Lovran. The concrete carbuncles of Communist Yugoslavia are best blanked out entirely.

North European styles prevailed in painting, too. Paris Academy-trained **Vlaho Bukovac** (1855–1922) earned a crust by portraiture of Zagreb aristocrats, but seems to really enjoy himself with the light Impressionism of later works; there's a gallery in his Cavtat birthplace. When not casting civic bronzes, **Ivan Rendić** (1849–1932) busied himself chiselling Secessionist memorials for Croat magnates (it was a great age for cemeteries), typically the marble maidens draped over tombs in Mirogoj (Zagreb), Supetar (Brač) or Orebić. But really the 20th century belongs to **Ivan Meštrović** (1883–1962), the colossus of Croatian art whose eclectic *pot pourri* of Rodin-inspired Romanticism, Secessionism, stylized Art Nouveau, dabbling in chiselled Byzantium and even folk motifs, won international acclaim. Muscular public bronzes of national heroes in Split and Zadar reveal his passion for the unity of southern Slavs, a conviction which landed him in an Ustaše jail in 1941 until a papal rebuke allowed him to flee to America, where he stayed until his death despite all Tito's sweet talk. What underpins Meštrović's patriotic swagger is sentimentality, whether an expression of a love for nation or family, whose portraits charm in retrospective museums in Split and Zagreb.

Topics

04

Glagolitic Script

In the mid-9th century, Prince Rastislav of Moravia (now in the east Czech Republic) confronted a thorny problem. In an age when secular and sacred power were bedfellows, he ruled a Slavic nation yoked to the liturgy of Frankish priests. He turned for aid to Byzantine emperor Michael III, who commanded monks Constantine (aka **Cyril**) and **Methodius** to devise a Slavic *New Testament* to oppose the Germanic priests' Latin text. Baffled at how to translate Latin sounds into a tongue with mouth-filler phonetics, the multilingual saints started from scratch. The brothers devised a 38-character alphabet, drawn with a nod to Greek and Samaritan Hebrew, then in AD 863 the missionaries sailed for the Balkans and into history as the apostles of the Slavs.

Their journey from the Adriatic seaboard up through Bulgaria and Serbia spread a runic script christened, appropriately, from the Old Slavonic for 'word' (*glagol*) and whose name translates, with poetic licence, as 'signs that speak'. Students of St Cyril tailored the shapes into the **Cyrillic** that is still in use almost verbatim in Russia, Serbia and Bulgaria, and also tutored Croatian priests, who planed off the characters' more fanciful swoops to create an angular version of the script.

And now our story really begins. The dissemination of Glagolitic was too much for the Latinate archbishops in Split. Theirs was a city founded by refugees of the Roman east Adriatic capital Salona, their allegiance sworn solemnly to Rome, and they were incensed at the adoption of Glagolitic in Mass, less because of the language's linguistic merits than the fear that it could damage attempts to reassert the powerful Latinate see of Salona in defiance of Bishop Grgur, the spiritual father of Nin and by proxy of Slavic Croatia. Wary of a schism, Pope John X called synods in Split in AD 925 and 928, and both times Grgur was outvoted, outnumbered by the Split bishops. Worse, he was humiliated first by the abolition of his see then by the cod conciliatory offer of the backwater bishopric of Sisak in Slavonia, an indignity he refused. Our Slavic champion vanished from the pages of history, and the early medieval church, never a religious mafia to tolerate renegades, drove Glagolitic underground. It survived in strongholds such as Krk, although not before the island's rebel leader was dragged in chains to Split then tortured and executed for daring to evict his Latin bishop. Indeed, the nation's oldest Glagolitic tablet, the *Baška tablet*, today reduced to mere foyer furniture of the Strossmayer Gallery of Old Masters in Zagreb, was chiselled in Baška in defiance of the ban some time around AD 1000. The Split bishops called another synod in AD 1060 – next in line for persecution were beards.

Rome relented eventually. In 1248, Pope Innocent IV, fearful of losing the Slavs to Byzantium, gave bishops in Senj the nod to preach in Glagolitic, and Croatia became the only country in Christendom privileged to use its own language and script in liturgy. Glorious days, these, for the young nation. Enthused scribes inked the **Vinodol Codex** of 1288, an official deed which handed much of the Kvarner Gulf to Krk-based superpower the Frankopan dukes, and a rare secular example of Glagolitic. The nation's first printed book was a **Glagolitic missal** (1483), its text groomed by scholars in Roč, Istria, and during the 16th century the see of Senj churned out treatises using the new-fangled printing presses imported from

Germany. In 1562 renegade Croat priests exiled to Tübingen, Germany, printed a Glagolitic New Testament, much to the chagrin of the Vatican, which was forced to reply with its own missals printed in a script it saw as defunct.

Rome may have grudgingly looked at the bigger picture and tolerated Glagolitic as being to the benefit of the Catholic Church. Not so the Venetian Republic. Unable to outlaw a script sanctioned by the pope himself, yet suspicious of a secret code which surely concealed dark plots of rebellion by recalcitrant priests, the Republic unleashed cultural war, spreading agitprop against its use and taking punitive measures against stubborn monasteries. It was a policy characteristic of a ruler with an autocratic streak, and one continued by the Habsburgs when they marched west to fill the power vacuum left after La Serenissima's bright star fell in 1797.

Some members of the Croatian clergy clung to their letters into the early 1800s, but in truth Rome had won long, long ago. As the 10th-century bishops understood – and Martin Luther was to point out centuries later – the word was power, and those three centuries that established the primacy of the Latinate church banished Glagolitic and a strong Slavic church to the wilderness along with Grgur Ninski; even hopes for a strong nation, say some historians, arguing the vote was a bodyblow from which the fledgling Croatian monarchy never really recovered. Unable to bed down, the script never spread beyond the insular sacred sphere, and certainly no secular writers ever penned in Glagolitic; even Marko Marulić, Renaissance poet and father of Croat literature, used Roman characters. There was a flutter of interest in the late 1800s, when the Croatian National Revival placed Glagolitic on the nation's altar, a talisman of Croat resistance to imperialists, a symbol of Slavic pride, but it was mere posturing, the celebration of an alphabet few of its advocates could even read, and by the late 19th century the Croats' enigmatic script had withered and died. Or almost. In 1999, cinemagoers goggled at a weird alien text in IMAX flick *Alien Adventure* – used by extraterrestrials the Glagoliths, under the leadership of one Cyrillus.

Tribes and Stereotypes

Every nation has its tribes. Britain has its Yorkshiremen and its Geordies, its Cornish and its Cockneys (to name but four), France its Bretons, America its Californians or its Texans. And although united under the banner of national independence, Croatia is no different. Ask delicately and Croats are happy to indulge in a gentle poking of fun at their nation's regional quirks. Stereotypes, of course, but ones which, like all platitudes, harbour a tiny grain of truth.

So, the inhabitants of continental **North Croatia** are Saturday's children, with work to do; dependable, hard-working country folk, they say, sweetened by the sort of rustic sentimentality which celebrates the twee *licitarsko srce*, iced lovehearts traditionally exchanged by local sweethearts, as a symbol of the Zagorje. They have a soft spot for folk traditions, nowhere better illustrated than in Slavonia, which stages the most eye-popping jamborees in the country. Whisper it, but there are hints of the Austrian and Hungarian genes stirred into the Balkan stock after centuries beholden to neighbours, whether Hungarian-Croat kings or Habsburgs.

Though also with a weakness for traditions, **Istrians** are Thursday's children, with far to go; forward-thinking and progressive, 10 years ahead in national trends, say other Croats with impressed exasperation. This is the region which welcomed the bucket-and-spade brigade of package tourism before any other; the country in miniature which has pioneered agrotourism and small boutique hotels in the last decade, and which was first to woo foodies with a gourmet take on local cuisine and wine and olive roads mapped out by the regional tourist board. It has also pioneered green thinking, providing stations for gas-powered cars, and was even first in turning to Communism – miners in Labin declared themselves a Communist republic over two decades before Tito came to power in 1945.

And then we come to the **Dalmatians**, whose live-for-today, easygoing attitudes lead other Croats to make jokes about the Mexicans of Croatia (or, more rudely, *tovari*, donkeys). This is a tribe which takes its *korzo* promenade at dusk seriously, which has coined words just for hanging out with friends – *đir*, pronounced 'jeer' – and for a deliciously indolent mood of pure, sated contentment, *fjaka* ('feeaka'), which has no lexical equivalent under the damp grey skies of North Europe. Dalmatians are renowned for their good voices – this is, after all, the heartland of *klapa* song – and have a reputation of being fine spokesmen.

All good fun, if also to be taken with a pinch of salt. But Croatia has her historical tribes too. Take the **Vlachs**, a nomadic shepherd people descended, they say, from ancient Illyrian stock and who eked out a living in highlands of the Dalmatian interior. Also known as **Morlachs**, derived from the Greek *Mavrovlahoi* – the jury is still out on whether the *mavro* (black) refers to prized black wool, the tribal banners or, more contentiously, the darker skins of its south Slavic people – they horrified the urbane Venetians, who spouted all sorts of prejudicial tosh about the bogeymen inland; because they slept alongside livestock, the *morlacci* were little more than animals, no-good drunks who beat their wives and knew nothing about an honest day's work. Nor were Catholic Croats on the coast much more hospitable to a largely Orthodox race. The loathing was mutual, even into the early years of 20th-century Yugoslavia.

It was ever thus, as former priest **Alberto Fortis** recorded in *Travels in Dalmatia* (1774). Although the Paduan traveller-philosopher acknowledged that his Italian audience would know the Morlachs 'as a race of ferocious men, unreasonable, without humanity, capable of any misdeed', he painted a generous portrait that was embraced by a European intelligentsia giddy with the Enlightenment. Indeed, the movement's godhead, Goethe, Germanicized a folk song Fortis had transcribed and presented it as a ditty *Aus dem Morlackischen*. Fortis also set the tone of much of the description since, half Rousseau-esque noble savage, half anthropological curio. He wrote of the Morlachs' hospitality despite their crippling hardship; that beds, where they existed at all, were the sole right of husbands. He was wide-eyed at a belief system in which fairies, spells, witches and vampires were facts of life, and astounded by Morlach religious customs: he recorded that wives were denounced by their parents on their wedding day (and suffered a hefty clip from their husbands-to-be as a result), and that absolution for women often came as a rap with a cudgel. He was also touched to the core by a blood-sister oath he witnessed sworn before the high altar of the Orthodox church.

Dalmatia has its Morlachs; the Kvarner region is (in)famous for **Uskoks**. Theirs is a swashbuckling *Braveheart* of a tale, full of high-seas piracy and skulduggery by sneaky politicians, the blockbuster Hollywood never made. Scene one: the early 16th century. As Ottoman Turks push west, refugees from Bosnia and Croatia organize themselves into military units and fall back towards the coast. Vowing to reclaim their land for Christianity, the Uskoks (literally, 'fugitives') take up in the mountain pass fortress of Klis, near Split, and launch a stiff rearguard action until they are finally overwhelmed by superior forces in 1537. The Uskoks retreat again, to Senj, under the protection of the Habsburgs.

For six decades, it was a perfect match. The Uskoks were conscripted to stand on Emperor Ferdinand I's *Vojna krajina* ('military frontier') to slow the relentless Ottoman advance. What they really wanted was to resettle as farmers, but the Habsburgs were reluctant to lose their staunchest guards and played a canny game of politics, under-paying them to keep the Uskoks sharp. In desperation, the landlubbers took to sea in swift coastal rowing boats to plunder the caravels of the Turks who had dispossessed them. The Venetian Republic, feckless and immoral through excess and spiritual decline, had already signed an Adriatic non-aggression pact with the Ottomans and for a decade or so the Uskoks attacked only the Turkish fleet. But when the Venetians compounded their betrayal by sailing as convoy guards to protect their little eastern luxuries after 1566, they – and their coastal settlements – became fair game too.

With nothing left to lose, the Uskoks became the gangsters of the Adriatic. With the courage of desperados and the fearlessness of condemned men, they swept down on caravels, their boats painted as black as doom, their oars daubed blood-red, and plundered rich fabrics and jewels which reappeared around the necks of ladies in the Austrian seat of government in Graz. They weren't all romantic heroes. There was also considerable pillage for its own sake, especially so when European vagabonds and brigands joined for the spoils; one tale relates that nine Englishmen, including five nobility seeking adventure, were among an Uskok party hanged in Venice in 1612. Meanwhile, back in Vienna, the Habsburgs were delighted – two regional rivals harried without the deployment of a single imperial troop. Splendid.

Venetian diplomats complained, of course, but didn't dare risk open confrontation by squaring up to the Habsburgs. Instead they began a smear campaign, circulating bogeyman tales of Uskoks who ripped out and ate the still-beating hearts of their enemies until, after a particularly gross outrage in 1615, they prodded the Habsburgs into a corner. So began the **Uskok War**, a two-year skirmish that used piracy as an excuse for a scrap over Adriatic dominance until a Madrid peace deal formalized the regional power structure in 1617. The free-wheeling Uskoks were an anachronism in this new era of modern diplomacy. With the knotty Adriatic problem resolved, the Habsburgs agreed to burn Uskok boats, and resettled its problem children from Senj to Otočac, south, and inland to the Žumberak hills north of Karlovac. It was a political masterstroke: the Uskoks received the land they always wanted, and the Habsburgs transferred fighters to what was now their most vulnerable front line.

The Wicked Winter Wind

Behind the luxurious lifestyles in new boutique hotels or hideaway villas, there are age-old constants on the Croatian coast, and not just the fish and wine. Although steel has replaced wood and we now have weathermen with whizzy computer charts, winter winds remain the scourge they have always been for coastal communities. None is more feared or more famous than the *bura*. In the north Adriatic, a wisp of cloud spun along high peaks of the Velebit mountains is the first warning to batten down the hatches in readiness for three or four days' buffeting. First the facts. Cold and dry, the *bura* begins life as a northeasterly which whips across the plains of central and eastern Europe until it hits the mountains of the north Adriatic, where it is channelled, howling, through mountain passes in sudden unpredictable gusts. For four chaotic hours or so, the sea is marbled with spindrift and thrown into a nasty chop, ferries moor fast to the quay as 'sea dust', actually droplets of water, reduce visibility to dangerous levels, and all access to road bridges for Krk and Pag is suspended. High-sided lorries are toppled, boats capsized... and then, almost as suddenly, the wind drops, all is silent, and the air is as crisp and clear as the third day of Creation.

The *bura*, then, is a capricious wind, in temperament but also in history. Because of the *bura*, islands such as Pag and the east slopes of Rab are as bare as monstrous flints, their soils cold-blasted away after the Venetian Republic stripped woods for its palace piles and merchant caravels, and their settlements forced to seek shelter on western shores. The *bura* also gave the Uskoks from Senj the upper hand over the Venetian fleets. 'They have the help of the winds, the sea and devils,' shuddered one captain in a letter. A fine theory, but it was less black magic than local knowledge of the strongest wind in Croatia which aided the refugees-turned-pirates. When the wind, funnelled by a tight pass, crashed down and rampaged through the streets of Senj, it was folly to venture outdoors, said Italian Alberto Fortis in *Travels in Dalmatia* (1774). Though weighted with stones, roofs were ripped off houses, and horses laden with salt were upended in the market. No one dared cross open squares and even in narrow streets striplings and the infirm were liable to be slammed into walls. If desperate need drove some poor sailor to the harbour, even though he crawled on all fours, 'sometimes he rolls like a straw in the might of the wind'. A century earlier, Slovenian encyclopaedist Janez Vajkard Valvasor also marvelled at the *bura* in Senj, reporting sea waves breaking over the city walls to spray streets inside.

But the *bura* isn't all bad news. From a Makarska abbot, Fortis learned that, on the rare occasions when it blew steadily, the *bura* was 'most favourable when the grape vine is pestered with downy mildew'. And in his 15-volume *magnum opus The Glory of the Duchy of Carniola* (1689), the ever-inquisitive Valvasor acclaimed it a clean broom that blessed the people of Senj with healthy air and longevity. How else to explain the 124-year-old man that he met there? Nor is it only Senj villagers who have reaped benefits from the *bura*. Because it found shelter from the wicked winter wind behind the limestone slab of Mount Učka, Opatija blossomed into Croatia's first holiday resort in the 1880s, a winter retreat in which Habsburg high-rollers and the Central European arts élite avoided the bone-aching chill of Vienna.

Food and Drink

05

The Venetians may have retreated back across the Adriatic, and the Austrian Habsburgs slunk north, but both former rulers left behind a little piece of themselves in Croatia's contradictory cuisines. Pastas and risottos abound on coastal menus full of Mediterranean dishes, seafood is exquisite, and everything comes with a heady hit of herbs and garlic and soused in olive oil; but go inland, north and east, and instead tuck into rustic platters, where pork and paprika, goulash and beans nod to the rib-sticking fare of neighbours Hungary, Slovenia and Austria. Whatever you eat, however, the watchword of Croatian cuisine is honesty; some nations' chefs show off with algebraic recipies and high-falutin' sauces, but those of Croatia let good ingredients do the talking.

Eating Out

Wherever you are, **breakfast** (*doručak*) in Croatia is a wake-up call: a powerful hit of earthy Turkish coffee (*kava*) or Italian-style espresso, cappuccino or *bijela kava* (white coffee) in cafés and bars which open around 6am and will be busy with gossiping locals by 7. Few offer food, however, so visit bakeries (*pekarnica*) to find *burek*, an occasionally delicious, often stodgy snack of filo pastry stuffed with curd cheese (*sa sirom*) or minced meat (*sa mesom*). Do try it once – it's a Balkan favourite. *Pekarnica* usually bake jam-filled croissants for delicate morning stomachs, and hotels lay on the usual spread of bread rolls, jams, cheese and meats, usually ham and salami, plus cereal and scrambled eggs in more upmarket establishments. **Mid-morning** hunger pangs in Dalmatia are sated by *marenda*, usually cheap fillers such as veal goulash or stuffed peppers which, by rights, you should be able to eat with a spoon, say Dalmatians. It's usually prepared in a *gostionica* (*see* below), and can be so filling that it can serve as an early **lunch** (*ručak*), which is generally eaten at 1–2pm. What you have depends on where you are, but in all but the simplest *gostionica* you will be offered simple starters (*predjelo*) and occasionally *hors-d'œuvre* before a main course served with vegetables. Everything comes with a small bakery of bread. Croatians drink an *apéritif* of grape-based *rakija*, and wine and water wash everything down. **Dinner** (*večera*) is usually lighter, but many restaurants offer the lunchtime menu again for foreigners. Thrown into the mix countrywide are Turkish delights as **snacks**.

Types of Restaurant

In title, the ***restoran*** is the aristocrat of Croatian dining, where smart waiters in black-and-whites present extensive menus. In truth, a ***konoba*** is just as skilled at traditional local dishes, and a term which originally referred to a wine cellar has been hijacked by any establishment with an eye for folksy, whimsical décor. Simple snacks for everyday eating are served in a ***gostionica/gostiona***, which leads a double life as a bar, and every town has its **pizzeria**: unpretentious and excellent on the coast, where you can get thin-crust pizzas and cut-price pastas and usually the best salad in town. In a nation only just succumbing to burger chains, the **snack bars** are excellent – traditional Balkan fillers such as *ćevapi* (spicy meat rissoles), *pljeskavica* (a mixed-meat Croat hamburger) and *ražnjići* (shish kebab) served in pitta bread are tasty and high-quality.

Regional Specialities

Cuisine **on the coast** is typically Mediterranean – super-fresh and simple. Excellent first courses are *pršut*, similar to Italian prosciutto and whose slivers, smoked by family firms who jealously guard their secrets, dissolve in the mouth; and *paški sir* (Pag cheese), a tangy, hard sheep's cheese from Pag island. Both are pricey but worth it. *Salata od hobotnice* may also come as a starter, although this salad of octopus, potatoes and onion soaked with olive oil and a tang of vinegar is delicious as a light lunch, as is the list of appetizers bequeathed by the Venetians: pastas and simple but tasty risottos such as *crni rižot(o)* (blackened with squid ink), *rižot sa škampima* (shrimp) and *rižot frutti di mare* (seafood, usually mussels, clams, prawns plus occasionally squid or octopus). Always worth investigating is the Adriatic catch of the day, brought fresh from the boat and priced by weight and category: gourmet's choice are *bijela riba* (white fish) such as John Dory, mullet and gilthead bream; hake is cheaper; and bargain fillers are *plava riba* (blue fish) such as tuna and mackerel. Pick from a platter brought to the table and your fish is grilled (*na žaru*) over wood and dashed with olive oil, baked (*u pećnici*) or, if you really must, boiled (*lešo*). Connoisseurs can splash out on *jastog* (lobster), delicious when prepared simply, exquisite cooked *na buzaru*, in a rich tomatoey sauce with a splash of white wine and sprigs of fresh parsley. Mussels, shrimps and clams (*kućice*) are a treat with the same preparation. For a cheap eat, there's traditional fish stew *brodet* (or brudet), often served in the pan and best eaten with bread to mop up the sauce. The classic fishy side dish is *blitva*, a medley of spinach-style Swiss chard, potatoes and garlic.

If you prefer meat, for a break from charcoal-grilled steaks, *kotlet* (pork chops) and *miješano meso* (mixed meats), seek out the **Dalmatia** speciality *pašticada*, a rich dish of beef slow-cooked in wine, or *janjetina*, spit-roast lamb popular on sheep-rearing islands Pag and Rab and in inland Dalmatia. Throughout Dalmatia menus include dishes cooked under a *peka*: octopus, lamb and veal (*teletina*) is covered with a metal lid then heaped with charcoals in a cooking style Illyrian tribes would still recognize. Desserts are simple: creamy *torta* (gâteaux) or *palačinke* (pancakes) with chocolate (*sa čokoladom*) or jam (*sa marmeladom*) to fill the corners, plus *sladoled* (ice cream) or seasonal *voće* (fruit). Around Dubrovnik, keep an eye open for *rozata*, a local *crème caramel*.

Tastes are similar north in **Istria**, although this region enthralled by neighbouring Italy has stronger Latin accents in vegetable and bean soup *maneštra*, filling *njoki* (gnocchi), twists of *fuži* pasta and *mar e monte* (literally, 'sea and mountains') dishes of shellfish and mushrooms. Explore just a few miles inland and you'll discover spicy, fat *kobasice* (sausages), fingers of wild *šparoga* (asparagus) in season, and thick *gulaš* (goulash) sauce in inland hill towns. More than anything, though, Istria, a region renowned for its gourmet restaurants, is truffle (*tartufi*) country; highly prized by gourmets, they appear in autumn with everything from seafood to steaks.

Continental Croatians on the Hungarian and Slovenian borders prefer robust dishes of rustic portions. The classic **Zagorje** starter is *štrukli*, a doughy dumpling filled with curd cheese which deserves respect. Less filling is bean soup (*grah*), often with hunks of sausage and far more appetizing than the standard repertoire of watery *juhe* (soups). For main courses Zagreb locals make a special trip to Samobor to eat *češnjovka* (garlic sausage), and **Slavonia** indulges its passion for paprika in salami *kulen*. Slavonians also pour the paprika into freshwater fish stew *fiš paprikaš*, but this is an exception in an inland region with a taste for farmyard favourites: pork or a baffling variety of cuts and *gulaš*, duck (*patka*), *zagrebački odrezak* (Zagreb *Schnitzel*, actually veal *cordon bleu*), and Zagreb and Zagorje institution turkey (*purica*) ubiquitously served with *mlinci*, thin baked noodles, as *purica s mlincima*. *Kupus* (cabbage) and *kiseli kupus* (*sauerkraut*) are standard side dishes, as is *grah* (beans), but you may also find maize porridge polenta (*pura*) – just don't plan on fitting in the dessert of walnut or poppyseed cake as well.

Drinks

It is no surprise that **wine** (*vino*) is a part of everyday life in a country which basks in over 2,400 hours of sunshine in an average year and where vines have been tended as far back as Roman times. The Croatians keep tipples best drunk young for themselves, and no wonder: 70 per cent of the country's 620 wines are quality standard and only two bottles in 10 are plain old plonk.

There's an awful lot to explore. The finest tipples come from the Romans' former stomping ground, Dalmatia. Connoisseur's choice red wine (*crno vino*) is dingač, luxurious and velvety, which just outranks rich podstup. Both are produced on the Pelješac peninsula by growers who will pour you a glass straight from the barrel. Less classy but just as drinkable reds include full-flavoured plavac from Hvar and Vis; babić from Primošten; and Istrian teran, dangerously light and made for summer sipping. Istrian tourist authorities also gladly direct enthusiasts on tours of local wine- growers. Nobles among Dalmatian whites (*bijelo vino*) are pošip and grk from Korčula or žlahtina from Krk. Faced with greater temperature extremes, continental Croatia prefers hardy white grapes: you'll find full-bodied dry graševina, chardonnays, and light, elegant rizling (riesling) with a floral nose in Slovenia and Zagorje. More details on all these local wines are given in descriptive boxes throughout the guide. Croatians often dilute basic plonk to create *bevanda*, which slips down far too easily, as does soda water spritzer *špricer*. For a dessert tipple, look for sweet prosecco.

Croatia also turns its grape harvest into ***rakija*** or *loza*, a potent *eau de vie* tossed off as an *apéritif* with a salute of *Živjeli!* ('Cheers!'). It's also acceptable as a *digestif*, but better names on brandy bottles are *šljivovica* (plum), *travarica* (herbs), *medovina/medica* (honey) and *pelinkovac* (flavoured with juniper berries). Keep an eye out for regional flavours, too: Istrian *biska* is a taste of mistletoe, Zadar maraschino cherry tipple Maraska (*see* p.233) comes in a cabinet of flavours, and Samobor's *bermet* is aromatic and pleasantly bitter.

The Austro-Hungarian rulers who nurtured Croatia's taste for **beer** (*pivo*) instilled a taste for pale lagers, some with a hint of sweetness and all served chilled; ubiquitous national brands served in little (*malo*, 0.3cl) and large (*veliko*, 0.5cl) draughts or by the bottle are Ožujsko, Karlovačko and Laško. Zagreb's local brew is Tomislav, darker and rich in malt.

Croatian Menu Reader

Basic Terms

dobar tek *bon appetit*
živjeli! (or ***na zdravlje***) cheers!
doručak breakfast
marenda brunch
ručak lunch
večera dinner
Imate li stol? Do you have a table?
Je li u ujenu uključena usluga? Is service included?
jelovnik menu
konobaru/kanobarice waiter/waitress
račun, molim the bill, please
vegetarijanskih vegetarian
vilika fork
nož knife
žlica spoon
tanjur plate
čaša glass
ubrus napkin

Cooking Terms

kiseli pickled
lešo boiled
na žaru grilled
na buzaru flash-fried with white wine, garlic and parsley
peka slow-baked under lid covered in hot coals
pečeno baked
prženo fried

Predjelo/Juhe Starters/Soups

juha od fažola bean soup, Istria
graha bean soup
manestra Istrian bean and vegetable soup
paški sir sheep's cheese from Pag
pršut prosciutto ham
štrukli baked or boiled cheese dumplings
šunka ham

Meso Meat

bubrezi kidneys
čevapčići/ćevapi spicy meat rissoles
govedina beef
gulaš goulash
janjetina lamb
jetra liver
kobasica sausage
koljenica roast pork knuckle
kotlet (***ombolo***, Istria) pork chop
kulen spicy paprika salami (Slavonia)
kunić rabbit
miješano meso mixed grill
pašticada beef stewed in wine (Dalmatia)
patka duck
pljeskavica mixed-meat patty (Croatian hamburger)
piletina chicken
pršut smoked ham
punjene paprike peppers stuffed with meat
purica turkey
ramsteak rump steak
ražnjići shish kebab (usually pork)
sarma cabbage leaves stuffed with meat and rice
slanina bacon
svinjetina pork
teletina veal
zagrebački odrezak Zagreb *Schnitzel* (veal *cordon bleu* – stuffed with cheese and ham and fried in breadcrumbs)

Riba Fish

bakalar rehydrated salted cod
bijela riba white fish
brodet fish stew
crni rižot black (ink) risotto
dagnje/mušule mussels
fiš paprikaš spicy Slavonian fish stew
frutti di mare seafood (with risotto or pasta)
girice fried small fish (whitebait)
hobotnica octopus
inčun/srdele anchovies
jastog lobster
jegulja eel
kovač John Dory
kucice clams
lignje squid
lokarda/skuša mackerel
orada sea bream
ostrige oysters
pastrva trout
plava riba blue fish
rak crab
ribice whitebait
sardina sardines
sipa cuttlefish
škampi shrimps
školjke shellfish

Povrće Vegetables

ajvar red pepper and aubergine relish
blitva Swiss chard
gljiva/šampinjon mushroom
grah beans
grašak peas
kiseli kupus sauerkraut
krastavac cucumber, gherkin
krumpir boiled potato
kupus cabbage
luk onion
paprika peppers or paprika

polenta/pura polenta
pomfrit chips, French fries
rajčica tomato
repa turnip
riža rice
rižot risotto
rukola rocket
salata (zelena, mješana) salad (green, mixed)
šparoga asparagus
špinat spinach
tartufi truffles

Deserti Desserts

baklava syrupy Turkish pastry with walnuts
palačinke pancakes
pita od jabuka apple pie
rozata crème caramel (Dubrovnik area)
sa čokoladom with chocolate
sa marmeladom with jam
sladoled ice cream
torta gâteau

Voće/Orah Fruit/Nuts

ananas pineapple
badem almond
banana banana
breskva peach
dinja melon
grožđe grapes
jabuka apple
jagoda strawberry
kruška pear
limun lemon
lješnjak hazelnut
lubenica watermelon
marelica apricot
naranča orange
orah/ovina walnut
šljiva plum
smokva fig
trešnja cherry

Miscellaneous

burek (sa sirom/sa mesom) filo pastry (filled with cheese/minced meat)
češnjak garlic
čokolada chocolate
jaje (na oko) egg (fried)
kajgana scrambled egg
kajmak clotted sour cream
kruh bread
marmelada/pekmez jam
maslac butter
maslinova ulje olive oil
med honey
mljeko milk
ocat vinegar
papar pepper
šećer sugar
sendvič sandwich
sir cheese
sol salt
ulje oil
vrhnje cream

Pića Drinks

bevanda wine and water
čaj tea (herbal)
indijski čaj tea (Indian tea, i.e. British-style)
kava (sa mlijekom) coffee (with milk)
led ice
medovina honey brandy
pelinkovac juniper berry aperitif
pivo beer
rakija grape-based *eau de vie*
šljivovica plum brandy
sok/đus juice
špricer wine spritzer
topla čokolada hot chocolate
travarica herb liqueur
vino (crno, bijelo, roze, domaće) (red, white, rosé, house) wine
voda (mineralna, negazirana) (sparkling, still) water

Planning Your Trip

Average daytime temperatures °C/°F

	Jan	Feb	Mar	April	May	June	July	Aug	Sept	Oct	Nov	Dec
Dubrovnik	9/48	10/50	12/54	16/61	18/64	23/73	28/82	27/81	22/72	17/63	14/57	10/50
Split	8/46	9/48	12/54	15/59	19/66	24/75	29/84	28/82	23/73	18/64	13/55	9/48
Pula	7/45	7/45	10/50	14/57	17/63	22/72	27/81	25/77	21/70	16/61	12/54	8/46
Zagreb	0/32	1/34	7/45	13/55	17/63	21/70	25/77	24/75	19/66	12/54	7/45	2/36

When to Go

Climate

Croatia springs few surprises with its climate. The **coast** is Mediterranean: it basks in hot summers cooled by balmy sea breezes and lit by brilliant sunshine, and has mild, damp winters where temperatures rarely drop below 6°C. The **interior** is continental, with sweltering summers and chilly winters when temperatures fluctuate around freezing and snow is common on high ground.

Such is the climatic consistency, the prime issue for visitors is tourism. Peak season begins on the coast in **July** then finds top gear in early **August**: café life is at its most effervescent in cities such as Split and Dubrovnik, which stage summer festival cultural extravaganzas (*see* below), and the evening stroll (*korzo*) and alfresco nightlife is at its most animated. The flip side to this popularity is, of course, crowds. Dubrovnik teeters on the chaotic, small towns such as Rovinj can be claustrophobic, and relaxing sightseeing is wishful thinking in premier destinations. In summer, too, accommodation is at its most expensive and hard to find, and resort beaches, such as in Bol or on the Makarska Riviera, vanish beneath a patchwork of towels. Similarly, drivers can expect long queues for ferries and heavy traffic on the Magistrala coast road. Inland Croatia, however, dozes over summer, at its quietest in a period when landlocked Croatians flee to the coast.

Croatia is at its best in spring and autumn. By early **May** you can dip a toe in the Adriatic and in **June** you can still expect smiles from restaurateurs and hoteliers. More enticing still is **September**, when the sea is at its warmest. **October** is a mite cooler but rewards gourmets with truffle season in Istria, and walkers with pleasant midday temperatures and gorgeous colours in national parks. Dubrovnik will still be busy even in these shoulder months.

Grey skies and rainfall in **November** herald the beginning of a coastal winter season which lasts until April. Resorts pull down their shutters for the season, especially on the islands, where you will have to source private accommodation, although there are bargains to be found in those holiday hotels that remain open in Split, Dubrovnik and Zadar. Now, too, the chill *bura* wind (*see* **Topics**, p.44) blasts from the north-northeast for up to two weeks, interspersed by the warm *siroko*, which can bring squalls and high waves from the south. Inland, you can expect a dusting of snow from **December** to **February**, when skiers take to the slopes above Zagreb.

For sun-seekers, Hvar is the sunniest spot in Croatia year-round, followed by Split, Korčula, then Dubrovnik.

Festivals

Croatia stages everything from *avant garde* film festivals to village donkey races, from pilgrimages and colourful folk events to medieval pageants and techno music festivals. However, few common folk events unite the nation. Instead, as well as each town's impressive spread for the day of its own patron, staunch Roman Catholic Croatia uses its bewildering number of saints as excuses to host an event.

Important ecclesiastical days on the Adriatic are **Holy Week** before Easter, when processions of Catholic pomp parade through Hvar and Korčula, and **Assumption** (15 August), when crowds of thousands say prayers at Marija Bistrica, Trsat (Rijeka) and Sinj.

The year's major inaugural folk event is ***karneval*** (Carnival), a pre-Lent indulgence of costumed parades usually on Shrove Tuesday or the preceding weekend. It is at its most ebullient in Rijeka – a week-long revel that attracts tens of thousands – and at its bizarrest on Lastovo, whose festivities climax with a straw puppet, the *poklad*, being paraded through the village then ritually burned before the parish church. Other events worth a detour are held in Samobor and Split. Pag re-stages its event to take advantage of summer weather.

Summer is party time on the Croatian coast. In July and August a cultural jamboree of classical, folk and pop concerts and theatre is staged in almost every town on the Adriatic; the most prestigious is Dubrovnik's **Summer Festival**, and second billing goes to Split.

Just as much fun are the **small folk events**, whether boisterous donkey races in villages

Calendar of Events

February

3 Feast of St Blaise procession, Dubrovnik.

Sun before Shrove Tues Carnival parade stretching 5km, Rijeka.

Shrove Tues Sword dance and 'execution' of *poklad* dummy, Lastovo; folk dance and burning of Marko dummy, Pag; carnival processions, Dubrovnik and Split; Međimure *fašnik* folklore procession, Čakovec.

March

Good Fri Procession of holy brotherhoods and mystery plays, Korčula Town.

April

28 Kumpanjija sword dance, Blato (Korčula).

Late April (odd years) Music Biennale, new sounds in classical music, Zagreb.

May

From 1st weekend Week-long festival of tamburica bands, Osijek.

7 Feast of St Domnius procession, Split.

9 Knights' Tournament, Rab Town.

2nd Sun With an Accordion at Roč international accordian festival, Roč.

Mid-May Croatian One-Minute Film Festival, Požega.

June

1st week Dance Week, contemporary dance and theatre, Zagreb.

Mid-June Brodsko Kolo Folklore Festival, Slavonski Brod.

End June Eurokaz new international theatre, Zagreb.

July

July–Aug Dubrovnik Summer Festival arts beano; Split Summer Music and Theatre Festival, Zagreb Summer Festival, classical music; weekend classical music in Osor and Lubenice, Krk.

July weekends Klapa Festival, Omiš.

1st or 2nd weekend Motifs of Podravina naïve art and handicrafts, Kopravina.

1st week Đakovo Embroidery, Slavonia folk costume spectacular, Đakovo.

25 Kumpanjija sword dance, Čara (Korčula).

27 Knights' Tournament, Rab Town.

29 Moreška sword dance in full, Korčula Town.

Late July International Folklore Festival, Croatian and international round-up, Zagreb; Film Festival screenings, amphitheatre, Pula.

Late July–Aug Grožnjan Jazz Festival.

Last week International Film Festival, Motovun.

Last Sat Folk-singing Festival, Labin.

August

August Kamplin Jazz Festival, Krk.

1st weekend Techno and house music festival, Labin; village festival with Sunday donkey race, Tribunj; boisterous three-day folk fest, Sali (sometimes 2nd weekend).

1st Sun Sinjska Alka, medieval joust, Sinj.

5 Kumpanjija sword dance, Pupnat (Korčula).

14 Kumpanjija, Smokvica (Korčula).

15 Assumption pilgrimage gatherings, Marija Bistrica, Trsat (Rijeka), Sinj.

16 Moštra sword dance, Žrnovo-Postrana (Korčula).

Mid-Aug Tilting of the Ring, medieval joust, Barban.

September

Weekends Truffle day festivals, inland Istria.

1st weekend Golden Strings of Slavonia tamburica bands festival, Požega.

2nd Sat Subotina 2,000-egg truffle omelette cook-in, Buzet.

Mid-Sept weekend 'Grape Days' harvest festivals, Buje.

Mid-Sept World Theatre Festival, Zagreb.

Late Sept–early Oct Baroque Evenings, smart classical music concerts, venues in (and around) Varaždin.

December

6 Dec Boat-burning, Komiža.

such as Tribunj or Sali, Dugi Otok; or ubiquitous fishermen's festivals on the coast. They also offer a chance to sample folk traditions and music in their most relaxed environment.

On p.53 is a calendar of main events, but dates change; consult local tourist information boards (also via websites) or a searchable database on national authority site *www.croatia.hr* for up-to-date information.

National Holidays

See p.70.

Tourist Information

The quality of *turistički zajednica* varies hugely throughout the country; whereas offices in cities and popular resorts are goldmines of information, in some small towns you are better off prospecting in a **private tourist agency** whose hours are longer, and information more current. Private agencies also organize all-inclusive sightseeing trips to regional attractions; ubiquitous national players **Atlas** (*www.atlas-croatia.com*) and **General Turist** (*www.generalturist.com*) are consistently reliable.

Both official and private agencies can proffer advice about hotel and private accommodation and public transport; large offices may book accommodation or sell tickets to events. Most also provide area maps free of charge or for a nominal fee.

Most towns and resorts have a **tourism website**, with a database of current events, basic information and links to hotel accommodation. Almost all come in English, as do a laudable number of official government and organization sites. Dedicated city sites are listed in the text of this guide, useful sites for pre-visit searches are below.

Croatian National Tourist Board, Iblerov trg 10/4, 10000 Zagreb, **t** (01) 4699 333; *www.croatia.hr*.

Croatian Tourist Offices Abroad

UK: 2 The Lanchesters, 162–4 Fulham Palace Road, London W6 9ER, **t** (020) 8563 7979.

USA: 350 Fifth Avenue, Suite 4003, 10118 New York, **t** 800 829 4416/**t** (212) 279 8672/8674.

Useful Websites

www.croatia.hr Croatian National Tourist Board site, with good hotels database – the home country version is most comprehensive.
www.tzzz.hr Zagreb regional tourist board.
www.istra.hr Istria regional tourist board.
www.kvarner.hr Kvarner regional tourist board.
www.zadar.hr Zadar regional tourist board.
www.dalmatia-cen.com Dalmatia regional tourist board.
www.visitdubrovnik.hr Dubrovnik Riviera and islands tourism.
www.visit-croatia.co.uk Handy source of all information on all sides of Croatian tourism.
www.croatiabusinessreport.com English-language economic forum.
www.mvp.hr Croatian Ministry of Foreign Affairs site, with links to national embassies.
www.hic.hr Croatian news, some in English.
www.hr Directory with themed links.
www.croatiafocus.com Croatian news issues, including war crimes trails and the EU.

Embassies and Consulates

Croatian Embassies Abroad

UK: 21 Conway Street, London W1P 5HL, **t** (020) 7387 2022, *www.croatia.embassyhomepage.com*.

Ireland: Adelaide Chambers, Peter St, Dublin 8, **t** (01) 476 7181, *http://.ie.mfa.hr*.

USA: 2343 Massachusetts Avenue NW, Washington DC, 20008-2853, **t** (202) 588 5899. Plus consulates in Chicago, LA, New York, Pittsburgh, Seattle, Kansas City – contacts through *www.croatiaemb.org*.

Canada: 229 Chapel Street, Ottawa, Ontario K1N 7Y6, **t** (613) 562 7820. Consulate in Mississauga, *www.croatiaemb.net*.

Foreign Embassies in Zagreb

UK: Ivana Lučića 4, 10000 Zagreb, **t** (01) 60 09 100, *www.britishembassy.gov.uk/croatia*.

Ireland: Miramarska 23 (Eurocenter), 10000 Zagreb, **t** (01) 63 10 025, *irish.consulate.zg@inet.hr*.

USA: Thomasa Jeffersona 2, 10010 Zagreb, **t** (01) 66 12 200, *http://zagreb.usembassy.gov/*.

Canada: Prilaz Gjure Deželića 4, 10000 Zagreb, **t** (01) 48 81 200, *www.international.gc.ca*.

Australia: Centar Kaptol, 3rd floor, Nova Ves 11, 10000 Zagreb, **t** (01) 48 91 200.

New Zealand: Vlaska ulica 50A, 10000 Zagreb, **t** (01) 46 12 060.

Entry Formalities

Passports and Visas

Not yet a member of the EU (expected for 2011), Croatia nevertheless harmonizes entry regulations with the continent, so holders of full, valid EU, US, Canadian, Australian and New Zealand passports can enter for a period of up to 90 days without a visa. If you decide to explore longer, the simplest visa extension is obtained by nipping across the Italian or Slovenian border then re-entering. Other nationals must apply to embassies or consulates (*see* p.54) for a visa, which costs 260Kn (£32/€36/US$46) regardless of type.

Note that if you are travelling to Dubrovnik by road, you must cross a 20km section of Bosnia-Hercegovina, with the usual border checks. Visa requirements have been similar to Croatia for the last decade, but it's worth double-checking before you travel, at least until a proposed bridge that skips onto the Pelješac peninsula before the border is built.

Customs

Foreign travellers are exempted from duty for non-commercial goods carried as personal baggage up to the value of 30,000Kn, though it may be a good idea to declare flashy laptops on entry to save a brush with customs officials on departure. In addition, travellers are exempted from duty for: 200 cigarettes or 100 cigarillos or 50 cigars or 250g of tobacco; 1 litre of strong spirits; 2 litres of table wine; 2 litres of liqueurs (under 22%), sparkling wine or dessert wine; 500g of coffee; 50ml perfume; 250ml of toilet water. In addition, you can only bring in and take out up to 15,000Kn.

A tortuous bureaucratic process reimburses foreign travellers with VAT paid on goods all bought in the same Croatian shop and whose value exceeds 500Kn if they complete a PDV-P form on purchase and present the goods to customs (*carina*) on departure; *see* 'Money', p.56. Official Croatian customs website *www.carina.hr* publishes full information.

Disabled Travellers

Disabled **toilet facilities** are provided in most major bus and train stations, which are generally wheelchair-friendly, and **ramps** are on the increase in cities. In Zagreb, the **Zagreb Electric Tram Company** (ZET, **t** (01) 66 00 443, *www.zet. hr*) provides a free vehicle for disabled visitors plus one passenger. Elsewhere, those in wheelchairs will struggle – access to public buildings is limited and public transport is not accessible without help from a usually sympathetic population. **Ferries** provide no ramps and you will have to rely on a steward or crew member. Similarly only high-end or modern **hotels** offer disabled rooms or a lift; seek local knowledge from tourist information agencies and confirm all advice before booking.

For country-wide information, consult Zagreb-based advice organization the **Association of Organizations of Disabled People in Croatia** (Savez Organizacija Invalida Hrvatske, **t** (01) 48 29 394) or, better, seek advice before travelling from one of the organizations at home before you go (*see* box below).

Disability Organizations

Organizations in the UK

Access Ability, *www.access-ability.co.uk*. Information on travel agencies catering specifically for disabled people.

RADAR , 12 City Forum, 250 City Rd, London ECIV 8AF, **t** (020) 7250 3222, *www.radar.org.uk*.

Holiday Care Service, 7th floor, Sunley House, 4 Bedford Park, Croydon CR0 2AP, **t** 0845 124 9971, *www.holidaycare.org.uk*.

Can Be Done, **t** (020) 8907 2400, *www. canbedone.co.uk*. Specialist holidays.

Organizations in the USA

Mobility International USA, PO Box 10767, Eugene, OR 97440, **t**/TTY (541) 343 1284, *www.miusa.org*.

SATH (Society for Accessible Travel and Hospitality), 347 5th Avenue, Suite 610, New York NY 10016, **t** (212) 447 7284, *www.sath.org*.

Emerging Horizons, *www.emerginghorizons. com*. An international subscription-based online (or mailed) quarterly travel newsletter for people with disabilities.

Insurance and EHIC Cards

Croatia's reciprocal arrangement with the EU provides EU citizens with free consultation and emergency care on the presentation of a **passport** or **EHIC card** (apply at post offices); be aware that the arrangement does not cover medical repatriation, private care or dental treatment. If you have to pay for any treatment, get a receipt for reimbursement later. Non-EU residents may enjoy the same deal; in any case, **private medical insurance** is a sensible precaution. Remember that most policies levy a surcharge to cover 'dangerous sports' such as scuba-diving.

See also **Health and Emergencies**, p.69.

Money

Croatia is not expected to join the eurozone soon; the proposed date of January 2007 slipped past without event and talk of 2010 or 2011 is likely to go the same way.

The official unit of currency is the **kuna**, whose translation as 'marten' recalls the pelts used for barter until the name was stamped on Slavonian coins in 1256. Bank notes printed on one side with aristocratic rulers or poets and on the other with national landmarks come in denominations of 5, 10, 20, 50, 100, 200 and 500Kn, and coins bearing the inevitable scampering mammal come in values of 1, 2 and 5Kn. Each kuna divides into 100 lipa, available as pocket-filling 1, 2, 5, 10, 20 and 50 lipa shrapnel.

Exchange rates in December 2008 were: £1 = 8.3Kn; $1 = 1.5Kn; €1 = 7.2Kn. *See www.xe.com* for current rates.

Though stable thanks to its being index-linked to the euro, the kuna is not a fully convertible currency, so currency cannot be bought in advance at home and must be exchanged or withdrawn on arrival. In addition, you can only take 2,000Kn out of the country (although even banks of neighbour Slovenia groan when accepting them).

While it's a good idea to arrive with a fistful of notes (the most widely accepted non-Croat currency is the euro) to safeguard against failed ATM machines, carrying pocketfuls of cash is not the most prudent choice. Whether they come in dollars, sterling or euros, **travellers' cheques** (*putnički ček*) remain the most secure means of transporting money. These can be exchanged, like hard cash, at all major banks (*banka*) for a commission of 1% or at money exchanges (*mjenjačnica*) in larger post offices and major tourist agencies such as Atlas which typically levy 3% commission, and also at larger hotels which sting with commission of up to 5%.

That said, for a holiday it's easier to withdraw cash directly from an **ATM (cash dispenser)**. These are ubiquitous on the Croatian coast and in major inland cities plus motorway petrol stations, but evaporate in remote Slavonia. All have an English-language option. ATMs take major **credit cards** – Visa, MasterCard/EuroCard, Diners Club and to a lesser extent American Express – with a PIN. However, remember that interest accrues as soon as a withdrawal is made. Cheaper are **debit cards** affiliated to credit card operators and affiliates such as Plus, Cirrus and Maestro. Many banks charge for the use of their cards abroad; nominal but it soon adds up.

Major **credit cards** are widely accepted in towns and tourist centres, but most small *pensions* and restaurants demand cash.

Value added tax (PDV) charged at 22% on most goods and 8.5% reduced rate for food, books and accommodation, can be reclaimed by non-residents (except on alcohol and tobacco) if receipt/s on one day from one retailer exceed 500Kn; ask sales assistants to complete the relevant form, which is stamped by Customs at departure then mailed back to the store, and your refund will arrive within a year – probably.

Getting There

By Air

The best-served international airports in Croatia are Zagreb, Split and Dubrovnik, offering a convenient spread across the country; note that only Zagreb and Split are currently served year-round, with Croatia Airways. Fewer services also go to Pula, Rijeka, Zadar and, with changes, Bol on Brač island. Except in Pula, Croatia Airlines shuttle buses link airports to city centres; *see* relevant chapters for information.

UK Airline Carriers

UK and Ireland (Direct)

The proliferation in budget carriers means a corresponding increase in the quota of direct flights. Alongside these, a large number of national carriers fly indirect routes to Croatia via their host nations; among them are Adria Airways (Slovenia), Air France, Alitalia, TUIfly and SkyEurope (central Europe). Ryanair and easyJet (*see* below) fly to Italian ports to link with ferries to Croatia.

Aer Lingus, **t** 0818 365 000, *www.aerlingus.com*. Dublin to Dubrovnik.

British Airways, **t** 0844 493 0787, *www.ba.com*. Gatwick to Split and Dubrovnik.

Croatia Airlines, **t** (020) 8563 0022/0870 4100 310, *www.croatiaairlines.hr*. Heathrow to Dubrovnik, Pula, Zadar, Split and Zagreb; Gatwick to Pula, Split, Dubrovnik and Zagreb.

easyJet, **t** 0905 821 0905 (65p/min), *www.easyjet.com*. Gatwick to Split, and Bristol to Split.

FlyBe, **t** 0871 700 2000, *www.flybe.com*. Birmingham/Southampton to Split and Dubrovnik; Exeter to Dubrovnik.

Flyglobespan, **t** 0871 971 1440, *www.flyglobespan.com*. Edinburgh to Pula.

GB Airways, **t** 0870 850 9850, *www.gbairways.com*. Manchester to Dubrovnik (April–Oct).

Jet2.com, **t** 0871 226 1737, *www.jet2.com*. Leeds Bradford to Dubrovnik; Belfast International to Dubrovnik.

Ryanair, **t** 0871 246 0000 (UK),**t** 0818 303 030, (Rep. Ireland), *www.ryanair.com*. Stansted to Pula and Zadar; Dublin to Zadar. Stansted to Rijeka proposed 2009.

Thomsonfly, **t** 0871 231 4869, *www.thomsonfly.com*. Gatwick to Pula and Dubrovnik; Manchester to Pula and Dubrovnik; Birmingham to Pula.

Wizz Air, **t** 0904 475 9500, *www.wizzair.com*. Luton to Zagreb.

USA and Canada

For European connections only.

Air Canada, **t** 888 567 4160 (Canada), **t** 800 268 0024 (USA), *www.aircanada.ca*.

Air France, USA **t** 800 237 2747, Canada **t** 800 667 2747, *www.airfrance.us*.

American Airlines, **t** 800 433 7300, **t** 800 543 1586 (TDD), *www.aa.com*.

British Airways, **t** 800 AIRWAYS, *www.ba.com*.

Continental, USA and Canada **t** 800 231 0856, *www.continental.com*.

Delta, USA and Canada **t** 800 241 4141, **t** 800 831 4488 (TDD), *www.delta.com*.

Northwest Airlines, **t** 800 447 4747 (24hr), **t** 800 328 2298, *www.nwa.com*.

United Airlines, **t** 800 538 2929, **t** 800 323 0170 (TDD), *www.united.com*.

Discounts and Youth Fares

Under-26-year-olds with the relevant ID cards are eligible for discounts of around 25% on flights but also reductions on admission fees to museums, concerts and more. Most agencies can prepare a photocard ID such as an ISIC.

UK and Ireland

Budget Travel, **t** (01) 631 1111, *www.budgettravel.ie*. Dublin-based cheap deals.

Charter Flight Centre, **t** (020) 7814 0010, *www.charterflightcentre.co.uk*.

Just the Flight, **t** 08718 551 551, *www.justtheflight.co.uk*. Charter flight deals.

STA, **t** 0871 2300 040, *www.statravel.co.uk*. Budget travel old-hand with 80 branches around the UK.

Trailfinders, **t** 0845 050 5945, *www.trailfinders.co.uk*. A UK-wide independent.

USIT Campus Travel, **t** (01) 602 1906, *www.usit.ie*. Irish university-based travel agents open to all.

USA and Canada

Airhitch, no tel, *www.airhitch.org*; good deals on unsold seats for flexible travellers

STA, **t** 800 781 4040, *www.statravel.com*. Over 100 branches in the USA and Canada.

TFI Tours International, **t** 800 745 8000/**t** (212) 736 1140, *www.tfitours.com*. New York-based discount fares.

Travel Cuts, US **t** 1 800 592 CUTS (2887), Canada **t** 1 866 246 9762, *www.travelcuts.com*. Student travel giant, with branches throughout Canada and West Coast USA.

From the UK and Ireland

Bar Zagreb and Split, most direct routes from the UK are operated by the national carriers British Airways and Croatia Airlines from May to October. In the last few years the number of budget carriers that fill in the gaps has soared. This has also slashed prices and opened up formerly under-served destinations such as Zadar and Split. In addition, many budget carriers operate scheduled routes from airports outside the London area. Details in the box on p.57 are correct at the start of 2009 but this is one area where information dates rapidly – check the website to hunt for new routes and shop around. As ever, those who book ahead save money. Bear in mind, too, that most flights are May to October only.

Aer Lingus provides direct flights from Ireland from Dublin to Dubrovnik. For other desinations, it is fastest to travel via London or the hub of an international carrier, e.g. with KLM via Amsterdam.

Many scheduled airlines fly indirectly to Croatia, especially Dubrovnik and Zagreb, via another European city. Check out the national airlines, e.g. Alitalia via Milan, Malev via Budapest, Austrian Airlines via Vienna, KLM via Amsterdam, Air France via Paris.

For flights and price comparisons on the Internet, *see www.skyscanner.net*, *www.whichbudget.com* (claims to include all routes flown by budget UK airlines on a single site), *www.traveljungle.co.uk*, *www.opodo.co.uk*, *www.travelocity.co.uk*, *www.expedia.co.uk*, *www.aboutflights.co.uk*, *www.airtickets.co.uk*, *www.cheapflights.co.uk*, *www.ebookers.com*, *www.flightcentre.co.uk*, *www.lastminute.com* and *www.travelocity.com*.

From the USA and Canada

Because no scheduled airline currently operates direct routes from the United States and Canada to Croatia, Stateside travellers must fly to European travel hubs such as London, Frankfurt, Zürich or Paris, then connect with flights of European carriers.

In recent years there have been some charter operators flying direct to Croatia, but many routes have been cancelled. A full list of US and Canada airline consolidator agencies is published in the Tour Operators section of the Croatia Tourist Board website, *www.croatia.hr*.

Various airlines do fly to Venice, from where you can easily get to northern Croatia by train or ferry.

Check out the flight-booking sites *www.cheapflights.com*, *www.ebookers.com*, *www.hotwire.com*, *www.skyauction.com* (the eBay of US flights) and *www.travelocity.com*.

Italy–Croatia Ferries

Routes are year-round unless where marked.

Azzurra Line, t (00 385) (0)20 313 178, *www.azzurraline.com*. Bari–Dubrovnik (May–Sept).

Blue Line, t (00 385) (0)21 352 533, *www.splittours.hr*. Ancona–Split; Ancona–Stari Grad (Hvar) (July–Aug); Ancona–Vis (July–Aug).

Jadrolinija, t (00 385) (0)51 666 111, *www.jadrolinija.hr*. Ancona–Split; Ancona–Split–Stari Grad (Hvar) (July–Aug); Ancona–Zadar; Bari–Dubrovnik.

Larivera Lines, t (00 39) 0875 82248, *www.lariveralines.com*. Termoli to Korčula (June–Sept); Termoli to Lastovo (June–Sept); Termoli to Hvar Town (June–Sept).

SNAV, t (00 39) (0)71 207 6116, *www.snav.it*. Ancona–Split (mid June–mid Sept); Pescara–Stari Grad (Hvar)–Split (July–Aug).

Venezia Lines, t Italy (00 39) (0)41 2424 000, Croatia (00 385) 52 422 896, *www.venezialines.com*. Venice–Mali Losinj (July–Aug); Venice–Rabac (July–Sept); Venice–Pula (July–Aug); Venice–Rovinj (Apr–Oct); Venice–Poreč (Apr–Oct).

By Sea

Time-rich travellers can fly to Italian ports then catch ferries to Croatia, though you're unlikely to save money on a direct budget flight to Croatia. Ferries from ports – Ancona, Pescara and Bari – take around 8hrs and are overnight except in summer, when morning ferries travel across in a day. Also in summer are fast catamaran services from Venice to destinations in Istria. For all, return tickets for overnight journeys are usually cheaper than two singles. Be aware that crossings may reduce considerably to one ferry a week in winter (company websites publish timetable details) and also that deck passage is just that – all but the most masochistic traveller should find the extra euros for a reclining seat, couchette or cabin.

By Train

You can certainly get to Croatia by train, after crossing the Channel via the **Eurostar**; the trip is laudable, too, given the environmental impact of air travel. But the journey time is extremely long and costs around £360, about the same as a scheduled flight to Croatia with the major players and at least triple what you'll pay for a budget carrier.

If you want to check it out for yourself, or investigate the various **rail passes** available for UK, US or Canadian citizens travelling through Europe, see the **Rail Europe** website. Rail Europe handles bookings for all services, including Eurostar and Motorail, sells rail passes, and acts for many other continental rail companies. Long-distance rail advice website *www.seat61.com* is invaluable for planning, with details on travel from London to major destinations in Croatia.

Eurostar, **t** 08705 186 186, *www.eurostar.com*.

Rail Europe (UK), 178 Piccadilly, London W1, **t** 08708 371 371, *www.raileurope.co.uk*.

Rail Europe (USA and Canada), **t** 877 257 2887 (USA), or **t** 800 361 RAIL (Canada), *www.raileurope.com*.

By Coach

Only the most adamant non-flier would consider a bus to Croatia from the UK. **Eurolines** (**t** 08717 818181, *www.eurolines.co.uk*) operates routes year-round from London to Zagreb and Varaždin. Buses take around 35hrs, plus you can expect a 3- or 4-hour wait when you change buses in Frankfurt, and a return fare costs around £179.

By Train or Bus from Slovenia and Italy

In addition to ferries, **buses** from Trieste go to Pula in two hours (plus destinations along the Istria coast) and also to Zagreb daily. From Slovenia, six direct **trains** a day (plus four trains requiring one change) blast from Ljubljana to Zagreb (*c*. 2hrs 20mins) and two trains a day travel direct from Ljubljana to Rijeka (via Opatija, 2hrs 30mins), there are more trains which require one change.

Two **trains** a day travel direct from Venice (4hrs) and Trieste (3hrs 40mins) to Zagreb.

By Car

Driving to Croatia from the UK is not the ordeal it looks on a map, and is likely to save money on pricey car hire in the nation. In addition, a car journey, although longer, has far less impact on the environment than flying. See it as a mini-European tour and options abound en route: the Black Forest in Germany, the Alps in Austria and Switzerland or the little-known mountains of Slovenia; or Provence and north Italy, whose charms need no introduction and from where ferries shuttle across the Adriatic.

The fastest route is through the Channel Tunnel on **Eurotunnel** or across the Channel on a **ferry** to Calais; via Lille (E42), then Mons, Luxembourg, into Germany at Saarbrücken to pick up the E52 to Munich, into Austria at Salzburg, to Villach then Ljubljana (Slovenia), from where it's equidistant to continue south into north Istria or cut east to the Zagorje and Zagreb. Starting in London, the total distance to around 1,600km. Expect a total drive time of 16–18hrs – i.e. two days, with an overnight in Germany. The excellent Michelin website (*www. viamichelin.com*) provides a route breakdown, complete with road signs, road tolls, superb maps for each junction and for the overall route, plus current roadworks.

Crossing the channel is cheapest by ferry from Dover, where ferries leave every 45mins or so, no reservation is required; and is quickest via the Channel Tunnel. For ferries, check out *www.ferrybooker.com*.

Eurotunnel, **t** 08705 35 35 35, *www.eurotunnel.com*. Operates the shuttle through the Channel Tunnel, Folkestone to Calais.

P&O Ferries, **t** 08716 645 645, *www.poferries.com*. Dover to Calais.

Sea France, **t** 0871 663 2546, *www.seafrance.com*. Dover to Calais.

Speed Ferries, **t** 0871 222 7456 *www.speedferries.com*. Dover to Boulogne.

The route suggested above is almost entirely on motorways, all of which are free – except in Austria, when in theory you must buy a pass from border customs which lasts a week, despite only a 3hr transit. Even if you take your chances, keep some euros (or a credit card) handy for the road tunnels.

Motoring organizations can provide more information on routes and petrol prices.

AAA (USA), **t** (407) 444 4000, *www.aaa.com*.

AA (UK), **t** 08706 000 371, *www.theaa.com*.

Moto Europa, (Europe), *www.ideamerge.com/motoeuropa*. US-focused driving-abroad site.

RAC (UK), **t** 08705 722 722, *www.rac.co.uk*.

Getting Around

By Air

The reason to fly is the time saving; Zagreb to Dubrovnik in 50mins rather than 14hrs by bus. Zagreb is the hub for all internal flights.

Croatia Airlines (*www.croatiaairlines.com*) operates daily schedules from Zagreb to: Pula (1–2 per day, 50mins); Split (3 per day, 45mins); Zadar (1 per day, 50mins); Brač (Bol; Sat–Sun, summer-only, 1hr); Dubrovnik (4 per day, 55mins). As an idea of prices, a Zagreb–Dubrovnik single costs *c.* 400Kn, but can drop as low as 200Kn with promotions and advance booking, roughly the same price as that 14hr bus.

By Train

Not really. The priorities of the former Habsburg rulers are revealed in Croatia's railway lines. A network pioneered in the 19th century centres on Slovenia-linked Zagreb and is focused on the continental north and east of the country – former Habsburg territory. A single line snakes down the country's spine to Split, with branch lines to Rijeka and Zadar. A line from Rijeka threads north into Slovenia then Italy, to which a branch line descends through Istria and pauses in Pazin on its way to Pula. Note that Dubrovnik does not have a train station. Rail is very much the poor cousin to road transport as car ownership increases and the motorway improves – services on once-busy routes such as Zagreb–Rijeka have been slashed after Croatians discovered they could make the 4hr journey in just over half the time by car. A new breed of fast trains introduced in 2005 has halved travel times between Zagreb and Split, from a painful 8hrs to 4hrs 40mins. And national operator **Croatian Railways** (Hrvatske Željeznice; *www.hznet.hr*) hopes a government investment of 18m kuna over the 2008–12 period will woo back customers. Don't bet on it.

Trains (*vlakov*, singular *vlak*), though clean and smooth, are slower than buses on local routes but around 10% cheaper. Fastest are **InterCity** (IC) trains, which are air-conditioned and have first-class (*prvi razred*) and second-class (*drugi razred*) carriages. The drawback is they are also more expensive than **local passenger trains** (*putnički*), which dawdle through the countryside.

Tickets (*karte*, singular *karta*) are bought prior to travel from the booking office of the **train station** (*žljeznički kolodvor*), with a single ticket (*karta u jednom*) priced at exactly half that of a return (*povratna karta*) on all but some IC routes. High-end routes may also require a **seat reservation** (*rezervacije*), indicated on a **timetable** (*vozni red*) as *rezerviranje mjesta obvezatno*; **departures** are *odlazak*, **arrivals** are *dolazak*. Searchable timetable information is published in English on **Croatian Railways**' website, *www.hznet.hr*.

While **international rail passes** such as Euro Domino or InterRail – see *www.raileurope.co.uk* (UK) or *www.raileurope.com* (USA/Canada) – are valid on Croatian Railways trains, they are not really worth the expense if you intend to travel only within Croatia.

By Bus

The workhorses of Croatian travel, buses (*autobusni*) are operated by a profusion of private companies. The most comfortable are air-conditioned **intercity express buses**, which generally depart every hour. Since the price structure is by distance they may also work out cheaper (and certainly faster) than more frequent local buses, whose timetables are geared towards rush-hour needs of locals. **Buses on islands** co-ordinate with ferry arrivals; miss the one bus which waits at the dock then tours the island and you could be in trouble.

At large city **bus stations** (*autobusni kolodvor*), **tickets** are bought before boarding from private companies in a booking hall; routes are listed in booth windows. Since companies frequently ply the same routes, check tickets to confirm the bus company and platform (*peron*). Be aware that some companies offer discounts on a return ticket, and advance purchase is a wise precaution in peak season. For local buses, which are far less strict about timetables, simply pile on and pay the driver. Do this on municipal city buses and you will usually pay extra and be required to proffer the exact money – slightly cheaper tickets can be bought in advance from kiosks and newsagents. Note that all tickets must be validated on boarding in 'ticket cancellers'. The number of departures reduces at weekends – skeleton services are the norm on Sundays.

By Ferry

Ferries are the traveller's friend: cheap (at least for foot passengers) and with journeys often as enjoyable as the destination itself. Roll-on, roll-off ferries ply short hops on busy **mainland–island** routes such as Orebić–Dominče (Korčula) or Jablanac–Mišnjak (Rab) every 30mins–1hr, but most journeys will be on **scheduled ferries that link islands to each other and to hub ports** Dubrovnik (Elafiti islands, Mljet), Split (Brač, Šolta, Hvar, Korčula, Vis and Lastovo) and Zadar (Ugljan and Dugi otok). In peak season, you can expect around 2–4 ferries a day, depending on popularity, or almost hourly on short routes.

Be warned that locals' needs come before those of tourists – ferries to and from remote destinations can depart in the sort of early hours no holidaymaker should have to see.

National ferry company **Jadrolinija** (*see* p.58) operates most routes, bolstered by a clutch of private companies, especially in summer, when hydrofoils and catamarans provide faster travel times for foot passengers; bikes can be taken for a modest fee.

Whatever the company, **tickets** are bought before boarding from a company office or booth near the quay or, for ports which are little more than a quay, from kiosks, around 30mins before departure. Expect to pay 10–30Kn for a foot passenger and 60–250Kn for a car according to journey distance and vehicle size. As ever, crowds can be a problem in peak season; you could lose half a day queuing for a ferry on popular routes such as Stari Grad (Hvar) to Split. Buy tickets in advance wherever possible and even then expect to have to arrive up to 2hrs before the departure time if you are driving; most ferries operate on a first-come, first-served basis and protests about early purchase of tickets to a crew whose boat is full will be met with a stoic shrug. Seek advice from ticket sales staff about waiting times. Similarly, so heavy are August queues on short-hop routes to Rab or Korčula that drivers may have to wait for a ferry to make a return journey.

If you intend to take a car on key routes – the aforementioned Stari Grad– Hvar, for example – during the last weeks of July and first of August, consider pre-purchasing tickets before you go, to make the most of your precious fortnight. The Jadrolinija agent in the UK is London-based **Viamare, t** (020) 7431 0091, *www.viamare.com*.

Jadrolinija also operates a **coastal service** along the entire seaboard from Rijeka to Dubrovnik in 22hrs: destinations en route are Split, Stari Grad (Hvar), Korčula and Sobra (Mljet). Departures are daily in July–Aug, four times a week in shoulder months and twice a week in winter. Prices vary depending on the level of comfort – slumming it in on deck or in the bar; a reclining seat; couchette-style bunk beds; or private cabin. At the time of writing, deck passengers are permitted to linger in any destination for up to a week (validate ticket with the purser at each stop), making this an enticing option to tour Croatia's fabulous coastline. Double-check current information before you buy, however.

All ferries offer food – usually rather tired sandwiches and snacks on short routes, a cafeteria or restaurant on day-long or overnight sailings – and drinks in a cafeteria or (usually smoke-choked) bar.

By Car

Conditions vary widely on Croatian roads. Well-maintained, three-lane **motorways** (*autocesta*), indicated by blue signs and an A prefix (green and E for international routes), go north (A2 and A4), east (A3) and west (A6) of Zagreb and speed south (A1) through the country's inland – by the start of 2009 it was opposite Makarska,and was expected to cut into Bosnia-Hercegovina to pass Dubrovnik by 2010. In addition, motorway routes cut through central Istria from Rijeka via Pazin to Pula, and extend north from Pula to Slovenia.

Bar the busy Zagreb–Karlovac section, they are generally free-flowing and fast thanks to **tolls** charged by distance; collect tickets on joining, and pay on exit. As an idea of prices, Zagreb–Karlovac (39km) costs 16Kn and Zagreb–Zadar (254km) costs 105Kn. Tolls are also payable for the Krk bridge and the Učka tunnel from inland Istria to Rijeka.

Croatia's only other major artery is the coastal Jadranska **Magistrala** (B8), a beautiful

Car Hire

For an online price comparison, log on to *www.autosabroad.com*, **t** 0845 029 1945.

UK

Avis, **t** 0844 581 0147, *www.avis.co.uk*.
Budget, **t** 0844 581 9998, *www.budget.co.uk*.
easyCar, **t** 08710 500 444, *www.easycar.com*.
Europcar, *www.europcar.co.uk*.
Hertz, *www.hertz.co.uk*.
Thrifty, **t** 0808 234 7642, *www.thrifty.co.uk*.

USA and Canada

Auto Europe, **t** 888 223 5555, *www.autoeurope.com*.
Avis Rent a Car, *www.avis.com*.
Europe by Car, **t** 800 223 1516, *www.europebycar.com*.
Europcar, *www.europcar.com*.
Hertz, *www.hertz.com*.

scenic drive that starts at Rijeka and shows off Croatians' coastline and anarchic driving – bumper-hanging and blind overtaking are standard practice. Fast it is not, however, especially in summer, when the single carriageway clogs with traffic; ease your foot off the pedal, and enjoy the ride. Elsewhere, roads disregard identifying numbers but are generally good, although minor inland roads can be rough, especially in the war-damaged regions around Zadar.

Petrol stations (*benzinska stanica*) provide 95- and 98-octane unleaded and diesel from 7am to 7 or 8pm (till 10 summer), although those on international motorways and at the city fringes work 24 hours and generally have an ATM. Although petrol stations punctuate motorways approx every 40–50km, chances to fill up evaporate alarmingly elsewhere, especially if you venture away from the coast.

Driving in major cities is not for wimps – it's generally fast and aggressive. **Parking** is a headache in cities. Follow the usual blue P, but accept the wait will be long and the bill high – if your hotel offers the option of parking space (and most do in city centres or tourist town) accept it.

The **Croatian Automobile Club** (Hrvatski Autoklub) is a good friend to the foreign driver – it provides roadside breakdown assistance (**t** 987) plus up-to-date info on road conditions and ferries in English either on **t** (01) 464 08 00 or its website *www.hak.hr*.

If you have an accident, do not move the car but inform the police (**t** 92) immediately. Only when there is no (or virtually no) material damage should can you skip notification.

Rules and Regulations

Drivers are required to hold a full, valid national licence and if in their own vehicles must also keep to hand documents of registration and a certificate of third-party insurance (including a Green Card). Driving is on the right, overtaking on the left, and **seat belts** are obligatory for driver and passengers. Also compulsory is a reflective **hazard warning triangle** and a reflective sleeveless jacket. Using mobile phones while driving is forbidden. Croatia also requires that you drive with headlights on at all times, day and night, a sure-fire way to a flat battery for anyone in an old car without a 'lights-on' alarm. Trust us – stick a reminder note on to your steering wheel.

Speed limits (generally ignored) are 130kph on motorways (80kph if towing), 110kph on major roadways, 90kph outside built-up areas and 50kph in towns. Speeding fines rise according to the gravity of your offence. To wine-growers' and restaurateurs' prophecies of doom, the government in 2004 forbade drivers from touching a drop of alcohol.

Hiring a Car

Car hire is a costly business in Croatia. Although prices of international players, which are represented in all major cities plus tourist destinations and operate bureaux in airports, fluctuate with the seasons, you can expect to stump up 500Kn (£60/€70/US$90) per day for a basic two-door manual runaround, usually without air-conditioning, and a blanching 1300Kn (£160/€190/US$230) per day for a four-door estate with air-conditioning. On the bright side, prices usually (but not always) include tax, personal accident insurance and collision damage waiver (CDW); be warned, the last doesn't usually extend to tyres, wheels, the underside and the interior. Longer-term hire rewards with better day-rates. Shopping around with major firms before you travel will turn up special deals – expect discounts of up to 30%

for booking over a month in advance – and investigate Fly-drive deals with your airline. Local companies are often cheaper if you are not overly concerned about cosmetics. Bear in mind, too, that reservation is obligatory in peak season.

All hire companies require drivers to be over 21 (although some firms demand they be older) and to have held an EU or international driving licence for (usually) one year. Also remember that a passport, driving licence and credit card will be required. *See* box opposite for a list of car-hire operators; local ones are listed throughout the guide.

Where to Stay

All accommodation is subject to a **tourist tax** of approx 7Kn per person per night.

Hotels

Fearful of the concrete vandalism which blighted Spanish and Grecian coastlines, Croatia has pledged itself instead to small family hotels. These are increasing in number and generally have a touch of local character. Recent years have also seen an overhaul of the large resort hotels of Croatia's tourism boom of the 1970s and early 80s into sassy international-standard addresses at best, comfy but bland at worst. That said, there are still a few soul-sapping relics of socialism; that many towns' entire hotel stock passed from a state to a private monopoly has not helped matters.

In recent years there has also been a realization that tourists want to say in the cities themselves, a mental switch from holidays past that has large resort hotels often sited by a beach in settlements 2–5km away from town centres. Grading is by a star system best ignored: one-stars might have a TV but otherwise barely rate above a hostel; four- and five-stars are comfy international-class residences either of business style or, in the premier resorts, stylish luxury residences. In between is a lucky dip, especially at three-star level. Neither is it cheap: prices for a relatively modest room can shock in peak season. Hotels throughout this guide are divided into price categories; *see* box right. Note that the tourist tax is not factored in.

Private Rooms

Characterful, if a little frayed at the edges, and certainly cheaper, are **rooms in private accommodation** in of local owners – sometimes modern, occasionally refurbished stone cottages. Some room somewhere will be available year-round, meaning this is a good option for a free-wheeling holiday. They are also an excellent choice to stay in city centres. Tourist offices and private tourist agencies are your best source of rooms or you can knock on the doors of houses advertising *sobe* (occasionally *zimmer*). In popular destinations, a crack squad of pensioners meets buses or ferries; double-check locations before expressing an interest and confirm prices, ideally in writing to avoid linguistic confusions, and length of stay. However you locate a room, don't be shy about asking to view before you commit. Again, rooms are graded: basic category I rooms share facilities; category II are more comfy and are either en suite or share with one other guest; and top-of-the-range category III rooms are en suite, quietly plush and frequently preferable to a three-star hotel. Double room **prices** range between 140 and 300Kn and the only catch is a surcharge of 30–40% on stays of less than three nights.

Self-catering

A plethora of tour operators offer self-catering villa rentals, either alone or in packages with flights and perhaps car hire; *see* box on pp.65–6.

Unusual Accommodation

For true escapism, investigate so-called **Robinson Crusoe cottages**, back-to-basics dwellings, usually former fishermen's houses, generally without electricity or running water. This began in the pristine Kornati archipelago but has since spread to remote

Hotel Price Categories

For a double room with WC and bath or shower in July–Aug; breakfast not included.

expensive	€€€	over 1,000Kn / €137
moderate	€€	500–1,000Kn / €68–137
inexpensive	€	under 500Kn / €68

destinations elsewhere such as Vis, Lastovo, even Dugi otok. Cottages in the Kornatis can be sourced through agencies at launchpad Murter Town (*see* p.249) or book a flights and week-long package through London-based agency **Europa Skylines, t** (020) 7226 4460, *www.croatiafortravellers.co.uk* or Croat travel agencies (*see* p.66).

Other isolated retreats are in 11 **lighthouses**, many still working, which stretch the length of the Adriatic. Options range from mainland lighthouses at Makarska to quiet bays on Lastovo or distant islet specks such as Pelagruža; bookings for the basic apartments are through Croatian travel agencies or **My Croatia**; *see* pp.65–6 for both.

Agrotourism

Agrotourism (*agriturizam*) – also known as *seoski turizam* and *seljački turizam* – is the buzzword in inland Croatia. It emerged in Istria, whose enchanting hill towns seem purpose-designed for rural retreats in stone cottages, but nowadays you can find farm-stays in the Zagorje region, Lonjsko Polje area and also in Slavonia, especially around the Kopački rit national park – a few days in a farmhouse, usually with traditional furnishings and home cooking and wine is a chance to get under the skin of local culture and sample true home-cooking. All in all, one of the most appealing stays you will have.

Accommodation in Istria tends to be more holiday orientated – from rustic-chic hotels to working farmhouses via B&Bs; the latter pair often provide meals of hearty home cuisine on request. That in inland continental Croatia is principally of the farmstay variety.

The biggest agrotourism website is *www.seoski-turizam*, which covers destinations throughout Croatia and has pages in English. The Istrian regional tourist board, based in the tourist office at Pula, publishes a *Ruralni Turizam Agroturizam* booklet listing all options or visit its website (*see www.istra.com/agroturizam* (also via *www.istra.hr*; click on 'Accommodation'). Croatian tourist agencies are also a good source.

Camping

Autokamp abound on the coast, from large sites with bars and restaurants to charming family-run sites among the olives. Although some sites remain open year-round, most operate from May to September, costing 60–80Kn per person, 20–40Kn for a pitch and 30–50Kn for parking. Electricity is widely available for an extra 20Kn or so. Remember that the ground can be hard – a hammer or spare guy-lines to attach to trees is a good idea. The **Croatian Camping Union** (*www.camping.hr*) details official sites, including the handful in Slavonia. Lots more await on the coast.

Youth Hostels

Members of Hostelling International-affiliated organizations can stay in **Croatian Hostelling Association** (HFHS; *www.hfhs.hr*) hostels in Zagreb, Pula, Zadar, Dubrovnik, Krk, Veli Lošinj and Punat, basic but clean, all with dorm rooms, some with single and double rooms. Those in the latter three destinations are open from May to Sept only; prices for all others except Zagreb change by season; for example, a bed in Dubrovnik in July or Aug costs 110Kn, in Nov–April 75Kn. Half board and full board is also available at bargain rates. For full details and bookings, visit *www.hfhs.hr*.

UK: HI International Youth Hostel Federation, **t** (01707) 324170, *www.hihostels.com*. Also contact YHA, **t** 0870 770 8868, *www.yha.org*.

USA: Hostelling International USA, **t** (301) 495 1240, *www.hiayh.org*.

Canada: Hostelling International Canada, **t** (613) 235 2595, *www.hihostels.ca*.

Australia: AYHA, **t** (02) 9218 9000, *www.yha.com.au*.

New Zealand: Youth Hostelling Association New Zealand, **t** 0800 278 299 or 03 379 9970, *wwww.yha.co.nz*.

Naturism

Naturists benefit from dedicated beaches as well as 20 naturism resorts, including the largest in Europe, Koversada near Vrsar in Istria, all along the coast, denoted by the German acronym 'FKK'. Visit **Croatia Naturism** website *www.cronatur.com* for full details.

Specialist Tour Operators

In the UK and Ireland

In addition to the niche operators, many of the holiday giants such as **Thomson** (**t** 0871 231 4691, *www.thomson.co.uk*), **First Choice** (**t** 0871 200 7799, *www.firstchoice.co.uk*), **Saga** (**t** 0800 096 0074, *www.saga.co.uk*) and **Holiday Options** (**t** 0844 477 0451, *www.holidayoptions.co.uk*) provide package deals, mostly in the Dubrovnik area (many hotels are in resort settlements south), Makarska Riviera and, in Istria, package resorts such as Poreč and Umag. The following are package and independent operators; most independents will also offer to source flights.

Hotels and Villas

Balkan Holidays, t 0845 130 1114, *www.balkanholidays.co.uk*. Package deals in Istria, Makarska and Dubrovnik regions.

Bond Tours, t (01372) 745300, *www.bondtours.com*. A Croatia all-rounder, covering all the usuals and unusuals too – out-of-the-way resorts, Kornati 'Robinson Crusoe' cottages (*see* p.249), interesting small hotels plus boat cruises.

Bosmere Travel, t (01473) 834094, *www.bosmeretravel.co.uk*. Specializes in small hotels plus tours in traditional gulet motorboats and scuba trips.

Concorde Travel, t (01) 775 9300, *www.concorde-travel.ie*. Package deals from Ireland that cover every base throughout Croatia – hotels, activities, even pilgrimages to the Catholic shrine of Medugorje in neighbouring Bosnia-Hercegovina.

Croatia Gems, t 0871 855 1031, *www.croatiagems.com*. Interesting villas in Dalmatia.

Croatia Tours, t (01) 878 0800, *www.croatiatours.ie*. Dublin-based package agency with destinations from Istria to Dubrovnik plus activity packages and excursions.

Croatian Affair, t (020) 7385 7111, *www.croatianaffair.com*. Wide range of fly-drive villas and self-catering apartments.

Croatian Villas, t (020) 8888 6655, *www.croatianvillas.com*. Large range of classy villas for rent.

Europa Skylines, t (020) 7226 4460, *www.croatiafortravellers.co.uk*. Bespoke holiday packages: multi-centre holidays for island-hopping, plus 'Robinson Crusoe' cottages on the Kornati Islands (*see* p.249).

Hidden Croatia, t 0871 208 0075, *www.hiddencroatia.com*. Tailor-made packages for independent tourists, also offering a good selection of activities – sailing, sea kayaking, rafting – and Istrian gourmet tours.

My Croatia, t 0800 021 7771, *www.mycroatia.co.uk*. Classy small hotels plus villas from a boutique tourism outfit specializing in lesser-known destinations such as Lovran, the Pelješac Peninsula, Vis and Lastovo. Sailing and adventure holidays, too.

Peng Travel, t 0845 345 8345, *www.pengtravel.co.uk*. Packages in naturist resorts, Istria.

Style Holidays, t 0871 895 0095, *www.styleholidays.co.uk*. Country villas in Istria.

Vintage Travel, t 0845 344 0460, *www.vintagetravel.co.uk*. Rustic retreats in inland Istria.

Activity Specialists

Many all-rounders such as Hidden Croatia or Bond Tours (*see* above) also organize activity packages.

Activities Abroad, t (01670) 789991, *www.activitiesabroad.com*. Two-centre multi-activity packages in Hvar and Makarska Riviera, targeted at kids, so mum and dad can relax poolside.

Activity Yachting, t (01243) 641304, *www.activityyachting.com*. Bareboat charters out of Murter, plus live-aboard 'learn to sail' deals – international certificate exams, too.

Adriatic Holidays, t (01865) 516577, *www.adriaticholidaysonline.com*. Luxury yacht charter, with crewed yachts, traditional wooden gulets and motorboats, plus some smart villas.

Andante Travels, t (01722) 713800, *www.andantetravels.co.uk*. Guided archaeology tours; prehistory plus Roman treasures. Not scheduled annually, however.

Arblaster & Clarke, t (01730) 263111, *www.arblasterandclarke.com*. An annual upmarket gourmet tour; past trips have included wine tours of the coast and islands by superyacht, and foodie tours into Istria.

Dermot Cavanagh, t (028) 8778 4166, *www.dermotcavanagh.com*. The watercolour artist and presenter of BBC2's Awash with Colour series organizes all-inclusive tuition tours, painting the inspirational scenery of Istria.

Exodus, t 0845 863 9600, *www.exodus.co.uk*. Multi-activity weeks for grown-ups – walking, cycling and culture in Dalmatia.

Explore Worldwide, t 0845 013 1537, *www.explore.co.uk*. Cultural tours and vintage motorboat tours.

Headwater Holidays, t (01606) 720199, *www.headwater.com*. Off-the-beaten-track guided walking tours, *c*. 10km per day, into the Velebit Mountains then on to the islands, plus around Dubrovnik.

Martin Randall, t (020) 8742 3355, *www.martinrandall.com*. All-inclusive cultural tours, often incorporating Italy.

Nautilus Yachting, t (01732) 867445, *www.nautilus-yachting.com*. Yacht charter from Pula, Zadar, Split and Dubrovnik.

Page & Moy, t 0870 833 4012, *www.pagemoy.com*. Escorted cultural tours, Istria/Opatija.

Sail Croatia, t 0800 988 3347, *www.sailcroatia.net*. The UK's only Croatia sailing-charter specialist: bareboat, skippered, villa-and-boat deals from Dubrovnik.

Scuba-en-Cuba, t (01895) 624 100, *www.scuba-en-cuba.com*. Diving holidays from Korčula, based at Vela Luka and Lumbarda.

Skedaddle, t (0191) 265 1110, *www.skedaddle.co.uk*. Guided or self-guide cycling tours of inland Istria, travelling on off-road trails, accommodation in farmhouses.

Swim Trek t (0)20 8696 6220, *www.swimtrek.com*. Island-hopping with a full safety escort around the Šibenik archipelago and Kornati National Park area.

Voyages Jules Verne, t 0845 166 7003, *www.vjv.com*. Croatia only or as part of discerning culture tours of the Mediterranean, Aegean and Adriatic.

In the USA, Canada

Abercrombie & Kent, t 800 554 7016, *www.abercrombieandkent.com*. High-end self-guided 'Signature' tours to Croatia.

Croatia Travel Agency, t 800 662 7628, *www.croatiatravel.com*. The full range of holidays from a New York-based agent.

Remote Odysseys Worldwide, t 1 800 451 6034, *www.rowinternational.com*. Island-hopping between Split and Dubrovnik on a 105ft gulet (traditional-styled motorboat), with options for a visit to Venice.

Smithsonian Journeys, t 1 877 EDU TOUR, *www.smithsonianjourneys.org*. Lecturer-guided cultural tours by boat: a 12-day Mediterranean Grand Tour or a jaunt from Venice down the Dalmatian coast.

Travel Time, t 800 354 8728, *www.traveltimeny.com*. The old-hand in the USA is a one-stop Croatian shop – hotels, flights, Adriatic cruises, guided regional tours (Greece to Dalmatia, Vienna to Zagreb, for example).

Wilderness Travel, t 800 368 2794, *www.wildernesstravel.com*. A Dalmatian coast highlights cruise aboard a traditional yacht and adventures in Istria from an award-winning activities outfit.

In Croatia

Adriatica.net, t (UK) (020) 7183 0437, *www.adriatica.net*. A jack-of-all-trades Zagreb-based outfit: all the usual hotels alongside small family outfits, plus interesting lighthouse apartments, sailing holidays and Istrian agrotourism.

Atlas, t (00 385) 20 442 900, *www.atlas-croatia.com*. From hotels to activities to ferry tickets, the ubiquitous national agency provides all things Croatian.

GeneralTurist, t (00 385) 1 480 5562, *www.generalturist.com*. Efficient Zagreb-based agency for hotels and activities.

Practical A–Z

07

Conversions: Imperial–Metric

Length (multiply by)
Inches to centimetres: 2.54
Centimetres to inches: 0.39
Feet to metres: 0.3
Metres to feet: 3.28
Yards to metres: 0.91
Metres to yards: 1.09
Miles to kilometres: 1.61
Kilometres to miles: 0.62

Area (multiply by)
Inches square to centimetres square: 6.45
Centimetres square to inches square: 0.15
Feet square to metres square: 0.09
Metres square to feet square: 10.76
Miles square to kilometres square: 2.59
Kilometres square to miles square: 0.39
Acres to hectares: 0.40
Hectares to acres: 2.47

Weight (multiply by)
Ounces to grams: 28.35
Grammes to ounces: 0.035
Pounds to kilograms: 0.45
Kilograms to pounds: 2.2
Stones to kilograms: 6.35
Kilograms to stones: 0.16
Tons (UK) to kilograms: 1,016
Kilograms to tons (UK): 0.0009
1 UK ton (2,240lbs) = 1.12 US tonnes (2,000lbs)

°C	°F
40	104
35	95
30	86
25	77
20	68
15	59
10	50
5	41
-0	32
-5	23
-10	14
-15	5

Volume (multiply by)
Pints (UK) to litres: 0.57
Litres to pints (UK): 1.76
Quarts (UK) to litres: 1.13
Litres to quarts (UK): 0.88
Gallons (UK) to litres: 4.55
Litres to gallons (UK): 0.22
1 UK pint/quart/gallon = 1.2 US pints/quarts/ gallons

Temperature
Celsius to Fahrenheit: multiply by 1.8 then add 32

Fahrenheit to Celsius: subtract 32 then multiply by 0.55

Croatia Information

Time Differences
Country: + 1hr GMT; + 6hrs EST

Daylight saving from last weekend in March to end of October

Dialling Codes
Croatia country code 385

To Croatia from: UK, Ireland, New Zealand 00 / USA, Canada 011 / Australia 0011 then dial 385 and the number omitting the initial zero

From Croatia to: UK 00 44; Ireland 00 353; USA, Canada 00 1; Australia 00 61; New Zealand 00 64 then the number without the initial zero

Directory enquiries: 988

International directory enquiries: 902

Emergency Numbers
Police: 92
Ambulance: 94
Fire: 93
Car breakdown: 987

Embassy Numbers in Croatia
UK: (01) 60 09 100; **Ireland** (01) 63 10 025; **USA**: (01) 66 12 200; **Canada** (01) 48 81 200; **Australia** (01) 48 91 200; **New Zealand** (01) 46 12 060

Shoe Sizes

Europe	UK	USA
35	2½ / 3	4
36	3 / 3½	4½ / 5
37	4	5½ / 6
38	5	6½
39	5½ / 6	7 / 7½
40	6 / 6½	8 / 8½
41	7	9 / 9½
42	8	9½ / 10
43	9	10½
44	9½ / 10	11
45	10½	12
46	11	12½ / 13

Women's Clothing

Europe	UK	USA
34	6	2
36	8	4
38	10	6
40	12	8
42	14	10
44	16	12

Crime and the Police

Police t 92

The crime rate in Croatia is low to the point of complacency. Foreigners are welcomed everywhere, hotel room theft is unheard of, and violent crime a genuine shock: the petty crime rife on the other side of the Adriatic has not crossed the water. That said, exercise the usual precautions: leaving valuables unguarded in restaurants or bars is asking for trouble; lock cars, and hide valuables out of sight; and be aware that city pickpockets favour crowded public spaces such as rush-hour buses. In the event of a theft, report the loss to the police to receive your magic insurance number.

The police are courteous; businesslike to the point of being brusque, perhaps, but generally helpful, although their low level of English can overcomplicate brushes with the law. Be aware, too, that by law you are supposed to carry an official proof of picture identity at all times. In the event of a lost passport, also inform your embassy – make a photocopy the key information before you go.

No-go areas do not exist in Croatia except in isolated areas formerly on the front line of the Homeland War – eastern Slavonia, the border regions of Bosnia-Hercegovina between Zadar and Split, and rural districts around Zadar – where landmines, although largely cleared, remain an issue. In theory, skull-and-crossbones signs labelled 'MINE' forewarn walkers, but don't bank on it. Stick to footpaths and roads when exploring remote districts, in the far reaches of the Krka National Park towards Knin, for example, and resist temptations to wander around shell-torn, deserted villages inland. Consider local sensitivities before blurting opinions on the Croat–Serb conflict, especially in the aforementioned regions.

Eating Out

For Croatian foods and specialities, types of restaurant and a menu reader, *see* **Food and Drink**, pp.45–50. Restaurants throughout this guide are divided into categories according to the cost of a meal for one person, with an average-priced main course and a shared bottle of house wine. *See* box, above.

Restaurant Price Categories

For a meal (main, starter, plus glass of wine) for one person.

expensive	€€€	over 160Kn / €23
moderate	€€	110–160Kn / €15–23
inexpensive	€	under 110Kn / €15

Electricity

Mains voltage is 220V, 50Hz. British and Irish appliances require a standard two-prong, round-pin adaptor; North American appliances require a transformer.

Health and Emergencies

Ambulance (bolesnička kola) **t** *93*

Fire t 94

Accidents aside, Croatia is no health hazard. Standards of public health are high, tap water is drinkable everywhere and the most common complaint is sunburn. Two exceptions are worth noting: swimmers must keep an eye out for sea urchins on rocky shores – if you get spiked dig the spine out with a sterilized needle – and hikers in mountain woods should consider the vaccination for tick-borne encephalitis recommended by the US and British embassies. Inland, mosquitoes around lakes annoy rather than infect.

Medicines for minor illnesses plus first-aid advice can be sourced at **pharmacies** (*ljekarna*), whose staff work shop hours and can match medicines from generic names if you proffer relevant packets. For more complicated medicines, bring a prescription (*recept*) signed by your doctor. In cities, one *ljekarna* works the night-shift and Sundays, organized by rota; a list is posted on all pharmacy windows.

More serious complaints are treated at a doctor's surgery, best found through tourist information or a hotel concierge, or for emergencies and pressing health problems outside consultancy hours visit a hospital (*bolnica*) – only call an ambulance in a genuine emergency.

Adequate English is spoken by many doctors in Croatia, especially the younger graduates; embassies hold lists of fluent English-speakers.

National Holidays

1 Jan New Year's Day
6 Jan Epiphany
Mar/April Easter Sunday and Monday
1 May Labour Day
Early–mid-June Corpus Christi
22 June Anti-Fascist Resistance Day
25 June Statehood Day
5 Aug National Thanksgiving Day
15 Aug Assumption
8 Oct Independence Day
1 Nov All Saints' Day
25–26 Dec Christmas

Internet

Whether in dedicated cafés, tourist agency rooms or simply a bar with a terminal in a corner, you will have little problem going online on the Adriatic coast – expect to pay around 20–30Kn per hour. Inland Slavonia is another matter; options are severely limited.

Negotiating non-QWERTY Croat keyboards is a headache wherever you are. Fortunately, Croatia drops its letter accents in its web addresses.

The availability of wireless is increasing in stylish modern cafes and upmarket hotels. Many business hotels receive ISDN lines in their rooms, but an old-fashioned phone system means dial-up connections can be a headache. If you are up to negotiate modem settings changes, modernized telephone sockets are standard US RJ-11.

Music

On the Dalmatian coast you're bound to hear ***klapa***, a sort of barbershop quartet of four to eight singers who deliver sentimental songs about love, loss and the sea in a rich baritone – the Italian influence is just a whisper away.

In the Konavle region south, a small three-stringed ***lirica*** accompanies formal dance steps – seen on Sundays in Čilipi.

Folk song in Istria and to a lesser extent the Kvarner region is strange and discordant, based on a microtonal scale echoed by its instruments: ***meh*** (or *mih*) goatskin bagpipes with two chanters and no drone; ***rožnice*** (or *sopila*) like oversized oboes, always played in pairs and whose sound is so nasal, a local myth makes excuses about musicians bewitched into thinking it was melodious; and the ***curla***, two pipes played with a single mouthpiece.

In Slavonia you'll hear the most celebrated of Croatia's folk instruments, the lute-like ***tamburica***, a version of the Balkan *tambura* (itself derived from the Turkish *saz*) which comes in all sizes. Plucked or turbo-strummed, it is played in groups of anything from 5 to 50, and, as something of a national talisman, it has enjoyed a revival since 1990.

The Zagorje region north of Zagreb sways along to Viennese-style polkas and waltzes played on the **accordion**.

Opening Hours

The winter season is usually November to March, but is often decided on a whim depending on trade.

Shops

Business hours are 8am–8pm on weekdays and 8–2 or 3pm on Saturdays, except in major cities such as Zagreb and Split. City **supermarkets** also operate longer hours on Saturdays and sometimes open on Sunday mornings. During summer (June– Sept) shops pull down shutters for a 12–4pm pause, then operate later evening hours, some until 10pm in tourist locales, where many also open on Saturday afternoons. Large **department stores** usually work without a break. **Private tourist agencies** attempt to make a year's money in July–Aug by opening daily 8am– 10pm. Croatia's wonderful **markets** are usually morning-only affairs, typically 8–1, Mon–Sat, though some open on Sundays.

Banks and Office Hours

Banks usually open Mon–Fri 8–5 and Sat 8–12 or 1, except on the coast where some follow shop hours. **Offices and public services** are Mon–Fri 8–3 or 4pm.

Post Offices

Standard hours are Mon–Fri 7am–7pm, Sat 8–1 or 2, but village and island offices usually open only Mon–Fri 7–2. The main office in large towns and tourist centres may open in the evening until 9pm or later.

Museum and Galleries

The premier sights in cities such as Zagreb or Split operate strict hours, but opening times on the coast are unpredictable; in peak season many open daily (with a long siesta), but don't be surprised if a place is closed. Many museums, like hotels, close in winter.

Churches

City churches that open all day are the exceptions. Those with renowned artworks usually operate set opening hours, typically with a 12–4pm pause. Small ones in small towns and villages usually only open for Mass, whose sanctity you should respect – if possible, slip in discreetly as the last of the congregation leave or ask neighbours for the whereabouts of the key (*ključ*), usually in an adjacent house.

Postal Services

You can buy **stamps** (*marke*, singular *marka*) at *pošta* of the **HPT Hravtska**, announced by a yellow spiral with a stripy triangle on its tail, but it is far easier to purchase them from newsagents and tobacco kiosks, then pop postcards into canary-yellow post boxes; delivery within the EU takes around five days. Allow two weeks to send transatlantic. Letters are priced according to weight, airmail (*avionska pošta*) costs extra, and staff must inspect parcels before you seal them. At some post offices, too, you can also buy **telephone cards** (*see* p.73) and make international calls, and change travellers' cheques and money.

Sports and Activities

There are plenty of specialist operators offering usually week-long activity holidays; *see* pp.65–6 for details.

Rafting and Canoeing

Such is the allure of the coast that everyone forgets about the inland river gorges which starred in the best bits of the Winnetou Western movies of the 1960s. Tourist agencies in Zagreb (try **GeneralTurist**, Pile 1a, **t** (01) 480 5652/3) and Karlovac, as well as UK tour operators (see pp.65–6), organize whitewater rafting trips on the Kupa, Mrežnica and Dobra rivers, the latter with grade IV and V rapids when dams play ball. The Zrmanja and Krupa rivers in the Velebit Nature Park are two of Europe's beauties, with warm emerald waters and waterfalls in impressive gorges, while the Cetina river, accessed from Omiš, south of Split, provides a gentle drift past banks shot through with silver willow unless swollen by rain. Tourist agencies in both towns organize trips, usually at weekends, except in Omiš when trips run daily.

For all but hardcore rafters, the season runs from June to October; trips cost *c.* 250–300Kn per person. The Zagreb-based **Croatian Rafting Federation** (Rafting Savez Hrvatske), **t** (01) 618 3333; *www.riverfree.hr* (Croatian only) is the best centre for information. Canoes and kayaks hired by the hour are available for non-guests at coastal resort hotels. Splendid sea canoeing trips are organized around the Dubrovnik town walls and to the Elafiti islands by town agencies.

Diving

The cleanest waters in the Mediterranean – with exceptional transparency up to 40m – and the relics of 2,000 years of seafaring have propelled Croatia into a premier diving destination in Europe. Today, wherever there's a resort there's a **diving centre**, all of which offer lessons for beginners (*c.*250Kn per day) and trips to regional sites – typically 200–350Kn for a one-tank dive. **Equipment hire** is more tricky; most outfits rent kit on the proviso that you join them for a dive. The standard of English is generally embarrassingly high and most mainland centres open year-round. Divers with an internationally recognized qualification must buy a one-year **licence** (100Kn), available from diving centres or the harbour master's office – bring your all-important chit as proof of competence.

Sea temperatures in summer average 21–26°C at the surface, or a constant 16–17°C at 20–30m, and in winter range from 7–10°C. **Visibility** is best in the deep waters to the south; the shallow waters off Istria are more murky. Diving is strictly regulated in the nature parks of Brijuni, the Kornatis and Mljet, and to dive by anchored warships or within 100m of military facilities is asking for trouble.

Local aficionados bicker about Croatia's top 10 dive sites, but agree that the wreck of *Baron Gautsch*, a passenger ferry from 1914 near Rovinj, is at number one. For an overview of diving sites, visit national tourism website *www.croatia.hr* (Tourism PLUS section); it also has contact details of the ubiquitous local diving centres.

Fishing

To try your luck in Croatian waters, first buy a Ministry of Agriculture and Forestry **licence**, available from tourist information centres and agencies for 60Kn, 150Kn or 250Kn (1 day/3 days/7 days) to cover a two-piece rod with up to three hooks or a spear-gun. Restrictions apply in national sea parks of Kornati, Brijuni and Mljet, and inland in Krka. Also be aware of catch size minimums and fishing seasons, which vary per species on rivers; in theory you'll receive all that information with the licence, or consult *www.croatia.hr*.

The full haul of Adriatic fish awaits offshore, either caught from rocks or on trips organized by agencies in major resorts (*c.* 300Kn per day), while in inland rivers you can expect trout and grayling. Worth a special mention is the **Gacka river** just south of Otočac (30km west of the Plitvice Lakes National Park), a name which turns Croatian fishermen misty-eyed about the superb fly-fishing for both brown and rainbow trout.

Hiking and Climbing

Search and rescue: 9155

Emergency: 112

Officially, the first pleasure walk was in 1838, when a party of nature-lovers, among them Croatian *ban* Josip Jelačić and Saxon king Friedrich August II, embarked on a botany expedition up outcrop Klek near Ogulin. Whatever the truth, many parts of Croatia are best experienced on foot. In a country full of wilderness, whether alpine meadows or rugged limestone mountains, all levels of fitness are catered for. Starting in the north, there are easy rambles on **Mount Medvednica** just outside Zagreb, or better still wooded trails into the karst valleys of the **Samobor hills** 20km west. South of Karlovac, Klek itself offers a pleasant pause on the route south, or west near Rijeka is the little-explored **Gorski kotar** range, its goal **Veliki Risnjak** (1,526m), the hub of the Risnjak National Park. Further west, **Mount Učka** (1,401m), reached from Opatija and Lovran, offers picturebook views of sea and country from its summit.

And now to the big stuff. There are superb hikes in the Velebit range, whose limestone flanks ripple along the Kvarner Gulf coast: it offers wilderness hikes in the **Velebit National Park** behind Senj, and monstrous gorges in the **Paklenica National Park**, with easy day trips plus long hikes for the well prepared. There is also good walking to be had in the far reaches of the **Krka National Park**, though, because of minefields laid during the Homeland War, leaving footpaths is folly. Further south, **Mount Biokovo** (1,762m) behind the Makarska Riviera resorts is crisscrossed by paths linking stone hamlets. Hiking on the **islands** is in its infancy; mountain peaks on rugged Brač and Hvar are worthy targets.

Prime **seasons** are spring, early summer and autumn, and the standard **trail mark** is a red circle with a white dot in the centre, occasionally rethought as stripes. There is no network of **hikers' huts** (*planinarski dom*) for long trails, although a few are scattered in the uplands of key areas, maintained by local clubs and listed on the website of the **Croatian Mountaineering Association** (Hrvatski Planinarski Savez), **t** (01) 48 24 142, *www.plsavez.hr*. It also produces the most detailed maps, often available from local tourist offices or bookshops, or direct from its headquarters in Zagreb (Kozarčeva 22; *open Mon 8–6, Tues–Fri 8–3*). The Croatian branch of the national tourist board website publishes written instructions for walking routes under its Toursim PLUS section. The Croatian Mountaineering Association also offers advice on **free climbing routes**: limestone gorges in the Paklenica National Park are the most celebrated destination for rock-huggers (see p.217), with over 500 graded routes to tackle.

Sailing

Search and rescue: 9155

Quite simply, a joy. Winds in summer are gentle, tides minimal, there are 1,185 islands to explore, deep, clear seas and deserted bays in which to drop anchor for a night of glorious isolation, and mooring at harbours lined by restaurants and modern marinas. Summers are governed by the *maestral* wind, a whisper in the morning which picks up in afternoons as land–sea convection currents kick in. In winter, sudden blasts of the north *bura* wind (*see* **Topics**, p.44) can make things exciting, and the late-autumn–spring *siroko* tests light-displacement boats with long swells, but shelter is never far away.

The principal cruising grounds are **north Dalmatia** (including the Kornati islands); **south Dalmatian islands** (including Dubrovnik); and the **Istrian west coast** and **Kvarner Gulf**. A large range of companies – including major players such as **Sunsail** (*www.sunsail.com*) and **The Moorings** (*www.moorings.com*) – offer yacht flotilla and bareboat charters to skippers, who must have a recognized basic qualification (RYA Dayskipper, for example). Many offer a rent-a-skipper deal for those without a qualification, and holiday companies offer fully crewed holidays where you can do as little or as much as you like; *see* pp.65–6 for a selection of operators. Or for a taster of what's on offer, look at **ClubAdriatic** (*www.clubadriatic.com*), a sailing supermarket (motorboats too) of skippered and bareboat options in Croatia.

Skippers receive a pre-charter briefing of local hazards and best anchorages, and for pre-planning can turn to yachties' friend websites: *www.adriatic-navigator.com* is packed with local info, from berthing charges and marina/harbourmaster contacts to local facilities. The website of Croatia marina giant **Adriatic Croatia International** (*www.aci-club.hr*) details facilities at (and publishes charts of) its 21 marinas dotted along the coast.

Skiing

Snowfall is not sufficiently reliable to support a skiing holiday. Nevertheless, seize the moment (usually in December or January) as Croatian skiers do and you can find pistes on Sljeme (1,032m; *www.sljeme.hr*), summit of **Mount Medvednica**, north of Zagreb, and at **Bjelolasica** (1,392m; *www.bjelolasica.hr*) near Ogulin, southwest of Karlovac, where the Croatian Olympic Centre has eight runs of 150m–1,700m, most of medium difficulty. A third ski resort is at Platak, *www.platak.hr*, 30km from Rijeka. Ski lifts, hire and lessons are available at all.

Windsurfing

Although there are rigs to rent all along the coast, the destinations for serious surf bums are **Bol**, on the island of Brač, and **Viganj** near Orebić on the Pelješac peninsula, host to the World (1989) and European (1990) championships and Croatia Windsurfing Championships in July. Both funnel the summer *maestral* wind, at its strongest in the afternoon (up to Force 5), through narrow channels with calm waters, ideal for beam-reach blasts. Your best bet for a salt-water speed fix in Istria is at **Fažana** or on Cape Kamenjak, a peninsula south of Pula that is exposed to all winds.

Centres at all these places **hire equipment** between May–Oct (near Fažana, in Bi-Village tourist resort) – expect to pay 250–350Kn a day – and offer lessons.

Telephones

Telephone boxes only accept magnetic-strip **telephone cards** (*telekarta*), which are sold at post offices and newsagent kiosks in credit units (*impulsa*) of 25, 50, 100, 200 and 500. Peak rates are between 7am and 10pm, when a 13Kn, 25-*impulsa* card will barely let you squawk hello and mention the weather before it cuts you off if dialling abroad. Rates are 5% lower from 4 to 10pm, and Sunday is deemed off-peak (50% off). For international calls, head to the **phone booths** in post offices, which have more favourable rates. **Hotel telephones** can raise a huge bill.

Croatia employs GSM 900/1800 standard for its **mobile phone network**, compatible with the rest of the Europe and US tri-band phones, but not with the North American GSM 1900/900. Coverage, which extends across most of the country, is excellent if phones are set to roam operators automatically to source the strongest signal. Your service provider will switch on international access on request either free or for a nominal charge, but will charge *you* huge amounts for incoming calls as well as outgoing. If you are away for any length of time and you have a phone that is not locked to a network, invest in a local SIM card from main operators VIP or T-Mobile; for your 250–300Kns you get a local number, plus around 100Kn of credit, topped up with pay-as-you-go cards. Within Croatia, mobile numbers all begin with 09.

To **call Croatia from abroad**, dial 00 then the country code 385, omit the first zero of the area code, then dial the number.

To **call abroad from Croatia**, dial 00 then the country code (UK 44; Ireland 353; USA and Canada 1; Australia 61; New Zealand 64) then dial the number, again omitting the first zero of the area code.

Local directory enquiries: t 988.
International directory enquiries: t 902.
Weather and road conditions: t 060 502 502.
Croatian Angels (state-operated tourist info, late Mar–mid Oct): t 062 999 999.

Time

Croatia is within the Central European Time zone: one hour ahead of GMT, six hours ahead of Eastern Standard Time and nine hours ahead of Western Standard Time.

Clocks go forward one hour on the last Sunday of March, and back one hour on the last Sunday of October.

Tipping

Service is not usually included in the price of drinks or food. Tips are not demanded – and there's certainly no need to pay for poor service – but standard practice is to leave change that rounds up to a convenient figure. As a rule of thumb, 10% is standard practice in smart restaurants. Change can be left for bars and cafés if you are feeling benevolent. Taxi drivers will expect a small tip – again, round up to a convenient figure. A few kunas tip is courteous after guided tours.

Toilets

Public toilets are clean and hygienic, but few and far between. Train and bus stations have maintained public facilities (*zahodi* or *WC*) which charge a couple of kunas. Men should enter ***Muški***, women ***Ženski***, hence occasionally M and Z, but more commonly twee pictures of urinating toddlers or a shoe and stiletto. Bar and café owners will usually let you use their facilities, although it doesn't hurt to express your relief with an espresso.

Zagreb and North Croatia

Continental Croatia was always a nation apart. Unlike Latin-looking Dalmatia, its people were content to embrace Hungarian protection in 1102, ushering in nearly 800 years beholden to Central European powers. The reminders are everywhere in a region that is closer to Budapest than Dubrovnik. Whether in the folds of the Zagorje hills or among nodding sunflowers in Slavonia, whether in the well-aired grid of Zagreb or in villages of the Turopolje, as cosy as an East European fairytale, the palette is for pastels not honey-hued stone, and glossy cockerels strut before ramshackle farmhouses among the cornfields. Here, too, Baroque churches bud onion domes rather than campaniles, and on menus there's gutsy stuff of pork and paprika.

08

Don't miss

1. **Ivan Meštrović sculpture and naïve art**
   Gradec, Zagreb **p.87**
2. **Hills, frescoes, wine and charm**
   The Zagorje **p.99**
3. **Highly elegant Baroque town**
   Varaždin **p.108**
4. **Waterbird wonderland**
   Kopački Rit Nature Park **p.122**
5. **Fairytale stork villages**
   Lonjsko Polje Nature Park **p.132**

See map overleaf

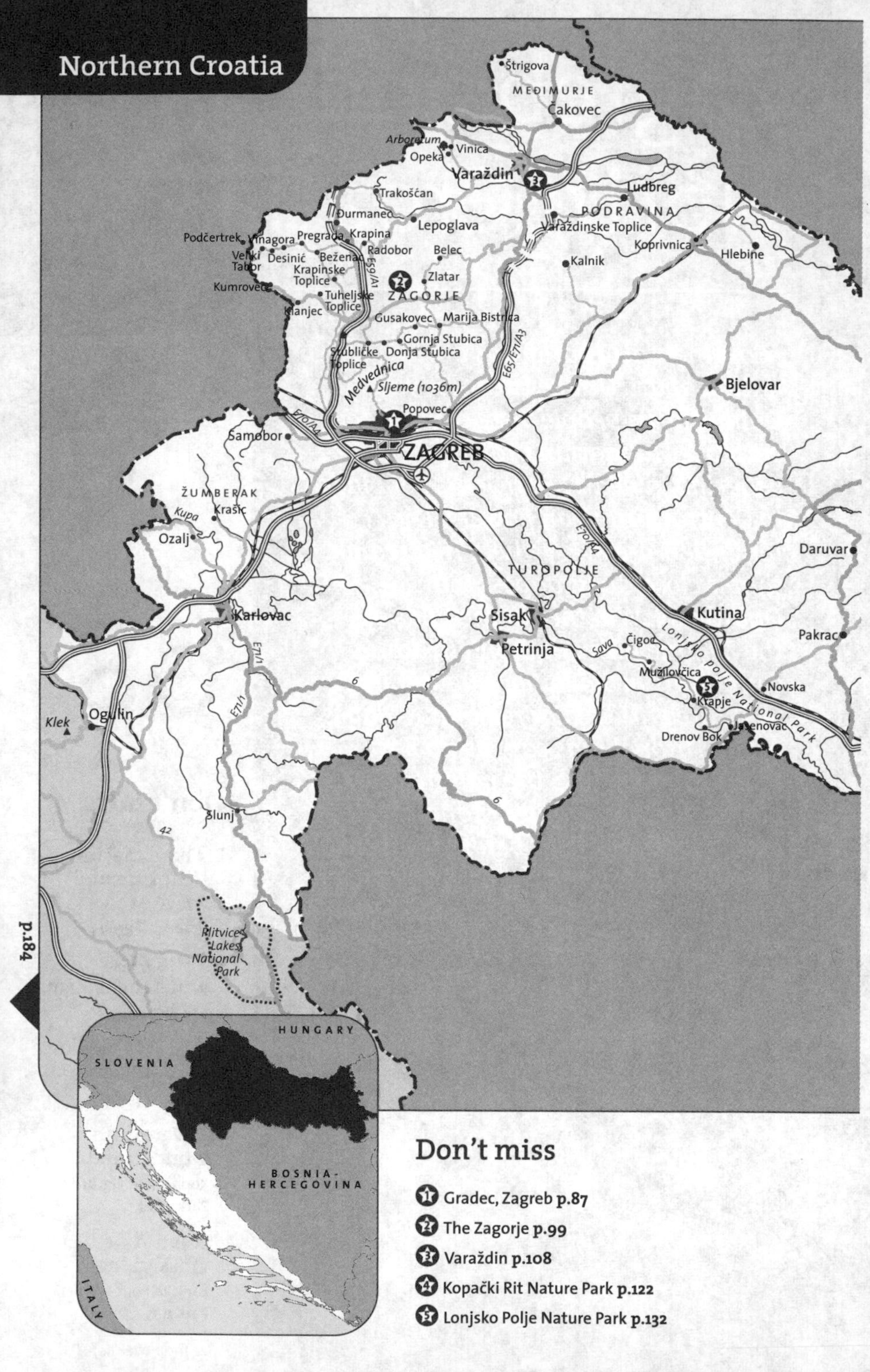
Northern Croatia
Štrigova
MEĐIMURJE
Čakovec
Arboretum
Vinica
Opeka
Varaždin
Ludbreg
Trakošćan
PODRAVINA
Đurmanec
Lepoglava
Varaždinske Toplice
Podčertrek
Vinagora
Pregrada
Krapina
Koprivnica
Hlebine
Veliki Tabor
Desinić
Radobor
Bežanec
Belec
Kalnik
Krapinske Toplice
E59/A1
Zlatar
Kumrovec
ZAGORJE
Tuheljske Toplice
Klanjec
Gusakovec
Marija Bistrica
Gornja Stubica
Stubičke Toplice
Donja Stubica
E65/E71/A3
Medvednica
Sljeme (1036m)
Bjelovar
Popovec
E70/A4
Samobor
ZAGREB
ŽUMBERAK
Kupa
Krašić
Ozalj
E70/A4
Daruvar
TUROPOLJE
Karlovac
Sisak
Kutina
E71/1
Petrinja
Sava
Čigoć
Lonjsko Polje National Park
Pakrac
Mužilovčica
Novska
6
Krapje
Klek
Ogulin
E71/1
Jasenovac
Drenov Bok
6
Slunj
42
1
Plitvice Lakes National Park
p.184
HUNGARY
SLOVENIA
BOSNIA-HERCEGOVINA
ITALY
Don't miss
1 Gradec, Zagreb p.87
2 The Zagorje p.99
3 Varaždin p.108
4 Kopački Rit Nature Park p.122
5 Lonjsko Polje Nature Park p.132

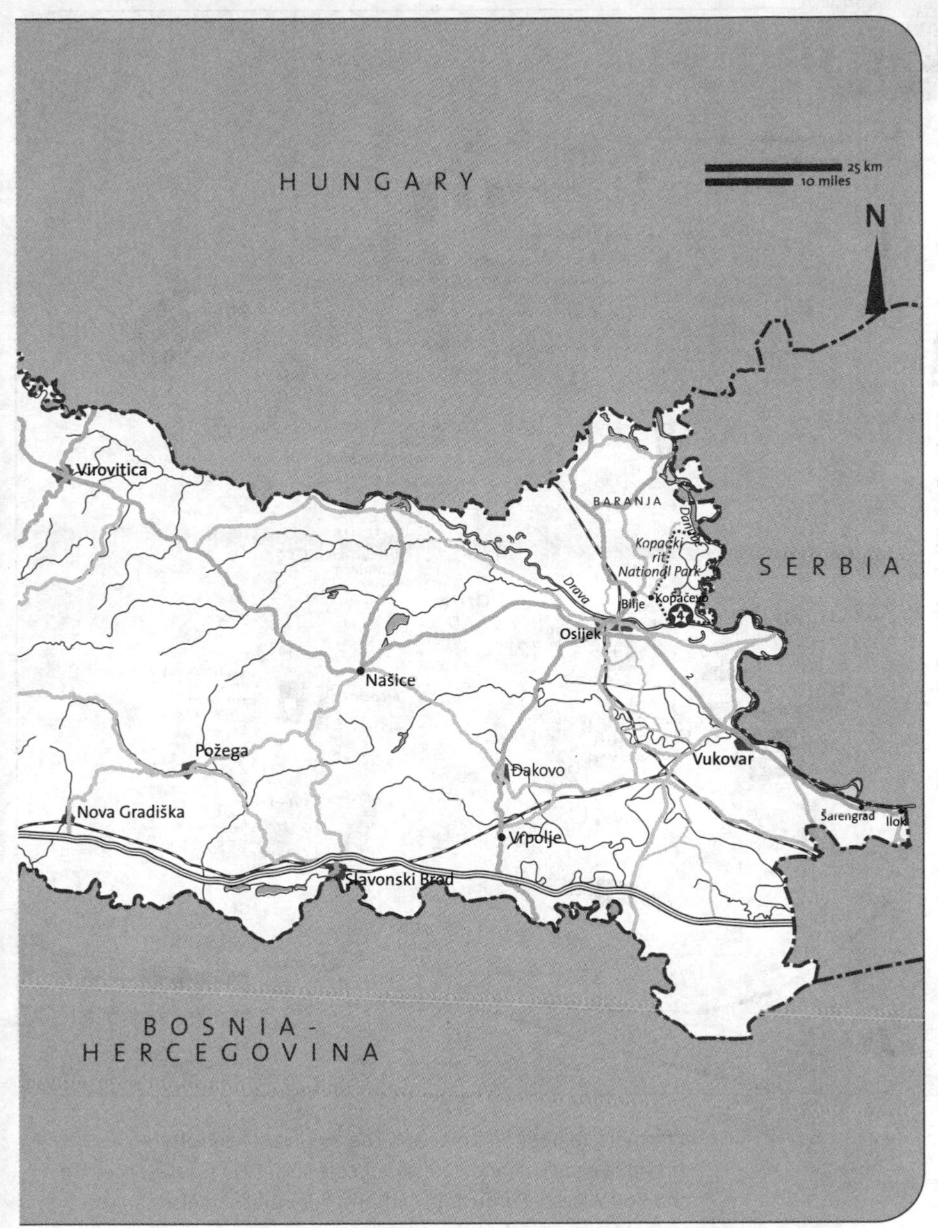

Zagreb

Few cities confess their multiple personalities as readily as Zagreb. Side by side in Croatia's contradictory capital are an enchanting Baroque kernel and a formal dollop of grandiose Mitteleuropa. Walk barely 300 yards from the bucolic patter of

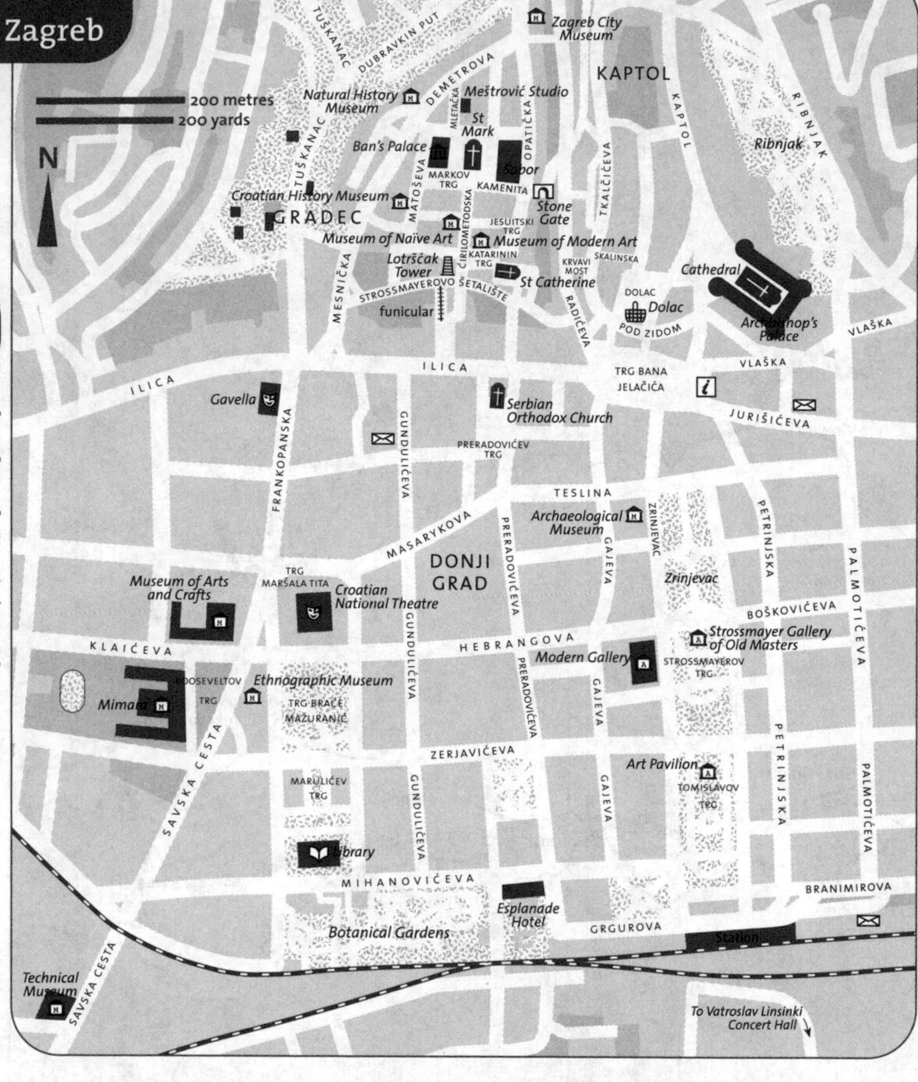

a farmers' market on Dolac and the air rings to the city-slicker gossip of a stylish (and dedicated) café society in Preradovićev trg and Bogovićeva. Confusing, perhaps, but what can else can you expect from a capital where Central Europe meets the Balkans?

Into this cultural hotpot the Mediterranean adds its own ingredient, a generous pinch of easygoing attitude which belies a headcount that hit one million some time around 2000. When Croatia goes to the polls today, nearly a quarter of its population cast their votes in the capital. Yet part of Zagreb's appeal is that you'd never know it. Whether in the well-aired grid of the

19th-century lower town or the cosy antique alleys above, whether browsing the independent shops of arterial high street Ilica or bar-hopping in the nightspots of Tkalčićeva, Zagreb is that rare breed, a capital on a human scale. A 'spiritual victory over urbanization', Rebecca West called it when she visited in the 1930s. 'From the way gossips stand in the street it is plain that everybody knows who is going to have a baby and when.'

Finally woken from the nightmare of its history, and shiny with the optimism of new prosperity at the head of a newly independent country, Zagreb still allows itself plenty of time for gossip in its cafés. And even if it can't boast the cultural colossi of some European capital, nor claim to be as dazzling or fizzy as some of its coastal cousins, it should be applauded for that.

History

Archaeologists point to finds from a late-Bronze Age settlement and evidence of 8th- and 9th-century Slavic forts on the twin hills of the upper town, but Zagreb prefers to begin its narrative in 1094, when Hungarian king Ladislas I founded a bishopric to take in hand his borders and 'return to the path of truth those who have strayed into idolatory'. An ecclesiastical community around the king's cathedral claimed and christened hillock Kaptol (a corruption of Capitolium), while a Hungarian garrison set up camp on Gradec opposite. Just over a century later, in 1242, Mongols reduced them both to smoking ruins, delivered a *coup de grâce* by stabling horses in the cathedral, then saddled up and rode out in search of fresh loot.

Doubtless King Bela IV meant well, but the Croat-Hungarian ruler's Golden Bull regeneration plan for Gradec – elevation to a royal free town in return for 10 soldiers in every battle and a bountiful dinner table on every royal visit – raised hackles in Kaptol. This was an era when the church claimed dominion over purses and politics as much as souls, and the medieval siblings bickered ceaselessly about land and customs duty. In fits of pique, Kaptol would excommunicate the entire populace of Gradec, which responded with sharp steel and fire, and the communities only put their differences aside during the two-week trade fairs that filled both their coffers three times a year. Hostilities reached a head in 1527 when the pair squabbled over claims to the Croatian throne between Ferdinand Habsburg and Hungarian king Ivan Zapolja. Gradec backed the winner, and this time it was Habsburg troops and Spanish mercenaries who looted the Kaptol bishopric.

It took the newly crowned emperor to knock heads together. When Turkish forces pressed in on all sides, the bitter foes agreed a truce and steeled themselves to face an enemy who was already camped

Getting to and around Zagreb

By Air

Domestic carrier Croatia Airlines operates services to Pula, Rijeka, Zadar, Split, Bol (Brač, summer-only) and Dubrovnik; *see* pp.56–8, for international connections.

All flights touch down at Pleso International Airport, **t** (01) 45 62 222, *www.zagreb-airport.hr*, 17km southeast of the city and linked by a Croatia Airlines bus to the main bus station (30Kn) every 30mins between 7am and 8pm and at other times to co-ordinate with flights (bus information, **t** (01) 633 1999, *www.plesoprijevoz.hr*). Expect to pay 200Kn for a taxi.

By Train

The 19th-century train station where Orient Express travellers disembarked (and James Bond met an agent in *From Russia with Love*) is at the base of Tomislavov trg, a 15min walk due south of the central square Trg bana Jelačića. Zagreb boasts a timetable that's the best in the nation, though trains remain a poor relative of buses. *See* 'Getting to...' sections for relevant destinations; *see* pp.58–9 for international routes.

By Bus

A 20min, 1km plod east along Branimirova from the train station takes you to the bus station, southeast of the city centre on Držićeva, linked to Trg bana Jelačića by tram 6. The good news is that buses from Zagreb will take you almost anywhere you want to go in Croatia: you can expect around 5 or 6 long-haul services a day to tourist favourites in all corners of the nation and hourly services to major towns such as Rijeka, Pula, Zadar and Split. Local routes are listed in relevant destinations, international links on p.59.

By Car

Driving in Zagreb is not for wimps – it's fast, aggressive and involves negotiation of an infuriating one-way system. The capital also has a parking problem, so it's worth reserving a place at your hotel. Street parking on meters (Mon–Fri 7–9, Sat 7–3) is priced by zone, with a maximum stay of 1hr in the centre and 2hr in zone two. Meters provide no change, so it's often cheaper and more convenient to buy 'Parkirna karta' tickets from newsagents and kiosks for display on the dashboard. Long-stay car parks offer better value: try those at Langov trg, at the triangle of Ribnjak a block east of the cathedral, and Nova Vas at the north end of Kaptol.

For car hire (all the major players also operate at the airport): **Hertz**, Vukotinovićeva 4, **t** (01) 48 46 777; **Budget**, Kneza Borne 2 (in the Sheraton hotel), **t** (01) 45 54 943; **Europcar**, Pierottijeva 5, **t** (01) 48 28 383; **Dollar/Thrifty**, Pleso bb, **t** (01) 62 65 333.

By Tram

The compact upper town (Gornji grad) doesn't demand top-grade shoe leather, but for rainy days and getting back to hotels public transport provider **ZET** (*www.set.hr*) runs trams between 4am and 11.45pm; in theory night trams take over in the wee hours, in practice walking can be faster than waiting and night trams represent a new route map to grapple with, as the tourist information city maps feature only a day map.

A single ticket bought from the driver costs 10Kn, or 8Kn from post offices and ZET kiosks located at major stops and termini; and a one-day ticket which lasts till 4am is 20Kn. All tickets must be validated in ticket cancellers on boarding: inspectors have heard all the excuses and simply issue on-the-spot 150Kn fines; while foreigners may receive a little leeway, they may also have their passport number taken to ensure a fine is paid within 8 days (after which it rises to 200Kn) or simply be marched to a police station via an ATM. Buy a **Zagreb Card** (*see* p.94) and you won't reach into your pocket for either 24 or 72hrs. Most trams pass through transport hub Trg bana Jelačica, just below the old town, and location of the tourist office.

By Taxi

Fleets of taxis gather outside the bus and train stations and at central ranks at the north end of Gajeva, just south of Trg bana Jelačića, and by the National Theatre on Trg maršala Tita. In theory, they charge a flat fee of 19Kn, plus 7Kn/km except at night, when 20 per cent is added to the bill. Advance bookings can be made with **Taxi 970**, **t** 060 80 08 00.

Getting to Mount Medvednica

Tram 14 from Trg bana Jelačića terminates at Mihaljevac, where you can change to a municipal bus for the summit, Sljeme; departures are every 1½hrs daily (6am–10pm). If the cable car is operational again – contact tourist information in Zagreb (*see* p.94) – tram 15 from Mihaljevac goes to Dolje, from where a short path leads to the **cable car** (signposted Žičara). Formerly, it departed on the hour from 8am to 8.30pm daily. A **footpath** from Zagreb street Dubravkin put (northwest of Gornji grad) also ascends north through wooded suburbs to Medvedgrad (*c.* 1hr 40mins).

---

on the Sava river's far bank and whose relentless advances from the north, south and east had affected both their bank balances.

With the once-powerful kingdom of Croatia whittled down to a sliver of its former size, power was centralized in Zagreb, a catch-all moniker for the twin settlements 'behind the hill' of Mount Medvednica. In 1557, it was first mentioned as capital and seat of Croat parliament the *sabor*, and by 1621 the *ban* (viceroy) had made it his permanent address. But, just as Zagreb was making itself comfortable on the nation's throne, history dealt a body blow. Plague, fire and rebellions of exasperated peasants and bit-part aristocrats compounded centuries of economic stagnation during Turkish incursions, and Habsburg empress Maria Theresa, an iron-fisted autocrat who dismissed Croatia as a mere buffer zone to keep the Ottomans at bay, turned her attention to matters closer to home. Besieged by such a battalion of sorrows, the *Sabor* shifted north to Varaždin in 1756, and had Croatia's new capital not gone up in smoke in 1776 (*see* 'Varaždin', p.109) – Zagreb could have been just another footnote in Croatian history.

Instead, given a second chance, the capital came of age. As nationalist sentiment grew in the mid-1800s, Zagreb intellectuals at the epicentre of the Croatian National Revival movement furiously penned prose and poetry to fire Slavic pride across Croatia. And, as the maturing city commissioned architects Friedrich von Schmidt and Hermann Bollé (conveniently overlooking their Austrian nationalities) to dream on to the plain below the old town all the grand architecture and tree-lined boulevards requisite for a Central European power, so it knuckled down to its responsibilities as a champion of national culture: the Academy of Arts and Sciences appeared in 1866, then in rapid succession a permanent opera and university (1870 and 1874); so impressive was the new national theatre (1890) that Emperor Franz Josef cut the ribbon.

The painful birth of Yugoslavia after the First World War simply replaced the Austro-Hungarian overlords for those in Belgrade – perhaps the reason why the first Croatian movie, *Matija Gubec* (1919), filmed here, celebrated a Peasants' Revolt leader of 1573. Nor were conditions much improved after the Second World War, during which local Communist sympathizers had nurtured nationwide resistance to Nazi stooge Ante Pavelić and his Fascist Independent State of Croatia headquartered in their midst. In name, post-war Zagreb was capital of a new socialist republic. In practice, it still played second fiddle to Belgrade. A more pressing concern for mayor Većeslav Holjevac was the inflow of rural refugees dispossessed by Communist nationalization. To accommodate the new arrivals, Zagreb infested itself with the shoddy concrete carbuncles which blight Novi Zagreb, south of the Sava, to this day.

Despite Zagreb-based movement the Croatian Spring having been a thorn in the side of the Communists since 1971, and apart from Belgrade's botched assassination attempt to blunt a president who had been one of the sharpest, Franjo Tuđman, in a 1991 air raid on the presidential offices, Zagreb emerged unscathed by the Homeland War. It could swallow the economic nosedive caused by the conflict; harder to stomach afterwards was Tuđman's skewed vision of democracy. Faced with evidence of corruption in the ranks of his Hrvatska demokratska zajednica (HDZ; Croatian Democratic Unity) Party, the capital's voters gave the president the cold shoulder in the post-conflict elections of October 1995. Never a leader to conceal his autocratic, far-right leaning, he retorted by invoking his prerogative to refuse the opposition's choice of mayor, an authoritarian streak which was far too close to the heavy-handed Communist tactics of old for many observers and which led to widescale protests.

But now, with Tuđman entombed beneath black granite in Mirogoj cemetery since December 1999, priorities have changed. Political navel-gazing is out, European partnerships are in, and gentrification has arrived, bringing with it a spread of international chain stores. Whether among the businesses which tot up balance sheets in glass-and-steel towers in the southwest financial district, or the politicos and fashionistas who gossip in cafés, Zagreb is gazing towards the European Union, which Croatia hopes to join in 2011; for the first time in centuries it is forging its own destiny.

The Upper Town (Gornji Grad): Kaptol and Gradec

Trg Bana Jelačića and Dolac

Zagreb relates that it was christened after a chance encounter between a viceroy and a local girl. '*Mandušo, zagrabi!* (scoop)' ordered the thirsty noble, pointing to the stream that ran between them. Never mind the prosaic truth that '*zagreb*' probably refers to nothing more romantic than the city's location below Mount

Medvednica, a fountain does indeed gush from the Manduševac spring now buried beneath the flagstones of **Trg bana Jelačića**, Zagreb's spiritual heart, set between the historic upper town (Gornji grad) and grand lower town (Donji grad). The square, conceived in 1641 as a marketplace for an upper city where space was at a premium, was paved by 1765, then fringed with Viennese Secession showpieces a century later to create Zagreb's equivalent of Times Square; in this main theatre for public revels, trams on seven routes rumble backstage, locals rendezvous beneath a clock tower in the wings, and at centre stage national hero *ban* Josip Jelačić charges into history.

Not that the history of the Croatian favourite is a tale of glory. Hoping to appease flickers of nationalist sentiment fanned by European revolution, the Austrian administration elevated the popular garrison commander Jelačić to *ban* in 1848, and the nation's new leader marched on anti-Habsburg forces in Hungary, hoping to curry favour for Croatian independence. But his good turn for the Habsburgs was forgotten, his demands brushed aside, though the Austrians still felt able to unveil Viennese sculptor Antun Fernkorn's wonderfully pompous bronze in the capital's heart in 1866, just seven years after Jelačić died. Nearly a century later, Josip Broz Tito was suspicious of a figure he viewed as a rabble-rouser, and in 1947 the newly declared Yugoslav president demanded the statue be removed from a square he had rechristened Trg Republike. Croatians weren't so quick to forget their glorious failure, however. Amid a crescendo of calls for Croatian independence from Yugoslavia, President Franjo Tuđman pulled off a public relations coup in 1991 when he restored the statue – now symbolically facing south to Belgrade – into a square that he had returned to its former title.

Keep your eyes high to spot a corner relief of figures with muscles like polished walnut by Croatia's finest 20th-century sculptor Ivan Meštrović as you walk north to **Dolac**. Moments from the grand airs of its main stage, Zagreb suddenly bursts out with a farmers' market that sprawls good-natured chaos across a piazza ringed by cafés and cheap-eat restaurants; fruit and vegetables, olives and nuts are piled on stalls, women in aprons hawk homemade cheeses wrapped in soggy cloths, and on a second tier stallholders tout chunky wooden toys, lacy tablecloths and embroidery.

Kaptol

The rustic sentimentality evaporates in Kaptol, northeast of Dolac. Zagreb made its debut here in 1094 as a bishopric of Hungarian king Ladislas – the hill was named after medieval canons of the cathedral chapter. The main street, still claimed by

Catholic institutions, retains an air of quiet formality thanks to a parade of Baroque erected after a fire reduced earlier buildings to ashes. Showpiece residences include Nos.9 and 28 and, at the south end, barely able to restrain its swagger, the 1730s **Archbishop's Palace**. The residence of Bishop Juraj Branjug rings the neo-Gothic **cathedral** (Katedrala Marijina Uznesenja) which follows to the letter Gothic's guiding principle of guiding eyes to heaven with two filigree spires that punctuate Zagreb's skyline like exclamation marks. Viennese architects Friedrich von Schmidt and Hermann Bollé sketched the 345ft-high steeples to crown a cathedral rebuilt after an 1880 earthquake reduced to rubble the Gothic original, itself a replacement for a Romanesque church levelled by marauding Mongols in 1242. Scraps of medieval fresco in the south aisle, nearby Renaissance choir stalls inlaid with cartoony saints and plait motifs handed down from medieval style books (incorporated today on the bands of policemen's caps), and a Baroque pulpit like a pagoda, survive in a lofty interior whose scale reveals the Austrians' aspirations for their Central European capital. Look, too, at the rear of the south aisle for the Ten Commandments on a 1941 tablet that celebrates 1,300 years of Croatian Christianity in an alien-looking Glagolitic script (*see* **Topics**, pp.40–1) – and also in the north aisle for Archbishop Alojzije Stepinac, who kneels ecstatic before Christ in a Meštrović relief which marks his tomb. In 1988 the late Pope John Paul II beatified the Croatian church leader, whose criticism of oppression under Tito's newly empowered partisans earned him 16 years' hard labour until the regime shifted him from prison to house arrest in December 1951. His effigy reclines in a glass sarcophagus behind the altar. Far more cheerful are Fernkorn's gilded *Virgin and Child*, who swoon on a pillar before the cathedral.

Outside, you can walk around the former **ramparts** which abut Vlaška. A section of 15th-century **defence wall**, that ringed a cathedral then on Christianity's ramparts as Europe's most easterly church, borders Ribnjak park to the northeast. Grassy scoops recall the 'fishponds' that christened it.

From Tkalčićeva into Gradec

When engineers filled a stream in 1898, Potok (brook) became **Tkalčićeva** and preserved a villagey street of 18th- and 19th-century houses to give camera-shutter fingers cramp; a parade of lovingly restored town houses once owned by workers in a street of textile mills. Today this is prime bar-hopping territory, and on warm summer evenings there's almost no space to stroll. Off the south end of Tkalčićeva, **Blood Bridge** (Krvavi most) recalls the vicious border wars between formative settlements Kaptol and Gradec (*see* below). Bloody skirmishes were commonplace as the sacred and secular rivals wrestled to be the local power.

Krvavi most links Tkalčićeva to parallel **Radićeva**, at the northern end of which is the **stone gate** (Kamenita vrata). The sole survivor of a quartet of town wall gateways has found its second wind as a shrine for a 16th-century statue of the Virgin, found without a singe among the ashes of a gate destroyed by a 1731 blaze, and who now quietly works miracles from a niche. Or so walls covered in plaques exclaiming *Hvala Marijo* (Thank you, Mary) entreat you to believe; an ever-present congregation testifies to the locals' enduring affection.

Beyond is **Gradec**, a genteel district of Baroque alleys and squares that barely recalls its roots as the Hungarian garrison town King Béla IV of Hungary rebuilt after the 1240s Mongol rout, then fattened up into a royal free town. You can also enter its pocket of lanes via a funicular off Ilica (*see* below). Just beyond the stone gate is Croatia's second-oldest **pharmacy** on the corner of Kamenita vrata – Dante's grandson Niccolò Alighieri once dispensed cures from this mid-1300s chemist's shop.

Markov Trg

The physical and symbolic heart of Gradec, Markov trg seems far too charming to be Croatia's political power base. While other parliament buildings aspire to induce awe, the **Sabor** on the east flank reveals itself as a modest palace (1910); from its balcony, Croatia declared emancipation from Austro-Hungarian rule on 1 December 1918, and behind its stately neoclassical façade politicians ratified the 25 June 1991 split from the Socialist Yugoslav republic. Retaliation came on 7 October 1991, when Yugoslav jets dropped bombs on the **Ban's Palace** (Banski dvori) opposite, the government administrative and reception building fashioned from two Baroque palaces for Habsburg-appointed Croatian viceroys. The Yugoslav republic's clumsy attempt to assert authority – and, say some observers, to assassinate Croatian president Franjo Tuđman – only prompted Croatia to sever all links with Belgrade, but then, the square has always been a venue for expressions of political might. Here in 1573 peasant revolutionary 'king' Matija Gubec was crowned with a band of white-hot iron before he was quartered; local lore claims the stone head which gazes mournfully from the corner of Ćirilometodska on the south side of Markov trg is his portrait.

For all the square's elegant Baroque buildings, none stands a chance beside the explosion of colour on centrepiece **St Mark's Church** (Crkva svetoga Marka). The Austrians unwittingly created a

Zagreb icon when they patterned ceramic roof tiles into two coats of arms: a united shield of the Kingdom of Croatia (red and white check), Dalmatia (three lions) and Slavonia (a marten); and the city of Zagreb. Their shot of cultural adrenaline, injected during rigorous renovation in the 1880s, was just the latest in a history of home improvements which also added an awkward Baroque tower to the 13th-century parish church christened after the St Mark's Day fairs held in Gradec's main square; a snapshot of the Gothic original remains on a south portal crowded with biblical bigwigs. Inside, gloomy Croat kings strike a pose among biblical personalities in muscular 1930s frescoes by painter Jozo Kljaković, and the ever-present Meštrović adds powerful Crucifixion and Pietà bronzes.

Around Katarinin Trg

Museum of Naïve Art
*Hrvatski muzej navine umjetnosti; **t** (01) 48 51 911, www.hmnu.org; open Tues–Fri 10–6, Sat–Sun 10–1; adm*

South on Ćirilometodska is the quirky **Museum of Naïve Art**. Enthused by Rousseau-esque concepts of 'primitive' integrity, Professor Krsto Hegedušić mentored self-taught daubers in the Slavonian village of Hlebine (*see* pp.117–18) to form the 'Hlebine School', demeaned as 'peasant' then 'primitive' art until Croatian politicians proposed the more flattering 'naïve' in 1994. Although not the cerebral fare of expressionism or surrealism, despite the museum's protests, there is still much to admire in glass-on-oil works by Ivan Generalić, as vivid and fizzy as cartoon cell acetates. The Hegedušić protégé's bucolic scenes of fairytale whimsy are far more charming than second-generation superstar Ivan Večenaj – thick globs of blood and tortured trees in *Evangelists on Calvary* are the stuff of which Grimm nightmares are made. Look, too, for works by Ivan Lacković Croata, a star among later Hlebine painters, whose lapses into twee melancholy are forgivable for his exquisite draughtsmanship.

Lotršćak Tower
Kula Lotršćak; open Tues–Sun 11–8; adm

Ćirilometodska opens into **Katarinin trg**, guarded on the south by the **Lotršćak Tower**, a relic of 13th-century defences named for the 'Robbers' bell which rang to warn locals of city closing time. A yarn relates that a cannonball loosed from the Romanesque tower at Turkish forces camped across the Sava river obliterated the pasha's chicken dinner and so demoralized the prince that he had second thoughts about raising his scimitar against Zagreb. Never mind that Ottoman forces never launched an assault on the capital (although they razed villages on the other side of the Sava during the mid-1500s), a cannon has blasted above rooftops at midday sharp since 1876 – be warned, it's loud. The tower also provides temporary art exhibitions and superlative views from its turret, just topping those from promenade **Strossmayerovo šetalište**

Funicular
runs every 10mins 6am–midnight; 4Kn

Museum of Contemporary Art
Muzej suvremene umjetnosti; www.mdc.hr/msu; closed at present; consult tourist office (p.94) for up-to-date information

below. In front of the tower is the terminus of Zagreb's **funicular** from Ilica; its dinky carriages first huffed up by steam in 1871.

The excellent **Museum of Contemporary Art** on the north side of Katarinin trg is closed pending a move to new premises in Novi Zagreb by 2010.

Closing the east side is Jesuit **St Catherine's Church** (Crkva svete Katarine), modelled on Rome's Il Gesù in 1620. Its outward public decorum drops no hint of the bewitching interior; walls are iced with sugar-sweet pink and white stucco in intimation of spiritual ecstasy through decorative excess in Zagreb's Baroque treasure. Concerts of classical music here are a joy. Almost overpowered by the candy walls, frescoes of Catherine with the pagan philosophers she dared to out-debate play *trompe l'œil* tricks behind the main altar; his war of words lost, furious Emperor Maxentius answered the patron saint's impudence by torturing her on the spiked wheel she holds outside, and which christened the spinning Catherine Wheel firework.

Galerija Klovićevi Dvori
t (01) 48 51 926, www.galerijaklovic.hr; open Tues–Sun 10–8; adm

After nearly two centuries of being press-ganged into military service until 1945, Baroque **Jesuit monastery** the Klovićevi dvori on adjacent Jezuitski trg is enjoying its freedom as a **gallery** for international blockbusters and a lovely courtyard venue for concerts of the Zagreb Summer Festival.

North of Markov Trg

Croatian History Museum
Hrvatski povijesni muzej, t (01) 48 51 900, www.hismus.hr; open Mon–Fri 10–5, Sat–Sun 10–1; adm

17 Meštrović Atelier
Atelje Meštrovic; Mletačka 8; t (01) 48 51 123, www.mdc.hr/mestrovic; open Tues–Fri 10–6, Sat–Sun 10–2–6; adm

Croatian Natural History Museum
Hrvatski prirodoslovni muzej; open Tues–Fri 10–5, Thurs till 10pm, Sat 10–7, Sun 10–1; adm

One block west of Gradec's central square, on Matoševa, the ritzy Baroque Rauch mansion is a suitably grand setting for questions of Croatian history posed by temporary exhibitions in the **Croatian History Museum**. The doyenne of Gradec museums, however, is the **Meštrović Atelier**. Flushed by the success of the first one-man show in the Victoria and Albert Museum in London, Croatia's finest modern sculptor treated himself to the Mletačka town house in which he crafted 20 years of bronzes – including the bronze Indians in Chicago's Grand Central Park – until persecution by Ustaše Fascists forced him into exile in America in 1942. Even models of more swaggering public works relax in the house, which preserves Meštrović's dusky frescoes and furniture. The sculptor who shaped swaggering Croat icons such as Bishop Grgur Ninski in Split, on show in miniature as a study, also reveals unexpected tenderness in a lovely bronze of his second wife Olga breast-feeding their son Tvrtko. It's a treat – not something which can always be said of the stuffed mammals and geology displays in the **Croatian Natural History Museum** a block north on Demetrova. There's an enjoyably musty corridor of *fin-de-siècle* specimen jars and the world's largest haul of Neanderthal finds, unearthed in Krapina (*see* pp.103–4).

Zagreb City Museum
*Muzej grada Zagreba; Opatička 20, **t** (01) 48 51 361, www.mgz.hr; open Tues–Fri 10–6, Thurs till 10, Sat 11–7, Sun 10–2; adm*

Last up in this cultural quarter, squirrelled away in the back streets is the **Zagreb City Museum**, which chronicles local history from days when Zagreb was a twinkle in the eye of 7th-century BC settlers to modern triumph in the Homeland War, in the 17th-century Convent of the Poor Clares. Rooms that re-create 19th-century shops from high street Ilica or famous artists' studios are particularly appealing. And, for once, captions that describe the museum's various artworks and weapons, costumes and city models are also in English.

The Lower Town (Donji Grad)

After the *rubato* of winding alleys in the upper town, Donji grad comes on as strict four-four time due to its grid of streets planned by late 19th-century Habsburgs, one element in their aspiration to elevate Zagreb into a cultured city that could hold its own among European capitals, a sort of metropolitan *My Fair Lady*. The pencil of urban architect Milan Lenuci didn't stray far from the ruler, but he softened his formal plan with a U of leafy squares dubbed, inevitably, Lenuci's Green Horseshoe.

From Trg Bana Jelačića to Zrinjevac

The border of the Lower Town is **Ilica**, Zagreb's longest street and shopping parade. Dive south as it blasts west from Trg bana Jelačića and you reach **Preradovićev trg**, christened in honour of romantic poet Petar Preradović at its centre but nicknamed Cvjetni trg (flower square). A few lonely florists' stalls recall the now-banished market in a square abuzz with the gossip of a dedicated café society – visit at weekends and it seems all Zagreb has descended to sup and pose here and in adjacent Bogovićeva. On the north side is the **Serbian Orthodox Church**, its congregation seriously depleted by recent history, its interior scented by incense and full of shimmering icons steeped in mystery.

Lenuci confesses his hankering after the elegant parks of European *grandes dames* in his first green creation, **Zrinjevac**, two or three blocks to the southeast. *Fin-de-siècle* strollers who took the air probably marvelled at the reinvention of a cattle fairground into a handsome park (1872) where you can almost hear the swish of Sunday-best silk skirts or the click of ebony walking canes. Structure in late 19th-century Zagreb's favourite promenade comes from busts of Croatian luminaries, a wrought-iron bandstand and a bizarre fountain like stacked gyroscopes, a whim of Hermann Bollé, freed from the architectural straitjacket of the neo-Gothic cathedral. A daffodil-yellow paint-job highlights the **Archaeological Museum** on the park's west flank. Despite impressive national

Archaeological Museum
*Arheološki muzej; Trg Nikole Šubića Zrinskog 19, **t** (01) 48 73 101, www.amz.hr; open Tues–Fri 10–5, Thurs till 10, Sat–Sun 10–1; adm*

artefacts which start at prehistory and peter out at invasion by medieval Tartars, the crowds clot the two rooms of Egyptian mummies, one prized for the world's longest script of Etruscan text, inked on bands that cocooned the body. The star exhibit is far more modest: so highly does Croatia treasure the *Vučedol Dove*, a tubby bird-shaped vessel crafted by Bronze Age settlers near Vukovar, Slavonia, that it is celebrated on the 20Kn note. The courtyard café doubles as a Roman lapidarium.

Strossmayerov Trg and Tomislavov Trg

At the centre of the park is the **Academy of Science and Art**, a brick pile founded in 1884 by Bishop Juraj Strossmayer in between denouncing papal infallibility (in the end he grudgingly commended the pope's 'remarkably good Latin') and promoting Croatian nationalism (he argued that its tinder box of resentments was preferable to foreign rule); Meštrović portrays the benefactor behind his creation, his head crowned by tufts of hair like Mercurial wings. Later acquisitions have expanded the bishop's private gallery to 120 canvases and turned it into the **Strossmayer's Gallery of Old Masters**, whose star players are Venetians such as Tintoretto, Bellini and Carpaccio. Brueghel and van Dyck fly the flag for the Flemish, and El Greco adds a dainty *Mary Magdalene*. Security guards will permit you to ponder for free the *Baška tablet* (*c*.1100) in the foyer; Croatia's most celebrated slab, etched in the unusual liturgical script Glagolitic (*see* pp.40–1), was discovered on the island of Krk (*see* p.207).

Strossmayer's Gallery of Old Masters
Strossmayerova galerija starih majstora; **t** *(01) 48 95 117, www.mdc.hr/strossmayer; open Tues 10–1 and 5–7, Wed–Sun 10–1; adm*

Zigzag west and the **Modern Gallery** on the corner of Hebrangova has reopened, after protracted renovation, with temporary exhibitions of Croatian art from 1850 to 1950 in 16 rooms. There are more in the **Art Pavilion**. One of the pioneers among European prefab buildings, moved brick by iron girder to Zagreb two years after it was showcased at the Budapest Millennium Exhibition in 1896, it now hosts passing exhibitions. You can't miss it – it's canary-yellow. Yet more art – mostly modern – is in the **Croatian Association of Artists** on Trg Žrtava Fašizma, east of here along Ruđera Boškovića. As intriguing as the contemporary exhibitions is the building itself, a creamy limestone rotunda designed by Meštrović.

Modern Gallery
Moderna galerija, **t** *(01) 49 22 368; open Tues–Sat 10–6, Sun 10–1; adm*

Art Pavilion
Umjetnički paviljon, **t** *(01) 48 41 070, www.umjetnicki-paviljon.hr; open Mon–Sat 11–7, Sun 10–1; adm*

Croatian Association of Artists
HDLU, **t** *(01) 46 11 818, www.hdlu.hr; open Tues–Fri 11–7, Sat–Sun 10–2; adm*

The south arm of the park is the manicured lawn of **Tomislavov trg**, named in salute to the first king of the fledgling Croatian state. The 10th-century ruler brandishes his sceptre southwards at the neoclassical train station, which was briefly in Europe's spotlight when royalty, diplomats and the bourgeoisie en route to Istanbul disembarked from the Orient Express. Those high rollers bedded down in the **Hotel Regent Esplanade** (*see* p.95) moments west of the station, whose luxurious Art Deco foyer remains the 'triumph of architecture and crafts' it was lauded as, when its doors opened in April 1923. Appropriately, the hotel's first registered guest was a Herr Glück (Mr Luck).

Botanical Gardens, Technical Museum and Ethnographic Museum

Botanical Gardens
Botanički vrt; Mihanovićeva; open Mon–Tues 9–2.30, Wed–Sun 9–6

For an intermission in the lower town's high culture-fest, there's the **Botanical Gardens** at the base of Lenuci's horticultural horseshoe (*see* p.88), with naturalistic gardens and pea-green ponds speckled by waterlilies. State archives now fill the former **university library** opposite, an architectural hotch-potch, with window stripes and stern owls shouldering globes, toys with Viennese Secession. **Marulićev trg**, behind, honours Split Renaissance poet Marko Marulić, who penned the first epic in Croatian, *Judita*. Not that you'd guess from the bronze by Meštrović – the author slumps in an armchair as if dozing after a heavy lunch.

Technical Museum
Tehnički muzej; ***t*** *(01) 48 44 050, www.mdc.hr/tehnicki; open Tues–Fri 9–5, Sat–Sun 9–1; adm.* ***Mine shaft:*** *guided tours Tues–Fri 3, Sat–Sun 11.* ***Study of Nikola Tesla:*** *guided tours Tues–Fri 3.30, Sat–Sun 11.30.* ***Planetarium:*** *guided tours Tues–Fri 4, Sat–Sun 12*

Never mind official opening hours, the **Technical Museum**, on Savska, a detour southwest, is all about timing. Plan carefully and you can explore historic fire engines, central Europe's oldest driving machines and a hall crammed with the usual modes of transport – automobiles, aeroplanes, a dinky submarine swiped from the Italians in 1942 – before you join tours which: burrow into a 1,000ft **mine shaft**; conduct electricity experiments in a mock-up **study of Nikola Tesla**, a Croatian-born Serbian inventor who pioneered the alternating current (Tesla coils still power many radio sets) and whose theories about a ray capable of obliterating a 10,000-strong squadron at 250 miles made him a favourite with sensationalist editors; or star-gaze in a **planetarium**. A dry section on geology is highly missable if you're pushed for time.

Ethnographic Museum
Etnografski muzej; ***t*** *(01) 48 26 220, www.etnografski-muzej.hr; open Tues–Thurs 10–6, Fri–Sun 10–1; adm*

North, the penultimate building block of Lenuci's horseshoe Trg braće Mažuranić is home to the **Ethnographic Museum**, with African sculptures and sleepy Buddhas brought home as souvenirs by explorers in the late 1800s, but best visited for displays which delve into Croatia's own corners: lace like spider's webs from the island of Pag; Sunday-best folk costumes which celebrate the country's cultural mishmash; and ritzy Slavonian scarves threaded with gold.

Mimara Museum
t *(01) 48 28 100, www.mimara.hr; open July–Sept Tues–Fri 10–7, Sat 10–5, Sun 10–2; Oct–June Tues–Sat 10–5, Thurs till 7, Sun 10–2*

Mimara Museum, Art and Crafts Museum and Trg Maršala Tita

If the small fleet of school group coaches on Rooseveltov trg doesn't give the game away, the imposing neo-Renaissance building declares the **Mimara Museum** the heavyweight of Zagreb (and Croatian) museums, stuffed with the private treasures amassed by Ante Topić Mimara. Possibly. Intrigue still surrounds not only the art collector's identity – some claim the Dalmatian peasant-farmer's son adopted 'Mimara' as a *nom de plume* while studying under Italian portrait painter Antonio Mancini, others that Mirko Maratović stole the identity of First World War battlefield victim Ante Topić, then tagged on Mimara as a sly nod to his own name – but also how the shadowy art collector acquired such a rich century-spanning collection. 'The master swindler of Yugoslavia,' hiss critics, alluding to allegations that Mimara used a post-war ruse of Yugoslav repatriation to swipe art snatched by the Nazi élite. Other art detectives list forgery alongside theft on Mimara's crime sheet. Either way, the flamboyant collector donated his hoard to the nation and was paid royally by a government convinced it had struck a bargain for a 3,600-strong *œuvre* of canvases and *objets d'art* it valued at a billion dollars. In 1987, the ribbon was snipped, champagne corks flew and the Zagreb Louvre opened its doors, only for critics to denounce as fakes many of its Michelangelos, Rembrandts and Botticellis. Croatian authorities are reluctantly addressing the claims, and many canvases have been downgraded to 'School of...' to be on the safe side. Of course, the museum holds no truck with such slander, and sets aside a top-floor homage to its benefactor, who smiles from his death mask (and no wonder since the government threw a Zagreb penthouse into the deal). And whatever the truth, there's an astonishing range of art and objects here. Ancient Egyptian glass, Persian rugs and Far East objects spice the ground floor with exotica while above china and fiddly ivory reliquary boxes feature in a millennium of European applied arts. The disputed artworks are on the second floor – big-name canvases which span from almond-eyed Byzantine icons to French Impressionists such as Renoir and Manet, genuine or otherwise.

Museum of Arts and Crafts
Muzej za umjetnost i obrt; **t** *(01) 48 82 111, www.muo.hr; open Tues–Sat 10–7, Sun 10–2; adm*

There are no authenticity problems in the **Museum of Arts and Crafts** a block north. Its stylistic tour through the decorative arts begins in the 1400s with stolid Gothic furniture, then perks up in rooms crammed with frothy Renaissance objects. Don't miss a Mary altar from the village of Remetinec in a room of devotional sculpture – statuettes of the willowy Virgin are a press release of her good deeds; building cathedrals, protecting lambs, etc. – before you inspect heavy historicism inspired by Austria and Italy above. Arts and Crafts furniture and elegant Tiffany lamps, plus a gallery of 1960s poster art, provide light relief. Worth a peek in their own right are the atrium and staircase of the museum's ritzy neo-Renaissance palace, a design of the ever-industrious Hermann Bollé. The museum flanks the west side of **Trg maršala Tita**, western tip of Lenuci's horseshoe and a square with a swaggering centrepiece, the **Croatian National Theatre**. Viennese architects sketched its columns and cupolas in 1894, then knocked up the neo-Baroque pile at a lightning pace to impress Emperor Franz Josef, who cut the ribbons at the 1895 opening. Overlooked but more enchanting before it is Meštrović's sculpture *Well of Life* (1905) – it's no surprise that its luxurious eroticism came from the imagination of a 22-year-old student.

Outside the Centre

Maksimir Park and Lake Jarun

Maksimir Park
3km east of the centre; trams 12 and 7 (heading to Dubrava), 11 and 12 (to Dubec) from Trg bana Jelačića

Ask about the easiest escape from city centre summer crowds and most locals will direct you to **Maksimir Park** or the artificial lake of Jarun. Closer to the centre, 20mins' tram ride east, lies the park. Zagreb archbishop Maksimilijan Vrhovac gets his name on the map for creating the first public promenade in southeast Europe, a modest French-style garden in 1784. But the real debt is owed to his successor. Enamoured by naturalistic English-style gardens, Archbishop Juraj Haulik incorporated an existing oak wood and expanded the 45-acre progenitor to create today's 780-acre expanse of meadows, woods and lakes, perfect for a stroll. If there are better places for a summer picnic, Zagreb is keeping them secret.

Zoo
t (01) 23 02 198, www.zoo.hr; open daily summer 9–4, winter 9–3; adm

An avenue of trees channels arrow-straight alleys past Croatia's largest **zoo** and adjacent 19th-century whimsy the **Echo Pavilion** towards romantic belvedere building the **Vidikovac** (1843), now a café with a view – expect to wait for a table at weekends. A contemporary **Swiss chalet** nestles among woods nearby, while thick woods and less-populated meadows are reached by taking paths north of the belvedere.

Lake Jarun
4km southwest of the centre; trams 17 and 5 (to Prečko or Jarun) from Trg bana Jelačića and Kvaterinkov trg respectively; get off at Staglišće or Jarun

During the breathless days of high summer, head instead to the cool waters of **Lake Jarun**. Even if local nickname 'the sea' is rose-tinted for a 2km long lake scooped out beside the river Sava for the 1987 World University Games, a shingle beach and string of cafés and restaurants on the south shore have a coastal-resort fizz on sun-soaked summer weekends. Bring a towel, too – there's fine bathing in sheltered waters.

Mirogoj Cemetery
2km northeast of the centre; bus 106 from the cathedral or tram 14 east (to Mihaljevac) from Trg bana Jelačića, then 10min walk from Gupčeva zvijezda (stop 4)

Mirogoj Cemetery

So beautiful is one of Europe's finest cemeteries, goes the quip, its occupants fare better than some of the living. Hermann Bollé would be quietly thrilled. The architect who designed much of Zagreb's Habsburg-era cityscape turned his attentions to a burial ground for the expanding city in 1876 and created a fortress-like necropolis whose walls are crowned with cupolas and pierced by a gateway which tempers sombre stolidity with grace. Don't be put off – Mirogoj's leafy park is a serene spot with mixed-denomination tombs; Communist partisans honoured with five-pointed stars lie beside Orthodox Jews named in Cyrillic, and Muslim headstones like obelisks lie next to Christian. Family mausoleums beneath evocative colonnades on either side of the entrance feature funerary sculpture carved by some of Croatia's finest: Ivan Rendić's 1872 mourner in billowing skirts, who lays a flower on the simple sarcophagus of Slavophile poet Petar Preradović (he of the central square); or the stooped Jewish patriarchs that Robert Frangeš Mihanović shaped for the Mayer family vault. Famous deceased include Stjepan Radić, Croatian Peasant Party founder whose demands for national independence were silenced by an assassin's bullet in the Belgrade parliament, and Croatia's first non-aristocrat *ban* (viceroy), Ivan Mažuranić. And then there's Franjo Tuđman; church bells tolled countrywide and jets flew over Mirogoj in December 1999 when Croatia's first president was entombed in a black granite crypt on the doorstep of the Christ the King Church.

Mount Medvednica

The nature playground in Zagreb's back garden is 'Bear Mountain'. On summer Sundays, an army of Zagreb pensioners dons walking boots to tramp thickly wooded slopes while families idle in meadows over a picnic, and in winter skiers swish down slopes (ski hire available at Sljeme summit). Be warned: the nature park, protected by parliamentary decree since 1981, is also Croatia's busiest at weekends.

The uplands lie just free of Zagreb's northern suburbs (easily combined with a visit to Mirogoj cemetery) and were once linked by a 4km cable car; formerly operated by municipal transport provider ZET, it was suspended indefinitely at the time of writing but consult the tourist office (p.97) for current details. In its place is a bus service (*see* 'Getting to Mount Medvednica', p.81); or you can reach the 1,100m summit on a footpath from the lower cable car terminus (approx 2hrs). You can't miss the top – a TV tower spikes the summit despite the best efforts of the Yugoslavian People's Army in 1991. From here an adjacent belvedere provides a sensational panorama north over the Zagorje, a fairytale carpet of villages and forest which on gin-clear days stretches to the Slovenian Alps.

Shrine of Our Lady of Sljeme
Sljemenska kapelica; open Tues, Thurs, Sat and Sun 11–3

Turn right from the cable car's upper terminus and across a steep meadow is the boxy **Shrine of Our Lady of Sljeme**, which sports quotes from Byzantine, Romanesque and Gothic, an academic's 1932 salute to a millennium of Croatian Christianity.

Fortress Medvedgrad
open daily 7–10

Fortress Medvedgrad provides different views over Zagreb and a goal for exploration 5km southwest of Sljeme. If the chunky medieval fortification seems a mite immaculate it's because Croatia celebrated its emancipation from Yugoslavia by rebuilding a stronghold against Mongol raids to support the Shrine of the Homeland, a modern glass-and-stone altar where a flame burns to heroes who fell for Croatian liberty. To save a return to Sljeme, a road threads downhill to suburb Šestine, from where bus 102 trundles back to Zagreb centre.

ⓘ Zagreb ›
Trg bana Jelačića 11, **t** *(01) 48 14 051/052/054, www.zagreb-touristinfo.hr; open Mon–Fri 8.30–8, Sat 9–5, Sun 10–2*

Tourist Information in Zagreb

The helpful central **tourist information office** provides excellent free city maps, can book hotels and entertainment tickets and sells the **Zagreb Card** (24hr, 60Kn; 72hr, 90Kn; also from most hotels), a three-day pass for public transport plus 50% discounts on museum entries and 10–20% reductions in selected shops and on car hire.

Addresses

Be aware that inconsistency between maps and street signs is the rule rather than the exception in Zagreb, whose casual disregard for a standard between colloquial names (on maps and postal addresses) and official names (on street signs) demands intuition from visitors; for example, eastern park Strossmayerov trg is interpreted on the ground as Trg Josipa Jurja Strossmayera, north–south street Gajeva is rendered on street signs as Ulica Ljudevita Gaja, and Trg Nikole Šubića Zrinskog becomes, bewilderingly, Zrinjevac. Good luck.

Festivals

Zagreb enjoys itself in summer. Trg bana Jelačića is centre stage of the **Folklore Festival** (Međunarodna smotra folklora, *www.msf.hr*), a five-day jamboree over the last or penultimate weekend in July, when Croatian folk groups, plus a few international acts, twirl and toot in colourful costume.

More highbrow music and dance are provided by: the **Contemporary Dance Week** in the first week of June; the **Summer Festival** which woos international stars of classical music between mid-July and mid-August; and the **Zagreb Biennial**, which celebrates contemporary classical music every odd-numbered year.

Shopping

Central high street **Ilica** lays out a window display of independents and chain stores in *fin-de-siècle* shop-fronts. Fashion boutiques plus the occasional antiques shop and gallery line **Radićeva**, which extends north off **Trg bana Jelačića**. For example, **Galerija Bil Ani**, Radićeva 37, pioneered in Croatia the Lilliputian ceramic models of streets and buildings of Zagreb, Dalmatia and Istria.

For more fashions, explore smart boutiques in grand arcade the **Oktagon** off Ilica, or go to **Croata**, Kaptol 13, and pick up a silk tie from the country of its birth: inspired by the neckwear of a crack Croat regiment he inspected in 1635, fashion-conscious French king Louis XIV knotted bright silk handkerchiefs '*à la Hrvat* (Croat)', and cravats caught on.

Foodies should sample Dalmatian *pršut* (prosciutto), sold by the slice (or leg), and browse a wonderland of tasty treats – fiery *rakija*, olive oils, sheep's cheeses from Pag island – at

Natura Croatica, Preradocićeva 8, and **Devin**, Hebrangova 23. Fine Croatian wines are available from exclusive *vinoteka* **Bornstein**, Kaptol 19; grasiner, kraviner and chardonnay plonks of local vineyards come straight from the barrel at a cellar *vinarija* opposite (Kaptol 14) – bring an empty water bottle if you want to take some home. **Alorgitam**, Gajeva 1, stocks a passable range of international media and books. Nearby Croatia Records, Bogovićeva 5, has all the CDs of Croatian crooners and rock bands you could wish for, alongside some international acts.

Markets

A daily market on **Dolac** (*7–3*) hides folksy traditional fabrics, wicker baskets and charming, naïve wooden toys beyond its fruit and veg, and a Sunday antique and flea market (*8–2*) on **Britanski trg**, off Ilica, is all tatty, cheerful fun. Early birds can even pick up a bargain.

★ Regent Esplanade >>

Football

Croatia's most successful football team, **Dinamo Zagreb** (*www.nk-dinamo.hr*), a regular name in the Champion's League tournament, play in the 40,000 Maksimir Stadion opposite the eponymous park east of the centre (tram 12). Tickets for Saturday games can be picked up from the gate for as little as 30Kn in a season that runs from mid-August to late-May, with a two-month break from January. The stadium also hosts Croatian international games – advance purchase from the tourist office is a must.

Where to Stay in Zagreb

Put this on the expense account, because Zagreb accommodation is not cheap. Budget hotels are in short supply and their few rooms are snapped up quickly in peak season. Hotels are clustered south of the centre around the train station and unless you pay the top rate are generally uninspiring, business-orientated ones.

Expensive (€€€)

Arcotel Allegra, Branimirova 29, **t** (01) 46 96 000, *www.arcotel.at/allegra*. From Austrian chain Arcotel, Zagreb's first design hotel has streamlined design and colourful fabrics with funky portraits of big names in arts and philosophy. The target market is business executives who like high-tech toys – all the rooms boast flat-screen TVs, DVD and CD players and internet connections.

Palace, Strossmayerov trg 10, **t** (01) 48 14 611, *www.palace.hr*. Not in the same league as the Regent Esplanade, but the oldest hotel in Central Europe, Orson Welles's favourite in Yugoslavia that was created from a central 1891 palace, has a reassuringly stuffy appeal, its lobby all vintage walnut panelling, brass fittings and leather chairs. Elegant rooms are modernized to four-star standard and have marble bathrooms.

Regent Esplanade, Mihanovićeva 1, **t** (01) 45 66 666, *www.regenthotels.com*. A lengthy refurbishment has done nothing to dilute the glamour of this Zagreb *grande dame*, fashioned to serve the Orient Express and whose marble lobby is fit for an Agatha Christie whodunnit. Luxurious rooms (de luxe are worth the extra money) maintain the nostalgia: fabrics are delicious shades of plum and moss, and rich chocolate woods are lit with hints of gilt. Croatian–Mediterranean fusion food in restaurant Zinfandel's is first-class and Zagreb locals say the *štrukli* of its bistro is the best in town. The connoisseur's choice.

Sheraton Zagreb, Kneza Borne 2, **t** (01) 45 53 535, *www.sheraton.com*. Five-star facilities in a hotel that's everything you expect of the American chain; it's pricey – as expensive as the Regent Esplanade without the bygone glamour – but reliable.

Moderate (€€)

Central, Branimirova 3, **t** (01) 48 41 122, *www.hotel-central.hr*. Unspectacular but competitively priced businessman's choice 50yds east of the train station.

Dubrovnik, Gajeva 1, **t** (01) 48 18 499/446, *www.hotel-dubrovnik.htnet.hr*. The best of the mid-range hotels, not nearly the 1980s throwback mirrored glass façade suggests and with an unbeatable location in the thick of Zagreb's buzzy café scene. Rooms are plush if rather anonymous four-stars, bathtubs are available on request; the best face onto the main square.

Ilica, Ilica 102, **t** (01) 37 77 522, *www.hotel-ilica.hr*. While not to everyone's taste, the chintzy glamour here is anything but boring, compensation for en-suite rooms where there's no room to swing a suitcase. Location is good, however, as is the price – just the wrong side of inexpensive.

Jadran, Vlaška 50, **t** (01) 45 53 777, *www.hoteljadran.com.hr*. Clean and modern(ish) en-suite rooms have satellite TV in a dated three-star worth considering for its central position 400 yards east of the cathedral.

Pansion Jägerhorn, Ilica 14, **t** (01) 48 33 877, *www.hotel-pansion-jaegerhorn.hr*. Rather pricey for the minimal facilities of its 13 rooms, but with a good location, two minutes' walk from the central square and at the foot of steps to the Upper Town.

★ Pod Grickim Topem >>

Inexpensive (€)

Sliško, Supilova 13, **t** (01) 61 94 210, *www.slisko.hr*. Simple en suites in a friendly cheapie two minutes from the bus station – handy for early starts and late arrivals.

Eating Out in and around Zagreb

Zagreb

Expensive (€€€)

Baltazar, Nova Ves 4, **t** (01) 46 66 999. High-end traditional dining from a Zagreb culinary king: the eponymous rustic tavern prepares a superb stuffed rump steak and a menu of perfectly grilled meats; and **Gašpar** is a classy fish restaurant furnished with antiques and palms. You may have to wait for a table in its wine bar christened – what else? – **Melkior**. *Closed Sun*.

Okrugljak, Mlinovi 28 (tram to Mihaljevac), **t** (01) 46 74 112. A star-studded clientele make the trek north for the acclaimed spit-roast lamb, choice dish on an upmarket menu of traditional dishes elevated with modern nuances. The rustic dining room is elegant, the wine list sensational. Book at weekends.

Paviljon, Tomislavov trg 22, **t** (01) 48 13 066. Sophisticated dining in the ground floor of the 19th-century Arts Pavilion – expect the likes of steak with Istrian truffles and gorgonzola, and sea bass tinted with saffron and basil on a bed of fried rocket. *Closed Sun*.

Expensive–moderate (€€€–€€)

Dubravkin put, Dubravkin Put 2, **t** (01) 48 34 970. A stylish, award-winning restaurant where fish is expertly grilled or flavoured with scampi sauces and seafood is exquisite; try Dalmatian favourite *jastog na buzaru* (lobster in garlic, tomatoes and white wine).

Pod Grickim Topem, Zakamarijeve stube 5, **t** (01) 48 33 607. Folksy charm – a cosy wood-panelled dining room and friendly, attentive service – meets top-notch Croatian cuisine of fresh fish and succulent slivers of beef at the top of the funicular; reservations recommended, especially for a terrace table for a panorama which sweeps over Zagreb. Worth every lipa. *Closed Sun eve*.

Moderate (€€)

Dida, Petrova 176, **t** (01) 23 35 661. A tiny piece of the Dalmatian coast wafted inland to Zagreb, 100 yards west of park Maksimir. Rustic charm abounds in a snug stone dining room of chunky beams and rustic knick-knacks, there is all sorts of fish and seafood to explore. A gem. Book at weekends.

Ivica i Marica, Tkalčićeva 70, **t** (01) 48 28 999. A quietly classy rustic place on Zagreb's bar strip that's named after Hansel and Gretel. Its traditional all-organic dishes won it the accolade of Zagreb's best traditional restaurant in 2007.

Maškin i Lota, A. Hebranga 11a, **t** (01) 48 18 273. An excellent lazy-paced cellar restaurant that's smart enough to feel like dinner but without any of the formalities. The menu is strong on fish and seafood – specialities include octopus slow-cooked in a *peka* – but includes turkey or veal stuffed with *pršut* (prosciutto) and sheep's cheese. *Closed Sun.*

Stari Fijaker, Mesnička 6, **t** (01) 48 33 829. A taste of tradition inland Croatia-style – thick winter-warmer soups plus meat-feast plates of beef, pork, veal and venison – in an enjoyably old-fashioned dining of traditional tablecloths ruled by waiters in black-and-whites.

Vinodol, Teslina 10, **t** (01) 48 11 427. Spit-roast lamb and *peka* dishes are the choice in this reliable restaurant one block south of Trg bana Jelačića, with a candlelit courtyard for summer evenings.

Moderate–inexpensive (€€–€)

Kerempuh >

Kerempuh, Kaptol 3, **t** (01) 48 19 000. Super-fresh inland Croatian cuisine at the back of the Dolac market, with a daily menu prepared from whatever the chefs have bought from stalls that morning. Popular with everyone from lunching executives to shoppers, and terrace tables have a grandstand view over the market. *Closed Sun eve.*

Inexpensive (€)

Boban, Gajeva 9, **t** (01) 48 11 549. Ever-popular cellar restaurant launched by Croatian World Cup footballer Zvonimir Boban, with Italian dishes in large portions and an extensive menu of salads.

Mount Medvednica >
Bliznec bb, Zagreb, **t** *(01) 45 86 317, www.pp-medvednica.hr; open Mon–Fri 8–4; Zagreb tourist offices also stock free maps which mark footpaths and mountain bike trails through the park*

Mount Medvednica

Okrugljak, Mlinovi 28 (left fork just before Mihaljevac terminus), **t** (01) 46 74 112 (€€€). A member of Zagreb's culinary élite. *Booking essential at weekends.*

Šestinski lagvić, Šestinska cesta bb, **t** (01) 46 74 417 (€€). North Croatian specialities served on a wonderful terrace or in a dining room which oozes bucolic charm in a restaurant situated downhill from the Medvedgrad fortress.

Zlatni medved, Sljeme; no tel (€). A busy and cheerful Alpine-style chalet at the summit which rustles up no-nonsense fillers: bean soup *grah*, sturdy pork cutlets and thick stews.

Cafés and Bars in Zagreb

Zagreb takes its café society seriously and loses entire weekends over a *kava* in café-bars of Bogovićeva and Preradovićev trg. Bar-hopping venue of choice is Tkalčićeva, northwest of Trg bana Jelačića.

Bulldog XL, Bogovićeva 6. Ever-busy café thronged at weekends and with a frequently boisterous bar inside at the centre of Bogovićeva.

Charlie, Bogovićeva 1. Long the doyenne of Bogovićeva cafés, this is a haunt of politicians and movers in the pedestrianized strip.

Gradska kavana, Trg bana Jelačića 10. Reassuringly old-fashioned café even if it largely screens off views of Zagreb's main square.

Hemingway, Tuškanac 1. Dress to impress in this slick 'n' stylish cocktail bar which is favoured by Zagreb's fashion-conscious.

K&K, Jurišićeva 3. A cosy bohemian retreat just off the main square, crammed with photos of prints of old and new Zagreb. *Closed Sun.*

Kaptolska klet, Kaptol 5. A refined take on the beer hall, with stucco and heavy beams and a menu (€) of robust local fare.

Maraschino, Margaretska 1. Hip central hangout over two floors, both rammed at weekends. It's named after the Zadar-made cherry brandy that laces many of the bar's cocktails.

Millennium, Bogovićeva 7. Death by chocolate. Or ice cream. Or gelato or great clouds of cream on Zagreb's café strip.

Molokai, Katarina trg 3. Mellow funk sounds and a symphony of wicker, wood and chiffon in a laidback lounge bar in the Upper Town.

Sedmica, Kačićeva 7a. Bohemian rendezvous of Zagreb's young glitter-arty that does all it can to remain a secret – look for a sign above a residential door. *Open Mon–Sat from 8pm, Sun from 5pm.*

Entertainment and Nightlife in Zagreb

The visitors' cultural bible is the monthly pamphlet entitled *Events & Performances*, available free from the tourist office.

Aquarius, Aleja Matije Ljubeka bb, Jarun, *www.aquarius.hr*. Twisted house and techno beats, plus hip hop and disco in the bar of Zagreb's premier nightclub, a 2,000-capacity venue with two dance floors and a summer garden. Get there on trams 17 and 5.

BP Club, Nikole Tesle 7, **t** (01) 48 14 444, *www.bpclub.hr*. A cosy jazz bar-club which swings on gig nights but is also a treat for a smart evening drink.

Croatian Music Institute (Hrvatski glazbeni zavod), Gundulićeva 6, **t** 48 30 822. Chamber music recitals and virtuoso soloists.

Croatian National Theatre (Hrvatsko narodno kazalište), Trg maršala Tita 15, **t** (01) 48 28 532, *www.hnk.hr*. The Habsburgs' neoclassical *grande dame* is the prestigious venue for classical theatre, ballet and opera from Croatian big names, as well as international visitors.

Gavella, Frankopanska 8, **t** (01) 48 48 552, *www.gavella.hr*. Excellently staged and less stuffy theatre staged alongside visiting productions, occasionally in English.

Saloon, Tuškanac 1, **t** (01) 48 34 903, *www.saloon.hr*. A hip hangout for Zagreb's dressed-up glamour set, with a record box of disco, soul and funky house tunes and central location, one block west of Gradec. Better still, the bar prices don't asphyxiate.

Sax, Palmotićeva 22, **t** (01) 48 72 836 *www.sax-zg.hr*. Blues, swing and occasional rock acts play to an enthusiastic crowd every night.

Vatroslav Lisinski Concert Hall (Koncertna dvorana Vatroslav Lisinski), Trg Stjepana Radića 4, **t** (01) 61 21 166/167/168, *www.linski.hr*. Orchestral extravaganzas in the main auditorium, home to the Zagreb Philharmonic; ensembles and jazz in the small hall.

North of Zagreb: The Zagorje and Varaždin

From Zagreb, most visitors hurry to the coast and leave Croatia ignorant of the Zagorje, a folksy fairytale as enchanting as its *licitarsko srce*, the iced gingerbread lovehearts exchanged by whimsical sweethearts. Wandering 19th-century poet Antun Gustav Matoš saluted this region north of the capital to neighbouring Slovenia as the guardian of the nation's soul; and when poet Antun Mihanović waxed about 'fields kissed by sunshine' and 'oaks whipped by wild winds' in *Lijepa naša domovino* ('Our Beautiful Homeland'), adopted as the national anthem in 1891, he had in mind the landscapes near the border town of Kumrovec. Only foreigners remain in the dark. But if this book were a beauty contest the Zagorje would be there in the final. It has enchanting hummocky hills, their shoulders draped with woods, their crowns capped by staccato spires and castles, and it has quirky art galleries and museums. Its churches feature some of Croatia's most exquisite Baroque frescoes, while its capital, Varaždin, is the nation's Habsburg Baroque stage set. And, as if to balance the appeal of every cultural site, there are thermal spas and wine routes, and delicious ravioli-like *štrukli*, as mouth-filling as the local dialect, *kajkavski*, christened, appropriately, after the local word for 'what?' (*kaj*).

The Zagorje

Along the Stubica Valley to Marija Bistrica and Belec

27 The Zagorje

Stubičke Toplice
V. Šipeka 24, ***t*** *(049) 282 727; open Mon–Fri 8–3, Sat 10–3*

Thermal pools
open May–Sept daily 7–7; adm

Museum of the Peasants' Revolt
Muzej seljačkih buna; ***t*** *(01) 049 587 880, www.mdc.hr/msb/index.htm; open daily April–Sept 9–7; Oct–Mar 9–5; adm*

The road which hairpins down the north slope of Mount Medvednica (*see* p.93) just north of Zagreb emerges from woods into hills of the Stubica valley. In each country added to their imperial register, the ancient Romans were quick to sniff out a thermal spa, and antique foundations reveal that here they wallowed in the calcium- and magnesium-rich waters of **Stubičke Toplice**, a cure town since 1776 which came into its own after 1811, when Zagreb bishop Maksimilijan Vrhovac treated himself to the **Maksimilijaneum bath-house** and lured the Zagreb élite to promenade in its gardens and attend concerts in its cultural hall. No ballgowns are required for today's visitors, here for rheumatism and spinal disease hospital treatments or to idle alfresco in **thermal pools**.

Six kilometres east, **Gornja Stubica** seems far too sleepy to be the hotbed of dissent which sparked a 1573 Peasants' Revolt and filled the Stubica Valley with villagers' battle cries. Before he was captured and crowned with hot lead in Zagreb, leader Matija Gubec is said to have whipped up yokel resentment against feudal overlords underneath the lime tree in front of the parish church of St George, a story not so much told as droned in the **Museum of the Peasants' Revolt** in the Oršić Palace 2km north. A few rooms of furnishings nod to the Zagorje nobility that Gubic hoped to displace.

More intriguing is Croatia's favourite Marian shrine, **Marija Bistrica**, a place so venerated that it was forced to change its name. Until the 17th century, the unprepossessing village was plain Bistrica, but on 15 July 1684 the parish priest heeded a mystical woman in blue and liberated a Black Madonna that had been bricked up in a niche of the village church in 1650 as Turkish troops drew near. Restored to the altar the next day, the early Gothic statue promptly cured a noblewoman's paralysed daughter. The Catholic hierarchy hailed it a miracle, and pilgrims flocked here, egged on by Pope Benedict XIV's decision to grant indulgences to those who confessed and took communion in the church. After the Croatian parliament declared Bistrica a shrine in 1715, life for the village was never the same again.

If you believe the stories, in its inaugural century the 15th-century statue, swathed in a dress on the main altar averaged a miracle a

month (1,109 in 98 years) and confirmed its credentials in 1880 by surviving a blaze that reduced the interior of the church to ruins on the eve of the Feast of the Assumption. Refurbishment provided an excuse to enlarge, and Hermann Bollé, liberated from the Zagreb cathedral, designed an engagingly esoteric number, its original Baroque spiced by a dollop of light-hearted neo-Gothic in a soaring spire and flutter of turrets, and dignified by neoclassical pavilions and an embracing colonnade. The latter shelters votive frescoes like PR shots of the Virgin's past miracles. *Hvala Marijo* ('Thank you, Mary') plaques testify to 20th-century marvels. For the best view of the ensemble, cross the amphitheatre built for Pope John Paul II's beatification of recalcitrant archbishop Alojzije Stepinac on 3 October 1998 – a good thing too, since nearly a million of the faithful braved rain to witness the event – and ascend, good pilgrim, past stations of the cross chiselled by Croatian sculptors, to the summit of Calvary Hill.

There's religious mania of a different kind in **Belec**, 18km northeast of Marija Bistrica via **Zlatar**, a likeable small market town, busy with quiet purpose. Although it is a frump on the outside, Belec's church of **St Mary of the Snows** (Crkva svete Marije Snježne) lets rip inside with an explosion of Baroque glitz, a sensory overload in jade, dusky pink and gilt, as affluent as you'd expect of an interior funded by north Croatian aristocrats to shore

Getting to and around the Zagorje

This is a region best seen with your own transport – buses go to and from Zagreb, but moving between destinations on public transport is fiddly.

Buses from Zagreb go to **Marija Bistrica** (15 a day), and hourly to **Zlatar**, from where it's a 5km walk or a taxi ride to **Belec**.

To **Kumrovec** and **Klanjec** there are 3 buses a day from Zagreb and more frequent trains, usually requiring a change at Savski Marof.

To reach **Veliki Tabor**, take a bus to **Desinić** (8 a day) then walk 2km west.

There are buses from Zagreb approx every 90mins, and trains (change at Zaprešić), to **Krapina**, and buses approx every 90mins to **Krapinske Toplice**. From Varaždin (*see* pp.108–12) there are 2 buses a day to Krapina. Buses approx every 2hrs connect Krapina to Krapinske Toplice. Rare buses from Zagreb go to **Lepoglava**, but it is more easily reached by bus and train connections from Varaždin. 6–9 buses a day go to **Trakošćan** from Varaždin.

---

up their place in heaven. This is Baroque at its most joyful, where every surface seems to move before your eyes. At centre stage, church founder Countess Keglević kneels before a benevolent Virgin in illusionist frescoes from the impeccable palette of Ivan Ranger, a Pauline monk who found gainful employment throughout northwest Croatia. But even the Tyrolean master's supreme achievement is blasted into the background by the mid-1700s furniture: a high altar impossibly squeezed into the apse, ablur with chubby cherubs, fey saints and swooning angels; a pair of tasselled side altars; and a fabulous pulpit on which Israelite revellers have blasphemous amounts of fun around their golden calf. The church is locked except for Sunday Mass – ask at the house directly behind it for the key (*ključ*).

Kumrovec and Around

When Kumrovec couple Franjo and Marija Javeršek celebrated the birth of their son Josip Broz in 1892, who would have imagined that 61 years later their hamlet would be restored then preserved as the **Old Village Museum**.

Old Village Museum
Muzej Staro selo; **t** *(01) 049 225 830, www.mdc.hr/kumrovec; open daily April–Sept 9–7, Oct–Mar 9–4; adm*

Today, twin titles as the birthplace of the father of Yugoslav Communism and Croatia's finest open-air museum ensure that the village on the Slovenian border receives more than its fair share of visitors, although even peak-season crowds are nothing compared with the 10,000 who arrived en masse to pay homage when Josip Broz Tito died in 1980 (*see* **History**, pp.30–1).

On a lane of pastel cottages painted in duck-egg blue and apple white, there's no missing **Tito's boyhood home** thanks to the bronze by Antun Augustinčić (*see* below) in the front garden of the dictator striding into history. In his semi-autobiography *Tito Speaks*, the Yugoslav father-figure waxes lyrical about his mother baking *štrukli* or villagers swapping yarns about the 1573 Peasants' Revolt around the heater of his boyhood home. The ceramic stove remains as a centrepiece to rooms of humble furniture as he knew them, bar one which documents his rise from Second World War Partisan leader – his 1944 uniform is set in a glass case like a relic – to world statesman, beaming in photographs alongside Nehru, Nixon and JFK.

Beyond, the immaculately restored cottages strung out along a brook offer an unashamedly rose-tinted look at Zagorje pastoral life in the late 1800s: there's a blacksmith's workshop full of tools; the village's oldest cottage is reinvented as a toymaker's workshop, oozing charm in colourful clutter; and the buntings are up and the bride looks nervous in tableaux of a Zagorje wedding.

In high summer, when Kumrovec's lanes disappear beneath tour groups, pretty **Klanjec** 6km east continues to daydream undisturbed. What raises it above a coffee stop are the sculptures that Antun Augustinčić donated to his birthplace in 1970, now displayed as the **Antun Augustinčić Gallery**. Forgive the drab presentation and there's much to enjoy in three rooms of works by the 20th-century sculptor who studied in Zagreb and Paris, from busts or stylized reliefs with a whiff of former mentor and Croatian art giant Ivan Meštrović, to swaggering monuments such as the *Peace* bronze created for the United Nations building in New York. Appropriately, Augustinčić is buried beside his wife in the sculpture park outside beneath his bronze *Carrying the Wounded*.

Antun Augustinčić Gallery
t (049) 550 343, www.mdc.hr/augustincic; open April–Sept daily 9–5; Oct–Mar Tues–Sun 9–3; adm

Five kilometres northeast lies **Tuheljske Toplice**, whose 33°C mineral waters made it a favourite of the Romans and respiratory and rheumatic patients alike. Leave them to their treatment centre and either join the spa-goers caked in skin-softening fango mud in the country's largest spa centre or wallow in four **outdoor pools** with water chute slides for the kiddies – big and little.

Outdoor pools
open May–Sept 7–7; adm

Veliki Tabor

ⓘ **Veliki Tabor**
t (049) 343 963, www.velikitabor.com; open daily April–Sept 10–5; Oct–Mar 9–3; adm

You'll spot Veliki Tabor before you see the signposts. The Zagorje's mightiest castle hunkers down as a brooding silhouette of towers and walls on a hilltop 10km north of Kumrovec. Close up, the oldest residential building in continental Croatia – a fortified pentagonal from the 12th century onto which Ratkay nobility grafted Gothic bastions as Turkish troops approached in 1502 – is showing its age. The exterior is riven with cracks in all the wrong places despite interminable restoration that has been the bane of all recent owners. One was Croatian painter Oton Iveković, who probably thought he'd snapped up a bargain when he bought the castle for 100,000 crowns at an auction in 1919, harbouring romantic notions of a faux baronial lifestyle. High maintenance costs put paid to those, and in the Second World War the castle was handed to Franciscan nuns as an orphanage and in latter years was a meat-smoking factory. The last decade has seen the completion of the handsome Renaissance courtyard and a central palace, which holds odds and ends of archaeological merit. By the time you read this, the surrounding rooms may also have been restored, some with Renaissance frescos as a backdrop for period displays. Keep an eye open for a skull uncovered in 1982 which castle owners would love to believe is that of Veronika, a peasant beauty who was murdered by former castle owner Count Herman II of Celje to end his son's absurd infatuation with a mere village girl. His legal argument that she had bewitched his Friedrich into marriage was thrown out by soft-hearted judges, who proclaimed love the noblest of emotions. Poppycock perhaps, but a good enough yarn to justify christening an opposite hilltop the **Hill of Sin** (Grešna gorica). Indeed, the views of the Zagorje's green carpet unrolled beneath are sufficient reason to visit the castle.

East to Krapina

Between Veliki Tabor and Trakošćan Castle (*see* p.106), the Zagorje is full of rustic charm. Antique tractors chug through a chequerboard of shaggy cornfields and nodding sunflowers; south-facing slopes are striped with vineyards and dotted with family-owned *klet* (wine cellars); and churches cap every hill, a defence strategy against Turkish raids rather than a hankering to be near God, whatever the local legend claims. The residents of **Vinagora** took no chances and added a defence wall and gate towers to their Baroque parish church, perched above the vines on a hilltop eyrie 4km east of Desinić. Although there are rich Gothic furnishings in the interior, the church is usually locked and the main reason to visit is the view – in the Zagorje's fairytale landscape, this is a panorama from Jack's beanstalk.

Continuing 4km further, you reach the administrative hub of **Pregrada**, snuggled into the hills at its back and dominated by its peach and cream neoclassical church – twin-spired, oversized and nicknamed, inevitably, the 'Zagorje Cathedral'. Appropriately, its organ was intended for Zagreb cathedral until the capital's ecclesiastical authorities decided that it was too puny and sold it to Pregrada in 1854 for 600 florins.

Krapina

A bit too small to be dynamic, a bit too large to be laidback, Krapina is the closest it gets to urban life in the central Zagorje. However much it goes about the business of being the region's administrative and cultural capital, or points to its role as the birthplace in 1809 of Ljudevit Gaj, the writer and politician who spearheaded the Croatian independence Illyrian Movement and is honoured by a statue on the main square of a jaded late Baroque core, Krapina is doomed to the earliest chapters of Croatian encyclopaedias. Its first mention is as the mythic 'cradle of the Slavs', the town where brothers Čeh (Czech), Leh and Meh are said to have walled up their sister Vilina for betraying a plot to overthrow Roman oppressors, then fled and inadvertently founded the Slavic nations (Bohemia, Poland and Russia). Less spurious is its acclaim as the home of 'Krapina Man', a robust proto-human spin-off which loped among caves 100,000 years ago. Zagreb pulled rank and cherry-picked the best bits of the world's richest ever haul of Neanderthal finds for its Croatian Natural History Museum (*see* p.87) and all Krapina has to show for the bones and tools archaeologist and palaeontologist Dragutin Gorjanović Kramberger unearthed in 1899 are some disappointing fossils and skull fragments, on show in musty display cases in the **Evolution Museum** – a new museum is promised for 2010. Far more fun are the lifesize bronzes of Krapina Man which strike action poses outside the half-cave where Kramberger made his discovery, opposite the museum; follow signs north of the centre for *Nalazište pračovjeka*.

Evolution Museum
Muzej evolucije; **t** *(049) 371 491, www.mhz.hr; open April–Sept daily 9–5; Oct–Mar Tues–Sun 9–3; adm*

In the town centre there are temporary exhibitions in the **City Gallery**, but the best art hereabouts is frescoed in the pilgrimage **Church of the Holy Mother of Jerusalem**, 2km east in the suburb of Trški Vrh. Although locals funded the Baroque church (1750–61) to treasure a miracle-working gold Madonna and Child, a pilgrim's souvenir from Jerusalem now swamped by a gloriously over-the-top high altar, it's the exuberant Baroque furniture and frescoes which capture the heart. Once inside, you are led through an encircling cloister painted with a votive slideshow of late 18th-century miracles and into a joyful intimation of paradise through Baroque excess: wall-to-wall frescoes, gilded altars and a sweet little organ on which angels strum lutes and thump drums.

City Gallery
Galerija grada Krapine; Magistratska 25; open Mon–Sat 10–1

Church of the Holy Mother of Jerusalem
Crkva Majke Božje *Jeruzalemske; Trški Vrh; check the location of the key with supermarket staff behind the church; the current incumbent is in adjacent pink house, Trški Vrh 85*

Continuing east towards Radoboj, the road bumbles through farm villages to **Gorjani Sutinski**. A pitted lane threads north from the centre, then climbs east to the parish church of **St Jacob**. It's nothing special after its almost total destruction in the Second World War, but there are spectacular views of the Zagorje laid out to the south.

Krapinske Toplice

A mineral spa has transformed Krapinske Toplice into an enigma; a relaxed resort and an oversized casualty ward in equal measure. Blame Jakov Badl. In 1863 the Croatian wine salesman was so impressed by the natural hot pools which cured his heart condition that he permanently stabled his horse to promote mineral springs as a cure-all to a spa-crazy Austro-Hungarian public. The postwar Communist authorities, who frowned on such frivolity, reshaped the Viennese-style resort into a medical centre, and today cardiac and post-operative patients, rheumatics and those with serious muscle injuries while away the hours between their next dip in the 39–41°C hydrocarbonate-, magnesium- and calcium-rich waters of Jakov's hospital pool on benches in his central park, while resort goers idle in cafés.

Badl now rests beside his wife in a mausoleum on the hill **Sv. Marija Magdalena** (a path ascends beside the hospital), the start of marked trails which loop around the locale to show off gorgeous views north to hills cloaked in vineyards and freckled by terracotta roofs. And Krapinske Toplice is also rediscovering its sense of fun. Two outdoor – but rather grubby – **spring water pools** welcome pleasure-seekers for a splash around in salty 33°C waters, and by 2010 an adjacent indoor pools of a private investor should be ready for year-round bathing.

Spring water pools
open May–Sept daily 8–8; adm

East to Trakošćan

Lepoglava, 22km northeast of Krapina, is famous for lace and the lock-up. The town is proud that its lace-making school won a Paris World Exhibition Gold Medal in 1937, and throws a lacy jamboree on the last weekend in September. A **lace gallery** displays and sells local pieces; prices start at 50Kn and go up to 10,000Kn for highly worked large examples. You'll find it signposted off the main road in the town centre opposite the Pauline **monastery** that commands the west end of a drab centre. When the order was outlawed in 1786, the Baroque building became a **state prison** where any political revolutionary worth the title spent years behind bars. In 1929 Josip Broz Tito did time in solitary here for bomb-making. Then, as Yugoslav dictator, he trumped up charges to incarcerate his own critics, most famously Archbishop Alojzije Stepinac, who served five years of a 16-year hard labour sentence before the Communists acknowledged that their mock trial for Nazi collusion had created a martyr and confined the recalcitrant priest to house arrest in his home town of Krašić. Not that the Yugoslav father learned by his mistakes. To world condemnation and howls of protest from Amnesty International, in 1982 he jailed future Croatia president Franjo Tuđman for 'maliciously and falsely representing socio-political conditions in Yugoslavia' in an interview with a foreign journalist. With the head-spinning logic of a real-life *1984*, the state prosecutors explained that the political dissident was incarcerated for speaking out because, actually, all Yugoslavians enjoyed full freedom of expression.

Lace gallery
Galerija čipke; open Tues–Sat 9–1

A new prison now incarcerates inmates behind the monastery, which was returned to the Varaždin diocese in 2001; this means you can again admire the dignified Baroque façade of the **Church of the Blessed Virgin Mary** and, on the rare chance it's open, marvel at a choir and chancel arch dappled by the frescoes of Pauline monk Ivan Ranger and a garden of stucco seeded by A. J. Quadrio, who was the Italian master responsible for Zagreb's charming St Catherine's Church.

Church of the Blessed Virgin Mary
Crkva Blažene Djevice Marije; ask for the key (ključ) at adjacent prison office or visit after Sunday Mass

Nine kilometres northwest of Lepoglava lies **Trakošćan Castle**. 1930s author Rebecca West dismissed the Zagorje's most celebrated castle as 'Balliol on a sugar-loaf hill'; 'a vast building executed in that baronial style which owed so much more to literary than to architectural inspiration, having been begotten by Sir Walter Scott', she railed. Juraj Drašković would have been quietly delighted, because defence was the last thing on the mind of the 19th-century count when he rebuilt a medieval pile gifted to his ancestors for their stout resistance to Turkish incursions in the 1500s.

Trakošćan Castle
t (042) 796 281, www.mdc.hr/trakoscan; open daily May–Sept 9–6, Oct–April 9–4; adm

If West was scathing of the too-perfect sugar-white turrets and set-square castellations which make the castle the Zagorje's most popular attraction, she was incensed by its neo-Gothic interior: 'big in accordance with the vulgar idea that bigness is splendid; documentary proof that German influence had meant nothing but corruption [to Croatia]'. It's certainly walloping stuff – all swaggering carved portals, absurdly oversized mantelpieces and the inevitable hunting trophies and suits of armour. The object is to think of it not as the genuine article, but as an Austro-Hungarian-styled paean to a romantic notion of medieval chivalry. The private living quarters furnished with family hand-me-downs are relaxed after the public show-offs below, even daring to hint at arty bohemia in a room hung with idealized portraits of peasant women by Julijana Erdödy-Drašković, Croatia's first academy-trained female painter. 'Exactly what is meant by the French word *niaiserie*,' West huffed. Even if you don't make the full 5km circuit through grounds landscaped in natural English style, there's a lovely view of the castle from the opposite side of a lake on which pedalos potter – one for the photo album.

ⓘ Marija Bistrica >>
Zagrebačka bb (just north of church), t (049) 468 380 or t (049) 301 010, www.info-marija-bistrica.hr; open Mon–Fri 9–4, Sat–Sun 12–5

Festivals in the Zagorje

Krapina trills Zagorje folk songs in local dialect *kajkavski* during its September **Kajkavian Festival**.

Where to Stay and Eat in the Zagorje

Marija Bistrica

Dioniz, Trg Pape Ivana Pavla II, **t** (049) 469 103 (€). If you don't fancy *kobasice* (sausages) and pork cutlets, pizzas

ⓘ **Tuheljske Toplice >>**
Gajeva 4, **t** *(049) 556 224; open Mon–Fri 8–2, Sat 10–2*

and pastas are passable in the central square – Zagorje speciality *štrukli sa sirom* (cottage cheese pockets, like large ravioli) will fill the corners.

Lojzekova hiža, 6km west of Marija Bistrica, signposted off Gusakovec road, **t** (049) 469 325, *www.lojzekovahiza.com* (€). A rustic charmer which hits all the right notes: a menu of home cooking – delicious fat sausages and steaks in rich mushroom sauces – and a peaceful setting. It also has a handful of farm-style simple rooms (€), all crisp white sheets and pine-clad walls.

Kumrovec

Kod starog, Josipa Broza 24, Kumrovec, no tel (€). Light bites for a summer's day opposite Tito's house – cold platters of meats and cheeses are served with hunks of bread, there are fat local sausages to sample and Zagorje favourite *štrukli* (baked cheese dumplings), all washed down with a cheerful homemade wine.

Stara Vura, Josipa Broza 13, Kumrovec, **t** (049) 553 137 (€). Hearty Zagorje cooking prepared in country portions in the village's best restaurant, located 100yds right of the entrance; pick from a small menu of trout for a light lunch. Be warned: it can be swamped by tour groups, so you should expect to wait for a terrace table in peak season.

Zagorsko Klet, Staro selo, no tel (€). Offers homemade cakes, *štrukli* and cheese in the cellar of an 1887 farmhouse.

ⓘ **Krapinske Toplice >>**
Zagreba¬ka 4 (beside bus station), **t** *(049) 232 106; open Mon–Fri 8–3, Sat 8–1*

ⓘ **Klanjec >**
Trg A. Mihanovića 2 (main square), **t** *(049) 550 235; open Mon–Fri 8–5, Sat 8–1*

★ **Vuglec Breg >>**

Klanjec

Zelenjak, Risvica 1 (2km west of Klanjec), **t** (049) 550 747, *www.zelenjak.com* (€€). The locals' choice for a slap-up meal is this semi-formal restaurant on the Kumrovec road, where the finest chef in the area prepares upmarket Zagorje fillers such as veal steaks in thick sauces laced with homemade cream and sausages with maize mash. Business-style **rooms** (*Inexpensive*) make up in three-star comforts what they lack in character.

Tuheljike Toplice

Terme Tuhelj, Ljudevita Gaja 4, **t** (049) 203 750, *www.terme-tuhelj.hr* (€). All rooms are on the cosy side, but half of the 92 here are modern and quietly stylish after a refurbishment, and the old-timers are adequate. The price includes access to three pools.

Desinic

Trsek, Trnovec Desinićki 23, **t** (049) 343 464, *www.trsek.hr* (€). A peaceful agrotourism farmhouse retreat, signposted 1km east of Desinić centre, with a garden full of livestock and blissful views from the balcony of its en-suite accommodation, simple but homely. Breakfast 20Kn extra. In the evening, Zagorje dishes are rustled up in a restaurant as traditional as a menu which includes turkey with noodles and fat homemade sausages.

Grešna gorica, Taborgradska 3, **t** (049) 343 001, *www.gresna-gorica.com* (€). Touristy but sweet place signposted 1km east of the castle: its wooden dining room decorated with embroidered tablecloths oozes bucolic character and the garden looks across to the silhouette of Veliki Tabor. The menu features regional dishes prepared from local farm produce: Grandpa Eduarda's Zagorje cheese, pork steaks stuffed with ham and homemade cheese or veal 'prepared the old-fashioned way'.

Krapinske Toplice and around

Aquae Vivae, Antuna Mihanovića 2, **t** (049) 202 202, *www.aquae-vivae.hr* (€€). A fallback spa hotel in the centre, fairly frumpy but just about worth its three-star status.

Vuglec Breg, Škarićevo 151, Lepjci (4km north of Krapinske Toplice), **t** (049) 345 015, *www.vuglec-breg.hr* (€€). A former hamlet on a hilltop, now a sophisticated agrotourism retreat with views over the Zagorje wine hills, its four cottages renovated to provide apartments with bright rustic style and mod cons such as flatscreen TVs. The centrepiece is a classy restaurant, ***Pri Kleti*** (€€), that prepares gourmet regional cooking from locally sourced ingredients – half- and full-board deals are worth investigating. There are also a wine cellar, tennis and riding facilities for guests.

Pečenjarnica, Toplička 6, **t** (049) 232 206 (€). Tasty mixed grills, steaks and cutlets in the town's best restaurant, located on the main road behind the park.

Krapina > *Magistratska 11,* ***t*** *(049) 371 330; open Mon–Fri 8–3, Sat 8–12*

Krapina

Croatia Krapina, A. Mihanovića 1, **t** (049) 370 547 (€). If Pod starim krovovima (*see* below) is full – and it probably will be in summer – this drab motel on the motorway east of the centre is a last choice.

Pod starim krovovima, Trg Ljudevita Gaja 15, **t** (049) 370 536 (€). A central *pension* with modest en-suite rooms: fork out an extra 100Kn to upgrade to a suite-sized three-bed room. The restaurant prepares strange cuts of pig plus cutlets and *Schnitzels* in country portions.

Pizzeria Picikato, Magistratska 2, no tel (€). Pizzas and pastas served in a courtyard.

Trakošćan

Coning Trakošćan, Trakošćan 5, **t** (042) 796 495, *www.coning-turizam.hr* (€€). A comfy, if characterless, two-star of the Coning chain, bland but well located bang opposite the castle. Its **restaurant** (€€), the only one near the castle, is a carnivore's heaven; try roast duck stuffed with a mixture of wheat and liver instead of steak.

Varaždin and the Međimurje

After the intimacy of the Zagorje hills, the endless agricultural plains beside the Drava river can induce agoraphobia. The lure of Croatia's far northern reaches, however, is not its waterway but the regional – once national – capital of Varaždin, with a bite-size Baroque centre. Nearby rival Čakovec and its castle won't detain you long but serves as a gateway to the sparsely populated Međimurje, an island of the Pannonian plain carved out by the Drava and Mura rivers, with wine country tucked in its nook.

Varaždin

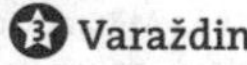

Greatness nipped in the bud characterizes the town of Varaždin. Its proximity to the Austro-Hungarian power-players first elevated it to aristocrat, then crowned it Croatian capital in the mid-18th century. Though now living in reduced circumstances, Croatia's best-preserved Habsburg town refuses to relinquish all her yesteryear grand airs. It's Bach not Bob Dylan that buskers play in front of Baroque palaces painted in smart shades of duck-egg blue, *café au lait* and pale grey, and it's the Zagreb élite who now pay homage to Varaždin in September during a three-week classical music beano. Varaždin also has all the zip of a university town ruled by bicycles – 22,000 of them, or 2.3 for each resident, at the last count.

Getting to and around Varaždin

Buses and slower trains run hourly from Zagreb to **Varaždin**. Long-haul buses from Varaždin go daily to Zadar, Rijeka, Pazin and Split. Being so close to the northern border, Varaždin has good international connections as well: there are daily buses to Nagykanizsa, Hungary, and Maribor, Slovenia, and daily trains to Budapest Déli.

As the regional travel hub, Varaždin is well connected to local towns by bus – every 30mins to **Čakovec**, hourly to **Ludbreg** and **Koprivnica**, two a day to **Krapina** – and there are frequent trains to Koprivnica via Ludbreg. Ludbreg and Koprivnica buses stop at **Aqua City** on request; 16 buses a day go to **Vinica**.

History

Although the Romans marched between colonies in these northern reaches, Varaždin begins its tale in 1181 as 'Garestin', which beat Zagreb to become the first 'royal and free town' in Croatia (1209) – a nod of gratitude by King Andrija II for local support during his imprisonment. After a battering by Ottoman Turks in 1242, this town on the ramparts of Christendom fortified itself around its progenitor castle to become a garrison centre and residence of choice for military top brass. Then as the Turkish threat receded in the 1600s, it grew fat on the profits as a staging post from Hungary. By the end of the century the military boom town was being gentrified by the cutting-edge Baroque palaces of resettled nobility and merchants. Cultural life flourished, and in 1756 continental Croatia's brightest star received its Oscar moment, crowned capital of Croatia, Slavonia and Dalmatia by Empress Maria Theresa during an administrative reshuffle of the Austro-Hungarian Empire. For 20 years Varaždin lived it up on the nation's throne. 'There, the latest kinds of shiny carriages, silver dishes, handsome liveries, couriers and French chefs could be seen,' tutted Count Adam Oršić, scandalized at a culture of decadence and 'perilous luxury'. 'Excellencies and women had expensive goods supplied from Vienna. Expenditures on mistresses were large. Women led luxurious lives, the latest and most expensive jewellery was ordered and it was hard to distinguish a chamber-maid or a middle-class woman from genuine ladies.'

Varaždin's fall from grace is worthy of Hollywood. On 25 April 1776, a blaze on an outlying farmstead – the story goes that a yokel tripped over a sow and dropped his pipe into a haystack – spread into the city walls, and the inferno raged for three days and reduced 80 per cent of the city to a smoking ruin. Three months later, a vicious storm delivered the *coup de grâce* and the Croatian *ban* (viceroy) and parliament returned to Zagreb, closely followed by the nobility. Small wonder Varaždin founded one of southeast Europe's oldest volunteer fire brigades, in 1864.

Patched up and humbled, Varaždin knuckled down to become a prosperous textile centre – local football team Varteks is christened after its textile factory, Croatia's largest – and contented itself with being a regional power. It was not disturbed by the Homeland War, despite the potentially destabilizing presence of a large Yugoslav People's Army (JNA) base, although this is largely thanks to Vladimir Trifunović: rather than risk bloodshed between his 300 troops and Croat fighters, the JNA general surrendered his garrison in September 1991 without a shot being fired. Belgrade, which preferred its Serb heroes glorious in death to magnanimous in life, was incensed. 'We needed you dead,' rebuked the military masterminds, and handed down a 15-year prison sentence.

Around Trg Kralja Tomislava

More than any monument, Varaždin's showpiece is its UNESCO-listed Baroque core, all pedestrianized and best explored from main square Trg kralja Tomislava. It remains a centre stage of town life it has always been, with an audience of terrace cafés and a backcloth of a tubby **town hall** (1523) bearing the coat of arms and spiked with a clock tower, a post-blaze pick-me-up added in 1791. The ball beneath the clock face indicates the weather forecast – gold for good, black for poor. Visit on Saturday and there are actors too – Varaždin's *purgari*, the **city guard** formed in 1750 as the town found its stride, march in full dress uniform. The creamy grandee on the square's east flank is the **Drašković Palace**, erected in the 18th century by the aristocrats of Trakošćan fame, and from 1756 the residence of Croatian *ban* Count Franjo Nadasdy and *de facto* meeting place of the *sabor* (parliament) during Varaždin's stint in the political driving seat. A *chocolateria* opposite preserves a pre-blaze Holy Trinity stucco ceiling – you can't miss it due to a bare-breasted mermaid outside that announces the imported goods of its former merchant owner.

City guard
parade at the town hall April–Oct Sat 11–12

Just east lies the **Cathedral of the Assumption** (Katedrala Uznesenja Marijana), built by Jesuit monks in the 1640s. If the whitewashed interior of its early Baroque barn seems plain, it also provides a blank canvas for a headspinning high altar shoehorned into a space the width of the nave and ablur with saints preaching in niches. An Assumption of the Virgin altarpiece never stands a chance. A block behind is the **town park**, created in place of southern defence walls torn down in the 1800s. Somewhere among its clipped lawns and specimen trees you'll find a bronze of 19th-century lecturer Vatroslav Jagić, a homage from his home town, which would have been more flattering had workmen not bodged a repair to his left leg, now shorter than the right, and had a Zagreb sculptor not dressed the founder of Slavic studies in a woman's coat that buttons on the left.

Franjevački Trg

While state and civic power-brokers claimed Trg kralja Tomislava, Franjevački trg, off its corner, was the address that all 18th-century merchant nobility aspired to. Their mansions play architectural one-upmanship on the spacious thoroughfare, a shoulder-to-shoulder parade of carriage-width portals surmounted by family coats of arms. None can match the swagger of the rococo **Patačić Palace** (1764) at the east end, whose grandiose portal makes the *ban*'s front door seem like a tradesmen's entrance. Now a sober branch of the Austria Bank, Count Franjo Patačić's address was, during capital decades, a whirl of glittering high society until his expensive lifestyle forced him to put the lot under the hammer.

Beyond, the 17th-century Franciscan **Church of St John the Baptist** (Crkva svetog Ivana Krstitelja) spiked by the highest tower in town (54.5m), has a late Renaissance carved pulpit, a shock of gold in an otherwise muted interior shaded in rusty browns and old ivory. Outside on a plinth is a miniature of Ivan Meštrović's Split colossus *Grgur Ninski* (*see* pp.275–6), whose lucky big toe grants wishes when rubbed. You might need one to get into the Franciscans' adjacent **pharmacy**, open for church hours in theory but not always in practice. Its joy is a low roof, daubed with frescoes of the elements and four continents from the brush of Pauline monk Ivan Ranger.

Entomology Museum
Entomološki muzej; ***t*** *(042) 210 474); open Tues–Sun 10–6; adm*

Artistry of another kind is on display in the restrained neoclassical Herczer Palace. For all its didactic title, the appeal of the **Entomology Museum** is as aesthetic as it is scientific in displays of over 4,500 creepy-crawlies displayed like a Victorian naturalist's sketchbook; butterflies and delicate mayflies waft in formation above pressed grasses, there are honeycombs like fragile sculptures between glass panes and a display of the vintage cigar- and matchboxes in which 19th-century entomologist and museum founder Franjo Koščec squirrelled away his prizes. Who would have thought creepy-crawlies could be so charming? A gem.

The Castle and Around

From the museum, Uršulinska threads north past its **Ursuline church** (Uršulinska crkva) pretty in pink and with a slender Baroque spire topped with an onion dome, then past charming lane Padovčeva to a **castle** (*stari grad*) immortalized on the 5Kn note. Only a square tower by the entrance remains of the stronghold Varaždin constructed in haste in the mid-16th-century, when the know-how of Italian architect Domenico dell'Allio transformed a front-line defence against Ottoman Turks into a galleried Renaissance fortress within a moat. Before they left its halls in the 1760s for a spanking new palace on Kapucinski trg, the powerful Erdödy counts heaped up earthworks and tacked on further bastions to create today's hybrid, caught between fortress and palace. Its **museum** spins through local history using the usual props – weaponry, guild signs and municipal treasures – and occasional sidetracks on to local heroes, before it fast-forwards through five centuries of interior décor upstairs. Here, too, off a first-floor corridor, you'll discover the intimate **chapel of St Lawrence**, a rare nugget of original Gothic.

Museum
t (042) 658 754; open Mon–Fri 10–5, Sat–Sun 10–1; adm

Across a drawbridge guarded by a 16th-century watchtower, Stančićev trg is boxed in by the medallioned slab of the Palača Sermage, a 17th-century nobleman's treat to himself which houses French and Dutch works, so-so oils of the Canaletto school and a peer book of stuffed-shirt aristocrats as the **Gallery of Old and New Masters** .

Gallery of Old and New Masters
Galerija starih i novih majstora; t (042) 214 172; open Tues–Fri 10–2, Sat–Sun 10–1; adm

Going the other way from the castle via Hallerova aleja you reach the **town cemetery**. Bewailing the 'lugubriousness' of European cemeteries where 'the presence of death and our own paltriness is bitterly felt', cemetery head Hermann Heller vowed to create 'a park of the living'. In 1905 his formal garden of sculpted firs and coppiced deciduous trees screened off the last tomb-slab, and Varaždin had a new park for a Sunday stroll.

Around Varaždin

In the humidity of high summer, locals head to **Aqua City**, 5km west of the centre on the Koprivnica road. A dressed-up name for a former gravel-pit lake fringed by reeds and willow, perhaps, but Blue Flag-quality water, shingle beaches where pedalos and canoes are available for hire, and the requisite beach bar and restaurant, mean the 'Varaždin Sea' can be oversubscribed to the tune of 6,000 people on breathless weekends. Escape the worst of the crowds on lawns on the left-hand side.

Aqua City
always open

For more secluded relaxation, there's the **Opeka Arboretum** 2km south of **Vinica**, an oversized village with aristocratic pretensions and a clutch of Baroque summer mansions 18km west of Varaždin. The 19th-century park that Count Marko Bombelles landscaped with lakes and exotic trees from the Americas and the Far East is protected as Croatia's finest arboretum; it's a wonderful spot for a stroll, whether along a nature trail or among greenhouse blooms of its horticultural school.

Opeka Arboretum
open daylight hours

Čakovec

Although Čakovec was christened after a 13th-century tower of Count Dimitar Čak, its history is bound up with that of the Zrinski family, one of the most colourful of Croatian clans, who sat on the throne four times during the two centuries that their page-turner of a story (*see* box, above right) gripped the nation.

Zrinski Tales

Fortunes began to change for this northern outpost in 1546. When it suited their imperial strategy, the Habsburgs were quick to reward success, and, with Ottoman Turks hammering at the gates, Emperor Ferdinand gifted Nikola Šubić Zrinski the minor borderland castle of Čakovec in appreciation for his defensive successes and a heroic intervention at Pest which spared imperial blushes in 1544. Cultural life in this Međimurje capital blossomed alongside its larger-than-life warlord-poets, who honoured sharp steel and brave deeds and met memorable deaths, few more celebrated than that of Nikola Šubić himself.

In a last-ditch defence of a frontier castle at Szigetvár in 1566, Nikola Šubić Zrinski rode out with a single garrison to meet the entire Turkish host led by Suleyman the Magnificent. It was a massacre, of course, but an end worthy of an epic poem, in this case penned a century later by his great-grandson Nikola VII Zrinski, a multilingual poet and no mean warrior himself – in 1643 he chased the Ottoman host east to Osijek and recaptured every Croat stronghold on the way. The Zrinski name became the toast of Europe. The pope struck a medal in salute, the Spanish rey sent a Golden Fleece and the Sun King provided a French peerage. Čakovec, as the Zrinski capital, basked in reflected glory.

Emperor Leopold chipped in with a princehood, but a relationship already strained by the Habsburg refusal to hunt down the retreating Ottomans was put beyond repair when the Turks won a slice of Hungary in a 1664 peace deal. Before he died in Čakovec woods attempting to finish off a wild boar armed only with a hunting knife, Nikola VII Zrinski had nurtured a conspiracy of Croatian nobles. Now brother Petar took up the cause alongside brother-in-law Krsto Frankopan, and the duo secretly touted the Hungarian-Croat crown around France, Poland and finally to mortal enemy Turkey in a desperate bid to secure backing for a rebellion. Word of the plot leaked out and, having failed spectacularly to rally local support, the conspirators hurried to Vienna to swear their fealty. Leopold was in no mood for clemency and swiftly beheaded the duo in Wiener Neustadt on 30 April 1671.

The tale doesn't quite end there. The shocking end of the Zrinskis and Frankopans in 1671 was a body blow for dreams of Croatian emancipation – when Leopold delivered the lands of the two dynastic superpowers to acquiescent foreign nobles, he swept away the future for an independent nation and set in its place an élite of foreigners. And it was a disaster for Čakovec, too: Viennese troops plundered the family seat down to the cheese in its larder and, with its spiritual fathers gone and in the hands of Habsburg stooges the Althan counts from Czechoslovakia, the Međimurje capital sank into relative anonymity – and, worse, into the shadow cast by rising star and rival Varaždin.

Museum of Međimurje
*Muzej Medimurje; **t** (040) 313 285, www.mdc.hr/cakovec; open Tues–Fri 10–3, Sat–Sun 10–1; adm*

What Zrinski artefacts Čakovec saved after the Viennese raids – a stone bust of the ill-fated Petar, municipal decrees and the tomb slab of Nikola Šubić, for example – are housed in the **castle**, set aloof from the town in a mature park, a Baroque courtyard mansion (built after a 1738 earthquake) behind Zrinski-built Renaissance bulwarks. Elsewhere in the **Museum of Međimurje** there are finds from an Iron Age necropolis in Goričan, including an asko vessel decorated with long-horned cattle, devotional paintings and 19th-century *objets d'art*, and displays of regional folk costume and crafts – look for a cabinet of nightmarish animal masks and costume dusted down for the Međimurje carnival, Čakovec 's pre-Lent revel.

Pleasant through provincial, the **town centre** merits little more than a coffee stop, although do look at Hungarian architect Ödön Horvath's bizarre **Secessionist hall**, with its weird knobbles and red brick swirls, standing ostracised at the far end of the pedestrian centre on Trg Republike.

Međimurje Wines

After a bout of *phylloxera*, the scourge of vintners, family wine-growers introduced new vines alongside autochthonic varieties, although most wines to taste on the Međimurje wine road (*Međimurska vinska cesta*) are semi-dry to semi-sweet whites: expect *šipon*, named by Napoleon's acclaim '*C'est bon*!' and dangerously quaffable, *ranjski rizlig* (Rhine riesling), noble *pinot bijeli* (pinot blanc) and *pinot gris*, an aromatic sauvignon, chardonnay and a smooth traminer-like summer blossom.

Most of the 22 producers string along two routes – from Štrigova to Stanetinec in district Sv. Urban; and east of Štrigova on the Čakovec road – and in theory you can roll into anywhere that advertises its *vino*. Few, however, are as charming as **Lovrec** (Sv. Urban 133, **t** (040) 830 171, *www.hotel.hr/vino-lovrec*; open April–Nov daily). Call in advance and in a rustic beamed farmhouse, you will be led (in English) through a range of dry to sweet whites nurtured by a wine knight of Austria and Hungary, accompanied by nibbles of tangy cheeses and smoked pork. Bottles to take away cost 30–120Kn.

West into Wine Country

Global warming hasn't always been bad. Ten million years ago it dried up the Pannonian Sea and replaced it with gentle hills of mineral-rich sandstone and clay. It also created a warm, balanced climate with moderate rainfall. First-century Romans paused in their conquering of Pannonian and Celtish tribes to earn a tidy *denarius* from local grapes – the Roman writer Pliny saluted Međimurje wines for their profits as much as their taste – and this last corner of Croatia to the west of Čakovec remains wine country.

As well as being a diminutive wine town as sweet as its traminer grapes, tiny picturesque **Štrigova** may be founded over the Roman town Stridon, say some scholars. Their academic rigour substantiates an old tale that encouraged locals to dedicate a Baroque parish church to the antique town's most famous son, **St Jerome**, glorified inside by the illusionist frescoes of the ever-industrious Pauline monk Ivan Ranger.

Festivals in and around Varaždin

Highlight of the Varaždin social calendar is the **Baroque Evenings**, a three-week festival of classical music in the cathedral and Erdödy Palace from the middle of September. You can buy tickets at T-Tours (*see* p.115) or the ticket office at Cesarčeva 1, **t** (042) 212 907.

Before that, the **Špancirfest** timewarps back to the 18th century for the last week of August, when lots of costumed performers and craftsmen take to the squares and streets.

An otherwise anonymous town, Čakovec sparks into life on the weekend before Lent for **Carnival** (*fašnik*) – there are processions of animal masks and *pikač*, walking haystacks with beehive heads, in a festival whose pagan roots are just a whisper away.

ⓘ **Varaždin >**
*Ivana Padovca 3, **t** (042) 210 987, www.varazdin.hr, www.tourism-varazdin.hr; open April–Oct Mon–Fri 8–7, Sat 9–5; Nov–Mar Mon–Fri 8–4, Sat 10–1*

★ **Zlatna Guska >>**

ⓘ **Čakovec >**
*Kralja Tomislava 1, **t** (040) 313 319, www.tourism-cakovec.hr; open Mon–Fri 8–7, Sat 8–1*

ⓘ **Međimurje >**
*Ivana Mažuranića 2/111, Čakovec, **t** (040) 313 090, www.tzm.hr*

Where to Stay in and around Varaždin

Varaždin

Istra, Ivana Kukuljevića 6, **t** (042) 659 659, *www.istra-hotel.hr* (€€). Opened in 2006 and currently the only old-town hotel in Varaždin. Though comfy and with inoffensive soft business style, four-star rooms are rather over-priced for attic accommodation above a restaurant. No faulting a location just off the main square, mind.

Varaždin, Kolodvorska 19, 290 720, *www.hotelvarazdin.com* (€€). Good-value, small, business-styled three-star opposite the train station. Most rooms have futuristic massage power-showers.

Turist, Aleja kralja Zvonimira 1, **t** (042) 395 394, *www.hotel-turist.hr* (€€–€). The businessman's favourite three-star. Standard rooms are poor value compared with the Maltar (*see* below); business class is comfy and modern if a mite bland.

Pansion Maltar, Prešernova 1, **t** (042) 311 100, *www.maltar.hr* (€). Good-value if functional rooms, all en suite, in a friendly *pension* near the Turist.

For rooms in private houses, contact tourist agency **T-Tours**, I. Gundulića 2, **t** (042) 210 989.

Čakovec

Aurora, Franje Punčeca bb (behind bus station), **t** (040) 310 700 (€€). Ten suite-style rooms in this family hotel are priced just the wrong side of inexpensive. Dated but comfy and spacious.

Park, Zrinsko-frankopanska bb (main road opposite the park), **t** (040) 311 255, *www.union-ck.hr* (€). Small modern rooms for visiting Hungarian businessmen. Not the dreary tower block it looks from outside, but still nothing special.

Medimurje

Monika, Železna gora 118, **t** (040) 851 304 (€). A chirpy three-star motel on the Štrigova–Čakovec road. Three-star facilities in six simple but bright rooms.

Eating Out in and around Varaždin

Varaždin

Zlatna guska, J. Habdelicva 4, **t** (042) 213 393 (€€). Marvellous faux medieval dining in a cellar restaurant that's long been the finest in town and has appeared in Croatia's 'Top 100'. The menu of the 'Golden Goose' aspires to banqueting splendour, with baronial-themed dishes of freshwater fish and meats such as steak with truffles.

Zlatna Ruke, Ivana Kukuljevića 13, **t** (042) 320 065 (€€). Another cellar place, but the 'Golden Hands' aspires to hip metropolitan style in decor and menu that adds international flavours to local fare.

Domenico, Trg slobode 7, **t** (042) 212 017 (€). Fifteen styles of pizza plus tasty homemade pastas on one of the nicest terraces, beside the park.

Grenadir, Kranjčevićeva 12, **t** (042) 211 131 (€). A traditional dining room of starched white tablecloths and antique dressers sets the tone for a good-value menu of continental Croatian fare: pork chops and trout. *Closed Sun eve.*

Ritz, Franjevački trg 4 (€). A corner café on the main square whose terrace is perfect for people-watching. Cellars beneath hold a lounge bar – think leather sofas stuffed between Baroque pillars and house beats.

Čakovec

Restoran ribiji, Kralja Tomislava 2, **t** (040) 312 688 (€€). A menu of sea bass, trout, crab and zander to explore and a dining room hung with nets in a speciality fish restaurant. An adjacent sister bistro (€) rustles up passable pizzas and pastas.

Medimurje

Terbotz, Železna gora 113, **t** (040) 857 444, *www.terbotz.hr* (€€). A Baroque country manor nearby with a fine restaurant of Međimurje cooking and wine cellar.

East of Varaždin: Into the Podravina

Varaždinske Toplice

The first stop on the trail east towards Podravina's typical farming hamlets is Varaždinske Toplice. Every passing tribe has paused to wallow in the two million litres of 58°C sulphurous waters which gush every day in Croatia's oldest spa town: the Illyrian Jasi in the 3rd century BC, Roman spa aficionados, medieval bathers in 'Toplisse', owned by Zagreb bishopric Kaptol, 18th-century spa-goers seeking miracle cures, 19th-century patrons of one of the Central Europe's most renowned health spas, and now rheumatic pensioners. Only the Goths were unimpressed.

Clouds of steam still waft over the Romans' 3rd-century Aquae Issae, whose **ruins** lie above today's town beyond an arch fashioned from chunks of a *nymphaeum* unearthed in 1865: two half-lions, half-fish, antique icons of thermal waters, and a shrine carved with a coquettish nymph, all supported on an inscribed slab. The site itself is just about recognizable as a central pool before a forum, the knobble studs actually worn pillars, and a baths complex that is still undergoing excavation.

The best finds – a prized marble Minerva, goddess of wisdom, who once stood in her own temple, 2nd-century skinny-dipping nymphs and a bestiality of mythical water creatures – are displayed in a **museum** in the central **castle**, the town's heart, which appeared in the 14th century as the fortress of Kaptol bishops until it gentrified into a palace (and the first spa) after the cessation of Turkish raids in the 1600s. Its church of **St Martin** features marble masterpieces from Croatian Baroque's finest sculptor, Francesco Robba, and a 1765 organ whose looks are as sweet as its acclaimed tone.

Museum
*Zavičajni muzej; **t** (042) 633 339; open Mon–Fri 9–2, Sat 9–12.30; adm*

In view of their illustrious history, today's two **pools** sequestered downhill as part of the Minerva hotel complex are a disappointment, though Olympic in size and with a fun-pool and water chutes for the kiddies.

Pools
open June–Sept daily 8–8; adm

Ludbreg

A sidetrack south of Varaždinske Toplice, the B24 winds lazily up and over the uplands of Kalničko gorje to **Kalnik**, site of a medieval castle which crumbles romantically on a bluff and provides picture-postcard panoramas over rolling hills.

Head east of Varaždinske Toplice and the hills flatten as you amble through farming hamlets of orchards and slatted corn barns to reach **Ludbreg**, agri-market hub and centre of the world. Or so narrates a Roman legend about its being the *centrum mundi*, a conceit the town maintains to this day on a main square of concentric rings. Every bit as dubious is a local priest's deathbed

Getting to and around the Podravina

Varaždinske Toplice is linked to Varaždin by frequent buses every 45mins; **Ludbreg** is linked to Varaždin and Koprivnica by buses every 30mins and trains every 1hr 30mins.

To **Koprivnica**, 7 buses a day and 8 trains a day go from Zagreb, and there are hourly buses from Varaždin. **Hlebine** is connected to Koprivnica by 4 buses a day.

---

claim that his Mass wine transmogrified into blood in 1414, but, backed by the full weight of Catholic authority and Pope Leo X's bull acclaiming a miracle in 1513, it is gospel truth for over 100,000 pilgrims who congregate for the first Sunday in September. The focus of Holy Sunday is an **outdoor chapel** just outside the town centre, built 255 years late by the Croatian parliament in 1994 as a morale-booster for a nation undergoing a traumatic birth. The Holy Blood of Christ, Croatia's greatest relic for believers, is revered in a gold monstrance in the central Baroque **Church of the Sanctuary of the Trinity** (Crkva presv. Trojstva), where images of the startled priest and Leo X processing in papal garb narrate the miracle.

Koprivnica and Hlebine

And so at last into the Podravina, the northern strip of continental Croatia planted with nodding sunflowers and cornfields, which is bordered to the north by the Drava river, suffering senility in its final stages and fragmenting into oxbow lakes and aimless backwaters, and to the south by the lush agricultural slopes of Bilogora.

At their base is western transport axis **Koprivnica**, a 30,000-strong town whose national renown is eclipsed by that of the Vegeta dehydrated stock produced by local food giant Podravka. Yet, cocooned within drab suburbs, this free royal town, founded in 1356 and rebuilt after it was put to the torch by 16th-century Turks, turns on the Central European charm in a handsome main square, **Zrinski trg**, all manicured flowerbeds and parterre hedge-swirls in front of a **park** of specimen trees and the obligatory wrought-iron bandstand.

Town gallery
Galerija Koprivnica; Zrinski trg 9, **t** *(048) 622 564; open Tues–Fri 10–1 and 5–8, Sat–Sun 10–1*

Town museum
Muzej grada Koprivnice; Trg Leandera Brozovića; open Mon–Fri 8–2, Sat 10–1; adm

The **town gallery** hangs temporary exhibitions of regional art, often picked from archives of Hlebine naïve artists (*see* below), while, on the southwest fringes of the park, the **town museum** displays church silver alongside an enjoyable rummage through 19th-century furniture, Sunday best china and costumes rescued from attics of the local bourgeoisie. There are also two rooms of photos and war trophies to celebrate the 1991 capitulation of local Yugoslav People's Army's troops without a fight.

Koprvinica is a bus change and 13km from **Hlebine**, the cradle of Croatian naïve art. The modern village in which 19 private *ateliers* tout homespun images has come a long way from the hamlet where academic painter Professor Krsto Hegedušić stumbled upon the daubs of farmlads Ivan Generalić and Franjo Mraz in 1930. In their unfussy, immediate style, he recognized a Croatian response to the soul-searching about artistic integrity which had elevated Rousseau to the toast of Paris and sent Picasso off studying African masks. So, having refined their raw talent with a crash course in art basics and encouraged a return to the oil-on-glass format practised in votive folk art, Hegedušić proudly presented his protégés' works to Zagreb alongside works of the socialist art group Zemlja ('The Earth').

From social documentary, the second-generation painters of the **Hlebine School**, today comprised of around 200 artists in neighbouring towns and villages, veered towards fantastical themes, and it's largely their archives which rotate in the **Hlebine Gallery** opposite a central café. Ivan Generalić's brand of rustic magic realism is on permanent display in a back-room retrospective of large works from the 1970s, as vivid as cartoon acetates. More works plus those of his son Josip Generalić, who died in December 2004 and had a weakness for beaming his pop music heroes into Hlebine, are in their **studio** five minutes' walk away and a naïve Stations of the Cross wraps around the church of **St Catherine** (Crkva sv. Katarine).

Hlebine Gallery
*Galerija Hlebine; **t** (048) 836 075; open Mon–Fri 10–4, Sat 10–2; adm*

Studio
*Galerija Josip Generalic; **t** (048) 836 071; open by appointment (or try your luck); adm*

ⓘ Ludbreg >>
*Trg sv. Trojstva 14, **t** (042) 810 690, www.ludbreg.hr; open Mon–Fri 7–3*

ⓘ Koprivnica >>
*Trg bana J. Jela¬ica 7, **t** (048) 621 433, www.koprivnica.hr; open Mon–Fri 8–2, Sat 8–12*

ⓘ Varaždinske Toplice >
*Trg slobode 16 (in castle), **t** (042) 633 133, www.toplice-vz.hr; open July–Aug daily 7–7; Sept–June Mon–Fri 7–3*

Festivals in and around the Podravina

Varaždinske Toplice revels in cultural events and street performers during **Lovrečevo**, usually the 2nd week in August, and a bizarre union of funfair and religious fever grips **Ludbreg** near the first Sunday in September.

Koprivnica stages a hurrah of folk tradition during **Motifs of Podravina** (Podravski motivi): there's art for sale in the world's biggest naïve art fair, displays of crafts and costume, and regional cuisine, including production of a half-kilometre sausage. It is traditionally on second weekend of July, but has been moved forward to the first in recent years.

Where to Stay and Eat in and around the Podravina

Varaždinske Toplice

Minerva, Trg slobode 1, **t** (042) 630 431/831, *www.minerva.com* (€€). Acceptable if bland accommodation in a rather tired resort hotel of socialist Yugoslavia vintage, favoured by an elderly spa clientele. There's free entrance to the pools and a sauna, though.

The tourist office lists rooms in private accommodation.

Ludbreg

Črn-Bel, Vinogradska bb, **t** (042) 819 177 (€€). A semi-smart restaurant, perched above the Vinogradi road with country views from its terrace and the finest menu in town. Try chef's pride *odrezak črn-bel*, local beef with a sauce of mushrooms and ham and bacon, or platters of the owner's homemade cheeses.

Koprivnica

Kralauš, Zrinski trg 8, **t** (048) 622 302 (€). A marvellous local favourite on the main square, its cobbles worn shiny from over two centuries of use as a beer cellar. A regional menu of sausages and *grah* (refried beans), *gorički gulaš* (Hungarian-style beef and potato goulash) and *jelenji paprikaš* (venison stew with paprika) changes every century or so.

Podravina, Hrvatske državnosti 9, **t** (048) 612 015, *www.hotel-podravina.hr* (€). A modest but modern(ish) two-star hotel, rescued by a central location one block west of Zrinski trg.

Podravska klet, Starigrad bb, **t** (048) 634 069 (*moderate*). Upmarket rusticity and country portions in a cottagey charmer 5km south off the B2 to Bjelovar. Start with mushroom soup with buckwheat, smoked local cheeses or a farm-produced *meso iz lodrice* (smoked pork), then try *teletina na pekarski* (veal baked with potatoes), the house special on a menu of sausages and steaks.

Slavonia

For Croatia and tourists alike, this is frontier country. Guardian on the nation's ramparts, Slavonia stood watch on the eastern flank of the Habsburgs' *Vojna Krajina* (Military Frontier) and still bears the scars from a turbulent history, whether inflicted by Ottoman Turks camped here until the late 17th century or, more visibly, by Serbian forces who tried to annexe its oil-rich fields in 1991. This is a tourist frontier, too – few visitors explore its minor towns and villages strung out like toy towns along the road. Yet there are attractions in this region wedged between Hungary and Bosnia-Hercegovina, not least a colourful patchwork of shaggy cornfields and swaying sunflowers on a fertile alluvial plain. And the regional tourist board is eager to promote its spas and cycle routes. Although overtaken by recent history, the main town of Osijek retains a whiff of propriety in wide streets of confident Habsburg architecture, and has a Baroque kernel far too picturesque to have been a barracks. It also serves as a launchpad for the Kopački rit Nature Reserve, a remnant of the swampy wetlands which appeared every autumn until the Sava, Drava and Dunav (Danube) were tamed. Elsewhere are mild-mannered market towns Požega and Đakovo, a paean to provincial bliss with modest architectural sights.

Eastern Slavonia: From Osijek to Ilok

Osijek

Few towns have felt the bite of Slavonia's history of conflict as deeply as Osijek. It's hard to believe today, but just 175 years ago the region's largest town outranked Zagreb in population. In 1829, when the nation's capital was only 8,000-strong, the 9,200 residents In the capital of Slavonia looked forwards to a prosperous future, drip-fed wealth by international trade routes that have proved a double-edged sword.

It was the presence of one, the Drava river, that persuaded 1st-century AD Romans to found a shipping base and garrison town

Getting to and around Eastern Slavonia

Two trains a day arrive in **Osijek** from Požega and 7 or 8 a day from Đakovo. 6 buses a day go to Osijek from Zagreb; there's 1 a day from Varaždin and frequent buses from Đakovo and Požega.

Tram 1 (10Kn single) links Trg Ante Starčevića to Tvrđa. The Kompa ferry – more a glorified raft – shuttles between Gornji grad and the zoo and Copocabana beach on the opposite bank (daily May–Sept 9–8, Apr and Oct 9–6; 5Kn).

Frequent local buses from Osijek go to **Bilje**, after which it's a 3km walk to the entrance of **Kopački rit Nature Park**. Buses travel to **Vukovar** from Osijek approx every 90mins, from where 8 buses a day proceed southeast to Ilok.

---

near the riverbank, later upgraded to full *civitas* status as Colonia Aelia Mursa, home of get-rich-quick merchants and retired generals. And it was the strategic location which caught the eye of Sultan Suleyman the Magnificent in 1529. Having snatched Osijek, he gathered its minarets and mosques tight within stone walls and directed every Turkish infantry unit bound for the western front over an oak bridge, built by 25,000 labourers and which snaked eight miles above the Drava's marshes as a wonder of the Ottoman world.

Back in Habsburg hands in 1687 without so much as a broken roofslate – Turkish citizens fled before the oncoming imperial army and Nikola Zrinksi of Čakovec fame torched the celebrated bridge – Osijek was rebuilt as military HQ Tvrđa (from *tvrđava*, fortress), strongest of strongholds on the Slavonian Military Frontier. It also acquired a new civic centre 1.5km upriver, Gornji grad ('upper town'), which remains the town's core, with residential district Donji grad ('lower town') east of the fortress. The sprawl of modernity has filled in the gaps united by statute in 1809, but Osijek retains a spacious, easygoing appeal.

The latest attempt at annexation landed a particularly heavy blow. Mere hours after the fall of Vukovar in November 1991 (*see* p.124), Yugoslav People's Army (JNA) troops marched on a panic-stricken Osijek. Acceptance of a UN peace deal by Serbian president Slobodan Milošević spared the town the hammering suffered by its sister, but the war wounds inflicted by Serbian artillery shells lobbed over the river during a 10-month bombardment from the Baranja region to the north are still evident. Other scars may prove more difficult to heal. Icy relations with next-door neighbour Serbia have frozen the drip-feed of international trade – and finance – to the Slavonian capital, which now pins its hopes of a revival on a transport corridor from the coast to Central Europe.

Until that happens, Osijek finds itself at a loose end. Tvrđa got off lightly in the destruction, but is a far cry from the cosmopolitan hub it was in the 1800s. Elsewhere, for all its formal parks graced with statues and its streets of Habsburg mansions, Osijek has the air of a former power left behind by the rush of history.

Gornji Grad

Osijek's self-confidence of old is still palpable just off Gornji grad's main square, **Trg Ante Starčevića**, in the neo-Gothic parish church of **SS Peter and Paul** (Crkva sv. Petra i Pavla), a red-brick behemoth, whose 90-metre-high spire like a ballistic missile was dwarfed only by that of the cathedral in Zagreb when it was finished in 1898. The Viennese stained glass and frescoes in the Osijek '*katedrala*' were first in line for restoration after 1995; the war-wounded 19th-century buildings on **Županijska**, opposite, still cry out for attention. McDonald's funded repairs of the smart town theatre as a *quid pro quo* for restaurant space.

East of Trg Ante Starčevića, continuing beyond high street Kapucinska, is **Europska avenija**. Art Nouveau and Secessionist grandees compete for attention on the wide thoroughfare which links Gornji grad to Tvrđa, the faded fantasies of Habsburg worthies on what was the most desirable address in Osijek. Among them is the **Gallery of Fine Arts**; set in its own 19th-century palace and displaying 18th- and 19th-century Austro-Hungarian landscapes plus a smattering of modern Croatian works.

Gallery of Fine Arts
Galerija likovnih umjetnosti; Europska avenija 9, ***t*** *(031) 251 280, www.mdc.hr/glu_osijek; open Tues–Fri 10–6, Sat–Sun 10–1; adm*

Tvrđa

Cocooned from the modernity of Gornji grad away to its west by a large park, Tvrđa is the part of Osijek everyone comes to see, a Baroque timewarp knitted together by cobbled lanes which is at its most alluring in lamplight and on balmy summer evenings. Approach this 'open-air museum' by way of Europaska avenija – you can also reach Tvrđa on a riverfront stroll east along the Šetalište kardinala Franje Šepara, a mouthful locals ditch in favour of '**Promenada**' – and you'll pass a horseshoe foundation among surrounding lawns, the last relic of the **walls** which girdled the city during 161 years of Turkish occupation. The Ottomans' fortifications were mined as a quarry of pre-cut stone to create defence walls punctuated by seven bastions during the Habsburg revamp which beamed a Dutch-style fortress into these Central European flatlands. These walls themselves were ripped down on all but the river side in 1923; it would have been sooner had Emperor Franz Josef I not pooh-poohed complaints that the stone girdle hindered trade and expansion and slapped a preservation order on the town.

The heart of Tvrđa's neat grid is Trg svetog Trojstva, once the nerve centre of Slavonia's *metropolis urbs*, now quiet except at weekends, when the artisans' houses on the south side are prime bar-hopping territory. In the centre, the Holy Trinity and assorted saints pose atop a boiling 1730 **plague pillar**, erected in votive thanks for a clean bill of health by a general's wife who had lost her husband to an epidemic two years earlier. It is flanked by the

18th-century **wells and pumps** of the first water supply system in Slavonia.

The imposing slab on the north flank of the square was the **Military Headquarters of Slavonia**, now demobbed and its Renaissance dress uniform tatty and threadbare in places; at its shoulder is the porticoed **city guard house**, capped with a Moorish-style observation post which gave the fortress commander a grandstand view over goings-on. Also on the square is Tvrđa's sole cultural institution, the **Museum of Slavonia**, with Bronze Age odds and ends and chunks of Roman tomb slabs, plus temporary exhibitions of town history.

Museum of Slavonia
Muzej Slavonije; ***t*** *(031) 250 730, www.mdc.hr/osijek; open Tues–Fri 9–2, Sat–Sun 10–1; adm*

A lane threads off the northeast corner of Trg sv. Trojstva to **Trg Jurja Križanića**. Here the conquering Austrians said prayers in the reconsecrated Kasim-pasha mosque, until a parish church was erected on its foundations in 1725 by Jesuits. With a point to prove, they built the twin-towered Baroque hulk which still awes surrounding alleys – it's no surprise that **St Michael's Church** (Crkva sv. Mihovila) is pledged to the victorious defender of the Christian Church.

On the north bank of the Drava, the lawns and pool of town 'beach' **Copacabana** provide a place to sunbathe and swim in summer. Rio it is not, however.

Kopački Rit Nature Park

4 Kopački Rit Nature Park
Park Prirode Kopački Rit; ***Warning:*** *although the park has been swept for the landmines laid when this was a front line in the Homeland War, always stick to the paths and take heed of skull-and-crossbones signs*

Before the mighty Danube was tamed and channelled and became just another river, seasonal wetlands pooled at the tributary confluences of its 2,840km run to the Black Sea. Although 81 per cent have dried up for good since the beginning of the 20th century, the elbow where the Drava rushes into the Danube, causing it to back up and burst its banks, is protected as the Kopački Rit Nature Park, one of the most important wetland habitats in Europe, whose marshes and pools choked by lilies and fringed by semi-submerged white willow are a modern Eden of birdlife. Especially in spring and early autumn, a spotter's book of waterbirds arrive to fatten up and breed in the largest spawning ground in the middle Danube, stocked with frogs and 44 varieties of fish, including carp, zander, pike and huge catfish. Grey heron and cormorants, spoonbills, terns and white stork stalk pools in their thousands – the few pairs of rare black stork and white-tailed eagle are more elusive – while in oak woods to the north of the park are wild boar and red deer. Everywhere are 17 varieties of mosquito, all of them hungry.

Boat tours
summer only, times vary; currently July–Aug Tues–Fri 11 and 3, Sat–Sun 11, 1 and 3

Your best chance of seeing reclusive wildlife is on the **boat tours** which potter through the centre of the wetlands to the Drava. The tours leave from a **park information centre** 3km east of Bilje and just north of **Kopačevo**, one of the most idyllic villages you'll find in Slavonia, whose core of slender Hungarian-style houses placed end-on to the lane seems caught in some hazy soft focus of timeless summers. Alternatively, armed with pamphlets from the kiosk or **park administration office**, located at the eastern edge of **Bilje** (*see* p.125) in an 18th-century hunting lodge that imperial commander Prince Eugene of Savoy gifted himself for routing Ottoman Turks, you can take to a boardwalk from the kiosk or drive along a road which cuts west then north, pausing in car parks to amble along paths that explore more interesting and secluded habitats.

Follow the road north past weekend fishermen and a fork slices east to **Dvorac Tikveš**, a 19th-century hunting villa enjoyed by Josip Broz Tito, battered by Serbian troops and which has long been slated for conversion into a hotel. The fields further north are scattered with the care-worn villages of the **Baranja**, one of Croatia's richest agricultural lands, wedged between Hungary and Serbia and farmed peacefully by peoples from all three countries until 24 August 1991, when Serbian tanks rolled over the border to 'liberate' the 25 per cent Serbian population. The Croatians fell back across the Drava, the Hungarians fled north, and the defiant few who remained or crept back between 1992–6, when the region was marshalled by Belgian troops of the United Nations, were subject to blatant ethnic cleansing. A veneer of normality has returned, but trust remains elusive.

South of Osijek: Vukovar to Ilok

Once a mildly prosperous town on the Danube, **Vukovar** is now famous for all the wrong reasons. Before 1990, its visitors came to saunter along a rustic Baroque high street or to strike deals with industrial rubber manufacturer Borovo. A Croat–Serb community (44 and 37 per cent) lived harmoniously on the banks of the Danube. And then came the bellicose statements and brinkmanship which ratcheted up tension in late 1990. In April 1991, a tit-for-tat exchange in a Serb-dominated suburb escalated, then spiralled out of control until the provincial town was caught in the most brutal siege of the Homeland War (*see* box on p.124). Once just a modest success story, Vukovar became a Croatian Stalingrad, placed on the nation's altar as 'the symbol of Croatian suffering,

Croatian resistance, Croatian aspirations for freedom' (Franjo Tuđman, 1997).

The town was reintegrated into the bosom of the nation in 1998, and restoration work has patched up many buildings shattered by bombs or spattered by shrapnel and added shiny glass and steel cubes thanks to UNESCO funding. Indeed, Vukovar is looking forward sufficiently to have constructed a business hotel in 2005. Harder to patch up is the psychological damage. If Osijek has been emotionally scarred by its experience on the front line, Vukovar is in counselling. A veneer of normality has returned in a majority Serb town, but the mass graves and murder are not easily forgotten, and tensions remain.

On sunny days, passing visitors may barely notice and, bar a ghoulish fascination for a few war derelicts with stoved-in roofs

The Siege of Vukovar

April 1991: after Croatia declared its independence, Vukovar divided along ethnic lines, Croatians for a free mother country, Serbs in the suburbs for Yugoslavia. An uneasy peace was maintained until agitators ratcheted up the tension by firing three rockets into the Serbian district of Borovo Selo, an act in which Gojko Šušak, future defence minister of president Franjo Tuđman's HDZ party, was implicated. Retaliation came swiftly on 1 May, when two policeman were kidnapped in the suburb. The next day a bus-borne cavalry of police rookies from Osijek were ambushed during a rescue attempt, resulting in 15 deaths and public outrage when rumour spread that the bodies were mutilated. Forces of the Yugoslav People's Army (JNA) interposed, ostensibly to keep the peace, and Vukovar was never the same again...

On 24 August 1991, surrounded by 50,000 troops and Serbian paramilitaries and flanked by tanks, Vukovar was hit by the first shell in the opening salvo of a full-scale military assault that was to last 87 days. As refugees took their chances with Serbian snipers and fled west through cornfields, on a thin thread of communication, a rag-tag army of police and national guard troops bolstered by around 1,000 volunteers with hunting rifles mounted a desperate defence. By early September, Vukovar was battered and reduced to a 15,000 population but still free and standing. Then the JNA tightened the net and seized outlying villages. On 14 September Vukovar disappeared from view as a week-long assault by troops and tanks spearheaded southeast on the Osijek road, later dubbed the 'tank graveyard', and a brutal air assault began.

Reports from a lone Croatia Radio journalist in his home town crackled across the airwaves, but all lines of communication had been cut by early October, when around 5,000 shells a day pulverized the centre into ruins. The remaining residents – the wounded, elderly or children – disappeared underground with tins of food and meagre water supplies, their plight, like Vukovar's, largely ignored by an international community aghast at the siege of Dubrovnik. Some commentators accused Zagreb of sacrificing Vukovar to reinforce the image of Croatia as a victim of Serbian aggression, a claim Tuđman disputed by pointing out that forces on other fronts were already at full stretch. After three weeks of fierce street-to-street combat, the town fell on 18 November. Civilians emerged from the dark and Croats were exiled or fled to the town hospital hoping to be evacuated in the presence of international observers. Instead, as TV footage documented a Serbian paramilitary unit chorusing, '*Biće mesa, biće mesa, klaćemo Hrvate*' ('There will be meat, there will be meat, we're slaughtering the Croats'), JNA troops entered the hospital the following day and removed around 400 patients, staff and soldiers, dumping around 260 bodies in a mass grave in Ovčara 4km southwest. Three JNA officers, the 'Vukovar Three', finally stood before the UN war crimes commission in The Hague in October 2005. All pleaded not guilty. It is said that 2,642 people are still missing. The media spotlight shifted long ago, but Vukovar is still coming to terms with its past.

and blank window sockets, the town's only real sight is the **Eltz Palace**, its Baroque in bad shape on thoroughfare J. J. Strossmayera and home to the **town museum**, with temporary exhibitions plus town treasures finally returned from Belgrade.

Town museum
Gradski muzej; **t** *(032) 441 270; open Sept–July Mon–Fri 7–3, adm*

East, through a central square lined by glass newcomers, off which a white cross to Vukovar's fallen defenders is placed like a provocation on the riverbank opposite the Serbian border, and uphill beyond a high street of porticoed Baroque town houses in various stages of construction and destruction, is the **Franciscan Monastery of SS Philip and Jacob** (Franjevački samostan Filipa i Jakova). It was reduced to a shell by Serbian bombadeers who deliberately trained their sights on churches to obliterate monuments of Croatian culture, but was then so immaculately rebuilt (in 2000) that you can barely see the joins in its intimate cloister – not something that can be said about the ice-cream cone water tower beyond, ravaged and punched by shell holes.

A **memorial cemetery** to victims of the war puts human names to the tragedy east, just beyond the once-ravaged suburbs, and more sobering still is the one in **Ovčara**, beyond. Then the mood lightens among vines, sunflowers and corn stalks as the B2 bowls southeast to the village of **Šarengrad**, its huddle of rustic houses, lorded over by a Baroque Franciscan monastery, war-scarred but at peace and pretty.

The end of Croatia's eastern road is **Ilok**, famous for wine – traminer and graševina whites cultivated on the Fruška Gora slopes – and for walls – the crenellated fortifications which guarded a 16th-century Turkish town and inspired town marketeers to dub Ilok a 'Dubrovnik of the Danube'. You can also spot scraps of the hammam baths abutting the walls and a lone Moorish pavilion before the Baroque mansion of Habsburg commander Duke Odescalchi, much-remodelled and now a down-at-heel home for the archaeology and ethnography displays in the **town museum**. A better reason to visit is for an epic panorama out over the flat plains of Serbia and a castle restaurant with local tipples.

Town museum
closed for restoration

ⓘ Kopački Rit Nature Park >
Petefi Šandora 33, Bilje, **t** *(031) 750 855/752 321 (reservations), www.kopacki-rit.com; open Mon–Fri 8–4*

Festivals in Eastern Slavonia

Osijek resounds to the sound of furiously strummed *tambura*, a sort of Croatian lute, for the **Tamburaški** festival held around the 1st weekend in May.

Activities in Kopački Rit Nature Park

Andrija Bekina, Ritska bb, Bilje, **t** (031) 740 571, mobile **t** 091 570 1063. English-speaking fishing trips in Kopački rit and Baranja.

Adventure Team, **t** (031) 735 750, mobile **t** 091 210 1212, *www.baranya-adventure.com*. Canoeing trips in the park, plus off-road and hiking tours in the Baranja region.

Where to Stay in Eastern Slavonia

Osijek > *Županijska 2, t (031) 203 755, www.tzosijek.hr; open Mon–Fri 7–4, Sat 8–12*

Osijek

Osijek has no time for cash-strapped travellers – if you're on a tight budget consider guesthouses and private accommodation in nearby Bilje (*see* below).

Central, Trg Ante Starčevića 6, **t** (031) 283 399, *www.hotel-central-os.hr* (€€). Priced just the wrong side of inexpensive, this central hotel is a little dated but offers good-value, modest accommodation.

Osijek, Šamačka 4, **t** (031) 230 333, *www.hotelosijek.hr* (€€). A former Yugoslav tower block that's had a style makeover to create a slick glass-skinned four-star with a touch of retro modernist chic to its decor in public areas, and superb river views, not least from its 14th floor spa.

Waldinger, Županijska 8, **t** (031) 250 450, *www.waldinger.hr* (€€). Understated luxury and plush furnishings nod to the Secession-era vintage of this small modern four-star near the cathedral. Prices are at the higher end – more modest and cheaper is a three-star *pension* (€) in the garden.

Bilje > *Kralja Zvonimira 10, t (031) 751 480, www.tzo-bilje.hr; open Mon–Fri 8.30–4.30*

Bilje and around

Sklepić, Kolodvorska 58, Karanac, **t** (031) 720 271, *www.sklpeic.hr* (€). Lovely agrotourism accommodation on the Sklepić family farm 20km north of Belje near the Hungarian border. Expect rustic antique furnishings, log fires, carriage rides and charm by the cart-load.

Vukovar > *J. J. Strossmayera 15, t (032) 442 889; open Mon–Fri 7–3*

Vukovar

Lav, J. J. Strossmayera 18, **t** (032) 445 110, *www.hotel-lav.hr* (€€). A smart glass and marble newcomer on which Vukovar pins hopes of a revival. Business-style rooms have four-star mod cons and the best international cuisine in town is rustled up in the restaurant.

Ilok > *Trg Nikole Ilo¬kog bb, t (032) 590 020; open Mon–Fri 8–3*

Ilok

Dunav, Julija Benešića 62, **t** (032) 596 500, *www.hoteldunavilok.com* (€€). A relaxed family hotel newly opened to provide mod cons with the traditional appeal of antique styled rooms and a riverside location. Its restaurant offers the full range of freshwater fish dishes.

Eating Out in Eastern Slavonia

Osijek

El Paso, Zimska luka, **t** (031) 230 500 (€). River views and an Italian menu on a houseboat on the Drava (Danube), rethought into a cheerful modern trattoria just north of Trg Ante Starčevića.

Slavonska kuća, Kamila Firingera 26, **t** (031) 208 277 (€). Fishy Slavonian specials are the choice in this cosy Tvrđa local: there are smoked fish sausages *riblja kobasica*, grilled carp and perch and steaming bowls of *riblji paprikaš*, a freshwater fish stew with a fiery bite of paprika. The décor of rustic knick-knacks is as charming as the service.

Bilje and around

Komoran, Podunavlje bb, Kopački rit, **t** (031) 753 099 (€€). Locals' choice for a splurge is this former hunting lodge in Kopački rit, country-smart in style and with an upmarket menu of game steaks, venison and wild boar stews and freshwater fish. Try house speciality *šaran na rašljama*, carp speared on a forked branch and roasted over an open fire.

Zelena žaba, Ribarska 3, Kopačevo, **t** (031) 752 212 (€). There's a spicy *čobanac* (paprika-flavoured stew) plus fish such as *smuđ* (pike-perch) and a world of *palačinke* (pancakes) for dessert in this modest bar-restaurant, south of the park entrance.

Vukovar

Vrške, Parobrodska 3, **t** (032) 441 788 (€€). Enjoy lunch on the terrace or snug rooms of this lovely fish restaurant and the war seems just a rumour. The menu is full of smoked and grilled freshwater fish – try the carp (*šaran*) – and the location beside the Danube is a charmer.

Cafés and Bars in Osijek

Osijek takes its café- and bar-hopping seriously. For weekend coffee take your pick from the cafés that line the Drava riverbank. Drinking is in the Tvrda, where students bounce between bar-clubs on Franje Kuhaca at the back of the main square.

Waldinger, Županijska 8 (€€). The coffee house of the hotel, a classy marriage of modern art exhibitions and a vintage moustache-wax atmosphere. Stop for coffee, fresh gâteaux and sticky pastries.

Entertainment in Osijek

Croatian National Theatre (Hrvatsko narodno kazalište), Županijska 9, **t** (031) 220 700, *www.hnk-osijek.hr*. Classical music and theatre in the splendid galleried auditorium of the *grande dame* of Osijek cultural life.

Southern Slavonia: Požega to Đakovo

Požega and Našice

Too many decades protected from cold north winds by the Papuk highlands and snuggled into the wooded Babja gora hills at its back have made Požega drowsy, but it wasn't always so. During the 19th century, the provincial market town was acclaimed the 'Athens of Slavonia', a title which probably says more about contemporary Slavonian cultural life than the impact of its social reformist scholars and artists. Nevertheless, their efforts buffed up the finest Baroque townscape in central Slavonia, for which Požega can thank Luka Ibrišimović Sokol. The moustachioed Franciscan friar liberated Požega from 150 years of Turkish rule on 12 March 1688. The victory, achieved in a murky dawn fog, remains a day of public holiday, and the local hero, his cassock sleeves rolled up for business, sheaths a sword and tramples a Turkish crescent – no place for diplomacy, this – on a plinth before the ostentatious late Baroque lemon-coloured **St Theresa's Church** (Crkva sv. Terezije).

You'll find the church one block northeast of the main square **Trg sv. Trojstva**, which slums it as a glorified car park ringed by a beauty parade of Baroque town houses with pastel stucco. At the western end of the square, the grey-blue hulk of the **Church of the Holy Spirit** (Crkva sv. Duha) with attached **Franciscan monastery** narrates local history better than any building in town: its current 1850s incarnation is founded on a 13th-century original erected when the town was just a glint in history's eye – a panel in the outside wall reveals medieval stonework – and it served as a mosque under Turkish occupation.

Town museum
*Gradski muzej; entrance on Matice Hrvatske, **t** 034 272 130, www.gmp.hr; open Mon–Fri 9–2; adm*

Before it stands a **votive column** which salutes the Holy Trinity of the square's name, built in 1749 after Požega finally staggered from its plague sick bed; sculptor Gabriel Granici used 2,000 eggs to cement the marble sand. Here too you'll find the grey triangle of the **town museum**.

Getting to and around Southern Slavonia

To **Požega**, there are 5 buses and 1 train a day from Zagreb. From Požega to Osijek, buses run 6 times a day, stopping in **Našice**, and to **Slavonski Brod** 4 times a day. **Đakovo** is linked to Osijek by frequent buses and 8 trains a day and to Slavonski Brod by hourly buses.

Slavonski Brod is connected to Zagreb by trains and buses approx every hour, and to Vukovar by infrequent buses.

Among its modest haul of archaeology and odds and ends of town history and ethnology, is the star piece, a Romanesque portrait of the Holy Trinity, three alien faces sharing six oval eyes, among reliefs which once wrapped an abbey of St Michael in nearby Rudina.

A sidetrack down Županijska opposite the museum reveals the swaggering **County Palace**, reshaped into a three-towered pile when Požega found its stride in the mid-19th century – in 1847, councillors here became the first in Croatia to use their mother tongue for official business. Otherwise across the east side of the square is the Gothic **St Lawrence's Church** (Crkva sv. Lovre), the oldest in town, its sanctuary frescoed with mysterious 13th-century saints and bashful angels.

From Požega the B51 takes its time towards Osijek, ambling through tidy Slavonian villages strung out like picture-book toy towns, their slender houses laid end-on to the road and where all family life is conducted in a central room or on a communal veranda. Just over the Krndija hills, tail end of Slavonia's Papuk 'mountain', is a good halfway coffee-stop: **Našice**, cosy in woods and vineyards and whose grandest manor, the country seat of the Pejačević family, houses ethnography and family furniture as a **regional museum**.

ⓘ Našice
*Pejačevićev trg 4, **t** (031) 614 951; open Mon–Fri 8–3*

Regional museum
Zavičajni muzej; open Mon–Fri 8–3, Sat 9–12; adm

Slavonski Brod

An alternative route east from Požega skirts the Bosnian border, past **Slavonski Kobaš**, a classic Slavonian village where storks perch on chimneys, then blasts along the *autocesta* towards **Slavonski Brod**. A long-serving frontier town, it sits uncomfortably in a skin of rapid Yugoslavia era industrial expansion and only recalls its folk roots during the **Brodsko kolo** festival. It retains a few records of its military service too, the most impressive being the 18th-century **Brod Fortress** dug by dashing Habsburg hero Prince Eugene of Savoy after he had driven Turkish forces back across the border in 1691. When its geometric star of moats and bastions modelled on the latest strategic thinking from France was completed in 1735, 4,000 troops stood guard over a town of only 1,573 civilians. Only demobbed in 1994, the fortress is slowly being repaired from damage inflicted by Serbian shells, but you can clamber over its

Brod Fortress
*Tvrđava Brod; Galerija Ružić; **t** (035) 411 510, www.gugsb.hr; open Tues–Fri 10–2 and 4–7, Sat–Sun 10–2; adm*

earthworks, and visit the west wing of the central cavalier, housing quirky bronzes that 20th-century sculptor Branko Ružić donated to his home town plus modern art.

The Ottomans' three-street settlement on the bank of the Sava has vanished beneath a new centre 300m east of the castle, whose focus is café-crammed **Trg I. B. Mažuranić**. A riverside stroll along Šetaliste braće Radić ends at a **Franciscan monastery** (Franjevački samostan), Slavonia's largest church, whose conception a year after the reconquest shows in a building which dithers between a fortress, with walls 2m thick, and a sanctuary, with a lovely garden cloister. Inside lies a pair of lavish Baroque altars of the Crucifixion and Resurrection, aflutter with cherubs. Opposite, a block back from the river, the **Regional Brod-Posavlje Museum** displays local history, regional archaeology and Slavonian handicrafts.

Regional Brod-Posavlje Museum
Muzej Brodskog Posavlja; **t** *(035) 447 415, www.muzejbp.hr; Mon–Sat 10–1 and 5–8, Sun 10–1; adm*

Đakovo and Vrpolje

Equidistant from Slavonski Brod, Našice and Osijek, the mild-mannered market town of **Đakovo** advertises its star attraction long before you arrive. On these vast flats of the Slavonian plain, the twin towers of the **Cathedral of St Peter** (Katedrala sv. Petra) can be seen for miles; 'two ardent flames of love, lighting for faith and fatherland in order to greet the coming traveller,' painter Izidor Kršnjavi gushed. The 'love' comes from Bishop Josip Juraj Strossmayer, because it was the charismatic 19th-century leader, a man who enchanted all who met him and was passionate about Croatian independence, who commissioned this goliath of Slavonia's ecclesiastical buildings, an apt gesture perhaps for a settlement which had ruled as the regional bishopric since the late 13th century.

He must have been thrilled as the red bricks of Viennese architect Baron Friedrich Schmidt's minster inched above Đakovo's low-rise roofscape between 1866 and 1882. This is cathedral as statement, a vast historicist hulk which draws on the architectural authority of seven centuries for its declaration of religious might: neo-Romanesque portals and 84m spires, neo-Gothic rose windows and, just to top things off, a dainty neo-Renaissance cupola that buds over the transept.

Those muscular looks belie a pleasant interior of floral wall paintings like Liberty prints, and frescoes that narrate the patron saint's life; father-and-son team Alexander and Ljudevit Seitz took their designs from Friedrich Overbeck, leader of the Nazarene school of artists, who strove for high art by aping Old Masters in Rome (and generously acquiesced to German rulers picking up their hotel bills).

A bronze of the good bishop, who is entombed within, stands outside the cathedral and a few sheafs of his writings are displayed as the **Strossmayer Memorial Museum** in the bishopric palace at the cathedral's left shoulder. It stands on the corner of main drag, **Papa Ivana Pavla II**, usually known as the **Korzo** (stroll) by locals due to its promenade of cafés and bars. All but ignored at the end is the **Church of All Saints** (Crkva svih svetih). Despite a new façade, this domed cube, its cupola painted midnight-blue and boiling with stars, is just a whisper away from its origins as the 16th-century mosque built when advancing Turks claimed Đakovo.

Strossmayer Memorial Museum
Spomen muzej; open Mon–Fri 8–6, Sat 8–1.30; adm

Go right before it, then left onto Anta Starčevića, and you come to the seat of the 19th-century regional government, now home to the **Regional Museum of Đakovo**, a well-presented wardrobe of unusual folk costume, none stranger than the flower-speckled hats tufted with feathers that sword-wielding women don on Whit Sunday in Gorjani 9km north. Alongside this taster of the eye-popping **Đakovo Embroidery** folk jamboree (*see* 'Festivals in Southern Slavonia', below) is a model which lets you peer into all those traditional Slavonian houses you have passed; and so-so displays of regional archaeology.

Regional Museum of Đakovo
*Muzej Đakovštine; **t** (031) 813 254, www.muzej-djakovstine.hr; open daily 9–1; adm*

Đakovo's international fame is as a breeder of **Lipizzaner horses**. Mature whites and brown colts of the thoroughbred, the choice of royals and the Spanish Riding School in Vienna, are put through morning paces in stud farm **Državna ergela lipicanaca**, 10 minutes' walk from the cathedral at the end of Matje Gupca – you're free to wander around the stables and watch. With reservation you can also go for a spin (*see* p.131).

South of Đakovo, **Vrpolje** is nothing to look at, but gets a mention in Croatian art books as the 1883 birthplace of Ivan Meštrović. So inordinately fond of this anonymous village was the sculptor that he gifted it his *Mother and Child* in 1958, the first exhibit gathered for a **gallery** of 30 of his works.

Gallery
Spomen galerija Ivana Meštrovića; open daily 7–2; adm

Festivals in Southern Slavonia

On the first weekend of September **Požega** hosts the delightfully named **'Golden Strings of Slavonia'**, a national get-together for *tambura* bands, a native instrument halfway between a lute and a mandolin. In May, international film-makers visit Požega for the most popular jamboree, the **Croatian One-Minute Film Festival**.

Slavonski Brod turns on the charm during the country's oldest folklore festival **Brodsko kolo**, a June jamboree of festive horse and cart parades, traditional song and dance, and local belles in folksy garb for Slavonia's own Miss World.

Đakovo pulls rank on this with **Đakovo Embroidery**, one of Croatia's leading folk spectaculars, held in the first week of July, when the town becomes a giant stage for a wonderland of traditional Slavonian costume, dancing and song. Well worth a special trip if you are in north Croatia.

Activities in Southern Slavonia

Đakovo: Lipizzaner stud farm **Državna ergela lipicanaca**, Augusta Šenoe 45, **t** (031) 813 286, provides riding and four- and two-in-hand carriage jaunts; expect to pay around 60Kn for 45mins and reserve in advance (largely Croatian-language only, so ask hotel/tourist information staff).

Where to Stay and Eat in Southern Slavonia

ⓘ **Požega >**
*Trg sv. Trojstva 1, **t** (034) 247 900, www.pozega-tz.hr; open Mon–Fri 8–3, Sat 8–1*

Požega

Grgin Dol, Grgin dol 20, **t** (034) 273 222 (€). A little tired and frayed at the edges, but adequate and comfortable accommodation in a three-star west of Trg sv. Trojstva.

Tomislav, Vjekoslava Babukića 25, **t** (034) 273 226 (€€). One of the few proper restaurants in Požega – though the bars on high street Cehovska will rustle up *ćevapi*. Start with Slavonian paprika sausage *kulen*, then pick from a menu of freshwater fish and steaks, washed down with local graševina or traminer whites.

ⓘ **Slavonski Brod >**
*Trg pobjede 30, **t** (035) 447 721, www.tzgsb.hr; open Mon–Fri 7–8, Sat 7–2, Sun 8–12; kiosk at fort 15 June–15 Sept; open same times*

Slavonski Brod

Residencia Uno, Šetalište brače Radić 6, **t** (035) 415 000, *www.uno-brod.hr* (€€). A dollop of bygone charm in a 19th-century riverfront house. Characterful furnishings, occasional antiques and floors laid with Turkish rugs in six spacious rooms (singles are a little poky). Just the wrong side of inexpensive.

Brod, Petra Krešimira IV 1, **t** (035) 440 515 (€). If that's full, this is adequate although stuck in a frumpy 1970s timewarp.

Slavonski podrum, Dr Andrije Štampara 1, **t** (035) 444 856 (€€). Walk five minutes beyond the monastery and you'll find this beamed country house, as traditional as its menu of sturdy meats and *kulen*.

Uno, Mikole Zrinskog 7, **t** (035) 442 107 (€). Wood-fired pizzas and pastas in a restaurant oozing rustic charm, whether in the beamed house of cheery check tablecloths and farm knick-knacks or on a verdant terrace.

Đakovo

Croatia-Turist, P. Preradovića 25, **t** (031) 813 391 (€€). Đakovo's finest chef prepares a Slavonian menu in an address that Croatian gourmets have twice rated in the nation's top 100. There are homemade *kulen* spicy fillers *čobanac od junetine* (veal goulash) and *grah s kobasicom* (sausage and fried beans) and the house special is fried trout or carp. Also has 15 chintzy **rooms** (€).

Southeast of Zagreb: The Turopolje and Lonjsko Polje

Up against Bosnia-Hercegovina in the south of North Croatia's buffer zone are the rolling plains of the Turopolje and the flats of the Lonjsko polje. This is an area wrestled over by Ottoman Turks and Habsburgs for two centuries and in the 1990s it was a front line in the Homeland War, under control of Serbian forces, whose ethnic cleansing was a shameful return of the discrimination pursued in a Second World War concentration camp in Jasenovac. Fortunately, such horrors are a world away in the tumbledown stork villages of the Lonjsko Polje Nature Park, one of inland Croatia's most charming corners, barely an hour southeast of Zagreb but where plump geese honk in farmyards and floppy-eared indigenous pigs root in the woods.

Getting around Southeast of Zagreb

There are frequent buses and trains usually every hour from Zagreb to **Sisak**. From here, a limited daily bus service links to **Čigoć**.

South to Sisak

Restless and hungry, Zagreb eats into the fields to its south at frightening pace before the suburbs slip away and the B30 ambles through villages with large wooden *kurija* houses and shingle-roofed churches built of 17th-century oak and adorned with folk carving. The most enchanting are in hamlets west of the road, hidden like secrets in a mazy nest of lanes which twist through beech forest and low hills. However, the easiest to locate is **St Barbara's Chapel** (Kapela sv. Barbare) in **Velika Mlaka**, 2km before **Velika Gorica**, an anonymous Zagreb satellite rescued by regional ethnology exhibits in the **Museum of the Turopolje**. It's located on town square Trg kralja Tomislava, in a Baroque hall where Turopolje aristocrats once hammered out municipal policy.

ⓘ **Velika Gorica**
Matije Slatinskog 11, ***t*** *(01) 62 22 378, www.tzvg.hr; open Mon–Fri 7.30–3.30*

Museum of the Turopolje
Muzej Turopolja; ***t*** *(01) 62 21 325, www.muzej-turopolja.hr; open Tues–Fri 9–4, Sat–Sun 10–1; adm*

Relentless industrialization under Tito has also robbed **Sisak** of its charms, and the regional powerhouse with the largest ironworks in Croatia now barely bothers to reminisce over its history. The earliest evidence of this in the centre, before the parish church, as a section of **wall** from Siscia, a Roman city which emerged from the ruins of Celtic Segestica, vanquished by 12,000 crack legionnaires of Emperor Octavius. For a few centuries, 40,000 citizens raised Siscia's game to that of thriving provincial capital and it got fat from two ports at the confluence of the Sava and Kupa rivers – the port authority of Sisak still governs shipping on the rivers Kupa, Sava, Krka and the Plitvice Lakes. Textbooks complain that the Goths and Slavic Avatars ruined Croatia's Roman cities, but latter-day Croatians were just as quick to plunder, and many of Sisak's antique bricks ended up in the walls of its 1540s **castle** (*stari grad*), standing guard over the rivers' confluence 2.5km south of the centre. As every schoolchild in Croatia can tell you, on the plain in front of this fortress the Habsburgs dealt a hammer blow to Ottoman territorial aspirations (and consolidated their own land-grab) during the Battle of Sisak on 22 June 1593. Despite this illustrious history, the trianglular fortress linked by tower-like bastions is only now being renovated – consult tourist information for visits – and it's left to a **town museum** to narrate the tale, alongside displays of Roman relics from Siscia and colourful ethnography.

Town museum
Gradski muzej; Kralja Tomislava 10; ***t*** *(044) 811 811, www.muzej-sisak.hr; open Apr–Sept Tues–Fri 10–6, Sat–Sun 9–12; Nov–Mar Mon–Fri 7.30–3.30; adm*

Lonjsko Polje Nature Park

Around 25km south of Sisak, the north bank of the Sava river suffers a mid-life crisis on its journey from Slovenia and fragments into purposeless meanders and ox-bow lakes. Strung out for 30km

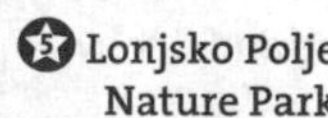

alongside is a string of enchanting ramshackle wooden villages, as picturesque as a folk tale, that are preserved as part of the 506km sq Lonjsko polje Nature Park.

The centrepiece of its rustic carpet – a patchwork of deciduous forest, meadows speckled with July wildflowers and wetlands fed by the Sava – is **Čigoć**, a one-lane village of tumbledown two-storey houses, their balconies and eaves patterned with carving, their oak build and external staircases a defence against flood. It's impossibly picturesque, even more so from late March to late August, when white storks migrate to Europe's first stork village to fatten up in marshes teeming with fry and frogs. They breed in the same nest with the same partner as the year before, then lumber back to South Africa. In a good year, storks outnumber villagers by 200 to 120 and, at the last count in 2005, 45 of their ungainly mud-and-twig baskets, up to 2m across and weighing up to a ton, were balanced on village roofs. Their threat as a beam-cracker is dealt with by hard oak and soft hearts – Posavina folklore relates that a nest on a roof is good luck.

Nature trails from Čigoć forage into opposite woods past the Tišina (quiet) oxbow lake (approx 30mins) or explore pasture and woods behind the village to an old pigsty (1hr). Enthusiastic rangers in a **park office** proffer advice on routes and also sell tickets to a private **museum** of bygone farming equipment rescued from Posavina farmsheds by the Susić family, as keen to demonstrate the family loom as they are to show off three generations of embroidery; tickets can also be bought at the museum.

Park office
*Čigoć 26, **t** (044) 715 115; open Mar–Nov daily 8–4; second centre at Krapje 1, mobile **t** 098 222 086; open Apr–Oct, times vary*

Museum
Čigoć 34

Consult the park office too about **wildlife tours** to see semi-wild Posavina breeds such as the Turopolje pig, a floppy-eared, long-snouted porker said to make delicious sausages, and stocky Posavina horses descended from an ancient breed of working horse. Your best bet to see them on your own is on a path which explores behind **Mužilovčica**, 7km east of Čigoć and a mite more modern, but picture-postcard-pretty as it hugs an oxbow lake choked by lilies and fringed by willow boughs and swaying reeds. It has its own **ethno-museum** and a swallow population at its most impressive in November when around 6,000 birds muster for migration. **Krapje**, designated an Architectural Heritage village due to its traditional wooden farmhouses turned end on to the road, and **Drenov Bok**, beyond, have few visitors and no one to impress, so are a mite more scruffy. Between them is the **Krapje Dol** – park wardens at Čigoć co-ordinate visits to one of the largest spoonbill reserves in Europe.

Ethno-museum
Mužilovčica 72; adm

Jasenovac

A rough lane heads on east towards border village Jasenovac, forever tarnished by its association with Croatia's largest Second

World War concentration camp of the Croatian Nazi Ustaše party. Between 1941 and 1945, non-Catholic POWs – Orthodox Serbs, Jews, Roma and Muslims – plus political opponents of the Nazi stooges were incarcerated as slave labour for a brickworks, or tortured and murdered with a barbarism fuelled by a religious and racial bigotry that shocked even the Nazis. Hitler's Zagreb representative, General von Horstenau, called it 'the epitome of horror', and a shocked German transport officer wrote home that it was 'the most horrible of camps, which can only be compared to Dante's *Inferno*. That the true scale of genocide in the 'Balkan Auschwitz' remains unknown is not helped by the reluctance of previous governments to confront the dark secret of a Nazi past and politicos' readiness to prod a raw nerve whenever it suited their purpose. Postwar Communist spinners mourned up to a million dead. In the late 1970s, future Croatian president Franjo Tuđman, an apologist for the far right with barely hidden ultra-nationalist leanings, railed at statistics he said had been inflated to exaggerate national guilt, and insisted that only 40,000 had died. A decade later, some Serbian media alluded to the camp to drum up anti-Croatian feeling as Yugoslavia imploded. Current estimates place the murdered between 60,000 and 97,000.

Guards razed the camp in 1945 as Tito's partisans approached, and today only a giant concrete tulip marks the site of the brickyard, planted in 1966 by Serbian architect Bogdan Bogdanović as a symbol of hope after suffering. 'A flower symbolizes life, it neither threatens nor offends anybody, and it does not call for revenge or hide the truth,' he said diplomatically. It says much about the camp's continuing power to divide that Croatian prime minister Ivo Sanadar repeated these words during a ceremony in March 2004 which celebrated the camp's renovation after war damage wrought by retreating Croatian Army forces in September 1991 and Serbian shells in 1995. There is a **museum** of photographs and moving personal histories.

Museum
t (044) 672 033, www.jusp-jasenovac.hr; open Tues–Fri 9–5, Sat–Sun 10–4

History clearly had it in for the village. Its core is war-scarred and quiet, as though still in shock from its 1991–5 occupation by Serbian Yugoslav People's Army troops and its later recapture by Croatian forces. A tank rusts by a former border crossing into Bosnia-Hercegovina just free of the outskirts, and skull-and-crossbones signs in nearby fields warn of landmines. No wonder the graffiti here reads 'Peace'.

If you visit this region via the A3 *autocesta* from Zagreb, you should pause in **Kutina**, a forgettable capital of the Moslavina with dull low-rise blocks but a head-spinning pilgrimage church, **St Mary of the Snows** (Snježna Marija), which offers a taster of heaven through the prism of Baroque excess: a riotous Holy Sepulchre high altar crammed into a sacristy and wall-to-wall frescoes.

Where to Stay and Eat Southeast of Zagreb

ⓘ Sisak > *Rimska bb, t (044) 522 655, www.sisakturist.com; open Mon–Fri 8–3*

ⓘ Lonjsko Polje > *Čigoć 26, t (044) 715 115, www.pp-lonjsko-polje.hr; open daily Mar–Nov 8–4. Second centre in Krapje 1, mobile t 098 222 086; open Apr–Oct, times vary*

★ Ravlić >>

Sisak

Panonija, I. K. Sakcinskog 21, **t** (044) 515 600, *www.hotel-panonija.hr* (€). Bland although adequate business-style accommodation.

Cocktail, Dr Starčevića 27, **t** (044) 549 137 (€). There's a pleasant terrace and an Italian–Croatian menu – risottos and spaghettis, steaks and a small platter of fish – in this central family restaurant.

Lonjsko Polje

Agrotourism apartments and farmhouse rooms are the only accommodation, and will provide guests with meals: contact the park office for more options or knock on doors wherever you see signs advertising '*sobe*'.

Iža na Trem, Čigoć bb, **t** (044) 715 617 (€). Four rooms, homely and cosy with antique country furniture and roofs lined with heavy beams, in a converted barn of the Sever family's farm in central Čigoć.

Jozin Budžak, Krapje 76, **t** 611 202 (€). Modern-ish apartments softened by simple furniture and traditional embroidered linen.

Ravlić, Mužilovčica 72, **t** (044) 710 151 (€). A lovely ramshackle farmstead with a handful of rustic-style rooms plus lunches of *kulen* (paprika sausage), and home-smoked meats or fresh fish plucked from the river (*book ahead*). Its French- and German-speaking owner also provides riding and fishing trips. A gem.

West and Southwest of Zagreb: Samobor and the Žumberak

Drive west of the capital for just 20 minutes and Zagreb's high-rise suburbs slip into the rear-view mirror; ahead are the thickly wooded hills that cradle Samobor, the address every capital commuter aspires to, whose Baroque kernel is as sweet as its gooey custard tart, *Samoborske kremšnite*. It's also the most handy base for day trips into the Žumberak-Samobor Nature Park (Park prirode Žumberak-Samoborsko gorje), snuggled into Slovenia's shoulder and popular with walkers for its carpet of beech and chestnut forest, sub-Alpine meadows, and karst scenery where steep valleys are dissected by rushing streams fed by 337 springs. Southwest are the villages of the Žumberak, isolated and secretive, and where getting lost is all part of the fun. It is best approached from Karlovac, which comes on tough, then relaxes into Baroque.

Samobor

Officially, Samobor is under the jurisdiction of Zagreb. Thankfully, you'd never know it. Though just 22km west of her big sister, the small town snuggled among wooded slopes hums with a provincial prosperity that's a world away in atmosphere; in the central square alone, old-fashioned grocers display tins in neat rows and the Gradna brook chuckles in a corner. Small wonder that Samobor is a favourite weekend jaunt for Zagrebers, bringing with them gentrification and a number of stylish cafés.

Getting to and around Samobor and the Žumberak

Buses from Zagreb arrive in **Samobor** every 20–30mins.

Transport hub **Karlovac** is well linked in all directions. Trains leave every hour for Zagreb and Ogulin, and 3 times a day to Rijeka. In addition, a weekend tourist train, the Karlek, shuttles between Zagreb and Ogulin from mid-June to Sept. Buses go hourly to Zagreb, Plitvice (via Slunj) and Rijeka and less frequently to Pula (8 per day), Split (6 per day) and Zadar (2 per day), plus there are daily connections to Rovinj, Rab and Pag.

Five local buses a day head north from Karlovac to **Ozalj**.

You'll find the best in the heart of the town, **Trg kralja Tomislava**, lined by the smart Baroque town houses – plus one Art Nouveau newcomer topped by angels – which replaced a townscape reduced to ashes in 1797. If you want to sample local delicacy *samoborske kremšnite*, a thick slab of custard between flaky pastry, this is your place. For intellectual nourishment there's the **Samobor Museum** west of the square. The streamside villa that houses its collections was formerly the home of composer Ferdinand Livadićev, and musty displays of town documents, hunting weapons and gloomy local dignitaries perk up (slightly) in period rooms where the advocate of Slavic independence and promoter of the national tongue composed the 1883 rallying cry 'Croatia Has Not Yet Fallen'.

Samobor Museum
Samoborski muzej; ***t** (01) 33 61 014; open Tues–Fri 9–3, Sat–Sun 9–1; adm*

Look, too, for a large model of 1764 Samobor as a cosy village before the blaze, barely recognizable were it not for the Baroque parish church of **St Anastasia** (Crkva svete Anastazije), whose primrose-yellow bulk still commands the east end of Trg kralja Tomislava. Opposite, on Jurjevska lane, there's Viennese china and so-so art in the private **Marton Museum**. Otherwise you can head uphill from the church up to a path just beyond the cemetery that picks its way through woods towards the 16th-century chapel of **St Anne** (Kapela sv. Ane). Stations of the cross count down the ascent to a sister chapel of **St George** (Kapela sv. Jurja), beyond which a path threads away through the trees. In theory it leads to **Stari grad** (literally, 'old town'), the ruins of a 13th-century castle isolated on a western spur. However, easier access to a castle (no entry) that is mailed in ivy after it was abandoned by 18th-century feudal counts is on a gravel path along the hillside west of St Anne.

Marton Museum
Muzej Marton; www.muzej-marton.hr; open Sat–Sun 10–1; adm

The Žumberak

While Samobor's slopes are full of walkers, the slumbering Žumberak is barely disturbed. Deep in the hush of wooded valleys or perched on defensive hills are hamlets overlooked by cartographers, their communities too busy scratching out a living from cornfields, vines and livestock to think about tourism. Most are descendants of Greek Orthodox and Catholic Uskoks, refugees from Ottoman advances in south Croatia who were resettled between 1530 and 1617 (*see* **Topics**, p.43). The move was a masterstroke by the Habsburgs, at once repopulating their estates desolated by Turkish raids and ensuring fealty by forcing the new arrivals to recognize papal supremacy.

Bar the smoke and mystery of Greek Orthodox icons in churches ubiquitously locked outside of Mass, cultural sights are as thin on the ground as accommodation options. But with a full tank of petrol and a good map you could lose a happy day exploring this living ethnographic museum of villages stuffed with ramshackle wooden haybarns and wine presses.

ⓘ Ozalj/Krašić
*13km northeast of Ozalj, Krašić 102, **t** (01) 62 70 91; open (in theory) Mon–Fri 10–4*

Castle
***t** (047) 732 271; open Mon–Fri 8–3, Sat–Sun 11–2; adm*

Without your own transport, southern agricultural centre **Ozalj** is the most accessible destination, providing views of hills crowned by spires and a **castle**, whose trawl through regional history salutes former owners the Frankopans and Zrinskis, warrior-aristocrats of Croatia's most noble stock until brothers-in-law Fran Krsto Frankopan and Petar Zrinski hatched a madcap scheme to overthrow the emperor and were swiftly executed for their folly in 1671 (*see* 'Čakovec', pp.112–13). There are scimitars left behind during Turkish incursions among its dry exhibits, and good views from the castle's rocky perch over the Kupa river – the mock-Gothic castle beneath is actually an HEP dam.

Etno-park Ozalj
erratically open

Cross the Kupa and walk 2.5km east, past cottages furnished with yokel knick-knacks in the open-air **Etno-park Ozalj**, and **Trg** is a taster of the charmingly dilapidated farming villages beyond, its sagging barns crammed with hay, its hush broken only by the glossy cockerels which strut in every yard.

Karlovac

Karlovac's fate is to be on the way to somewhere else. Located at the nation's crossroads,it is a place you go through, not to, and curious visitors who pause for a look are unlikely to be wooed by first impressions. Karlovac, famous for ubiquitous Croatian beer Karlovačko, which accounts for a third of the nation's three million hectolitre output, comes on tough in the suburbs littered with small industry.

Although it's also fairly scruffy in the pedestrianized centre, the strict grid within a six-point star moat has curiosity value. Only military minds could conceive such regimented precision, and in this case it was those of Habsburg strategists, who christened a 1579 garrison town on the Ottoman frontier after Karl II. Trade replaced tactics as Turkish troops were driven south, and the fort restyled itself in Baroque, got portly on profits after its accreditation as a royal free town in 1781, then grew so fat that it had to remove its town walls in order to splurge outwards in the 19th century. Heady days, those, for a town with a population half that of Zagreb, when Croatia's three continent-to-coast routes passed through its centre corn and wheat, from Slavonia and Posavina, came west to Karlovac's distribution node via the Kupa river.

In a twist of fate Karlovac found itself back on the front line in the 1990s, this time facing the Yugoslav People's Army, whose advance finally stalled in Turanj, 3km south. The suburb's buildings still bear shrapnel wounds – many were razed entirely – and two have been left in ruins as a backdrop for a **Museum of the Homeland War** (Muzej Domovinskog rata), a small roadside collection of armoured vehicles, tanks and field guns gathered around the fuselage of a downed Yugoslav Air Force MiG-21 jet.

The artillery shells also damaged Karlovac's centre within a moat now planted as a park of chestnut trees. To the east of main drag **Radićeva**, the late Baroque nobles' palaces which box in **Trg bana Josipa Jelačića** suffered particularly badly, and, bereft of shops or cafés, the former main square is overlooked except those who visit its **Church of the Holy Trinity**, which springs a surprise with a smart 17th-century interior whose low barrel vaulting is painted in froth-free Baroque.

Town museum
Gradski muzej; Strossmayerov trg 7; t (047) 615 980, www.mdc.hr/karlovac; open Tues–Fri 8–3, Sat–Sun 10–12; adm

A block north you'll find the **town museum**. After some musty Illyrian and Roman archaeology, there are scale models of a burgeoning town and rooms of furniture and cultural relics of the prosperous 1800s. There's also a small ethnographic section of wicker baskets, jewellery and festive whites worn by the region's villagers – look too for a photo of *lasenj* grass raincoats, worn into the 20th century. The museum's artwork is at Ljudevita Šestića, known as the **Vjekoslav Karas Gallery**, including works by its eponymous local dauber infatuated with the German Nazarenes he met in Rome.

Vjekoslav Karas Gallery
Galerija Vjekoslav Karas; open Tues–Fri 8–3, Sat–Sun 10–12; adm

West along the Kupa river for 30 minutes is **Dubovac Castle**. Once the hilltop stronghold of the Frankopan counts, a dynastic superpower based on the island of Krk, the triangular galleried structure is in limbo – plans to convert into a youth hostel seem to have been ditched. The **guard tower**, under the protection of the town museum, provides marvellous views north to the Žumberak's woody hummocks and on a clear day east to Mount Medvednica behind Zagreb.

South of Karlovac

Beyond the agricultural plains south of Karlovac are hills topped with a fuzz of woods. The road southwest follows the river Mrežnica then cuts inland to reach **Ogulin**, spawned from a late 15th century castle of a Frankopan prince and christened, apparently, in dubious Latin after a chasm (*ob gula*) where the river Dobra vanishes into the gloom of Croatia's longest cave system. The hanging cavern is opposite a **castle** with an impressive foreguard of towers and a reputation as the prison where Josip

Broz Tito served seven months for Communist agitation in 1933, a tale told alongside the usual archaeology and ethnology displays in its **museum**.

Museum
t (047) 522 502; open Tues–Sat 8–2; adm

Another section of the museum features the flora and fauna of **Klek**, the knobble of rock which juts above woods of the Velika Kapela range west of Ogulin. A party of aristocratic nature-lovers, among them Croatian *ban* Josip Jelačić and Saxon king Friedrich August II, embarked on a botany expedition in 1838 and became the first to scale the 1,181m summit, clearly dismissive of warnings about the black arts. Seventeenth-century Slovenian Renaissance man Janez Vajkard Valvasor recorded that Ogulin locals heard the cackles of an international coven of witches whooping it up on Klek on stormy nights. As silly is a yarn that the 200m vertical rock face cracks every 100 years to reveal a snake atop a dowry of ducats, actually a princess who can be restored by the kiss of a brave youth. Clearly none has been tempted yet. More worrying than sorceresses and serpents are the vertiginous sections you'll encounter on the climb – maps and guides are available through tourist information offices. You can walk from Ogulin (3hrs) to the trail-head, but far better is to start from **Bijelsko**, 7km west, from where it's a 40min walk to a mountain hut for the ascent.

Also from Karlovac runs the arterial B1, which forges a route inland ever south towards the Plitvice lakes (*see* pp.224–5) then down into Dalmatia. Just over 50km south is **Slunj**, nothing special in itself but worth a pause for satellite settlement **Ratsoke**. Prettily sited beneath a gorge carved by the Korana river, the 17th-century mill village is a miniature wonderland of cascades, rapids and waterfalls. Apparently, the highest, Bak, was more impressive still until the road bridge above took a bomb on the nose in the 1990s and sent a rock crashing into the gorge. You can potter about former mill buildings to peer into stone fishpools and stream-fed barrel 'washing machines'. As good a reason to stop is for the fresh trout that is prepared in many *pension*-restaurants.

ⓘ **Slunj**
Brace Radica 7, **t** *(047) 777 630, www.tz-slunj.hr; open (in theory) Mon–Fri 8–3*

Festivals in Samobor and the Žumberak

Lazy-paced Samobor is anything but during **Carnival** (*Samoborski fašnik*), held since 1827 on the weekend before Shrove Tuesday.

Though merged as **Karlovac**, former settlements Gaza and Banija still build rival bonfires – and large ones at that – for **St John's Day** (23 June), now with added fireworks. For 10 days in late August (usually from last Sat) the town enjoys processions and boozy revels to celebrate its famous beer.

Sports and Activities in Samobor and the Žumberak

Samobor has two breeds of visitor: those who idle, and those who **hike** the Samoborsko gorje hills. The tourist office stocks maps and can advise on easy strolls in the national park that begins 6km west, or visit the Žumberak-Samobor National Park information centre in **Slani Dol**, **t** (01) 332 76 60, *www.pp-zumberak-samoborsko-gorje.hr*, 10km west of Samobor, which has information on walks and fauna.

Where to Stay in Samobor and the Žumberak

ⓘ Samobor ›
Trg kralja Tomislava 5, **t** *(01) 33 60 050, www.tz-samobor.hr; open Mon–Fri 8–7, Sat 9–7, Sun 10–7 (Sat–Sun till 5 in winter)*

Samobor

Samoborski slapovi, Hamor 16 (3km west), **t** (01) 338 40 61 (€€). Accommodation in the 'Samobor Waterfall' is comfortable if a little bland; come instead for a setting among woods and the excellent chef.

Golubić, Obrtnička 12, **t** (01) 336 09 37 (€). A handful of rooms in a family *pension*, well located behind the central square.

Livadić, Trg kralja Tomislava 1, **t** (01) 33 65 850; *www.hotel-livadic.hr* (€). Old-fashioned elegance and country charm abound in Samobor's premier address on the main square; expect honey-coloured parquet and antique rugs in plush rooms furnished in 19th-century style and a friendly welcome. The cafe's classy too.

ⓘ Karlovac ›
Petra Zrinskog 3, **t** *(047) 600 606, www.karlovac-touristinfo.hr; open June–mid-Sept Mon–Sat 8–8, Sun 9–1; mid-Sept–May Mon–Fri 8–3, Sat 9–1*

Karlovac

Korana, Perivoj Josipa Vrbanića 8, **t** (047) 609 090, *www.hotelkorana.hr* (€€). Plush rooms and a pool, sauna and massage centre combine to make this stylish address by the river south of the centre the best in the area. It's excellent **restaurant** (€€) prepares top-notch pork, veal and game specials. A balcony overlooking the river is idyllic for summer evenings.

Carlstadt, Vraniczanyeva 1, **t** (047) 611 111, *www.carlstadt.hr* (€). A super-central business-style three-star in a side street opposite the tourist office.

ⓘ Ogulin ›
Bernardina Frankopana 2, **t** *(047) 532 278, www.tz-grada-ogulina.hr; open Mon–Fri 8–3*

Ogulin

Klek, Otok Oštarijski, **t** (047) 819 120 (€). The only option in the area, nothing special, passable three-star accommodation 3km south of the centre. Otherwise, try Bjelolasica (*see* p.225).

Eating Out in Samobor and the Žumberak

Samobor

Samobor sausages (*češnjovke*) are best munched with local mustard then washed down with *bermet*, an aromatic, slightly bitter local tipple whose wine-based recipe is guarded by a family firm. You can buy a bottle (plus jars of mustard) from a factory outlet at Stražnička 1a (off Trg kralja Tomislava).

Pri staroj vuri, Giznik 2, **t** (01) 33 50 548 (€€€–€€). A charming dining room cluttered with the 'old clocks' of its name sets the tone for a traditional menu. Smoked sausages are served with *sauerkraut*, baked pork comes in a spicy red wine sauce and local trout is laced with Riesling and garlic.

Samoborska pivnica, Šmedhenova 3, **t** (01) 33 61 623 (€€). Good old-fashioned cellar bar-restaurant with platters of sausages.

U prolazu, Trg krala Tomislava 6 (€). Terrace tables to people-watch and Samobor's best *samoborske kremšnite* on the main square.

Karlovac

Pod starimi krovovi, Radićeva 8–10, **t** (047) 615 420 (€€). Chef's specials in the locals' choice for a central sit-down dinner are anglerfish in salmon sauce and rump steak in cranberry sauce. Shame about the uninspired modern dining room.

Ogulin

Sabljaci, Jezero bb (2km south), **t** (047) 535 434 (€€). The best summer lunch in the region – an idyllic location on the shore of Lake Sabljaki with scallops, steak and trout.

Istria

Istria, the heart-shaped locket at the Adriatic's throat, is a continent in miniature. Stylish coastal resorts lie within a short drive of rustic hamlets to make this one of Croatia's most rewarding touring regions. Yet if anything flavours this rich cultural stew it's Italy: signs are bilingual, and you'll hear a twisted Italian spoken in the streets. It should probably come as no surprise to learn that the Romans and the Venetians as well as latter-day Italians had a hand in local history.

Today, Croatians know Istrians as the most go-ahead of their tribes. A coast that has had more practice at package tourism than any other part of Croatia does have its concrete cubes, but there are far more boutique hotels or rustic agrotourism properties. To add to its sybaritic appeal, Istria is the best-kept foodie secret in Europe, stuffed with slow-food restaurants, local wines and olive oil. It's as if the Romans never left.

09

Don't miss

1. Superb Roman amphitheatre
   Pula **p.143**
2. Enchanting Italianate port
   Rovinj **p.154**
3. Byzantine mosaics
   Basilica, Poreč **p.159**
4. Idyllic hill town
   Grožnjan **p.166**
5. Fine medieval frescoes
   Beram **p.175**

See map overleaf

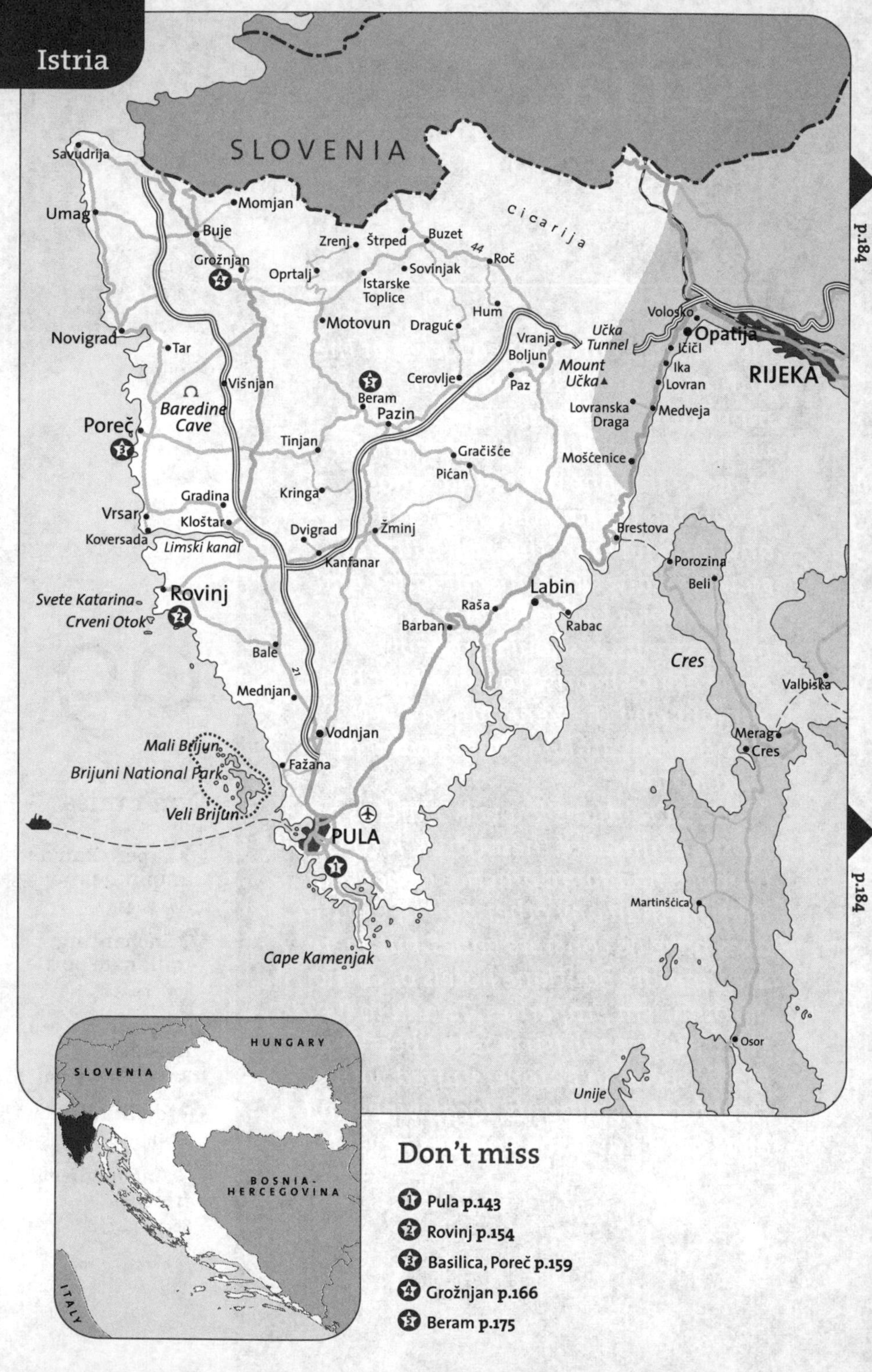
Istria
SLOVENIA
Savudrija
Umag
Momjan
Buje
Grožnjan
Zrenj
Štrped
Buzet
Cicarija
Roč
Oprtalj
Istarske Toplice
Sovinjak
Hum
Novigrad
Tar
Motovun
Dragué
Vranja
Učka Tunnel
Volosko
Opatija
Ičići
Ika
Lovran
RIJEKA
Boljun
Mount Učka
Paz
Cerovlje
Višnjan
Baredine Cave
Beram
Pazin
Lovranska Draga
Medveja
Poreč
Tinjan
Gračišće
Pićan
Mošćenice
Kringa
Gradina
Vrsar
Kloštar
Koversada
Limski kanal
Dvigrad
Žminj
Kanfanar
Brestova
Porozina
Beli
Svete Katarina
Rovinj
Crveni Otok
Raša
Labin
Barban
Rabac
Bale
Cres
Valbiska
Mednjan
Vodnjan
Merag
Cres
Mali Brijun
Brijuni National Park
Fažana
Veli Brijun
PULA
Martinšćica
Cape Kamenjak
Osor
Unije
HUNGARY
SLOVENIA
BOSNIA-HERCEGOVINA
ITALY
p.184
p.184
Don't miss
1 Pula p.143
2 Rovinj p.154
3 Basilica, Poreč p.159
4 Grožnjan p.166
5 Beram p.175

Pula

Even if the tale that the Colchians, pursuing Jason and his Golden Fleece, founded the town rather than return to King Aeëtes empty-handed is just swords-and-sandals bluster, Pula (Pola) has reason to pride itself on its ancient history. During prestigious concerts, crowds still roar in the world's sixth largest Roman amphitheatre, the prize of Croatian antiquity; locals go to market beneath a classical gateway that features in Michelangelo's sketchbook; and one of the finest Roman temples you'll see lends class to the showpiece Forum.

For these antique treasures, Istria's capital can thank the Romans. In the 1st-century BC, they occupied an Illyrian hill fort, and within 200 years the new star on the Adriatic stage, Colonia Julia Pollentia Herculanea, was a thriving commercial and administrative centre. Success proved short-lived, however. Signed up with the Venetian Republic from 1150, Pula atrophied, devastated by plague and its port neglected as Italian ambitions turned elsewhere. A population reduced to just 600 probably breathed a sigh of relief when the fall of the Venetian Republic in 1797 ceded their town to the Austro-Hungarians, who masterminded Pula's second golden age as the Habsburgs' naval powerhouse on the Adriatic. Shipbuilding and a commercial harbour still bring a no-nonsense, workaday grit to a city which encouraged industry under Tito. They also mean that Pula, home to over half of Istria's population, is no beauty compared with tourist towns elsewhere in the region. No matter. Nowhere in Croatia except Split rivals Pula for antiquities – the real reason to visit.

The Amphitheatre

(1) The Amphitheatre
Amfiteatar; open daily summer 8–8, winter 9–5; adm

No monument symbolizes Roman Pula like its amphitheatre. The 145m ellipse expanded over the course of a century from a modest arena under 1st-century BC Emperor Augustus to the sixth largest Roman stadium in the world – the story goes that Emperor Vespasian was badgered by his Pula-born girlfriend Cenida to build a 23,000-seater despite the fact that Pula's Roman population never topped 5,000. The stadium, which shaded its spectators with *velarii* (canvas sails) strung across 30m-high walls, was renowned for gladiatorial combat. Wild animal bouts took their place when this was outlawed. But when even that was made a criminal offence after the 7th century, it was looted for pre-cut limestone by locals. Most of the stone terraces have therefore morphed into local houses. Nevertheless, the outer shell of arches still stamps its authority on the shoreline, and for that Pula owes a debt to Gabriele Emo. In 1583, the senator put the brakes on the plans of the Venetian senate to ship the entire amphitheatre across the Adriatic stone by stone; the enlightened local son is honoured with a plaque inside. It's worth circling the rhythmic tiers of arches before you enter to marvel at gladiator's-eye views from the floor of the amphitheatre, now host to blockbuster concerts not bloody contest. A musty **museum** of wine and olive presses and crusty amphorae, displayed in the cellars where animals were caged and gladiators prepared, is a disappointment by comparison.

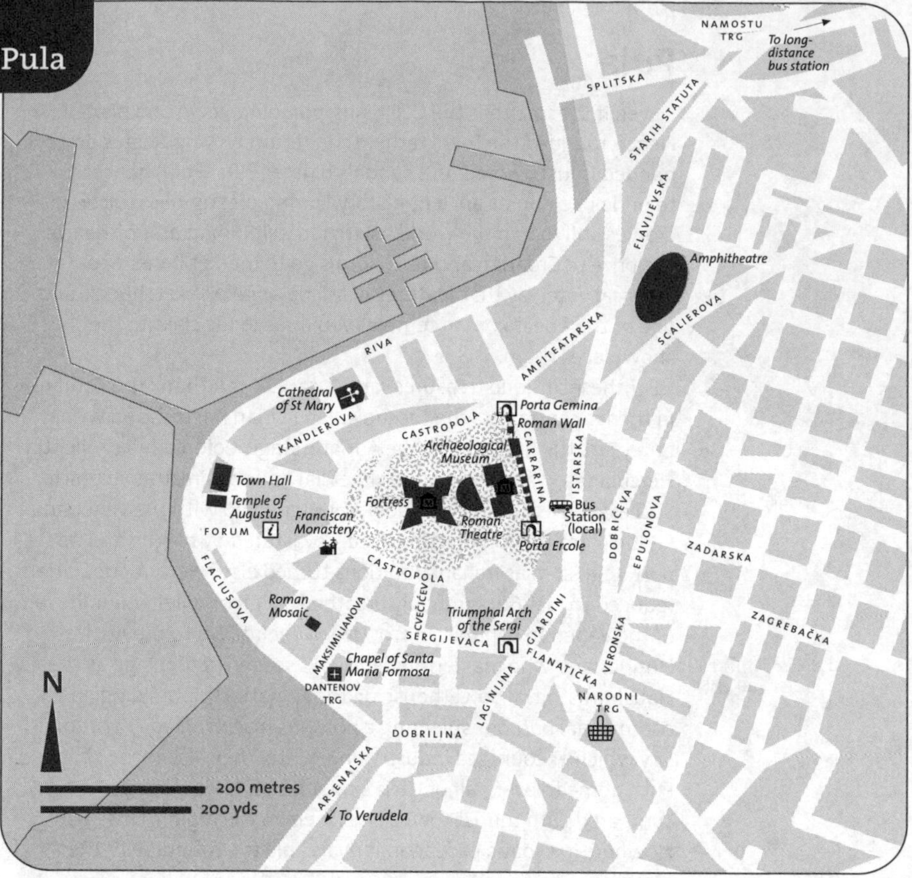

The Romans padded out to the revels through the AD 2 city gateway **Porta Gemina** (Dvojna vrata) nearby on Carrarina, called the Twin Gate because of its double arches, which punctuates a section of Roman wall patched up over the centuries with whatever came to hand; among its bricks you'll uncover lozenges of Roman column and chunks of carved tablet. The 1st-century BC fortification is matched at the other end by the **Porta Ercole** (Herkulova vrata) – but it takes a keen imagination to conjure Hercules's head and raised club from the weathered blobs of stone at the apex.

Getting to and around Pula

By Air

From the UK, Croatian Airlines and Ryanair fly to Pula airport, 6km northeast of the city. Croatian Airlines schedules regular flight connections from Zagreb at least daily. Taxis are the only means of transport from the airport to Pula centre; expect to pay 200Kn.

By Sea

Venezia Lines catamarans nip across the Adriatic from Venice in 3hrs mid-May–mid-Sept (*see* p.58). Ferries link to Mali Lošinj and Zadar 5 times a week in summer, and once a week in winter. The port is just outside the walls of the old town.

By Train

Direct trains go to Pazin (6 per day), Buzet and Roč (4 per day). The train station is 1km north of the amphitheatre on Koldovorska.

By Bus

Buses travel daily to Koper, Portorož and Piran (Slovenia); 4 times a day to Trieste; and daily to Venice (Italy). There are long-distance bus routes to: Rijeka, Opatija and Zagreb (hourly); Split (5 per day); Šibenik (4 per day); Zadar (3 per day); and Dubrovnik and Varaždin (daily). The main buses connect to destinations throughout Istria. On the west coast there are links every 45mins–1hr to Fažana, Vodnjan, Bale, Rovinj, Poreč and Umag, plus to Novigrad (5 per day). Buses go inland to: Pazin (8 per day); Buje and Svetvinčenat (5 per day); and Buzet (2 per day). Connections are approximately hourly to Labin.

Pula's pedestrianized city centre is compact enough to wander around. Buses 1 (to Stoja), 2 and 3 to southern suburbs (note: 2a and 3a continue to the package hotels on the Verudela peninsula) start from the main bus station at 43 Istarska, although the stops in central street Giardini are more convenient. A single zone 1 ticket to Verudela costs 6Kn from the driver or 10Kn for a two-journey ticket from kiosks.

By Car

For car hire (the major players also operate at the airport): **Hertz**, Hotel Histria, Verudela, **t** (052) 210 868; **Avis**, Starih statuta 4, **t** (052) 223 739; **Budget**, Carrarina 4, **t** (052) 218 252; **Tref**, Splitska 1, **t** (052) 223 124.

The Forum and Cathedral

The focus of Roman civic life – and modern café life, come to that – is the **Forum** at the heart of the antique town. The Romans' flanking arcades have long gone, but the **Temple of Augustus** (Augustov hram) remains, imposing architectural authority on the square through powerful Corinthian columns and a massive gable crown. Augustus, founder of the Roman Empire, would probably be delighted that the AD 2–14 homage erected during his lifetime still stands as one of the world's finest Roman temples, albeit a mite tatty having been rebuilt following bomb damage in 1945. After earlier use as a Christian church and later a granary it now houses a **lapidarium** of Roman sculpture. Its lost twin, the Temple of Diana, is just visible in outline where it was incorporated into the back wall of the adjacent **town hall** (Gradska palača), built using Roman masonry in the 13th century and tinkered with by architects of the Renaissance , who tacked on a loggia, and the Baroque period, who stripped former frills away again. A Gothic staircase is remembered like a scar on the north end wall. You'll pass it en route to the **Cathedral of St Mary** (Katedrala sv. Marije). A 4th-century church was erected symbolically over a Roman temple to lay the foundations for today's architectural jumble: a core Romanesque

Lapidarium
open May–Sept Mon–Fri 9–8, Sat–Sun 10–3; adm

basilica, tweaked by Gothic architects then pepped up with an Italianesque Renaissance façade. To round things off there's a 3rd-century AD Roman sarcophagus used for a high altar, a highlight in an otherwise ascetic three-nave interior.

The Archaeological Museum and Fortress

Pula made its debut on the conical hill which rises above the Forum and which every ruler has shaped into a defensive stronghold: a Roman *castrum* replaced the Illyrians' 1000 BC hill fort; medieval feudal rulers lorded it over town from a castle at the summit; and in the 1630s the Venetians gazed across the bay from a fortress, designed by French defence supremo Antoine de Vile and modernized by succeeding Austro-Hungarians.

Monastery of the Franciscan Order
Franjevački samostan; open June–mid-Oct daily 10–12 and 2–4; adm

Archaeological Museum
*Arheološki muzej Istre; **t** (052) 218 603, www.mdc.hr/pula; open May–Sept Mon–Sat 9–8, Sun 10–3; Oct–Mar Mon–Fri 9–2; adm*

En route from the Forum you ascend via the 13th-century **Monastery of the Franciscan Order**, whose vows of poverty meant that anything other than a barn was far too great an extravagance. A charmingly haphazard lapidarium rambles through the Roman and medieval finds in its cloister. Pula's real sculptural prizes, however, are in the **Archaeological Museum** on the other side of the hill. Staircases and corridors are stuffed with sculpture from the Roman city: cavorting cherubs and grinning dolphins, furiously bearded gods and sombre funeral snapshots carved on the slabs that once lined the amphitheatre road. Elsewhere there are worthy but musty display cases of 4th-century BC spiral jewellery and weapons exhumed from Illyrian graves on hill fort Nesactium, 7km from Pula, near the airport. More Roman exhibits are on the top floor: a gorgeous 1st-century alabaster funerary urn, a marble bust of Agrippina Minor, Nero's mother, and saucy pictures on terracotta oil lamps. Behind the museum are remnants of a 2nd-century **Roman theatre** (Malo rimsko kazalište) – with the right eyes you can conjure from its crumbling walls a crescent of seating, the orchestra space and the pit from which scenery was hoisted.

Historical Museum of Istria
*Povijesni muzej Istre; **t** (052) 211 566; open daily May–Sept 8–8, Oct–April 9–5; adm*

The Venetians shifted limestone blocks from a larger Roman theatre to create their hilltop cannon **battery** (*kaštel*), later tweaked by Austro-Hungarians as a link in a 12-strong chain of defences that made the Habsburg naval stronghold one of the best-protected towns in 19th-century Europe. As the **Historical Museum of Istria** the fortification has little to recommend it – meagre exhibits of the Habsburg port teased out over three rooms which perk up briefly in commemorative mugs of a magnificently moustachioed Emperor Franz Josef I. For the views over Pula, however, its bastions are unbeatable.

Along Sergijevaca

The Roman era high street, Sergijevaca, threads away off the Forum as Pula's main shopping street to conclude at the **Triumphal**

James Joyce in Pula

One of the strangest soujourns in Croatian literary history is James Joyce's stint in Pula. It was also one of the briefest. The man who would redefine literature arrived with future wife Nora Barnacle in October 1904 as nothing more than an English teacher at the Berlitz School. Instantly he hated the place. Pula, he sniffed, was 'a naval Siberia', one he suffered for just five months before demanding a transfer to Trieste. Pula's loss may have been culture's gain. With so little to divert him, the Irish author had completed chapters 12 and 13 of *Stephen Hero* by December and also worked up the aesthetic principles for its successor, *Portrait of the Artist as a Young Man*, which he set down in the 'Pola Notebook'. By March 1905 he was away – small wonder associate Tatjana Arambašin Slišković mused: 'He did not forget Dublin, he was often there in his thoughts.'

Arch of the Sergi (Slavoluk Sergijevaca; 30 BC). And triumphal it certainly is. On the Forum side of the monumental late-Hellenistic gateway, one Slavia Posthuma Sergii crows over her family's role in the Battle of Actium (a 31 BC Roman-on-Roman spat which Octavian, later Emperor Augustus, won after Cleopatra left the fray, trailed by Mark Antony), with a vainglorious boast and wealth of reliefs. Small wonder the gate appeared in the sketchbooks of Michelangelo and Inigo Jones. The reclining bronze figure who ponders its chariots and winged goddesses Nike and Victoria outside **Caffé Uliks** (Ulysses) is James Joyce, a few steps from the building in which he received £2 a week for drumming English grammar into Austro-Hungarian naval officers (*see* box above).

Pula also made a deep impression on the poet Dante. He witnessed the city in the 13th century beset by plague, and was sufficiently shocked to place the former Roman graveyard that lay outside the Sergi arch in his fifth circle of Hell (Canto IX). Fortunately the site is no longer 'uneven with the array, on every hand, of countless sepulchres', though the author is honoured with **Dantenov trg** a block south of Sergijevaca. Incidentally, the square's **post office** features a startling mosaic-clad Futurist staircase by Bologna architect Angiolo Mazzoni. A block west from the square, marooned in a small park, part-time gallery the **Chapel of Santa Maria Formosa** is all that remains of a basilica of a 6th-century Benedictine abbey whose walls are incorporated into adjacent houses. The marble ornamentation and columns of the Byzantine basilica which christened the church the 'Magnificent' (*formosa*) were swiped by Venice for the San Marco basilica, some of its mosaic is on display in the Archaeological Museum (*see* opposite).

Post office
open Mon–Fri 7–8, Sat 7–2

Chapel of Santa Maria Formosa
Kapela Marije Formoze; opening times vary

Somehow still *in situ* across a car park north is a **Roman mosaic** (Rimski mozaik), revealed when an apartment took a bomb on the nose during the Second World War. The 3rd-century floor mosaic from an nobleman's villa depicts beaming brothers Amphion and Zethus as they tie Dirce to the horns of an enraged bull in revenge for maltreating their mother Antiope, who had been seduced by Zeus.

South of the Centre: the beaches and Cape Kamenjak

Aquarium
open April–Sept daily 9–7; Oct–Mar Sat–Sun 11–5; adm

Cape Kamenjak nature reserve
open daily May–Sept 7–9; adm for cars; other months no times

Clad in a coat of pine forest, its shingle beaches lapped by clear seas and boasting a clutch of splendid restaurants, the Verudela peninsula 3km south of the city centre is as close as it gets to a beach resort in Pula. A headland track loops around an Austro-Hungarian fort which houses a lacklustre **aquarium** of Adriatic sealife and ambles past the best town beaches. Proximity to the resort hotels also makes them the busiest, however.

If you have your own transport, drive 10km south to cherrypick a cove on **Cape Kamenjak nature reserve**, a deeply notched finger of land that pokes into the pristine Adriatic from the bottom of Istria. The 3.5km peninsula is one of the last secrets of Istria; a mosaic of green fields, meadows speckled in spring by white and yellow heather flowers and aromatic Aleppo pines, washed by the cleanest seas in the area. Small wonder its *terra magica* was prime real estate for the villas of moneyed Romans. The peninsula gateway is Premantura, a village-resort served by bus from Pula. Windsurfing is very popular here.

Tourist Information in Pula

ⓘ Pula ›
*Forum 3, **t** (052) 219 197, www.pulainfo.hr; open June–mid-Sept daily 8am–10pm; mid-Sept–May Mon–Sat 8–8, Sun 9–8*

The **tourist information office** offers advice about accommodation, and provides city maps which mark bus routes and major hotels and extend south to the Verudela peninsula. It also has details about wine and olive oil routes throughout Istria.

Festivals

Even if not the celebrity honeypot which lured stars such as Richard Burton, Elizabeth Taylor and Sophia Loren, the highlight of Pula's social calendar remains a **Film Festival** in July, when the amphitheatre fills and a smattering of international releases are premiered beneath the stars.

Shopping

Central high street **Sergijevaca** offers a mixed bag of shops, while east of Giardini Flanatička is the principal high street for modern chains. The superb morning market on **Narodni trg** off here has all you could want for a picnic. Otherwise **Saxa**, Kandlerova 28, and **Zigante Tartufi**, Smareglina 7, sell Istrian goodies such as olive oils and truffles, wines, *rakija* and fruit brandies.

Sports and Activities

Cape Kamenjak is celebrated for its excellent windsurfing due to its being exposed to all wind conditions.

Windsurfing Centar Prementura, mobile **t** 091 512 36 46, *www.windsurfing.hr*, on the beach at Prementura hires kit (from 70Kn/hr) and offers lessons.

Where to Stay in Pula

Pula is well stocked with small hotels, boasting a couple of characterful central options and some classy boutique numbers to the south. The usual package hotels are by the beaches of the Verudela peninsula, 4km south of the centre; book through **Arenaturist**, Splitska 1, **t** (052) 529 400.

Galija, Epulonova 3, **t** (052) 383 602, *www.hotel-galija-pula.com* (€€). Hotel-restaurant off Flanatička opened in 2005, with 10 rather smart en-suite rooms, all three-star – good value.

Histria, Verudela, **t** (052) 590 000, *www.arenaturist.com* (€€). The best of the package holiday hotels on the Verudela peninsula and the only one open year-round. Proximity to beaches (plus a pool) and large four-star rooms with panoramic balconies compensate for an anonymous, sprawling complex.

Milan, Stoja 4, **t** (052) 210 200, *www.milan1967.hr* (€€). Another classy family-run number with an excellent restaurant (*see* below), near the harbour 1km south of the centre. It has an eye for designer style in its 12 rooms, all en suite, with air-conditioning and satellite TV.

Riviera, Splitska 1, **t** (052) 211 166, *www.arenaturist.hr* (€€). A *grande dame* from Pula's Austro-Hungarian past opposite the amphitheatre; a little tired, but atmospheric nevertheless. Faded glories are recalled in the public areas; dated one-star rooms make up in space what they lack in mod cons. Ask for a balcony and harbour view.

Scaletta, Flavijevska 26, **t** (052) 541 599, *www.hotel-scaletta.com* (€€). Smart Italian-styled modern rooms of pale woods and stainless steel fittings in a friendly family hotel with an excellent restaurant (*see* below). The central location near the amphitheatre is excellent but can suffer traffic noise.

Valsabbion (hotel) >

Valsabbion, Pješćana IX/26, **t** (052) 218 033, *www.valsabbion.hr* (€€). Not just a laid-back boutique hotel near the Marina Veruda – small and family-run, with four spacious suites (€€€), double rooms and a terrace with superb views over the bay – but also a beauty and spa centre (love that rooftop pool) and gourmet restaurant (*see* below).

Omir, Serda Dobrica 6, **t** (052) 210 614/218 186 (€). Compact but comfy simple rooms in a decent cheapie off Giardini.

Eating Out in Pula

Three of the restaurants in Pula's small hotels would rank among the top 10 in any gourmet pick of Istria, and feature in a list of the finest in Croatia – central restaurants are disappointing by comparison. Cheap pizza joints and grills line Kandlerova.

Valsabbion (restaurant) >

Valsabbion, Pješćana IX/26, **t** (052) 218 033 (€€€). On the Verduela peninsula and crowned king of Croatian restaurants twice and consistently voted Istria's number one. Gourmet 'slow food' is on a super-fresh menu that changes with the seasons; from frogfish in vine leaves or a sensational scampi *carpaccio* to mixed game in autumn. Year-round, a classy dining room unites antiques and modern style, and service is immaculate. *Closed Jan.*

Milan, Stoja 4, **t** (052) 210 200 (€€€–€€). Another effortlessly classy number in Istria's top five, where a master chef does creative things with fish and there's live jazz piano in the dining room. It's located 1km from the centre, midway between the city and beach.

Vela Nera, Veruda Marina, Pješćana uvala bb, **t** (052) 219 209 (€€€–€€). Just around the corner from Valsabbion, its big selling point a terrace that looks above the yachts and a relaxed vibe – delightful on lazy summer evenings for Adriatic fish grilled or roasted to perfection. Try chef's special baked sea bass with chickpeas and tomatoes.

Kantina, Flanatička 16, **t** (052) 214 054 (€€). On the high street behind the daily market with a terrace bar and a cellar restaurant that comfortably unites old and new – think rough stone walls meets interior design. The menu is above-average Istrian fare such as steaks with truffles and good salads.

Kažun, Vrtlarska 1 (off Mutilska from Trg Republike), **t** (052) 223 184 (€€). Pula's finest *konoba*, named after a stone shelter, prepares a menu of quality rustic dishes as authentic as it gets. Try homemade *kobasice u vinu* (sausages in wine) or thick goulashes and ragoûts of game or beef, all washed down with an Istrian merlot or teran.

Scaletta, Flavijevska 26, **t** (052) 541 599 (€€). Two venues in one: a laidback Pavilion and a dining room opposite that's smart without being stuffy. Quality Italian stuff either way – ravioli stuffed with scampi in a truffle sauce or seafood risotto with saffron and dried grapes, plus gourmet pizzas in the Pavilion – and a central location to boot.

Dva Ferala, Kandlerova 32, no tel (€). Traditional bar-cum-restaurant that's a credit to its breed (and not nearly as intimidating as its patrons would have you believe). Solid *kotlet* (pork cutlets), simple fish dishes such as *girice* (whitebait) and snacks such as *čevapi* are on the menu and there's a bargain *marenda* (lunch menu).

Cafés and Bars in Pula

Café Cvajner, Forum 2. That's Kunstcafé (art café) Cvajner, to give it its full title. Sticky pastries and coffee served in an arty café perfect for people-watching, with Renaissance fresco in a grand interior.

Caffé Uliks, Trg Portarata 1. Aka 'Café Ulysses' in honour of James Joyce, whose bronze is outside the building where he gave English lessons by the Sergei arch. Style alludes to Viennese Secession.

E&D Verudela 22. By the resort hotels above the seashore promenade, this hip bar-restaurant (€€) arranges terrace seating around a small pool and segues into a lively lounge bar in the evenings. Recommended.

Up the West Coast

Istria's west coast is no stranger to tourism. Both aristocratic Romans and Josip Broz Tito had luxury holiday homes on the Brijuni islands, and in his *Memoirs* Giacomo Casanova pined for the long, languid nights of wine and women he'd enjoyed in Vrsar. Mass tourism arrived here early, too, as towns like Umag might now lament.

Fortunately not even the 1980s bucket-and-spade brigade in Yugoslavia's holiday playground could kill off the deep roots of tradition and history. For every package resort, there's a *kažun* shepherd's shelter in southern Istria, a grey stone beehive among rust-red soil and silver olives, or a honey-hued pin-up such as Rovinj, a slice of La Serenissima wafted across the sea. And the shimmering mosaics of the Basilica of Euphrasius counter every concrete ziggurat in Poreč. You'll also find more rustic agrotourism hotels in this part of Istria than in any other strip of Croatia. Being first isn't always such a bad thing.

Brijuni National Park

In 1885, accompanied by his children, a retired Pula naval officer and a hamper of roast chicken, peaches and wine, Paul Kupelwieser hired a Fažana fishing boat to reach the uninhabited island of Veli Brijun for a picnic. The Austrian industrial magnate clearly liked what he found, because eight years later he signed the title deeds and began to transform an island abandoned due to malarial mosquitoes into a resort. While German bacteriologist and Nobel Prize winner Robert Koch sorted out the bugs, Kupelwieser busied himself clearing scrub to create a nine-hole golf course (today expanded to 18 holes) and built villas and luxury hotels to lure the cream of European high society. And lured they were: Austro-Hungarian heir Franz Ferdinand, German emperor Wilhelm II and

Getting to and around Brijuni, Vodjnan and Bale

Frequent buses shuttle 9km north of Pula to village Fažana, departure point for ferries to Veli Brijun. It can only be visited on tours organized by the National Park; some larger hotels offer packages (*c.* 260Kn) which include coach transport to Fažana and often lunch. In addition, private boats from Pula harbour operate 5hr trips to the National Park (*c.* 200Kn), either for a picnic on little sister Mali Brijun or a panoramic tour around the archipelago; note that these do not land on Veli Brijun. The only way to explore the island at leisure is by an overnight stay in one of two linked hotels, or find private accommodation through the tourist board in Fažana.

From Pula there are hourly buses to Vodnjan and hourly buses to Rovinj which stop at Bale. Buses to Vodnjan stop at the back of town, west of Narodni trg; to Bale in the main square below the old town.

---

author Thomas Mann all lazed in the name of recuperation at the élite health resort.

The war which doomed the era's idle aristocracy also did for the Austrian's playground – in 1930 his son Karl committed suicide on an island he had bankrupted himself trying to revive – and Veli Brijun only revived when it caught the eye of Yugoslav dictator Josip Broz Tito. Two years after his victory parade into Zagreb in 1945, the Partisan leader commandeered the island, treated himself to an official residence, the **Bijela Vila** (White Villa), and, when not tending the vegetable plots of his summer retreat, entertained heads of state; slotting together the multi-nation economic and political jigsaw of the Non-Aligned Nations Movement, or bathing in the limelight of celebrity guests such as Sophia Loren, Gina Lollobrigida or Elizabeth Taylor and Richard Burton. (Recent visitors have included the Princess of Monaco, model Naomi Campbell and Formula 1 CEO Bernie Ecclestone.) If future leaders have seemed less enthusiastic about the residence, which is still officially in government hands, at least they have good reason: Veli Brijun was designated a public national park three years after Tito's death in 1980.

National Park tour
available in English; five per day July–Aug 210Kn, June and Sept 200Kn, April–May and Oct 170Kn; one per day Nov–Mar 125Kn; tickets from Fažana park office (see p.153), includes ferry; advance booking essential in peak season

Two of Kupelwieser's hotels overlook the **harbour**, from where you join a tourist road-train for a **National Park tour**. These potter north through parks whose manicured lawns are clipped by the descendants of the Austrian's deer to reach a **safari park**, created in 1978 for the menagerie of animals gifted to Tito by world leaders; Queen Elizabeth II's Shetland ponies are a poor show compared with elephants Sonny and Lanka presented by Indira Gandhi. The tours then head south past Tito's White Villa (still under guard) to pause at the remains of a 2 BC Byzantine castle whose walls enclose the foundations of a 15th-century settlement abandoned because of the plague.

Back at the harbour, you can embark on a whistlestop tour of Istrian ecclesiastical art through Kupelwieser's reproductions of medieval frescoes housed in his rebuilt **St Germaine church** (Crkva sv. Germana). Far more intriguing, however, is the nearby exhibition '**Tito on Brijuni**'. A floor of stuffed animals, deceased gifts from world leaders, is highly missable, but there's much to enjoy in photos above of the republic's father-figure, beaming when dressed in swimming trunks or pottering in his garden in casuals, then attired in state regalia to greet the jet set and political leaders. Poor Kupelwieser is all but forgotten in a room that chronicles the 19th-century creation of Veli Brijun resort.

Vodnjan and Bale

Until 19th-century Austrians gave Pula a happy ending to its story, **Vodnjan** (Dignano) was the largest town in southern Istria. Don't worry – a city it is not. The Gothic palaces on central square **Narodni trg** hint at former greatness, and a rummage through dusty side alleys of a surrounding warren reveals quietly crumbling Renaissance mansions. However, the town's fame today is for its mummies, star exhibits of over 370 relics plucked from 250 saints. 'The phenomenon of Vodnjan... The biggest attraction in Istria' trumpet the leaflets which promote the second-largest hoard of ecclesiastical relics outside the Vatican, indicating that there's still life in a 13th-century fad so feverish that St Francis in his dying days hired bodyguards to prevent a rival town whisking him away from Assisi to secure his relics.

Church of St Blaise
Crkva svetog Blaža; ***t*** *(052) 511 420; open July–Aug Mon–Sat 9–7, Sun 2–7; Sept–June by request to priest or call ahead; adm*

The desiccated saints are revered in the **Church of St Blaise**, a Venetian wannabe with a pair of superlatives; it is Istria's largest church, copied from Andrea Palladio's San Pietro in Castello, and it boasts its highest campanile (63m), modelled on St Mark's in Venice. Pay your entrance fee and you are ushered through a heavy velvet curtain to a space behind the altar, stacked with glass cases like a sacred natural history museum. Illuminated in their coffins at stage front are those parchment-brown bodies. Of the medieval trio still quietly working miracle cures, Blessed Leon Bembo is the best preserved and most revered. While the 12th-century curate and ambassador to the Venetian doge was reduced to a cripple by torture during religious riots, his capacity to cure the sick from beyond the grave led to his exhumation in 1320. Above him, crowned with a garland, is St Nikoloza Bursa, a miracle- working nun from Koper whose grave wafted the odour of sanctity – crushed violets, apparently – in the mid-1500s. The third is St Johannes Olini, a 13th-century Venetian priest dedicated to plague victims. Look, too for, a twisted scrunch of sinew, allegedly the shoulder and backbone of St Sebastian. Revered in monstrances like oversized specimen jars and displayed like an ecclesiastical apothecary, an old curiosity shop of relics is on display in the church's **Collection of Sacral Art**. Curators direct you towards a 15th-century gold monstrance with the undecayed tongue and lower jaw of St Mary of Egypt, a repentant Alexandrian prostitute of the 5th century who wandered the desert for 47 years on a diet

Collection of Sacral Art
open same times as church above; adm

of herbs. There's also a 14th-century polyptych by Paolo Veneziano, which depicts Bembo in action and which once served as his coffin lid. Clearly, the clerics who commissioned the Venetian artist had an astute grasp of PR – like a canny politician, the beatified priest cures sick babies and is acclaimed by nobility on his death bed.

Vodnjan isn't the only place with miracle cures. Drive north on the B21, turn left towards the hamlet of **Mednjan** and locals say you'll shudder, have a hot flush or feel a sudden chill as underground 'energy circles' perform their magic. It's a New Age spin on an age-old tale, one that led the **Church of St Fosca** (Crkva sv. Foška) to be sited on its own in a field where the good vibrations are strongest – a miracle cure for those with leg disease, they say, which is presumably why crutches are left outside.

Enchantment of another sort is to be found 11 miles north of Vodnjan in **Bale** (Valle). This hilltop settlement with Roman roots (Castrum Valle) was almost deserted by an Italian population after Istria's 1945 repatriation to Yugoslavia, and is just beginning to wake up to the fact that it's everyone's idea of what a rustic Italian idyll should be. There are picture-postcard images everywhere you look beyond the **Soardo-Bembo Palace**, manor stronghold of a 15th-century Venetian built beside a town gate bearing the Republic's Lion of St Mark. Channelled by crumbling grey stone houses, a cobbled street spirals up to the neo-Baroque **Church of the Visitation**, with a crypt lapidarium chock-full of medieval masonry. Early medieval wicker designs tie stone knots on slabs and, at the rear, Bale's own saint, a 14th-century friar, the Blessed Julian, stands on an altar cobbled together from five centuries of tomb-slabs. His remains are venerated in a chapel right of the main altar of the church, entered via the lapidarium.

Church of the Visitation
entry at rear of church; open summer daily 8–2 and 3–6; adm

Festivals in Vodjnan and Bale

An **Istrian craft and food fair**, bursting with rustic atmosphere, rolls into **Vodnjan** on the first Sat of every month.

Bale stages the '**Bale Night**' of folk dance in traditional costume on the first Sat of Aug.

Where to Stay and Eat north of Pula

Brijuni and Fažana

Brijuni hotels style themselves as a cut above, which explains their high prices.

Neptun-Istra, Veli Brijun, **t** (052) 525 807 (€€€). Thomas Mann bedded down in founder Paul Kupelwieser's vintage harbourfront hotel, overpriced for its dated décor and worth it only for a lazy getaway to better explore the island – ask about riding trips or bicycle hire.

Marina, Riva 2, Fažana, **t** (052) 521 071, *www.marina-fazana.com* (€€). Designer style in a small harbourside hotel opened in 2007 – rooms are on the small side, but perfectly adequate.

Feral, Trg Stare Škole 1, Fažana, **t** (052) 520 040 (€€). This is the best of the eateries on Fažana harbour, traditionally styled and with a reliable menu of fish; good salted anchovies in a rich savoury sauce.

ⓘ Brijuni National Park >
*Brijunska 10 (harbourfront), Fažana, **t** (052) 525 888, www.brijuni.hr; open Mon–Sat 8–8, Sun 8–3*

ⓘ Fažana >
*Riva 2, **t** (052) 383 727; open summer daily 8–8*

Vodnjan >
Narodni trg 3, **t** *(052) 511 700, www.istria-vodnjan.com; open June–Sept Mon–Fri 8–3, Sat–Sun 9–12; Oct–May Mon–Fri 8–3*

Bale >>
Rovinjska 1, **t** *(052) 824 270; open July–Aug daily 8–8; Sept–June Mon–Fri 9–1*

Stancija Negričani >

Vodnjan

Stancija Negričani (7km northeast), **t** (052) 391 084, *www.stancija negricani.com* (€€). An idyllic agrotourism address signposted 1km before Dvišići on the Barban road. Nine rooms come from the boutique-rustic school of décor, furnished with antique beds and wardrobes and overflowing with character. Throw in a swimming pool and stables, an excellent **restaurant** with a super-fresh menu of local produce (*open to non-guests on reservation*), charming owners and a peaceful location deep in the Istrian countryside and you have, quite simply, one of the premier addresses in Istria. *Reservations essential in summer. Breakfast extra.*

Vodnjanka, Istarska bb, **t** (052) 511 435 (€€). No signs and hard to find – it's opposite a car park at the back of Vodnjan – but one of the gourmet addresses of the region. Subtle Italian flavours abound on an inventive menu – squid-ink black ravioli with white wine and prawns or sauces of *escargot*, ham, truffles, asparagus and mushroom to cover homemade *fuži* and *njoki* – and the dining room is modern-rustic with a twist. *Closed Sun and Jan.*

Bale

Kamene priče, Kaštel 57, **t** (052) 824 231 (€). Four apartments each catering for two or three in a stone house just inside the town gate of Bale's crumbling kernel.

Istra, Trg La Musa bb, **t** (052) 824 396 (€€). Cook confides that her *maneštra*, an Istrian stew of meat and veg, is special in this easygoing restaurant on the main square of the lower town. She also prepares homemade *njoki* and a rich *fuži* with game goulash.

Find agrotourism rooms and apartments through tourist agency **Amfora**, Trg La Musa bb, **t** (052) 841 773–5, *www.amfora-turist.hr*.

Rovinj

Rovinj

Lovely and uncomplicated, Rovinj (pronounced 'Roveen'; Rovigno) is Istria's pin-up. The appeal of this medieval port is not intellectual but sheer good looks; a corner of former owner Venice (1283–1797) wafted across the Adriatic. Shoehorned into an old town huddled into an oval – a reminder that Rovinj existed on an island until it was connected to the mainland by Habsburg engineers in 1763 – is an absurdly picturesque medieval warren. Look back from the harbour or islet of Svete Katarina (*see* p.156), and the town appears like one of the romantic watercolours sold in its streets: on the seafront jostle houses in earthy Italian shades which seem to have ripened in the sun, and crusty terracotta roofs heap up to a mighty church. Of course, being everyone's favourite It girl has its down sides – too many admirers and August prices. But high summer brings a riviera fizz to an increasingly stylish restaurant and bar scene. That sophistication is achieved without selling out accounts for much of Rovinj's charm.

Town museum
Gradski muzej; **t** *052 816 720, www.muzej-rovinj.com; open Tues–Sun June–Sept 10–2 and 6–10, Oct–May 10–1; adm*

Start at main harbourside square **Trg maršala Tita**, lined with cafés. At the back of the triangular square, a Baroque palace has been gutted to house the **town museum**, a fairly musty display of Roman odds and ends plus scraps of stone rescued from 9th-century Carolingian church St Thomas's on the ground floor. Above is a small gallery of largely Italian Old Masters, the highlights

Getting to and around Rovinj

Venezia Lines plies a summer **ferry** route from Venice to Rovinj that links to Poreč.

Hourly **buses** link Pula to Rovinj. Up-coast connections go to Poreč and Novigrad (4 per day) and daily inland routes go to Buje and Buzet; more frequent inland links (4 or 5 per day) go to Kanfanar and Labin. Long-haul bus routes include Zagreb (7 per day) and Rijeka (6 per day), plus daily services to Varaždin and Split. The bus station is on Trg Na Lovki; walk 300m west to the old town or 100m south on Vladimira Nazora to locate the harbour.

North of Rovinj, buses from Pula and Rovinj to Poreč stop at the **Lim Channel** and **Vrsar** on request.

---

among some flashy Renaissance works the simplicity of Giovanni Bellini's 15th-century *Madonna and Child with Saints* and a lovely contemporary *Adoration of the Magi* by Bonifazio de Pitati. Going the other way around the square, on the harbourfront, you reach **Batana House**, a mini multimedia museum in honour of the traditional *batana* fishing boats crammed into the inner harbour outside. The design, derived from Venetian Republic craft that worked the Venetian Lagoon, is renowned for its seaworthiness rather than its comfort – one theory has it that the name comes from the Italian verb *battere* (to beat or thrash) as the flat-bottomed boats pounded against the waves.

Batana House
Kuća o batani; open June–Sept daily 10–1 and 7–10; Oct–Dec and Mar–May Tues–Sun 10–1 and 3–5

However, there's no better museum than the old town itself, reached via the Baroque **Balbi arch**, christened after the family whose coat of arms features beneath a growling Lion of St Mark, emblem of the Venetian Republic. Beyond is the old town's spine street, **Grisia**, thronged in summer and almost impassable in mid-August when it becomes a free-for-all outdoor art gallery during the **art fair**. Follow it uphill and eventually you reach Rovinj's crowning glory, the Baroque bulk of **St Euphemia**. Facts – or at least Christian records – say that Rovinj's patron saint was thrown to the lions of Constantinople amphitheatre in 304 for daring to denounce the pagan gods of Emperor Diocletian. Legend takes up the tale at this point, with a story that Euphemia's stone sarcophagus washed up at Rovinj's harbour on 13 July 800. It was hauled uphill by a boy and some oxen, strengthened, they say, through divine intervention when the town's horses proved too feeble. Academics suggest that fishermen smuggled the marble sarcophagus out of Constantinople during the purges of Emperor Nicefor. Either way, the 6th-century marble box lies in state behind the right altar, surrounded by oils of the saint's legend, and she is depicted as a wind vane on the 60m **campanile** modelled on St Mark's, Venice. You can ascend a tight whorl of steps for views from its balcony, or simply soak in head-spinningly gorgeous coastal views from the terrace before the church – magic at sunset.

Art fair
usually second Sat in Aug

St Euphemia
Crkva sv. Eufemije; open daily July–Aug 8am–10pm, April–June and Sept–Nov 10–6

Campanile
adm

Away from these showpieces, Rovinj reveals her charms to those willing to get to know her properly. There's little to see but much to enjoy if you follow your instincts in the streets beneath the church:

cobbled alleys trickle like tributaries downhill to the harbour, winding through tightly packed medieval and Renaissance houses whose unique chimneys were thrust skywards during a population explosion that converted every spare room into living quarters.

Aquarium
Akvarij; open mid-April–Oct daily 9–8; adm

East of the old town, at Obala Giordano Paliaga 5, the **Aquarium** has brought Adriatic aquatics onto dry land since 1891. For a glimpse of the real thing, there are shingle beaches on Zlatni Rt, a wooded headland 1km south of the centre, and on pine-shaded islets **Sveta Katarina** (St Katherine) and **Crveni otok** (Red Island) opposite the old town, both reached by a hourly ferry from the harbour and marina.

North to Poreč

Hearsay has it that when life became too hot in the Caribbean, buccaneer Sir Henry Morgan sailed dropped anchor in the **Limski kanal**. Allegedly Morgan, who ended his days as governor of Jamaica, found refuge with former Uskok pirates who had looted Dvigrad 5km inland (*see* p.178), then holed up in adjacent hamlet Mrgani. However enticing a yarn this is, it should be taken with an admiral's pinch of sea salt, although, ironically, the fjord-like inlet was a location for Hollywood Viking movie *The Long Ships* (1964), starring Richard Widmark and Sidney Poitier. Archaeologists are happier to support the story that the Romans anchored in the narrow body of water which pokes a finger inland 4km north of Rovinj. Boat tours from Rovinj, Vrsrar and Poreč wind into the 12km channel whose steep slopes are riddled with caves. One of the obscurest of Catholic saints, Romuald from Ravenna (*c.* 950–1027), is said to have lived here as a hermit – tours of the 105m cave known for its mouse-eared bats operate from mid-June to mid-Sept through the tourist office at **Kanfanar**. Most visitors stop only for seafood – fine oysters, mussels, gilthead and sea bass are served in restaurants here.

ⓘ **Kanfanar**
t (052) 825 221

Packed tightly on the channel's north headland, the genteel small town of **Vrsar** (Orsera) huddles above its harbour in pastel shades around the hilltop church of **St Martin** (Crkva sv. Martina), with light-hearted frescos. It may well have been the vista of sea and islets from its **campanile** that inspired 13th-century Poreč bishops to build the adjacent *castrum* as a holiday home, their summer visits doubtless accompanied by much local grumbling, since a 1577 document relates that locals were 'obliged to carry the bishop's luggage without any charge whenever the bishop is coming to the castle or is leaving it'. Casanova also spent his holidays here, and luxuriated in languid nights of Refošk wine and women if his memoirs are any guide. The 17th-century Venetian

Campanile
open summer daily 9–7; adm

gigolo would be titillated that one of Europe's largest naturist resorts, **Koversada**, lies a few kilometres south.

You reach the old town via the **Sea Gate** above the harbour, the last of those that once punctuated the town walls and whose ubiquitous Lion of St Mark paws a closed bible – the book would usually be open at PAX TIBI MARCE EVANGELISTA MEUS, but this was deemed bad taste for a tribute sculpted during war. Just before the gate, the **Church of St Fosca** contains Petro Ferrari's image of the martyr and town protector getting it in the neck beneath murderous skies, the eye-catcher among so-so Italian Baroque daubs plus vestments and prize texts; while beside the harbour the **Church of St Mary by the Sea** (Crkva sv. Marije od mora) preserves 16th-century frescoes in a Romanesque basilica. Views over the iselt archipelago beyond are magic at sunset.

Church of St Fosca
Crkva sv. Foške; open summer Fri–Wed 9–11 and 5–8, Thurs 9–11

The Venetian Republic prized Vrsar limestone for its Renaissance palaces and churches. A 20th-century admirer of high-quality *pietra di Orsera* was the sculptor Dušan Džamonja. Miniatures of his organic shapes, on display in New York's Modern Art Museum and held in the Tate collection in London, are scattered like alien eggs of bronze and iron in a **sculpture park** where the Macedonian artist beavered in his studio, 2km north on the Poreč road.

Sculpture park Džamonja
open Tues–Sun June–Aug 9–8, Mar–May and Sept–Oct 9–7, Nov–Feb 9–5

Activities in and around Rovinj

In 1914 the Austrian passenger steamer *Baron Guasch* hit a mine southwest of Rovinj and disappeared beneath the waves in 10 minutes to create one of the world's premier dive sites at 40m. Advanced divers can visit the site year-round with **Diver Sport Centers** in Villa Rubin, 3km south of Rovinj near the Polari campsite, **t** (052) 816 648. It also runs excursions to easier dive sites.

Bike hire is available from **Bike Planet**, opposite the bus station at Trg na Lokvi 3. The tourist office has maps of routes that follow tracks deep into the surrounding countryside.

ⓘ Rovinj >
Obala Pina Budicina 12 (harbourfront), **t** *(052) 811 566, www.tzgrovinj.hr; open daily June–Sept 8–10, Oct–May 8–3*

Where to Stay in Rovinj

Hotel chain Maistra owns most of the town's hotel stock, which is far from cheap in season. Source private rooms at **Natale-Lokva**, Carducci 4, **t** (052) 813 365, by the bus station.

★ Angelo d'Oro >

Angelo d'Oro, Vladimira Švalbe 38–42, **t** (052) 840 502, *www.angelodoro.hr* (€€€). The premier address is this boutique hotel of just 24 rooms, created from a bishop's palace. On the north side of the old town, it's an effortless marriage of four-star mod cons, Baroque architecture and antique furnishings. Breakfast is served on a garden terrace – a hideaway second only to the rooftop loggia – and the **restaurant** (€€€) ranks among Rovinj's finest.

Istria, Sv. Andrej (aka Crveni otok), **t** (052) 802 500, *www.maistra.hr* (€€€). Another pricey Maistra resort hotel, this on pretty St Andrew's island. Style is designer, with spa and wellness facilities, and first class.

Katarina, Svete Katarine, **t** (052) 804 100, *www.maistra.hr* (€€€). Pricey but you're paying for the splendid atmosphere of an Austro-Hungarian-vintage resort hotel on a palm-filled islet opposite the harbour. Deluxe doubles are worth the extra.

Monte Mulini A Smareglia bb, **t** (052) 636 000, *www.maistra.com* (€€€). Reopened in 2008 after refurbishment, a bayside resort hotel on the Zlatni rt headland 2km south that adds a dollop of swish designer style to the town's hotel stock.

Adriatic, Obala P Budicin bb (on Trg maršala Tita), **t** (052) 815 088, *www.maistra.com* (€€). Simple rooms in a small Austro-Hungarian era hotel that's superbly located before the harbour on the main square.

Mofardin Agroturizam Veštar 4, 7km south of Rovinj, **t** (052) 829 044 (€€). A step back into timeless rustic Istria on an farmhouse a stone's throw from the sea. Rooms in the old house have antique hand-me-down furnishings (those in a new building are more modern), the garden is idyllic and there's home produce in a restaurant (€€). Agrotourism at its finest. *Reservations essential.*

Eating Out in and around Rovinj

Rovinj

Monte, Montalbano 75, **t** (052) 820 203 (€€€). Gutsy Istrian cuisine elevated to gourmet heights – fillet steak in a sauce of local truffles and red wine, *ombolo* (loin of pork) with an almond, fig and Malvazija white wine sauce – plus creative seafood dishes from a Gault & Millau-recognized rustic-chic address near the cathedral. *Closed Nov–Feb.*

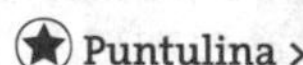

Puntulina, Sveti Križa 38, **t** (052) 813 186 (€€€–€€). First-class, creative Italian cuisine in the most inspiring location in the island, its terrace hanging above the sea on the south side of the old town. One for a splurge. *Booking recommended. Closed Wed, and Dec–Feb.*

Dream, J Rakovca 18, **t** (052) 830 613 (€€). A sweet and quietly stylish trattoria in an old stone house that brings a touch of class to the bars area behind the harbour. Also has international dishes.

Giannio, Via A. Ferri 38, **t** (052) 813 402 (€€). Don't be fooled by a dining room of benches and stone walls; this is acclaimed as a seafood address, where sole comes with truffles, and conger eel and scorpion fish star alongside bream and bass. *Closed Mon.*

Toni, Driovier 3, **t** (052) 815 303 (€€). Good-value pastas such as a fusilli with scampi and truffles in a highly respected, unfussy Italian. *Closed Wed.*

Veli Jože, Sveti Križa 1, **t** (052) 816 337 (€€). A little more pricey than the average *konoba*, but more upmarket, too, with a marvellously cluttered bosun's locker of an interior. *Pečena janjetina* (roast lamb) served with potato is delicious (better still with an Istrian red wine) or try *bakalar in bianco* (dried cod in white wine sauce). Touristy but essential. *Closed Jan–Feb.*

Limski Kanal

Viking, Limski kanal, **t** (052) 448 223 (€€€–€€). Forgive a terrace of plastic tables and chairs and enjoy the seafood: oysters served on ice, pasta with scampi and mushrooms and super-fresh fish. Gourmets rate it above neighbour **Fjord**, **t** (052) 448 222, which has finer views.

Vrsar

Trošt, Obala maršala Tita 1a (waterfront), **t** (052) 445 197 (€€). Veal and fish slow-cooked under a *peka* are the choice in Vrsar's premier address; don't be fooled by a drab exterior. For a light bite, *tjestenina sa šparugama, tartufima i pršutom* (tagliatelle with asparagus, truffles and *pršut* ham) is outstanding.

Cafés and Bars in Rovinj

As well as these options, there's a strip of bars behind the harbour area opposite the old town.

Marea, Vladimira Švalbe 34. Shoebox-sized bar with a menu of nibbles and a terrace inches above the sea on the north side of the old town – perfect for a mid-morning *marende*.

Puntulina, Sveti Križa 38. A wine bar beneath the restaurant of the same name, its terraces scattered over several levels just above the waves.

Valentino, Sveti Križa 28. Not the cheapest, but there are no better spots for a sundowner than the terrace of this tiny place beyond the harbour.

Viecia Batana, Trg maršala Tita 8. Pastries and coffees in a café on a central square – the locals' choice.

Poreč

Poreč (Parenzo) does all it can to put you off. Statistics of 700,000 visitors a year and 30 satellite hotel and villa complexes don't bode well for those unhappy with mass tourism. Nor are first impressions good in a town that has long wooed the tourist kuna. One Pietro Kandler penned the first town guidebook in 1845, and a drip of 1950s visitors became a flood when the bucket-and-spade brigade arrived in their thousands in the 1980s. Venetian Gothic patricians' houses are reinvented as boutiques, and the cobbled lanes have more than their share of touristy *konobe* and tacky souvenir shops. Then, just when you've written it off, Poreč pulls an ace from its sleeve, the UNESCO-listed Basilica of Euphrasius, and all is forgiven. For all its plastic-fantastic sheen, Poreč's roots run deep, and it remains on Istria's must-see checklist.

The Basilica of Euphrasius

The Basilica of Euphrasius
Eufrazijeva Bazilika; open daily 7am–8pm

The end of the 5th century: the barbarians are hammering at the gates of Rome and imperial artists are lazy from centuries of excess. In a gamble to inject a shot of cultural adrenaline into a tottering empire, Emperor Justinian looks to the brilliance of art of the ancient world. A vain hope, as history proved, but it was during the full flowering of Justinian's *reconquista* in the mid-6th century that Bishop Euphrasius arrived at what was a minor town on the fringe of a dying empire.

Campanile
open daily 7–7; adm

Bishop's Palace
open daily 10–5; adm

You enter his religious complex, in the centre of Poreč old town, via the square **atrium**, a courtyard patched up in the 19th century by Austro-Hungarian emperor Franz Josef and whose walls are studded with medieval religious carving and bishops' tomb-slabs. At its back is the octagonal **baptistry**, empty except for its tub sunk into the floor like a Byzantine Jacuzzi, and a doorway to ascend a 35m **campanile** for a view of fluttering terracotta roofs. An adjacent 6th-century **Bishop's Palace** displays mosaics from the Oratory of St Maurus, the 4th-century forerunner of Euphrasius's more glitzy basilica, none more famous than the image of a toothed fish, a clandestine symbol of faith in an era when Christians were amphitheatre fodder and prayers were said in secret cellars. Today it has been adopted as a Poreč mascot. Also here is a minor lapidarium and above, off the ceremonial hall of the 1690s palace, is a small collection of late Gothic devotional artwork from inland Istria.

And so the basilica. Bishop Euphrasius was a vain man. He swears in a mosaic inscription in the apse that his pious dedication lifted the three-nave basilica from earlier ruins: 'Here at first was a shaken and ruined temple in danger of falling down, and it was not strengthened by sure power. It was narrow and was not

Getting to and around Poreč

In summer, Venezia Lines operate a high-speed **catamaran** to Venice and to Rovinj.

As a major resort, Poreč is well-connected by **bus**: hourly services run to Pula and approx every 90mins to Rovinj, plus there are 6 services a day to Umag, Novigrad and Rijeka. Inland, 8 buses a day go to Pazin (the nearest train station), 5 a day to Buje and a limited service goes to Buzet. Long-haul routes go to Zagreb (6 per day). The bus station is at Rade Končara 1, 5mins' walk east of the centre behind the marina: Boze Milanovića leads direct to Trg slobode.

Eight buses a day link **Novigrad** with Poreč and **Umag**; Poreč services stop in **Tar**. Novigrad bus station is a 500m hike from the centre: follow the only road west.

embellished with gold and the dilapidated roof was held together by grace. When the concerned priest Euphrasius, devoted to the faith, saw that his seat was in danger of collapsing under the burden, with a holy intention he forestalled the ruination and to make the ruined building more firm he demolished it; having laid the foundations he raised the summit of the temple.' A fine story, but one that puts a top-spin on the truth, because the bishop enlarged a 4th-century shrine: exhibit A is the geometric mosaics by the main portal.

Yet whether narcissistic or simply authoritative, Euphrasius had impeccable taste. Yes, he stamped his monogram on every capital along an otherwise bland **nave**, but you can forgive his faults when you stand before the shimmering gold skin of mosaics which cover the **apse**, as luxuriant and brilliant as those in Ravenna and full of the smoke and incense of the Byzantine East which inspired them. Among the doe-eyed martyrs and saints in the **vault**, including Poreč martyr and patron St Maurus, the tonsured bishop stands with a model of his creation on the Virgin's right-hand side – small wonder that the pope later excommunicated him for his effrontery – while beneath are charming cartoony scenes from the Annunciation and Visitation, and a sash of mother-of-pearl and semi-precious stones, set here and there as Roman tridents and dolphins. Overshadowed but just as impressive is a 13th-century ***ciborium***, glittering with its own sheen of mosaics. The ensemble can be lost in the gloom in late afternoon – visit in the morning light or better still for evening mass.

Down the Decumanus

The rest of Poreč is an anticlimax after such a showstopper. Having batted aside an Illyrian tribe, 1st-century Romans planned the streets, which still lay a tidy grid on to the peninsular old town. Just as two millennia ago in Colonia Julia Parentium, the spine-street is the **Decumanus** (Dekumanska), ruler-straight from open square **Trg slobode**, the Forum (see below). A pentagonal **tower** at the edge of the square, built over earlier Roman and medieval watchtowers when the Venetians bolstered the fortifications in 1447, marks the start of the old town and, near it, the Sinčić family's

District Museum
*Zavičajni muzej; **t** (052) 431 585; open June–Sept Mon–Sat 10–1 and 6–10, Sun 10–1; Oct–May only through the tourist office (see p.163); adm*

Baroque palace, home to the **District Museum**. Istria's oldest museum has a passable collection of Roman ceramics, busts and bric-a-brac and a room of carved slabs – look for a toga-clad Roman harvesting olives in a region which remains famous for one of Europe's premier oils, produced near Tar (*see* below). Above Baroque salons are hung with the usual portraits of bishops and bigwigs, sombre and sour-faced and not nearly as dashing as Gian Rinaldo Carly, who steals the show in the Turkish threads he wore as a Venetian government interpreter in the Ottoman court.

The town saves saves its grandest Venetian Gothic mansions for the centre point where the Decumanus intersects with the **Cardo**, the urban cross-street to which all Roman town planners adhered. A little further south, on the edge of **Park M. Gupca**, a balconied building, of stolid 13th-century Romanesque, houses occasional summer art exhibitions, then the Decumanus opens into **Trg Marafor**, centre stage of Roman Poreč as the Forum and with scrappy remains of **temples**, possibly to Mars and Neptune, located in a park on the left-hand side. It's backed on the north by the last strip of **medieval defence wall**.

Sveti Nikola
boats summer 7–11 every 30mins; 15Kn return

It's not a spot to swim, however. For a dip, take a boat from the harbour to island **Sveti Nikola** – a sea of sizzling flesh.

North of Poreč

Baredine Cave and Tar

Baredine Cave
*Jama Baredine; **t** (052) 421 333, www.baredine.com; open July–Aug 9.30–6; May–June and Sept 10–5; April and 1–15 Oct 10–4; adm*

Not technically on the coast, but only an 8km detour east towards Višnjan, is the **Baredine Cave**, with five caverns and a gallery of limestone sculpture moulded over the millennia into passable approximations of the Leaning Tower of Pisa, the Virgin and a snowman. Guides revel in the yarn of a 13th-century milkmaid cast into the caves and calcified after the mother of local lord disapproved of her son's sweetheart, although more intriguing exhibits on the 40-minute tours are specimens of *Proteus anguinus*, a blind amphibian which spends its century of life skulking in the total darkness of north Croatian and Slovenian caves. Sadly, science has disproved the 18th-century conviction that it was dragon spawn, and a modern nickname of the 'Human Fish' owes more to its pigment-free pink skin than its newt-like looks. The latest attraction here is a climbing and caving centre – **Speleolit** runs abseil trips and potholing adventures into the caverns.

Speleolit
***t** (052) 421 333, www.baredine.com; open daily 10–5; reservation essential; abseiling 40Kn, potholing 350Kn*

Nearly 2,000 years ago, when Roman patricians led a life of ease in *villae rusticae* and an imperial *castrum* appeared on every peninsula, Istria was the source of the finest olive oil in the empire – only Istrian oil was deemed of sufficient taste and purity to

ⓘ **Tar**
*Istarska 8a, **t** (052) 443 250; open June–Sept daily 8–9; Oct–May Mon–Fri 8–3*

Obitelj Žužic
*Istarska 5, **t** (052) 443 141*

appear on the emperor's table. The best of the best was and still is pressed from groves north of Poreč around **Tar** (Torre); pick up a bottle from a prize-winning producer at **Obitelj Žužic**. Tar still remembers the unannounced visit of Pope Pius VII in 1800, related as an inscription on the gable of its parish church of **St Martin** (Crkva sv. Martina). The pontiff was less enthusiastic – the stop was enforced because his frigate *Bellona* was storm-bound – although at least he could enjoy views over fields and out to sea from Tar's perch on a plateau. Locals say that on crisp winter days they can see the campanile of St Mark's in Venice.

Novigrad

Beyond Tar, the road leaps over the Mirna river to arrive in **Novigrad**. Amiable and easygoing, it's a small-fry resort that has yet to suffer the crowds elsewhere on the coast, another reason to go alongside its first-class restaurants. A new marina suggests change is on its way. The reason that Novigrad is a place in which to idle, not intellectualize over culture, is largely down to history. Crowded on to a hook-shaped peninsula (an islet until the 18th century), the old town quietly prospered as an exporter of oak to Venetian Republic shipyards until 1687, when Turkish forces landed a blow so devastating that tourist authorities now direct their visitors to a single remaining pair of Venetian Gothic windows that are everyday elsewhere on the coast. You'll find them on old town main street Velika ulica, a few doors down from a dusky pink late Baroque noble's mansion, now home to modern art exhibitions as the **Rigo Gallery**. Notwithstanding sections of crenellated **medieval town wall** that stutter before the *mandrač* (inner harbour), other pre-wrack relics – Roman graves and Romanesque ecclesiastical carving – are well dispayed in a gallery-like **Lapidarium** on main square Veliki trg. Also here is the **Church of St Pelagius** (Crkva sv. Pelagija), located by a campanile which punctuates the skyline like an exclamation mark. Despite the church's demotion in 1831, when the bishop swapped seats, locals insist on honouring the basilica a *katedrala*, and there is an ecclesiastical swagger about its Venetian Baroque altarpieces and altar on which pouting cherubs steal all the attention from the town's oldest relic, Istria's only Romanesque crypt. Inevitably it is usually locked.

Rigo Gallery
*Rigo galerija; **t** (052) 726 582, www.galerija-rigo.hr; open Tues–Sun 10–12 and 5–8; adm*

Lapidarium
*Muzej-museo Lapidarium; **t** (052) 726 582, www.muzej-lapidarium.hr; open Tues–Sun June–Sept 10–1 and 6–10, Oct–May 10–1 and 5–7; adm*

For a quick dip, swim off the nearby seafront **promenade** which replaced the town walls. **Pebble beaches** and **concrete platforms** front two large package resort hotels 1km southeast.

Umag and Savudrija

According to legend, there was once a Mediterranean fishing village at this northern gateway into Istria. You could almost believe it, too, on a tiny teardrop peninsula where the Romans founded Umacas in the 1st century, and where late-Gothic stone houses are crammed around the 1750s parish church of **St Mary**. Like all good tales, this one has a moral. **Umag** (Umago) got greedy for tourist kunas. She cocooned herself within boxy hotels and tourist complexes, handed over her streets to souvenir shops and poured concrete over her pebble beaches. Persevere into her heart and you can glimpse what she was before she got tough and had a charm bypass, but unless you're here for the Croatia Open tennis tournament in mid-July, you would be far better advised to push 7km north to **Savudrija** (Salvore), named, they say, because King Otto, 12th-century son of Emperor Barbarossa, Germany's real-life King Arthur, evaded his enemies in a cistern after a naval battle, hence *Salvo re*. Although the village is no stranger to tourism – and is changing fast, the largest development yet a five-star Kempinski group resort, **Adriatic Istria**, new in summer 2009 – it's low-key around a Blue Flag beach (turn left at signs in Bašanija), a notch among pine woods where fishing boats are strung high on log davits.

ⓘ Poreč > *Zagrebačka 8,* **t** *(052) 451 293/458, www.porec.hr; open Mon–Sat 8–8, Sun 8–1*

Where to Stay in and around Poreč

Poreč

Most hotels are in outlying satellite complexes – the three-stars listed here are central.

Isabella Castle, Sv Nikola, **t** (052) 465 100, *www.valamar.hr* (€€€). Perhaps the most romantic address in town, an Italianate aristocrat's castle secluded among the trees of St Nicholas islet in Poreč bay. Noble features such as marble floors and high windows compensate for dated décor. Regular boats shuttle from the harbour.

Filipini, Filipini bb (4km east), **t** (052) 463 200, *www.istra.com/filipini* (€€). Two rooms and four apartments in a rustic retreat signposted off the road to Pazin. Parquet floors, rough plaster walls and the occasional antique provide yesteryear charm to complement the modern service. Breakfast on the terrace is a delight.

Hostin, Rade Končara 4, **t** (052) 408 800, *www.hostin.hr* (€€). One of Poreč's smaller hotels, hidden from the waterfront by a screen of trees. Accommodation, though bland, is spacious, plus there's a gym, sauna and plunge pool.

Jadran Residence, Obala maršala Tita 15, **t** (052) 465 100, *www.valamar.com* (€€). Cheaper than the nearby Neptun with smaller rooms; dated though none the worse for it – ceilings are of Austro-Hungarian height, for example – and with views to Sv Nikola islet from the best rooms.

Neptun, Obala maršala Tita 15, **t** (052) 400 800, *www.valamar.com* (€€). Modest but comfy small hotel with the most central location in town, beside the harbour. Air-con is promised as part of an update mooted for the summer 2009 season.

Source private accommodation from tourist agencies (more from the tourist office): **General Turist**, Obala maršala Tita 19, **t** (052) 451 188, *www.generalturist.hr*; **DI-Tours**, Prvomajska 2, **t** (052) 452 018, *www.ditours.hr*; **Istra-Line**, Partizanska 2, **t** (052) 432 339.

Novigrad

Nautica, Sv Anton 15 (marina), **t** (052) 600 400, *www.nauticahotels.com* (€€€). A five-star newcomer (2005) by the marina. Style is nautical luxury – think dark woods, brass and ship's wheel bedheads – in rooms with terraces over the yachts outside. There's also a gourmet restaurant,

Navigare, and a marina lounge bar – a sign of the way Novigrad is going.

Cittar, Prolaz Venecija 1, **t** (052) 757 737, *www.cittar.hr* (€€). An independent small hotel on a coastline of conglomerates, and it shows – this friendly, three-star fronted by the medieval town wall, is a homely place of modern fabrics, wicker and parquet floors. Sister hotel **Villa Cittar**, Sv. Antona 4, **t** (052) 758 780, *www.cittar.hr* (€€), opened in 2008 and has tasteful modern style and a rooftop Jacuzzi.

Source private rooms via agency **Montakso, t** (052) 757 603, in the bus station on Murvi.

Umag

San Rocco ›

San Rocco, Srednja 22, Brtonigla (11km east of Umag), **t** (052) 725 000, *www.san-rocco.hr* (€€€). A luxurious four-star which proves agrotourism is not all rustic chic. Stone walls and chunky beams abound in the 12 rooms of this renovated house; 'premier' rooms are a mite larger than 'classic'. It also has a terrace and pool for lazy days, a small spa and an excellent wine cellar and a gourmet Istrian restaurant. Small wonder it was voted Croatia's best small hotel in 2007.

Novigrad ››
*Porporella 1, **t** (052) 757 075, www.istra.com/novigrad; open summer daily 8–8, winter Mon–Fri 8.30–3.30, Sat 9–1.30*

Savudrija

Adriatic Istria, t (052) 708 526, *www.kempinski-adriatic.com* (€€€). Five-star Kempinski group resort, opening in summer 2009.

Villa Rosetta, Crvena uvala 31, **t** (052) 725 710, *www.villarosetta.hr* (€€). Tasteful modern hotel with a spa and calm neutral rooms of oak parquet overlooking the bay.

Ask about private rooms in Savudrija from *pension*-agency **Lido**, Istarska 38, **t** (052) 759 562, which also itself offers five basic **rooms** (€) moments from the beach.

Eating Out in and around Poreč

Poreč

Dvi murve, Grožnjanska 17, Vranići, **t** (052) 434 115 (€€€). An upmarket *konoba* signposted off the road to Vrs, 3km north of the centre. The style is elegant rustic, the cuisine exquisite, with fish dishes such as a *carpaccio* of sea bass alongside game, and the wine list is sensational. *Closed Jan.*

Sv. Nikola, Obala maršala Tita 23, **t** (052) 423 018 (€€€). There's a touch of Riviera glitz to this gourmet address opposite the marina. Fish menus change but are always exquisite: a carpaccio of scampi, frogfish and octopus, black tagliatelle with lobster flavoured by lemon, orange and brandy; lobster with black truffle shavings. Far from cheap but the classiest place in town.

Peterokutna kula, Dekumanska 1, **t** (052) 451 378 (€€€–€€). Touristy though atmospheric dining in a 15th-century Venetian tower with a great terrace.

Istria, Bože Milanovica 30, **t** (052) 434 636 (€€). *Jastog sa rezancima* (lobster with tagliatelle) comes recommended in a fish restaurant whose ordinary looks belie a good reputation.

Ulixes, Dekumanska 2, **t** (052) 451 132 (€€). Atmospheric dining in a nicely tatty rustic-styled courtyard or stone dining room – a world away from the tourist joints outside.

Novigrad

Damir & Ornella, Zidine 5, **t** (052) 758 134 (€€€–€€). An upmarket *konoba* with a stone dining room that's Istria-renowned for dishes of sushi-style fish. *Reservation recommended. Closed Mon.*

Mandrač, Mandrač 6, **t** (052) 757 120 (€€€–€€). One of the slickest numbers in town, with a large terrace by the inner harbour and a talented chef who prepares fresh fish and steaks. *Closed Mon–Fri Dec–Feb.*

Čok, Sv Antona 2, **t** (052) 757 643 (€€). Lobster with noodles or homemade fusilli pasta with truffles are on the Istrian menu of this old-fashioned family *konoba*. Find it near the roundabout before the inner harbour. *Closed Wed.*

Vitriol, Ribarnička 6, **t** (052) 758 270 (€). Waterside bar at the back of the old town that's easily the best in town, with a colourful maximalist style and bossa nova sounds. Just add sunset.

Umag and Savudrija

Buščina, Buščina 18 (5km north of Umag), **t** (052) 732 088 (€€€–€€). On the road to Koper, this garden *konoba* ranks among Istria's best for upmarket traditional fare. *Closed Tues.*

Lanterna, Svjetioničarska bb, Savudrija, **t** (052) 759 365 (€€). Beside the lighthouse of its name, with grilled fish and seafood and a terrace beside the sea.

Cafés and Bars in Poreč

Comitium Bar, Trg Marafor 15. The best bar in Poreč by a long shot spreads beneath a mimosa tree beside the ruins of a medieval house. If you can bear to go inside, you'll find wood floors, cocktails and laidback, lounge sounds.

Entertainment in Poreč

Classical music concerts held in the church and atrium of the Basilica of St Euphrasius are usually held on Friday between mid-June and late August.

There's more music (usually first Sun in June) for the **Naš kanat je lip**, a meeting of traditional Istrian and Kvarner vocal choirs, bolstered by national and international guests, plus July and August **jazz** in the District Museum's back yard.

Inland Istria

After the crisp sea-blues and villa-whites of the coast, inland Istria is shaded in the rusty reds and slate greys of soil and stone. And, unlike its breezy neighbour, this is a region only just waking up to tourism. For the moment, the 'Croatian Tuscany' is one of the nation's better kept secrets. Yet it's as enchanting as a child's picture-book. Hills are topped with a medieval huddle of stone houses and a spire, defensive high ground occupied since Neolithic times, and valleys ripe with pumpkins and cornfields are shot through with the silver of olive and willow.

Pulled between Venetians and Austro-Hungarians for five centuries, then part-abandoned after 1945, when its large Italian population fled after Italy grudgingly returned to Yugoslavia a territory it had claimed as spoils of war in 1920, Istria's inland towns and villages have an ancient, care-worn appeal. There are the acclaimed beauties such as Motovun, arty near-sister Grožnjan or under-rated truffle capital Buzet. There are rollicking medieval frescoes the colour of teran red wine stains in the tiny churches of Beram or Dragué, and there is Hum, a town so small that it took a myth to explain it. But this is a region to explore. Off main routes, clocks have stopped in a timeless landscape of small-scale agriculture, lush and languorous in summer, misty and romantic in autumn when crisp nights boil with stars. With a good map and a full tank of petrol, you can spend happy days on back roads you'll share only with antique tractors and find hamlets omitted from even the most detailed plans. You'll get lost, of course, but maybe that's half the point.

Northern Inland Istria

Buje

Maps show that just 12km separates the tourist fleshpots of Umag from agri-centre **Buje** (Buie), but the distance in character is a century or more; nowhere better defines Istria's split personality. Although the town with Roman roots is now off-watch after centuries as the 'Guard of Istria' over a trade crossroads, the views from the old town jumbled up on a hilltop, which made it so strategically important, are the same.

The aptly named street **Belvedere** marks out a circuit of panoramas over the green vineyards of Istria's premier wine country (*see* box, p.168) and out to the sea, a come-hither blue threaded with silver glints. It also traces the outline of the fortifications that once protected the old town above, a Venetian-era warren of dilapidated grey stone houses and interesting corners whose alleys thread uphill to the parish church of **St Servolo** (Crkva svetog Servula). Adjacent to a **campanile** that spears the sky at the hill's 222m summit, the Baroque church is studded with pillars and a funerary stele swiped from a temple which stood as crowning glory of the Romans' town Bulleae. Bar a frilly portal, the unfinished façade lends it a rather down-at-heel appearance, much like the adjacent late Gothic Venetian frescoed mansion.

Buje keeps its culture near the town gate, below: the **Ethnographic Museum** showcases folk culture and handicrafts by local artisans, and in the nearby **Church of the Madonna of Mercy** (Crkva Majke Milosrđa) there are Venetian Baroque altarpieces.

Ethnographic Museum
*Etnografska zbirka; **t** (052) 773 075; open (in theory) June–Sept Tues–Sun 9–12 and 6–8; Oct–May through the tourist office (see p.172); adm*

From Grožnjan to Motovun

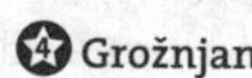
Grožnjan

While Buje is too preoccupied with its fields to bother with appearances, **Grožnjan** (Grisignana) fits into the timeless landscape like an old shoe. A film set of cobbled alleys and flowerboxes where cats doze in sunny corners, the honey-hued hill village 13km east seems too perfect to be true. And in a sense it is. Not so long ago the region's most enchanting village was a near-ruin, virtually abandoned to its fate by an Italian population who departed in 1945. Its fortunes revived when it lured artists with studio space in a newly declared *grad umjetnika* ('town of artists') in 1965 – 27 *ateliers* and galleries now welcome browsers. The establishment of the Croatian Jeunesses Musicales, a summer youth music school led by world-renowned tutors, consolidated the transformation, and today Grožnjan is probably more radiant than ever. Gentrification, of course, but of the best kind. Indeed, while time is measured here in wine, coffee and cat yawns, the problem in summer is over-popularity.

Getting to and around Northern Inland Istria

Without your own transport this area is fiddly to explore. Buses connect **Buje** to Poreč (5 per day), Pazin (3 per day) and Pula (4 per day). 4 buses a day ply inland from Novigrad to Buje. One bus a day links Buje to **Buzet**, via the Mirna valley, and two Pula–Buzet buses loop along the valley, pausing at **Motovun**; you'll have to hike uphill from all stops. 3 buses a day go direct from Pazin to Motovun. Conveniently, Buje's *ad hoc* bus station is the crossroads by Istarska – and the tourist office.

Buses to **Buzet** connect to: Pula (2 per day), Rijeka (5 per day), Novigrad (2 per day), Umag (4 per day) and Poreč (3 per day) and Buje (1 per day). All coastal buses pass **Istarske toplice**, as do buses to Buje. The Rijeka-bound buses pass **Roč**, which can also be reached by train from Pazin (change at Lepoglava, station *c.* 1km north). Buzet's bus station is by the garage on the main road beneath the old town. Its train station 3km northeast of the centre is on the Pula line (7 per day).

There's no transport to **Hum** and **Kotli**, although it's only a 3hr stroll to Hum from Buzet; vague sketch-maps are available from the tourist office.

Most of the charm of Grožnjan is in browsing for ceramics and art in the shuttered lanes. But there are cultural monuments, too. On a postcard-perfect little square, the Baroque **Church of SS Vitus and Modestus** conceals impressive altars; one, donated in 1800 by a storm-bound Pope Pius VII stuck in Tar (*see* p.162), is said to have mysterious powers to heed the prayers of the devout. Down the alley to the church's left there's a Renaissance **loggia** (1557) where corn was stored and judges and councillors of the Venetian Republic deliberated. It hosts above the only professional exhibtion space, **Gallery Fonticus**. Sidetrack south off its tiny square for a **belvedere** which affords views down the lush Mirna valley. Otherwise, outside the town gate at the loggia's shoulder – the **Porta Maggiore**, last of two entrances in medieval walls which once guarded the village – the diminutive Renaissance church **SS Cosmas and Damian** (1554) has folksy carved pews and 1960s artwork by Croatian artist Ivan Lovrenčić.

Gallery Fonticus
t (052) 776 131, www.gallery-fonticus-groznjan.hr, opening times vary

For an image of Grožnjan past, take the B44 east along the Mirna valley, here lush and open, and after 3km turn left and bounce up a dirt track to **Završje**, which slips down a hillside, lost in dreams of what might have been before it was deserted by an Italian population who knew it as Piemonte. A handful of families linger on, and the swagger of the oversized Baroque **Church of the Blessed Virgin Mary** (1794) testifies to former self-confidence. But a settlement with a leaning tower of Istria (a 22m belfy) is retreating from the public gaze behind a veil of ivy. One for connoisseurs of ruins. **Motovun** (Montona), 5km east of the turning for Zavrišje, might sometimes wish it could also drift forgotten. This is the most celebrated of Istria's medieval hill towns, its thread of dusty grey stone and terracotta zigzagging up a conical hill to a fortified kernel that's everybody's idea of a romantic rustic town. Its looks sometimes prove its undoing: defensive hilltop or no, in peak season Motovun is besieged. Expect full car parks (at the bottom of the hill) and hotels throughout high summer, especially in the last week of July, when the Motovun Film Festival rolls into town.

Istrian Wine

Istria has always known a thing or two about wine. The ancient Greeks named an Istrian bay after the fine wine produced there (*kalavonja*), and 1st-century Romans pruned vines on its sun-soaked southern slopes. Although family wine-makers tend grapes throughout this continent-in-miniature, with bauxite-rich red soils along the seaboard and white soils, heavy with clay, inland, the majority of vineyards are in the northwest, around Buje and northeast of Poreč below the Mirna river. First in everything as usual, the regional tourist board has mapped out wine roads (*vinska cesta*; sketch plans from tourist offices) of nearly 70 cellars and wine-makers.

Autochthonic varieties are the secrets to exploring Istrian tipples. You'll have no trouble tracking down *malvazija*, a ubiquitous white thought to have been introduced by the ancient Greeks, whose abundant growth and resistance to disease have made it a regional favourite. In poor years it can be rather flat, but a good vintage, rich in sugar and with around 12 per cent alcohol, has a bouquet of summer blossom and a fresh, balanced flavour that's dangerously quaffable with fish and seafood. A white for connoisseurs is the *muškat* grown on slopes around Momjan, 5km northeast of Buje, gold in colour, with a nose of wild clover and a sweetness that goes well with desserts; locals say with a twinkle in their eye that it has aphrodisiac powers.

Not so *teran*, a red which kept Livia, wife of Emperor Augustus, in rude health until she was 82, according to Roman encyclopaedist Pliny the Elder. In recent times Austrian apothecaries sold it as a health cure, and until the late 1950s some country doctors prescribed a glass of the iron-rich tipple to pregnant mothers. This is a robust farmer's wine, strong on personality, heavy with fruit, which tradition decrees should be as black as fresh hare's blood. Best drunk young, it's well-paired with *pršut* ham and complements sausages and pork. No-nonsense plonks can be cheek-suckingly tart, however, which is probably why it is often served warm with sugar, olive oil, a pinch of pepper and crouton floats as *supa*. Subtype *Refošk* is just as dark, but more lively and fruity – no wonder it was the holiday tipple of Casanova.

Still, Motovun is a splendid ensemble piece. A grandee among Mirna valley hill towns, it counts Renaissance composer Andrea Antico and Formula One driver Mario Andretti among local sons. It has a noble foyer, too, a double **gate** in its 13th-century town walls. Stroll beneath a leonine plaque of former owner Venice and the **upper square** is charming, shaded by chestnut boughs and laid with a well which once tapped an underground water cistern, topped up by rainwater channelled by stone gutters left over from the 1400s. Adjacent to the Baroque **Church of St Stephen** (Crkva sv. Stjepana) at its back, the castellated Romanesque-Gothic **campanile** appears to actualize one of the quintet of towers on the town shield, a stage flat for a medieval heraldic drama. Motovun's greatest treat is its medieval **fortifications**. Make a circuit of the ramparts and see the finest panoramas of the Mirna valley there are; a sweeping vista over teran and malvazija vineyards and the thick Motovun Forest. You get to nose into Motovun's back gardens too. A road north, opposite Motovun, hairpins up through that truffle-hunter's paradise, where Giancarlo Zigante stumbled across his monster mushroom (*see* box, p.171), past the **Church of St Helen** – its adjacent water well is stopped by a boulder to prevent all the water of the world gushing out and drowning the Mirna valley, apparently.

Slalom further uphill and you plateau out at **Oprtalj** (Portole). The antidote to Motovun's crowds turns on the charm around a Venetian **loggia** like a summer pavilion, with a lapidarium of contemporary masonry and pleasant country views. However, behind its town walls it is quietly falling to pieces, depopulated by the double whammy of Italian emigration and coastal jobs. An aristocratic portal, a turbaned head at its apex, fronts the Baroque **Palazzo Portole** behind the parish church of **St George** as a testament to better days, which may return soon – it has been buffed up as a stylish agrotourism villa. As you leave Oprtalj, peer through an iron grille for 16th-century frescoes said to be of St Anthony of Padua in the diminutive **Chapel of St Rock**. The best views hereabouts are from hamlet **Zrenj** (Stridone), 1km north of Oprtalj then a jolting 4km east on a dirt track. Villagers in a hamlet named as one of St Jermone's many birthplaces say they see more hilltop spires from their eyrie than anyone else in Istria.

Palazzo Portole
through Villas Forum, ***t*** *(052) 375 600, www.villasforum.com*

East to Buzet

After the gentle slopes of its open west course, Istria's longest river, the Mirna, becomes more secretive upstream. Wooded slopes and escarpments press tight as the valley narrows, crowned by centuries-old stone hamlets – worth a detour. Midway along is **Istarske toplice** 7km east of Motovun, sited beneath a limestone crag. Distraught that her virtue had been slandered, a local girl beseeched St Stephen for a curative spring to prove her chastity, then hurled herself from the 85m bluff. Or so goes a tale to explain the Sveti Stjepan (St Stephen) thermal waters enjoyed by two millennia of holidaymakers: first the Romans, now elderly Croatian and Slovenian rheumatics, who wallow in sodium- and sulphur-rich waters so potent that doctors prescribe only one half-hour dip a day The ugly resort hotel is nothing special, but has diversified to provide spa cures, including an acclaimed fango mud pack. For more activity, climb a goat-trail to a 19th-century chapel at the cliff summit dedicated to the good saint. Mercifully, the views out to the valley gaze beyond the hotel.

A right turn 4km east labours up through woods then emerges in sleepy **Sovinjak**, aged to the colour of old ivory. They say that surrounding vineyards cultivated the Puccinum, an antique variety of the iron-rich red teran, which Roman empress Livia Drusilla quaffed exclusively;and the hamlet of **Sovinjsko polje** 1km beyond is the home of celebrated *konoba* Toklarija – reservations are as essential as ample time to savour gourmet Istrian fare (*see* p.173).

Buzet

Istria's self-declared *grad tartufa* ('truffle town') is often given the cold shoulder by tourists in the stampede to Motovun. It wasn't always so. After the Venetian military governor of Istria shifted his seat inland in 1511, blossoming Buzet, hub of the regional administration, was the destination of every passing stagecoach. Its star fell with that of the Republic in 1797, and it takes the right eyes to see former glories in the old town, an island of care-worn stone and cobbles caught in a temporal back-eddy above modern Buzet beneath – being overlooked isn't always a bad thing. You arrive in the town to the Baroque parish **Church of the Blessed Virgin Mary**, its size a statement of optimism from when it was completed two decades before the Republic's demise in 1797. In neighbouring streets, signs highlight noble portals and heraldic crests adorn 18th-century *palazzi*, the *pieds-à-terre* of Venetian aristocrats whose ghosts flit just out of sight in silks and wigs.

Heart of the old town is lovely **Trg Vela šterna** ('large well') boxed in by Renaissance artisans' houses and shaded by chestnut trees like a film set for a whimsical romance. Its centrepiece is a Baroque fountain stamped with the Venetian lion and a Venetian captain's crest. The **little well** (*mala šterna*) to match the large is one block west outside the contemporary small **gate** (1592), which breaches what remains of the **fortifications**, worth exploring for views west down the Mirna valley and east towards the Ćićarija uplands that sweep northwest into Slovenia and southeast to Mt Učka. Another reason to find the gate is to locate the **Regional Museum** a block south, with displays of weird Glagolitic tablets (*see* pp.40–1) and a traditional kitchen, all housed in a 1639 palace. The stone Baroque postbox on its left was for 'Denoncie Secrete' – a slot by which the public could accuse corrupt officals in secret.

Regional Museum
Zavičajni muzej;
***t** (052) 662 792; open*
Mon–Fri 11–3; adm

Around Buzet: Roč and Hum

Hotels are rare in this part of Istria, and Buzet's duo make it a handy base for forays into surrounding villages. Beyond Štrped, 3km northwest, **Salež** proudly boasts the last 'shame pillar' in Istria, a bizarre column just about recognizable as a man sporting a fez. Villagers nickname him 'Berlin' and say he entered their hamlet in 1769 in a cart pulled by six oxen and trailed by 18 virgins clad in white. They are less forthcoming on whether miscreants are still shackled to the 2m-high obelisk.

Roč, peering over a stone wall which has protected it since the 16th-century, is equidistant east of Buzet but draws on a far more illustrious heritage. It's hard to believe today, but in the 15th century it was the academic centre of Glagolitic literature and printing (*see* pp.40–1); Roč's scholars groomed the text of the nation's first printed book, a 1483 Glagolitic missal. Out of nostalgia, it still hosts workshops for students in July, probably not nearlys as fun as the irrepressible accordion jamboree *Z armoniku v Roč* (With an Accordion at Roč). At other times Roč dozes behind its

Truffles

Discovered by Romans, the preserve of élite gatherers during five centuries of Venetian rule, then reserved exclusively for imperial dinner plates in the Viennese Royal Palace, the truffle (*tartuf*) is Istria's gastronomic delicacy, and the forest around Oprtalj, Livade and Buzet is one of Europe's most bountiful hunting grounds. Come late September, around 3,000 truffle-hunters – and three times as many dogs trained since puppies – comb the damp woods of the Motovun Forest to root out the whiffy gourmet fungus from among oak roots.

Peak season is September to early November, when the local obsession intensifies to near mania. Choose any weekend and there will be some sort of Truffle Day (Dani tartufa), whether the folksy bonhomie of Buzet's Subotina festival on the second Saturday of September, when 10kg of truffles are stirred into a 2,000-egg omelette, or the tastings and 'most beautiful truffle' awards which lure connoisseurs to Livade. Tourist information centres and the regional tourism website *www.istra.hr* list all events.

Istria's prize fungal globes are its black truffles, a favourite of French chefs, and gourmet-choice white truffles, both of which grow to the size of an apple – usually. However, on 2 November 1999, while walking his dog Diana, Giancarlo Zigante unearthed a 1.31kg monster the size of a small pumpkin. Accredited by the *Guinness Book of Records*, the largest truffle in the world was cast in bronze, then scoffed by 100 guests, and Zigante cashed in on his new-found fame by styling himself Istria's 'truffle king'. His restaurant in Livade is obsessed to the point of offering truffle ice cream, and his chain of shops, Zigante Tartufi – now as far afield as Germany, Japan and America, *www.zigantetartufi.com* – stock an array of truffle goodies plus regional olive oils and wines. Find them in: Pula (Smareglina 7), Buje (Trg J. B. Tita 12), Grožnjan (Gorjan 5), Motovun (Gradiziol 8), Livade (Livade 7) and Buzet (Trg Fontana).

main gateway, which holds a lapidarium of Roman tombstones. Beyond, stone houses are laid out on parallel streets around the three-nave parish church of **St Bartholomew** and its 26m tower. For all its impressive Gothic, Roč's smaller churches have the treasure: the **Church of St Rock** near the large gate has medieval frescoes; and the 12th-century **Church of St Anthony**, with an asymmetric belfry, is graffitied inside with characters of the Glagolitic alphabet, an aide-memoire for former students.

Church of St Anthony
Crkva sv. Antuna; if locked, consult the Ročska konoba for whereabouts of the church keys (ključ)

More letters from the unusual religious script that's more alien than ecclesiastical line the road which dives south off the B44, 500m west of Roč. Scattered along the 7km **Glagolitic Alley** (Aleja glagoljaša) en route to Hum are 11 alphabet characters shaped from concrete by Croatian sculptor Želimer Janeš. Arranged like pagan standing stones, the letters are arranged in groups to represent key events in the development of the Byzantine script, which only fell out of favour in the late 1800s (*see* **Topics**, pp.28–9). Midway, a track forages right to **Kotli**, a quiet corner among woods christened after the 'hollows' in the stone river bed. Tourism is slowly resuscitating this tumbledown village, deserted in the 1950s after the last of its millers threw in the flour sack. Although a water wheel turns in one renovated mill, most visitors come to lark about in a necklace of pools.

So small is **Hum**, its 20 occupants have had to invent a legend. By the time the giants of old had completed the other towns in the

Mirna valley, they explain, there was hardly any stone left. But, in this age of Tourist Man, Hum has found itself a promotional angle as the self-proclaimed 'smallest town in the world', a Lilliput city of walls and watchtowers with an oversized parish **Church of the Assumption of Mary** (Crkva Blažene Djevice Marije), built in 1802 when Hum was a settlement over 100-strong.

Do look at the pictorial calendar of seasonal chores imprinted on the town gate's copper doors, their handles shaped like the horns of indigenous Istrian *boškarin* ox, before you look at the 12th-century frescoes in the cemetery **Chapel of St Jeronim**. Time has stopped in this atmospheric nook, daubed in Romanesque and Byzantine frescoes of the Annunciation, Crucifixion and Deposition the colour of red wine, and whose air of ancient secrets is only heightened by the Glagolitic graffiti scratched by an early priest. Its key is held by the Humska *konoba* (*see* p.174) just outside the gate, worth a visit for its mistletoe-flavoured *Humska biska*, a powerful *rakija* the *konoba*'s owner swears was once distilled by Istrian Celtic Druids. His secret recipe was passed on by Hum's late parish priest, a renowned herbalist, and locals say it does wonders for their blood pressure. You can pick up bottles, plus wines and souvenir Glagolitic script penned by local schoolchildren, in Hum's gallery-*vinoteka*.

ⓘ **Buje >>**
Istarska 2 (in town hall beneath old town), **t** *(052) 772 122, www.tzg-buje.hr; open June–mid-Sept Mon–Fri 8–6, Sat 8–1*

Festivals in Northern Inland Istria

Buje celebrates the **wine harvest** with parades, music and, of course, a bottle or three during 'Grape Days' (Praznik grožđa) held over a weekend in mid-Sept. In **Grožnjan**, musicians of the Croatian Jeunesses Musicales stage alfresco **concerts** from late June to mid-Aug, and the village swings to to 16 concerts a day during an **International Jazz Festival**, usually in late July. **Motovun's** pride is the **Motovun Film Festival**, with international art house and endless bubbly during a prestigious get-together of Croatian high society (last week of July). Year-round, there's a traditional **crafts and produce fair** on the 3rd Mon of the month. **Buzet** celebrates its title as truffle capital with **Subotina** on the 2nd Sat in September, with a giant omelette prepared on Trg Fontana. It also hosts a traditional **crafts and food fair** on the 3rd Thurs of the month. **Roč** succumbs to folksy nostalgia during the delightfully named ***Z armoniku v Roč*** (With an Accordion at Roč), an international convention of diatonic accordion players on the 2nd Sun in May. On the 1st or 2nd Sat in June, **Hum** elects its mayor using a curious medieval custom of casting votes by notching a stick. Expect traditional music and food too.

Where to Stay and Eat in Northern Inland Istria

Buje

The swish San Rocco agrotourism hotel is 4km south of Buje in Brtonigla; *see* p.164.

Volpia, Volpia 3 (3km north of Buje), **t** (052) 433 635 (€€). Off the road to Koper (Slovenia), this was Croatia's first agrotourism hotel, a friendly, family-run place which oozes modern-rustic charm. Expect to eat in, too – fine seasonal dishes from all-local produce are offered.

Konoba Morgan, Bracanija 1 (5km south), **t** (052) 774 520 (€€). One of the finest *konobe* you'll visit in Istria thanks to a young restauranteur, who does creative things with traditional gamey Istrian fare such as wild boar (*vepar*) with polenta or roast farm cockerel (*pečeni pijetao*). Expect age-old, slow-cooking methods and subtle cosmopolitan touches, all served in a garden signposted off on the road to Novigrad. *Closed Tues.*

Olivia, Via Giuseppe Verde 9, **t** (052) 772 050 (€€). Good seafood and pastas with truffles.

Pod voltum, Ante Bibića, **t** (052) 772 232 (€). Just uphill and a little less upmarket, sturdy Istrian rustic fillers such as *njoki sa gulašom* (gnocchi with goulash) plus the usual steaks near the museum.

ⓘ Grožnjan >
above old-town loggia, **t** *(052) 776 131, www.tz-groznjan.hr; open June–mid-Sept Mon–Fri 8–8, Sat 8–1*

ⓘ Buzet >>
Trg Fontana 7, **t** *(052) 662 343, www.buzet.hr; open summer Mon–Fri 8–3, Sat 8–1; winter Mon–Fri 8–3*

Grožnjan

Černac, V. Gortana 5, **t** (052) 776 122, *www.groznjan-grisignana.hr/app-cernac* (€). Country charm in the Černac family's two private apartments (sleeping 2 and 3).

Pintur, M. Gorijana, **t** (052) 776 397 (€). Central family guesthouse – two doubles and a single – opposite Bastia restaurant.

Bastla, Svibnja 1, **t** (052) 776 370 (€€) Wait for a table in the courtyard of this restaurant named for a mythic river-horse in the Mirna. The menu features homemade pastas plus fish and langoustines in summer, and locally distilled *digestifs* of *medica* (honey) or *travarica* (herb) brandy.

ⓘ Motovun >
Andrea Antico bb (main square), **t** *(052) 681 758; open June–mid-Sept Mon–Fri 8–8, Sat 8–1*

Motovun

Kaštel, Trg Andrea Antico 7, **t** (052) 681 607, *www.hotel-kastel-motovun.hr* (€€). Modern(ish) accommodation in an 18th-century building at the heart of Motovun's old town. Never mind the comfy but average décor, just enjoy the views out over roofs to the Mirna valley. *Reservation recommended in summer.* Its **restaurant** prepares an Istrian cookbook – dishes such as *maneštra* and pasta with jugged venison – all served on the showpiece square.

★ Toklarija >

Mondo, Barbakan 1, no tel (€€€). Truffles abound in a lovely address before the town gates, with a modern palate and an eye for rustic chic. Beef and lamb dishes have a twang of New World accents.

Zigante Enoteka, Livade 7 (1km north of Motovun), **t** (052) 664 302 (€€€). Elegant without being intimidating, the flagship restaurant of Croatian truffle king Giancarlo Zigante (*see* p.171) is one of the nation's gourmet addresses. No surprise that there are truffles with everything: lamb with goose liver, lobster, plus for dessert – what else? – truffle ice cream. A sister *gostiona* opposite is cheaper and faster.

Pod Voltun, Trg Josefa Ressala 6, no tel (€€). Touristy but atmospheric and reliable dining 'under the vaults' of the inner gate. Game and turkey specials are on offer.

Istarske Toplice

Mirna, Istarske toplice bb, **t** (052) 603 000, *www.istarkse-toplice.hr* (€). The spa resort hotel provides guests with modest, cheerful accommodation and a free pass to the outdoor pool.

Buzet and Roč

Plans are afoot for a small boutique hotel in Buzet, possibly due to open in 2010 – ask in the tourist office. Families in Roč provide inexpensive rooms: look for signs for '*Sobe*' or book through the office tourist.

Fontana, Trg Fontana 1, Buzet, **t** (052) 662 615, *www.hotelfontanabuzet.com* (€). A drab and just about acceptable Yugoslavia-era two-star on the square beneath the old town.

Ročska konoba, Roč bb, **t** (052) 666 451 (€€). Go for house specials in this village-centre *konoba*: an omelette of wild asparagus and mushrooms or seasonal truffles, or *pršut* delicately fried in olive oil. Start with a nip of home-distilled *biska* (mistletoe) or *medica* (honey) *rakija*.

Stara oštarija, Petra Flega 5a, Buzet, no tel (€€). On the square before the parish church, modern style meets updated recipes from granny's cookbook in an old-town trattoria. Great valley views from the conservatory. *Closed Tues.*

Sovinjsko Polje

Toklarija, Sovinjsko polje 11, **t** (052) 663 031 (€€€). Gastronomic Istrian cuisine

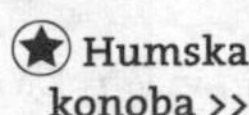

Humska konoba >>

in a refurbished oil mill, lovingly prepared from the finest seasonal ingredients by a master chef. After an *apéritif* of Poreč champagne, expect *maneštra* soup, *fuži* with mushrooms, veal carpaccio with tangy cheese and, in season, fresh truffles in gourmet 7- and 10-course taster menus; book 4 days in advance for the latter and be ready to swallow a bill of 900Kn per person. *Reservations essential. Closed Tues.*

Hum

Humska konoba, Hum 2 **t** (052) 660 005 (€€). It's worth lingering in Hum to dine in this lovely *konoba*. There's a menu of homemade *kobasice* (sausages) and *ombolo* (smoked pork), and idyllic country views from its terrace. Start with local speciality mistletoe brandy, *Humska biska*. *Closed Mon–Fri in Jan–Feb*.

Central Inland Istria

Pazin

Poor Pazin. The large and rather scruffy town at Istria's heart – the bullseye is marked by a marble obelisk near Trošti 3km south – is the regional capital and the hub of public transport, yet most of its visitors pause just long enough to change buses. Such is the price of being a plain Jane among country belles, a fact enthusiastic tourist authorities seem to acknowledge tacitly in their eagerness to promote Pazin as an activity destination: a destination for walkers on a web of marked countryside trails, a gauntlet for ace free-climbers on routes which include the toughest in the country (the drily named Zarečki krov, 'Easy Ride', graded 8b+), and a destination for freshwater anglers to try their luck for pike, chub and trout. Consult the tourist office about all.

Yet Pazin has deep roots and literary friends, both on display at the far end of a **high street** which only perks into life when a giant traditional fair sets up its stalls (*see* 'Festivals'), and off which the parish church of **St Nicholas** (Crkva sv. Nikola) has smudgy Old Testament frescoes (1400) in the vaults of its Gothic sacristy. Pazin germinated from the **castle** (*kaštel*) at the far end of the high street, first documented in 983 as a gift of Emperor Otto II to Poreč bishops. It is thanks to this much-strengthened hulk on a spur that, when much of Istria fell to Venetian forces, Pazin remained tantalizingly out of reach; it was captured by Republican troops just once and was re-taken before the year was out. Inside the 16th-century courtyard stronghold is the **Istrian Ethnographic and Pazin Museum**, a bright, well-displayed romp through Istrian folk costume – woolly socks and hemp garments donned by villagers on the windswept highlands of Ćićarija to the northeast, and embroided Sunday-best coats everywhere. There's also a collection of Istrian instruments – a *mih* wineskin bagpipe and an oboe-like *roženice*, an instrument with a whine so nasal that Istrians excuse it with a legend about a sorceress who bewitched a musician into

Istrian Ethnographic and Pazin Museum
Etnografski muzej Istre i Muzej grada Pazina; **t** *(052) 622 220, www.emi.hr; open 15 May–15 Oct Tues–Sun 10–6; 16 Oct–14 May Tues–Thurs 10–3, Fri–Sun 11–4; adm*

Getting to and around Central Inland Istria

As a central regional capital, **Pazin** has impressive connections. Trains link approx hourly to Pula and less frequently to Buzet. There are bus connections to: Pula (9 per day), Poreč (8 per day), Rijeka (7 per day), Rovinj (5 per day), Buzet and Motovun (both 3 per day). Long-distance routes go to Zagreb (seven per day), Osijek and Varaždin (daily). The bus and train stations are west of the centre, reached by following the tree-lined promenade Šetalište Pazinske gimnazije. Mountain bikes can be hired for 740Kn per day from **Matić**, Lovrin bb, 1.5km southwest towards Žminj, **t** (052) 621 119.

South of Pazin, this is a region for your own transport. **Kanfanar** is served by trains every 90mins from Pula and Pazin and linked by buses to most coastal towns. One bus a day travels from Pazin to Labin via **Gračišće** and **Pićan**.

thinking it was melodious – plus a mock-up of an open kitchen and agricultural tools plucked from farm sheds.

We promised you literary connections, and both stem from the rust-stained **gorge** behind the castle which plummets 130m and swallows the river Pazinčica. It has been promoted as Dante's inspiration for the gate to his *Inferno* – not so far-fetched, argue the theory's supporters, because the poet found refuge in a monastery of St Michael (there's one 1km northwest of Pazin) and shared a mutual friend with Heinrich II, who acquired the castle from Poreč bishops. Harder proof is available for the gorge's walk-on part in Jules Verne's 1885 novel *Mathias Sandorf*. For the 27th of his famous literary *Voyages Extraordinaires*, the French writer had his eponymous hero escape the dungeons of Pazin castle, scale down the cliff then bob off into the darkness, emerging 30km southwest and six hours later in the Limski kanal. Verne was not a writer to let facts stand in the way of a good story – the river actually reappears east as the spring of the river Raša near Pićan – and his enthusiasm for Pazin was probably sparked by illustrations of Charles Yriarte's 1878 *Les Bords de l'Adriatique*; he also nods nominally to the Pazin official, Count Esdorff, who explored the cave by boat in 1858, according to Yriarte. Verne never actually paid a visit – he made do with a snapshot of the landmark sent by the town mayor, Giuseppe Cech – but Pazin celebrates its advocate with the 'Around Pazin in 80 Minutes' bike race on the last weekend of June. Either way, a signposted walk from the museum descends to make a nature circuit around the Pazin pit.

Beram

Never mind that Beram is one of Istria's oldest settlements – built over an iron age hill fort and prehistoric necropolis – nor that its timewarp village clustered on a hilltop above cornfields was mentioned before Pazin in 911. Its place in the encyclopaedias is justified by what are arguably the finest – and certainly the most famous – **frescoes** in Istria. Nothing to look at from outside, the minor cemetery church of **St Mary of the Rocks** (Crkva Majke Božje

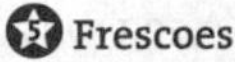

na Škriljinah), below the village 600m north, is an artistic hurrah inside, a wall-to-wall, late-Gothic pictorial Bible painted in 1475 for the benefit of illiterates.

Its artist, Vincent of Kastev, probably copied his designs from those in Pazin's St Nicholas church. But he brought a far higher level of artistry to his work, and a wry eye for local colour. Just as outside, castles and villages crown every hilltop in an *Adoration of the Kings* like the medieval procession of a vintage Hollywood blockbuster; right of the portal, blind Fortune spins the wheel of fate; and above it, a celebrated *Danse Macabre* fizzes with character. A skeletal piper with a pair of Istrian *mih* (wineskin bagpipes) leads a procession of grinning skeletons and a procession (in strict pecking order) of the 15th-century's great – a bishop, king, noblewoman and a farmer – and not so great – a knight, beggar and, bringing up the rear, a merchant hoping to buy his way into Heaven with a stack of gold coins.

The key (*ključ*) for the church is held at house No.22 or 23, although a steady trickle of visitors means the incumbent rarely leaves the church in summer months; during the off season, consult Pazin's tourist office if you get no reply.

East of Pazin: Dragué and Boljun

Although there is a string of enticing waterfalls and bathing spots if you stroll east along the Pazinčica river, none impresses like the **Zarečje waterfall** (Zarečki krov). One of the largest falls in Istria, and the only one active in the driest summer, it drops a curtain of water off a riverbed shelf to a lake 10m below, providing locals with a favourite spot for a summer dip and free-climbing. Find it on a 14km **circular trail** which loops through gorgeous countryside or on an unmarked footpath which leads north off the main road approximately 500m before a viaduct 2km east from Pazin.

Circular trail
Pazin tourist office (see p.179) has leaflets showing routes

At Cerovlje, a left fork follows a tributary then meanders north from the valley floor. Even in a region with more than its fair share of charmers, **Draguć**, strung out along on a defensive ridge, is a gem, a village so impossibly picture-postcard pretty that it had a fleeting career in the movies during the 1980s. You have to pinch yourself to believe that lights and cameras are not just out of sight in its rough cobbled lanes. Action is confined to elderly locals exchanging gossip on a bench. Alongside enchanting looks, the reason to visit lies at the far end of the village, past the town square and ramshackle wooden farms. On the hilltop spur you'll find the **Church of St Rock** (Crkva sv. Roka), a one-pew chapel frescoed in the 1530s with a pictorial Bible in earthy shades of rust and moss. A dog runs, spooked by the vision of Gabriel in an Annunciation set in a shady grove; in a medieval pageant of Adoring Magi, pages and squires ride from the wings to the stable where a shaft of light spotlights the child; and the boy Jesus stands dignified after a clip around the ear for preaching in the temple. The key (*ključ*) for this unrestored Beram (*see* left) is kept in a house on the village square; at the time of writing, it's No.20. Ask, too, for the key for the Romanesque cemetery church of **St Eliseus** (Crkva sv. Elizija), whose less well preserved frescoes are inspired by Byzantine art.

Over the Rijeka–Pula *autocesta* from Cerovlje, a minor road burrows east into wooded countryside few tourists ever see. Past **Paz**, the valleys open into agricultural flatlands of the **Boljunsko polje**, a 'field' that stretches south to the coast squeezed by the slopes of Istria's highest mountain, **Mount Učka** (1,401m). It is christened after the village of **Boljun**, guarded by grizzled medieval fortifications and ramparts from its era as a stronghold on a strategic trade route. Glagolitic script squiggles (*see* **Topics**, pp.40–1) adorn the belfry of the Romanesque parish church of **SS Cosmas and Damian** by the entrance, beyond which are a 16th-century wheat storehouse and loggia on the town square. Take a road north (towards the Učka motorway tunnel) through the village of Vranja to **Brci**, then walk through woods on a footpath (on the right) and you reach **Vela draga**, a protected nature park punctuated by weird pillar-like stalagmites left behind from a vanished cavern.

Gračišće and Pićan

Impossible to imagine today, but 15th-century **Gračišće** bore comparison with Pazin as a garrison town in the buffer zone between the Habsburg and Venetian empires. Left only with its fortifications, the sleepy village beyond the town gate is a medieval cocoon forgotten by modernity. Evidence of grander days is here, though. Take the **Salamon Palace**, a hybrid of Venetian Gothic windows and leonine balcony, extended up in Renaissance style, now slowly falling into ruin. It opens a dilapidated square with medieval artisans' houses and the **Church of Our Lady on the Square** (1425; Crkva sv. Marije na Placu), whose frescoed Magi adore the Christ child (and Joseph grumps). Councillors and judges hammered out civic policy in its local government office – the Gothic **loggia** – and adjudicated traders' measurements of wine, oil and grain in the stone bowl hollowed like cook's cups just outside. Meanwhile, local women hammered nails into the church's mortar: a well-placed nail and a heartfelt prayer here was said to cure female sterility. It still does, judging by some of the shiny tacks embedded in the mortar.

Behind the church, a coat of arms announces the **chapel** where bishops from Pićan (*see* p.178) prayed during their summer holidays in Gračišće; a curious choice given the villages' proximity, although options are limited when your diocese holiday brochure only contains of 10 villages. Lanes beyond twist through tumbledown medieval stone houses – note the outside staircases to leave ground floors as stables or cellars – to the Baroque parish church of **St Vito**, which has one of the finest vistas in Istria; a magnificent sweep across wooded slopes and hilltops to Mount Učka and even Creš on clear days.

To stretch your legs, take to the **Path of Sv. Šimun**. A 11.5km loop through wood and meadow, this marked path begins by the town gate, passes the **chapel** of its namesake St Simon and pauses midway at the **Sopot waterfall**, which plumes into a chalk-blue lake secreted away behind cliffs.

Three kilometres south through the vineyards lies **Pićan**. When this, the next spire south of Gračišće, rose over a Roman *castrum* some time around AD 520, it is said that the Catholic world celebrated its fifth bishopric, this lasting until the 18th century. The parish church contains the relics of that first bishop, St Nicefor. Visit, however, for another fine view east towards Mount Učka from its belvedere.

Kanfanar and Dvigrad

Although united by history and location, these villages are as different as night and day. **Kanfanar**, 18km southwest of Pazin on the A8 *autocesta*, is a missable agricentre with a must-see cattle fair called Jakovlja. On the Saturday nearest St Jacob's Day (25 July) farmers haggle over prices of *boškarin*, a stocky indigenous ox with ancient looks, musicians dust down their Istrian *mih* (wineskin bagpipes) and *roženice* (a sort of nasal oboe), and much wine is drunk by all.

The town was founded in the mid-17th century by refugees from **Dvigrad**, 2km north on a minor road just clear of western Kanfanar. A siege by Uskok pirates who snuck up the Limski kanal 5km west was the final blow in a battalion of sorrows – plague, taxes and clashes between Austrians and the Venetian Republic – which assaulted the town. They say, the last citizen packed up in 1630 and Dvigrad crumbled into a haunting ruin. Defence walls and watchtowers are veiled in ivy, and houses slowly collapse on streets laid with flagstones worn smooth over the centuries. With some imagination, you can trace the layout of an early three-nave basilica at the rear.

There are worthwhile detours in this region, a landscape coloured red and grey by bauxite-rich soil and ancient dry-stone *kažun* shelters like beehives. Six km southwest of Kanfanar, **Svetvinčenat** insists on promoting its **castle**, of an Italian noble family, to the detriment of Istria's finest Renaissance **square**, with a neat loggia and town well and the tidy trefoil façade of the **Church of the**

Assumption. The castle opens only to concert-goers during a summer jazz festival; the 16th-century church contains Italian Baroque altarpieces.

North of Dvigrad via Barat, leafy hamlet **Kringa** is quiet after a nervous 17th century when a *vukodlak* prowled – in his encyclopaedic tome *The Glory of the Duchy of Carniola*, Slovenian polymath Janez Vajkard Valvasor relates that the local priest saw off a vampire with a hawthorn spike in 1672. From here it's 4km on a bumpy lane to **Tinjan**, renowned for blacksmiths and electing its mayor by flea. Apparently, villagers chose their official from the hopefuls who laid their beards onto the stone table behind the parish church. The flea hopped into one and its owner duly received the chains of office for a year. Whether Tinjan continues to uphold its electoral practice is unclear.

Festivals in Central Inland Istria

Pazin hosts one of Istria's largest **traditional crafts and food fairs** on the 1st Tuesday of the month. The last weekend of June sees a **bike race** as part of the town's Jules Verne Days.

Gračišće hosts a **harmonica festival** on the second Sun of May, a warm-up for **Vldova**, a festival in honour of village patron St Vito on 15 June; expect all the usual stalls, music and donkey races. Make a detour to visit **Kanfanar** for a **folk festival** and fair of *boškarin* ox, held on the Sat before or after St Jacob's Day (25 July).

Where to Stay and Eat in Central Inland Istria

ⓘ Pazin ›
Franine i Jurine 14, **t** *(052) 622 460, www.tzpazin.hr; open June–Sept Mon–Fri 9–7, Sat 10–1; Oct–May Mon–Fri 9–3, Sat 10–1*

Pazin

The helpful Pazin tourist board advises on and books agrotourism accommodation.

Lovac, Šime Kurelića 4, **t** (052) 524 324 (€). The only hotel in town is a tired two-star, heartsinkingly dated, with thin carpets and boxy beds. Its **restaurant** is popular with locals, however, for lunchtime fillers of steaks or pastas in thick meaty sauces, and has spectacular views of the gorge.

Draguć and around Boljun

Gržinić, Draguć 35, **t** (052) 665 105 (€). Three rooms and one apartment in the B&B of the English-speaking Gržinić family. Breakfasts come with Guido's honey.

Dol, Gologorički dol 6, **t** (052) 684 625, mobile **t** 098 415 522 (€). True escapism on a working farm in a valley where time has held its breath; find it downhill from Gologorica off the Cervolje–Boljun road. The English-speaking owners also offer riding lessons. *Reservations essential.*

Boljunska konoba, Boljun bb, **t** (052) 631 100 (€). A *konoba* renowned for fresh wild mushroom dishes. Otherwise, the menu is super-fresh and sourced locally, – washed down with carafes of good plonk. *Open after 3 and all day Sun; closed Tues.*

Gračišće

Agrotourism property **Dol** (above) is 7km away; turn left at Zajci south of Pićan then take the second left towards Gologorički.

Poli Luce, Gračišće 75, **t** (052) 687 081 (€). Charm in abundance in the four rooms (three doubles, one single) of the Marino *konoba's* B&B, with medieval stone walls and beams, and antique furnishings from the 'granny's house' school of décor.

Marino, Gračišće 75, **t** (052) 687 081 (€). A snug rustic *konoba* that's a credit to the name and serves some of the finest cuisine in the Pazin area. Start with *pršut* ham or *maneštra* soup, then pick from *fuži* pasta, fat homemade *kobasice* (sausages) and a rib-sticking *ombolo* (pork loin). *Closed Wed.*

Kanfanar

La Casa di Matiki, Matiki 14 (3km east of Kanfanar), **t** (052) 846 297, *www.matiki.com* (€€). Drive to Žminj then right towards Pula to locate this four-apartment agrotourism property with a small pool. The bright rooms are simple but modern, and owner Sonja serves her homemade jams and bread for breakfast on the terrace.

Tinjan

Điđi, Tinjan 17, **t** (052) 626 106 (€€). One of the finest and most charming gastronomic addresses in central Istria. *Njoki* and *fuži* come with game and truffles (*s divljači i tartufima*) and there are specialities slow-baked under a *peka*. *In winter, closed until 4pm Mon–Sat (Sun open 12–12).*

The East Coast: Labin and Around

Labin

Istria's east coast is bypassed by most visitors to Istria. Yet the coast road is a slice of slow travel compared to the motorway; a looping scenic drive between Pula and Rijeka with holm oak on one side and the Adriatic on the other. **Labin** lies roughly at the midway point, though does little to suggest you break the journey in its modern suburb Podlabin (literally 'beneath Labin'). But don't let that put you off. Exploitation of seams to fuel Austro-Hungarian expansion peaked under Italian occupation in 1942, when 10,000 miners hacked out over a million tonnes of coal and Podlabin sprawled beneath the hilltop old town. By then, working-class Labin was established in the national consciousness as a dyed-in-the-wool socialist after the miners came out on strike in 1921 and declared they were taking over production. The 'Labin Republic' was quashed in a month. Since the last mine shut in the 1990s – a minehead just east of the old town still bears the crossed hammers and 'TITO' legend of its Yugoslavian heyday – Labin has re-evaluated its old town. Nowadays it proclaims itself an '*Art Republika*', host to a vibrant arts scene after cheap studio space was offered to homegrown artists. At the same time it has restored its Baroque core into a kernel shaded in ochre and terracotta. It has probably never looked so lovely.

You approach the Old Town from **Titov trg**, ringed by broad sycamore trees and the 16th-century **loggia** where Venetian Republic court and council met. Above is the **Uskok gate**, named for a victory over the feared Uskok pirates – a yarn to be taken with a generous pinch of sea salt relates that 800 pirates turned in fright when confronted by cauldrons full of iron cutlery bouncing downhill and a river of oxblood. Through this front door in the medieval walls, the centuries fall away as you follow a river of cobbles upstream into **Stari trg**. A sidetrack left explores to Labin's

Getting to and around the East Coast

Hourly buses between Rijeka and Pula stop at all east coast destinations. One bus a day travels from Pazin to **Labin** via Gračišće and Pićan. Labin's bus stop is on the main drag in lower suburb **Podlabin**, about 20mins' walk to the Old Town. Buses from Labin link to **Rabac** approximately hourly.

---

most interesting *ateliers*, while up the stairs of main street **1 Maja**, the **Church of the Blessed Virgin Mary's Birth** (Crkva rođenja Blažene Djevice Marije) wears its history on its façade: a Gothic rose window and a Venetian lion, a symbol of Labin's submission to the Republic. The bearded patriarch is Antonio Bollani, a Venetian senator and Labin mayor in 1616–17, who is honoured for seeing off further Uskok raids.

National Museum of Labin
Narodni muzej Labina; ***t*** *(052) 852 477; open May–Sept Mon–Fri 10–1 and 5–7, Sat 10–1; Oct–May Mon–Fri 7–3; adm*

Town gallery
Gradska galerija Labin; ***t*** *(052) 852 464; open Mon–Fri 10–3, Sat–Sun 10–1*

The square's scene-stealer is the balconied Battiala-Lazzarini ducal palace, host to the **National Museum of Labin**. Never mind the Illyrian pots and crusty Roman amphorae, old kitchenware and folk costume with a predilection for sensible socks – all is eclipsed by a lovingly crafted recreation of a coal mine. To a soundtrack of rumbling trucks and rattling machinery, you stoop through a network of low-lit tunnels, propped up by heavy beams and littered with rusty machinery. A **town gallery** opposite the museum hangs exhibitions of contemporary art.

Campanile
open (in theory) summer daily 9–12 and 1–7; adm

Heading uphill on 1 Maja you'll reach the **Fortica** cannon bastion, with a vast panorama of sea and cypresses. Similar views plus those of Labin's roofscape are available at 35m up in a nearby **campanile** on the rare chance it's open. If not belvedere Šetalište San Marco just off Titov trg beside the loggia offers more views.

Memorial Collection of Matija Vlačić Ilirik
Memorijalna zbrika Matije Vlačić Ilirik; open May–Sept Mon–Fri 10–1 and 5–7, Sat 10–1; Oct–May Mon–Fri 7–3; adm

Ulica Giuseppine Martinuzzi (left off Stari trg) hosts several ateliers of the modern art revolutionaries of Labin's *Art Republika*. On its corner you'll find the **Memorial Collection of Matija Vlačić Ilirik** dedicated to a local Lutherian (born 1520) who studied under Martin Luther in Germany. Copperplate images of his tomes, which railed against Catholicism, are the only highlights of an inexcusably dull display – one lambasts the pope astride a sow, almost flattering compared with an image of the pontiff as a scaly woman with an ass's head. Though accused of heresy, Ilirika lived to the age of 55 by shuffling between German university towns. The great-uncle who urged him to go was less fortunate – he ended up at the bottom of the Venice lagoon for daring to preach Protestantism.

Around Labin

Visitor centre
due to open in 2009

Labin re-states its artistic aspirations in the **Dubrova Sculpture Park**, 2km north of the centre on the Rijeka road; look for the glass cube **visitor centre**. Its field of scattered monoliths was chiselled by international artists of the annual Dubrova Mediterranean

Sculpture Symposium; the annual prize-winner gets to extend the world's most eccentric road that slices through the centre.

If Labin is all about culture, **Rabac** 3km east of Labin is about fun. Members of the Mining Society took their vacations in what was a fishing village snug in a woody inlet, and is now the largest resort on the Istrian east coast. There's a pleasant beach, though, and Blue Flag-quality seas.

South of Labin, **Raša** is a curio. It is Istria's newest village, having been built as a miners' settlement by the Italians, and it is one of its most distinctive, being a complete ensemble of Thirties Futurist architecture. Mussolini himself laid the foundation stone of its church to **St Barbara**, patron saint of miners, which was designed as an upturned coal truck and has a miner's lamp for a steeple. Five kilometres further south, **Barban** offers little reason to pause except, perhaps, the Venetian Baroque altarpieces in the parish **church of St Nicholas** on the main square. Or at least not until a mid-August weekend, when it hosts the 'Tilting at the Ring' joust, like that of Sinj in Dalmatia (*see* p.285), but crowd-free.

Church of St Nicholas
Crkva sv. Nikole; on the main square; locked outside of Mass

Festivals in Labin and Barban

Labin stages the **Labinski konti** folk-singing festival on the last Sat in July, before it holds one of the largest techno and house music parties in Istria the following week. **Barban** holds a superb **joust** in mid-Aug.

Where to Stay and Eat on the East Coast

ⓘ Labin >
*Titov trg 10, **t** (052) 855 560; open June–Sept Mon–Sat 8–9, Sun 10–1 6–9; Oct–May Mon–Fri 9–4*

Labin

There are no hotels in Labin – you can find private accommodation through **Veritas**, Svete Katarine 4, **t** (052) 852 758, *www.istra-veritas.hr*.

Kvarner, Šetaliste San Marco bb (behind post office), **t** (052) 852 336 (€€). Terrace views over the surrounding hills and a menu of fish and homemade *fuži, njoki* and *krafi* with game sauces and cheeses.

Dubrova, Dubrova bb, **t** (052) 885 054 (€€). Locals' choice for a slap-up celebration is the smart address by the Sculpture Park: steaks laced with truffles, pastas or Istrian cold platters.

Velo Kafe, Titov trg 6 **t** (052) 852 754 (€€–€). The core of the community is three venues in one: café, cellar pasta joint and hip upstairs restaurant.

Rabac

Villa Annette, Raška 24, **t** (052) 884 222, *www.villaannette.hr* (€€€). Sophisticated small boutique hotel with a dozen suites furnished in a relaxed minimalism – stylish without ever showing off. Also has a pool and a restaurant that prides itself on 'slow-food' menus.

Around Labin

Palača Lazzarini-Battiala, Sv. Martin (10km west of Labin), **t** (052) 856 006, *www.sv-martin.com* (€). Fairly dated but adequate apartments in a Baroque country mansion. *Breakfast and heating extra.*

Agropansion Partner, Bratulići 17 (9km south of Barban), **t** (052) 544 400, *www.agroturizam-istra-partner.com* (€€). Rough beams and stone walls in a lovely restored agrotourism complex buried deep in the countryside; turn off 7km south of Barban at Manjadvorci then cut back north for 2km. *Full board offers an Istrian menu; breakfast is extra.*

The Kvarner Region

The bura *(bora) wind has traditionally been the scourge of the Kvarner region. Folk tales tell of people blown to their doom by the northeasterly wind that howls through mountain passes in winter. It also picked clean the bones of the Kvarner islands after the Venetian Republic stripped their forests for its ships and palaces. But the* bura *is not all bad news. Because it was sheltered in the lee of Mount Učka, Opatija blossomed as Croatia's first resort, still going strong as the hub of a verdant riviera whose Habsburg looks have been spruced up by recent renovation.*

No such charm in Rijeka. The Kvarner's gritty capital is every bit as bad as Croatia's largest port, every bit as good as a gateway to the idyllic holiday islands of Krk and Cres. The regional dynamo also launches the Magistrala coast road on its long slalom south around spurs of the Velebit mountains whose eastern slopes define the border of the region – keep going and there are plunging karst canyons and waterfalls in the nation's two favourite nature parks, Paklenica and Plitvice.

10

Don't miss

See map overleaf

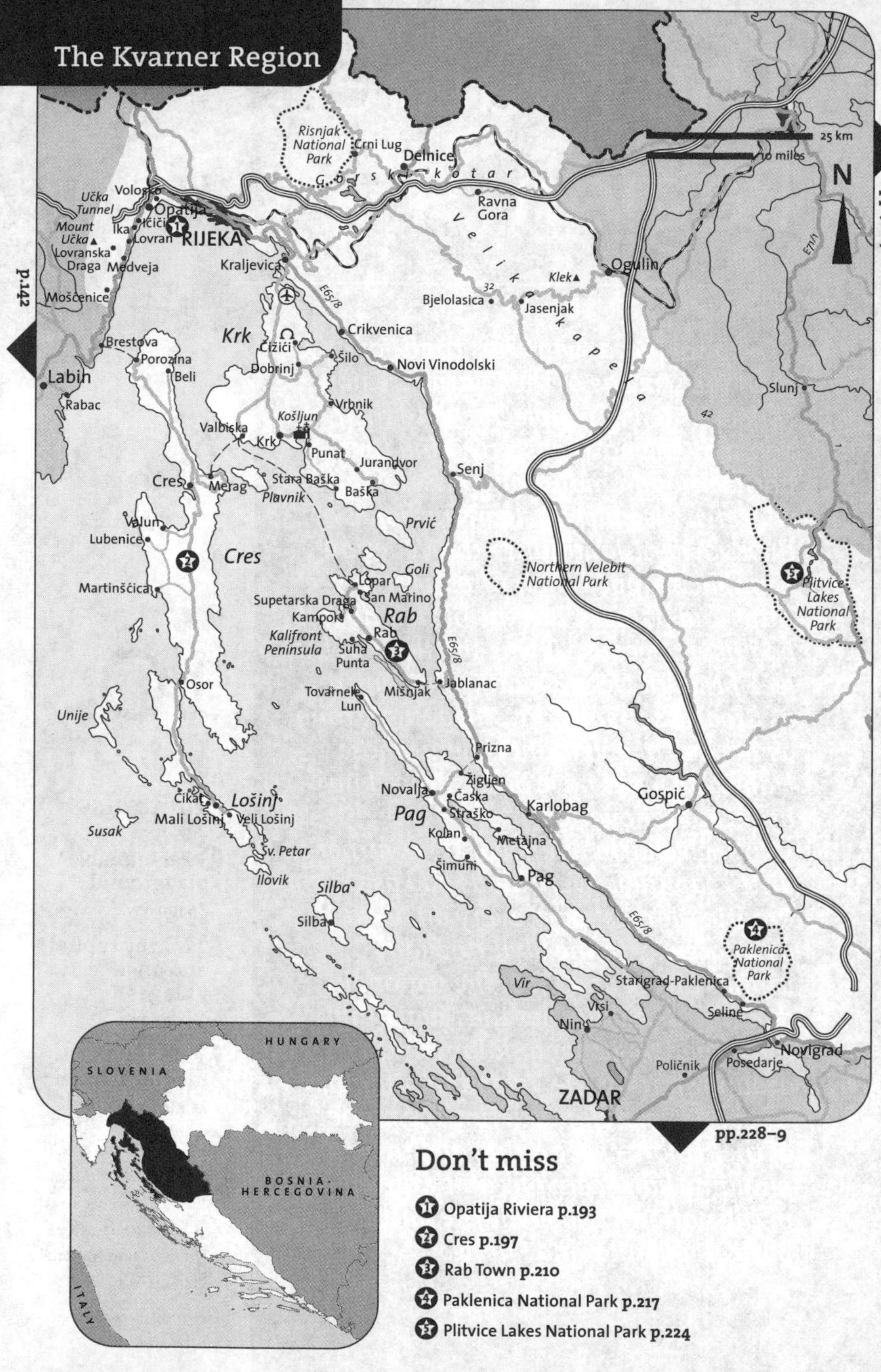
The Kvarner Region
Risnjak National Park
Crni Lug
Delnice
Gorski kotar
Ravna Gora
Velika kapela
Učka Tunnel
Volosko
Opatija
Ičići
Ika
Lovran
RIJEKA
Mount Učka
Lovranska Draga
Medveja
Mošćenice
Kraljevica
E65/8
Klek
Ogulin
Bjelolasica
Jasenjak
Crikvenica
Krk
Čižići
Šilo
Dobrinj
Novi Vinodolski
Brestova
Porozina
Beli
Labin
Rabac
Vrbnik
Košljun
Valbiska
Krk
Punat
Jurandvor
Senj
Cres
Merag
Stara Baška
Baška
Plavnik
Prvić
Valun
Lubenice
Cres
Goli
Northern Velebit National Park
Martinšćica
Lopar
San Marino
Supetarska Draga
Kampor
Rab
Kalifront Peninsula
Rab
Suha Punta
Tovarnele
Lun
Mišnjak
Jablanac
Osor
Unije
Prizna
Žiglijen
Novalja
Časka
Čikat
Lošinj
Mali Lošinj
Veli Lošinj
Pag
Straško
Karlobag
Gospić
Susak
Kolan
Metajna
Sv. Petar
Šimuni
Pag
Ilovik
Silba
Silba
Slunj
Plitvice Lakes National Park
Paklenica National Park
Starigrad-Paklenica
Vir
Vrsi
Seline
Nin
Novigrad
Posedarje
Poličnik
ZADAR
25 km
10 miles
N
p.142
pp.76–7
pp.228–9
HUNGARY
SLOVENIA
BOSNIA-HERCEGOVINA
ITALY
Don't miss
1 Opatija Riviera p.193
2 Cres p.197
3 Rab Town p.210
4 Paklenica National Park p.217
5 Plitvice Lakes National Park p.224

Rijeka

On Croatia's fairytale coastline, Rijeka is something of an ugly sister. While Split and Zadar are all creamy stone mansions and idling streets, this industrial city is one of grimey Socialist apartment blocks, cargo hulks and cranes of the country's largest port. There's not even a beach. So, Rijeka is unlikely to be any visitor's favourite town. What it does have is energy – while most Istrian or Dalmatian towns daydream, dynamo Rijeka thrums as the country's third largest city.

For that, it can thank Austria. The Habsburgs snatched the port for an Adriatic base in the 15th century before the Venetian Republic could add yet another name to its list of acquisitions on Croatia's coastline. They transformed the fledlging city into their principle sea-port on the Adriatic, establishing a shipbuilding industry that limps on today alongside Rijeka's role as the hub of Croatian ferry routes. In the 1860s, they passed it to their similarly landlocked partners, the Hungarians. At the same time, the town acquired much of its Austro-Hungarian looks.

The Italians claimed it eventually, however. In 1918, at Versailles, the Italians demanded Rijeka in compensation for the Allies' reneging on the 1915 Treaty of London; their sweet-talk about Dalmatian spoils had bribed Italy into the war. They even proffered a population census to prove Rijeka was majority Italian – a statistic achieved by ignoring the Croatian 25 per cent in the suburb of Sušak. While the French and British prevaricated, Italian warrior-poet Gabriele D'Annunzio seized the initiative with a blackshirt army in 1919 (*see* box, p.190), and although the mini-dictator was soon ousted by an embarrassed Italian government, he inspired Il Duce to goose-step into town in 1922, a smash-and-grab raid Yugoslavia was forced to legitimize through the 1924 Treaty of Rome, which delivered Istria to Italy. The city, like the region, was only returned to Yugoslavia after the Second World War.

Allied bombardiers reduced Rijeka to a woebegone widow of the Adriatic, and Tito wreaked some vandalism of his own in the form of now rusting industrial detritus. Yes, Rijeka has more than its fair share of grim Socialist realism, but the city core retains heirlooms from its Hungarian heyday – in streets such as the Korzo you can almost sense the ghosts of 19th-century Budapest. As appealing is that Rijeka is catagorically not a tourist town – this is a vigorous city, gritty, fast-paced and dynamic, with quality restaurants, a great bar scene, and no tourists for miles.

Around the Korzo

Fattened with late 18th-century prosperity, Rijeka burst beyond the stone girdle of its defence walls and replaced its moat with the

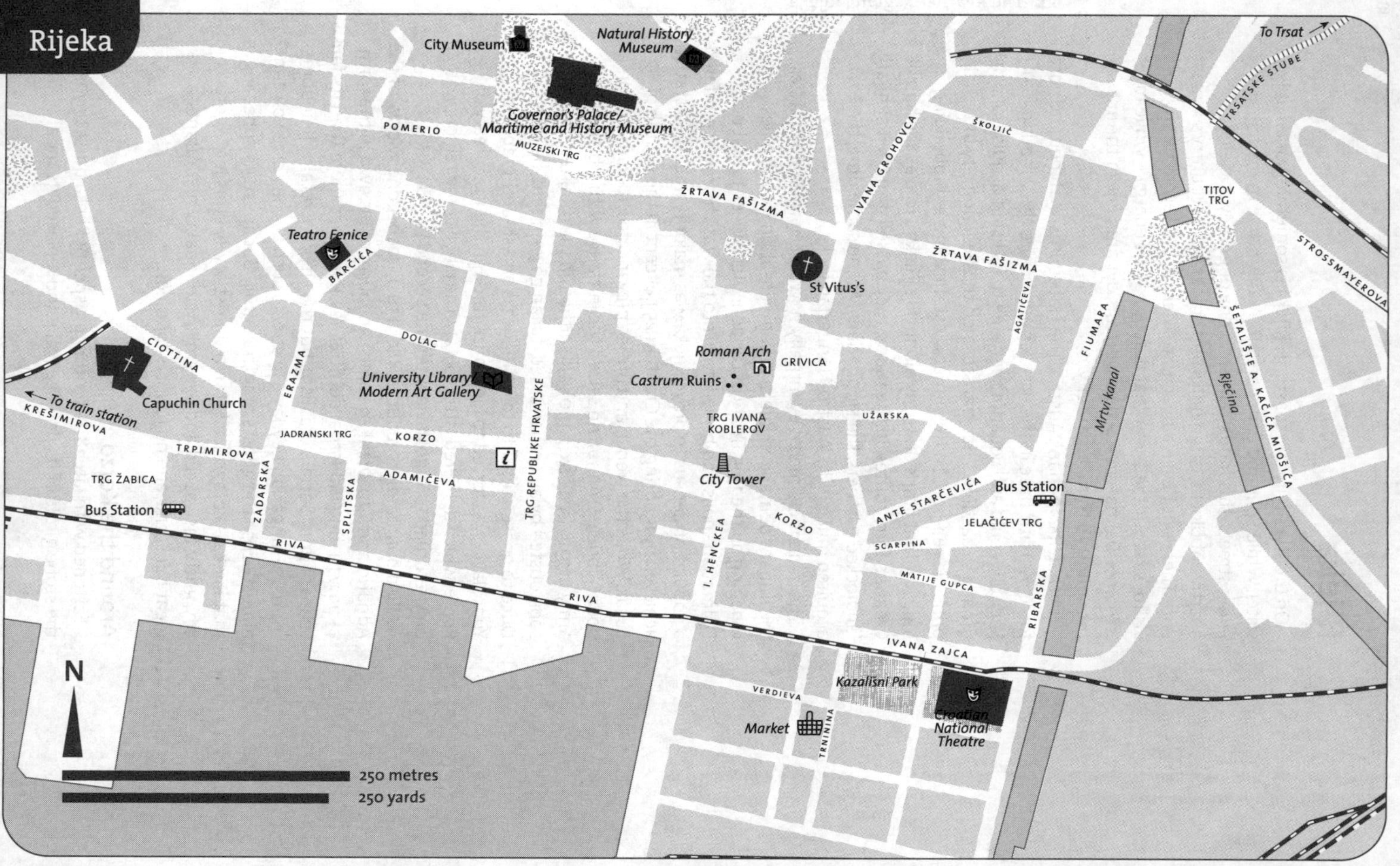
Rijeka
City Museum
Natural History Museum
Governor's Palace/ Maritime and History Museum
POMERIO
MUZEJSKI TRG
ŽRTAVA FAŠIZMA
IVANA GROHOVCA
ŠKOLJIĆ
To Trsat
TRSATSKE STUBE
TITOV TRG
STROSSMAYEROVA
Teatro Fenice
BARČIĆA
St Vitus's
ŽRTAVA FAŠIZMA
AGATIĆEVA
FIUMARA
Mrtvi kanal
Rječina
ŠETALIŠTE A. KAČIĆA MIOŠIĆA
CIOTTINA
Capuchin Church
To train station
KREŠIMIROVA
ERAZMA
DOLAC
University Library/ Modern Art Gallery
Roman Arch
GRIVICA
Castrum Ruins
TRG IVANA KOBLEROV
UŽARSKA
TRG REPUBLIKE HRVATSKE
JADRANSKI TRG
KORZO
TRPIMIROVA
TRG ŽABICA
ZADARSKA
SPLITSKA
ADAMIĆEVA
City Tower
Bus Station
ANTE STARČEVIĆA
Bus Station
JELAČIĆEV TRG
KORZO
SCARPINA
I. HENCKEA
MATIJE GUPCA
RIBARSKA
RIVA
RIVA
IVANA ZAJCA
Kazališni Park
VERDIEVA
Market
TRNININA
Croatian National Theatre
N
250 metres
250 yards

Getting to and around Rijeka

By Air

Croatia Airlines and budget operator Ryanair operate schedules from the UK. Three Croatia Airlines flights a week link Rijeka to Zagreb.

Rijeka airport is 25km south on Krk island opposite, 3km south of the island bridge. Buses operated by Autotrolej co-ordinate with flights to take you to the local bus station on Jelačićev trg (20Kn) and leave from the same stop 90mins before departures. A taxi should cost around 200Kn, but fares can hit 300Kn depending on the time of arrival.

By Sea

Jadrolinija ferries run between Dubrovnik, Rijeka and Bari (Italy). They ply a long-distance route to Dubrovnik via Split, Hvar and Korčula 5 times a week in summer; 2 services a week call at Zadar and 1 a week stops at Mljet. Jadrolinija also operates daily summer services to Cres and Mali Lošinj (car ferry and passenger-only catamarans) and catamarans to Rab and Novalja (Pag). The Jadrolinija head office is opposite the harbour at Riva 16.

By Train

Daily international trains link to Ljubljana, Budapest and Munich. Three trains a day link Rijeka to Zagreb. The train station is 300m west of the centre on Krešimirova.

By Bus

Two buses a day connect Rijeka with Ljubljana and Trieste in Italy. Buses twice a week link to Berlin (Mon, Fri), Sarajevo (Fri, Sun) and Međugorje (Thurs, Sat).

Non-stop long-distance buses link with: Zagreb (2 per day), Zadar (4 per day), Split (3 per day), Pula and Dubrovnik (2 per day), plus hourly connections to all stop at destinations on the way. Major Istrian bus links include: Poreč (5 per day), Rovinj (4 per day), Pazin (7 per day) and Buzet (4 per day). To the Kvarner gulf islands there are bus routes to: Krk (town) (10 per day), Cres and Mali Lošinj (4 per day), Rab (2 per day) and Pag (2 per day). Frequent buses connect to Opatija and Lovran.

The main bus station is 100m west of the centre on Trg Žabica. Local buses to Opatija and Trsat go from Jelačićev trg on the edge of the centre's east flank. Central Rijeka is eminently walkable. The hop-on, hop-off tourist bus loops from Jadranksi trg to Trsat and nearby resort Opatija three times a day. Tickets (48hr, 35Kn) can be bought from the driver or from the tourist office.

By Car

Squeezed against the coast by a mountain that funnels traffic into the centre, Rijeka has a traffic problem. Your best bet for a parking space in the centre is the open-air car park beside the harbour, alongside the Riva.

For car hire (the big names also operate at the airport), try: **Hertz**, Riva 6, **t** (051) 311 098; **Avis**, Riva 8, **t** (051) 311 135; **Dollar/Thrifty**, Riva 22, **t** (051) 337 917; **Budget**, Trg 128. brigade Hrvatske vojske 8, **t** (051) 214 742.

By Taxi

Taxi ranks are at the train station, the bus station on Trg Žabica and on Matije Gupica near the National Theatre. To book a taxi, call **t** 051 345 610.

Korzo, the old town's spacious high street lined by peeling candy-coloured Viennese Secession-era and Art Nouveau mansions. The early defence fortifications ended up as filler for the moat, leaving only the **City Tower** (Gradski toranj), the seafront gateway that greeted medieval sailors. Austrian emperors Leopold I and Charles VI, shameless drama queens both, pout above a double-headed imperial eagle on its rebuilt Baroque upper sections. The fabulously mustachioed Charles has good reason to look smug – it was his elevation of Rijeka to free port in 1719 that catapulted the city into the economic big league.

Pass like the merchants of old through an arch and you enter the **Old Town** (Stari grad), a rather optimistic description for a tatty hotchpotch of patched-up old-timers and ugly glass and concrete postwar additions on **Trg Ivana Koblera**. Hard to believe, but you now stand where Rijeka made its début as Roman garrison town; a chunky stone arch in an alley off the square's north side is all that's left of Tarsatica.

Northeast is square **Grivica**, dominated by the splendid **St Vitus's Church** (Crkva svetog Vida). Eager to reclaim a congregation from the Reformation in the 17th century, the town's Jesuits revived the legend of one Petar Lončarić, a gambler so frustrated at his luck during a hand of cards in 1296 that he hurled a stone at the order's crucifix. The wooden effigy of Jesus bled and the player was swallowed whole into the ground – a dubious tale which nevertheless allowed the Jesuits to proclaim their Gothic crucifix miraculous and pursuaded one Countess Ursula von Thanhausen to stump up funds for today's rotunda church, modelled on Santa Maria della Salute in Venice. The money-spinning Gothic crucifix hangs in pride of place. Incidentally, the cannonball embedded near the portal was a gift from the British during the Napoleonic wars.

Around Jadranski Trg

Museum of Modern and Contemporary Art
Muzej moderne i suvremene umjetnosti; **t** *(051) 492 611, www.mmsu.hr; open Tues–Sun 10–1 and 5–8; adm*

Mali Salon
same times as above

Glagolitic Exhibition
Izložba glagoljice; **t** *(052) 336 911, www.svkri.hr; open Mon–Fri 8–3; adm*

Just off the centre of the Korzo on **Dolac**, the **university library** opposite the Grand Hotel Bonavia hosts exhibitions in the **Museum of Modern and Contemporary Art**. There's a second gallery space, **Mali Salon**, at Korzo 24. The library also houses a superb **Glagolitic Exhibition**, a collection of manuscripts and tablets in Glagolitic script, not extraterrestrial for all its looks, but actually the Greek-based alphabet of medieval Croatian ecclesiastics (*see* pp.40–1). Reservations are recommended. Even without one, the building's foyer is worth a visit for its replicas of celebrated frescoes from Istrian churches: Beram's *Danse Macabre* (*see* p.176) and the medieval pageant of Draguć.

West to Jadranski trg, dominated by a pair of Rijeka landmarks: on the south flank, the late 19th-century **Adriatic Palace** is the swaggering Historicist headquarters of the Jadrolinija ferry company, with a quartet of sailors striking preposterous heroic poses on the Riva side; and on the west flank of the square a Futurist Italian towerblock of the 1930s, the **Rijeka Skyscraper**, whose stack of cubes is mocked by locals as a 'chest of drawers'. Head north up Erazma Barčića and you'll reach the protomodernist **Teatro Fenice** (1913), a former theatre caught between geometrical Secession and early Futurism that's now a scruffy cinema.

A block west of Jadranski trg, looming over a bus station, the Capuchin church of **Our Lady of Lourdes** (Kapucinska crkva) is a neo-Gothic surprise in Rijeka's modern cityscape. Inspired by a visit to France, Bernardin Škrivanić, Superior of the Capuchin monastery, nurtured plans for Rijeka as a pilgrimage centre when his homage to Lourdes began to rise in 1900. His enthusiasm wasn't matched by his funds, however, and the project stalled until one 'St Jochanza' loosened locals' purse strings by miraculously sweating blood. The church finally stood in all its Venetian neo-Gothic glory by 1929, 16 years after the showman saint was arrested for fraud.

Along the Riva

Lined by the grand offices of Hungarian shipping magnates, the port-front **Riva** is a missed opportunity. Yes, there is a string of hip cafés and bars, but oh, the traffic: four lanes, ceaseless. A multi-million euro refurbishment of the waterfront opposite is promised. Schedules are not. Walk east into **Ivana Zajca** for the main **market**, where a wonderland of cheeses and pastries, breads and meats is crammed into two 1880s pavilions; a sister pavilion (1914) stocks fresh fish beneath a frieze of Adriatic sea life.

On the far side of an adjacent scruffy park, the **Croatian National Theatre** (1885) keeps up appearances as the *grande dame* of cultural life under the Hungarian rulers. Its formal public airs relax inside a **concert hall** adorned with frescoes by Gustav and Ernst Klimt, one of the first commissions for the brothers' short-lived company before Gustav flew solo.

Concert hall
viewing by appointment or during concerts

Further east lies the grubby river Rječina. Between the world wars, it demarcated the Italy–Yugoslavia border after the Treaty of Rome cleaved the city in two in 1924: while Rijeka stagnated at the farthest reaches of the Italian kingdom, rival **Sušak**, today a mere suburb, flourished as a Yugoslav border town. No passports are now required to follow the west bank of the adjunct Mrtvi kanal to reach **Titov trg**, gateway to Trsat (*see* below).

The Museums

Above the pedestrianized centre, across arterial route Žrtava fašizma, the **Governor's Palace** (Guvernerova palača) is a stocky neo-Renaissance pile erected in 1869 by the Hungarians to awe the locals. They weren't the only ones who were impressed – Italian Gabriele D'Annunzio commandeered the palace as a personal headquarters during his mini dictatorship in 1919 (*see* box, p.190). The Hungarian palace is today on show as the **Maritime and History Museum**. The exhibits – a salute to Rijeka's port above, with nautical knick-knacks such as model ships, navigation equipment and oils of barques, and a ground-floor display of rustic regional crafts – are overshadowed by the decorative splendour of the rooms themselves, their gloriously over-the-top revival interiors as the Hungarian governors knew them.

Maritime and History Museum
Pomorski i povijesni muzej; ***t*** *(051) 553 667, www.ppmhp.hr; open June–Sept Tues–Fri 9–8, Sat 9–1; Oct–May Tues–Fri 9–4, Sat 9–1; adm*

Gabriele D'Annunzio: Italy's first dictator

Versailles 1918: the Allies stall as Italy demands Fiume (literally 'river', the Italian translation of Rijeka) as the spoils it was promised for joining the Great War. Statesman Vittiorio Orlando makes a lot of bad noise but, as the least powerful of the victorious Big Four, his protests go unheeded. Back in Italy, war pilot, poet and unrepentant Fascist Gabriele D'Annunzio followed the progress with growing frustration.

With the sulky withdrawal of the Italian delegation from the Paris Peace Conference, the self-declared Superman spurred into action. In August 1919, two months after the Treaty of Versailles had been signed in the Hall of Mirrors, he rounded up a few hundred black-shirted *arditi* and marched on Fiume. He took it unopposed on 12 September 1919 to proclaim himself commandant of the 'Reggenza Italiana del Carano' (Italian Regency of Carnaro). For a heady year during his occupation, D'Annunzio stood on the balcony of the Hungarian Governor's Palace each night to deliver orations and watch firework displays. The *arditi* silenced dissenters in his proto dictatorship with overdoses of castor oil.

In the end he went too far and declared war on Italy itself. This was too much for premier Giovanni Giolitti. D'Annunzio's bluster jeopardized a diplomatic deal with Yugoslavia to establish Fiume-Rijeka as a free state shared by both nations. Giolitti ordered the battleship *Andrea Doria* to attack Rijeka, and D'Annunzio's reign ended as swiftly as it began. The free state, meanwhile, came to naught – D'Annunzio's great rival, Benito Mussolini, leaned on the Yugoslav government and Rijeka was divided at the river Rječina in 1924.

More museums are at the palace's shoulders: on the left, the **Rijeka City Museum** hosts temporary exhibitions of local history; and behind the palace to the northeast there are so-so displays of Adriatic geology and sea life in the **Natural History Museum**.

Rijeka City Museum
*Muzej grada Rijeke; **t** (051) 336 711, www.muzej-rijeka.hr; open Mon–Fri 10–1 and 4–7, Sat 10–1; adm*

Natural History Museum
*Prirodoslovni muzej; **t** (051) 553 669, www.prirodoslovni.com; open Mon–Sat 9–7, Sun 9–3; adm*

Trsat

Off the north side of Titiov trg, a Baroque **gateway** with a relief of the Virgin indicates Rijeka's own stairway to heaven. At the top of the Trsatske stube steps – carved as an act of devotion by a military captain in 1531 – lies the pilgrimage centre of **Trsat**. As you climb past votive chapels on its 538 steps, spare a thought for the devout believers who ascend on their knees during holy of holy days 10 May. Bus 1 or 1a from the stop on Fiumara or the city tourist bus (*see* p.187) also ascends.

On 10 May 1291, puffed angels charged with spiriting the Nazareth Tabernacle away from invading heathens paused for a breather in hilltop village Trsat, now, like Sušak, swallowed into Rijeka's sprawl. Believe the hype and God's removal men whisked the house of the Virgin and Joseph on to Loreto, near Ancona, Italy, three years and seven months later, and Rijeka could only commemorate the spot with the **Church of Our Lady of Trsat** (Crkva Gospa Trsatske). Not that it did too badly out of the event. In the sanctuary of a largely Biedermeier replacement for that 13th-century progenitor church, an icon of Mary hung with votive beads has been quietly working miracles since its donation in 1367, Pope Urban V's gift to console Trsat for its loss.

Evidence of its power fills the **Chapel of Votive Gifts** (Kapela zavjetnih darova), squirrelled away off the Baroque cloister of the adjacent **Franciscan monastery** and which makes up in personality for what it lacks in ecclesiastical pomp. Paintings of doe-eyed Madonnas who interceded for accident victims or recent Homeland War casualties, embroideries of storm-tossed ships, even crutches presumably tossed aside after a miracle cure, hang on walls inked with grateful graffiti.

Trsat Castle
Trsatska gradina; open Apr–Sept daily 9–midnight; Nov–Mar daily 9–3

Roman guards first kept a keen eye out for barbarians from a frontier watchtower here; then medieval Frankopan counts, Croatian aristocracy from the island of Krk, saw the strategic potential of the hilltop location and created **Trsat Castle**, which is reached via a lane opposite the church. Tramp its walkways and towers, which offer Rijeka's finest views across the Kvarner Gulf to the humps of Krk and Cres, and you can understand why Irish-born Austrian Field Marshal Count Laval Nugent fell for its charms and restored sections of the castle in neo-Gothic as a museum for his war booty and paintings. The eccentric commander also created the Doric temple at its centre; his '*mir junaka*' (haven for heroes) family mausoleum. Incidentally, in 2004 a schoolboy on an outing pulled an interesting slab from the castle's undergrowth and discovered one of the earliest tablets of Glagolitic script in Croatia – keep your eyes peeled.

Tourist Information in Rijeka

ⓘ Rijeka >
Korzo 33, **t** *(051) 335 882, www.tz-rijeka.hr; open 15 June–15 Sept Mon–Sat 8–8, Sun 9–2; 16 Sept–14 June Mon–Sat 8–8*

An enthusiastic **office** at the hub of pedestrianized high street Korzo provides free detailed maps and city tourist information booklets.

Festivals

Rijeka lets rip during Croatia's biggest **Carnival** (*karneval*). A week of parties climaxes on the Sunday before Shrove Tuesday with the International Carnival Procession, a noisy, 5km parade of costumes, floats and, bringing up the rear, traditional *zvončari* – young bucks from surrounding villages, costumed in sheepskins, who clang bells to frighten evil spirits.

Shopping

The main high street is the **Korzo**. You'll need to hunt away from its chain stores to find the city's famous souvenir: jewellery depicting city mascot the *morčić*, Rijeka's take on the Venetian *moretto* (a moorish figure with a white turban) popularized by Austrian aristocrats of the 1800s – including Empress Maria Anna. **Mala Galerija** (*closed Sun*), Užarska 25, sells enamel and gold brooches and earrings of the figure. For folksy sculptures and *objets d'art*, try **Poklon galerija**, Strossmayerova 6c.

Where to Stay in Rijeka

While Rijeka's hotel stock has improved exponenetially in recent years thanks to investment by stakeholder the Jadran group, most hotels and restaurants are on the Opatija Riviera 15km west.

Grand Hotel Bonavia, Dolac 4, **t** (051) 357 100, *www.bonavia.hr* (€€). A modern luxury four-star in the heart of Rijeka, which exudes relaxed comfort in business-style rooms of tasteful fabrics and deep, spongey carpets. Its fine dining restaurant, **Kamov**, is one of the city's gourmet addresses.

Jadran, Šetalište XIII divizije 46, **t** (051) 216 600, *www.jadran-hoteli.hr* (€€). As close as it gets to a resort hotel in Rijeka, with its own patch of beach and modern rooms after total renovation in 2005. The caveat is a location 1km east of Rijeka in suburb Pećine (bus No.2).

Kontinental, Šetalište A. Kačića-Miošića 1, **t** (051) 372 008, *www.jadran-hoteli.hr* (€€). Undergoing a much-needed refurbishment at the time of writing to upgrade its 1970s timewarp and two-star standards into a hotel in keeping with its late 1800s building. Well located in the centre opposite the stairway to Trsat.

Neboder, Strossmayerova 1, **t** (051) 373 538, *www.jadran-hoteli.hr* (€€). Top-to-bottom renovation has scrubbed up a grubby tower block east of the centre, still a mite pokey in its rooms though good value for modern business style. Great views from the upper storeys, too.

Eating Out in Rijeka

Feral, Matije Gupca 5b, **t** (051) 212 274 (€€€–€€). A cellar-style *konoba* hung with fishing nets that is highly rated for its fish and seafood. House speciality shellfish are worth investigating, including *gratinirane jakopske*, scallops *gratinés* prepared with white wine, tomato and cheese. *Closed Sun.*

Trsatika, Šetalište Joakima Rakovca 33, Trsat, **t** (051) 217 455 (€€). Lovely spot for a long lazy lunch opposite the pilgrimage church. A large menu strays from lamb to pizza via Krk's *šurlice* pasta with stew, but the reason to visit is the panorama over the Kvarner Gulf from the terrace.

Zlatna školjka, Kružna 12, **t** (051) 213 782 (€€). More pricey than other places but the semi-smart nautically styled 'Golden Shell' off the Korzo has a good reputation for dishes such as *jastog na buzaru* (lobster in white wine, tomatoes, garlic and parsley). A cosy sister restaurant opposite serves pizza and pasta among fishing décor. *Closed Sun.*

Na Kantuna, Demetrova 2, **t** (051) 313 271 (€€–€). Great little fish bistro in the port area that serves a daily menu in generous portions. It's hidden away southeast of the market. *Closed Sun.*

Pod Voltun, Pod Voltun 15, **t** (051) 330 806 (€). Simple gutsy dishes such as *bakalar gulaš* (cod goulash) or homemade sausages in red wine ensure a steady stream of locals to this friendly choice beside a car park west of St Vitus's church. Daily specials are reliable and cheap.

Cafés and Bars in Rijeka

Cafe As/Pommery, Trg Republika Hrvatska. The former is a traditional brasserie, the latter a 'champagne bar' with wicker loungers. Both are side by side on the pedestrianized central square.

Capitano, Riva 10. A touch of class among the Riva café-bars, with a gents' club feel to its old-world interior of brass and polished wood.

Celtic Caffe Bard, Grivica 6a. Quirky, unpretentious bar over two levels by St Vitus's Church where it always feels like 2am. Guinness on tap, naturally.

Hemingway, Korzo 28. The hip Croatian chain provides a bar with wow factor – modern glamour in a Habsburg mansion, ideal for morning coffee as much as cocktails.

Indigo, Stara Vrata. Funky retro-modernist bar-club by the Roman arch whose Pop Art stylings – like being in a Barbarella film set – are posey but still succeed. A restaurant serves fusion food and rocks to DJs at weekends. *Closed Sun.*

Opium Buddha Bar, Riva 12. Clubby lounge bar in scarlet and black that's always popular when DJs spin at weekends. Look out for the enormous iguana (in a glass tank, fortunately).

The Opatija Riviera

Opatija

1 The Opatija Riviera

Although it was christened after a 1420s Benedictine abbey (*opatija*), now hidden as the kernel of the seafront **St James's Church** (Crkva sv. Jakova), Opatija (pronounced 'O*pat*eeya') dates its birth to 1844. Seeking a retreat from his balance sheets, Rijeka tycoon Iginio Scarpa fell in love with the nearby fishing village and treated himself to **Villa Angiolina**, a grand holiday home named for his deceased wife and screened by a park of exotics. Here he softened up his business partners with luxury, and cultivated relations with élite Habsburgs such as Austro-Hungarian empress Maria Anna, wife of Ferdinand I. However, it was railways not regents which elevated Opatija to the St-Tropez of Central Europe. In 1882 the Society of Southern Railways pioneered a link from Rijeka to Budapest and Vienna, acquired Scarpa's villa and in two years knocked up the eastern Adriatic's first luxury hotel, today **Hotel Kvarner**. Life in Opatija was never the same again. Lured by the microclimate of a resort protected from blasts of cold north wind the *bura*, a Who's Who of Central Europe flocked to promenade and play in the fashionable winter playground: Gustav Mahler toiled over the re-orchestration of his Fourth Symphony while recuperating from an operation; Anton Chekhov escaped Russian gloom to stroll in the sunshine; dancer Isadora Duncan found inspiration in Opatija's fluttering palm leaves; and James Joyce idled over coffee in the Hotel Imperial (and did precious little else, apparently). Just a decade after its début, Opatija was chosen to host a historic meeting between Austrian emperor Franz Josef and German emperor Wilhelm II in 1894, a trip the former must have enjoyed, since he returned 10 years later with Swedish king Oscar.

A recent revamp has seen Opatija reinterpret its past with modern spa hotels as it edges towards modern sophistication, the first update of a resort which has relied on an older clientele of conservative tourists for decades. Yet there remains a hint of old-fashioned gentility about Croatia's oldest resort. The architecture helps. Viennese Secession and the villas of the moneyed élite, line parts of **Maršala Tita**, the arterial road. And Scarpa's Villa Angiolina remains in its **park**; a confection of sugary stucco surrounded by specimen plants from Japan, South America, Australia and China. In theory the tycoon's neoclassical interior – a joy of frescoed ceilings, Corinthian capitals and marble floors – is open as a **museum** with displays that trace the resort's history. It also hosts classical music concerts in summer.

Museum
open summer Tues–Sun 10–6

Opatija's favourite activity, though, remains promenading. And the promenade of choice is still the **Lungomare**. The 12km seashore

Getting to and around the Opatija Riviera

Bus 32 from Rijeka goes to **Opatija** via **Volosko** in approx. 25mins, then on south to **Lovran** and **Medveja**. Tickets can be bought from the driver or kiosks at the bus station in Rijeka.

For a taxi in Opatija, call **t** (051) 711 366.

footpath, named for the lungs of sea air you get en route, was completed in 1889 to coincide with the resort's launch as a spa and recuperation resort to the European élite. It remains a treat, with lush Mediterranean planting and a string of swimming spots that are far more enticing than the concrete Lido by the villa at the start.

Volosko and Lovran

Follow the coastal path 2km north, past parks of cypresses, pines, magnolia and palms, and you reach **Volosko**, still looking like a fishing village despite being swallowed into Opatija's sprawl. It's arguably more charming than its neighbour, a cosy pocket of alleys which trickle down past villas to an inner harbour crammed with fishing boats. It's also emerging as a gourmet destination for those in the know.

Just as delightful is lovely **Lovran**, 6km south of Opatija, beyond villages Ičiči and Ika, a 1½–2hr stroll (or you can catch a bus) past the palatial holiday homes of Austro-Hungarian grandees; Viennese Secession architect Carl Siedl sketched much of their Venetian neo-Gothic at the turn of the century. Bays and notches in the coast provide opportunities for a dip on the way, although the best beach of the riviera is 2km beyond Lovran in **Medveja**, a crescent of shingle backed by restaurants and cafés.

Quietly reinventing itself as a boutique tourism resort, Lovran today offers a glimpse of Opatija before it sold out to large hotels. Many of the *fin-de-siècle* Habsburg-era **mansions** are preserved in all their yesteryear glory as classy small hotels for a romantic splurge. The leafy village is christened after laurel trees (*lovor*), and poetry is wholly appropriate for the medieval kernel, a tiny kasbah-like warren of houses huddled tight as if still girdled by a long-gone defensive wall. On Trg sv. Jurja, the Gothic parish church **St George's** (Crkva sv. Jurja) has contemporary frescoes by local painters in its chancel. The village's patron saint spears his dragon in an early 19th-century tympanum on the mansion opposite the church, upstaged by the century-older Mustaćon on the same square, whose scowl and fabulous moustache were intended to scare evil sprites.

Mount Učka

Lovran is also the most convenient base camp for an assault on **Mount Učka**, Istria's highest mountain, which backs the east seaboard, preserved as the 160 square km **Učka Nature Park** (Park prirode Učka). Behind the Old Town, a path threads uphill: first through villas and chestnut trees, then partially terraced slopes where the mountain's limestone bones show, to emerge from deciduous woods below Vojak, a 1,401m peak crowned with a viewing tower. And what a view: on clear days a 360-degree panorama sweeps northeast past the urban smudge of Rijeka, round to Krk and Cres out in the Adriatic and west to the Italian Alps, then inland across the wooded slopes of inland Istria, where a spire and village crowns every hilltop.

You can cut out half the ascent by driving to scattered mountain hamlet **Lovranska draga**, or there's a rough road which begins at **Veprinac**, inland from Opatija, to the summit. Tourist information centres at Opatija and Lovran stock maps, or consult the **park office** in Lovran.

Park office
Liganj 42, t (051) 293 753, www.pp-ucka.hr; open Mon–Fri 7–3

Where to Stay on the Opatija Riviera

ⓘ Opatija >
Maršala Tita 101, t (051) 271 310, www.opatija-tourism.hr; open summer daily 8–9 (till 8 shoulder months), winter Mon–Fri 8.30–3.30, Sat 9–2

Opatija

Villa Ariston, Maršala Tita 179, **t** (051) 271 379, *www.villa-ariston.hr* (€€€). Six plush rooms and two suites in a gorgeous Habsburg confection 1km west of Opatija which has hosted a Who's Who of Habsburgs, assorted Kennedys and Coco Chanel. Cuisine in the gourmet restaurant is Croat-international, that in the dining room elegant Biedermeier.

Milenij, Maršala Tita 109, **t** (051) 202 000, *www.milenijhoteli.hr* (€€€). Super-central five-star that, if not as charcterful as other options, has tasteful modern Italian style and faultless service. For old-fashioned luxury there's a garden villa.

Mozart, Maršala Tita 138, **t** (051) 718 260, *www.hotel-mozart.hr* (€€€). Of all the hotels in central Opatija, the Art Nouveau Mozart is most evocative of the resort's heyday, a 26 room residence which sells itself on five-star comfort and period style rather than flashy fittings. Nice spa and garden, too.

Miramar, Ive Kaline 11, **t** (051) 280 000, *www.hotel-miramar.info* (€€€–€€). Set in its own gardens on the seafront and with a private beach, an Austrian-owned 200-bed resort hotel created from a Belle Époque hotel, Villa Neptun. Style is relaxed and modern, sea views are omnipresent.

Astoria, Maršala Tita 174, **t** (051) 706 350, *www.hotel-astoria.hr* (€€). After complete restoration of a historic building in 2005, Opatija has its first design hotel; think blonde woods and tones of olive and cream. Most rooms have a balcony and guests have access to a hotel spa nearby.

Kvarner, Park 1, **t** (051) 271 233, *www.liburnia.hr* (€€). The *grande dame* which kickstarted Opatija's trajectory, now rather past its prime – polystyrene ceiling tiles are inexcusable in an 1880s vintage building. Still, the proportions are grand and the décor inoffensive in dated but comfy rooms.

Palace-Bellevue, Maršala Tita 144–6, **t** (051) 271 811, *www.liburnia.hr* (€€). Two competitively priced old-timers under one banner, both a mishmash of *fin-de-siècle* pomp in public areas – the Palace foyer is a marvel – and spacious, old-fashioned rooms. Those of the Palace are a mite more modern.

Opatija, Trg V. Gortana 2/1, **t** (051) 271 388, *www.hotel-opatija.hr* (€). Another

Habsburg hotel that's seen better days, this central place is a good choice for bygone character on a budget. Facilties include a tennis court and a small pool.

Rooms in private houses (€) can be sourced through tourist agency **Katarina Line**, Maršala Tita 71/1, **t** (051) 272 110.

Lovran >
*beside harbour, **t** (051) 291 740, www.tz-lovran.hr; open May–Sept Mon–Sat 8am–8pm, Sun 8–12; Oct–April Mon–Fri 9–4*

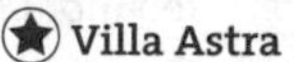
Villa Astra >

Lovran

Villa Astra, V. C. Emina 11, **t** (051) 294 400, *www.lovranske-vile.com* (€€€). A neo-Gothic confection built in 1905 for Italian aristos, now an effortlessly classy five-star Historic Hotel of Europe whose six individually decorated rooms blend old and new – some retain their ceramic heaters. It styles itself a holistic retreat as much as a luxury hotel, with both pilates sessions and breakfast on the seafront terrace. There's also a pool, and a first-class *à la carte* restaurant. The connoisseur's choice.

Villa Eugenia, Maršala Tita 34, **t** (051) 294 800, *www.villa-eugenia.com* (€€€). Beautifully modernized in 2003 and now flooded with natural light, this 1910 Secession villa oozes luxury, a union of Biedermeier-style furnishings and chic bathrooms of frosted glass and stainless steel. Balconies are on floors one and two.

Lovran, Maršala Tita 19/2, **t** (051) 291 222, *www.hotel-lovran.hr* (€€). A good-value three-star fashioned from two villas with quietly plush rooms in shades of cream.

Eating Out on the Opatija Riviera

Opatija

Bevanda >

Bevanda, Zert 8 (by harbour) **t** (051) 712 769 (€€€). A glamorous restaurant with a seafront terrace that's as much about chic style as its fine fish menu. A flagship address of Croatia, it is far from cheap – lobster is a cool 750Kn – but this is as much about the experience as the cuisine. It also has a slick champagne and caviar bar beside the waves. *Booking essential for both.*

Mali Raj, Maršala Tita 191 (2km south of centre) **t** (051) 704 074 (€€€–€€). Excellent lobster and grilled fish served on a terrace with great sea views – ideal for a lunch spot midway along the Lungomare path.

Istranka, B Milanovića, **t** (051) 271 385 (€€–€). A taste of tradition in a traditionally styled *konoba* located uphill above the harbour road.

Pizzeria Sardegna, E Kumičića 9 (by post office), **t** (051) 603 048 (€). A charming Italian-owned pizzeria off the main drag; highly rated by locals.

Volosko

Le Mandrać, harbour, **t** (051) 701 357 (€€€). Deniz Zembo, one of Croatia's gastro stars, has wowed the critics with dishes that are daring without ever showing off. He fuses Istrian cuisine with Japanese or modern European flavours to create menus from whatever is freshest. Style is all sybaritic sophistication – a slick glassed terrace and metro chic furnishings; staff are charming.

Plavi podrum, harbour, **t** (051) 701 223 (€€€). Rather upstaged by its neighbour, this is a classy charmer nevertheless, with a marvellous terrace beside the inner harbour. Expect the likes of shrimp risotto with Istrian truffles and champagne and octopus on a creative menu that's strong on fish.

Lovran

Kvarner, Maršala Tita 68, **t** (051) 291 118 (€€). Grilled fish and meats served on a terrace overlooking the Lovran harbour.

Najade, Maršala Tita 69, **t** (051) 291 866 (€€). The finest menu in Lovran and the loveliest terrace in town, inches from the sea with views of villas and woods. Find it through an arch just south of the tourist office.

Buffet Stubica, Stari grad 25, Lovran, **t** (051) 293 412 (€). Almost opposite Kvarner is this tiny *konoba* crammed with the trophies of its champion fisherman owner: expect a small menu of simple fish – *girice* (whitebait) and *lignje* (squid).

Cafés and Bars in Opatija

Café Wagner, Maršala Tita 109. A Biedermier-styled café in the centre with one of the finest sea-terraces in town.

Hemingway, Zert 2. Opatija's best nightspot is this grown-up cocktail bar and bistro spread over three spaces by the harbour. DJs lay down party house beats at weekends and in an associated club, **Seven**, at Maršala Tita 125.

Monokini, Maršala Tita 69. Funky retro-styled bar and café that attracts a more arty crowd than the fashionistas in the Hemingway.

The Kvarner Gulf

Cres and Lošinj

Having yoked fire-breathing bulls, sowed a field with dragons' teeth and overcome the warriors which rose from the furrows to snatch the Golden Fleece from under the nose of a sleeping dragon, Jason passed this way on his journey home to Iolchos. King Aeëtes had other ideas. Incandescent with rage at the loss of his prize *and* his daughter to our dashing hero, he sent his son Apsyrtus in pursuit. Medea, starry-eyed with love for Jason, hacked off her brother's limbs, which transmogrified into the Absyrtides, the slivers now known as Cres ('tsress') and Lošinj ('losheen').

Ancient myth aside, it was either Illyrian tribes or the 1st-century Romans who hacked out a shipping channel to begin this tale of two islands. It's hard to believe today, but the Cres village of Osor developed into a regional star on that waterway, first as a Roman port, then as a medieval bishopric until it was snuffed out by the double-whammy of the Venetian Republic and pestilence. Lošinj's turn came under the Austro-Hungarians. While Cres returned to fishing after the fall of the Venetian Republic, Mali Lošinj grew as a shipbuilding port with a sideline in tourism that indirectly spawned the package hotels which make this the islands' largest resort. Cres remains a late developer; outside its mazey capital, ancient villages shrug at mass tourism and busy themselves instead with fishing, olives and sheep.

Cres

Cres Town

Cres

Stagnation isn't always a bad thing. Because Cres Town repaired fishing nets while Mali Lošinj sprouted cranes, it retains an idyllic Italianate town at the heel of its sock-shaped inlet. Nor is the island's largest settlement just renowned for looks – Renaissance palaces and noblemen's crests testify to the era when it was the seat of the Venetian Republic governor and bishop who had fled from Osor (*see* pp.199–200).

Getting to and around Cres

Jadrolinija **ferries** from mainland port Brestova (33km south of Rijeka) go to Porozina, Cres, every hour, and ferries from Valbiska, on Krk, go to Merag, Cres, approx every 90mins. Expect queues in peak season. In addition, commuter **catamarans** travel from Rijeka to Cres town and Martinšćica, Cres.

Buses from Cres Town connect to Rijeka (4 per day) and Zagreb (2 per day). Island buses ply the main north–south road between Cres town and Mali Lošinj 8 times a day. Connections to villages off this road are limited to 2 or 3 a week.

Italy seems wafted over the Adriatic around the *mandrač* (inner harbour), the most enchanting introduction to Cres there is, especially in late afternoon when its pastel houses glow as if ripening in the sun. The town's big cultural sight is the Petrić Palace, a beautifully restored Venetian Gothic palazzo a block back from the harbour behind the Cres restaurant. It opened in 2006 after a decade of renovation as a **town gallery** and is slated as a venue for the **town museum** (Cerski muzej), possibly by 2011. In the mean time save your attention for the harbourside heart of town, **Trg Frane Petrića**, with a 16th-century **loggia** where Republic court and council conducted public business and wrongdoers were chained to a pillory to be shamed in public. Today, it hosts a morning fruit and veg **market**.

Town gallery
open May–Sept Tues–Sun 9–12 and 8–10, Oct–Apr 10–12

Through the contemporary **main gate** at its shoulder, one of a trio of gateways in the former defence walls, Cres turns on the charm in a maze of lanes which teases with dead ends or springs surprises with sudden stamp-sized piazzas. Shoehorned into **Pod urom** square (literally 'under the clock') beyond the gate is the diminutive Gothic-Renaissance hybrid **St Mary of the Snows**; its name hails a miraculous snowfall in May, its interior holds Venetian altarworks. It's also always locked outside Mass.

Until the town museum reopens, Cres's only repository of culture is a **Franciscan monastery** southeast of the centre – its museum, with a modest hoard of oils of Franciscan heroes and Baroque furnishings, is worth a visit as much for a peaceful cloister that's usually open at all times.

Franciscan monastery
t (051) 571 217; adm

Beli

A car or stamina is required to explore around the capital. Just two buses a week from Cres Town twist 12km north along the island's spine then slalom through woods to Beli, a poem of ancient limestone and light on a 130m-high cliff, crumpled as if braced for the *bura* wind which cold-blasts this shore in winter. After decades of decay, one of the oldest settlements on Cres is enjoying a second wind (in summer) due to a beach at the end of a very steep road and the native griffon vulture (*see* p.218). Conservation work of the **Caput Insulae Ecology Centre** supports around 70 pairs in the area – their numbers waned with that of

Caput Insulae Ecology Centre
*Eko-centar Caput Insulae; **t** (051) 840 525, www.supovi.hr; open summer daily 9–8, winter daily 9–7; adm*

sheep carcasses when local sheep-farmers threw in the crook. You can't count on spotting one of the brown vultures on the 5–7km nature walks mapped out by the centre, but a few recuperating birds lope around an aviary.

Valun and Lubenice

Famous for an 11th-century Glagolitic tablet in its parish church, **Valun** southwest of Cres is tiny and uncomplicated, a place to idle in harbourside *konobe* or swim from beaches you'll have to yourself outside of peak season. A 6km dogleg southwest is **Lubenice**, less to do with watermelons (*lubenice*) than the cold winter winds which chill this hamlet on a 387m eyrie; the name, they say, is Latin *hibernicius* ('wintry') chewed by over two millennia. Unemployment not ill winds have been its downfall, and the medieval town is dilapidated through depopulation around its square and rustic-Gothic parish church, which is being restored by a Rijeka arts collective and hosts exhibtions in summer. An elderly 25-strong population rises 20-fold during classical concerts on Friday evenings in high summer.

Osor

Lubenice's tale of woe is nothing compared to that of Osor. An impressive drive south, past the **Vransko jezero** reservoir then over bare limestone hills, descends to the oldest settlement in Cres. It stands beside the narrow Kavuada channel that divides Cres from Lošinj, carved as a short-cut between Italy and Dalmatia by Illyrians or Romans. Hooked up to this mercantile drip-feed, Osor (Apsoros to the ancient Greeks) bulked out into a 1st-century Roman settlement of a few thousand citizens, then matured into a medieval bishopric with its own cult saint, St Gaudencius. The obscure 11th-century hermit-bishop cast out snakes from Cres before himself being banished to Rome by a local nobility jealous of his influence. Gaudencius had the last laugh – he miraculously drifted home across the Adriatic in his coffin.

Under the Venetians, Osor was the island capital, and 17th-century cartographers depict it crowded with palaces and spires. In truth, it had ceded power to Cres a century earlier and was already a ghost of its former self, weak from malaria and plague, its life-blood trade leached by sea routes to the Americas. And so Osor lives in its dotage, cocooned in a hush as an arty museum-village with repro' sculpture by the likes of Ivan Meštrović in its lanes. There's also the **Church of the Assumption** (Crkva Uznesenja), a Renaissance cathedral in looks if not title after its demotion in 1828. Its altar has the relics of the religious hero who washed up on Osor's shores – you'll also see him frowning at a snake on a Venetian altarpiece.

Also on the cobbled kernel square is the contemporary Venetian **town hall**. Sculpture from Osor's Roman and early medieval years is showcased in the porch, where the government made civic announcements, as the **Archaeological Museum**. The patricians' debating hall above has models of the walled Venetian town in its heyday.

Archaeological Museum
Arheološki muzej; open summer daily 10–12 and 7–9; adm

Bishop's Palace
opening times erratic; adm

The **Bishop's Palace** on the opposite side of the square holds more Roman reliefs and medieval carving, but may not be open; otherwise you can walk north of the centre beyond the walls to the ruins of a 15th-century **Franciscan monastery**, a replacement for Gaudencius's 1005 church which blossomed into a centre for the Glagolitic text (*see* **Topics**, pp.28–9) that is inscribed on its lintel. Bring your swimming costume – it's beside **Bijar Bay**.

Festivals on Cres

Arty **Osor** and **Lubenice** both host classical music evenings – the former (**Osorske večeri**) from mid-July to mid-Aug in the Church of the Assumption, the latter on the village square on Friday evenings in July and Aug; programme information can be obtained from Cres and Mali Lošinj tourist information centres.

Where to Stay on Cres

ⓘ **Cres Town >**
Cons 10 (by bus stop off harbour), **t** *(051) 571 535, www.tzg-cres.hr; open July–Aug daily 8–10; June and Sept daily 8–12 and 3–8; Oct–May Mon–Fri 8–3*

★ **Bukaleta >>**

Cres Town

Kimen, Varozina 25, **t** (051) 571 161, *www.hotel-kimen.com* (€€). Modest though acceptable rooms in Cres's only hotel, a resort hotel overlooking a bay 1km north of the centre. There are plans for an upgrade for 2009.

Private **rooms** (€) via **Putnička agencija Croatia**, Cons 10, **t** (051) 573 053.

Eating Out on Cres

Cres Town

Riva, Riva creskih kapetana 13, **t** (051) 571 107 (€€€–€€). The slickest of the harbourside places, with a good choice of Adriatic fish presented for inspection.

Al Buon Gusto, Sveti Sidar 14, **t** (051) 571 878 (€). Squirrelled away in the Old Town is this snug *konoba*, with a passion for bygone days and a wide-ranging menu.

Bleona, Šetaliste 20 aprila 24, **t** (051) 571 203 (€). Portions are large and prices low in an old-fashioned locals' choice.

Osor

Bonifačić, Osor 64, **t** (051) 237 413 (€€). Fresh Adriatic fish plus pastas in a surprisingly stylish garden *konoba* buried behind the main square.

Livio, Osor 30, **t** (051) 237 242 (€€). The décor gives away a hunting infatuation, and this *konoba* prepares thick game-fest *lovački gulaš* (hunter's goulash) and a rich dish of Dalmatian-style rabbit.

Loznati

Bukaleta, Loznati, signposted 4km south of Cres, **t** (051) 571 606 (€€). A rustic restaurant famous for preparing the best lamb dishes on the island; *janjeći žgvacet* (lamb stew) or *janjetina u krušnoj peći* (lamb slow-cooked in a *peka*) is served with hunks of homemade bread. *Closed Nov–April.*

Lošinj

Mali Lošinj

The largest island town in Croatia, Mali Lošinj should thank its stars for steamships. A late starter, it put on a spurt of growth after it shifted from an eastern bay and developed a dock that fronts today's town. By the 19th century, as an Austro-Hungarian port, its warehouses handled more cargo than any other in the Adriatic except Trieste. Then along came steamships and the days of its sail clippers were numbered. So, while Trieste today is exhaust-choked and gritty, Mali Lošinj, a resort since the 1890s, retains a hint of yesteryear propriety among the captains' houses stacked up behind its sheltered inlet.

Compared with Cres and Osor, Mali Lošinj comes on as ship-shape and Bristol fashion along its harbourfront promenade, **Riva lošinjskih kapetana**. Behind its palms and cafés, at Vladimira Gortana 35, the **Art Collections** hangs the bequests of two local collectors: Cres-born Zagreb Academy of Arts professor Andro Vid Mihičić went in for home-grown 20th-century painting; Giuseppe Piperata, an Italian physician, had a soft spot for Baroque pastoral idylls plus second division French and Dutch daubers. By summer 2009 it should also hold the *Apoxyomenos*, a bronze of a Greek athlete fairly twanging with youth, who scrapes off the grime of physical competition. Archaeologists speculate that the 2000-year-old life-size bronze, which has undergone protracted restoration after it was found off Veli Lošinj in 1999, was thrown overboard to lighten a ship during a storm.

Art Collections
Umjetničke zbirke; ***t*** *(051) 233 892, www.public.carnet.hr/art-collections-losinj; open June–Sept daily 10–12 and 7–9; Oct–May Mon–Fri 10–12; adm*

For a swim, head to **Čikat Bay**, a pine-trimmed crescent 3km west of the centre. Don't expect it to yourself – the big resort hotels are also here.

Veli Lošinj

Only in name is Veli Lošinj the 'large' to Mali Lošinj 's 'little'. While its sister grew on shipping in the mid-1800s, Veli Lošinj, a former residence of sea captains, emerged as a winter getaway of Viennese grandees. Habsburg archduke Karl Stephan took the air from **Villa Seewarte** (Morska staza), a health spa for respiratory illness since 1892, and in 1856 the ill-fated archduke Maximilian Habsburg changed from holiday casuals into official suit to lay the foundation stone of the harbour breakwater.

The Croatian Tourist Board's tidiest town of 2008 centres on its **harbour**, ringed by a colourful mosaic of small houses and a pink Baroque barn, actually the church of **St Anthony the Hermit** (Crkva sv. Antuna). Local captains picked up its masterclass of Italian art – Venetian Bartolomeo Vivarini dabbles in emergent Renaissance in its prize *Madonna with Child and Saints* (1475) left of the portal.

Getting to and around Lošinj

Ferries travel to Mali Lošinj from Pula and Zadar (both 5 per week) and daily **catamarans** timed for commuters ply a route from Rijeka to Mali Lošinj via islets Susak and Unije.

Buses from Veli Lošinj, via Mali Lošinj, travel north through Cres Town to Rijeka (4 per day) and Zagreb (2 per day). Buses going only to Cres Town run 8 times a day.

Museum
open June–Sept daily 10–12 and 7–9; Oct–Nov daily 10–12; adm

Lošinj Marine Education Center
Kaštel 24; ***t*** *(051) 604 666, www.blue-world.org; open summer daily 9–12 and 5–9; winter Mon–Fri 10–12*

The oversized chesspiece opposite is a Venetian **fortification** erected in 1455 to make Uskok pirates from Senj think twice before attacking (*see* p.215); it contains a modest **museum** of nautical memorabilia and a gallery.

The pristine seas off Lošinj and Cres are one of the last Mediterranean habitats of bottlenosed dolphins – learn about them and other local sea life at the **Lošinj Marine Education Center** by the harbour. It can put you in touch with reputable local firms that offer approved dolphin-watching trips. Its charity, Blue World Institute of Marine Research and Conservation, also welcomes enthusiasts for 12-day volunteer programmes (you'll find current information on their website) – expect data entry as well as dolphin-spotting, however.

Susak and Ilovik

That the harbour of Mali Lošinj looks its tidy best from the sea is one more reason to take a trip to the islands west of Lošinj. Reached by Jadrolinija ferry or private excursion boats from Mali Lošinj harbour, **Susak**, 9km west, is the most popular destination for day-trippers. Most come hoping to see the island's *po lošinsku* folk costume, a rakish pairing of shocking pink or crimson tights with a multicoloured tutu. It's rarely dusted off even on high days, and more common among elderly women is everyday *po susačku* ('of Susak'), black stockings and embroidered navy skirt at sensible knee-length. A low-lying sand island with an archaic dialect and an ageing population – a wave of emigration after Socialist collectivization in 1948 saw many islanders settle in Hoboken, New Jersey – Susak asks only that its visitors idle with a glass of local plonk: Suscan and Susac reds, rosé Trojiscina and white Krizol, cultivated from the vines which cloak the island. For a stroll you can visit the village's parish church of **St Nicholas** (Crkva sv. Nikole). Hearsay claims the 12th-century 'Veli Buoh' (Great God) crucifix washed up on the island's shores.

They are almost crowded compared with those of verdant **Ilovik**, famous for flowers and eucalyptus trees. Every passing tribe – Illyrians, Romans, 12th-century Benedictine monks, Venetians, then Croats in the 1700s – has dropped anchor in the sheltered waters behind the islet of Sv. Petar. The latest arrivals are yachties, who swell a population reduced to 100 after two-thirds of the population emigrated to America. Those who remain survive on the simple things that God provides – fishing, sheep and tourists. Beaches can be found in either direction of the village: north 500m or 2km south to the isolated **Paržine** cove, protected when north winds blow.

Activities on Lošinj

Diver Sport Center (DSC), t (051) 233 900, *www.diver.hr*, on the Čikat peninsula, Mali Lošinj (near Bellevue hotel). Highlights include dives to the 60m Austro-Hungarian steamship *Tihany*, sunk in 1917 and lying with amphorae by its stern, and to the 'cathedral', a magical 80m cave illuminated by shafts of sunlight.

Where to Stay on and around Lošinj

ⓘ **Mali Lošinj >**
Riva lošinjskih kapetana 29, t (051) 231 884/547, www.tz-malilosinj.hr; open early June–mid-Sept Mon–Sat 8–9, Sun 9–1; mid-Sept–early June Mon–Fri 8–3

Mali Lošinj

Apoksiomen, Riva lošinjskih kapetana 1, **t** (051) 520 820, *www.apoksiomen.com* (€€€). The most expensive and most desirable address in Mali Lošinj, fashioned from a refurbished 19th-century shipping office on the quay. Cheerful décor and marble bathrooms in large rooms; port views are worth the extra.

Mare Mare Suites, Riva lošinjskih kapetana 36, **t** (051) 232 010, *www.mare-mare.com* (€€€). Four-star boutique residence on the harbour with a taste for Caribbean colours in eight rather funky modern suites, each with a large terrace. Nice hot tub on the roof, too.

Aurora, Sunčana uvala, **t** (051) 232 222, *www.losinj-hotels.com* (€€). The best of the Jadranka group resort hotels after a recent upgrade, with all the facilities you'd expect of a four-star and a location by the beach.

Villa Favorita, Sunčana uvala, **t** (051) 520 640, *www.villafavorita.hr* (€€). Personal service and plush furnishings in a classy four-star hotel carved from a Habsburg villa near a quiet beach. The best getaway in town.

Villa Alhambra, Čikat bb, **t** (051) 232 022, *www.losinj-hotels.com* (€). A passable if frumpy cheapie in a Habsburg villa.

Lošinjska Plovidba, Riva lošinjskih kapetana 8, **t** (051) 231 077, *www.losinjplov.hr*, can source private **rooms**.

Veli Lošinj

Punta, Šestavina bb; **t** (051) 662 000, *www.jadranka.hr* (€€). A package holiday three-star of the Jadranka chain, just around the bay from the town; the sea is 50m away.

See also **Villa San** ('Eating Out').

Susak and Ilovik

Private accommodation is in short supply. With luck, the tourist office or private agency **Lošinjska plovidba** may find you a bed.

Eating Out on Lošinj

Mali Lošinj

Corrado, Sv. Marije 1, **t** (051) 232 487 (€€€–€€). Lošinj lamb goulash and stuffed squid prepared in a garden *konoba*.

Bonito, Spiridona Gopčevića 37, no tel (€€). A modern restaurant behind the Riva; try gnocchi with shrimps and truffles for a light meal or a gastro-tour of starters and fish mains for a blow-out (€€€).

Lanterna, Sv. Martin 71, **t** (051) 233 625 (€). Just a simple *konoba* on the bay 1km east of the centre where Mali Lošinj began, perhaps, but romantic nonetheless. Simple fresh fish dishes and meaty snacks at bargain prices.

Veli Lošinj

Marina, Obala maršala Tita 38, **t** (051) 236 178 (€€). A lovely spot for a lazy alfresco fish lunch at the far end of the harbour – terrace tables look down into the village.

Villa San, Garina 15, **t** (051) 236 527 (€€). Grilled fish and island lamb served among garden palms on a terrace. Also a clutch of basic but clean **rooms** (€); no.8 has a balcony overlooking the harbour.

Krk

In his *Iliad*, Homer salutes the Kourete, an Illyrian tribe with good sea legs and a merchant's nose for deals in amber; and that prolific ancient Greek Ptolemy knew of Fulfinum, scraps of whose walls lie in Sepen Bay on the northwest tip of Krk (pronounced Kirk, with a rolled 'r'). In 49 BC Julius Caesar lost a sea battle to Pompey nearby, off today's Omišalj, and the Romans founded capital Curicium on an island they acclaimed an *insula aurea* (golden island). Fast-forward and the island becomes a stronghold first of Byzantine Glagolitic script, then, in 1118, of the Frankopan dukes (*see* box, p.113), a dynastic superpower whose strong arm reached across North Croatia until their headquarters was reclaimed by Venice in 1480. Krk, then, has deep roots.

Remember that when you arrive, because the Krk bridge which leapfrogged 2km from the mainland via islet Sv. Marko in 1980 brought with it industry and overspill from Rijeka; there's an oil terminal and Rijeka's airport near the package hotels of Omišalj, and the island's capital has expanded over surrounding hills. All good for Krk's pockets, of course – this is the only Croatian island not to have atrophied from depopulation – but less so for its appearance in the north of the island, at least. Visit for the capital's cosy old town, for one of Croatia's most famous beaches, or for wine-village Vrbnik or dozy Dobrinj, which is tailor-made for lazy afternoons.

Krk Town

Capital Krk Town compacts 100 per cent of an island's history into a fraction of its space. On its sheltered, west-facing bay, 1st-century Romans nurtured a minor port into a town that a 4th-century tomb-slab sculptor was moved to hail a *Splendissima Civitas*; Frankopan dukes masterminded a conquest of the Kvarner region from its grizzled stronghold; and in the last 30 years, the modern capital has sprawled with a casual disdain for urban planning.

The pocket-sized Old Town remains as intimate as ever behind medieval **fortifications** erected by the Venetians with whatever came to hand; in the seafront bastion, framed by their tomb-slab, a Roman couple peer out at *korzo* strollers on the quay-side, one millennium gazing at another. This harbour gun battery is 100m from the main **City Gate**, the *magna porta*, guarded by a stocky late 15th-century **watchtower** that bears an inverted 24-hour clock on its Vela placa side. Other furniture in Krk's foyer includes a hexagonal Renaissance **fountain** with plaques of Krk's awesome twosome, the lion of the Venetian Republic, whose flag first flew above Krk in 1180, and town patron St Quirinus, an obscure Sisak bishop tossed into a river with a millstone around his neck in AD

Getting to and around Krk

All **flights** to Rijeka land on Krk, at the airport 2km from Omišalj.

Year-round **car ferries** from Lopar, Rab, go to Baška, Krk (5 per day in summer), and from Merag, Cres, to Valbiska, 6km west of Krk town (12 per day in summer).

Hourly **buses** link Rijeka with Krk town and there are 7 a day from Zagreb (via Karlovac). Island bus connections link Krk town to: Punat (hourly), Baška (7 per day), Vrbnik (2 per day) and Dobrinj (daily).

---

390. The Roman martyr hovers above the waves, cradling a model of Krk, on each of the town's trio of gates.

The eastern **Upper Gate** which breaches the longest extant section of medieval wall is at the far end of cobbled alley **J. J. Strossmayera**, the narrow high street which angles off **Vela placa** and plies straight through the centre. Right off here lies the **Cathedral of the Assumption**. The catwalk of multicoloured Roman columns that prop up the nave reveal older roots than the Romanesque arches of the basilica let on. Look on one capital and you'll see two birds plucking fish from a font, an early Christian allegory of the Eucharist carved on a column that has been recycled from a forerunner 5th-century Oratory, itself built over a Roman spa. Although there are a few murky Venetian altarpieces to peer at, the pick of Krk's ecclesiastical treasures is in the campanile of the adjacent **Church of St Quirinus**, displayed in a low-lit Romanesque chapel built for Krk bishops, and later reserved exclusively for Frankopan counts. The last of them, Duke Ivan Frankopan, commissioned a star piece altarwork from a Venetian craftsman in 1477, a two-layer lucky dip of assorted saints like chocolates wrapped in gold foil. Look, too, for a Nicolo Grassi work of Our Lady of the Rosary for an image of 18th-century Krk wave-washed and enclosed within walls.

Cathedral of the Assumption
Katedrala Uznesenja; open daily 9.30–1

Church of St Quirinus
Crkva sv. Kvirina; open May–mid-Sept daily 9.30–1; adm

They say condemned prisoners were led for last rites in St Quirinus from a courthouse in the square tower of the **Kamplin citadel** behind the cathedral. Its crenellated walls and round tower stamped with the Lion of St Mark for the *Aureae Venetorum libertati* ('golden liberty of Venice') are more impressive from the sea as the Frankopans' grizzled 14th-century stronghold. Your best view of it is from the headland east of the Old Town, by happy coincidence on the way to Krk's best cove for a dip, **Dražica**.

Punat and Košljun

East of the capital, laid-back resort Punat more or less ignores its hillside old town of small houses above cave-like wine cellars, preferring to devote its energies to a modern **waterfront** where captains hustle for custom to the offshore islet of **Košljun** (*taxi boats, 20Kn*). Franciscan monks took no chances with temptation and built their 15th-century **monastery** on an islet first occupied by a Roman villa. Their bare barn of a basilica is a blank canvas for an

Monastery
t (051) 854 017; open (in theory) year-round Mon–Sat 9.30–6, Sun 10.30–12.30 (in practice on request in winter); adm

eye-popping *Last Judgement* on which a Who's Who of Christianity – Moses with his tablets, St Lawrence with the grill on which he was griddled by Rome – wait to enter Heaven, politely ignoring the sinners who roast below. Tear your eyes from this, the largest moveable painting in Croatia, gifted in 1654 by Krk's Venetian administrator Nikola Dandolo, and there's a lovely high altar polyptych (1534), as crisp and luminescent as the Mediterranean light known to its Venetian artist Girolamo da Santacroce, who was paid a bonus for hitting his deadline. They say its image of St John the Baptist is a clandestine portrait of Ivan VII Frankopan, included in allegory because the last Krk Frankopan was in the Venetians' bad books for losing a battle with the Hungarians in 1480. Never an administration to forgive failure, the Republic called in its lease of Krk island to the Frankopans after that defeat, and Ivan's daughter Katarina, depicted as St Catherine with the wheel on which she was tortured (and which named the firework), ended her days in Venice in 1520. On her death, she was laid beneath a tombstone to the left of the main portal, so fulfilling her dying wish to be at peace in a church completed through her 1,000-ducat bequest – until the *arditi* of Gabriele D'Annunzio (*see* box, p.190) disturbed her grave in search of Frankopan treasure four centuries later.

A tortured Expressionist *Stations of the Cross* by Croatian painter Ivo Dulčić is a taster for the artwork in the adjacent **Chapel of St Bernadine**: spidery pen and ink drawings by naïve artist Ivan Laković-Croat and a relief of the tonsured patron with the IHS tablet with which he always preached. They say the dour-faced portrait of the 15th-century Siena missionary was chiselled during his lifetime.

Also on the islet is a **museum** with a joyful collection of good old-fashioned bric-a-brac; there's everything here, from old banknotes, gramophones and typewriters to pickle jars of animal freaks and a dusty boa constrictor propped in a corner. There are displays of folk costume and photocopies of a rare late 16th-century *Ptolemy Atlas* stored in the safe. More curios – tiny chapels and Baroque statuary – line the footpaths that crisscross through the islet's pine woods.

South to Baška

Drive south of Punat and shingle beaches flank the road which twists along the contours of limestone hills whose tops are cold-blasted by the chilly *bura* wind. The best beach in these parts is **Stara Baška**, 8km from Punat and 1km before its eponymous resort. Locate it by a roadside nose-to-tail with parked cars.

Even non-beach-bums should venture south, however. For a start there's the lush **Baška Valley**, sheltered from the *bura*'s blasts and watered by the hyperbolically named Vela rika ('grand river') to seem like a lost world in this region of barren limestone. There's also **Jurandvor**, midway down the valley. In 1851, priest Petar Dorčić peered closer at the markings on a slab that divided the choir from the congregation – which had once been used as a grate for shepherds' fires – and stumbled upon the prize of Croatian archaeology, the *Baška tablet* (Bašćanska ploča). Zagreb pulled rank and demanded the earliest Glagolitic text (*see* pp.40–1) – a tedious passage about land donation by Croatia's first-named ruler, King Zvonimir – for its Academy of Science and Art (*see* 'Zagreb', p.89), where it slums it as foyer furniture. Local efforts to hide the 11th-century tablet came to naught, which is why the **Church of St Lucy** (Crkva sv. Lucije) has been palmed off with a replica.

So to the beach. A straggle of modern development announces **Baška** and one of the finest shingle crescents in the Adriatic; a 2km sweep, hemmed in by rugged hills and barely visible beneath a sea of sizzling flesh for a month from mid-July. Before it became a fleshpot and number one destination for Krk's sun-seekers, Baška earned a crust as a port. The kernel fishing village remains a charmer, its minuscule houses stacked up above the harbour like a ceramic model. Quieter bays notch the coast beyond the harbour, none as idyllic as **Vela luka**. Take a marked footpath (maps from tourist office) inland by naturist campsite FKK Bunculuka and tramp 6km over limestone slopes as white as bleached bones – their vineyards withered after Yugoslav nationalization – and you reach a lovely bay served in summer by a *konoba*. Taxi-boats make the trip from Baška harbour in season. **Mala luka** nicks the coast 1km behind; less romantic, but less busy too.

Vrbnik and Dobrinj

Vrbnik receives far too many coach groups for claims about a medieval timewarp to hold much water. Nevertheless, there's charm in abundance in the cobbled lanes which wriggle through vine-slung houses to 50m-high cliffs on the east coast. There are grand Baroque altars, too, in the parish church of **St Mary** (Crkva sv. Marije), funded perhaps by the treasure which was unearthed during building, according to a dubious local tale. An adjacent building houses a **sacred museum**. Medieval Vrbnik was known as a lively ecclesiastical centre, as famous for its Glagolitic colleges

Sacred museum
open summer only; times vary

Vrbnik Wine

Vrbnička žlahtina wine is cultivated on the Vrbničko polje plain west of the village. Such is the renown of its autocthonic dry white that Vrbnik is quietly transforming itself into a wine village, and craggy locals hawk their homemade plonk in every other doorway. For tastings, visit the rustic *vinarija* of one of Krk's finest restaurants, Nada (see p.209), or go direct to the maker 1km west of Vrbnik: family producer Katunar, t (051) 857 393, *www.katunar.com*, cultivates an award-winning žlahtina and light *frizzante* wines perfect for summer evenings.

as for the intellect of its priests – Vrbnik son Cardinal Josip Bozanić was appointed archbishop of Zagreb cathedral in 2003. Nowadays its everyone's favourite wine town, celebrated for Vrbnička Žlahtina white (*see* box, p.207). There's a small beach 100m east of the village old town.

North of Vrbnik, through vineyards and the village of Risika and straight across a crossroads, hamlet **Soline** is named for the salt panned since Roman days until 15th-century Venice halted production of a 'white gold' superior to that skimmed from its pans in Pag. It's now visited for mud liberally applied as a fango skin treatment – look for cracking grey figures at the end of the shallow bay to source the ooziest goo. You can make an excursion beyond **Čižići** on the bay's north side to the 110m **Biserujka Cave**, christened after a booty of pearls (*biser*) hidden there by smugglers and with impressive stacks of stalacmites.

Biserujka Cave
open daily July–Aug daily 9–6; June 9–5; Sept 10–5; April, May and Oct 10–3; adm

Left at the crossroads before Soline, **Dobrinj** drifts out of time on its defensive ridge, a one-street village that feels more like the hill towns of north Istria than the resorts on the coast. It has a similar artistic bent too. A **Sacred Art Museum** treasures a Glagolitic salutation to Dobrinj (1110), deeds of gift of the 'Illustrious Dragoslav', and a 14th-century Venetian silk altar cloth; the golden thread of its *Coronation of the Virgin* was embroided by Kaja Frankopan herself. There's also modern art in the private **Galerija Infeld**. Both are off an idyllic square shaded by sycamore boughs, before which an **Ethnographic Museum** houses everyday bric-a-brac from granny's shed. Don't leave without gazing over the vista from the **Church of St Stephen** (Crkva sv. Stjepana) at the square's opposite end.

Sacred Art Museum
Sakralna muzejska zbirka; open (in theory) summer Mon–Fri 9–12 and 6–9; adm

Ethnographic Museum
Etnografski muzej; open summer daily 9–12 and 6–9

Festivals on Krk

Krk stages **classical music concerts, opera, drama and ballet** in the cathedral, Frankopan castle and in the monastery of Košljun, Punat, in July and Aug. The castle also swings to international jazz acts for the one-week **Kamplin Jazz Festival** in mid-Aug. Also in Krk is the late August traditional jamboree, the **Festival of Folk Traditions**.

Where to Stay on Krk

Krk Town

Koralj, Vlade Tomašića bb, **t** (051) 465 300, *www.valamar.com* (€€€). The best of Krk's package hotels has quietly plush accommodation after a revamp. Better still, it's moments from the town's cleanest cove for a swim.

Marina, Obala hrvatske mornarice bb, **t** (051) 221 128, *www.hotelikrk.hr* (€€€). The waterfront gets the glamorous-style hotel it has long deserved after renovation of this central two-star in 2007. Most of the 10 rooms or suites have sea views or a balcony; style is very glossy – all black lacquer and sumptuous fabrics. There's a hip harbour lounge bar, too.

Dražica, Vlade Tomašića bb, **t** (051) 644 755, *www. hotelikrk.hr* (€€). If the Koralj is full try this standard three-star nearby; it's bland but clean.

When the package hotels fill up in summer, source private **rooms** (€) through **Autotrans**, **t** (051) 222 661, in the Trg bana Jelačića bus station.

ⓘ Krk >
Krk island office: *Vela placa 1 (staircase beside clock tower),* **t** *(051) 221 414, www.tz-krk.hr; open Mon–Fri 8–3, Sat 8–1, Sun (summer only) 9–12*
Krk Town office: *Obala Hrvatske Mornarice bb (harbourfront),* **t** *(051) 220 226; open April–Oct daily 8–9; Nov–Mar Mon–Fri 8–3*

★ Marina >>

ⓘ Punat >
Pod topol 2 (by bus station), **t** *(051) 584 860, www.tzpunat.hr; open summer daily 8–9; winter Mon–Fri 8–3*

ⓘ Baška >
Kralja Zvonimira 114, **t** *(051) 856 544, www.tz-baska.hr; open daily July–Aug 8am–9pm, mid-May–June and 1–15 Sept 8–3*

ⓘ Vrbnik >>
Placa vrbničkog statuta 4 (main square), **t** *(051) 857 479, www.vrbnik.net/tz; open summer only, times erratic*

Punat

In 2010, the tired Punat Park, **t** (051) 854 024, *www.falkensteiner.com*, in the centre is slated to reopen after complete renovation as a glossy member of the Falkensteiner group.

Kanajt, Kanajt 5, **t** (051) 654 340, *www.kanajt.hr* (€€). The summer residence of the Krk bishops, now a pleasant small hotel by the marina: comfy, tasteful and modern(ish).

Source private **rooms** through **Marina Tours**, Obala 81, **t** (051) 854 375, *www.marina-tours.hr*.

Baška

Zvonimir, Baška bb, **t** (051) 656 810, *www.hotelibaska.hr* (€€). Walloping four-star flagship of the Hoteli Baška conglomerate's concrete package holiday hotels behind the beach, renovated in 2003 into bland but inoffensive accommodation.

An abundance of tourist agencies offer private **rooms**: try **Primaturist**, Zvonimirova 98, **t** (051) 856 132, *www.primaturist.hr*, in the village.

Eating Out and Drinking on Krk

Krk's culinary quirk is *šurlice*, pasta tubes traditionally shaped around a knitting needle – they say no girl could marry till she had mastered the trick – then served with thick goulash (*gulaš*) and seafood.

Krk Town

Corsaro, Obala hrvatske mornarice 2, **t** (051) 220 084 (€€). A small menu of fishy delights plus rich *šurlice* pastas in a harbourfront restaurant with chunky bench seating and a cosy stone-walled dining room.

Frankopan, Trg sv. Kvirina bb, **t** (051) 221 437 (€€). One of the prettiest locations in town, beneath the campanile of St Quirinus, with the full Adriatic menu – fresh fish and seafood, grilled steaks and spaghettis.

Galija, Frankopanska 38, **t** (051) 221 250 (€€). An old house off the main strip (so quieter than the seafront places) that doubles as a *konoba* and pizzeria.

Casa di Frangopani, Obala hrvastke moranice, no tel (€). Clubby lounge bar on the harbourfront that bustles to a hip young crowd and gets busy in the evenings when DJs play for a cocktail clientele.

Volsonis, Vela placa 8, no tel (€). Atmospheric bar in a fortification on the main square, spread over several spaces and with DJs and hammocks.

Punat

Marina, Puntica 7, **t** (051) 654 380 (€€). By common consent the marina restaurant is the finest in town, serving up a wide variety of upmarket seafood and fish dishes plus island lamb and *šurlice*.

Ribice, 17 Travinja 95, **t** (051) 123 854 (€). A tiny menu of fishy treats fresh each day plus cheese and *pršut* and an idyllic terrace beneath vines and fig boughs. *Eves only*.

Baška

Cicibela, Emila Geistlicha bb, **t** (051) 856 013 (€€). Good seafood in a modern restaurant with stone walls and a penchant for ropework behind the famous beach.

Pirun, Palada 92, **t** (051) 864 061 (€€). At the farthest end of the harbour, so this friendly restaurant is quieter. There's all the usual fish plus a good selection of charcoal-grilled steaks.

Vrbnik

Nada, Glavača 22, **t** (051) 857 065 (€€€–€€). The finest fish and seafood on Krk, super-fresh, grilled and baked to perfection by an expert chef – simplicity is a virtue here. Its cosy stone cellar is a rustic *konoba* (€) for nibbles of *pršut* and tangy ewe's cheese (*oučji sir*) washed down with local wines – there are tables before the cliffs too. Staff here can direct more serious wine buffs 100m to a *vinarija* off east–west street Gospoja.

Dobrinj

Zara, Dobrinj 71, **t** (051) 848 250 (€). A quiet *konoba* on Dobrinj's square that's perfect for a lazy lunch of mum's home-cooking: try *šurlice* pasta tubes with goulash.

Rab

Rab gives the mainland the cold shoulder with an eastern flank of bare rock picked clean by the biting *bura* wind. But the Romans had good reason to christen a 2nd-century BC settlement here Arba (green, wooded) because Rab is the lushest of the Kvarner Gulf islands. Sheltered behind a mountain windbreak lies a verdant plain of vineyards, *maquis* and olives, plus sun-soaked Rab Town, as seductive as a holiday daydream and the repository of a millennium of island culture. And as if to balance the appeal of every ecclesiastical masterpiece in the island capital, some of Croatia's most enticing coves notch Rab's intricate coastline, an appeal to hearts over heads so persuasive that in 1938 British king Edward VIII removed the royal trunks.

Rab Town

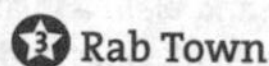

Rab is built of stone which is sometimes silver, sometimes at high noon and sunset rose and golden, and in the shadow sometimes blue and lilac, but always fixed in restraint by its underlying whiteness.

So wrote author Rebecca West of a town she fell for in the mid-1930s, when Rab, after centuries of lean years, was at last optimistic about its future. Like most settlements on the Croatian coast, the capital passed between Illyrians, Romans and Byzantine Slavs until 1409, when it was bought for a snip by the Venetian Republic as one lot in the 100,000 gold-coin sell-off of Dalmatia. Once a self-governing Byzantine city-state known as a silk trader, Rab now found itself subject to a disdainful absolutist ruler which practised subjugation through starvation. Already weak from two bouts of plague in the 15th-century, it atrophied as Venice took its cut, the doge demanding 10lb of silk a year, the church creaming off tributes of produce. The town's head-count was hammered from 5,000 at the end of the 14th century to a 2002 official statistic of 592. Indeed, Rab's future only started looking up in 1887, when it cashed in on a benign climate and the fat wallets of stressed Austrians.

Stagnation isn't always a bad thing, however. Because Rab had no funds for home improvements, it preserves a lovely **Old Town**; 'closer to reminiscence than reality', sighed Victorian English architect T. G. Jackson. As cosy as a village, as graceful and as weighty as a city, Rab crowds on to the peninsula where it grew up. At the farthest tip is the original Roman settlement, an overlooked corner christened **Kaldanac** that never really recovered from mid-15th-century plague; the windows remain blocked with the stone with which Rab entombed its sick.

Getting to and around Rab

Ferries from mainland port Jablanac connect to Mišnjak, Rab, every 30mins. From Baška, Krk, ferries chug to Lopar, Rab, 5 times a day in summer. Also in summer, two **catamarans** a day between Rijeka and Novalja, Pag, stop at Rab Town. A limited Rapska Plovidba Line service shuttles in summer up to 3 times daily between Rab Town and Lun (Tovarnele), Pag.

Rab Town is connected by **bus** services to Rijeka via Jablanac and Senj (2 per day) and Zagreb (summer only, 4 per day). On the island, bus services link Rab Town to Lopar (approx hourly) and Kampor (7 per day).

Mansions and Palaces

Behind Kaldanac is the larger Gothic and Renaissance quarter **Varoš**, the business end of Rab Town, whose three long alleys linked by staircases hold all the interesting sights.

You'll probably enter from **Trg svetog Kristofora**, the first of two squares beside the harbour. Step from its modern paved expanse into central thoroughfare **Srednja ulica** and the centuries fall away. Stone fern leaves curl up pilasters and cupids drape laurel buntings over the crest of some forgotten aristocrat on the balconied patricians' mansions which speak of Venetian ambition, a little tatty in places, but 'no more than what a great emperor might permit in the homelier corners of his palace', defended West. One noble remembered with affection is local son Markantun de Dominis (1560–1624), a maverick physics scholar and archbishop of Split (*see* box, overleaf). He was born in the grand Gothic **Dominis-Nimira Palace** on the right as you enter from the square.

The street widens at its far end into a stamp-sized piazza. Opposite the Venetian council's **loggia** (1509), today a café, an alley threads to **Trg Municipium Arba** facing the harbour. Now ringed by cafés, it was always centre stage of Rab's municipal drama, a spotlight for the Venetian rector. He issued proclaimations from a leonine balcony on the Gothic **Rector's Palace** on the left, north side of the square.

The Churches and a Beach

Ecclesiastical authorities built all the town churches on the upper street of Rab Town, aloof from the mercantile commerce below. Of the four spires which define the town's skyline, the local favourite is the 25m **Great Bell Tower**, a 12th-century symphony in stone whose crescendo of arches rests on Roman foundations. Rab's most beautiful bell tower is also its highest, its belvedere providing the best views there are over the town and coast. Local legend attributes the sweetness of its bell to the gold and silver which citizens threw into the casting pot. Pope Alexander II himself paused in Rab in 1177 to consecrate the adjacent **Church of St Mary the Great** (Crkva sv. Marije Velike), whose façade is striped in pale grey and rose marble, and spanned with blind Romanesque arcades. Only a *Pietà* (1514) above the portal darkens the mood.

Great Bell Tower
Veli zvonik; open May–Sept daily 10–1 and 7.30–10; adm

Markantun de Dominis (1560–1624)

As with many a focused brainbox, the fate of Rab's most famous son was to be as naïve as he was intellectual. A Jesuit-educated physics scholar, Markantun de Dominis broke new ground, pioneering theories of light diffraction and the moon's influence on tides that were lauded by Newton. Descartes and Goethe also admitted their debts. The Catholic Church was less enthusiastic about the enquiring mind of a man who became the archbishop of Split, a maverick who confessed gleefully that he always read banned literature on the grounds that it must harbour seeds of truth. Small wonder that church authorities also outlawed his 1616 *Scogli del Cristiano Naufragio* (*The Rocks of Christian Shipwreck*).

Assured of a warm welcome by Sir Henry Wotton, Venetian ambassador and author of 'You Meaner Beauties of the Night', Dominis took his anti-papal views to England in 1616, a coup for Protestant King James, who seated him fifth at his dinner table and consecrated him Dean of Windsor in 1617. Dominis found peace for six years, just long enough to consolidate in print the modern use of the word 'puritan' and to denounce Rome in his weighty tome *De Republica Ecclesiastica*, before he left to make peace with Rome and denounce Anglicism. At first he was received sympathetically by Pope Gregory XV but, after the pontiff died in 1623, Dominis, having burned his bridges with Catholicism and Protestantism and been blacklisted by the Inquisition, was in a corner. He ended his days awaiting trial in dungeons of the castle of Sant'Angelo. The Inquisition, not to be cheated of its heretic, exhumed his corpse three months after his death and burned his body and works on Rome's Campo dei Fiori on 21 December 1624.

Until it was defrocked in 1828 the parish church was a cathedral – locals still refer to it as the *katedrala* – which helps explain the elegance of its interior; they say a master 8th-century sculptor chiselled its ciborium from a single block of marble.

Next stop along Rab's sacred spine street is **St Andrew's Church** (Crkva sv. Andrije), with a stumpy Romanesque campanile, beyond which is the **Church of St Justine** (Crkva sv. Justina), its campanile capped by an onion dome like a bishop's mitre. Napoleon gave its Benedictine nuns the boot in 1808 and the convent church (1572) now hosts the **Museum of Sacred Art** containing the skull of St Christopher, a gift from Constantinople made in AD 809, apparently. Its gold reliquary box relates the martyrdom of a saint beheaded by Romans after their firing squad of 40 archers was porcupined by its own arrows, redirected by God. Rab elevated the saint to town protector for answering its calls to thwart a 15-day siege laid by Italian Normans in 1075. The Italians slunk away empty-handed – for the time being.

Museum of Sacred Art
Muzej sakralne umjetnosti; ***t*** *(051) 724 805; open June–Sept daily 10–12 and 6–8; adm*

The last campanile of the quartet is a 13th-century plain Jane attached to the shell of the 7th-century **Basilica of St John the Evangelist**. Its belvedere provides another glorious roofscape, its basilica ruins hold a lapidarium of headstones and carvings. There's more so-so stonework in another lapidarium at the end of the street beside **St Christopher's Church**, crammed into a corner of the Venetians' medieval defence walls. The staircase by its side cuts west across a corner of the **Komrčar Park** to reach seaside footpath **Šetalište Odorika Badurine**, with a string of platforms along its length where you can stop for a dip in super-clear waters.

Basilica of St John the Evangelist
Bazilika sv. Ivana Evanđeliste; open summer daily 9–1 and 6–8; adm

St Christopher's Church
Crkva sv. Kristofora; open in theory summer daily 10–1 and 7–9; adm

A 3km stroll west along the footpath, you reach the monastery of **St Euphemia**, its church a typically Gothic juxtaposition of ethereal painted ceiling and tortured crucifix.

St Euphemia
Samostan sv. Eufemije; open June–Sept Mon–Sat 9–12 and 4–6; adm

Around the Island

After the capital's culture, Rab kicks off its shoes on some of Croatia's finest beaches: to the west are rocky coves, to the north sand fine enough for castles.

Closest to Rab are the pine-backed shingle stretches of the **Frakanj peninsula**, whose wooded finger pokes out south of Rab town, a 4km walk around bay Sv. Eufemija or take a taxi-ferry from Rab harbour. By car, turn off the Kampor road towards the **Suha Punta** tourist complex, from where a track leads east to nudist beach **Kandarola**. It was on this pine-fringed shore, while on a 1936 Adriatic cruise with Wallis Simpson that scandalized Britons (and titillated Europe and America), that British King Edward VIII derobed. Rab officials turned a blind eye and the beach received a nickname, Engleska plaza ('English Beach'), not to mention a reputation for skinny-dippers.

The island's most secluded bays lie in the scalloped coastline of the **Kalifront peninsula** to the west – follow footpaths through its pine woods to discover rocky south coast coves straight from the pages of glossy tourist brochures. **Čifnata** is a seductive little notch of turquoise and pine green just two bays west of Suha Punta, though it can be busy.

The bays of the **Lopar peninsula** are busier still, because Rab's northwest knobble boasts lovely beaches serviced by two dull resorts: **Lopar**, port for summer catamarans to Krk; and to its east **San Marino**, which claims to be the 4th-century birthplace of St Marin, the stonemason who sailed to Italy to seek his fortune and accidentally founded the snug city-state of San Marino there. Its visitors come for sand, not saints. Fronting the bay is 1.5km family favourite **Rajska plaža** (Paradise Beach), while more secluded bays **Sahara** and **Stolac** are reached on a path which loops around the headland. Crowd numbers and swimming costumes lower the further you go.

Naturists also christened **Goli otok** ('bare island'), in the innocent days before the islet east of Lopar became a prison for political dissidents under Josip Broz Tito. It was less the 'Croatian Alcatraz' billed by private tourist agencies who organize visits than a Yugoslav *gulag* where torture was routine and labour hard for Stalinists sentenced without trial during Informbiro purges of 1948–55. After relations with Russia normalized in 1956, they were joined by non-political dissidents of the Yugoslav regime, their names still graffitied on cells and quarry walls of a prison decommissioned in 1988.

Festivals on Rab

Rab Town pulls on doublet and hose for the **Rab Knights' Tournament**, a medieval extravaganza with 1365 roots, revived in 1995. The main event is a contest of crossbow marksmanship on 9 May and again on 27 July, day of town patron St Christopher and climax of the preceding two days of **Fiera Medieval Days**, when the squares and streets become a film-set of medieval costume and crafts.

Where to Stay on Rab

Rab Town

Rab Town > *Trg Municipium Arba 8, **t** (051) 771 111, www.tzg-rab.hr; open summer daily 8–10; winter Mon–Fri 8–3*

Ros Maris, Obala Petra Krešimira IV, **t** (051) 778 899 (€€€). Designer style and rich tones of chocolate, ruby and calico from a stylish newcomer on the harbour. Has a good restaurant and a spa.

Arbiana, Obala Obala Petra Krešimira IV 12, **t** (051) 776 306, *www.arbianahotel.com* (€€). Handsome 1920s hotel renovated in 2006 to offer classic elegant style on the harbourfront. Some standards look over the bell towers, spacious superiors on the upper floors get sea views.

Imperial, Palit bb, **t** (051) 724 544, *www.imperial.hr* (€€). Rab's first hotel, a Habsburg number of the 1890s, has benefited from refurbishment to introduce modern style and air con. It's well located between the old town and beached in the Komrčar Park.

Istra, M. de Dominisa bb, **t** (051) 742 276, *www.hotel-istra.hr* (€€). A well-priced small hotel on the harbour – the best simple, comfortable en-suite rooms boast harbour views from their balconies.

Source private **rooms** from **Atlas**, Biskupska draga bb 2, **t** (051) 724 585, *www.atlas-rab.com*, and **Numero Uno**, J. de Marisa 22 (beside Hotel Istra), **t** (051) 724 688.

Lopar Peninsula

Lopar > *Lopar bb (junction with San Marino road), **t** (051) 775 508, www.lopar.com; open summer daily 8am–9pm*

Find **private accommodation** through tourist agency **Numero Uno**, **t** (051) 775 073, adjacent to Paradise beach.

Eating Out on Rab

Rab Town

Ana, Palit 80, **t** (051) 724 376 (€€€–€€). A talented chef peps up old favourites such as grilled Rab lamb or Adriatic fish in a salt crust with subtle flavours in this smart new town restaurant. One of the island's finest addresses, according to locals.

Rab, Kneza Branimira 3, **t** (051) 725 666 (€€). A little touristy, perhaps, but still a charming *konoba* which oozes homespun rusticity in a balconied interior full of cosy nooks and decorated with rough-plastered walls, heavy beams and tiled roofs. Try island lamb or veal slow-cooked under a *peka*.

Santa Maria, Dinka Dokule 6, **t** (051) 724 196 (€€). Fish and seafood – *škampi na buzaru* is rich and gutsy – plus a world tour of grilled steaks in a classy establishment which claims the courtyard of a 14th-century mansion just off the old town square.

Kod Kineza, Kneza Domagoja bb, no tel (€). Good honest simple cooking in a cellar *konoba* hung with fishing nets – tasty fish and squid, grilled and soused in olive oil, and country fillers such as roast lamb and roast knuckle of veal.

Paradiso, Stjepana Radića 2, **t** (051) 771 109 (€). A long-standing tourist favourite thanks to its courtyard setting, this offers a large menu of tasty pizzas and pastas.

Riva, Biskupska draga bb, no tel (€). A down-to-earth *konoba* off main square Trg Municipium Arbe, with a cosy stone interior. Expect a changing menu of simple tasty fare: *girice* (small fish, like whitebait) or *lignje na žaru* (grilled squid).

Supetarska Draga

Zlatni Zalaz, Supetarska draga 379, **t** (051) 775 150 (€€€–€€). One of the island's best eateries, located a few km before Lopar. Sweeping panoramas over the coast accompany fish or, with luck, leg of lamb. A joy at dusk, for the eponymous 'golden sunset'. It also has 14 **rooms** (€€).

Down the Mainland Coast: Rijeka to Senj

Crikvenica and Novi Vinodolski

Unwilling to accommodate her guests, Rijeka is also reluctant to see them go. Half-hearted road signs and heavy traffic in the city's industrial suburbs conspire to make the drive out a chore. Finally free and bowling south along the Magistrala (B8) opposite Krk, you arrive at **Crikvenica**, pioneered in the 1890s as a holiday riviera for well-to-do Austro-Hungarians. Although the benign climate that lured them remains, protected as the town is from the north winds by the Velebit mountains, Crikvenica now earns a crust as a budget family resort, and it knows its market. The neglected Secessionist villas by the harbour offer sepia-tinted snapshots of bygone days but little in the way of cash-flow, and Crikvenica prefers its hotels big and blocky. Even a 16th-century Pauline monastery is slumming it as the Kaštel hotel, and the only reason to stop is for the Blue Flag-quality shingle beaches north of the centre linked by the Lungomare footpath.

Novi Vinodolski 9km further south seems to have had a similar charm bypass. Yet a town whose straggle of modern suburban blight puts the 'Novi' (new) into the name has history, too, as the location for the 1288 signing of the *Vinodol Codex*, a prize of Croat Glagolitic (*see* **Topics**, pp.40–1) that ceded regional power to Krk's Frankopan dukes. A photocopy is in their 13th-century **castle**, hidden among a crowd of crusty terracotta roofs in the hillside old town, as part of a **museum**, also containing displays of folk costume, some of it donned for the '**wheeldance**', a reel performed on the square to ballads of brave deeds. While here, peer in at the **Cathedral of SS Philip and James** (Katedrala sv. Filipa i Jacobva) for a quietly extravagant Baroque interior.

Museum
open summer Mon–Sat 9–12 and 7–9, Sun 9–12; adm

'Wheeldance'
usually Sun, Mon and Tues; times vary, consult tourist office (see p.217)

Senj

'God guard you from Senj hands,' the Venetians would say in the late 1500s. Small wonder. From this scruffy small town sheltered behind Krk, one of Croatia's most notorious historical tribes, the **Uskoks** (*see* **Topics**, p.43), rowed forth to bedevil the Republic, the scourge of every Venetian town on the Kvarner seaboard, the nightmare of every caravel captain. 'They could, whenever they wanted, make the northern wind blow,' wrote one, referring to Uskok local knowledge of the mast-cracking *bura*, at its fiercest where it howls through a pass above Senj. Another captain was more blunt: 'They have the help of the winds, the sea and devils.'

For six decades, Senj was the pirate hideout everyone knew about but no one could loot, guarded above by the **Nehaj Fortress**. A keen

Nehaj Fortress
Tvrdava Nehaj; **t** *(053) 885 277; open daily July–Aug 10–9, May–June and Sept–Oct 9–6; adm*

Getting to and around the coast from Rijeka to Senj

All buses between Rijeka and Dalmatia stop at **Crikvenica, Novi Vinodolski** and **Senj**.

strategist, Uskok captain Ivan Lenković requisitioned the stone of surrounding churches and monasteries to build the 3.3m-high walls of the sturdy castle (1558) which kept watch over the old town – and sea lanes – from a southern hill. Do look at leftover chunks of ecclesiastical carving on the ground floor before you ascend to a **museum of the Uskoks**, a tale told with unrestrained boasts about 'unconquerable Uskoks', hissing at the sneaky tricks of double-crossing diplomats, and a display of Uskok costume that is every inch pantomime brigand. Uskok coats of arms on the **cannon deck** impale rather more Turkish heads than seems necessary, but the views from the **belvedere** are the same ones as when guards watched for passing ships and sympathizers' smoke signals along the coast.

You'll also get a good view over Senj **old town**, gathered into a tight oval as if still belted by the crenellated **walls** which continue to protect the north flank. It's a lived-in kernel that's fairly scruffy in places, even on the central **Cathedral of St Mary** (Katedrala sv. Marije), tailored in Romanesque fabric then patched and darned in Baroque and concrete by subsequent generations. Carved tombstones inside tell a similarly eclectic tale, but it's rarely open outside Mass. The pick of the Senj bishops' treasure is in an adjacent **museum** anyway – 15th-century Glagolitic missals compiled when Senj was a hub of ecclesiastical printing, and the front door keys of Klis (*see* pp.283–4) near Split, scene of the Uskoks' last stand. Senj isn't all about Uskoks though, as a **town museum** one block towards the seafront in a Gothic patrician's mansion is at pains to point out. Perhaps, but its mediocre lapidarium and Roman sea-bed finds do little to convince you that the Uskoks didn't provide the most gripping chapter in the town's chronicle.

Museum
Sakralna baština; ***t*** *(053) 883 109; open 15 July–Aug Mon–Sat 9–12 and 6–9; Sept–14 July Mon–Fri 7–3; adm*

Town museum
Gradski muzej; ***t*** *(053) 881 141; open 15 July–Aug Mon–Fri 7–3 and 6–8, Sat 10–12 and 6–8, Sun 10–12; Sept–14 July Mon–Fri 7–3; adm*

Northern Velebit National Park

Spectacular karst scenery, well-maintained footpaths and fauna that includes brown bears and wild horses make the little-known 109 square km Northern Velebit National Park (Nacionalni park Sjeverni Velebit) an alternative to the Paklenica National Park further south (*see* below). The star features of this park, which was founded in 1999, are the **Hajdučki** and **Rožanski kukovi**, limestone 'ledges' bored by 150 caves, such as **Luke's cave** (Lukina jama), over 1km deep, reached via the Premužić trail. Hiking information, accommodation in three mountain lodges, maps and park tickets can be sourced at the **National Park office** in Senj.

National Park office
Obala kralja Zvonimara 6, Senj, ***t*** *(053) 884 552, www.np-sjeverni-velebit.hr; open Mon–Fri 7–3; park tickets 1–3 days 30Kn*

ⓘ **Novi Vinodolski >>**
Kralja Tomislava 6, **t** *(051) 244 306, www.tz-novi-vinodolski.hr; open July–Aug daily 8–8; Sept–June Mon–Sat 8–3*

ⓘ **Crikvenica >**
Trg Stjepana Radica 1, **t** *(051) 241 867; open July–Aug daily 8–10; Sept–June Mon–Fri 8–3, Sat 8–1*

ⓘ **Senj >>**
Stara cesta 2 (on main road at north end of centre), **t** *(053) 881 068, www.senj.hr; open July–Aug daily 8–8; Sept–June Mon–Fri 7–2*

Where to Stay and Eat in and around Senj

Crikvenica

Vali, Gajevo šetalište 35, Dramalj (2km north of Crikvenica), **t** (051) 788 110, *www.hotelvali.hr* (€€€). A rare moment of class among the spirit-sapping package tourism, a small luxury hotel that's stylish and modern, its 21 rooms flooded with light through windows which look across to Krk. *Booking essential.*

Amor, Frankopanska 35, **t** (051) 242 017 (€€€–€€). Walls are hung with canvas sails and black and gold palms sprout in the dining room of the ritziest address in town, with a menu of fine grilled Adriatic fishes and seafood.

Novi Vinodolski

Lucija, Vinodolska, **t** (051) 245 755 (€€). All the usuals plus a few surprises for culinary explorers – try the homemade black gnocchi filled with Parmesan.

Senj

Hotel Libra (*www.hotel-libra.hr*), a central four-star with a pool and gym on the main road, is scheduled to open for summer 2009.

Art, Kralja Zvonimira 15, **t** (051) 884 377, *www.coning.hr* (€). A functional two-star hotel, part of the Coning chain; harbour views compensate for basic accommodation.

Stari Grad, Uskočka 12, **t** (051) 885 242 (€€). Large portions of lunchtime fillers – charcoal-grilled steaks, fish, pizzas and pastas – in a cheerful little *konoba* behind the cathedral.

Paklenica National Park

④ Paklenica National Park

If you have a head for hairpin bends, you'll find the Magistrala coast road which clings to the spurs south of Senj is one of the most spectacular in Croatia: on one side the cliffs of Rab and Pag, as bare as cut flints, on the other the rippling muscular flanks of the limestone Velebit mountains.

The southern highlights of a range which stretches back to Bosnia-Hercegovina in peaks of around 1,500m is the **Paklenica National Park** (Nacionalni park Paklenica), created in 1949 to protect the most spectacular limestone scenery in Croatia, a wonderland of gorges and bluffs beloved by climbers, draped in flora which morphs from beech forest via black pine to sub-alpine scrub. In far reaches, brown bear, lynx and chamois roam. Late July marks the annual migration of Tourist Man, who arrives by the hundred for a month's stay.

He rarely explores the whole 150km network of paths; most visitors are content just to pull on trainers for the 2hr tramp up showpiece gorge **Velika Paklenica**, cut like a giant axe-cleft in 1,300ft cliffs. The entrance is 3km inland, signposted at the south end of **Starigrad-Paklenica** (100km south of Senj, 38km east of Zadar). Beyond the **ticket booth**, a path ascends past some cliff bunkers – early 1950s refuges tunnelled for military top brass when relations between Russia and Tito's Yugoslavia hit a new low, now an exhibition centre and tourist shops – into a canyon squeezed tight by vertiginous cliffs. After 40 minutes, a sweaty

Ticket booth
one-day ticket 40Kn, 50Kn with Manita Pec cave; three-day ticket 80Kn, five-day ticket 120Kn

Getting to Paklenica National Park

All buses between Rijeka and Dalmatia stop at **Starigrad-Paklenica**, starting point for the Velika Paklenica gorge, and, 2.5km southeast, at **Seline**, entrance to the Mala Paklenica.

ascent to the right climbs around the back of **Anić kuk** for epic views from the top of a 716m bluff.

Through lush forest, 1km further on, past a right-hand fork which loops back through Mala Paklenica (*see* below), a stiff zigzagging path ascends to the cave **Manita peć**, hung with stalactites. A path behind the cave rewards those who continue to ascend east (*c.* 1hr) to the peak of **Vidakov kuk** and a vast panorama over islands Pag and Rab, as bare as pumice stones in the shimmering Adriatic, at 806m. Back on the main path, 2km above the cave fork, is lunch-stop Lugarnica, above which a mountain hut (*see* 'Where to Stay') serves as a launchpad for more adventurous hikes into the alpine meadows of the high wilderness Upper Velebit; the park office (*see* 'Tourist Information') sells good maps.

Manita peć
open July–Sept daily 10–1; June and Oct Mon, Wed and Sat 10–1; May Wed and Sat 10–1; April Sat 10–1; adm

For a challenge you could make a circular loop back via rugged sister gorge **Mala Paklenica**, the 'little' to Velika Paklenica's 'large', though it's not a route to take lightly – you'll need walking boots, a map and compass, water and experience. Shops at the entrance of the Velika Paklenica sell walking maps (*c.* 50Kn). The reward for your rock-hopping is a chance to spot a rare protected griffon vulture, an impressive brown bird with a wingspan up to 3m, that looks as disreputable as a drunk. A path which picks through boulders descends to coastal village **Seline**, 2.5km south of Starigrad-Paklenica and, by happy coincidence, fronted by shingle beaches. Allow 6hrs for a full circuit from the car park through both gorges to Seline.

Activities in Paklenica

Paklenica is the premier **climbing** destination in Croatia. Rado Sport, mobile **t** 099 220 5009, *www.radosport.hr*, based in hotel Alan, runs organized trips, alongside 4WD 'Foto Safaris' into the mountains. Outdoors shop Igla Sport nearby (behind a central IDA garage) has a decent stock of climbing gear.

Park ornithologists lead one-day and half-day **bird-watching expeditions** for groups. The park office will know if you can tag along with one – note that binoculars are not provided.

ⓘ Paklenica National Park >>
Dr F. Tuđmana 14a (400m before entrance, near Alan hotel), Starigrad-Paklenica, ***t*** *(023) 369 155/202/803, www.paklenica.hr; open Mon–Fri 8–3*

Where to Stay and Eat in Paklenica

Paklenica National Park

Planinarski dom Paklenica (Paklenica Mountain Hut), **t** (023) 213 792 (€). Dorm beds for 45 hikers in a mountain hut with a kitchen. Since both blankets and beds are in short supply, your own sleeping bag and reservations are advisable. *Open weekends only Dec–Apr.*

Lugarnica, a 2hr walk from the car park, no tel (€). Stock up on grilled sausages, sandwiches, water and coffee for the return journey in a former forester's hut, snuggled among woods and located beside a chuckling stream. *Closed Nov–Mar; closed Mon–Fri April, May and Oct.*

Starigrad-Paklenica

Alan, Dr Franje Tuđmana 14, **t** (023) 369 236, *www.bluesunhotels.com* (€€). Renovated in 2005, this is a large three-star of the Blue Sun group, located before the beach, with a pool and good spa centre.

Vicko, Jose Dokoze 20, **t** (023) 369 304, *www.hotel-vicko.hr* (€€). A mite chintzy in places, yet all rooms in this family three-star hotel are comfy. Seafront sister hotel **Depandanse** (€€€; same tel) has more modern style and bright, spacious rooms.

Ranja, Dr Franje Tuđmana 105, **t** (023) 359 105 (€). Modest rooms in a trekkers' choice near the park entrance, which offers year-round park jeep tours.

Roli, Stipana Bušljete 1, **t** (023) 369 018 (€€). A good choice for a relaxed evening meal, with a haul of fresh fish and a pleasant terrace sheltered from the main road. Also has **rooms** (€).

Dalmacija, Sv. Jurja 9 **t** (023) 369 018 (€). Follow a path off the central market to find this laid-back, café-restaurant with a peaceful seafront location. Mixed meat grills, fish, risottos and pastas.

ⓘ Starigrad-Paklenica > *Trg Tome Marasovica 1 (opposite harbour), **t** (023) 369 255, www.rivijera-paklenica.hr; open July–Aug daily 8–9; Sept–June Mon–Sat 8–1*

Pag

However you arrive, Pag comes on as austere and magical as the desert. Drive north from the mainland across the Pag Bridge (Paški most), the easiest access from Zadar to the south or the Paklenica National Park (*see* pp.217–18), and a stark landscape whose trees were stripped for Venetian galleons and palace piles shimmers in the heat haze. Arrive by ferry at eastern port Žigljen (from the mainland directly east) or Lun at the far north tip (from Rab island) and the jagged scenery cold-blasted to bare pale pink rock by the *bura* wind seems more Martian than Mediterranean.

What thrives on this tough island are sheep, which outnumber Pag's 8,000 population by over three to one and whose diet of wild sage, thyme and rosemary seasoned with sea salt flavours the tangy cheese of Croatian connoisseurs, *paški sir*. If Pag has a leitmotif, it's salt. Its lagoon-like inlets are more saline than those anywhere else in the nation, and pocket-sized Pag Town, officially part of north Dalmatia, shifted ground to safeguard its salt pans. The pumping, thumping antidote to the Renaissance capital's air of past glories is Croatia's answer to Ibiza, Zrće beach, and Novalja, more interested in resort tourists than a Roman past. But there are also secrets hidden away on the longest island coastline in Croatia – visit with your own transport and you'll discover a magical beach, Ručica.

Pag Town

Yes, its 33,000-ton yield still represents two-thirds of Croatia's total output, but after centuries of obsession, Pag is thinking beyond salt. Thanks to the 'white gold' skimmed from the pans which cover three square km of a murky lagoon, Pag prospered on

Getting to and around Pag

Hourly **ferries** cross year-round from Prizna on the mainland (12km north of Karlobag) to Žigljen, Pag, and a limited Rapska plovidba Line service shuttles between Rab town and Lun (Tovarnele), Pag (3 times a day in summer, winter daily). **Catamarans** shuttle daily in summer from Rijeka to Novalja, via Rab Town.

Buses link Pag Town with Zagreb (6 per day), Zadar (4 per day) and Rijeka (2 per day). Eight buses a day ply the main road between Pag Town and Novalja.

---

the opposite bank to its present position, its success sealed by tax breaks after its elevation to a free town in 1244. And it was because of the wealth accumulated through trade in high-mineral-content salt that it was sacked by mercenaries of the Zadar bishops in 1393, a robust response to centuries of chess-match diplomacy by Pag's ambassadors.

Venice also had protection of salt assets in mind when it realized its new (1403) acquisition's vulnerability to Turkish fleets, and eyed up a new green-field site on the east bank. Parish records narrate that at 3pm on Saturday 18 May 1443, the foundation stone of the parish church was laid to a mass chorus of hymns. An hour later, stonemasons began work on a Renaissance new town from the drawing-board of Dalmatian superstar architect Juraj Dalmatinac, who designed a neat fishbone of streets ringed by fortifications (removed on all but the northeast flank in the late 18th century). In 1474, Pag packed its bags, formed a line behind a treasured sculpture of the Virgin and processed to its new home.

Dalmatinac's **ducal palace** (Knev dvor) has been restored as an exhibition space on **Trg kralja Petra Krešimira IV**, the main square of an old town whose looks belie its age – a weakness for pebbledash obscures the character of many buildings. Here, that progenitor basilica of **St Mary's Church** (Crkva sv. Marije) remains the centrepiece, a Romanesque barn built as a cathedral until political bickering got in the way. Its façade is enlived only by a lovely lunette of Mary sheltering Pag's citizens who are dressed in Renaissance robes – an image copied from its old town church that Pag couldn't bear to leave – and a Renaissance rose window like a doily, an apt flourish for a town with a lace obsession. Local lore has it that merchants from Mikena, ancient Greece, taught local women the stitches, and Austro-Hungarian empress Maria Theresa prized Pag lace so highly that she retained a Pag lacemaker at the Viennese court. Samplers are showcased in a **Lace Museum** on the square, more modest pieces are sold by old women, busy in doorways in Kralja D. Zvonimira. Aficionados say authentic Pag lace is woven with a needle from stiff thread – if a sampler flops when lifted, the thread is inferior.

Lace Museum
open mid June–Aug daily 8–10; expect to pay at least 250Kn for a small piece

For a stroll, head across the causeway from the town waterfront. On the isthmus at the front of the former salt pans are the 17th-century salt warehouses whose size says all you need to know about the scale of the salt industry. Beyond the complex is the shingle **town beach** (*gradska plaža*), a modest strip and often busy, but far more enticing than swampy **Lokunja pools** behind. The pools' gloopy mud allegedly soothes rheumatic joints and cleanses the skin of those who bake in it for two hours, but they have a terrible smell. The quietest beaches in the vicinity fringe the inlet northwest of Pag, reached by turning right from the bridge: pretty Bošana after 4km or Konjsko.

A 2km walk to the left, progenitor settlement **Stari grad** ('old town') opposite the all-important salt pans crumbles among bamboo rushes beneath the ruins of a **Franciscan monastery**. Its church features the original humble lunette of the sheltering Queen of Heaven, who also ensures the monastery's well in an adjacent courtyard never dries during the worst droughts, according to a legend. The church itself is locked except for two days when all Pag pays homage: on Assumption (15 August) villagers carry its statue of the Virgin to the parish church of Mary, then process back again on the nativity of the Virgin Mary (8 September).

North to Novalja and Beaches

A road which winds through *bura*-blasted hills passes north through **Šimuni**, a minor resort sheltered in an inlet, then **Kolan**. Eventually you'll wind up near **Zrće**, a magnificent sweep of fine shingle beach, 2km southeast of Novalja (*see* below). Quiet it is not, however, or at least not in July to early September. For this is Croatia's very own Ibiza, and from mid-afternoon Balearic-style commercial house music pumps out from the alfresco beach-clubs of Zagreb superclubs Aquarius, Kalypso and Papaya. Unlike in the Balearics, all are free.

Such is their popularity, a regular bus service shuttles in summer from **Novalja**, making the small resort the liveliest on the island in high summer. The Romans would marvel. In the 1st-century they established a settlement here, and created a kilometre-long aqueduct that burrows underground, aerated by nine vents, a technical feat locals disparage as the **Talijanova buža** ('Italians' hole'). A section of the tunnel is open as part of the **town museum** at Kralja Zvonimira 7, an otherwise hit-and-miss attempt to portray island life – there are folk crafts, costumes and wine-presses, plus a pile of crusty Roman amphorae salvaged from a 1st-century BC wreck.

Town museum
Gradski muzeja; ***t*** *(053) 661 160; open Mon–Sat 9–1 and 6–10; adm*

Novalja's town beaches are small beer compared with those nearby – a strip of concrete platforms and bare rock to the north, a grubby crescent of sand south before the hotel Liburnija. Take a path from the latter that cuts west across a headland to **Straško**, a long ribbon of white shingle hemmed by green pines and a turquoise sea of Blue Flag quality. But on an island with the nation's longest coastline (270km), the antidote is not far away. Drive east of Novalja, past **Caska beach**, quieter sister beach to Zrće with a sunken Roman city offshore – remains of a sewage system bigger than that of ancient Rome in the bay have inspired some historians to hypothesize that this was home to a 30,000-strong city – and the road winds on to **Metajna**. The end of the road (literally) is **Ručica beach**, with smooth pebbles, super-still waters and views south to Pag's bare eastern flanks. Lunch in a wonderful *konoba* then stay till dusk – cliffs blush pink, only gulls break the silence and you'll pinch yourself that you're on the same island. Pure magic.

Going north of Novalja is to enter another world again; a dry landscape littered with boulders, sage and twisted olive trees. Fishing village Jakišnica is an appealing goal for explorations, with a couple of relaxing restaurants in the bay.

Festivals on Pag

Pag Town stages one of Croatia's most enjoyable **Carnivals** on the three days before Ash Wednesday, and again for tourists around 27 June, with masked balls and *tanac* dancing – a costumed line-dance whose steps are passed down the generations – accompanied by much music and wine on the main square. The Easter event culminates in the cremation of Marko, a puppet scapegoat for every ill Pag suffered in the last year.

Where to Stay on Pag

Pag Town

Plaža, Marka Marulića 14, **t** (023) 600 855, *www.plaza-croatia.com* (€€€–€). Facing the old town and near the town beach, a large four-star resort hotel with a pool.

Pagus, A. Starčevića 1, **t** (023) 611 309, *www.coning.hr/hotelpagus* (€€). The closest hotel to the old town, just a 5min walk from the town centre. Nothing special but this three-star is modern(ish) spacious and efficient.

Toni, Dubrovacka 39, **t** (023) 611 370 (€€). A low-key pension above a small beach north of the old town, with simple Mediterranean-styled rooms and a nice lazy atmosphere.

Biser, A. G. Matoša 8, **t** (023) 611 333, *www.hotel-biser.com* (€). Just up from the Plaža and a bit of an Eighties throwback, but with air-conditioning and satellite TV in 20 en-suite rooms and a good restaurant.

You can source private **rooms** (€) at **Mediteran**, Nazora 12, **t** (023) 611 238, or **Sunturist**, Šetalište grada Carbonere 1, **t** 612 060.

Šimuni

Villa Olea, Šimuni 101, **t** (053) 697 439, *www.villaolea.hr* (€€). Modern two- and four-bed accommodation in an apart-hotel 10km north of Pag Town, most with their own terrace. A pleasant spot to drop off the map for a few days.

Novalja

Boškinac, Novaljsko polje bb (4km east of Novalja), **t** (053) 663 500, *www.boskinac.com* (€€€). The best address on the island by far is this classy hotel with nine rooms (plus two suites). The mood is elegant yet friendly, the style contemporary and cool softened with antiques, and the location is in a lush valley of vineyards – boutique tourism at its best. It also boasts a top-notch slow-food restaurant (*see* p.223). Worth every lipa.

ⓘ **Pag Town >**
Trg Petra Krešimira IV bb, **t** *(023) 611 286, www.pag-tourism.hr; open May–Oct daily 8–7; Nov–April Mon–Fri 8–3*

ⓘ **Novalja >>**
seafront, **t** *(053) 661 404, www.tz-novalja.hr; open summer daily 7–11; winter Mon–Fri 8–3*

★ **Boškinac >>**

Loža, Trg Loža 1, **t** (053) 663 380, *www.turno.hr* (€€). The best in Novalja, perhaps, but overpriced for a spirit-sapping Yugoslavia relic. Worth it only for seafront location.

You can source private **rooms** from agencies **Aurora**, Slatinska bb, **t** (053) 663 493, *www.aurora-travel.hr*, or nearby **Navalija Kompas**, Slatinska bb, **t** (053) 661 102, *www.navalija-kompas.hr*.

Jakišnica

Luna, Jakišnica bb, **t** (053) 654 700, *www.luna-hotel.hr* (€€€–€€). The latest hotel venture in Pag, an airy four-star resort opened in 2007 with tasteful décor, provides a shot in the arm for the island's accommodation. On the water, it also has various pools, cocktail bars, and a spa. It also stays open longer than most hotels on the island and is a bargain out of season.

Eating Out on Pag

Pag's delicacies are Parmesan-like sheep's cheese *Paški sir*, pricey, but worth paying extra for, and lamb self-seasoned with herbs and salt. Light white wines cultivated in northeast valleys are žutica and gegić. Get hooked and the *vinarija* of hotel Boškinac is bursting with good things: wine, an excellent fig *rakija*, *paški sir*, *pršut* and anchovies in olive oil.

★ Kanjan >>

Pag Town

Smokva, Golija bb, **t** (023) 611 095 (€€). Start with island cheese then tuck into *paška janjetina* (Pag lamb) on a terrace littered with rustic knick-knacks and which gazes out across the bay.

Bodulo, Van grade 19, no tel (€). An old-fashioned *konoba* that's a credit to the name: snug, simple and with a small menu of basic meat and fish dishes.

Novalja

Boškinac, Novaljsko polje bb (4km east of Novalja), **t** (053) 663 500 (€€€). The finest slow food, whether in a classy terrace restaurant over vineyards or a rustic *konoba* beneath. Menus created from the freshest ingredients change with the seasons, but expect catch of the day grilled to perfection, or Pag lamb and veal seasoned with island herbs. *Booking recommended.*

Steffani, Petra Krešimira IV 28, **t** (053) 661 697 (€€). A touch of style among the bland touristy restaurants, this bistro-restaurant rustles up fish plus roast octopus and a tasty *škampi na buzaru*.

Račica Beach

Kanjan, Račica beach, Metajna, **t** (mobile) 091 502 4349 (€€). Escapist heaven in a truly marvellous *konoba*, with bags of atmosphere and terraces scattered on cliff ledges. Call at least 2hrs beforehand to reserve specials *paška janjetina* (Pag lamb) or *hobotnica pod pekom* (octopus slow-roasted under a *peka* lid). A gem.

The Kvarner Highlands

Risnjak National Park and Bjelolasica

Technically, this region belongs to the Kvarner area, but it's another world compared with the salty air and crisp light of the coast. Bear, lynx, chamois and roe deer roam the woods of the **Risnjak National Park** (Nacionalni park Risnjak), 30km northeast of Rijeka, a highland karst plateau at the west end of the **Gorski kotar** range, whose exposed spine rises to a mountain centrepiece, **Veliki Risnjak**, a 1,526m challenge to keen hikers. Those as sturdy as their walking boots can locate the trail for the 6–7hr trek near the park entrance at **Crni Lug**, 9km west of Delnice. Ramblers can pick up

Getting to and around the Kvarner Highlands

To **Risnjak**, trains on the Karlovac–Rijeka run stop at **Desnice**, from where irregular buses connect to **Crni Lug**. Without your own transport, **Bjelolasica** is a headache: irregular buses run from Ogulin to Jasenjak, and the 4km after is on foot.

All Zagreb buses going south to Dalmatian cities (e.g. Zadar and Split) stop at **Plitvice** on request – expect a connection every 30mins. Buses shuttle non-stop between four stops on the lakes' east shore: ST1, a 15min walk from entrance 1; ST2 by Entrance 2; ST3 by Lake Galovac; and ST4 at the north end of Lake Prošćansko. In summer, mountain bikes can be hired from a kiosk at ST4 (60Kn per half-day, 90Kn per day).

---

the **Leska education trail** (Poučna staza Leska), a gentle 4.5km loop through mixed forest and meadows scattered with wild flowers in late-spring. Everyone will find a bed, food and walking information in a small motel which houses the park office.

Spearing inland southeast from the Gorski kotar are the **Velika kapela** and **Mala kapela** ranges, where villages colonize what space they can find in valleys. This is largely undiscovered country, known only to outdoor types at the **Croatian Olympic Centre Bjelolasica** (Hrvatski olimpijski centar Bjelolasica), an all-year sports centre 17km west of Ogulin (*see* p.138) and Croatia's largest ski resort, though the superlative is more impressive than the snowfall – December and January are your best hope. There's access to seven pistes graded from easy to difficult and 150–1,700m in length. Tuition and ski hire are available from a ski school in the complex. A handful of adventure sports outfits here also offer kayaking and rafting trips.

Plitvice Lakes National Park

Plitvice Lakes National Park
Nacionalni park Plitvička jezera; open summer daily 8–8 (or dusk), winter daily 8–3; adm daily Apr–Oct 110Kn, Nov–Mar 70Kn

Over-compensating for the dearth of tourists elsewhere in the highlands is Croatia's number one tourist attraction. In peak season, 8,000 visitors a day amble around the Plitvice Lakes National Park's chain of 16 emerald-turquoise lakes, linked by waterfalls and burbling cataracts, and trimmed with a hem of dense pine woods. In early August, queues snake back from the ticket kiosks by 9am. Yet Croatia's first national park (1949) remains worth its UNESCO World Heritage listing; visit in autumn and you'll have a necklace of lakes set in gold and ruby beech leaves all to yourself.

The busiest area of the park is that with its showstopper lakes by **Entrance 1** (Ulaz 1) – this is also the best starting point to see waterfalls at their most impressive as you walk upstream. **Entrance 2** (Ulaz 2) is 3km further south, midway along the lake chain (*car parks at both*). Put aside 5–6hrs for a full one-way tour – thankfully, buses shuttle you back to the entrance in 30mins (*see* above).

The waterfall with wow factor is **Veliki slap** ('big waterfall'), the park's largest. A minor Niagara in spring, it lies a short stroll from

Entrance 1, just above the point where the lakes funnel into the Korona river gorge after their 161m stepped descent. Follow a path south around lakes fringed with trout to the **Velika kaskada** ('great cascade'). Its mossy steps provide the best geology lesson there is on the park's formative travertine (or tufa) stone, dissolved limestone sedimented over the millennia onto moss and algae as barriers that dam the lakes, like a limescale-furred kettle element on a super-grand scale. More cataracts lie beyond, past the **Slap Milke Trnine**, a minor waterfall named to honour an 1897 opera singer who stumped up 1,902 crowns to preserve the park. The halfway point is **Lake Kozjak** (Kozjak jezero), the park's largest lake with a busy café/restaurant on its shore.

Ferries
every 30mins, included in ticket price

Rowing boats
from 60Kn per hour

Electric **ferries** glide 2.3km across Kozjak to Entrance 2, launch pad for the upper lakes in the reverse S-bend chain. A kiosk at this point rents **rowing boats.** Above lie a series of basins linked by the largest series of cataracts in the park – a thick band at the head of **Lake Galovac**, lovely chokers of pools at either end of **Lake Gradinsko** – before the footpath arrives at the highest and last lake, **Lake Prošćansko** (Prošćansko jezero). Take the path which forges uphill through woods on the west (right-hand) bank of the upper lakes and you are rewarded with picture-postcard views. Better still, there are no crowds.

Barac caves
Baračeve špilje; open June–Aug daily 9–7; **t** *(047) 782 113, www.baraceve-spilje.hr; May, June and Sept daily 10–6; Apr and Oct Fri–Sun 10–4; adm*

The limestone sedimented out above ground had to come from somewhere – see where in the **Barac caves**, a series of halls and galleries carved by water over the aeons and hung with stalactites and bats. It lies 11km north of the Plitvice lakes, signposted east off the main road.

ⓘ Bjelolasica >>
www.bjelolasica.hr

ⓘ Plitvice Lakes National Park >>
kiosks at both entrances, **t** *(053) 751 015, www.np-plitvicka-jezera.hr*

ⓘ Risnjak National Park >
www.risnjak.hr

Tourist Information in the Kvarner Highlands

Tourist information for Risnjak National Park and Bjelolasica is also available in their hotels.

Activities

For **skiing**, **t** (047) 562 118, *www.bjelolasica.hr*.

Where to Stay in the Kvarner Highlands

Risnjak National Park

Motel Risnjak, Crni lug, **t** (051) 836 133 (€). Basic accommodation and hiking advice in a nine-room motel near the walking trails. *Booking recommended*. Its restaurant rustles up rich fillers to sate big appetites – such as venison steaks in mushroom sauce.

Bjelolasica

Bjelolasica, Vrelo bb (4km north of Jasenak), **t** (047) 562 118 (€€). Drive 17km west of Ogulin to find this resort for hikers and skiers. Not much in the way of luxuries, but acceptable chalet-style accommodation and super-central for the slopes.

Plitvice Lakes National Park

Three park-managed hotels are located near Entrance 2 (all *www.np-plitvicka-jezera.hr*) – *booking recommended in season*. Villagers offer beds (€) in their houses north of the lakes: look for 'rooms' signs (also *sobe*, *zimmer*).

Jezero, **t** (053) 751 400 (€€€–€€). The park's flagship hotel, refurbished over the last few years into a comfy if overpriced stay for what is, in truth, a fairly average three-star. All rooms come with balconies over the park.

Plitvice, t (053) 751 100 (€€). Although a touch business-bland in style, this is the best of the bunch for value for money, with all modern comforts and suite-style superiors that are larger (yet cheaper) than standards in the Jezero. Some rooms have a balcony.

Bellevue, t (053) 751 700 (€€). Just the wrong side of inexpensive and with drab décor and wardrobe-sized bathrooms to match.

Eating Out in the Kvarner Highlands

Plitvice Lakes National Park

Cafés at each bus stop sell drinks and snacks.

Lička kuća, Entrance 1 (€€€–€€). A cookbook of Croatian cuisine from the restaurant of the country's biggest attraction: there's everything here, from Zagorje turkey steaks to Dalmatian *pršut*, Slavonian *kulen* to *peka* dishes and fresh grilled trout or local favourite, spit-roast suckling pig, all served in a folksy log cabin.

North and Central Dalmatia

As famous as the spotted dogs bred there in the 1400s, Dalmatia is the bit of Croatia everyone knows. It has Croatia's longest, whitest beaches and the cleanest seas in the Mediterranean, which lap a constellation of islands that spray down the mainland like a comet trail. Dalmatia also has the nation's most enchanting Italianate towns, whose looks are modelled on those of the area's former owner, the Venetian Republic.

It's tempting to suggest that the Italians left behind their spirit as much as creamy stone palaces. If continental Croatia is thorough and industrious after its centuries under the Austrian Habsburgs, Dalmatia's coastal strip seems imbued with a Mediterranean mindset both in the Latin fizz of its cities and in an easygoing manner which leads Croatians to stereotype Dalmatians as laidback. A cliché, of course, but one that harbours a grain of truth. Is it just coincidence that continental Dalmatia, a highland repopulated after late-medieval Turkish incursions by east Balkan migrants, feels almost like another country?

11

Don't miss

See map overleaf

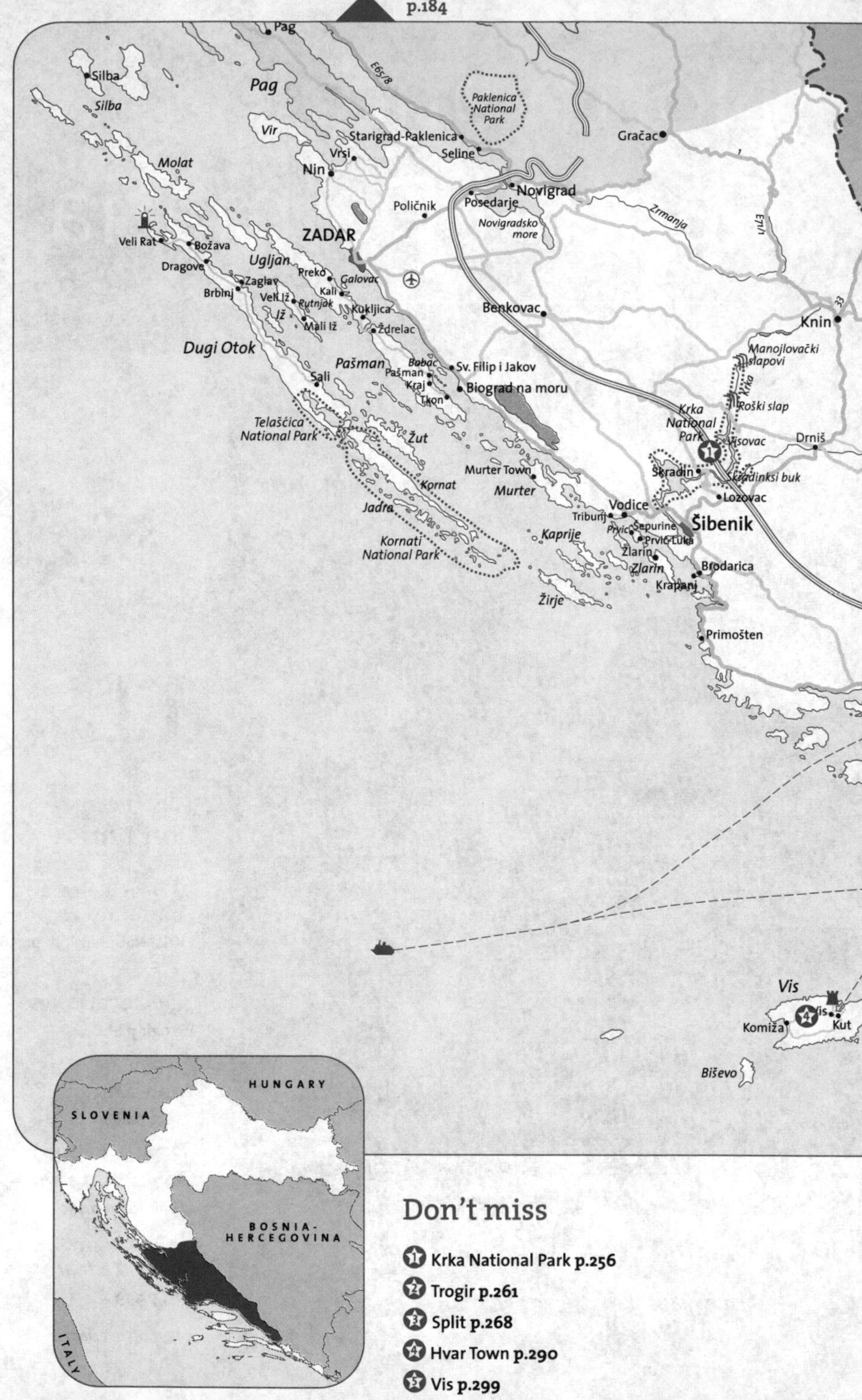
p.184
Pag
Pag
Silba
Silba
Vir
Molat
Starigrad-Paklenica
Seline
Vrsi
Nin
Paklenica National Park
E65/8
Gračac
Novigrad
Posedarje
Poličnik
Novigradsko more
Zrmanja
E71/1
1
ZADAR
Veli Rat
Božava
Dragove
Ugljan
Preko
Galovac
Kali
Zaglav
Brbinj
Veli Iž
Rutnjak
Iž
Mali Iž
Kukljica
Ždrelac
Benkovac
Knin
33
Dugi Otok
Pašman
Babac
Pašman
Kraj
Tkon
Sv. Filip i Jakov
Biograd na moru
Manojlovački slapovi
Krka
Roški slap
Sali
Telašćica National Park
Žut
Krka National Park
Visovac
Drniš
Murter Town
Skradin
Skradinski buk
Kornat
Murter
Lozovac
Jadra
Vodice
Tribunj
Prvić
Šepurine
Prvić-Luka
Šibenik
Kaprije
Kornati National Park
Zlarin
Zlarin
Brodarica
Krapanj
Žirje
Primošten
Vis
Vis
Komiža
Kut
Biševo
HUNGARY
SLOVENIA
BOSNIA-HERCEGOVINA
ITALY
Don't miss
1 Krka National Park p.256
2 Trogir p.261
3 Split p.268
4 Hvar Town p.290
5 Vis p.299

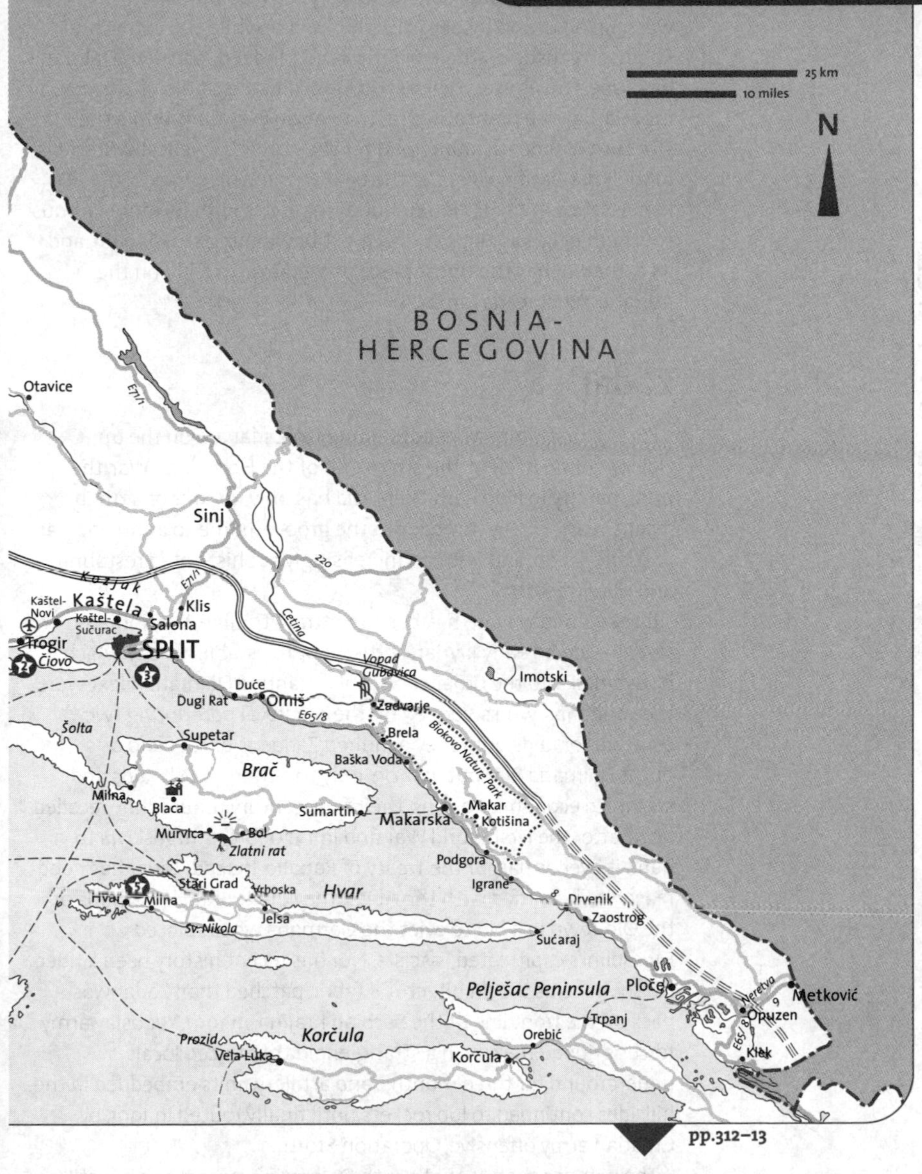

Northern Dalmatia

Though relegated to the back of Dalmatia's tourist brochure, our northern region has a stew as rich and complex as its heavenly *brodet*, flavoured with everything Dalmatia is famous for. Mixed-up and much-beleaguered regional capital Zadar narrates two millennia of regional culture in a two-hour loop around its Old Town. Spend the same time on a ferry from its port and you'll wash up on unspoilt specks like Iž or Silba, while you can play at Robinson Crusoe on the Kornati Islands. Indeed, northern Dalmatia has superlatives everywhere you look. Nin, the cradle of Slavic Croatia, has the first cathedral the nation ever built, while the star turn of Šibenik, launchpad for the nation's loveliest waterfalls in the Krka National Park, is the country's most spectacular Renaissance minster. Honey-hued Trogir vies with its more famous southern belles as the nation's most bewitching small town, and its cathedral has the finest piece of medieval carving on the Adriatic. Who needs fame?

Zadar

For the first time in decades, things in Zadar are on the up. Having found itself at the sharp end of the Homeland War, the principal city in Northern Dalmatia has only got out of a rut in recent years. Finally it is back in the groove, home to a thriving bar and café scene, and with an increasingly sophisticated restaurant and hotel sector.

It seems Zadar's fate has been to attract trouble. The Romans swept aside an early Illyrian settlement to establish a city which blossomed into the Croat capital of Byzantine Dalmatia. Next were the Venetians, who swooped on the medieval port during two centuries of raids until they acquired Zadar as part of a 10,000-ducat Dalmatia buy-out in 1409, only to suffer Turkish raids and strangled economics during their four-century tenure. Italy recalled 'Zara' after the First World War and in 1920 forced Yugoslavia to hand it over as part of the Treaty of Rapallo. Indeed, Zadar has good reason to be miffed with the Allies: they obliterated two-thirds of the Old Town in a bid to evict the Germans who replaced Mussolini's capitulated Fascists. Nor has recent history been kinder. No sooner was the architectural fabric patched than Zadar was back on the front line of the Serbian Krajina. In 1991, Yugoslav army forces gripped the city in a stranglehold that forced locals underground for three months, and artillery units embedded in the hillsides continued to lob rockets until finally routed in 1995 by Croatian army offensive, Operation Storm.

The wonder, then, is that north Dalmatia's largest town is still so appealing. While the architecture is patchy in places, the historic kernel still packs in an intriguing mishmash: Roman relics stand beside Croatia's prize jewel of Byzantium, and a splendid clutch of Romanesque churches graces the lanes of a compact centre crowded on to a peninsula.

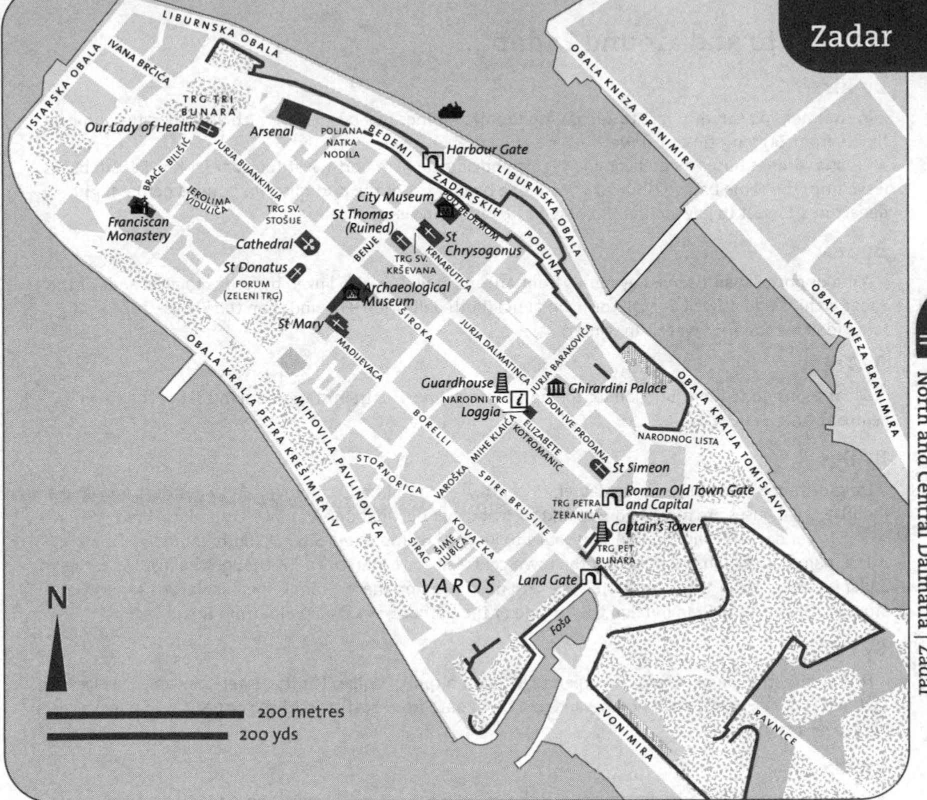

The Forum and the Church of St Donatus

Its official title is Zeleni trg, but 2000 years of habitual use guarantees that Zadar's central square will forever be the **Forum**. A casual litter of sarcophagi and chunks of carved pediment betray the Roman roots of what was the largest public space in the eastern Adriatic, a 95m by 45m square ordered by Emperor Augustus to aggrandize his 1 BC–AD 3 Roman settlement. The flanking porticoes, temples and shops fell victim to fire, earthquake and the declining fortunes of the Roman colony, but a lone decorative column remains at the back of the square, saved from destruction by centuries of use as a pillory. The miscreants shamed in public until 1840 probably cared little about the Corinthian capital, nor the trio of Roman god masquerons that pull faces on a wall behind that demarcates the position of the Capitolium temple on the Forum's west flank.

St Donatus
Crkva sv. Donata; open summer 9–9, shoulder months 9–3; closed Nov–Mar; adm

Much of the Forum's Roman masonry went into the 9th-century church of **St Donatus**, a powerful rotunda that is a city icon. Look at the base of the the largest Byzantine church in Croatia and you'll see inscriptions to '*Augustate*' carved on sacrificial altars

Getting to and around Zadar

By Air

In summer, you can fly direct to Zadar with Croatia Airlines (*see* pp.56–8), which also operates domestic flights from Zagreb 3 times per week.

Croatia Airlines buses meet incoming flights and shuttle 9km northwest to Zadar (20Kn). Return buses leave from the same bay, on Liburnska obala one block west of the port gate, 1hr 20mins before flight departures. Expect to pay around 180Kn for a taxi to/from the airport.

By Sea

A major port, Zadar is served by ferries from Ancona, Italy. It is also linked by ferries to all islands of the Zadar archipelago as well as Mali Lošinj and Pula (both daily Mon–Fri), and is on the Rijeka–Dubrovnik route (daily in summer, weekly in winter).

By Train

Zadar trains go to Knin, junction for the north–south line. The train station is 1km east of the town centre at Ante Starčevića 1.

By Bus

Long-distance direct buses go to Zagreb (6 per day), Pula, Split and Dubrovnik (all 3 per day), and Rijeka (hourly). Local buses are more frequent and stop at other destinations en route. Other local links go north to Pag (5 per day) and Nin (hourly); and south to Biograd na moru and Šibenik (both hourly).

The main bus station is 1km east of the town centre at Ante Starčevića 1. Although the historic kernel of Zadar is easy to stroll, the resort hotels are 5km northwest on the Puntamika peninsula; bus 5 goes via stops on Obala kneza Branimira on the far side of the harbour; tickets are 6Kn from the driver.

By Car

For car hire (the major players also operate in Zadar airport): **Dollar/Thrifty**, Hotel Kolovare, Bože Peričića 14, **t** (023) 315 733; **Hertz**, Vrata sv. Krševana (old town gate from port), **t** (023) 254 301; **Sidro**, Jadranska cesta bb, **t** (023) 343 916.

By Taxi

Taxis wait in the port area: for advance bookings call 023 251 400. A **rowing boat-taxi** (*barkarijoli*, 5Kn) links either side of the port area between the wharf and breakwater to save a 20min walk around the harbour.

---

embedded alongside Roman columns as the foundations, while inside an impressively ascetic interior, a pair of Corinthian columns help support the upper gallery, and slabs of tablet from the Roman temple invoke deities Juno and Jupiter. Dedicated to wandering Irish saint and local bishop St Donatus, the church, deconsecrated in 1798, has found a second wind as a concert hall thanks to superb acoustics.

Southwest of the Forum is waterfront boulevard **Obala kralja Petra Krešimira IV**, a mouthful locals dismiss in favour of the more manageable title **Riva**. Walk to its far western end and soft chords sigh from a sea organ that is powered by waves. At sunset they are accompanied by a light show from an installation in the pavement. The 22m 'Greeting to the Sun', created by sea organ artist Nikola Bašic, feeds off wave energy to ripple lights through 300 multi-layered glass plates. All in all, the best spot for 'the most beautiful sunset in the world', as Alfred Hitchcock would testify (*see* box, above right).

Cherry Brandy

Film director Alfred Hitchcock loved Zadar. Its sunset was more beautiful than that in California, he said; nowhere were women more beautiful. Notoriously fond of a tipple, he added that 'Nothing is better than the Maraschino liqueur', thereby joining illustrious company with a taste for Zadar's cherry brandy. Tradition relates that in the 16th century Zadar began to distil its own version of the cherry liqueur brought home by sea captains as a souvenir of Venice; Dominican monks created a full-flavoured liqueur sold in apothecaries as Rosolj, a derivation of *ros solis* (sun dew). Large-scale production began after an 18th-century entrepreneur read that town patron St Anastasia had dreamed of cherry tree orchards on the Ravni kotar plains behind Zadar. Whatever the truth behind the sales pitch, his *apéritif* was such a success that every passing dignitary kept a bottle in the sideboard. Napoleon Bonaparte and Russian Tsar Nicholas I were fans, and King George IV was so partial to a snifter that he diverted war fleets to pick up crates for his London *pied-à-terre*, Buckingham Palace. Even that model of decorum, Queen Victoria, ordered stocks for her cellars in 1871. The Maraska factory still operates on the harbour north bank. Get hooked on the liqueur in your cocktails and there's an outlet at Mate Karamana 3.

Archaeology and Church Art

Archaeological Museum
Arheološki muzej; ***t*** *(023) 250 516, www.amzd.hr; open Apr–Sept Mon–Sat 9–2 and 5–9; Oct–Mar Mon–Sat 9–2; adm*

Zadar's museums flank the east side of the Forum. The town's sculptural prizes are in the **Archaeological Museum**. Beyond musty Neolithic displays on the top floor are spiral jewellery and ceramics brought home by merchant Liburnians from Greece and Italy, while finds from Roman Zadar are displayed on the first floor below: grave slabs and a 1st-century statue of Emperor Augustus. Look, too, for a model of the Forum which makes sense of today's remnants before you examine ground-floor eye-catchers chiselled by medieval sculptors of the fledgling Croatian nation. Highlights among a stylebook of national wicker and plait motifs like Celtic knotwork (still on the band of policemen's caps) are a cartoon-strip of Christ's early life carved for 11th-century illiterates and swiped from nearby chapel St Nedilice, and a 10th-century *ciborium* with lions, griffins and peacocks.

Permanent Exhibition of Church Art
Stalna izložba crkvene umjetnosti; ***t*** *(023) 250 496; open summer Mon–Sat 10–1 and 6–8, Sun 10–1; winter Mon–Sat 10–12 and 5–6.30; adm*

Arguably the doyenne of Zadar museums is the **Permanent Exhibition of Church Art**, in the adjacent Benedictine convent of the Church of St Mary. It's popularly known as 'The Gold and Silver of Zadar' due to its beautifully presented display of ecclesiastical treasure. An 11th-century reliquary of St Isidore's arm spiralled with gold filigree catches the eye among sensitively lit gold and silver, studded with outrageous gems like booty from a vintage swashbuckler, as does a quirky reliquary which looks like a model piano for Liberace, but is actually a receptacle for St Mark's shoulderblade. There are paintings upstairs: look for prized Adriatic icon the *Benedictine Madonna* (*c.* 1300); Lorenzo Luzzo's wonderful *Assumption of the Virgin* (1520), in which she fixes the viewer with a steely gaze as she is hoisted heavenwards by a flutter of angels; and an elegant polyptych of St Martin donating his cloak to the beggar, the vision of 15th-century Venetian Vittore Carpaccio. Sculpture includes a crowd of bashful Gothic saints, who once evaded the eyes of the Zadar cathedral congregation atop a rood screen – and don't leave without exploring the tiny **Chapel of St Nedilice** (Crkvica sv. Nediljice) hidden away beyond Romanesque-Byzantine sculpture on the ground floor.

Though founded two centuries after St Donatus (1066), centuries of tinkering have added tweaked the adjacent **Church of St Mary** (Crkva sv. Marije) into an encyclopaedia of styles, erudite stuff for the architecturally literate – behind a swoopy Venetian Renaissance façade, Roman pillars march down a nave frothed with rococo plaster but which preserves original Romanesque lines.

The Cathedral and Southwest Zadar

Campanile
open summer Mon–Sat 10–5; adm

Picture-postcard views over the Forum – and Zadar – are available from the belvedere of the **campanile** on the piazza's north side. For all its looks, the cathedral bell tower is a relative newcomer to the skyline; until a Vienna committee agreed the plans of British architect T. G. Jackson in the 1890s, the 15th-century original was a single storey, stalled through lack of funds. Small wonder the conservative Austro-Hungarians approved of the design – he copied it from the cathedral in Rab.

The campanile stands at the back of the cathedral, a replacement for a Christian basilica smashed in 1202, when the Venetians sacked Zadar with a force of Crusaders en route to Palestine. Pope Innocent III was furious. Explaining his excommunication order, he railed that the Venetian Doge, Henrique Dandolo, had 'bloodied [his] hands, plundered a city, ruined churches, pulled down altars'. Its replacement is the 13th-century **Cathedral of St Anastasia** (Katedrala sv. Stošije), with a perfectly balanced Romanesque **façade** of blind arcades punched with Gothic rose windows. Carving wreathes the central portal – birds and animals that pick at grapes, an angel climbs a ladder to swipe eggs from a nest and a cat stalks a mouse on the lintel. Within lies a lofty **nave** whose alternating capitals and neat arcades look almost Tuscan, a Gothic *ciborium* (1332) and medieval choir stalls. The cathedral's prize possession, secreted away in the left aisle, is a simple marble casket that holds the bones of its patron. The remains of the 4th-century martyr beheaded by Emperor Diocletian were presented to Bishop Donatus in the 9th century as a vote of thanks for his diplomacy in quelling a spat between Frankish emperor Charlemagne and the Byzantine Empire.

West of the cathedral, Jurja Bijankinija culminates in the **Church of Our Lady of Health** (Crkva Gospe od zdravlja), a Baroque nave tacked on to a 1582 circular chapel like a grotto, on one side of triangular park **Trg Tri bunara**, named after the three wells on its north side. Explore south on alley Braće Bilišić to discover the 13th-century **Franciscan monastery** (Franjevački samostan). The story goes that the construction of the Order's oldest monastery in the eastern Adriatic was inspired by a visit of St Francis himself. While the church is nothing special – a barn-like space seemingly not recovered from a stint as a military hospital – its cloister is lovely, lined with epitaphs of Zadar nobles.

Along the City Walls

'Zadar', saluted 13th-century Frenchman M. Villehardouin, 'is a city surrounded with tall walls and high towers. It is useless', he declared with finality, 'to look for a greater and richer city.' The defences admired by the chronicler of the Fourth Crusade were beefed up in the 1560s by Venetians to counter the Ottoman threat, thereby creating the largest city-fortress in their republic. And just in the nick of time, too – the final brick had not long been laid when there began a two-year Turkish siege during the 1570–71 Cyprus Wars. The walls' massive bulk still guards the city's northern flank beside the port, a road on top providing a promenade ramparts. En route from central Zadar, it's worth a detour to Trg Sv. Krševana for the Romanesque **St Chrysogonus** (Crkva sv. Krševana); its exterior is lined with twisted columns like old-fashioned candy sticks and a sash of blind arcade wraps around the apse. If it's open, scraps of 12th-century fresco in two side apses enliven a stark interior in awe of a Baroque high altar (1701). **St Thomas's** opposite fared less well – tellers from the Zagrebačka banka sit among its late 5th-century columns.

And so to the walls. The main gateway beyond St Chrysogonus is the **Harbour Gate**, erected in 1573 to celebrate the Christian victory over the Turkish fleet in the Battle of Lepanto. Travellers departing from Zadar are blessed by principal city protector St Chrysogonus on horseback above a section of ceremonial Roman arch; a growling Venetian Lion of St Mark informs arrivals from the port just whose town they're in.

One upshot of the Allied bombs that obliterated housing was that they cleared space for Zadar's wonderful daily **market**, which spreads produce from the agricultural hinterland across a small square hard against the walls. Walk southeast along the defences (ascend via steps on Poljana Natka Nodila a block west), or follow them east on Pod bedemom, and a crack squad of silver-haired sellers tout cheeses and fruits, homemade olive oils, wines and *rakija*, or crocheted dollies and tablecloths.

Narodni Trg and around

As Zadar developed into a medieval commercial power, city fathers created **Narodni trg** as a mercantile reply to the ecclesiastical Forum – a focus for council and commerce alike. The sixteenth-century city **loggia**, the municipal courthouse, is a

Loggia
open Mon–Fri 9–12 and 5–8, Sat 9–1

city gallery exhibitions and stands opposite the former city **guardhouse** (1562), its Venetian design rather spoilt by an Austro-Hungarian **clock tower**. No wonder the bust of the Venetian governor, with a beard like a doormat, frowns in a niche. The balconied window begging for a Shakespeare love scene on the north side belongs to the Gothic **Ghirardini Palace**.

South off Narodni trg on Mihe Klaića lies the **Varoš** district, a cat's-cradle of medieval alleys that hosts the city's best bar district. Otherwise go east to the Baroque church of **St Simeon** (Crkva sv. Šimuna), rebuilt in in the 17th century. To explain the adoption as city patron of an apostle said to have held Christ in the Temple, a tale relates how a dying Venetian merchant, storm-bound in Zadar, confided to monks that he had buried St Simeon's relics nearby for safe keeping. The brothers exhumed the relics and were blessed by visions. On the saint's gilded casket, a no-expense-spared extravaganza that Queen Elizabeta of Hungary commissioned from a Milanese silversmith in 1381, the monks dig furiously and St Simeon displays the Christ child (a scene taken from a Giotto fresco in the Arena Chapel, Padua). Another story claims that the queen ordered the casket to atone for stealing a finger of the saint, although, if so, she took the same opportunity to remind locals about the triumphant entry her husband Louis Ier of Anjou made into Zadar 23 years earlier; the Hungarian-Croat king swaggers on the right-hand panel, probably a canny piece of sloganeering on behalf of a ruler who was waging a losing battle against Venetian ambitions on Zadar. Visit on the feast day, 8 October, and the mummified saint is exposed to hear the prayers of locals.

Around Trg Pet Bunara

A hotchpotch of Roman columns from the Forum stands as a sentry over the Decumanus, the Romans' longitudinal artery that now marches through central Zadar as streets Elizabete Kotromanić, Široka and Jurja Bijankinija. An echo of the Roman city can also be seen in the remains of their **gateway** which are being excavated on Trg Petra Zoranića.

Behind it, **Trg pet bunara** is christened for its five wells (*pet bunara*) which tapped a new cistern from 1574. This supplied the city with water until the mid-19th century, when the square enjoyed a fleeting heyday as fashionable promenade. Doubtless its surprise elevation was aided by General Welden – the Austro-Hungarian officer seized on a rare outbreak of peace in 1829 to create the first public park in Dalmatia atop a pentagonal bastion which abuts the square. Earlier defences – a chunk of crenellated 13th-century defence wall – hang on the shoulder of the medieval watchtower, the **Captain's Tower**, opposite. It hosts art or

Captain's Tower
Kapetanova kula; open Mon–Sat 10–1 and 5–8; adm

photography exhibitions and offers views from its summit. South lies the **Land Gate** (Kopnena vrata), a muscular Venetian gateway with a pediment of cattle skulls and flower buds. Its fierce Lion of St Mark represents the most forceful stamp of Venetian rule on the Dalmatian coast; city patron St Chrysogonus on the keystone never stands a chance.

It stands beside the **Foša harbour**, shaped from the former city moat and crammed with fishing boats. From here, coast road **Zvonimira** continues southeast, and central Zadar eases into residential district **Kolovare**, fronted by a thin strip of beach, restaurants and cafés that get more laid-back the further you go.

Tourist Information in Zadar

ⓘ **Zadar >** *Corner of Narodni trg and Mihe Klaica,* **t** *(023) 316 166, www.zadar.hr; open June–Sept daily 8–12; Oct–May Tues–Sat 8–8, Sun–Mon 9–3*

The helpful **tourist office** offers free maps of Zadar and the locale which extend to the Puntamika peninsula, and gives advice on regional day trips.

Where to Stay in Zadar

Most hotels are on the **Puntamika peninsula** 5km northwest of the centre. Here you'll find the resort giants, which have come a long way from Socialist roots thanks to massive investment by the Austrian Falkensteiner chain (*www.falkensteiner.com*); it will open a five-star leisure resort, Punta Skala, **t** (023) 492 909, for summer 2009. Most are located in the Borik complex, a tourist enclave low on character but big on amenities and located before a small shingle beach.

Bastion, Bedemi zadarskih pobuna 13, **t** (023) 494 950, *www.hotel-bastion.hr* (€€€). Off the north side of Trg Tri bunara, this is the design hotel that Zadar has long deserved, opened in 2008 and incorporating a medieval bastion into its fabric. Style is hip retro-maximalism with room for faux antiques. There's also a splendid spa, and an à la carte Mediterranean restaurant, Kaštel.

President, Vladana Desnice 16, Puntamika, **t** (023) 333 696, *www.hotel-president.hr* (€€€). Small four-star in the Borik area whose traditional décor is in the sumptuous vein – think tones of old gold and ruby set off by walnut and cherrywood in rooms; those on the third floor boast coastal views. Its restaurant, **Vivaldi**, prepares an international menu.

Club Funimation Borik, Majstora Radovana 7, Puntamika, **t** (023) 206 636, *www.falkensteiner.com* (€€€–€€). Kiddie-friendly resort that divides between the main complex and a quieter – and more stylish – Garden Wing Adriana for couples, all wicker furnishings and neutral shades of calico and *café au lait*. Excellent spa facilities for indulgence.

Villa Hrešc, Obala kneza Trpimira 28, **t** (023) 337 570, *www.villa-hresc.hr* (€€€–€€). Design-led small hotel on the harbour's north shore which prides itself on personal service and an excellent restaurant. Rooms and apartments are furnished in modern Italian style, the best with views across to the Old Town, a 20min walk away.

Kolovare, Bože Peričića 14, **t** (023) 211 017, *www.hotel-kolovare.com* (€€). Above the beaches of the same name and a little pricey, but close enough to the Old Town to be worth considering after a revamp in 2004–5 to update a Socialist-era hotel.

Venera, Šime Ljubića 4a (off Kovačka), **t** (023) 214 098, *www.hotel-venera-zd.hr* (€). Yes it's basic and, though en suite, rooms are tiny. But this is a good-value cheapie in a quiet alley in the thick of the Varoš bar district.

Private **rooms** (€) in the historic kernel can be booked through tourist agencies **Aquarius**, Nova vrata (gateway at top of Jurja Barakovića), **t** (023) 212 919, and **Miatours**, Vrata Svetog Krševana, **t** (023) 254 300/400.

Eating Out in Zadar

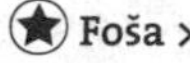

Foša, Kralja Dimitra Zvonimira 2, **t** (023) 314 421 (€€€–€€). A highly rated restaurant, with fish specialities in a former guard house beside the Land Gate that has been refurbished as a minimalist dining room. Not cheap, but this is glamorous dining, not least on a splendid terrace beside the Foša harbour.

Kornat, Liburnska obala 6, **t** (023) 254 101 (€€€–€€). Long the best place in town, with a style that's traditional without being stuffy, and a menu that's creative without ever showing off – expect the likes of lamb in a rosemary sauce, monkfish laced with Istrian truffles. It's at the northwest end of the harbourfront.

Niko, Obala kneza Domagoja 9, Puntamika, **t** (023) 337 888 (€€€–€€). A Zadar institution before the Puntamika marina, and the locals' choice for a Sunday slap-up feast. Choose from a changing catch-of-the-day platter or indulge in a seafood menu of favourites such as *jastog* (lobster) and *škampi na buzaru* (scampi cooked in garlic and white wine).

Trata, Jerolima Vidulića 5, no tel (€€). Signposed off in the side streets at the back of the Forum is this friendly *konoba* with a lovely garden and traditional menu: rich *brodet* (Dalmatian fish stew) is served in old-fashioned clay bowls, and local wines are on the list.

Zadar, Obala kralja Petra Krešimira IV bb, **t** (023) 212 182 (€€). An unremarkable menu is forgivable by a terrace on Zadar's best promenade, offering the best views in town across the bay to Ugljan.

Žvelti barbor, Ispod dvorina, Bokanjac (5km northeast), mobile **t** 098 403 322 (€€). Just five tables in a stone house and the best *peka*-cooked octopus (*hobotnica pod pekom*) you'll eat, say locals in-the-know. All food is brought in to order, so reserve a day before. As authentic as it gets.

Dva ribara, Blaža Jurjeva bb, **t** (023) 213 445 (€). From the Foša team, this long-time favourite has gone hip with a slick minimalist interior. The menu remains more traditional: thin-crust pizzas plus homemade pastas in large portions.

Stomorica, Stomorica 12 (€). Simple fish snacks and traditional boozing in a snug *konoba* whose patrons are liable to burst into song after a few glasses of homemade plonk. A gem.

Cafés and Bars in Zadar

Zadar likes its café society. It is well served on the Old Town squares – Narodni trg is a mite more stylish than the Forum – while the bar scene lies in lanes of the Varoš district, centred around Kult bar on Stomorica.

Arsenal, Trg Tri bunara 1. Once a historic warehouse, now a stylish multi-role venue: a slick cocktail bar and restaurant, a concert hall which hosts bands and DJs. Also has an art space and a fine-wines outlet.

Galerija Djina, Varoška 4. Drinking den of choice for an older bohemian crowd is this arty café-bar at the edge of the Varoš district, with bench seats outside and a photography or art exhibiton within.

Garden, Bedemi Zadarskih Pobuna bb. An eclectic set-list of chilled beats takes in nu-jazz, dub and Latin, perfect for comfy loungers atop the city walls of this hip alfresco bar and club opened in 2004 by members of British reggae band UB40. *Summer only*.

Maya Pub, Liburnska obala 6. The name gives away this as a mixed number, part hippy chic exotica, part spacious boozer. There are DJs at weekends and a port-side terrace with egg-shaped seats from which to watch the ferries go by.

Around Zadar

Nin

Forget Zagreb, roll over Split. If anywhere can stake a claim to be the cradle of Croatia it is Nin. Some time in the early 7th century, Croats arrived at the ruins of Roman peninsula port Aeona and ended a protracted 1,000-mile migration from somewhere near Ukraine. For 400 years Nin was the capital of a fledgling Slavic nation, the seat of its first kings and, from the 9th century, see of Croatia's highest Slavic bishop, Grgur Ninski. Small wonder poet Vinko Nikolić acclaimed it 'the Croatian Bethlehem'. Seized by the iron grip of Venice in 1382, Nin became a mere salt-worker, exploited but undefended and vulnerable to fleets of Ottoman Turks. They struck in 1571 and drew on again in 1646, when the Republic itself put Nin to the torch before falling back to Zadar. Racked by malaria, Nin vanished into obscurity.

The village which slumbers on an islet beside soupy salt marshes can barely have changed. Only the wide streets and ancient relics speak of former glories; both are reached via the **Donji most**, the 'lower bridge' of two, which crosses to a 16th-century **town gate** erected by Venice. The thoroughfare beyond leads to the 18th-century parish church of **St Ansel** (Crkva sv. Anzelma), christened in honour of an early Nin bishop. He waves hello with both hands on a Carolingian reliquary of his shoulderblade in the church's **treasury**, star piece of a hoard which testifies both to the power of Nin's bishops and the craft of Zadar's goldsmiths. Also in this old curiosity shop of St Ansel you'll see his head in a pirate-swashbuckler of a treasure chest, his jaw and arm, and a Gothic slipper which conceals his foot. Look, too, for one of Judas's 30 pieces of silver showcased in a 15-century monstrance (and never mind that the coin is from Rhodes).

Treasury
open 15 July–15 Sept Mon–Sat 10–12.30 and 5.30–9.30; adm

Behind St Ansel is a miniature of Ivan Meštrović's bronze in Split of Grgur Ninski (*see* pp.275–6), the Nin bishop who dared confront Rome at an AD 929 synod in Split and champion the use of Croatian Glagolitic in the liturgy. A more haunting testament to former glories is the dedicatory inscription to *župan* ('ruler') Godežav on the lintel of the nearby **Church of the Holy Cross** (Crkva sv. Križa). The AD 800 sheriff commissioned the first church Croatia ever built, as tiny as a matchbox, as atmospheric as a cathedral. Its *gravitas* so impressed British architect Thomas Graham Jackson in 1887 that he dubbed it 'the smallest cathedral in Christianity'. They say its pre-Romanesque Greek cross is placed so the setting sun on the feast day of St Ambrose, patron of Nin's Benedictine monks, spears through a window to illuminate the baptismal font.

Archaeology Museum
www.amzd.hr; open June–Aug Mon–Sat 9–10; May and Sept Mon–Sat 9–12 and 5–8; Oct–May Mon–Sat 8–2; adm

If its now-bare interior is locked, seek the key from the **Archaeology Museum**. At the end of Nin's main drag, it tells the

Getting around north and east of Zadar

Nin is linked to Zadar by frequent buses. There are no direct buses to **Novalja**: take one up-coast and alight at Posedarje, then join local services or walk 7km south beside the inlet.

tale of the early years – Liburnian pots and jewellery, Roman gods on votive altars and early Croatian carving – organized around a sleek Liburnian trading ship, a low-freeboard craft found in Nin harbour, where it may have been scuttled as a breakwater. Next door is a replica of the hexagonal font of the Holy Cross church in which 9th-century Croat king Višeslav accepted Christianity: 'Here the weak man is brought to light', its Latin inscription sermonizes. The original is in the Museum of Croatian Archaeological Monuments in Split (*see* p.278).

While here, look at the model of the Romans' temple of Diana, because only column stumps and chunks of carved lintel remain of the real thing behind the museum. South, the 13th-century barn of **St Ambrose's Church** stands beside a stretch of Venetian fortifications by the **upper bridge**. A town whose fortunes have always been bound up with salt, Nin hopes the 'white gold' which lured the Turks will also attract tourists – manufacturer **Solana Nin** leads tours around a checkerboard of pans first skimmed by Romans; a factory outlet retails bath and cooking salts. Find both by walking 200m away from Nin from the bridge.

Solana Nin
t (023) 264 021; open summer daily 11–6; adm

In days of yore, 11th-century kings rode 1km south after their coronation in Nin to present themselves before citizens from the dinky **Church of St Nicholas**, castellated in the 1500s when the octagonal tower doubled as a watchtower against the Turks. Although the church is always locked, the stroll through meadows off the Zadar road is pleasant, and the views when you get there are better still.

The counterpoint to Nin's culture is its beach, **Kraljičina plaža**, as superb as its panorama of the rippling Velebit mountains opposite. Walk past fishing boats tied to the quay to find a path that goes 2.5km north to one of Dalmatia's few strips of sand. Halfway there, you'll pass an inlet whose black mud has been applied as a skin cleanser and cure-all for everything from rheumatism to female sterility since Roman times. The stronger the stink, the more beneficial is Nin's free fango therapy, say the tourist authorities. Good luck.

East of Zadar

A mixed Serbian-Croat population and the strategic **Maslenica bridge** put Zadar's hinterland at the sharp end of the Homeland War. Already a source of dispute – a bitter 1990 local election between a 60 per cent Serb, 40 per cent Croat population in

Benkovac became a rallying carry for Croat rabble-rousers – the area flew under the Serbian flag as part of the Republic of Serbian Krajina, during which Serbian JNA (Yugoslavia People's Army) troops dynamited the Maslenica bridge in 1992 to sever the last stitch which bound Dalmatia and continental Croatia. Job done, they handed the area to UN peacekeepers, upholding a (theoretical) peace commitment made by Slobodan Milošević. The calm lasted until 1993. Beleaguered Croatian president Franjo Tuđman needed a morale-booster. On 22 January he ordered 6,000 Croatian troops across UN demarcation lines – killing two French soldiers in the process – to establish a pontoon bridge. Battle scars remain in an area where Serb strongholds such as Benkovac crumbled mere hours after the fall in 1995 of symbolic capital Klis (*see* pp.283–4). **Drače**, 6km south of Poličnik, is a ghost town after its Serbian population fled, its houses imploded and roofless, its walls sprayed with shrapnel. An eloquent spokesman for the tragedy of a war, all but invisible on the upbeat coast.

You'll pass it on the drive to **Novigrad**, a dozy fishing village stacked above an S-bend harbour that is quietly reinventing itself as a tiny resort. Guests come to laze on the small beach which fringes lake-like inlet the **Novigrad Sea** (Novigradsko more), to join a summer spree by boat up the **Zrmanja Canyon** river gorge, or to clamber up a staircase to view a panorama of the Velebit mountains from the ruins of a 13th-century hilltop **castle** (*fortica*). Queen Elizabeta of Hungary and Croatia was held and murdered here (1386–7), victim of a nobles' rebellion, and whiled away the long hours during her imprisonment by embroidering a gold vestment for the parish church.

Where to Stay and Eat north and east of Zadar

Nin

Zaton, 2km south of Nin off Zadar road, **t** (023) 280 280, *www.zaton.hr* (€€). The best and worst of the package resort experience – all the facilities and activities you could ask for, all the crowds of a holiday village with modern(ish) apartments among pine woods and near its own beach.

Source private **rooms** in Nin from the tourist information centre and opposite agency **Lotos**, Vila Velebita 2, **t** (023) 265 555, *www.lotos-nin.com*.

Branimir, Trg Višeslavov, **t** (023) 284 866 (€€€–€€). Nin's finest *konoba* is classy-rustic in style, with a terrace which overlooks the Church of the Holy Cross and a menu of top-notch local cuisine. Try a platter of white fish and crab cooked under a *peka*.

Sokol, Hrvatskog sabora, **t** (023) 234 442 (€€). Charcoal-grilled meats served in a courtyard restaurant near the Donji most bridge.

Novigrad

Agava, Elizabete Koromanić bb, **t** (023) 375 255 (€). A peaceful retreat with cosy and modern three-star apartments; book ahead to wake up to views of the Novigrad Sea.

Konoba Pece, Vinjerac bb (15km north of Novigrad), **t** (023) 275 069 (€€). Turn left before the Maslenica bridge to find a village *konoba* acclaimed by some gourmets to be the finest in the Zadar region. The fish is exquisite. *Booking recommended.*

ⓘ **Nin >**
Trg brace Radica 3 (before bridge to old gate), **t** *(023) 265 247, www.nin.hr; open summer Mon–Sat 8–8, Sun 9–12; winter Mon–Fri 8–4*

The Zadar Archipelago

Received wisdom says that Dalmatia's most enchanting islands are southern belles. There's truth there, of course, but, when Hvar, Korčula or Brač are besieged by admirers in summer, the overlooked islands just off Zadar drift at a slower pace. Whether on a quietly bohemian speck such as Silba, daydreaming Iž or Dugi otok, as dramatic as any Adriatic island in the Telašćica bay, these are sleepy islands to get off the beaten path – oases of rural tranquillity where mass tourism has yet to arrive. There's little to tick off on the must-see list, but perhaps that's a reason to visit.

Silba

Ever-pragmatic, the Romans christened Silba for its woods (*silva* in Latin), the Mediterranean black oak which cloak a 15 square km island that is 1½hrs by ferry, but decades in atmosphere, away from Zadar. What **Silba Town** takes from the regional capital is a pinch of bohemia. Occasional art exhibitions and jazz sounds (try Café Mik) give it a reputation as something of an easygoing cosmopolitan.

Quite a change for village formerly known for its sailors. In the 17th century, Silba experienced rapid development as a port on the Zadar–Venice route. Fast-forward a century and parish records name over 200 ship owners, whose 150 captains steered a 20,000-tonnage fleet to a pilot-book of Mediterranean ports. This was Silba's golden age, when the village at the pinched island centre spread to both coasts and was acclaimed, hyperbolically, a 'little Venice'. Austrian steamships took the wind out of Silba's sails – those sailors that didn't jump ship emigrated to the Americas – to leave only mementoes of grand days, captains' **mansions** in the verdant village or the six 17th-century **churches**, all but one abandoned to their fate for lack of restoration funds, the sailors' headstones in their graveyards carved with sailing ships. In better condition near the centre is a **watchtower** (*toreta*) with a spiral staircase that winds around its outside. They say one Captain Marinic built the 30m tower, so his wife could see the sails of his ship as he travelled to neighbouring islands. It is unclear whether she was besotted or suspicious.

Car-free and carefree, Silba is all about doing nothing, usually on the beach. Reached by a seafront path north of the ferry dock, **Tratica** and **Carpusina** offer shingle bays on which to lay your towel. More popular is **Šotorišće**, on the opposite coast with shallow warm waters and a bed of pure sand. Walk 4km (1½hrs) north and you'll reach the rocky **Pernastica bay**, yachtsmen's choice for plopping off side decks into the clear turquoise waters.

Getting to and around the Zadar Archipelago

Silba: one catamaran a day goes from Zadar, a Zadar–Mali Lošinj ferry stops in Silba twice a week (currently Mon and Wed) and one ferry a week (currently Sat) goes from Rijeka.

Ugljan and **Pašman**: hourly ferries from Zadar dock just south of Preko (Ugljan), and approximately hourly ferries go from Biograd to Tkon (Pašman). The pair are linked by a single road; buses are timed to the ferry schedule.

Iž: One car ferry a day from Zadar goes to Bršanj (1km south of Mali Iž) and two ferries a week (currently Fri and Sun) go to Mali Iž and Veli Iž. There are no buses: allow 40mins to walk between the two.

Dugi otok: regular Jadrolinija ferries weave through the archipelago to Brbinj, Sali and Zaglav (car ferries only to Brbinj) and a summer-only Miatours hydrofoil speeds to Božava. A bus meets ferries at Brbinj and trundles north to Božava and Veli Rat; another meets arrivals at either Sali and Zaglav to connect the two villages. Apart from that, only one bus a week links north and south Dugi otok. A single road traces the island's spine, and the only petrol station is at Zaglav, 5km north of Sali.

Ugljan and Pašman

Although an easy cross-channel commute to the office has transformed pockets of **Ugljan** into a mainland suburb, the 52km long sliver that lies 5km off the coast opposite Zadar retains a sleepy air, clad in the luxurious silver coat of its olive (*ulje*) namesake. Two millennia of oil-pressing by Illyrians, Romans and medieval Croatians christened Ugljan, whose first mention in print was the record of an 1106 donation of olive groves to a Zadar monastery.

You won't see many olive trees in **Preko**, a commuter centre literally 'across' or 'on the other side' of Zadar, where a marina opened in 2008 has joined modern houses to blot out the old stone mansions. The most verdant patch hereabouts is 80m offshore (taxi-ferries from harbour) on islet **Galevac** (aka Školjić), where pines and cypress trees as lush as a secret garden hide a 15th-century Franciscan monastery. Back on the main island, an excursion inland from Preko slogs uphill to the **Fortress of St Michael** (Tvrđava sv. Mihovil), a conspicuous shell built as a Venetian stronghold. The views west across the Zadar archipelago are worth the sweat of the 5km return journey – just.

Two kilometres south is **Kali**, which boasts of being home to the finest fishermen in the Zadar region. There were more, too, until two-thirds of the population emigrated to Panama in the late 1940s. Some of those who remain join their colleagues in **Kukljica**, 4km south, for the festivity of Our Lady of the Snow. On 5 August the local fleet chugs behind a statue of the Virgin bound for a small chapel to commemorate a miraculous snowfall in high summer four centuries earlier. Sheltered in a natural harbour, the hamlet serves as a hub for low-key tourism. Escape – if you need it – can be found on a network of paths which idle through a thick fuzz of pines; the best are a 15-minute stroll west: **Sabuša beach**, or the shallow waters of **Kostanj**.

Buses from Ugljan go south across a road bridge, past tiny Ždrelac, to **Pašman**, Ugljan's sleepy sister island, with its main city, also called Pašman, set on a pretty bay. If views out to the islet of **Babac** to accompany coffee don't suffice, walk 1km north to a shallow bay beyond pines for a dip. Sandy coves are to be found 2km south in hamlet **Kraj**, whose **Franciscan monastery** (Franjevački samostan) has an elegant – though rarely open – Renaissance cloister. However, the island's ecclesiastical star is the hilltop **Benedictine monastery of SS Cosmas and Damien**, near **Tkon** 3km south, a Gothic rebuild of an 1125 original built after the sack of Biograd on the mainland opposite (*see* p.247), whose treasure is a blood-red 14th-century crucifix.

Benedictine monastery of SS Cosmas and Damien
Sv. Kuzma i Damjan; opening times erratic; consult tourist information in Pašman

Iž

Snug between Zadar archipelago giants Ugljan and Dugi otok, Iž is an island for escapists. A handful of holidaymakers venture here in July and August, briefly rousing the 17.5 square km speck, but largely it slumbers beneath a thick blanket of Aleppo pine, figs and *maquis*, sustained by the simple things God provides – fish, and a herbal *rakija* locals swear is good for the heart. With no cultural boxes to nag the conscience, Iž is an island to indulge in simple pleasures – a stroll, a swim, an hour lost gazing over a bay.

Car ferries arrive in the bay of Bršanj, 1km south of **Mali Iž**, a handful of houses scattered in a cleft before the harbour. The 'big' to its 'little' is **Veli Iž** 4km north, the default capital of 470 villagers, gathered around a narrow harbour. On its far side, the small gallery-workshop **Iška keramika** displays pots and bowls which local Illyrians of two millennia earlier would recognize. In bygone days, Iž was renowned for terracotta wares hawked by local families around the markets of the Zadar region. The story goes that villagers dumped unsold pots rather than be branded poor tradesmen. Small wonder the trade has died out.

Iška keramika
behind the ferry dock; open summer Mon, Wed and Fri 10–12 and 7–9; adm

Most visitors top up their tans on a concrete platform in front of the hotel Korinjak, but far nicer is the bay of **Drage**. To get there, follow a seashore footpath from the hotel to locate the tiny harbour with clear waters and ample space to lay a towel. En route, diving outfit **Nauticus** rents snorkelling equipment. Locals prefer the gin-clear shores of pine-covered islet **Ratnjak**, 1km off Veli Iž; Nauticus runs occasional morning boats. Alternatively, you can take to a path from Drage through abandoned olive plantations to find a private cove on the island's north tip. On the way you pass the island's high-point, **Korinjak**.

Nauticus
mobile **t** *098 774 925*

Dugi Otok

A sliver of land 43km long, never more than 4.6km wide and coated in a thick fuzz of scrubby pine, 'Long Island' seems to have drifted through the centuries untrammelled by the events which raged on the mainland. Without freshwater springs, civilization – from Romans to Zadar Venetians fleeing Turkish raiders – established little more than a fingerhold on the largest island of the Zadar archipelago; indeed, its modern worry is depopulation. And, while Zadar's residents were sheltering underground from the hail of Serbian shells in 1991, Dugi otok's 1,800 inhabitants busied themselves with the Mediterranean mainstays of fishing, sheep-farming and vineyards. Even tourism, wooed in Zadar since the late 1800s, is a newcomer – and that, alongside the wild Telašćica Nature Park, is reason enough to visit.

Nearly half of Dugi otok's population call the main port of **Sali** home, but don't let that put you off, because this is a quietly handsome Mediterranean harbour which slumbers in the afternoon sunshine until the evening cool encourages a gentle *korzo* (stroll). The medieval salt pans which christened the island's largest village fell in importance compared with fishing, and in summer some Sali locals pause from their nets to catch tourists keen to embark on a spree to the neighbouring moonscape of the Kornati National Park to the south (*see* pp.248–9).

Most boats also wiggle through islets before the Kornati to the **Telašćica Nature Park** (Park prirode Telašćicz), but you can also reach this pristine 8km inlet scattered with islets by simply walking 3km south of Sali through olive groves (signposted before Sali if driving). Arrive by car and for once there's no need to explore off-track, because the views are sensational – the road wraps around the bay's east end, then cuts across to vertiginous cliffs on the park's wild south shore; their vantage point, up to 190m high and 10km long, offers spectacular views of an Adriatic speckled by sails. A number of nearby bays tempt you to pause for a dip; alternatively, the **Jezero Mir** lake rewards those who explore further southeast. Even if you refuse to believe the local tales about the salt water's curative properties, the lake is definitely a few degrees warmer than the bay.

In the northern half of Dugi otok, from **Brbinj**, just a dock and lone restaurant-*pension*, the island's only road idles north past hilltop village **Dragove**, which shimmers in the heat haze like a watercolour of terracottas and greens, to the fishing village of **Božava**, whose stone houses huddle around a pretty harbour lined with seasonal *konobe* and cafés. Beyond it, a path rambles around a rocky, pine-cloaked headland to swimming spots off rocks.

The best beach on Dugi otok, however, is **Sakarun**, a double-bill of aromatic pines behind and spectacular views down the island's rugged spine in front. Its fine-shingle crescent is signposted northwest of Božava on the road towards the village of **Veli Rat**. Continue northwest and the road peters out at an 1849 Austro-

Hungarian **lighthouse**, whose bricks were mortared with 100,000 egg yolks (and a considerable dollop of faith) and which overlooks a handful of notches for a dip.

ⓘ Dugi Otok >>
harbour, Sali, **t** *(023) 377 094; open May–Oct daily 8–12 and 5–8; Nov–April Mon–Fri 8–2. Also Božava,* **t** *(023) 377 607; open June–Sept daily 8–12 and 6–8*

ⓘ Silba >
office in village school, **t** *(023) 370 010, www.silba.net; open July–Aug Mon–Sat 7–12, Sun 8–11*

ⓘ Ugljan >
harbourfront, Preko, **t** *(023) 286 108, www.ugljan.hr; open July–Aug daily 8–1 and 3–9; June and Sept Mon–Sat 8–1 and 6–8; Oct–May Mon–Sat 8–2; there is also an office in Kukljica,* **t** *(023) 373 276, www.kukljica.hr; opening hours as Preko*

ⓘ Pašman >
seafront, **t** *(023) 260 155; open July–Aug daily 8–8*

ⓘ Iž >
on Veli Iž harbour, no tel; open July–Aug Mon–Sat 7–1 and 7–9, Sun 8–12; other times in summer erratic

Festivals in the Zadar Archipelago

All **Iž** turns out in traditional garb to sing folk songs and dance traditional steps for the **Feast of Iž** on July 29, which climaxes in the election of a 'village king' who rules for a year.

Sali, on **Dugi otok**, lets rip during the three-day romp **Saljski užanci**, held over the 1st or 2nd weekend in Aug. Expect all the usual japes: costumed parades, weird folk music played on animal horn trumpets, donkey races and crates of wine and *rakija*.

Where to Stay in the Zadar Archipelago

Silba

All the beds in Silba are in **private accommodation**. Arrange yours before arrival through tourist information or online at *www.silba.net*. Also through tourist agencies in Zadar.

Ugljan and Pašman

Bar two heart-sinking Yugoslavian relics, all the accommodation is in **private houses** (€): contact tourist information centres or ask at private agencies in each village. **Val Tours** in Biograd (*see* p.249) books isolated 'Robinson' cottages on Pašman.

Preko, Preko harbour, Ugljan, **t** (023) 286 041 (€). Basic and drab two-star, which gets the nod only for harbourside accommodation.

Zelena punta, Kukljica, Ugljan, **t** (023) 373 319, *www.coning-turizam.hr* (€). More drabness, this a tourist village whose Yugoslavia vintage shows in dated décor. It has a decent restaurant, though.

Iž

Hotel Korinjak, Veli Iž, **t** (023) 277 064, *www.korinjak.hr* (€). Vegetarian cuisine and New Age therapy of meditation and massages in the island's only hotel, bizarrely reinvented as a holistic centre. Compensation, perhaps, for the tatty en-suite rooms which are frayed at the edges.

Dugi Otok

Both tourist offices can advise about **rooms** (€) in private houses – true escapists should investigate daydreaming villages such as Dragove or Luka.

Sali, Sali, **t** (023) 377 049, *www.hotel-sali.hr* (€€). Air-conditioning, fridges and balcony views over a quiet bay come as standard in the 52 modest but comfy en-suite rooms of this hotel 5mins' walk from the harbour. *Closed Nov–April.*

Agava, Božava, **t** (023) 291 291, *www.hoteli-bozava.hr* (€). Standard package fare in a complex of hotels screened by pine woods by the harbour; adequate but unspectacular. *Closed Nov–April.*

Eating Out in the Zadar Archipelago

Silba

Žalić, **t** (023) 370 138 (€€). A cheerful *konoba* with bench seating in the shady courtyard of a seafront captain's mansion and a taste for everything from Dalmatian dishes to pizzas. Fresh catch of the day, spit-roast lamb and *peka* dishes are the pick.

Ugljan

Barba Tome, Kukljica bb, **t** (023) 373 323 (€€). Fresh fish, steaks sizzled over charcoal and the usual seafood risottos and pastas rustled up in a chirpy modern restaurant on the harbour.

Stari mlin, Kukljica bb, **t** (023) 373 304 (€€). Similar menu, but the atmosphere harks back a century in a snug stone dining room with a canopy of fishing nets.

Iž

Mandrač, harbour front, Veli Iž, **t** (023) 277 115 (€€). The locals' choice for a celebratory dinner is this snug *konoba* near the church, with a menu of whatever was caught the night before, grilled over charcoal.

No name, Mali Iž, no tel (€). Basic but bags of atmosphere, with dining on a terrace hung with fishing nets and a small menu of whatever fish the owner has in stock. A lovely spot to wait for your ferry.

Dugi Otok

Boxavia, Božava, **t** (023) 377 614 (€€). Simple bench seating and prime views over the harbour to accompany a house-special fish platter and tasty seafood delights, from simple grilled squid to rich *škampi na buzara*.

Kod Sipe, Sali, **t** (023) 377 137 (€€). *Hobotnica ispod peke* (octopus baked under a *peka*) is a chef's speciality in this lovely *konoba*; locate the stairs which ascend off the harbourside to find its cosy wood interior where locals put the world to rights, or the spacious alfresco dining area.

Marin, Sali, **t** (023) 377 500 (€€). This charming back-street *konoba* just off the harbour end prepares a small menu of tasty grilled meats, served in a snug dining room hung with nets or on a small terrace.

South from Zadar

Biograd na Moru

The royal seat of 11th-century ruler King Petar Krešimir IV and the coronation capital of Hungarian-Croat monarchs after 1102, Biograd na Moru should be a more interesting place. Its fate was to peak too early. As Biograd found its stride, the then queen of the Adriatic, Venice, took decisive action against a rival. In 1125 its warships razed Biograd to the ground, and it has never really recovered. The few citizens who slunk back from offshore islands and nearby Šibenik after the Venetian sacking suffered jangled nerves in this 15th-century outpost on the Venetian–Turkish frontier, then destroyed Biograd themselves in the mid-1600s rather than see it fall into Ottoman hands.

Robbed of architectural charm, Biograd has reinvented itself as a package tourism destination whose joy is its waterfront setting. Scraps of the past are on show in a seafront **town museum** on the seafront, whose curators rush you upstairs to view the cargo salvaged from a late 16th-century Venetian caravel. Although the bale of moss-coloured damask, the brass chandelier from Lübeck, Germany, and the etched glass goblets speak of Renaissance high living, more fascinating are the minutiae of daily life: scales with tiny weights, brass bells to dress waistcoats, packets of rusty cut-throat razors and leather-rimmed *pince-nez*.

Town museum
Zavičajni muzej; Krešimirova obala 22; open June–Sept Mon–Sat 9–12 and 8–10; Oct–May Mon–Sat 7–12; adm

For a swim, follow the seafront promenade south to pine-fringed **Soline beach**, whose sandy bed compensates for noisy bars and crowds. More towel space can be found on a shingle beach 3km north before **Sveti Filip i Jakov**.

Otherwise, Biograd is a place to depart from. Tourist agencies offer boat trips to Telašćica Bay and the 160m-high white cliffs of

Getting around south of Zadar

Hourly Zadar–Šibenik buses stop at all destinations on the Magistrala (E65/B8) coast road. **Murter** is linked by buses to Šibenik every 90mins and to Zadar twice a day.

Tourist agencies in Murter Town, Biograd, Zadar and Sali (Dugi otok) operate day trips (*c.* 250Kn), which include lunch, wine and the 50Kn entry into **Kornati National Park**.

Dugi otok (*see* p.244), usually misnamed as tours of the Kornati Islands. Granted, the trips afford glimpses south at the Kornatis' chain-like pumice stones but, at the time of writing, only agency Leut (*see* p.249) also zips around the back of the Kornati archipelago itself.

South of Biograd to Murter

The Magistrala road will take you 6km south of Biograd to **Pakoštane**, a quiet holiday resort with a beach, and also to **Lake Vransko** (Vransko jezero). Spoonbills, herons and ibis stalk the whispering reeds of Croatia's largest lake, 13km long and 3.5km at its widest, protected as a **nature park** (Park prirode Vransko jezero) and circled by a 30km cycle path; maps are available from the **park office** in Biograd. Follow the path to the northeast corner of the lake and you reach **Vrana**, doomed to sit on the front line of Croatia's battles – with the Ottoman Turks in 1537, who established a caravanserai, and with Serbian paramilitaries in 1992 – when all the villagers want is to be left in peace with their fields drained from swamps by Venetian expertise.

Park office
Kralja P. Svačica 2, above market at crossroads; ***t*** *(023) 383 181; open Mon–Fri 8–4*

Turn right off the Magistrala just beyond the lake's end and the B121 hops from the mainland to the island of **Murter**. Its main town, **Murter Town**, is the launchpad for trips to the Kornati National Park – long before you arrive, agency boards tout their day trips and 'Robinson' cottages (*see* below). The only reason to linger is **Slanica bay**, a pine-cloaked notch in the coast whose sandy bottom gives it that seductive tourist-brochure turquoise. You'll find it packed with the guests of an adjacent hotel southwest of the centre (also signposted off main road). **Čigrada**, further around the headland, lacks the shingle beach – swimming is off rocks – but also the crowds.

Kornati National Park

On the last day of the Creation, God desired to crown His work and thus created the Kornati islands out of tears, stars and breath.
George Bernard Shaw

Even if Shaw was being a mite hyperbolic (*see* left), few Croatian landscapes compare with the archipelago southeast of Zadar. Modernity is just a rumour on the islands scattered in a turquoise sea like oversized pumice stones. The reason for their popularity is, paradoxically, because of what there is not – trees. This is landscape as minimalism, reflective and serene. The islands were stripped of vegetation after Venetian aristocrats permitted shepherds from island Murter to fell their Mediterranean oak and pine to create pasture, today revealed by dry stone wall circles which crumble unused. Parched without freshwater streams, scoured by sheep, the islands withered.

The Venetians shrugged and handed over 90 per cent ownership to the Murterini, some of whom continue to eke out a living in summer grazing sheep, keeping bees and cultivating olives, figs and grapes. Many, however, have reinvented their 300 cottages which shelter in coves as so-called 'Robinson' (i.e. Robinson Crusoe) retreats, where stressed-out city-slickers potter around a humble stone house which lacks electricity and running water. Murter Town agencies offer the widest choice for week-long bookings, which usually start on Saturday. For €500 a week, you are shuttled by boat to your cottage, perhaps with a canoe to paddle, then left in solitude, your peace disturbed only twice a week to receive food supplies and gas for a stove and fridge. The **tourist office** can advise on agencies approved by the Kornati National Park: **Coronata**, **Kornatturist**, and **Atlas** all had the seal of approval in summer 2008. Nor is it only escapists who visit. The islands' astoundingly clear waters have seen them morph into one of Croatia's premier yachting destinations. For the first time in centuries their population is expanding as summer restaurants appear. Most day-trip captains loop around the back of the archipelago to show off the Kornati (literally, 'crowns'), 90m-high sheer cliffs which reared out of the sea after Africa bumped into Europe and tore a rift which begins in Istria and stretches somewhere into Middle Dalmatia. Bring your binoculars: peregrine falcons, shags and swifts perch on the crags.

ⓘ **Kornati National Park >**
Butina 3, **t** *(022) 435 740, www.kornati.hr; open summer daily 8–10; shoulder months daily 8–12 and 5–8; winter Mon–Fri 8–3*

Coronata
Žrtava ratova 17, **t** *(022) 435 089, www.coronata.hr*

Kornatturist
Hrvatskih vladara 2, **t** *(022) 435 855, www.kornatturist.hr*

Atlas
Hrvatskih vladara 8, **t** *(022) 434 999, www.atlas.hr*

Where to Stay and Eat south of Zadar

Biograd na moru

Adriatic, Tina Ujevića 7, **t** (023) 383 062, *www.ilirijabiograd.com* (€€). The only package hotel open year-round in Biograd, moments from the centre, now promotes itself as a style hotel. Its garden Lavender Bed Bar begs for a sundowner cocktail.

Source private **rooms** at **Leut**, Trg kralja Tomislava 2, **t** (023) 385 570, *www.leut.hr*, and **Val Tours**, Trg hrvatskih velikana 1, **t** (023) 386 479, *www.val-tours.hr*. Val Tours also books so-called 'Robinson' cottages in the isolated bays of Pašman and Žižanj, a speck at its toe of barely 1km square.

Fjaka, Bana J. Jelačića bb (off Kraljice Jelene), **t** (023) 384 366 (€€). Try a seafood special of octopus and shrimps slow-baked under a *peka* or fresh fish and steaks sizzled on a charcoal grill in a courtyard. One of the most pleasant spots for a lazy dinner.

Murter

Colentum, Put Slanice bb, **t** (023) 431 111, *www.hotel-colentum.hr* (€€). Try to ignore the uninspired package hotel style, and focus instead on the location of this three-star hotel on Slanica bay.

Tourist agencies find private **rooms**: *see* main text above.

Tic-Tac, Hrokešina 5, **t** (023) 435 230 (€€€–€€). A reassuringly old-fashioned restaurant behind the harbour and the locals' choice for posh nosh. Less is more on a menu that's strong on fish: monkfish tail in wine, anchovies on a bed of rocket and octopus with olive oil and coarse sea salt.

ⓘ **Biograd >**
Trg hrvatskih velikana 2 (courtyard behind main crossroads), **t** *(023) 383 123, www.tzg-biograd.hr; open summer Mon–Sat 8–12 and 4–8, Sun 8–12; winter Mon–Fri 8–2*

ⓘ **Murter Town >>**
Trg Rudina bb, **t** *(022) 434 995, www.tzo-murter.hr; open summer Mon–Fri 8–1 and 6–8, Sat 8–1; winter Mon–Fri 8–3*

Šibenik

On a coastline of Greek and Roman heritage, the Šibenik tourist authorities set their town apart as a Croatian thoroughbred founded some time in the 9th century. It was always thus. About 300 years after the settlement's birth, King Petar Krešimir IV founded a seat in Šibenik, an exercise in point-scoring to cock a snook at the more powerful rivals with Roman roots such as Zadar and Split.

All of Šibenik's gems are from its four centuries under Italian rule as property of La Serenissima. For a start, there are the late Gothic and Renaissance residences of former patricians, whose finely turned balustrades or coats of arms on the lintels show their class in a mazy warren of streets to explore. And there's the main reason to visit, which, fortunately for an industrial town which all but smothers its historic kernel, is a good one: the UNESCO-listed St James's Cathedral.

St James's Cathedral (Katedrala svetog Jakova)

St James's Cathedral
Katedrala svetog Jakova; Trg Republike Hrvatske; open daily 8.30–7

The Venetians instigated the building of the cathedral in 1402; it stalled almost immediately for want of funds but established a Gothic core enlivened with Italian gusto, at its liveliest around the **main portal**. Gloomy apostles glower from within an arch of twisted columns. Before you enter, look, too, at the **north portal**, with a pair of lions and a shamefaced Adam and Eve.

In 1441, bursting with ambition instilled by a new cash donation, the city fathers proclaimed Gothic passé, appointed Venice-trained architect **Juraj Dalmatinac**. Šibenik's ecclesiastical showpiece now inched into the skyline in Renaissance. Still there were problems. A lack of funds meant progress inched at snail's pace and forced Dalmatinac to seek a crust elsewhere on the coast – here chiselling an altar for Split's cathedral, there mapping out a new town for Pag, to become the country's most revered Renaissance architect.

The Croatian architect's superb **nave** tells the building's story as well as anything else: lower Gothic arches give way to Renaissance proportions that power to a high barrel-vault **roof**, nowhere more spectacular than at a crossing crowned by a cupola. Christopher Wren used to preach that 'nothing can add beauty to light' – Dalmatinac's Renaissance cap, flooded with sunshine like a revelation, suggests he was on to something. But if the cathedral body inspires the awe, it's his intimate **baptistry** to the right of the altar that is his enchanting masterpiece, a grotto-like nook whose low roof carved with angels and a furiously bearded Creator is caught between Gothic and Renaissance.

Like all great artists, Dalmatinac signed his work – outside on the north side a pair of plump cherubs hold a dedicatory text with the

Getting to and around Šibenik

A side track snakes off the main **train** line to link Šibenik to Split (change in Perković, 4 per day) and Zagreb (daily) via Knin. The train station is 1km southeast of the centre on Milete.

All north–south **buses** along the coast stop in Šibenik. Long-distance links north include: Zagreb (hourly), Pula (3 per day), Rijeka (hourly), Zadar (approx hourly), Split (hourly) and Dubrovnik (10 per day). Key local bus services link to: Murter (8 per day), Vodice (hourly), Skradin (6 per day) and Primošten (6 per day). The main bus station is 400m south of the centre off seafront Obala Hrvatske mornarice.

Ferries link Šibenik to destinations of the Šibenik archipelago (*see* pp.253–4).

---

legend '*Hoc opus cuvarum fecit magister Georgius Mathei Dalmaticus*'. He never saw his creation in its full glory – it was left to his Italian pupil **Nikola Firentinac** to mount the Florentine cupola and wow contemporary architects with his master's stone roof of tongue-and-groove slabs slotted together like parquet. However, Dalmatinac must have chuckled when he completed the 71 carved heads that wrap around the exterior of the three apses near his dedication. Hearsay says the portraits are of Šibenik locals who refused to stump up a donation for the cathedral – and none-too-flattering character studies they are, too.

Around the Town

The rest of Šibenik's is an under-rated proposition. If it's often overlooked, it's perhaps because the old town is not prettified for tourism, rather a lived-in streetscape where only carved portals and heraldic plaques suggest past glory. Pick up the details and there's much to enjoy. Dalmatinac as imagined by Ivan Meštrović stands on a plinth in Trg Republike Hrvatske outside the cathedral, one Croatian artistic giant saluting another at the heart of public life. Nearby, the square's Venetian **loggia** serves as restaurant (*see* 'Eating Out') while just off it, the **City Museum** is due to reopen in 2009 following a revamp of what was a fairly weary assortment of prehistoric scraps and early medieval finds showcased in an 15th-century palace of the Venetian rector behind the cathedral.

City Museum
*Muzej grada; **t** (023) 213 880, www.muzej-sibenik.hr; open summer Mon–Fri 10–1 and 7–9, Sat 10–1; adm*

More lovable is the church-gallery of **St Barbara**, just south of Trg Republike Hrvatske, down Kralja Tomislava. The showpiece of the four-century *œuvre* of religious art is a polyptych of the Madonna and (grumpy) Child by Blaž Jurjev Trogiranin, a master of the 15th century who imported Italian ideals of beauty across the Adriatic but could never quite overcome his weakness for willowy Byzantine figures with almond eyes.

St Barbara
Crkva svete Barbare; open summer Mon–Fri 9.30–12 and 6–8; adm

Cut uphill a block and you arrive on former medieval market **Krešimirov trg**. Rings which supported sailcloth shades donated by docked ships – by town dictate not ship captains' philanthropy – remain embedded in the **Church of St John** (Crkva sv. Ivana), a monastic church of an Order which excused its extravagance as a celebration of their saint. The brothers commissioned the cathedral's Nikola Firentinac to sculpt its fine Renaissance balustrade. Look, too, at a charming relief of the good friars humbled before their patron in a landscape of castles and galleons. The church's other claim to fame is for the first mechanical public clock in Šibenik (1648).

You'll need to return north, past **St Chrysogonus's Church**, a part-time gallery, to pick up street Sv. Luce heading off to the right. Following steps up, you'll ascend above the Old Town where it meets Strme Stube to reach the **Medieval Mediterranean Garden** of St Lawrence's Monastery. The recreation by one of Croatia's best landscape gardeners is designed as a cross and planted with fruit trees and medicinal herbs. It's worth a visit for its café – one of the most peaceful locations in town for a quiet drink. From here it's only a short haul up to the top of the hill for **St Anne's Fortress**, constructed by Venetians on the hill where Šibenik made its Byzantine debut, from where you receive a panorama over a roof-scape of rippling terracotta, the cathedral's barrel roof like a capsized hull below, to a bay scattered with islands.

Medieval Mediterranean Garden
open daily 8–7

St Anne's Fortress
Tvrđava sv. Ane; open daily 8–dusk; adm

ⓘ Šibenik >
*Obala dr Franje Tuđmana 5 (waterfront), **t** (022) 214 411/448, www.sibenik-tourism.hr; open June–Aug daily 8–8; May and Sept–Oct Mon–Fri 8–8, Sat–Sun 8–2; Nov–Apr daily 8–12*

ⓘ Šibenik region >
*Fausta Vrančića 18 (behind town office), **t** (022) 212 075; open Mon–Fri 7.30–3*

Where to Stay in and around Šibenik

There's just one hotel in Šibenik – local alternatives are in Vodice, Brodarica and islands Zlarin and Prvić.

Jadran, Obala dr Franje Tuđmana 52, **t** (022) 212 644, *www.rivijera.hr* (€€). A monopoly on accommodation means Šibenik's hotel is nothing special – two-star rooms are bland in décor and modest in size. A missed opportunity for a great waterfront location moments from the cathedral.

Solaris Resort, 5km south, **t** (022) 361 001, *www.solaris.hr* (€€). Four-star rooms in the renovated Ivan hotel are the pick of a gargantuan resort village on the beach with five package-holiday hotels.

Panorama, Šibenik bridge 3km north, **t** (022) 213 398, *www.hotel-panorama.hr* (€€). Adequate rather than admirable en-suite rooms by the bridge towards Vodice.

Book **private rooms** (most in neighbouring villages) from **Atlas**, Trg Republike Hrvatske 2, **t** (022) 330 232, *www.atlassibenik.com*.

Eating Out in and around Šibenik

Pelegrin, Jurja Dalmatinca 1, **t** (022) 213 701 (€€€–€€). New in 2007 and very classy, this place facing the cathedral is an effortless marriage of interior design and traditional charm. The menu similarly brings gourmet twists to traditional Dalmatian cooking, while tapas-style plates are made to graze. Vies with the Vijećnica for the title of the best wine list in town.

Uzorita, Bana Jelačića 50, **t** (022) 213 660 (€€€–€€). A rustic-styled place of late 1800s vintage 20mins' walk northeast of the centre, famous for *hobotnica ispod peke* (octopus slow-baked under a *peka*) and seafood.

Vijećnica, Trg Republike Hrvatske 1, **t** (022) 213 605 (€€€–€€). Semi-smart and just the right side of expensive, the restaurant in the Venetian town hall opposite the cathedral prepares grilled fish and seafood, plus cheaper pastas and risottos, and has tables beneath the town loggia.

Kanela, Obala dr Franje Tuđmana, **t** (022) 214 986 (€€). All the usuals in a laid-back *konoba*, the best choice on the waterfront.

Entertainment and Nightlife in Šibenik

Classical music concerts are staged in the **cathedral** in summer months; ask at the tourist office (or private agencies) about events in **St Nicholas Fortress** – concert-goers are shuttled to the Venetians' gun battery by boat.

One of Croatia's hippest nightclubs, **Hacienda**, is 8km west, near Vodice (*see* p.255).

The Šibenik Riviera

Vodice and Tribunj

After decades of promoting itself as the premier resort in central Dalmatia, **Vodice** has more or less destroyed itself. Gorged on package tourism, the fortified Venetian town which once supplied drinking water (*voda*) has bulked out into a Croatian *costa* resort, whose tacky *konobe* and souvenir shops crowd out the Baroque **Church of the Holy Cross** (Crkva sv. Križa). It can't even boast a good beach – sizzling holidaymakers jostle for space on concrete platforms that front the hotels on the headland right of the seafront. What Vodice does have is beds (and by the thousand), plus good ferry links to Šibenik and islands Prvić and Zlarin.

Tribunj, 3km west of Vodice, is no stranger to tourism either, but the difference is like night and day. The antidote to plastic tourism, its diminutive kernel on an islet linked by a stone bridge has ramshackle houses and old-world charm in spades, although a flashy new marina suggests change may be on its way. When you've tired of its lanes you can sit with a drink beside a couple of waterfront bars sunset-side or ascend behind the Old Town to the parish church of **St Nicholas**. Views north to the Kornati Islands (*see* p.249) are spectacular at sunset; those over Tribunj's roofs packed tight like a model are impressive at any time. For a swim, pine-clad bay **Sovlje** lies 1km west.

Prvić and Zlarin

It seems appropriate that the sort of jaunty ferry usually seen only in black and white films plies the route to Prvić and Zlarin, because these, the closest islands to Šibenik and Vodice, drift in some temporal back-eddy decades behind their near-neighbours – soporific and all the better for it. They also boast the best beaches in the area.

Embark at Šibenik and the ferry thrums out between the cliffs of the St Anthony Canal to the **St Nicholas Fortress**. Nervous of a Turkish pincer movement from Skradin inland, the Venetians built the most arresting gun battery in Croatia, a 16th-century triangular to guard Šibenik sea approaches which immediately proved its worth in the Ottoman Cyprus War (1570–73) and Candia War (1645–69).

Getting to and around the Šibenik Riviera

Ferries which shuttle from Šibenik to **Vodice** call at **Zlarin**, **Prvić Luka** and **Šepurine** (5 per day Mon–Sat summer). You could also reach **Prvić** by small motorboats for hire from Vodice harbour (*c.* 400Kn per day).

Hourly buses link Šibenik to Vodice.

Hire bicycles from Vodice tourist agency **Homberger**, Trg kneza Branimira 32, **t** (022) 444 109.

ⓘ **Zlarin**
*on harbour, **t** (022) 553 557; open July–Aug daily 9–12 and 6–9*

Museum of amphorae and ethnology
open summer daily 9–12 and 6–9

Although it is the most developed of the islands, **Zlarin**, 15 minutes out, is refreshingly low-key after Šibenik or Vodice. Visitors idle on the quay either side of the bay – a small pebble beach lies 10 minutes' walk north of the harbour – or browse the boutiques for jewellery crafted of Zlarin coral, a local trade which peaked in the 19th century as souvenirs for Austrians. **Centar Zlarinka** has a small **museum of amphorae and ethnology** to lure you to its workshop; nearby *atelier* **Viktor** makes no such pretence. Both are found at the back of the village.

Public records vouch that the 2.4 square km island of **Prvić** suffered overcrowding in the 15th century as the mainlanders found themselves at the sharp end of Turkish incursions. It's hard to believe today in erstwhile capital **Prvić Luka**, another 15 minutes by ferry beyond Zlarin. Atrophied by emigration – first in the late 19th century after its vineyards were struck by phylloxera, a blow for a producer of wines exported to France, Austria and the Vatican, then in the 1960s – it is dozy and quiet, a treat of escapist tourism with the most stylish small hotel in the region. If you time your visit to coincide with Mass in the parish church of **Our Lady of Mercy**, you can also pay homage at the **tomb of Faust Vrančić** (1551–1617), local son, lexicographer and general egghead (*see* box, below).

The island's single lane leads 1km through olives and cypress spears to **Šepurine**. The penultimate port before Vodice – or first depending on your direction – is as idyllic a fishing village as you could wish for, lived-in and comfy like an old shoe. Wooden boats nod in the harbour before a flagstaff pillar, swiped, they say, from Roman Salona near Split (*see* pp.282–3), and it's only the swallows

Faust Vrančić

In 1595 this Renaissance Man's Renaissance Man not only published a 25,000-word lexicon of Latin, Italian, German, Croatian and Hungarian, but he also produced a tome of over 50 mechanical contraptions, inspired by Leonardo da Vinci. European science marvelled at his *Machinae Novae*, its pages full of ingenious bridges, windmills with twisted blades like propellors, a tide-powered mill, and the pope was so impressed that he hired Vrančić to solve once and for all the problem of the Tiber floodwaters which bedevilled Rome. Like his hero, Vrančić dreamed of a *Homo volans* descending beneath a square-sail parachute. Unlike Leonardo, he trialled his design in Venice in 1617. It's unclear whether his death that year is related, but he is surely the only Renaissance polymath in Croatia honoured with a mural in his birthplace.

that chatter in the streets of shuttered houses behind the church of **St Roko**. There's a good **beach**, too, 100m before the ferry quay, its shingle fine enough for sandcastles.

Festivals on the Šibenik Riviera

On the first weekend in Aug, up to 15,000 spectators gather in **Tribunj** to celebrate Croatia's indigenous donkey, culminating on Sun in the **Trka tovara**, a rowdy donkey race around the village. Locals say their nearby donkey reserve was the world's first, but won't be drawn on whether it doubles as a race-donkey stable.

Prvić Luka >> *main street near supermarket, **t** (022) 448 083; open summer Mon–Sat 12–2 and 6.30–9, Sun 9–12*

Vodice > *Ive Čače 1a (one block west of the park), **t** (022) 443 888, www.vodice.hr; open June–mid-Sept Mon–Fri 8–10, Sat 8–8, Sun 9–7; mid-Sept–April Mon–Fri 8–3, Sat 8–1*

Tribunj > *Badnje bb (far side of islet bridge), **t** (022) 446 143; open July–Aug Mon–Sat 8–1 and 6–9, Sun 8–12; April–June and Sept–Nov Mon–Fri 8–2, Sat 8–12; winter times erratic*

Where to Stay and Eat on the Šibenik Riviera

Šibenik agencies and tourist information centres co-ordinate private accommodation in locations other than Vodice.

Vodice

Olympia, Ljudevita Gaja bb, **t** (022) 452 452, *www.olympiavodice.hr* (€€). At the upper end of moderate, justified by a recent upgrade to get a fourth star. Nevertheless, you're likely to find a bed in this seafront behemoth is the best of the package hotels. A quiet location adds to its appeal.

Source private **rooms** in Vodice from tourist agency **Nik**, Artina bb (harbour), **t** (022) 441 730.

Adria, Obala Matice Hrvatske, **t** (022) 441 543 (€€€–€€). The finest fish in town, say locals, served on the harbour front.

Santa Maria, Pamuković Kamila 9, **t** (022) 443 319 (€€). Just as you write off Vodice, there's this funky Croat-Mex restaurant, colourful, cluttered and defiantly idiosyncratic; a terrace opposite is more restrained.

Tribunj

Movie Resort, Jurjevgradska 49, **t** (022) 446 331, *www.themovieresort.com* (€€). Thankfully, the 28 rooms in this three-star are themed by name not modern décor style. A beach bar makes a stab at the Caribbean.

Luna, Podvrh 3, **t** (022) 446 359 (€€€–€€). Tribunj is renowned for the best seafood in the region – sample it in this swish modern restaurant near the town bridge. Chef asserts that his *brodet* is something special.

Roko, Težačka 16, no tel (€). A short menu of fish snacks – *rižoto od škampi* (scampi risotto) and *hobotnica na salatu* (octopus salad), plus fried catch of the day – and the best terrace in town, perched on the Old Town waterfront.

Prvić

Maestral, Prvić Luka, **t** (022) 448 300, *www.hotelmaestral.com* (€€). Rustic minimalism – bare stone walls, Japanese-style beds and mahogany parquet floors – in the best small hotel in the region, perfect for a bout of stylish escapism. *Booking recommended.*

Ribarski dvor, Šepurine (by beach), **t** (022) 448 511 (€€€–€€). A few tables inches from the sea and a terrace slung with vines are a lovely setting for a highly rated seafood joint. Catch of the day, plus *škampi* (shrimp) or *jastog* (lobster) *buzara* are worth investigating.

Val, Prvić Luka, **t** (022) 448 300 (€€). A 'Dalmatina' plate of *pršut* ham, domestic cheeses, salted sardines and olives is ideal for a light lunch, plus there are *peka*-cooked lamb and veal specials and interesting fish dishes on the terrace of the Maestral hotel.

Entertainment on the Šibenik Riviera

Hacienda, 2km east of Vodice, *www.hacienda.hr*. Up to 2,000 clubbers in summer party in one of Croatia's most stylish venues. Expect Ibiza-style deep and twisted house tunes, spun by Croatian names or passing international DJs. What's-on details from flyers in tourist information or on the website.

North of Šibenik

Krka National Park

Krka National Park
Nacionalni park Krka; open daily; June–Sept 95Kn; Mar–May and Sept 80Kn; Nov–Feb 30Kn

About 4km northeast of Knin, the Krka river emerges as a modest brook from a cave in the foothills of the Dinara mountains near Bosnia. By the time it processes out into an estuary near Šibenik 73km southeast, it has carved limestone gorges, idled in lakes and burbled over a waterfall featured in every national tourist board brochure. Fame means popularity, of course, and the lower regions of the 190 square km riverscape protected as the Krka National Park can be elbow room only in early August. No matter – this is a place seemingly tailor-made for loafing. Put aside an extra day or two if you want to explore the remote upper gorges.

National Park tour boats
daily Mar–Oct; included in ticket price

The principal park entry point is **Skradin**, a village at the head of the estuary that was seized in 1552 by Ottoman Turks plotting a push on Šibenik. Venice recaptured the village 122 years later and the latest invaders are tourists embarking on hourly **National Park tour boats** upstream to park showpiece the **Skradinski buk waterfalls**. Over the course of 800m, its 17 cascades tumble over travertine (tufa) steps laid by calcium sedimented on to algae and moss, then pour into a natural paddling pool. If you fancy a dip, this is the only place to enjoy it. The adjacent meadows are the stuff picnics are made of, after which you can take to footbridges that crisscross between islets thick with reeds and willow or ponder ethnology displays in old stone watermills. In 1895, six centuries after the first water wheels creaked, the Krka powered the turbines of an HEP plant and Šibenik home-owners had electric lights well before those in London, Frankfurt or Rome. Allow three hours for a return trip this far.

Boats
Mar–Oct only; 100–130Kn

From here a well-marked footpath leads to **Lozovac**, second entry point to the park and embarkation point for **boats** that continue upstream to inland destinations. The first is the **Visovac lake** (Visovačko jezero). It is named after the islet of **Visovac** in the middle, home to a Franciscan monastery founded in 1445 and now hushed behind a veil of poplars. Boats pause for 30 minutes, so you can ponder a modest gallery of Baroque devotional oils inside, a few antique Roman finds, plus, in the treasury, one of only three 15th-century illustrated *Aesop's Fables*. Allow two hours for a return excursion this far. Trips lasting three and a half hours continue up through the **Među gredama gorge** to reach the **Roški slap** waterfall, a minor epic of nature spread across 800m where the valley eases from gorge to gentle slopes. From here there's one more two-hour trip to be taken, this to Krka Monastery, a centre of the Orthodox diocese that has been rebuilt in Byzantine style, and onwards to the remains of a medieval fortress at Nečven. Be

Getting around north of Šibenik

On the main train line, **Knin** and **Drniš** are linked to Split (4 per day), Šibenik (daily, more with change at Perković) and Zagreb (5 a day).

Six buses a day link Šibenik and **Skradin** on weekdays, only two on weekends. With your own wheels, you can enter the Krka National Park at **Lozovac**, gateway for trips to the park's northern reaches. Nine buses a day link **Drniš** to Šibenik and Split (via Sinj) and 3 a day to Zagreb (via **Knin**) and Makarska. Buses shuttle between Drniš and Knin every 30mins.

---

warned that to complete all three trips in a day is a minor logistical triumph; consult park authorities for boat times.

With your own transport you can access remote wilderness regions further north. The Krka gorge is at its most spectacular at the **Manojlovački slapovi**, a set of four cascades which tumble (winter and spring only) at an elbow. The views are sensational. Good maps are a must, however – buy yours, and a National Park guidebook, from the **park tourist office** in Šibenik. Note, too, that park authorities insist you stick to the footpaths – the region was on the frontline of the Homeland War and fields may conceal uncleared landmines.

ⓘ Krka National Park > *Trg Ivana Pavla II 5, Šibenik, **t** (022) 201 777, www.npkrka.hr; open Mon–Fri 7–3*

Knin, Drniš and Otavice

You don't have to travel far inland from the Dalmatian coast to enter a world where the limestone bones show through lean soils and villagers eke out a living from sheep and agriculture. The Šibenik hinterland is more careworn than most, reeling from its recent past as the heartland of the Republic of Serb Krajina (Republic Srpska Krajina or RSK). Symbolic capital of the self-declared statelet – a conceit intended to split Croatia geographically, north from south, as much as ethnically – was **Knin**, which already knew a thing or two about conflict after 200 years on the Turkish–Venetian front line. War was all but inevitable when Milan Babić, the local party leader and erstwhile dentist, squared up to Zagreb and announced the RSK from Knin on 25 August 1990; the hostilities of the Homeland War ceased within hours of the reconquest of Knin on 8 August 1995. Just over two weeks after the success of Operation Storm (Oluja), President Franjo Tuđman, always a leader fond of theatrics, hopped off the 'Freedom Train' and, basking in the spotlight of global media, kissed a Croatian flag unfurled at the fortress on a rocky valley ridge high above Knin.

Fortress *open daily 7am–9pm*

An oversized standard flies to this day on the grizzled **fortress**, begun as a seat of 11th-century King Zvonimir then bolstered by the Venetians into continental Dalmatia's strongest fortress after the 1688 reconquest of Knin. Understandably, it's now a minor pilgrimage site for many Croatians. For others, apart from clambering over the fortress's looping ramparts and bastions moulded to the rock, or gazing east to the barren slopes of Dinara,

Croatia's highest mountain (1,830m) on the Bosnia border, Knin has little to offer. Tuđman rolled triumphantly into a town abandoned by its Serb citizens, and it remains depressed and grim.

Its surroundings suffered, too, ravaged by tit-for-tat destruction; Serbian paramilitary militia the 'Knindas' cleared 'Croatian' villages in 1991; Croats wreaked vengeance on 'Serbian' villages in 1995. Drive 25km south towards Drniš and you'll pass hamlets where only a few old couples struggle on among the shattered houses, the Serbs having fled east, the younger Croats west for jobs on the coast. Posters here salute General Ante Gotovina as a '*Heroj!*'. The Croatian commander who masterminded the recapture of Knin was himself seized in December 2005 after seven years on the run, allegedly protected secretly by high-up military. He stands accused of the expulsion of around 150,00 Serbian civilians from the vanquished RSK and the murder of at least 150 by The Hague War Crimes Tribunal, a touchy subject for many Croatians.

Agricultural centre **Drniš** is no stranger to conflict, either. A **tower-minaret stub** beside the parish church of St Roco and the Baroque church of St Anthony, fashioned from a grand mosque, recalls two centuries of Turkish occupation. The small town's fame nationwide is for its *pršut* ham – the best in Croatia, they say – and the **mausoleum of Ivan Meštrović**. Croatia's finest modern sculptor (1883–1962) built what he intended as a family tomb above his childhood home in **Otavice**, 10km east of Drniš. If its silent bear of a curator is there, do look inside for a typically stylised pot-pourri of world religions – a serene Buddha-head, Christ on a bed of lotus petals and four Evangelists with the stern aura of Byzantium – all carved in Art Nouveau. The effect is seductive, a meditation on the peace of death whose message was lost on Serbian troops: they vandalized the tomb of a Croatian icon and took for scrap the bronze doors embossed with portraits of the Meštrović family.

Mausoleum of Ivan Meštrović
Mauzolez Ivana Meštrovića; open (in theory) summer Tues–Sun 8–12 and 5–8; adm

The latest venture hereabouts is **Etnoland**, signposted off the road to Šibenik. It bills itself as a theme park, but don't let that, nor its scrubby expanse dotted with stone buildings, put you off. Its few buildings are an attempt to showcase traditional Dalmatian crafts and folk culture practised by workers in costume.

Etnoland
mobile **t** *099 22 00 200, www.dalmati.com; open daily Apr–Oct; adm*

Where to Stay and Eat north of Šibenik

There's also a café-restaurant (€€) at the Lozovac embarkation point for the Krka National Park.

Skradi

Skradinski Buk, Burinovac bb, **t** (022) 771 771, *www.skradinskibuk.hr* (€€). Modest en-suite rooms in a small three-star 300m from the ferry dock. Also four apartments.

Bonaca, Rokovačka 5, **t** (022) 771 444 (€€). Traditional cooking in a yachties' favourite above the ACI marina at the Krka Park entry village. Mussels, Skradin grey mullet (*cipal*) or thick eel broth (*brodet od jegulja*).

Drniš >
*Fra Nikole Ruzica bb; **t** (022) 219 072, www.sibenikregion.com; open Mon–Sat 8–4*

Knin >>
*Dr Franje Tudmana 24; **t** (022) 664 819, www.knin.hr; open Mon–Sat 8–3*

Drniš

Park, Stubište 1, **t** (022) 888 636, *www.hotelpark.hr* (€). Flowery fabrics, air-conditioning and satellite TV perk up the simple rooms of Drniš's central hotel. It also has a decent restaurant.

Gradska kavana, opposite Hotel Park, is a café which rustles up light bites with coffee.

Knin

Knin fortress, no tel (€). A limited menu of goulash and veal steaks plus a wonderful panorama east towards Dinara in a café-restaurant in the gatehouse.

South of Šibenik: Brodarica, Krapanj and Primošten

You're only just free of Šibenik's suburbs before you roll into **Brodarica**, an oversized village and port for **Krapanj** – for the princely sum of 5Kn, an hourly ferry shuttles you across a 100m channel to the smallest inhabited island in the Adriatic. The second superlative of this 0.36 sq km speck is sponges. In the heyday of the industry before the First World War, 400,000 Krapanj sponges a year were exported to soap backs in Italy, France and Germany, filling the pockets of 32 local divers. Nowadays, 10 divers net a modest 4,000kg per annum, a small portion of it for sale in a **sponge gallery** (*galerija od spužava*) at the southern end of the harbour.

Museum
open Mon–Sat 9–12; adm

A 17th-century Cretan friar named Antun was the first to teach villagers the knack of harvesting sponges, then done with a trident, between his devotions in a **Franciscan monastery** 10 minutes' walk north of the harbour. In his honour, it has a **museum** of spongey bits and bobs: a diver's suit slumped in a corner, Roman amphorae found on the sea bed. If it's closed – and it often is – you can make do with showcases of dried sponges in the cloister. Away from the island's one sight, Krapanj is workmanlike and practical, its fabric tatty and quickly patched with concrete in places. Clean waters for a dip are off a quay at the south end of the island.

A coast-hugging drive 19km south of Brodarica takes you to **Primošten**. Its best angle is actually from the south, where it stacks up on a teardrop headland beneath a spire, just like Istria's Rovinj. Close up, the small town which blossomed as a 16th-century islet refuge from Turkish forces – the channel was filled in after the Ottoman threat receded in the 17th century – is not quite such a stunner and, in streets which ascend to the parish church of **St George**, Primošten is more modern than it lets on around the harbour. Two things will detain you in the minor resort: a crescent of shingle lapped by clear waters on a headland thick with pines;

Getting around south of Šibenik

All north–south coast buses call at main road stops by **Brodarica** and **Primošten**. Direct connections from Primošten to Šibenik and Split leave every 30mins.

and the local plonk, babić. Apparently, the New York office of the United Nations hangs a picture of vines of Primošten's soft red wine. Sample it straight from the oak barrel in the *vinarija* of *konoba* **Barba Marko** on the main street, Put briga. You can't miss it – a crowd of locals will be putting the world to rights on benches outside.

ⓘ Brodarica/ Krapanj >
Krapanjskih spužvara 1, Brodarica (by main road junction), **t** *(022) 350 612, www.tz-brodarica.hr; open daily summer 9–12 and 2–3*

ⓘ Primošten >
Trg Josipa Arnerića 2, **t** *(022) 571 111, www.tz-primosten.hr; open summer daily 8–10; winter Mon–Fri 9–12*

Where to Stay and Eat south of Šibenik

Both tourist boards co-ordinate bookings of **private accommodation**, or in Primošten contact private agencies **Paduća**, Trg Stjepana Radića 1, **t** (022) 571 289, and **Dalmatinka**, Zagrebačka 8, **t** (022) 570 323.

Brodarica

Zlatna ribica, Krapanjskih spužvara 1, **t** (022) 350 300 (€€€–€€). Often in Croatia's top 100, this semi-smart restaurant prepares some of the finest fish in the region, cooked simply and to perfection. It's worth reserving to secure a table on a waterfront terrace. Also has 16 modern **rooms** (*moderate*), all en suite with the usual mod cons.

Primošten

Zora, Raduča bb, **t** (022) 570 048, *www.zora-hotel.com* (€€€). Among the pines on the headland and refurbished from Yugoslavia relic to a comfy, modern resort hotel that prides itself on a wellness centre. *Minimum three-night stay in peak season.*

Villa Koša, Bana Josipa Jelačića 4, **t** (022) 570 365, *www.villa-kosa.htnet.hr* (€€). Perfectly acceptable if unexciting small apartment-hotel, most of whose units look across the bay to the old town harbour opposite.

Bila Lučica, Rtić 3, Dolac (3km north), **t** (022) 571 753 (€€€–€€). A locals' favourite on the main road that serves the full catch of Adriatic goodness as waves lap the terrace.

Panorama, Ribarska 26, **t** 570 009 (€€). On the far side of the village, via the path uphill from the centre, a reliable seafood place that's all about its glorious seascape – wait for a table rather than sit inside. Also has a small pool to make a long lunch of it.

Torkul, Grgura Ninskog bb, **t** (022) 570 670 (€€). Octopus is the connoisseur's choice of the only *peka* dishes prepared in Primošten, served in a traditional good-value *konoba* before the Old Town. *Eves only.*

Nightlife south of Šibenik

Aurora, Kamenjar bb, Primošten, *www.auroraclub.hr*. Ibiza-style clubbing – four dance floors, palms and a pool – plus house beats from international DJs and Croatian big names in one of Croatia's hippest night-spots, 2km from the centre. Also has hip-hop and disco nights, foam parties and gigs.

Trogir

Trogir

Trogir is one of those golden-brown cities: the colour of rich crumbling shortbread, of butterscotch, of the best pastry.
Rebecca West, *Black Lamb and Grey Falcon*

Tiny and uncomplicated, Trogir has picture-postcard images everywhere you look. Yes, one of Dalmatia's most seductive small towns, shoehorned onto an islet between the mainland and the island of Čiovo, suffers from more than its fair share of tour groups; but explore the back streets or stay till dusk and there's magic in the air. Hard to believe, then, that Trogir was named Tragurion by Greeks in 220 BC after the goats (*tragos*, *koza* in Croatian) grazed on nearby Mount Kozjak. If there's also a hint of Venice about a warren the colour of old ivory it's because the Italian Republic snatched the trading town in 1420 and stamped its authority on it until 1797, an occupation that still rankled in the 1930s – more on that later.

The Venetians might point out that they protected Trogir from Turkish raiders with town walls, pierced on the mainland side by the **Land Gate**, a late-Renaissance arch from which 12th-century bishop and town protector St John of Trogir salutes visitors. Just inside it, a noble dynasty's Baroque palace houses a rather dull **town museum**, with Greek and Roman finds and 18th-century furnishings. Lovely courtyard behind, though.

Town museum
Gradski muze; **t** *(021) 881 406; open summer daily 9–12 and 5–8; winter Mon–Fri 9–2; adm*

The Cathedral of St Lawrence (Katedrala sv. Lovre)

The Cathedral of St Lawrence
Katedrala sv. Lovre; open daily July–Aug 9–8, Sept–June 9–5; adm

Your time is best spent, however, on the 13th-century main portal of the Romanesque Cathedral of St Lawrence. The prize of Croatian medieval carving (1240), looking better than it has for centuries after recent renovation, put author Rebecca West in mind of Dostoevsky: 'There is the same sense of rich, contending disorder changing oozily from form to form, each one of which the mind strives to grasp.' As with the Russian writer's books, the secret to reading master mason Radovan's **portal** is to see it as psychoanalysis. The figures who shoulder the carnival of sculpture on the outer ring – a typically medieval blur of reality, religion and folklore which jumbles everything from sheep to mermaids via bemused apostles – are 13th-century bogeymen: Jews, Turks and pagans. Move in one band and there's a calendar of seasonal chores: a burgher tends vines in spring, hunts a fleeing hare and slays a swine in October, then sizzles sausages with a cup of wine in November. And above all, in the lunette, Radovan stages Bible scenes. House curtains lift to a Nativity and Baptism at centre stage, the Magi and adoring shepherds peer on from the wings, while a sash at the top quickly recaps subplots of the Christian narrative for 13th-century illiterates. Like any great artist, the Middle Ages Slavic master signs his work, adding casually below the lunette that he is 'most famous in this art'.

Don't miss the **baptistry** (1467) left of the portal, by Andrija Aleši, pupil of Croatian Renaissance supremo Juraj Dalmatinac, before

Getting to and around Trogir

One Jadrolinija **ferry** a week (currently Friday) links Split and Trogir (then on to Drvenik Mali and Drvenik Veli); 3 ferries a day (2 on Fri) shuttle between Trogir and the Drvenik islands.

Buses link Trogir to Split (every 20min), Šibenik (hourly) and Zadar (hourly).

you enter the three-nave interior of a church largely completed in the 13th century, but whose **belfry** inched up over a further three centuries, a history neatly summed up by its transition through first-storey Gothic to Venetian Gothic then Renaissance. Climb it for lovely views across Trogir's jumbled roofscape.

For all its Romanesque dignity, the main reason to enter the church is the Renaissance **Chapel of St John of Trogir** (1480) in the east nave, by fellow Dalmatinac pupil Nikola Firentinac, which blazes with light like a revelation in the gloom. Sensitive statues of the Evangelists express all the humanist ambition of the Renaissance – the youthful St John is said to be a dedicatory portrait of the son of Koriolan Ćipiko, a figurehead of Trogir humanism who funded the chapel. They stand like serious schoolmasters beneath cherubs who scamper in and out of the gates of Hades, naughty schoolboys on an outing, too excited to formally represent immortality. The sacristy **treasury** (*riznica*) is a disappointment by comparison.

The Rest of Town

Ćipiko treated himself to Trogir's finest **mansion** opposite the cathedral portal, its façade dignified by Venetian Gothic windows. The story goes that his grandson, galleon captain Alvizo Ćipiko, snatched its cockerel (the original is in the town museum) from the bow of a vanquished Turkish ship during the 1571 Adriatic brouhaha known as the Battle of Lepanto.

Firentinac also carved the relief of *Justice* flanked by St Lawrence and St John of Trogir in the **loggia** opposite the cathedral, a 15th-century open-air courtroom still with the rusty chains to which miscreants were shackled. The sculptor's Lion of St Mark – a conspicuous blank in the loggia – fared less well. Citizens hacked out the Venetian Republic's icon after Mussolini declared that 'whichever place bears the sign of a lion with wings should belong to Italy' in 1932. Quick to make mischief, Il Duce raged at a 'clear expression of a mentality of hate', adding with menace, 'The lions of Trogir are destroyed, but in their destruction they stand stronger than ever as a living symbol – and a certain promise.' The Yugoslav government was forced into a formal apology. If Trogir hoped to restore local pride with the relief on the loggia's south wall of local son Petar Berislavić, a 16th-century Croatian *ban* (viceroy) and Zagreb bishop who battled against Italian rule and was killed fighting Turks in 1520, it must have been sorely disappointed with the uncharacteristically flaccid relief by 20th-century sculptor Ivan Meštrović. An adjacent **clock tower** that serves as a memorial to victims of the Homeland War also contains some early Christian sarcophagi. Trogir's hoard of ecclesiastical art treasures is hung in an adjacent palace as the **Pinakoteka**; at the time of writing there was talk about relocation to the cathedral. Look for a pair of 15th-century polyptychs by Blaž Jurjev Trogiranin, a pioneer of Italian styles on the east Adriatic; watched by angels and dour saints, the Virigin breastfeeds her Child, and the pair share a tender moment in the rose garden. More religious art – Madonna icons is hung in the **Convent of St Nicholas**. Its highlight is an intriguing 3rd-century BC relief of Kairos, the running Greek god of opportunity who must be seized or lost forever – dither and you'll only scrabble at his bald pate. Find it southwest of the square on **Gradska**, which emerges from the intimate Old Town via the sea gate in the town walls onto harbourside promenade the **Riva**. Follow this to its western end (i.e. turn right out of Gradska), and you'll reach the dumpy **Kamerlengo Fortress**, a 15th-century Venetian castle built to guard the sea approaches at what was the southwest corner of Trogir's island. A gun battery, the **St Mark's Tower**, now a shop of Croatian folk music, stood watch over the opposite northwest flank, which is why the **Gloriette** (1808) in between the pair is so admirable despite being nothing much to look at. The monument to glorify then-owner France formerly stood among the waves, linked to the island by a slim belvedere. Perhaps only a Frenchman, and one as enlightened as Dalmatian overlord Marshal Marmont, a man committed to the creation of an educated Illyrian utopia, could bring Trogir such gentle seriousness, such delight in small pleasures, as to build a wave-washed miniature neoclassical temple in which to play card games with his officers.

Pinakoteka
t (021) 881 426; open 15 June–15 Sept Mon–Sat 9–8, Sun 3–7; winter by reservation; adm

Convent of St Nicholas
Samostan sv. Nikole; t (021) 881 631, 2–3pm only; open summer Mon–Sat 8–1 and 3–7; winter through tourist information; adm

Kamerlengo Fortress
open daily June–Aug 8–10, April–May and Sept–Oct 10–6; adm

Beaches and Islands near Trogir: The Drveniks

Although intellectual, cultural and a beauty, Trogir has little time for idle hedonism. You can laze on pine-fringed shingle **Pantan beach**, beside a river estuary 1.5km east of Trogir, or join the crowds at the beach bars of **Okrug beach**, 5km from Trogir on the south side of opposite island **Čiovo** near Okrug Gornji.

For real peace, however, hop aboard ferries from the Riva (also from Seget, 3km west) bound for the **Drvenik islands** 13km offshore – barely populated and with little in the way of tourist amenities but much to offer for lazy rambles and quiet beaches. The finest is **Vela Rina**, a shingle crescent with turquoise water an easy stroll from the port of **Drvenik Mali**. Apart from a handful of guests and diners at the Vela Rina restaurant, you'll be on your own. Closer big sister island **Drvenik Veli** is more accommodating. Its main town of time-worn stone houses provides guests with a few fish restaurants and a 16th-century parish church with Baroque furniture and an altarpiece by Venetian painter Antonio Grapinelli. Once those avenues for diversion have been explored, you can follow footpaths over an island of long-forgotten olive plantations and black pines to reach sand and pebble beaches; the biggest are **Solinska** and **Drvenik**.

Festivals in Trogir

The highlight of Trogir's calendar is the **Summer Festival**, with performances of classical and folk music from early July to the end of August. Also worth investigating is the religious pomp that celebrates patron saint **St John** on 16 November.

Where to Stay in and around Trogir

Trogir is well served by small family hotels in the old town. Most provide parking for a modest price that's worth accepting. Source private **rooms** and **apartments** in Trogir and the Drveniks from **Ćipiko**, in the Ćipiko mansion opposite the cathedral, **t** 881 554, or **Sea Gate**, behind the Fontana hotel at A. Kažotića 5, **t** 797 710, *www.sea-gate.net*. Alternatively a number of restaurants on the far side of the harbour also provide rooms.

ⓘ Trogir >
Gradksa vrata 4 (beside town museum), **t** *(021) 885 628, www.trogir.hr; open June–Aug daily 8–9, otherwise Mon–Sat 8–7*

Trogir

Fontana, Obrov 1, **t** (021) 885 744, *www.fontana-trogir.com* (€€). The Old Town old-hand, rather overpriced for three-star rooms in need of a revamp. Focus instead on location on the Riva or that an extra 120Kn buys you a Jacuzzi.

Pašike, Sinjska bb, **t** (021) 885 185, *www.hotelpasike.com* (€€). One block back from the north shore car park (*free parking*), this *pension* has a taste for Biedermeier style in seven rooms with antiques and stone walls; the Trogir room is classiest. The restaurant is excellent too.

Tragos, Budislavićeva 3, **t** (021) 884 729, *www.tragos.hr* (€€). A home from home, all pine furnishings and bright duvet covers, in a family-owned *pension*-restaurant fashioned from a medieval house off the town square. At the restaurant, try a rich *pašticada* or lamb with beans.

Villa Sv. Petar, Ivana Duknovića 14, **t** (021) 884 359, *www.villa-svpetar.com* (€€). Snug medieval proportions and modern Mediterranean style – floaty drapes and mahogany parquet – from a friendly family place. The four rooms and an apartment include DVD players and plasma TVs.

Villa Sikaa, Obala kralja Zvonimira 13, **t** (021) 881 223, *www.vila-sikaa-r.com* (€€). Facing the Old Town from the opposite harbourfront, this swish four-star has the best morning views in Trogir.

Drvenik Veli

Mia, **t** (021) 893 038, *www.hotel-mia.tk* (€). Located above the port, with bargain-priced three-star rooms and five apartments, most with bay views. If forewarned, its owner will meet you at the port.

Drvenik Mali

Vela Rina, **t** (021) 884 888, *www.velarina.com* (€€). Twenty apartments in this beach restaurant a short stroll from the port.

Eating Out in and around Trogir

Trogir

Alka, Augustina Kažotića 15, **t** (021) 881 856 (€€€–€€). Fish specials plus a polyglot of steak styles or chicken with *pršut* in an award-winning restaurant which is highly rated for a formal meal. Wait for a table in a nearby terrace rather than suffer its stuffy interior.

Fontana, Obrov 1, **t** (021) 884 811 (€€€–€€). Less formal than the Alka but just as pricey thanks to an unbeatable location before the Riva, a lovely spot for a lazy alfresco lunch of high-quality seafood.

Škrapa, Hrvatskih mučenika 9, no tel (€). Chunky bench seating and checked tablecloths in this chirpy café at the top of Trogir's north–south spine – and the mixed fish plate (*miješana riba*) is delicious.

Drvenik Mali

Vela Rina, **t** (021) 884 888, *www. velarina.com* (€€). A beach restaurant a short stroll from the port.

Kaštela

The 1463 fall of Bosnia to Ottoman Turks sent a shock wave of panic rippling west. Dalmatia was stunned suddenly to find itself on the ramparts of Christendom, and the prosperous cities of Split and Trogir assumed they would be next on the Ottoman list. Not trusting to the preparations of an offhand Venetian Republic, many feudal aristocrats built themselves fortified residences on the bay which sweeps east between the two towns. As peasants on the slopes of Mount Kozjak moved to the coast for protection, seven villages gathered at the fortresses' feet; in later, more peaceful centuries they spread out, the aristocrats reworked their castles into summer retreats, and today Kaštela arches almost unbroken along the coast between Split and Trogir as a row of merged fishing villages.

For a day of easy strolling, take to the seafront promenade which links the villages, then return on buses which ply the Magistrala between Split and Trogir every 20mins. Don't forget your swimsuit – numerous bays line the 15km trip – and do stop for a glass of red wine. In 2001, DNA analysis pinpointed Kaštela as the source of zinfandel, the pride of Californian wine-producers. Locals just shrug and call their local plonk 'kaštelanski crljenak' (Kaštela red)

Starting from Trogir, head east past modern suburb Resnik and alight at **Kaštel Štafilić**. Beyond its harbour, a small fortress floats as if by magic in the bay, stunted at the first floor as its brother-builders breathed a sigh of relief after a Venetian–Turk peace deal halted building work in 1548.

ⓘ **Kaštel Novi**
Ante Beretina 1, **t** *(021) 232 044, www. dalmacija.net/kastela; open summer Mon–Sat 8–12 and 6–9; winter Mon–Fri 8–3*

It is just west of **Kaštel Novi**, a sleepy stone village which grew behind the progenitor harbourfront tower (1512) of Pavao Ćipiko, nephew of Trogir luminary Koriolan Ćipiko – the family zigzag crest informs land arrivals just which dynasty they are approaching. Behind, the parish church of St Roko has an octagonal Renaissance campanile, while near the main road off Lucijin put is one of the many oldest olive trees in Europe – this gnarled, 1,500-year-old contender (*Stara maslina*) was over a century old when the first Roman refugees from Salona straggled into the palatial ruins of what was to become Split, a smudge across the bay.

The 'old' castle (1493) to Kaštel Novi's 'new' is **Kaštel Stari**, a minor resort 1km east. For an all-round brainbox such as Koriolan

Kastela and Central Dalmatia

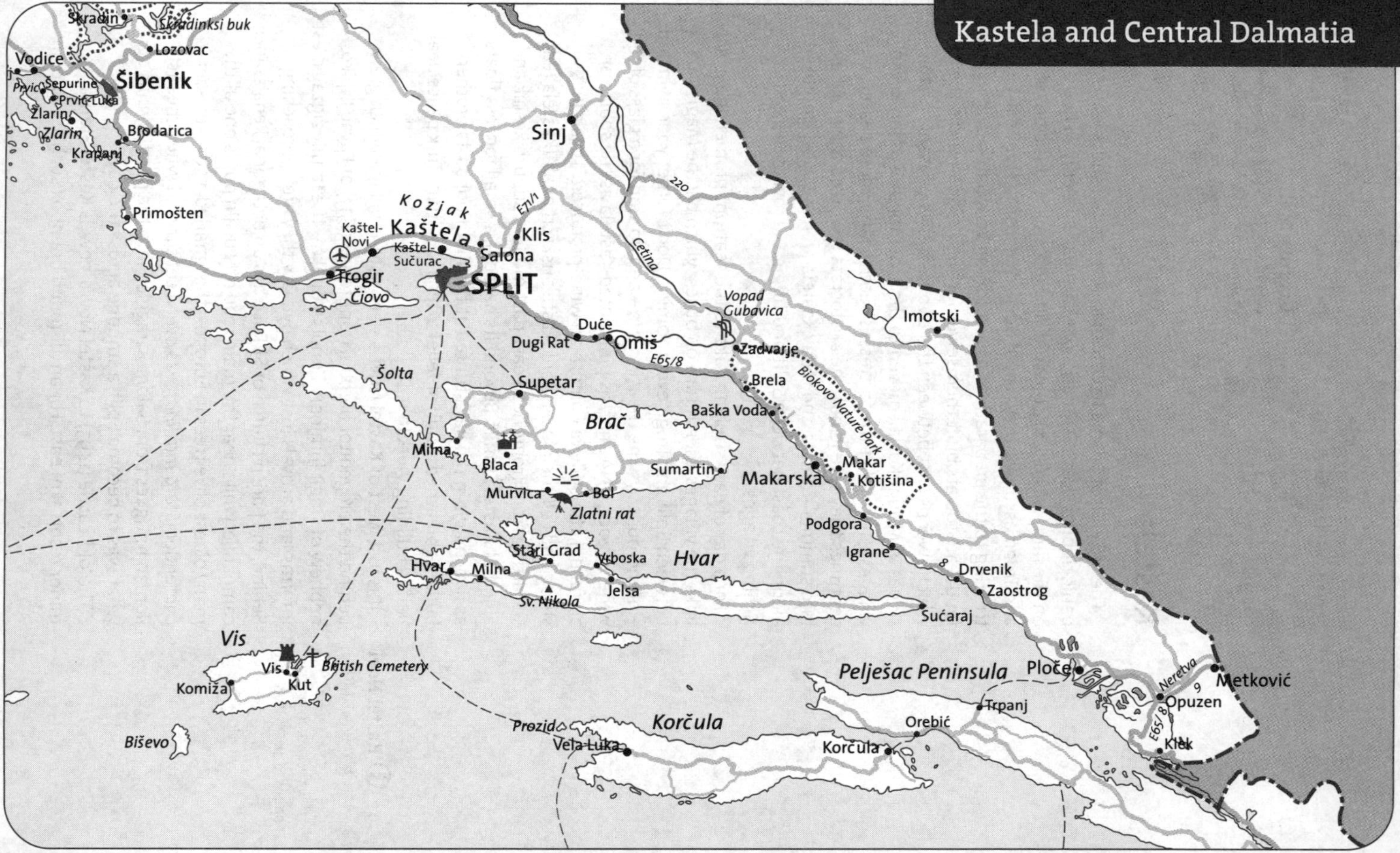

Getting to and around Kaštela

North–south coastal **buses** and the 37 bus between Trogir and Split ply the Magistrala behind Kaštela. Be warned: differentiating between the villages is tricky from the main road.

Ćipiko – writer, humanist and dashing army commander – it's an anonymous residence, aggrandized only by a balcony and that lightning zigzag. More appealing is the rustic market behind, where you can peer into the mansion's courtyard once linked to the market square by a drawbridge.

ⓘ **Kaštel Lukšic**
Dvorac Vitturi (castle), **t** *(021) 227 933, www.dalmacija.net/kastela; open summer Mon–Sat 8–12 and 6–9; winter Mon–Fri 8–3*

Museum
open summer Mon–Sat 8–12 and 6–9, Sun 6–9; winter Mon–Fri 8–3

The moated Renaissance palace in **Kaštel Lukšić** is the finest of the group, a stocky 1564 cube which juts into the sea, although not so sturdy that Trogir aristocrats the Vitturi brothers didn't demand a back door for a hasty getaway by boat. Restored rooms host an **art gallery** and a **museum** with temporary exhibitions on Kaštela themes, and also the tourist office. The nearby parish church treasures a sarcophagus-altar from the impeccable chisel of Juraj Dalmatinac, knocked off in 1445 while the Renaissance architect was busy with Split commissions, but it's never open. Never mind – the adjacent square is ideal for a coffee break and there's a strip of beach just east of the castle.

Next stop **Kaštel Kambelovac** is a soporific tangle of lanes gathered around a scruffy round tower where pigeons roost in murder holes intended for boiling oil. Your time is better spent at **Kaštel Gomilica** 1km beyond. Its core floats offshore on a 'tiny heap' (*gomilica*) of rock, a town in minature that's organised for defence; it's reached via a stone bridge and entry is via a gate tower pierced by loop- and cannonholes. **Kaštel Sućurac** is said to be the oldest of the group – it dates from a tower built in 1392 by one Archbishop Averold Gualdo from Split. Today the closest village to Croatia's second city is tainted by industry. Continue the 3km from Kaštel Gomilica and if you look hard you can make out the village kernel jutting into the sea, where the good archbishop's rebuilt late-Gothic summer palace backs onto the village square.

Where to Stay and Eat in Kaštela

Adria, F. Tuđmana bb, Kaštel Štafilić, **t** (021) 798 140, *www.hotel-adria.hr* (€€). On the main road 3km from Trogir, with smart accommodation for businessmen using the nearby airport.

Palace, Obala kralja Tomislava 82, Kaštel Stari, **t** (021) 206 270 (€€). An Austrian-style grandee from 1923 reduced to a tatty two-star. Good swimming in front of it, though.

Villa Žarko, Obala kralja Tomislava 7a, Kaštel Lukšić, **t** (021) 228 160, *www.villa-zarko.com* (€€). There are 16 chipper rooms in breezy blue colour schemes in this amiable small hotel with views over the bay. Just the wrong side of inexpensive.

Balenta Škola, A. Starčevića 45, Kaštel Kambelovac, **t** (021) 220 208 (€€). Try a rich *pašticada* beef stew or grilled fish selected from the morning's catch landed in the adjacent harbour, washed down with a carafe of local red *kaštelanski crljenak*.

Central Dalmatia

Central Dalmatia is *fjaka* country, a place to indulge the deliciously indolent mood of contentment that has no lexical equivalent under the damp grey skies of Northern Europe. Whether hanging out with the Armani set in chic Hvar Town, paddling in the shallows of a famous beach in Bol, or dropping off the radar on gourmet hideaway Vis, this central region is one in which to idle not intellectualize, where astounding architecture and rich culture are as much a part of the everyday as the gentle art of *rakija*-sipping at sunset. Holiday heaven, in other words.

Split, the gateway to these celebrated islands and the hub around which all else revolves, is far too much the most densely populated, hurly-burly and everything-you've-come-to-get-away-from part of Dalmatia to let you ease into daydreams, but don't let that put you off. It has antiquities by the ton around its honeycomb kernel, and offers the best museums and hippest boutiques in the region. It also has the most intoxicating shot of urban adrenaline you'll taste on this side of the Adriatic.

Split

An antique, modern, sprawling, crawling, grime-smeared, marble-veneered metropolis, Split is not nearly as well known as it deserves to be. Zagreb holds the reins of power, and Dubrovnik steals all the international limelight, but this, the nation's second city, the great anti-Zagreb, has the more intriguing personality. Whereas Dubrovnik protects its Baroque timewarp so fiercely that shop signs are outlawed in its streets, Split is antiquity as everyday. It is living history, where locals queue for a teller without batting an eye at the Roman columns which march across the bank, and designer frocks hang in the windows of medieval aristocrats' mansions. Even Split's Sunday best, the cathedral, is allowed to show signs of age.

Restoration – and the huge improvement in hotel stock – means Split is at last being recognized as a destination in its own right rather than just as a gateway to the islands. Indeed, by peak season its mazey, UNESCO-listed old town clogs to a standstill as Americans on cruise ships, and seemingly the entire Française metropolitaine, fill the shell of Emperor Diocletian's palace. The architecture astounds, of course. Yet antiquity is not really the point – or at least not the whole point. By all means go on a treasure hunt for the Roman remains, or pore over culture in some of Dalmatia's finest museums. But visit, too, for a sassy city fizzing

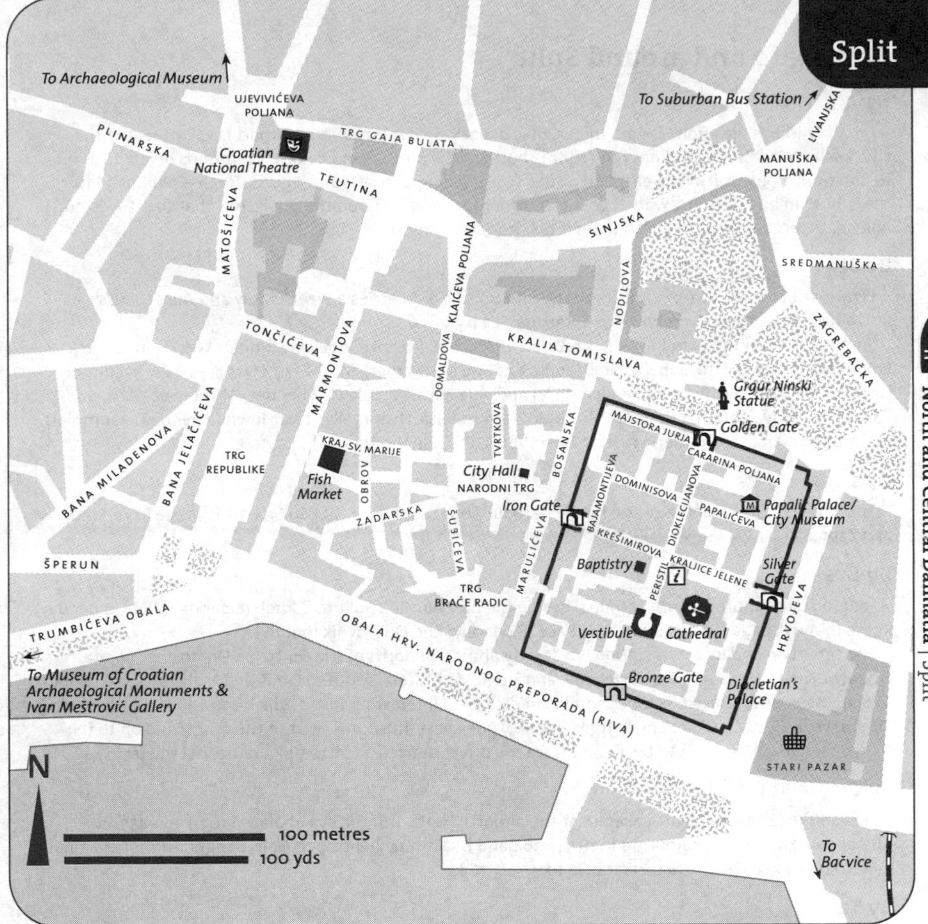

with metropolitan zip, its labyrinthine alleys chock-a-block with cafés and bars and hip boutiques.

A Brief History

From little seeds, mighty cities grow. The ground for Split's growth was prepared by Roman emperor Diocletian, who in AD 295 built a seaside retirement home an easy trot from the east Adriatic capital, Salona (*see* pp.282–3). No lowly bungalow for a 3rd-century Dalmatian despot who had masterminded the last great hurrah of the empire. Instead, the self-declared son of Jupiter treated himself to a designer *castrum*-cum-villa of creamy white stone quarried from Brač, with the latest security features – corner watchtowers, gateways and walls up to 28m, manned by an in-house garrison – and a small allotment for his cabbages. For eight years he pottered about his vegetable patch, rebuffing every entreaty to return to office, until he was laid to rest in a

Getting to and around Split

By Air

Croatia Airlines flies from Zagreb three times a week. Split international airport is 22km west of the city. A scheduled Croatia Airlines bus (30Kn) shuttles new arrivals and departees 90mins before take-off to and from a bus stop at the east end of the Riva. If you miss that, you can take Trogir–Split bus 37 to the suburban bus stop. Be aware if going to the airport from Split on the public bus that the stop is not named. Expect to pay around 250Kn for a taxi from the airport.

By Sea

Ferries sail year-round from Ancona, Italy, with up to 5 or 6 ferries a week in July and Aug. There's also a fast, 4hr catamaran service from Ancona. *See* p.58.

Split is a port on the Jadrolinija Rijeka–Dubrovnik coastal service (daily in summer, weekly in winter). From Split, ferries link to: Supetar, Brač (approx hourly in summer); Stari Grad, Hvar (3–5 daily in summer); Lastovo via Hvar Town (foot passengers only) and Vela Luka, Korčula (1–2 per day); Vis (1–2 per day); and Zadar (4 per day). Catamarans go to: Bol, Brač, then to Jelsa, Hvar (daily); Hvar Town (2 per day in summer); Lastovo (2 per day in summer) via Hvar Town, Vela Luka; and Vis (daily).

By Train

The station is south of the centre by the harbour. Four trains a day link to Šibenik (change in Perković) and Zagreb.

By Bus

Long-distance routes, from a terminal beside the harbour, link Split to Zagreb (8 per day), Pula (4 per day), Rijeka (hourly), Zadar (every 30mins), Plitvice (8 per day) and Dubrovnik (hourly).

The suburban and local bus station is a scruffy affair 1km north of the centre on Domovinskog rata. Frequent connections go north to Šibenik and Trogir via Kaštela, south to Omiš and Makarska, and inland to Sinj. The pedestrianized historic centre is riddled with interesting alleys which you will still be exploring after a week. Bus 12 (stop opposite Trg Republike) goes past museums west of the centre and on to the Marjan peninsula; tickets can be bought from the driver or from a tobacconist or newsstand (*tisak*).

By Car

For car hire (all agencies also operate at the airport): **Hertz**, Trumbićeva obala 2, **t** (021) 360 455; **ABC** and **ADEX**, Obala Lazareta 3, **t** (021) 342 364 and **t** (021) 344 344 respectively; **Budget**, Trumbićeva obala 12, **t** (021) 399 214; **ITR**, Obala Lazareta 2, **t** (021) 343 264.

By Taxi

Taxis congregate at either end of the Riva.

---

mausoleum in AD 313. For a few centuries the palace continued as an imperial holiday home for his successors, then it fell into ruin.

Revival came in AD 614. As barbarian Avars ripped through Salona on their smash-and-grab raid north, refugees straggled into the ruins, patched up the fabric of their adopted home, then safeguarded it in statute by accepting Byzantine authority in return for privileges as a free *commune*. Nurtured by the stability of the fledgling Croat kingdom and its port location, early medieval Split gradually fleshed out its Roman skeleton. By the time the Venetians added it to their title deeds in 1420, the neat grid designed by a Greco-Roman architectural partnership was bored by alleys like woodworm holes, while gaps in the antique fabric were crammed with buildings – 19th-century Austrian surveyors shelved the idea of stripping Split back to its Roman core when they realized it was only the medieval props stuffed into corners and columns that kept the palace upright. Robert Adam, the father of British neoclassical design, also looked past the later additions when he disembarked from Venice in 1757 to study the palace. The Venetian governor was highly suspicious of the foreign party busy sketching his city and even requesting to enter people's houses to inspect their walls, and denounced the Scottish architect and his draughtsmen as spies. The commander-in-chief of the garrison, a fellow Scot, assuaged his fears, and a good thing too, because the palace subsequently reappeared in Adam's plans for Georgian London and Edinburgh.

Pressing against its walls, Split burst out in the mid-1400s. The Venetians introduced Italian mansions and handsome piazzas, plus a ring of 16th- and 17th-century fortresses to repel the encroaching Turkish power. Later owners the Habsburgs also nudged Split's boundaries outwards in an otherwise forgettable 19th century and, having got a taste for expansion, the Splićani threw caution to the wind after 1945. Shipbuilding and rapid industrialization lured migrants from the tough inland regions. To accommodate the new arrivals, Split infested itself with the haphazard scatter of shoddy concrete carbuncles which blight its suburbs to this day. More refugees flooded in after the Homeland War, when Split suffered a half-hearted bombardment by the Yugoslav navy. Bloated into the giant of the Adriatic, Split still creeps ever outwards to jostle neighbours such as Solin, as bad as a large industrial city, as good as a sassy metropolis.

Around the Peristyle

Nowhere displays Split's early history so cleanly as the area around the **Peristyle** (Peristil), Diocletian's ceremonial courtyard at the crossroads of the east–west *decumanus* and north–south *cardo* which carved the palace into quadrants and are still hinted at on the modern street map. Corinthian columns and arches march along its sides – a grateful Renaissance architect incorporated them into the Grisogono-Cipci nobleman's palace on the northwest side to frame the *protiron* at its south end. Even a pair of Renaissance chapels stuffed beneath the gable cannot hush the declaration of authority made by the front door to Diocletian's palace building, and if it impresses today it must have positively swaggered when crowned by a sculpture of four horses. It doesn't stretch the imagination too far to visualize the retired emperor in robes stiff with gold and silk embroidery on his public balcony, gazing over subjects prostrate before the self-declared son of Jupiter.

The Peristyle is the main stage of celebrations for city patron St Domnius on 7 May and for operatic extravaganzas of the Split Summer Festival. Admire a black granite sphinx before the *protiron*, a spoil of war from Diocletian's AD 297–9 campaigns in Egypt and the only one of 11 not ritually smashed after his death, then ascend beneath its mighty loggia to reach the domed **vestibule**, once coated in mosaics and marble. The waiting room for ambassadors is the only room of Diocletian's palace intact above ground; you can piece together the rest of the imperial living quarters from the cellars below (*see* pp.274).

The Cathedral and Baptistry

Cathedral of St Domnius
Katedrala sv. Duje; open daily 7–12 and 5–7

Sidekick to the Peristyle, and holy of holies ever since Split made its début, is the **Cathedral of St Domnius**. Diocletian pooh-poohed the Roman custom of burial outside city walls as stuff for mere mortals and demanded instead a central octagonal mausoleum attended by an arcade of columns looted from Grecian and Egyptian temples. Unwisely as it turns out, because, nearly 200 years after his death in AD 313, his mortal remains vanished from their final resting place in mysterious circumstances. That was a minor slight compared with the final insult, however – 7th-century refugees from Salona hijacked the tomb of an emperor whose final years were characterized by Christian persecution and transformed it into a church to venerate the bones of St Domnius, the first bishop of Salona, martyred in the arena in AD 304.

Diocletian: Man and Myth

The son of slaves, born in AD 245, possibly in Salona, Diocletian rose rapidly up the army ranks from lowly legionnaire to commander. Appointed emperor at the age of 39, the native Dalmatian masterminded a ruthless conquest of Rome's persistent enemy, Persia, the last great triumph of the empire; and although he quartered an unwieldy empire to establish the Tetrarchy, a job-share among a minion Augustus and two Caesar underlings, he retained an iron grip on power. Diocletian, records history, was an autocrat, an emperor who introduced the model of the servile Persian court to Rome, who undermined the authority of the Senate and approved the most terrible persecutions of the early Christian church. A black-and-white bogeyman.

However, history frequently serves an agenda. Alongside the stereotype as the scourge of the Christian Church are glimpses of another Diocletian. In AD 301, he became the first emperor to retire, exchanging the hurly-burly of empire to 'grow cabbages' in his new palace. Begged to return by beleaguered successor Maximilian, who wrestled with a fractious empire as the tetrarchs squabbled, Diocletian told the ambassador, 'If you could show the cabbage I planted with my own hands to your emperor, he wouldn't suggest I replace the peace and happiness of this place with the storms of a never-satisfied greed.' So much for the portrait of the megalomaniac.

Even the old fallback of persecution may not hold water. Contemporary Palestine bishop Eusebius of Caesarea records that Christians enjoyed peace until the twilight of Diocletian's reign, when Galerius, tetrarch of the eastern empire, nudged the ruler into a vicious suppression which continued in his name. Our last recorded peep of Diocletian as he recedes from history's spotlight suggests magnanimity. When Christian masons refused to chisel a pagan statue of Aesculapius, god of medicine, for his palace, the ex-emperor accepted their faith with a sigh, and only imprisoned them for the minor public order offence of not atoning by sacrifice to Apollo.

Ascend the cathedral's steps, guarded by a pair of snarling Romanesque lions, to magnificent walnut **doors**, a 28-panel Bible cartoon strip for 13th-century illiterates by local son Andrija Buvina, which must have dazzled when painted and gold-plated, and enter an intimate **interior**. Diocletian's tomb in all its imperial pomp probably stood at the centre of the octagon beneath a shimmering skin of mosaics which coated the domed roof. A purge of pagan iconography stripped the mausoleum of both – a 13th-century Split archdeacon sagely noted an 'exorcism' of pagan spirits – but the Christians could not eradicate the dome's sash of Roman chariot-racing or hunting scenes, nor, wreathed by garlands and lauded by cupids, the reliefs of Diocletian and wife Empress Priscia.

One story claims that fragments of the emperor's ruby-coloured porphyry sarcophagus ended up in the 13th-century **pulpit**, whose slender columns bud into fabulous Romanesque capitals of tangled thickets where dragons and serpents lurk. Eclipsing even these is the 1448 **altar of St Anastasius**, on the cusp between Gothic and Renaissance and created by Juraj Dalmatinac, the architect behind the UNESCO-listed cathedral in Šibenik (*see* p.250). Its patron reclines with the millstone with which he was drowned by Diocletian after the cloth dyer, newly arrived from Aquileia in Italy and an innocent in Salona, daubed a cross on his front door. Split has adopted the Christian martyr as a second patron and venerates his bones behind reliefs of saints and a vicious relief of the scourging of Christ. Dalmatinac modelled his work on the 1427 **sarcophagus of St Domnius** on the opposite side of the cathedral; its dozing bishop and late Gothic baldachin are the work of a Milanese master, while the saint's sarcophagus before it dates from AD 2. The saint's remains are now in a whimsical Baroque altar by Venetian artist Giovan Maria Morlaiter stuffed into a chapel beside the St Anastasius altar.

Treasury
adm

Crypt
adm

Campanile
open (in theory) summer daily 8–8; winter times erratic; adm

The **choir**, tacked awkwardly on to the original building in the 17th century, has the oldest choir stalls in Dalmatia, carved with 13th-century hunters and craftsmen. The **treasury** holds reliquaries of saints Domnius and Anastasius, shimmering vestments and, in pride of place, the *Evangelarium Spalatenese* gospel, brought to Split with the first Christian refugees, and the oldest manuscript Croatia owns. Return outside the cathedral and you can descend to a missable **crypt**, or can ascend the 200ft-high **campanile** – its slender stacks, rebuilt to the original Romanesque-Gothic blueprint, stood complete in 1908 and were promptly denounced as charmless by locals.

Baptistry
Jupiterov hram; open same hours as campanile; adm

A passage directly opposite the cathedral steps threads to the cathedral **baptistry**, actually more recognizable as the **Jupiter Temple** that Diocletian erected to his adopted father. Roman gods Jupiter, Hercules, Sol and Nike as well as dogs and cherubs ornament its portal and, inside, a barrel vault is studded with flower buds and heads. For a period during Venetian rule (1420–1797) this was the ritziest prison imaginable. In better condition are the Romanesque interwoven knots and plaits carved on the cross-shaped 11th-century baptismal font, on which an enthroned Croat king, possibly Krešimir IV, brandishes his orb and crucifix over either a prostrate citizen or vanquished foe. The lanky *St John the Baptist* behind is a late work by Croatia's finest modern sculptor, Ivan Meštrović.

From the Peristyle to the Riva

Although largely razed above ground, the palace floorplan is fossilized underground in mirror-image as brick **cellars** (*podrum*) whose architectural integrity is intact due to centuries of use as a rubbish dump; they were only cleared in the 1950s. Descend the steps from the Peristyle, and you are in cellars which reflect the vestibule and connecting central hall, today a venue for touristy arts and crafts stalls. At the latter's end stretched the *cryptoporticus*, a promenade which wafted sea breezes into palace rooms and doubled as Diocletian's seafront promenade, interpreted below ground as a long corridor. If it's open for intermittent antiques markets, the eastern arm allows a glimpse into the cellars beneath the *triclinium* (dining hall). Otherwise, you can explore mazy Roman substructures off the *cryptoporticus*'s **western arm**, which illustrate the imperial reception hall (possibly a throne room) and a cluster of living quarters.

Western arm
open Mon–Sat 9–8, Sun 10–6; adm

You exit the cellars of the central hall through the **Bronze Gate**, the south entrance of the palace's quartet of gates that originally emerged onto the seashore. Today you arrive on to a harbourside boulevard titled Obala hrvatskog narodnog preporoda (Croatian National Revival Embankment). Even tourist authorities baulk at that mouthful and sensibly dub their palm-fringed promenade the **Riva**. Renovation in recent years has stripped the expanse of some of its lived-in shabby charm, imposing modern street furniture and shiny paving. But it remains the best spot to do as the locals do: study the papers over morning coffee, people-watch with a sundowner or join the *korzo* (evening stroll). Step back from the parade and you get a tantalizing glimpse of the seafront south wall of Diocletian's palace, a rhythmic parade of Corinthian columns and arches etched into Renaissance houses and punctuated with the definitive full-stop of a solid defence bastion at its southeast corner.

East and North of the Peristyle

Its flagstones buffed smooth by millions of feet – from Roman sandals to trainers – the *decumanus* (aka Poljana Kraljice Jelene) parades east past the cathedral and exits the former palace through Diocletian's former east gate, the **Silver Gate** which breaks arches along the flank of the palace. Just before it the **Vidović Gallery** displays colourful artwork by Emanuel Vidović, a locally born 20th-century painter. Beyond is Split's superb **market**, a wonderland of seasonal fruits and home produce – cheese, honey, olive oil and wine. The southeast quadrant of the palace, reached by the side of the Peristil hotel, has undergone serious renovation in recent years to improve what has long been a tatty, semi-derelict area of dark corners and washing lines. Beyond the swish hotel Vestibul, a restored stone building on the lane behind the palace front hosts the **Ethnographic Museum**, the latest addition to the city's museum scene, with Dalmatian folk costume, crafts and folksy antique furnishings.

Vidović Gallery
Galerija Vidović; **t** *(021) 360 155, www.galerija-vidovic.com; open summer Tues–Fri 9–9, Sat–Sun 9–4; winter Tues–Fri 9–4, Sat–Sun 10–1; adm*

Ethnographic Museum
Etnografski muzej; **t** *(021) 344 164, www.etnografski-muzej-split.hr; open July–14 Sept Mon–Fri 9–9, Sat 9–1; 15 Sept–May Mon–Fri 9–7, Sat 9–1; June Mon–Fri 9–2 and 5–8, Sat 9–1; adm*

Back to the Peristil. The north–south Roman *cardo* which linked the Roman city of Salona (*see* pp.282–3) to the Peristyle and divides the palace's east and west quadrants is known as **Dioklecijanova**, which excavates through Gothic and Renaissance houses dotted with the occasional courtyard mansion of the medieval élite. None is finer than the **Papalić Palace**, an aristocratic 15th-century pile on side street Papalićeva from the drawing board of Renaissance architect Juraj Dalmatinac. Its owner's star-and-feathers coat of arms in a frothy plaque on the portal leads into a lovely courtyard with a well and a tasteful loggia. The mansion itself hosts the **City Museum**, whose narrative of city history, told in Roman coins stamped with a bearded Diocletian, sculpture rescued from the cathedral exterior and medieval weapons, perks up in the first-floor festive hall. Beneath its painted ceiling, Split's Renaissance intellectuals enthused about the new philosophies from the other side of the Adriatic, which explains the salute to Marko Marulić – fired by the humanist ideals of Italy, the local poet renounced Latin to pen the first literary work in Croatian, *Judita* (1521).

City Museum
Gradski muzej; **t** *(021) 344 164, www.mgst.net; open summer Tues–Fri 9–9, Sat–Mon 9–4; winter Tues–Fri 10–5, Sat–Mon 9–4; adm*

Dioklecijanova culminates in the **Golden Gate** (Zlatna vrata). The monumental gate was the front door to the palace, and even if it has lost the statuary in its niches – and has been cloaked in scaffolding for a decade – it retains a hint of the swagger with which Diocletian impressed new arrivals from Salona. Originally his statue and those of his tetrarchs stood on four column bases atop the wall.

The wizard who hurls a spell from fingers like spiders' legs in front of the gate is actually **Grgur Ninski**, 10th-century bishop of Nin (*see* pp.239–40) who campaigned against Split bishops for the use of Slav over Latin in the liturgy. If the 1929 colossus cast by Ivan Meštrović to celebrate the millennium anniversary of the Synod of Split seems impressive here, it must have astounded in the Peristyle. Ever-opinionated author Rebecca West was incensed by Meštrović's work. 'A more ungodly misfit was never seen,' she complained. 'It reduces the architectural proportions of the palace to chaos, for its head is on a level with the colonnades.' You can see her point. So perhaps it was a good thing that Italian Fascists in the Second World War exiled the symbol of Croatian nationalism outside the walls. His big toe is said to be lucky if you rub it. The star-shaped fortification beyond a small park adjacent is the best-preserved **bastion** of five erected by the mid-17th-century Venetians.

The Rest of the Old Town

Feeling the pinch of its Roman shell, the medieval city burst beyond the palace walls to sprawl west over the centuries to Marmontova. Follow main trade route the *decumanus* through the west palace entrance, the **Iron Gate**, and you'll emerge in **Narodni trg**, a square clad in white marble that served as the epicentre of medieval government. For an aerial perspective of 'People's Square', nicknamed simply Pjaca, the Croatian spelling of piazza, ascend the steps just north of the Iron Gate. The route was trodden by expectant mothers, who prayed before a 13th-century icon in **Our Lady of the Belfry** church, named after the tower (1090) which caps the gate. The square would have been more lovely still had many of its Gothic-Renaissance mansions not been razed in the late 1800s. A few remain on the east flank: a Romanesque belfry with a 24-hour Renaissance clock; a Romanesque palace carved with cartoony reliefs of St Anthony, a devotee hiding in his skirts, and Adam and Eve; and a Renaissance balconied mansion living in reduced circumstances as a shop. The Austro-Hungarians also spared the loggia of the Gothic **City Hall**, today an exhibition space.

City Hall
Gradska vijećnica; open Mon–Sat 10–1 and 5–8

The sister of Narodni trg, **Trg braće Radić** a block south is commonly nicknamed Voćni trg ('Fruit Square') in memory of an earlier market, and stars a bronze of local hero Marulić poring over his poetry by the ever-dramatic Meštrović. The octagonal **tower** on its south side is a leftover of a 1453 garrison citadel Venetian rulers erected to safeguard the seafront from Turkish raids. West, there's a cosy medieval warren to explore before modernity returns with a jolt on the Old Town border of **Marmontova**. Split's shopping high street is christened in honour of French marshal Marmont, an acknowledgement of the Napoleonic governor of Dalmatia who modernized the city and carved out the Riva during Dalmatia's brief stint under French rule. Reinvented in the mid-19th century, his park became **Trg Republike**, flanked on three sides with neo-Renaissance buildings and dubbed the **Prokurative** in optimistic allusion to its Venetian role model, although it's a rather forlorn space next to the buzzy Old Town. More enjoyable is a lively morning **fish market** on Kraj sv. Marije opposite.

Museums North and East of the Old Centre

North of the historic centre, a modern city littered with apartment blocks is rescued from anonymity by one of Split's finest museums. Croatia's oldest, the **Archaeological Museum** 10 minutes' walk north of the centre on Zrinsko-Frankopanska, hoards the rich Roman pickings unearthed at Salona (*see* pp.282–3). Overlook the musty didacticism of its display cases and there are exquisite gold jewellery, glassware and votive statuettes of preening gods to discover. However, the fun is in an arcaded courtyard with a treasure hunt of sculpture to rummage through: Roman and early Christian sarcophagi, grave slabs carved with gloomy snapshots of their interred, and crowds of decapitated statues. Don't miss, in a roadside corner tower, an immaculate 3rd-century marble sarcophagus of Phaedra and Hippolytus; the hero displays a love letter from the amorous stepmother he spurned, she spreads gossip with her attendants stage left, while his troubled father Theseus waits in the wings musing on the accusations that his son made a move on his wife. Just as famous is a 4th-century sarcophagus in the opposite tower dubbed the Good Shepherd for its central relief and whose muddle of early-Christian with Roman imagery such as the gates of Hades has baffled scholars. Incidentally, the stadium of Hajduk Split football club lies not far beyond if you hope to join the most fanatical fans in Croatia (*see* box, below).

Archaeological Museum
*Arheološki muzej; **t** (021) 329 340, www.mdc.hr/split-arheoloski; open June–Sept Mon–Sat 9–2 and 4–8; Oct–May Mon–Fri 9–2 and 4–8, Sat 9–2; adm*

A couple of destinations like east of the old town. In residential district Radunica, in a 17th-century Venetian fortress at Glagoljaška 18, the **Maritime Museum** is a fairly dull salute to Croatian maritime heritage through Roman hydro-archaeology salvage and model ships. Far more enticing is Split's most central beach, **Bačvice**, 10 minutes' walk east of the port and the model of a city beach, with a smattering of cafés and bars nearby. Its shallow

Maritime Museum
*Pomorski muzej; **t** (021) 347 788; open Mon–Fri 9.30–8.30; adm*

Hajduk Split: Brazil in Dalmatia

The capital's football team Dinamo Zagreb may have more league trophies, but for passion you can't beat their great rival, Hajduk Split (*www.hnkhajduk.hr*). Christened for the romanticized bandits that fought the Ottoman Turks in the 1500s, Hajduk are a team about local identity and defiance – famously, Tito, newly installed as a post-war hero and impressed by the team's Dalmatian spirit, was turned down when he suggested Hajduk move to Belgrade as the official army team. The loyalty was well received by the fans. Wherever you go in Dalmatia, you'll see graffiti for the 'Torcida' or 'Torcida 1950', a nod to the year in which fans began to copy Brazilian 'torcidas' fan groups. They adopted the ultra-style antics, too, with a hardcore of fans wearing gangster-style bandana masks and igniting flares in the stands.

A match at Split's 35,000-capacity Poljud stadium in the north of the city is a must for any footie fan worth the name. Games are played at weekends in a domestic season that runs from mid-August to late May, with a two-month break from January. Tickets are available at the stadium gate for as little as 30Kn or in advance from team outlet FanShop Hajduk on Trogirska, a block north of the fish market and with all the logoed merchandise a diehard torcida could wish for.

waters are a favourite venue for games of *picigin*, a cross between handball and football's keepie-uppie that's played in a circle. Ubiquitously favoured by macho young men, it's also rather camp.

West of the Old Centre: Museum of Croatian Archaeological Monuments and Ivan Meštrovic Gallery

It's arguable that Split's premier museums are the pair that lie a 20-minute walk west of the old centre on the Marjan peninsula road, Supilova.

Museum of Croatian Archaeological Monuments
Muzej hrvatskih arheoloških spomenika; **t** *(021) 323 901, www.mhas-split.hr; open Mon–Fri 10–1 and 5–8, Sat 10–1; adm*

A giant sword thrust into the earth announces the Byzantine and medieval artifacts in the modern **Museum of Croatian Archaeological Monuments**. It takes up the baton from the Archaeological Museum to present Croatian sculpture from the Middle Ages, formative years for the young nation. So there are pre-Romanesque *ciboria* and 7th–12th-century plaques which tie plaits, an early medieval design loaded with national significance – police hatbands still use the woven Celtic-style motifs which may have been learned from the Illyrians.

Ivan Meštrović Gallery
Galerija Ivan Meštrović; **t** *(021) 322 988, www.mdc.hr/mestrovic; open May–Sept Tues–Sun 9–7; Oct–Apr Tues–Sat 9–4, Sun 10–3; adm*

Ten minutes further west along the coast road there's the **Ivan Meštrović Gallery.** Within the spacious 1930s villa and gardens of Croatia's most celebrated modern sculptor, family portraits charm reveal a tender side to the artist usually associated with muscular public works such as Grgur Ninski. The sculptor who gave Chicago Grand Park its equestrian Indians also turns in a taut *Job* (1946), racked as if by the traumas of the Second World War; opposition to the Fascist Ustaše and support for Yugoslav nationalism put Meštrović behind bars for five months until high-ranking Italian friends secured his release, allowing the sculptor to flee to America. For all its career-spanning *œuvre*, the gallery's prize is secreted a little way down the road in the Holy Cross Chapel of the **Kaštelet** (*open same times and ticket*). Meštrović revived a dilapidated 16th-century residence to create a gallery for his *Life of Christ* cycle (1950), a stylized New Testament that took nearly 40 years to complete and is lauded by critics as his finest work.

Marjan Hill and Šolta

Locals' choice for a Sunday stroll, the **Marjan Peninsula Nature Reserve** offers breathing space when summer crowds clot the Old Town. It's best accessed via residential district Veli Varoš, a former fishermen's and port workers district whose cobbled alleys feel another world from Croatia's second largest city. From café Vidilica uphill, an asphalt footpath with panoramas of the coast threads west past the **Chapel of St Nicholas** (Sv. Nikola) to the 15th-century **Church of St Jerome** (Sv. Jere), pressed hard against a cliff face in which medieval hermits pondered their faith in caves.

Split saves the finest views over the rugged coastline and islands for those who ascend the peninsula's highest peak, **Telegrin**, reached on a right-hand fork off the main path. Climb to its 178m summit then descend (also on paths from St Jerome) for a dip and a snack in **Bene Bay** at the western tip of the peninsula, after which you'll be grateful that bus 12 makes the return trip back to central Split.

For easy escapism, however, there's **Šolta**. The island offshore from the Marjan peninsula (regular ferries from Split) was Olynta, the isle of figs, to the Greeks. Under the Romans it was Solenta – sun island. Nowadays it's gone to seed; a backwater of olives, figs and rich red soils that produce a red, almost black wine. The reason to come is the beaches – from the quay at Rogač take a connecting bus either to fishing village Maslinica 7km west, with concrete platforms, or to a shingle arc that fronts Nečujam to the east.

Tourist Information in Split

Split > *adjacent to the cathedral on the Peristyle*, **t** *(021) 347 100, www.visitsplit.com; open Mon–Fri 8–8, Sat 8–1, Sun 9–1*

The **tourist information office** provides good maps, lists of departure times for all Split ferries and a contacts sheet of every telephone number and address you'll need, from diving and sailing schools to the car hire and consulates. Its free *Visit Split* booklet has monthly details of cultural and entertainment events.

It also sells the superb **Split Card** (35Kn; free if staying over 72hrs) which allows free or 50% discounts for all museums and galleries, 20% discounts on car hire and cheap deals on hotels and restaurants. Private agencies (*see* p.280) also stock the card.

Festivals

The Peristyle and squares of the Old Town ring to top-notch opera (traditionally Verdi's *Nabucco* and *Aïda*) and classical music and host dance and theatre during the mid-July to mid-Aug arts extravaganza the **Split Summer Festival**, while the Peristyle fills with religious theatre on **7 May** for the feast of patron saint Domnius.

Where to Stay in Split

The good news is that the hotel stock in Split has improved beyond measure in recent years, and there are now several options within the old town. The bad news is that little of it is cheap. The **Marjan**, Obala kneza Branimira 8; **t** (021) 302 111, *www.hotel-marjan.com*, decrepit flagship of the Socialist scene, is expected to reopen after a total overhaul in 2010.

Park >>

Park, Hatzeov perivoj 3, **t** (021) 406 400, *www.hotelpark-split.hr* (€€€). A touch of class from what has long been Split's premier address, in an 18th-century manor near Bačvice beach east of the port. With its airy public areas with marble floors, and hushed waiters, it's all about yesteryear elegance – the terrace is a joy for breakfast – though an upgrade is expected for 2010 to improve rooms and win a fifth star.

Marmont, Zadarska 13, **t** (021) 308 060, *www.marmonthotel.com* (€€€). A stylish boutique number, this opened in 2008 in a refurbished mansion just off Narodni trg. Sensual and sexy, its raw stone walls, black lacquer furniture and chocolate leather furnishings are glamorous without trying too hard. Bathrooms are huge, and a fabulous terrace to boot.

Peristil, Poljana kraljice Jelene 5, **t** (021) 239 070, *www.hotelperistil.com* (€€€). Superbly located beside the Silver Gate and incorporates chunks of Roman masonry into nine double rooms furnished with repro antiques. There's boutique service to match.

Vestibul Palace, Iza Vestibula 4, **t** (021) 329 329, *www.vestibulpalace.com* (€€€). Hidden behind the cathedral and Peristil hotel, the city's first design hotel is a fusion of Roman walls and modernist design. Very hip, very exclusive, though check room sizes of standard doubles – some are on the small side.

Adriana, Riva 8, **t** (021) 340 000, *www.hotel-adriana.hr* (€€). Crying out for a refurb, this is decent without being remarkable, its USP the unbeatable location on the Riva – all but two rooms have a harbour view.

Bellevue, Bana Jelačića 2, **t** (021) 345 644, *www.hotel-bellevue-split.hr* (€€). A Habsburg-era hotel that overlooks Trg Republike and whose décor is a Yugoslavia-era throwback. A good location but overpriced and barely worth its three stars.

Consul, Tršćanska 34, **t** (021) 340 130, *www.hotel-consul.net* (€€). Nothing special but a small, friendly three-star in a leafy residential street north of the centre; all rooms are spacious, some boasting a Jacuzzi.

Globo, Lovretska 18, **t** (021) 481 111, *www.hotelglobo.com* (€€). Four-star mod cons and quietly plush rooms in a business hotel one block west of the bus station and 10mins' walk north of the centre.

Slavija, Buvinina 2, **t** (021) 323 840, *www.hotelslavija.com* (€€). Not as slick as the reception promises, but well located one block east of Braće Radića nonetheless, off bar strip Dosud. Modern(ish) en suites above, cheaper rooms with basic pine décor below. Front rooms overlooking the bars can be noisy in summer. *Breakfast not included.*

Villa Varoš, Miljenka Smojina 1, **t** (021) 483 623, *www.villavaros.hr* (€€–€). A good cheapie away from the crowds in the locals' Varoš quarter west of the Riva. Run by a Croatian-born expat American, it has rooms and apartments.

Kaštel, Mihovilova širina 5, **t** (021) 098 973 8601, *www.kastelsplit.com* (€). A medieval house built into the palace walls, now a sweet little family *pension* with a simple funky style. Amenities in en-suite rooms and apartments include air-conditioning and satellite TV. Some have sea views too. *Breakfast not included.*

Jupiter, Grabovčeva širina 1, **t** (021) 344 081, *www.hotel-jupiter.info* (€). The cheapest beds in Split, which means rooms, although clean, verge on hostel-esque. Great location moments south of the Jupiter Palace, mind. *Breakfast not included.*

For **rooms** (€), try the tourist agencies: the most convenient are **Turistički Biro**, Riva 12, **t** (021) 347 100, and **Atlas**, Nepotova 4 (old town, up from Silver Gate), **t** (021) 346 333.

Eating Out in Split

Split's Old Town is not well served by restaurants. There's a handful in the lanes west of Trg Republike at the fringe of residential district Veli Varoš. For a quick snack on the go, join the queue of locals waiting for *ćevapčići* (spicy meat rissoles) from **Kantun Paulina**, opposite Pizzeria Galija.

Boban, Hektorovićeva 49 (parallel to Bačvice beach road Put Firula), **t** (021) 543 300 (€€€). The gourmet's choice, visited by prime ministers and luminaries such as Plácido Domingo. A well-priced menu of Croatian dishes adds Italian accents – *drob grdobine* (monkfish) grilled with bacon in a cream sauce; spicy lobster and tomato stew *jastog na brudet* with white wine and herbs – and the cellar is sensational.

Šumica, Put Firla 6, **t** (021) 389 897 (€€€). A smart restaurant that's as much about its seafront location in a small pine wood just west of Bačvice beach as it is a good seafood menu.

Noštromo, Kraj svete Marije 10, **t** (021) 091 405 6666 (€€€–€€). Chef's special *riblja plata*, a mixed plate of fishy treats, plus super-fresh catch of the day and seafood in a designer eaterie of blond wood and gleaming aluminium beside the fish market. *Tables are limited: book or wait.*

Kod Joze, Sredmanuška 4 (off Zagrebačka), **t** (021) 347 397 (€€). Hardly the secret it once was and tourists often outnumber locals, but this *konoba* charms nonetheless, its snug stone dining rooms unbeatable for atmosphere. A large menu covers all bases and risottos and pastas are cheap.

Varoš, Ban Mladenova 7, **t** (021) 396 138 (€€) In the Veli Varoš area and highly rated by locals for a slap-up dinner of speciality *peka* dishes – veal, lamb, octopus or squid slow-cooked beneath a lid heaped with charcoal.

Bistro Black Cat, Šegvićeva bb, **t** (021) 490 284 (€). Mexican, Thai, Indian, breakfasts, salads, even Croatian – a crowd-pleasing menu and a handy location in the lanes east of the port. *Closed Sun.*

Pizzeria Galija, Tončićeva 12, **t** (021) 347 932 (€). Split's finest pizzas cooked in a charcoal oven, plus tasty *antipasti* and pastas in sauces laced with cream and brandy, a block north of Trg Republike.

Šperun, Šperun 3, **t** (021) 346 999 (€). Even if it is rather over-run with tourists nowadays, this small Dalmatian buffet in the Veli Varoš area appeals for a good Dalmatian menu and bistro charm, as much as for its reasonable prices. A bar-bistro opposite from the same owner is a good spot to wait for a table outdoors.

Zlatna ribica, Kraj svete Marije 12, no tel (€). No airs or graces and precious few smiles in a snack bar beside the fish market. Daily specials on the blackboard bolster a short menu of small plates of *pržene lignje* (fried squid) or *miješana riba* (mixed fish platter). *Closes 9pm weekdays, 2pm at weekends.*

Zlatna Vrata Pizzeria, Majstora Jurja, **t** (021) 341 834 (€). If Galija has the reputation, this has the atmosphere, thanks to tables scattered in a Renaissance courtyard.

Cafés and Bars in Split

The Riva is crammed with cafés; it's a mite smarter at the western end, probably why locals favour east-end café **Slatice Bobis** for a gossip after market. You'll run out of stamina before you exhaust Split's superb bar culture. It is focused on two areas: Dosud, a block east of Mihovilova širina, with a young noisy crowd on the streets; and Majstora Jurja, arty and relaxed by day, hip and stylish by night.

Academia Ghetto Club, Dosud 10. A bit of a Split legend past a run of bars on Dosud. Arty, with occasional exhibitions in a courtyard and a grungey backroom.

Cafe-Bar St Riva, Riva 19. Wedged in front of the palace walls, with a terrace that offers grandstand views of the Riva beneath.

Gradska kavana, Narodni trg. Wicker seats and grandstand views for people-watching in one of Split's smarter cafés.

Po Bata, Šubićeva 2. Off the north side of Radićev trg and a great little bolthole where a young (p)arty set hold court. Slightly louche and all the better for it.

Porta and **Dante**, Majstora Jurja 4. In a small courtyard, the former is Twenties, brasserie-style bar with over 100 cocktails in its recipe book; the latter has a chunk of Gothic arch in a snug interior and a larger terrace. Both serve morning coffees and late-night drinks to Split's 30-something fashion *cognoscenti*.

Tri Volta (aka Diokleciajn), Dosud 9. A former prostitute hang-out deep in warren of the palace named for its three arches. Expect a crowd of sozzled old boys at the bar by 10am, and snacks of pršut.

Vidilica, Prilaz Vladimira Nazora. Deep chairs in which to enjoy the finest views over Split, from a belvedere on the Marjan peninsula path.

Žbirac, Bačvice beach. Lazy-paced beach bar, as handy for morning coffee as cocktails at sundown.

Nearby **Equador** bar-club lacks the charm but has views from its raised bar.

Entertainment in Split

What's-on **information** is best sourced from the *Visit Split* booklet from the tourist office – it also stocks local *Splitski Navigator* freesheet and flyers.

Croatian National Theatre (Hrvatsko narodno kazalište, or HNK), Trg Gaja Bulata, **t** (021) 344 999. Theatre, classical concerts and opera from the bastion of Split cultural life which co-ordinates the Summer Festival.

Master's, Osječka bb, **t** (021) 536 983. Currently club of choice for the Split *cognoscenti*, which attracts major-name national DJs.

Tropic Club Ecuador, Bačvice beach, no tel. Commercial sounds in a disco-bar overlooking the beach above the Ecuador bar.

Inland from Split

Salona

Salona
t (021) 211 538, www.mdc.hr/split-arheoloski; open May–Oct Mon–Fri 7–7, Sat 9–7, Sun 9–1; Nov–April Mon–Fri 9–3, Sat 9–2; adm

When Split was just a daydream in Emperor Diocletian's idle hours, Colonia Martia Julia Salona 5km inland was the thriving giant of the east Adriatic, a 60,000-strong metropolis on the Jadro river delta whose jurisdiction extended to the Danube. And then came the Avar and Slavic tribes. In AD 614 they delivered a knockout blow to what was a cosmopolitan, multi-faith Byzantine community; the refugees fled to the shell of Diocletian's Palace to found Split, and Salona was left to crumble to dust. Visiting in 1764, Edward Gibbon, author of *The Decline and Fall of the Roman Empire*, recorded that 'a miserable village preserves the name of Salona' and it was left to amateur archaeologist Father Frane Bulić to peel away the centuries in the late 1800s. The prize finds are in Split's Archaeological Museum (*see* p.277), but the foundation walls sketch the self-declared 'Cradle of Croatia' in fields which still seem half-forgotten. Keep your eyes peeled and you'll even spot Roman cart-tracks in the flagstones.

Your tour of the most important site of Croatian antiquity begins on the bus: en route to the site you'll see sections of a 9km-long **aqueduct** which channelled fresh water to Diocletian's retirement home, still in use thanks to 19th-century ingenuity. Beyond the site car park, crumbling walls outline the **Manastirine**, surrounded by a litter of sarcophagi showing its origins as an early Christian necropolis. A kernel chapel built as a requiem for first Salona bishop Domnius, martyred in Diocletian's amphitheatre in AD 304, sprouted private chapels of élite Salona Christians, then flowered into a 5th-century basilica, now ruined but whose columns still punctuate one of three naves. Entry is free up to this point. You'll pay to enter **Villa Bulić** behind, the base for excavations which is aggrandized with Roman grave slabs and statutory. In photos

Getting around Inland from Split

Buses from Split go every 20mins to **Salona** site entrance and hourly to **Klis** and **Sinj**. Sinj is also linked to Knin by 5 buses a day.

inside, the good father gazes across the site, and in the garden there are antique columns to support the rose and honeysuckle bushes in his garden.

Salona begins downhill, as walls which trace eastern suburb Urbs Nova Orientalis, episcopal centre of a city which kept alive the flame of Christianity despite persecution. The AD 313 Edict of Milan which forced pagan Romans to practise religious tolerance also emboldened Christians here to create a 5th-century **basilica**, a far cry from the cellar baths of the private house located below the site access stairs, in which they previously sang clandestine liturgies. Directly east of the basilica are ruins of the **public baths**, still with paths for their hot-water pipes.

Go south along a flagstoned lane then turn right at the five arches of a Roman bridge to find the main road *decumanus maximus*, or take to the walls for a guard's-eye view as you march south to reach the **Porta Caesarea**, an east gate that demarcates the Urbs Nova (New Town) from the Urbs Vetus (Old Town). Olive groves and vineyards have swallowed the old city on the other side of the Augustinian gate. Follow the walls past the outline of the **Kapulić basilica**, Salona's oldest cathedral, and you eventually reach the 2nd-century **amphitheatre** in what was the northwest of the city. It may be stripped of its terraces, but stand at the centre and you can almost hear an 18,000-strong crowd.

Klis and Sinj

This is border country, a little bit Mediterranean and a little bit Balkan in both character and location. A microcosm of Croatia, in fact. **Klis**, 9km inland of Split, has long been the key that opened Dalmatia's back door. From this strategic mountain pass the Romans set out from Kleisa to wallop the Illyrian Delmati tribe, and from AD 852 the knuckles of its rocky fist wore the fortresses of Croat king Trpimir, then Hungarian-Croat medieval monarchs, to prevent inland invaders sneaking towards the coast. This they did with ease until the arrival of the Ottoman Turks to a fortress then under Habsburg control. In 1536, with Bosnia conquered and his army idle after a pincer movement on Italy came to naught (the French pulled out after a papal wigging), Sultan Suleyman the Magnificent swung north up the Adriatic coast. At first Klis held out, bolstered by Uskok refugees who had been dispossessed from lands east and were commanded by Petar Kružić, the dashing captain who built the pilgrims' way to Trsat in Rijeka (*see* p.190). Heroic folk songs tell of a 'David and Goliath' battle between Kružić's page and a monstrous Turkish warrior called Bagora, and ballads salute brave deeds by Uskok raiding parties. But after 25 years, weakened and alone – the Venetian Senate advocated non-aggression to preserve its precious trade – Klis fell. The Uskoks' resolve finally crumbled when the Ottomans brandished the head of their captain skewered on a stick, and on 12 March 1537, having negotiated a surrender, they withdrew to Senj (*see* pp.215–16).

Fortress
Tvrdava; open summer Tues–Sun 7–7; winter Tues–Sun 10–4; adm

The Ottomans bolstered the **fortress** which hunkers down on a ridge in **Klis-Megdan**, core of Klis's three districts; **Klis-Varoš** is beneath, **Klis-Grlo** beyond. They also built the domed cube that seems every inch a mosque despite its conversion to Christianity by the Venetians, who liberated Klis in March 1648 after a gruelling 10-day battle. You'll find it – minus the minaret – at the heart of the three rings of defences with which the Venetians strengthened Klis, determined not to lose it for a second time, and which command a sweeping panorama west to Split, bristling with high-rises. Strongest of the strongholds was the inner **Bembo bulwark** near the church, thickest on its eastern inland walls and whose cannon-holes point over the pitch of local football team NK Uskok.

On the inland road south from Knin, **Sinj**, 21km north of Klis, is famous for the liturgies and lances of its finest hour. In August 1715, little Sinj, barely 500-strong, stared down, alarmed, at 50,000 Ottoman troops massed for a week-long siege beneath a hilltop stronghold (*stari grad*). Dysentery was the more likely cause, but the fact that the soldiers slunk away empty-handed on the Virgin's Assumption Day (15 August) was all the evidence the Sinj faithful needed of intercession by the Madonna, invoked by prayers to an icon removed for safe keeping from a Franciscan monastery. (One folk tale concedes the disease, but argues it was induced by Mary's transmogrifying of well water into blood.) Within days of the astonishing victory, a whip-round generated 80 gold coins to pay for a gold crown that the 16th-century *Sinjska gospa* (Our Lady of Sinj) wears in the **parish church** to this day. The pilgrims who gaze in silent reverence at the demure, Italianate Madonna somehow see beyond her frame of fruitcake Baroque. They arrive in their thousands on 15 August to witness the miracle-working icon being processed around town, the truly devout having made the pilgrimage to Sinj barefoot.

Parish church
open daily 7–12 and 4–8

Their fingers have worn to gold an image of the icon's lucky face on bronze church doors, which also show Turkish forces crumpling beneath a torrent of cavalry, a snapshot of Croatia's most boisterous folk pageant, the **Sinjska alka**. At 3pm sharp on the first Sunday in August, 17 local-born *Alkari* ('tilters'), fabulously outfitted in silk and silver brocade, process before the riderless horse of the vanquished Turkish pasha, and so begins the last medieval chivalric contest of the Venetian Adriatic, instigated in the early 18th century to celebrate Sinj's victory. The main interest for the 15,000 spectators is the jousters' three attempts to spear a 13cm metal ring, the *alka*, hung at 3.32m; consult the tourist office in Split for grandstand tickets. Seats or no, the joust is a splendid affair. Many participants groom luxurious moustaches for a pageant staged with all the swagger of a town fiercely proud of its tribe, caught between coast and continent. Much spit-roast lamb and wine is consumed by all.

From the road opposite the church on central square **Trg kralja Tomislava**, steps ascend towards the scene of Sinj's great triumph, a pine-clad perch all but forgotten, that gazes over a 270-degree panorama over the Sinjsko polje plain, littered, they say, with 10,000 corpses after the Ottoman retreat. Uphill from the other end of the square, a **Regional History Museum** has finds from Roman Aequum, 4km north, plus a Persian furniture in a 19th-century 'flirting room', all sensual rich woods and ivory inlay.

Regional History Museum
Muzej Cetinske krajine; **t** *(021) 821 949; open Mon–Fri 8–4, Sat 8–1; adm*

Where to Stay Inland from Split

Sinj

Alkar, Vrlička 50, **t** (021) 824 488, *www.hotel-alkar.hr* (€). Fifty simple rooms in Sinj's only hotel, a modest three-star.

Eating Out Inland from Split

Klis >
Megdan 57 (off conservatory of Café Belfast), **t** *(021) 240 578, www.tzo-klis.hr; open erratically*

Klis

Spit-roast lamb (*janjetina*) is Klis's delicacy, a savoury taste of the Balkans.

Perlica, Grlo 3, **t** (021) 240 004 (€€€–€€). Smartest of a trio of roadside lamb restaurants in Klis-Grlo east of the castle; its succulent speciality, priced by the kilo, revolves behind glass like some feast for Henry VIII's table.

Konoba Uskok, **t** (021) 240 148 (€). Opposite Perlica, more workaday in style.

Sinj

Sinj specialities include *arambaši*, minced beef, veal and lamb rolled in a *sauerkraut* cabbage leaf bound with *pršut* ham, and from June to Oct *žablji brudet* (a sort of frog *bouillabaisse*) or breadcrumbed frog's legs *pohane žabe*.

Ispod ure, Istarska 2, **t** (021) 822 229 (€€). Meaty roulade *arambaši* (*see above*) is prepared in Sinj's finest *konoba*, a snug charmer with a fetching stone dining room, just off the main square. The wine list is full of local varieties to ponder. *Open Sun from 4pm*.

Brač

The locals may grumble at the island's loss of identity during the annual invasion from the mainland, but after decades of depopulation Brač is finally looking forward. Before it accepted the tourist kuna (and an airport) in the 1960s, Dalmatia's third largest island was more famous for the white marble of its quarries: Brač stone was used for Diocletian's palace in Split, and the high altar of Liverpool's cathedral. Sadly it didn't put the white into America's White House whatever locals claim. This trade continues on a minor scale in the interior. Here Brač has a rock problem. It has it under control, packing loose stones into terraces or circular *bunja* (shepherds' shelters) among scrubby pine. In inland villages houses and vineyards go gently to seed, abandoned in the early 20th century by farmers ruined by phylloxera. Indeed, Bol might be a sleepy place were it not for two destinations on opposite sides of the island: ferry quay Supetar and Bol, site of the most famous beach in Croatia. That Supetar and solitude are both only an hour ferry ride from Split are equally good reasons to go.

North Brač: Supetar and Beyond

Most visitors arrive at the palm-lined harbour of main settlement **Supetar**. Long before it got the spillover from Split, it was christened after a 6th-century basilica to St Peter, scraps of whose mosaic lie before the replacement Baroque **parish church**. With that ticked off, the only cultural sights are the funerary sculptures in the **cemetery** beyond the harbour. The best were created for the élite families by Ivan Rendić (1849–1932), a local son who developed into one of the era's leading sculptors. He's also hard to pin down due to eclectic tastes: there's a tender *Pietà* is on the tomb of Mihovil Frasnović, Art Nouveau for that of Rinaldo Culić by the entrance, and a stodgy Byzantine-inspired mausoleum of the Radnić family. The centrepiece, not by Rendić, is the bell-shaped **Petrinović mausoleum**, crowned by a mourning angel. If it's open, you'll find inside an Art Nouveau ode to Resurrection and life in the interior. If not, there are more Rendić bronzes in the library (knjižnica) as the **Galerija Ivan Rendić.**

Petrinović mausoleum
open (in theory) summer daily 9–2 and 4–7; adm

Galerija Ivan Rendić
located before restaurant Vinotoka on Jobova off the harbour; open Mon–Sat 8.30–1.30 and 2.30–7.30

From Supetar, the main road tracks the coast 5km west to the village of **Sutivan**, then cuts into the scrubby uplands before descending to **Milna** 20km southwest of Supetar. After a whirlwind 19th century – a short-lived island capital under Russian protectorate during the Napoleonic wars and a late spurt building ships – it is now just a pretty fishing village in which to idle among a tangle of alleys at the end of a deep natural bay.

ⓘ Milna >
*main square, **t** (021) 636 233, www.milna.hr; open July–Aug daily 8–10; June, Sept Mon–Sat 8–1 and 3–8, Sun 8.30–12*

For culture, head east of Supetar to charming **Splitska**, retired after years as the export port of Brač stone, then 3km south, to

Getting to and around Brač

There are summer **flights** to an airport 11km east of Bol from Zagreb.

From Split, **ferries** go hourly to Supetar in summer (otherwise every 2½hrs) and summer **catamarans** shuttle from Split to Milna and Bol. Ferries from Makarska link to Sumartin on the eastern corner. Bol is linked to Jelsa, Hvar, by summer catamarans (passenger-only) several times a day. Private **taxi boats** also shuttle at frequent intervals. **Buses** meet all ferry arrivals at Supetar and Sumartin. Supetar is the hub of transport; every couple of hours ply routes west to Milna and south to Bol, two or three times a day inland to Škrip or east to Sumartin.

Hire **cars and scooters** from **Mjenjačnica, t** (021) 630 709, or **Atlas, t** (021) 631 105, at the Supetar harbour; you must book in summer.

---

reach **Škrip**, a haphazard sprawl of stone houses overlooked by modernity. It's a three-hour, 4km walk here from Supetar should you feel up to it. The island's oldest settlement, founded by ancient Illyrians, Škrip is at its most nostalgic around the Baroque **Church of St Helena** (Crkva sv. Jelene) – the village is said to be the birthplace of St Helena, mother of Constantine the Great – beyond which a 16th-century **tower**, fortified to withstand Turkish raids, houses a junkshop of island ethnology plus a relief of Hercules as the **Brač Museum**. Apparently, Diocletian's wife and daughter were laid in the museum's incorporated Roman mausoleum, built atop a Cyclopean wall circa 5000 BC.

Brač Museum
Bračkі muzej; key next door if locked; open summer daily 8–8; adm

South Brač: Bol and Around

Up and over the highlands of pine scrub, the south road from Supetar switches west and twists beneath mountain Draževac to **Bol**. This quiet fishing village was reinvented practically overnight when tourists discovered **Zlatni rat** (Golden Cape). There's no denying the allure of Croatia's most famous beach, a shingle finger which pokes into turquoise seas at the end of a pine-shaded promenade; the problem is finding space in August. The beach is also renowned for good kite- and windsurfing when afternoon winds funnel between Brač and Hvar (see p.288).

Bol village, meanwhile, gathers around its harbour. At its back the **Branislav Dešković Gallery** showcases works by Croatian sculptors such as Ivan Meštrović and Ivan Rendić plus Expressionist canvases. There's more art – a treasured Tintoretto *Madonna with Child* – plus ancient Greek coins and amphorae in the museum of the **Dominican monastery**, a 10-minute walk beyond the harbour. A small beach on its far side offers a quieter spot to lay out a towel.

Branislav Dešković Gallery
t (021) 635 270 open summer daily 9–1; adm

Dominican monastery
Dominikanski samostan; t (021) 778 000; open July–Aug daily 8–12 and 5–9, May–June and Sept daily 10–12 and 4–7; adm

Boards at the harbour tout trips to 'Pustinja Blaca' by boat, by far the easiest means of travel to the Glagolitic **hermitage** built in 1588 above **Blaca bay** as a defensive strategy against the Turkish fleets that battered Bol in the 16th century. Its last incumbent, Niko Miličević, an amateur astrologer with a passion for clocks, left behind some astronomical equipment and there are cells and a kitchen. Be warned that it's a 2km slog up from the bay – you might keep in mind the prospect of a view across to Hvar and a dramatic location beneath a vertiginous cliff.

Dragon Cave
above the hamlet; ask Bol tourist office for opening hours

In the same area there's **Murvica**, 5km west of Bol. Blaca monks are said to have carved the menagerie of monsters on the so-called **Dragon Cave** above the hamlet.

Another path ascends north off the main road just free of Bol's sprawl to **Vidova gora**, which feels every inch the highest peak (780m) of the Croatian islands if you climb its south-facing slope in full glare of the sun. Take plenty of water or, better still, make a right-hand turn 2km southeast of Nerežišće and drive up for the most astounding view on Brač: south over Zlatni rat to the slivers of Hvar, Korčula and the Pelješac Peninsula, and southeast to Vis humped on the horizon. A *konoba* operates at the summit in summer.

ⓘ Bol >>
far end of harbour, **t** *(021) 635 638, www.bol.hr; open July–Aug daily 8–10; Sept–June Mon–Fri 8.30–2 and 4–8, Sat–Sun 9–12*

ⓘ Supetar >
Porat 1 (opposite ferry dock), **t** *(021) 630 551, www.supetar.hr; open July–Aug daily 8am–10pm; Sept–June Mon–Sat 8–4*

★ Palace Deškovic >

Activities on Brač

Hire of windsurfing and kitesurfing kit in Bol is through watersports agencies on the path to Zlatni Rat. Try **Big Blue**, mobile **t** 098 212 419, *www.big-blue-sport.hr*, near the Bonaca hotel, or **Nautic Center Bol**, mobile **t** 098 222 842, *www.nautic-center-bol.com*, near the Elaphusa hotel, also home of the Dolphin Diving Center.

Where to Stay on Brač

Supetar

Villa Adriatica, Put Vele Luke 31, **t** (021) 343 806, *www.villaadriatica.com* (€€). A family-run hotel, refurbished in 2003 to provide modern accommodation as cheerful as the welcome. Also has a palm-shaded terrace and plunge pool.

Supetar tourist agencies book private **rooms**: **Mjenjačnica**, **t** (021) 630 709, or **Atlas**, **t** (021) 631 105, at the harbour.

Pučisća

Palace Deškovic, beside the church behind the harbour, **t** (021) 778 240, *www.palaca-deskovic.com* (€€€). High-end retreat that ticks all boxes: a renovated aristocrat's Renaissance palace, in a quiet coastal village east of Supetar and with a charming owner. It's beautifully furnished with a light artistic touch and antique furnishings in rooms. *Book a long time in advance.*

Bol

Elaphusa, Braška cesta 13, **t** (021) 306 200, *www.bluesunhotels.com* (€€€–€€). Large resort hotel of the Blue Sun chain near the famous beach, renovated top to bottom into neutrals and blond wood in 2007. *Good discounts out of season*.

Ivan, David Cesta 11a, **t** (021) 640 888, *www.hotel-ivan.com* (€€). Simple and spotless four-star accommodation – 8 doubles, 32 apartments – plus a pool 300m east of the harbour.

Kaštil, Frane Radića 1, Bol, **t** (021) 635 995, *www.kastil.hr* (€€). Smart modern style and a harbour location compensate for the cosy dimensions in Bol's best hotel, created from a fortification against Turkish raids and with a nice terrace of wicker loungers.

Source private **rooms** from **Boltours**, V. Nazora 18, **t** (021) 635 693, *www.boltours.com*.

Eating Out on Brač

Supetar

Palute, Porat 4, **t** (021) 631 730 (€€). All the usuals plus the largest harbour terrace.

Vinotoka, Jobova 6, **t** (021) 630 969 (€€). Still the finest food in town even if it has closed over its terrace of one of two dining rooms; there are tables outside in summer. Highly rated for its fish and authentic Dalmatian cuisine, but many dishes are prepared with Italian flavours.

Luka, Januarskih Žtrava 32, no tel (€). On the far side of the harbour, a new rustic-chic *konoba* which gets the sun over breakfast.

Bol

Gušt, Frane Radića 14, **t** (021) 635 911 (€€€–€€). Bygone rustic charm and the full Dalmatian kitchen. Be prepared to queue for an outside table in summer.

Miln, Ante Starićeva 11, **t** (021) 635 376 (€€€–€€). One of Bol's more atmospheric addresses, created from an old mill en route to the monastery. Coastal views from its garden terrace are magic at sunset.

Bars on Brač

Bol

Moby Dick, Loža bb. Laid-back terrace bar above the harbour with mellow grooves and chilled beers.

Veradero, Fraje Radića bb. Open-air cocktail bar at the heart of Bol, with all the wicker loungers and palms you could desire. DJs pick up a party atmosphere on summer evenings.

Hvar

No island in Croatia has to live up to hype like Hvar. Even without the tittle-tattle that appears in the gossip press every summer, statistics name it as the longest island in the Adriatic and the sunniest, basking in an average 2,724 hours per year. With poetic licence it is also the most fragrant, perfumed in its interior by clumps of lavender that add Impressionist blotches of dusty purple to a canvas of grey limestone, pine green and aqua flecked with silver sunlight. No wonder that Hvar is no stranger to tourism: sickly Austrians from 1868, lured to an island where the mercury rarely dipped below 8°C; pleasure-seekers to the 'Yugoslav Madeira' in the early 1900s; or inter-war visitors such as writer Rebecca West, who delighted in an island 'where the air is so sweet'. At the turn of this century, Hollywood film stars hid behind their designer sunglasses in Hvar Town cafés, and on our last visit the Croatian president was there on his holidays. It's been a long time since Hvar was a secret.

The first visitors in recorded history were the ancient Greeks, in 385 BC, who named their colony Pharos (today's Stari Grad) in honour of the islet off Alexandria. Its army commander Demetrius, a favourite of Illyrian Queen Teute, eased it into a flourishing town, then became too big for his boots and snubbed Rome. The imperial fleet duly appeared offshore in 219 BC. The Romans rechristened the island Pharia, which became Byzantine naval base Fara, a name 8th-century Slavs chewed into Hvar. Annexed by the Venetian Republic in 1240, the focus shifted east and new capital Hvar Town emerged, nurtured from 1420 as an east Adriatic reflection of La Serenissima's luminescence. It shines now as a Croatian St-Tropez, the ideal base for forays to Stari Grad, gentle Vrboska or laid-back port-resort Jelsa.

Getting to and around Hvar

Summer **ferries** go from Ancona, Italy, to Stari Grad. Stari Grad is on the Rijeka–Dubrovnik coastal ferry service (*see* p.61). From Split, **car ferries** go to Stari Grad (3–5 per day) , and regular ferries and **catamarans** from Split to Lastovo call at Hvar Town (no cars disembarking). In June–Sept, SEM catamarans also zip between Split and Hvar Town. A daily ferry shuttles between Split and Jelsa via Bol, Brač. From Drvenik (on the mainland south of Makarska), frequent ferries chug across to Sućuraj at the eastern tip of the island. Be warned: peak season queues to leave Hvar from Stari Grad are horrendous. Plan to arrive early, then make it a couple of hours earlier.

Local **buses** to the main towns meet ferries at Stari Grad. From Stari Grad there are buses to Hvar Town (9 per day both ways). From Hvar Town there are buses to Vrboska (5 a day), Jelsa (8 a day) and Sućuraj (1 a day).

Taxi-ferries from the harbour at Hvar Town serve south-coast beaches Milna, Zaraće and Dubovica. To explore nearby bays and the Pakleni islands at leisure, hire **motorboats** from the *mandrač* harbour; 500Kn peak season, 350Kn in shoulder months.

Car/scooter hire is through tourist agencies (*see* p.297).

Hvar Town

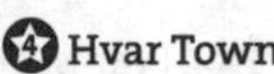
Hvar Town

The heart of the hype is Hvar Town. Just a small town, it is nevertheless the premier holiday destination in the country after Dubrovnik, one whose claim to be a glossy Croatian St-Tropez finally stands up to scrutiny after a massive upgrade of its hotels in 2008. And, like the French Riviera, you come to do nothing more complicated than eat, drink, tan and party. Crisp white shirts show off deep tans in the cafés of main square Trg sv. Stjepana, and the super-rich aboard super-yachts moor in the harbour.

Such is the whirlwind of hype that everyone forgets about the Renaissance backcloth hung by the Venetian Republic in a key staging post on the Oriental trade route. For two centuries Hvar was the golden child of the east Adriatic, a prosperous Renaissance trader where nobles and commoners shared equal rights, probably inspired by the shared woe of an Ottoman raid. In the run-up to the Battle of Lepanto off Corfu in 1571, Uluz Ali, the most daring of Ottoman corsairs, put Hvar to the torch on 17 August. Almost all of its kernel, the colour of pale honey and butterscotch, was built afterwards.

There's a dollop of art and culture, too. But, for all its good looks, Hvar is not one for cultural pilgrims so much as idle tourists, a place to people-watch, stroll a leisurely *korzo* at dusk or laze on the shores of the Pakleni islets just offshore. Enjoy.

Trg Svetog Stjepana

In this compact capital, a relaxed morning's sightseeing then a few more hours to mop up after lunch will tick off most sights in a day. Begin on main piazza Trg svetog Stjepana, lined with creamy late-Renaissance mansions; as bewitching when it glows with its own private sunset in late afternoon as when whitewashed in moonlight. Factual superlatives rank it the largest square in Dalmatia. You will probably be more impressed by its choice of cafés.

Sit on the wall of the ***mandrač*** (inner harbour) at the square's western end, spiked by Baroque pyramids and it narrates local history too. Two winged Lions of St Mark snarl as a centrepiece on the Venetian town hall **loggia** that fronts the Palace hotel on your left. Once you look, the Republic's icon is stamped everywhere in this former corner of government: a rescued duo are incorporated on the loggia's side; another paws St Mark's gospel on the belfry left over from the now-demolished Governor's Palace; one more is on the base of the flag pillar. This is Venice as statement, declaring who's boss in a town where the commoners dared to revolt. In 1510, led by one Matija Ivaić, the people swore on a cathedral crucifix to overthrow their aristocratic oppressors, an oath so terrible that it gave the crucifix's Christ a nosebleed and prompted weeks of mass self-flagellation that ended the revolt in Hvar Town before it even began. Not elsewhere, though. For five years Ivanić and his rebels, holed up in Vrboska, held control over most of the island. They even dared a second push on the capital, until Venice, fearful that the contagion of disobedience might spread elsewhere in Dalmatia, gathered a fleet and swatted aside the peasant rabble. Vrboska was plundered, and the rebels swung from the yard-arm.

Theatre
currently undergoing renovation

After a century of mutual bad feeling, in 1610 the commoners and the ruling oligarchy wiped the slate clean with a proclamation of equality, recalled on the **theatre** lintel by its foundation in '*Anno secundo pacisime*' ('Second Year of Peace'). In a display of equanimity, in 1612 Croatia's first theatre opened its doors to prole and aristo alike, the first theatre in Europe to do so, and a typically educated step from a town which had nurtured humanist aristocrat-poets such as Hanibal Lucić (1485–1553). The theatre claims the top floor of the stone barn on the other side of the *mandrač*, in fact the arsenal where Venetian war galleons were hauled out for repair. By 2010 you should be able to see into the boxy playhouse after its renovation. Until then, the balcony is the ideal viewpoint for the square, especially during the evening *korzo*. Prior to renovation, a **gallery** in the foyer before the theatre hung modern Croatian art and a winged dragon figurehead from a Hvar galleon which fought in the Venetian, Papal and Spanish fleet at the Battle of Lepanto.

The backdrop to Trg svetog Stjepana's ensemble piece is **St Stephen's Cathedral** (Katedrala sv. Stjepana), flanked by a campanile which rises in a crescendo of arches. Behind the loveliest late Renaissance façade in central Dalmatia, the cathedral is a bit of a disappointment. There are Venetian Baroque altarpieces lost in the gloom, late Gothic choir stalls, and a murky 15th-century *Pietà* by Spaniard Juan Boschetus crammed awkwardly into a later Italian work, and not nearly as mysterious as a 14th-century Venetian icon of the Virgin, one of the oldest in Dalamatia. The copy in the cathedral is smothered by an altar of overblown Baroque, so pop next door to see the incense and candlelight of the real thing in the **Bishop's Museum**. Other treasures of the Hvar bishops include a florid sarcophagus (1674) to host town co-patron St Prospero and an oil of the wall-girdled, wave-washed town in the 1700s, watched over by St Anne.

Bishop's Museum
*Biskupski muzej; **t** (021) 742 160; open summer Mon–Sat 9–12 and 4–6; winter via tourist information; adm*

North of Trg Svetog Stjepana

There's little to tick off, but much to enjoy, in the alleys terraced above the square. Here you'll find most of the aristocrats' stone mansions; the finest was never completed, and has always remained a shell with slender Venetian-Gothic windows. Inspired by the Hektorović family cow on its coat of arms, popular consent names it the **Hektorović Palace**, as the Hvar *pied-à-terre* of aristocrat-poet Petar Hektorović (*see* 'Stari Grad', p.294). Actually academics suggest instead it was built in 1463 by another branch of the family tree. Just uphill, a nameless noble announces himself with a rabbit that's got it in the neck.

Benedictine convent
*Benediktinski samostan; **t** (021) 741 052; open Mon–Sat 10–12 and 5–7; adm*

Continue up Ivanića, which opens out at a **Benedictine convent**, formerly the house where Hanibal Lucić penned his lyric dramas and now a **museum** of devotional oils and spiderweb lace doilies the nuns spun from agave fibres. They didn't have far to go for thread – agave bristle on the hill above, which has always been Hvar's refuge. The Illyrians camped here, as did the Romans and the Byzantine Slavs, and the Venetians built its 1551 **fortress**. Thanks to restoration – locals once claimed with a twinkle that fairies danced among the ruins at night – you can peer into a dungeon or look at Roman amphorae salvaged from ancient shipwrecks. The biggest attraction is the panorama of medieval fortifications, roofs and offshore Pakleni islets.

Fortress
Španjola; open daily summer 9–midnight, winter 9–8; adm

Turn left above the convent; lateral alley Bože Domančića threads west to the **Church of St Mark** (Crkva sv. Marka), whose campanile pokes above the rooftops west of the *mandrač*. The Dominican monks of the 17th century practised devotions in this secluded spot; visit now for showcases of **archaeology** from prehistoric to Roman.

Archaeology
*Arheološka zbirka; **t** (021) 741 009, www.mdc.hr/mhb; open summer 10–1 and 8–11; adm*

The Franciscan Monastery
*Franjevački Samostan; **t** (021) 741 193; open May–Oct Mon–Sat 10–12 and 4–7; Nov–April via tourist office; adm*

The Franciscan Monastery (Franjevački Samostan)

Channelled between palms and yachts, the **Riva** (aka 'Obala') quay tracks south off Trg sv. Stjepana to the Gothic Franciscan monastery, built through the bequest of the captain of the Venetian fleet, Piero Soranza. Its most famous prize is to be found off a cloister in the refectory. Academics attribute the 17th-century canvas of the **Last Supper** to Ravenna's Matteo Ingoli, but no one is really sure. Hearsay claims the Italianate work was painted by an artist who was nursed back to health by the monks after being dumped ashore by a Venetian captain. He sought live models in Hvar Town, they say, but was unable to cajole anyone to accept the role of Judas, which is why he sits with his back turned, his face invisible. Another thread to the tale has it that he planted the 300-year-old cypress tree in the garden behind the refectory, just like his hero Michelangelo had done in Rome. An equally enjoyable narrative goes that a Rothschild offered to buy the work for as many gold coins as would fit on the canvas. It fills the back wall.

A small **gallery** opposite hangs other devotional works, plus a rather joyless *Annunciation* panel by luminary 20th-century sculptor Ivan Meštrović.

Such is the fame of the monastery's epic canvas that its **church** is often overlooked. This is a shame, because, behind a sombre exterior with a portal lunette of the Virgin and Child by Nikola Firentinac, a pupil of Donatello who oversaw the completion of the Šibenik cathedral (*see* p.250), it's extraordinary stuff, nowhere more so than in the **choir screen** (1583). The prophets painted by Venetian artist Francesco de Santacroce hold their predictions like divine telexes beneath a kinetic Passion cycle (1607) by Martin Benetović, a local noble who penned comic verse in his spare hours and who depicts the Roman soldiers in the Betrayal as Croatia's arch-enemy, the Ottoman Turks. The most famous body buried beneath church flagstones is that of poet Hanibal Lucić, in pride of place before the high altar.

Around Hvar Town: Beaches and the Pakleni Islands

Bays scallop the shore west of the centre before the big hotels, reached around the **Šumica headland** opposite the inner harbour. The most developed is that before the Amfora hotel, where you'll find the Bonj les bains, a Thirties changing room renovated into a spa area. There's also a scrap of beach before the Franciscan monastery if you're desperate. A better option is to continue for 2.5km beyond the monastery to **Pokonji dol**, a lovely bay with smooth white pebbles and a pair of summer *konobe* to make a day of it. A footpath traverses its far headland to more beaches in **Mekićevica bay**, with its own *konoba*. Taxi-boats from the inner harbour shuttle frequently in summer, many continuing on to the wooded shores and shady coves of **Milna**, a small resort 5km from the centre.

Boat captains also advertise trips to the idyllic **Pakleni otoci**, an archipelago of islets christened by the *paklina* pine resin which sealed bygone boat timbers. **Jerolim** is for naturists; **Marinkovac** has two pine-fringed bays; and **Sv. Klement** has a good sandy beach, **Palmižana**, fringed by pine, lavender and rosemary. Long a favourite picnic spot of Hvar locals, it is the most developed bay of the archipelago, backed by a fine restaurant. From here, a footpath traces the islet's spine for 2km to reach **Vlaka**, a nest of lanes where Romans had summer picnics. All the islets have a seasonal restaurant.

Stari Grad

The road from Hvar Town dips down to follow the coast east, past **Milna**, and the abandoned hamlet of **Zaraće**, with good snorkelling, then cuts away inland at the pretty bay of **Dubovica** towards Stari Grad. The island's first settlement, ancient Greek Pharos, Stari Grad (literally 'Old Town') has long been in the shadow of Hvar Town. But change is in the air. Packed behind its harbour, Stari Grad is gentrifying rapidly. Tatty stone houses have been repaired, lanes smartened. Indeed, Stari Grad is slowly emerging as a bohemian alternative to chic Hvar Town, where artists' ateliers add to the appeal of its picture-postcard looks. The problem for now is a lack of accommodation.

Tvrdalj
t (021) 765 068; open June–Sept daily 10–1 and 6–8; adm

The town's big sight remains the **Tvrdalj**, that backs onto a harbourside piazza. Unlike so many of his aristocratic peers, Petar Hektorović espoused humanism in deed and print. With his home town left to its fate by the Venetians fretting over their capital, the author of 'Fishing and Talks with Fishermen', a manifesto for equality masquerading as a chronicle of a trip around the neighbouring islands, erected the 16th-century stronghold as a manor house and refuge for travellers and the poor – '*Pro Itinerantibus*' and '*Pro Pauperibus*', as two of the many multilingual plaques which stud the walls put it. Nor did his idealism stop there. The poet conceived his manor as a model of God's universe, where fish swam in a pond fed by sea water, humans were at ground level and doves fluttered above in a watchtower/loft. With a fishpond (still stocked with grey mullet) to feed stomachs, and walls studded with *bon mots* to fill minds, Hektorović also had sieges in mind. 'Remember that neither riches nor fame, beauty nor age can save you from death,' he moralizes by the pond, which must have been uplifting when Uluz Ali and his crew brandished their scimitars a year after the manor was completed in 1570. 'Know what you are and how you can be proud,' he adds by the foyer latrine.

Blankini Palace
t (021) 765 910; open summer daily 10–12 and 7–9; adm

Museum
open Mon–Sat 10–12 and 5–7.30; adm

What locals made of his maxim, 'The days flow by like waves and do not return', on the mansion's right-hand side is anyone's guess. Here, the **Blankini Palace** displays Greek and Roman finds from an antique shipwreck, plus maritime items, while a path on the other side of the Tvrdalj threads to a fortified **Dominican monastery**. Local lore has it that the Joseph of Arimathea on an *Internment of Christ* in its **museum** portrays Hektorović himself, an old man with a candyfloss beard who donated the canvas by Tintoretto, while the Mary Magdalene is said to depict the humanist's daughter. The museum's tomb-slabs are definitely from Pharos and Roman Pharia, that of Stari Grad's local hero is in the monastery church in front of the high altar.

There is more ancient history at the **Church of St Stephen** (Crkva sv. Stjepana) in the town centre: Greek blocks recycled from the gate of Pharos support its campanile, and Eros leans on an inverted torch, a symbol of death on a Roman tomb-slab mounted into a wall. Excavations continue 100m back towards the main road, behind the diminutive 6th-century **Church of St John** (Crkva sv. Ivana). There is a small **beach** west of the harbour, towards the ferry terminal, or you can swim from concrete platforms that front the hotels on the opposite headland.

Vrboska, Jelsa and Beyond

ⓘ Vrboska
*at bus station, **t** (021) 774 137, www.vrboska.info; open July–Aug Mon–Sat 8–12 and 6–9, Sun 10–12 and 7–8; Sept–June Mon–Fri 8–2*

Fishing museum
Ribarski muzej; open summer Tues–Sun 9–12 and 8–10; adm

Fortress-church of St Mary
Crkva-tvrdava svete Marije; open (in theory) summer Mon–Sat 10–12, 7–8.30; adm

Church of St Lawrence
Crkva sv. Lovre; open same times as Fortress-church of St Mary

Old salts in **Vrboska** say they can forecast the weather by the water level in the narrow inlet which snakes through the centre. For the village 6km east of Stari Grad had the champion sardine fleet on Hvar. At a loose end since a fish factory closed in 1977, Vrboska is left with a **fishing museum** on its harbour.

With its fleet gone, its quiet is broken only by the bells of **Fortress-church of St Mary**. Shocked into action by the sack of Vrboska by Uluz Ali in 1571, villagers bolstered the church with a crenellated tower and a bulwark like a stone destroyer. On the off-chance that it's open, you can ascend from the sacristy to peer over battlements on its rooftop and look in the apse for a 1737 grave of parson Petar Fabrić that sermonizes, '*Ne differas amice – hodie mihi cras tibi.*' ('You won't be different, friend – me today, you tomorrow.') Otherwise the nearby **Church of St Lawrence** hides a master-class of Venetian Old Masters. Skies and saints – Lawrence, flanked by John the Baptist and Nicholas – brood on a melodramatic high altar work that Vrboska would love to believe is by Titian, but which academics attribute to Paolo Veronese. Wishful thinking also assigned the *Our Lady of the Rosary* stuffed in a right-hand chapel to high Renaissance master Jacopo Bassano rather than his Mannerist son Leandro. The hosanna of nameless saints who ring his Madonna were summoned to clinch victory in the Battle of Lepanto.

The best **beaches** for a dip are on the other side of the inlet at the end of the peninsula. Quieter rocky coves scallop the north bank.

Compared with the indolence elsewhere, **Jelsa** comes on industrious and stolid around a Habsburg harbour built in the 19th century to serve a shipping industry. For a century while Hvar Town mouldered, Jelsa was the ascendant star of the island thanks to its deep-water port. Look beyond its 19th-century façade, however, and

Jelsa reveals deeper roots in alleys that conceal gems such as the lozenge-shaped Renaissance **Church of St John** (Crkva sv. Ivana), shoehorned into a tiny square of mansions like a set for an Italian operetta. You'll find it to the left off a café-filled **central square**, at whose back a staircase ascends to the **parish church**. The Habsburg administration added its neo-Baroque façade to smarten up a church that had been fortified in 1531; a prescient move, as it transpired, because 40 years later Uluz Ali's fleet appeared in the bay – only Jelsa and Hektorović's Tvrđalj thwarted the Ottoman corsair. The church's fortified tower are visible from the side and are painted on a Baroque altarpiece inside.

Two pine-fringed bays of deep turquoise beg for swimsuits: **Mina bay** 600m east of the harbour, and **Grebišće**, 500m further on beyond the Holiday campsite.

Away from the major settlements, Hvar island is rustic and sleepy. Long before **Humac**, 7km east of Jelsa, fell into ruin as a shepherd's settlement, prehistoric man loped around its limestone uplands. He bedded down five millennia ago in a **cave**, now on show to groups. South of Jelsa, a tunnel burrows through the rugged hills to south coast villages, isolated among vineyards, olive groves, lavender and rosemary. Largest and most modern of the quartet, minor resort **Zavala** has a decent beach, while **Sv. Nedjelja** 9km west is positioned below a cave that conceals remains of an Augustine monastery. It is also the launchpad for a walk up to Hvar high point **Sv. Nikola**, with views in all directions from its eyrie at 628m.

Cave
Grapčeva spilja, mobile **t** *091 523 9463 or via konoba Humac* *(see p.298)**; tours summer Mon, Wed and Sat 9am; adm*

Meneghello >>

Hvar Town >
Trg svetog Stjepana bb (in arsenal/ theatre), **t** *(021) 741 059/977, www.tzhvar.hr; open July–Aug daily 8–2 and 3–11; June and Sept Mon–Sat 8–1 and 4–9, Sun 10–1 and 6–8; Oct–May Mon–Fri 8–2*

Activities on Hvar

Hvar Adventure, off the Riva behind the arsenal, **t** (021) 717 813, *www.hvaradventure.com*, organizes trips to go sea kayaking, sailing, walking and rock climbing, plus combined adventure packages. Tuition is also available.

Where to Stay on Hvar

Hvar Town

Adriana, Hvar habour bb, **t** (021) 750 200, *www.suncanihvar.hr* (€€€). The only hotel with Riva views, reopened in 2008 as the luxury spa retreat for the beau Monde: think sexy white lacquer, frosted glass and marble. Has a first-rate spa, seawater pool and a hip terrace bar.

Amfora, Tonija Petrića bb, **t** (021) 750 300, *www.suncanihvar.hr* (€€€). Gargantuan 315-room hotel above a beach 1.5km west of the centre which reopened in 2008 as a grand deluxe resort, refurbished with an eye for Pop Art retro in (smallish) rooms. Astounding pools complex.

Meneghello, Palmižana, Sv. Klement islet, **t** (021) 717 270, *www.palmizana.hr* (€€€). A classy holiday village of stone villas, apartments and bungalows, set above the best beach in the area. Bohemian and artistic, from the exhibitions and fashion shows to stylish décor that dares to be quirky. Superb restaurant too. *Minimum stay one week.*

Riva, Riva bb, **t** (021) 750 100, *www.suncanihvar.hr* (€€€). Classy small hotel on the waterfront that styles itself a yacht harbour hotel. Understated sophistication reigns in a palate of red, grey, black and oiled teak, rooms have monochrome portraits of Fifties' film icons. Great restaurant and bar.

Palace, Trg svetog Stjepana bb (main square), **t** (021) 741 966, *www.suncanihvar.hr* (€€€–€€). Hvar Town's first hotel, of late-1800s vintage, does justice to its location after a refurb' in 2008. Calm, neutral elegance in high-ceilinged rooms, the best with a harbour view.

Park, Bankete bb, **t** (021) 718 337, *www.hotelparkhvar.com* (€€€–€€). Pleasant suites in modern Med style in a vintage building above the inner harbour (beside the Palace hotel). Sea views and under-floor heating throughout; some apartments also available.

Podstine, Pod stine, **t** (021) 740 400, *www.podstine.com* (€€€–€€). Sea views and tasteful rooms, most with a balcony, in a pleasant family hotel split over two blocks, 20 minutes' west of town above a beach.

Villa Nora, Matković Ante bb, **t** (021) 742 498, *www.villanora.eu* (€€€–€€). Small family hotel Hvar installed in an aristocrats' house uphill from main square in 2007. Homely rather than glamorous, four-star comforts and charming owners. Its Lucullus restaurant is rated, too.

Croatia, Majerovica bb, **t** (021) 742 400, *www.hotelcroatia.net* (€€). Old-world elegance in a relaxed villa set in a park beside the Amfora hotel. Nothing flash, just simple parquet-floored rooms with wrought iron balconies looking across the bay.

Dalmacija, Obala Ivana Lučića-Lavčevića bb, **t** (021) 741 120, *www.suncanihvar.hr* (€€). Acceptable if rather tired rooms rescued by a location overlooking the Franciscan monastery. Nice terrace for breakfast too. Still, only slightly cheaper than the Palace.

Private rooms (€) are your only chance of a cheap bed. They can be sourced via the tourist office website or try **Atlas**, **t** (021) 741 911, and **Pelégrini t** (021) 742 743, both on the harbourfront Riva.

Stari Grad

Arkada, Priko, **t** (021) 756 555, *www.stari-grad-faros.hr/hoteli* (€€). Best of an uninspiring bunch of package holiday hotels of the Helios group north of the inlet, this early 1980s timewarp has compact but clean and adequate accommodation.

Private accommodation (€) is available from **Mistral**, Grofa Vranjicanija 2 (near bus station).

Jelsa

Murvića, Sv Roko (behind bus station), **t** (021) 761 405, *www.murvica.net* (€). Charming small *pension* signposted as you enter town, behind whose garden terrace are home-from-home studios. A good restaurant features home produce.

Residence Romantica, Mala banda bb, mobile **t** 098 199 1698 (€). Modest but modern rooms above the central **L'Accento** restaurant, located just off the harbour.

Private accommodation (€) can be booked through tourist information centres and **Spes Tours**, over main bridge, Vrboska, **t** (021) 774 234, *www.spes-tours-vrboska.hr*; or **Atlas**, Obala bb, Jelsa (on harbour), **t** (021) 672 038, *www.atlas.hr*.

Eating Out on Hvar

Hvar Town

You'll run short of ready cash before a new place to eat in Hvar Town – prices in the many restaurants are above average. The Riva and Petra Hektorovića one block uphill from the main square are good places to browse. All the Pakleni islets have a restaurant in summer.

Gariful, Riva bb, **t** (021) 742 999 (€€€). Arguably the choicest dining experience on the Riva, preparing an upmarket Dalmatian menu of fish and meats where the charcoal grill sizzles at the far end of the harbour.

Luna, Petra Hektorovića 2, **t** (021) 741 000 (€€€–€€). A top-floor terrace open to the stars is the big draw of a funky restaurant which likes its colour. The must-have dish is lobster in a rich sauce of tomato, wine and brandy.

Macondo, Groda bb, **t** (021) 742 850 (€€€–€€). Hvar's finest address, according to many locals, and certainly a charmer, a homely stone

ⓘ Jelsa >>
Obala bb (north corner of harbour), t (021) 761 017, www.tzjelsa.hr; open July–Aug Mon–Sat 8–11, Sun 10–12 and 7.30–9.30; June and Sept Mon–Fri 8–2 and 3–8, Sat 8.30–2; Oct–May Mon–Fri 8–12

ⓘ Stari Grad >
kiosk at harbour end, t (021) 765 763, www.stari-grad-faros.hr; open summer Mon–Sat 8–10, Sun 9–1 and 3–7; winter Mon–Fri 8–1

dining room with a superb fish plate and lamb. Don't miss a fiery home-recipe *rakija* for an aperitif.

Yakša, Petra Hektorovića bb, **t** (021) 717 202 (€€€–€€). Hip modern style and quality international cuisine meets Renaissance architecture in a sophisticated new venture that raises the bar in Hvar. Pricey but a place to splurge.

Zlatna Školja, Petra Hektorovića 8, mobile **t** 098 1688 797 (€€€–€€). 'Slow food' pioneer Ivan Buzolić brings creative twists to Dalmatian plates; beef stewed with goat's cheese and capers or truffles; or squid in a sauce of wild oranges. Set menus are available 'for brave gourmets'.

Kod kapetana, Fabrika bb, **t** (021) 742 230 (€€). A reliable quieter option on the other side of the harbour with the full Dalmatian menu and views of the Riva.

Junior, Pučkog ustanka 4, **t** (021) 741 069 (€€–€). Simple restaurant of a fishing family; there's a three-style squid sampler and a seafood risotto that's one of the best you'll taste.

Pizzeria Mama Leon, Riva bb, no tel (€). The finest pizzas in Hvar on the corner of the buzzy Riva.

Stari Grad

Ermitaž, Priko, mobile **t** 091 542 8395 (€€). Rustic-stlyed *konoba* on the north side of the inlet whose terrace has views and interior has charm.

Jurin Podrum, Dolnja kuloa 24, **t** (021) 765 448 (€€). Arty bistro style and first-class island cooking in the nest of lanes behind the harbour. Expect the likes of tagliatelle with *pršut* ham and sage, or octopus and scampi buzara.

Stari Miln, behind Kerum supermarket, **t** (021) 765 805 (€€). New garden *konoba* from the owner of Jurin Podrum with a stylish modern-rustic dining room.

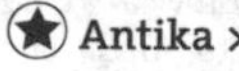

Antika, Cnr Dolnja kuloa and Ivana Gundulića, **t** (021) 765 479 (€€–€). Marvellous buffet and bar (opposite) at the heart of Stari Grad's arts scene that combine antique character and bohemian credentials. Good-value dishes are always fresh and prepared to order; character abounds.

Jelsa

Humac, Humac, 7km east of Jelsa, mobile **t** 091 523 9463 (€€). A rustic village *konoba* with *peka* dishes cooked on an open fire and anchovy-and-veggie pasty *viška pogača* washed down with homemade plonks. As far from Hvar Town chic as you can get, though do call beforehand.

Napoleon, Mala banda bb, Jelsa, **t** (021) 761 438 (€€). Meats seared on a charcoal grill come with lovely views across the harbour.

Nono, signed off Braće Batoš, Jelsa, **t** (021) 761 441 (€€). Home cooking and a canopy of vines in a tiny treat with a big welcome hidden in a southern back street (signs uphill from St John's). The chef prepares feasts of *odojak ispod* (suckling pig) or *hobotnica* (octopus) cooked under a *peka* given advance notice.

Cafés and Bars on Hvar

BB Club, Riva bb. Chic, metro and retro, spread before yachts in front of the Riva hotel.

Carpe Diem, Riva bb. The most prestigious and pricey cocktail joint in Hvar; reservations are essential to join fashionistas on its rattan sofas in high season.

Hula Hula Beach Bar, Majerovića. Around the next headland from the Amfora hotel, this is more a hangout than a cool beach bar; just a terrace with loungers and an in-the-know crowd.

Kiva, Fabrika bb. Unpretentious lively boozer in a sidestreet off the quay, around from the Palace hotel.

Pršuta Tri, Petra Hektorovića bb. Sweet antique-styled winebar with Dalmatian tapas – a quiet bolthole when other bars are heaving.

The Top Sky Club, Hotel Adriana, harbour. Staggering views of the waterfront opposite from the top floor – very glossy, very fashion.

Zimmer Frei, Groda bb (near the cathedral). Not as flash but perhaps cooler than Carpe Diem, where white cushions are spread on steps for a 30-something crowd.

Vis and Biševo

Few islands in Croatia seize the imagination like Vis. Its main settlements, Vis Town and Komiža, drift at yesteryear pace and use dialects which baffle each other let alone their fellow countrymen; semi-abandoned villages crumble in a rugged interior where vineyards cultivate acclaimed white Vugava and red Viški plavac wines; and some of the Adriatic's cleanest seas wash its beaches. A siren call of adventure can be heard even on the approach, when Vis rises on the horizon like some lost treasure island – which, in a sense, it was. A Yugoslav naval base that put Croatia's most isolated island off-limits to foreigners until 1989 also sheltered it from modernity and package tourism. In the last decade, yachties discovered it, and with them came some top-notch restaurants. So Vis is quietly transforming into a destination for exclusive escapists, a sort of Robinson Crusoe hideaway with a five-star chef. Croatians acclaim it as a retreat for those in the know; now foreigners are seeking it out – catch it while you can.

Vis Town

The isolated location which entices today saw Vis prized as a central Adriatic stronghold by a succession of rulers – Venetian, British, then Austrian. Later, it served as the headquarters of the Partisan struggle in 1944, when Tito masterminded strategies from a cave in Mount Hum (*see* below), while Allied Flying Fortress bombers dropped supplies onto emergency airstrips laid among vineyards. First to arrive, however, were the Greeks, some time in the 4th century BC. They founded Issa, a settlement which served as a springboard for colonization of much of the Dalmatian coast; it straggled on the northwest slopes above the main port Vis Town, strung out along the bay between the once-separate villages of portside **Luka** and residential **Kut**.

Next came the Romans, under whom Issa matured into a town of 14,000 citizens that Julius Caesar hailed as 'the most distinguished city in the area'. Snapshots of Vis's formative years are on show in a small but excellent **town museum** in a 19th-century Austrian fortification called Our Lady's Battery (Gospod baterija) a 10-minute walk east of the port (*left from ferry dock*). Spotlighted on the top floor, antique ceramics and a prize late 4th-century BC bust of the goddess Artemis, the chaste daughter of Zeus and Leto, speak volumes about a life where *luxe, calme et volupté* reigned supreme. Island handicrafts and 19th-century furnishings are below.

Town museum
Gradski muzej; open June–Sept Tues–Sat 10–1 and 6–9, Sun 10–1; otherwise on demand via tourist agencies; adm

To the right of the port, a few tombstones of the **ancient Greek cemetery** are ignored behind the municipal tennis courts, while further around the bay are scrappy remains of 1st-century

Ancient Greek cemetery
times vary, usually 4–8

Getting to and around Vis

Two or three Jadrolinija **ferries** and one SEM **catamaran** (summer only) per day shuttle between Split and Vis. Five **buses** per day go between Vis Town and Komiža, scheduled to coincide with ferry arrivals.

Roman baths
times vary, but usually open

Roman baths, their mosaic floors patterned with dolphins (at the rear) and swastikas, an ancient good luck symbol until hijacked by Hitler. Exhibit B of Roman Issa is the peninsular **Franciscan monastery** (Franjevački samostan) on a headland beyond the baths. Its 16th-century arc is founded on the marble blocks of a 2,500-seater amphitheatre, which was outside the city walls beside the Roman harbour – they say that slabs of the Roman's dock can be seen in the shallows at low tide.

Nineteenth-century funerary statuary in the **town cemetery** behind the monastery relates more recent history – a leonine epitaph salutes the sailors who fell defending Vis *'für Kaiser und Österreich'* in a clash with the Italian navy in 1866. The Italians lost. The clash was a re-run of one these shores had witnessed 55 years earlier. when, on paper at least, Vis was under French dominion. But the British ruled the roost, and with gleeful perversity governor Sir George Duncan Robertson promoted it as a haven for smugglers and pirates in order to harry French interests in the Adriatic (and also boost the island's population to 12,000 people). Already with no great love for the British, Napoleon was incensed by such underhand tactics and sailed on the island in 1811. He lost, too. But the British heeded the warning and quickly bolstered their Adriatic base with fortresses on either side of the harbour mouth. Take the road past the monastery, then fork right onto a dirt track and you reach the ruins of the **Fortress of George III**, a Union Jack still etched into the portal. It has crumbled into an evocative (if grubby) shell, capped by silver-green agave and forgotten among the pine trees. A more lasting legacy of the British is the Sir William Hoste Cricket Club, even if it was revived by an Australian Croat.

Back at the town museum. An easy walk east leads to **Kut** (literally 'corner'), a tangle of lanes of 16th-century vintage, aggrandized here and there by the Renaissance summer mansions of Hvar aristocrats. Finely turned balconies and balustrades are the giveaways. A dirt road peters out by the headland at a **cemetery** for the British servicemen who fell defending the island, first from Napoleon, then during the 1944 push on the Adriatic – their comrades were the only foreigners permitted access to Vis during its years as a Yugoslav navy base. Just behind it is the best **beach** in Vis Town.

Inland Vis and Komiža

Inland, Vis is another world. Lush and semi-overgrown, it is a landscape shaded by silver olive groves and virile green vineyards. With your own transport you can follow lanes that hairpin off into a wild and romantic landscape of pine and carob. Terraces of vines cascade down hillsides, blue coves wink around each corner and the air everywhere is drunk with the scent of wild rosemary and sage.

Head from Vis Town on the main road, which tracks west to east behind Mount Hum, and a bumpy side-track veers off suddenly towards the south coast: right at the T-junction is **Rukavac**, a few holiday homes, a pebble beach and a fringe of pine woods on a wide bay; left is **Milna**, a soporific hamlet above a sand beach (**Plaža Zaglav**) with intoxicating turquoise water in its shallows. The most dramatic beach on the south coast is Stiniva bay, sheltered behind a gap in cliffs – it's also tricky to find. Ask at tourist offices to locate its steep footpath, or join a boat trip with the tourist agencies.

Continue west on the main road, however, and you'll swing around Mount Hum then hairpin down into **Komiža**. The island's second settlement is a gem; a mite scruffy, perhaps, but as pretty a village as you'll find in Croatia, cradled behind a cliff which reaches into the sea. Whether for gossip over morning coffee or the *korzo* at dusk, life revolves around a harbour, behind which 16th- and 17th-century stone houses jostle for position. They were built by the Venetians, who also erected the stocky **Kaštel** (1585) fort that guards the harbour, slightly emasculated by an Austrian **clock tower**. Nowadays the fort houses a **Fishing Museum** which documents the sardine fleet that earned the village fame, its prize possession a reconstructed *falkuša*; others occassionally bob in the harbour. Until the 1950s, fleets sailed south of Komiža for the shoals off Palagruža (*see* below). The *falkuša* side-panels that raised freeboard for the 45-mile sail in open seas were removed during fishing to ease the hauling of the nets.

Fishing Museum
Ribarski muzej; open May–Sept Mon–Sat 10–12 and 7–10, Sun 7–10 only; adm

A stroll around the harbour behind the beach, the church of **Our Lady of the Pirates** (Gospa Gusarica) was christened, they say, because its icon of the Madonna miraculously washed up a few weeks after it was taken by pirates. Its odd shape – a trio of stone beach huts pressed tight – emerged as Komiža tacked on single-nave churches either side of the Renaissance original. The octagonal well outside introduces village protector St Nicholas, also honoured by the fortified **Benedictine monastery of St Nicholas** (Samostan sv. Nikole) uphill above town as you enter.

It's always locked but is worth a visit for views over Komiža's roofs out into the bay. One for the photo album at sunset. Visit on 6 December and you'll be joined by the entire village, turned out en masse for a boat-burning sacrifice to curry favour with its patron saint, also that of fishermen. Beaches in Komiža lie either side of the village, the best being that by hotel Biševo in front of Our Lady of the Pirates.

A track behind ascends to the summit of **Mount Hum** (587m), a stiff climb, but, oh, what a panorama of the glittering Adriatic: west to Jabuka, the weird pyramidal peak of a submerged volcano whose magnetism plays havoc with the compass of any ship rash enough to approach; and south to **Palagruža**, the Adriatic speck where Odysseus's pal Diomedes, the bravest of the Greeks who sacked Troy, sheathed his sword for good.

Biševo

Boat trips
c.90–110Kn depending on season

In appearance just another islet in the Adriatic, Biševo has nevertheless wooed tourists ever since its **Blue Cave** was billed as a Croatian Capri in 1884. **Boat trips** from Komiža and Vis are scheduled to arrive at the cavern for midday. Sunlight spears through a submerged side-entrance, water in the cave fluoresces lapis lazuli, and a crowd of tourists bobbing in boats coo in unison. Magic.

ⓘ Komiža >>
*harbour, **t** (021) 713 455; www.tz-vis.h; open summer Mon–Sat 8–12 and 6–10, winter Mon–Sat 8–2*

ⓘ Vis Town >
*opposite ferry dock in Jadrolinija office, **t** (021) 717 017, www.tz-vis.hr; open daily summer 8–8, winter Mon–Fri 8–2*

Where to Stay on Vis

Private Tourist Agencies

Vis Town: Ionios, Obala sv. Jurja 37, **t** (021) 711 532; or **Navigator**, Šetalište stare Isse 1, **t** (021) 717 786 (both near ferry dock).

Komiža: Nonna, behind harbour near bus stop, **t** (021) 713 500.

All the above can arrange private accommodation, scooter and bike hire, and organize tours to Biševo and diving trips.

Vis Town and Kut

Issa, Šetalište Apolonija Zanelle 5, **t** (021) 711 124 (€€). Functional package two-star from the same company as Tamaris.

Paula, Petra Hektorovića 2, Kut, **t** (021) 711 362, *www.paula-hotel.htnet.hr* (€€). Modern and friendly, this is the pick of the hotels, a small family hotel carved from a stone house with bucketloads of charm. It also offers an **apartment** (€€€), with a terrace overlooking the bay and a Jacuzzi.

Tamaris, Obala sv. Jurja 20, **t** (021) 711 350 (€€). An Austro-Hungarian-era place near the dock. Still stuck in the Socialist era décor-wise, but has high ceilings and creaky parquet floors – with luck you'll get a room with views over the bay.

Private tourist agencies (*see* left) co-ordinate **rooms** in private houses (€).

Komiža

Biševo, Ribarska 72, **t** (021) 713 729, *www.hotel-bisevo.com* (€€). Adequate rooms with fridges in Komiža's only large hotel, above its beach. Modest spa facilities.

Villa Nonna, Ribarska 50, **t** (021) 713 500 or mobile **t** 098 380 046, *www.villa-nonna.com* (€). Stone house between the harbour and beach, tastefully restored into seven modern studio apartments with feature stone walls. Kitchenettes and flat-screen TVs in each. All in all excellent value. The owners also rent a four-bed restored house.

Eating Out on Vis

You'll eat well in Vis. Drink well too – ancient Greek writer Athenaios acclaimed the wine of Issa the finest in the Adriatic. For a snack, pick up tomato, onion and anchovy bread *pogača*, prefixed *viška* or *komiška* depending on where you buy it.

Vis Town and Kut

Villa Kaliopa, Vladimira Nazora 32, Kut, mobile **t** 091 27 11 755 (€€€). Pricey, but the place for a romantic splurge. Fish is consistently excellent on a menu of cuisine that changes with the seasons and the Renaissance-style garden of palms is a delight for alfresco dining. *Eves only.*

Doručak kod Tihane, Obala sv Jurja 5, **t** (021) 718, Vis Town (€€€–€€). Vis's first hotel (1911) now run by its founder's great-granddaughter Tihana as 'Breakfast at Tiffany's'. Boutique old-world charm and a creative menu features island produce: veal in local honey and almonds, crab in a marmalade of island oranges and lemons. Great terrace.

Kantun, Biskupa Mihe Pušića 17 (€€). On the seafront by **Doručak kod Tihane**, this is a large lazy-paced bistro with a nice line in artistic décor: chunky tables, art on the brick walls and a jazz soundtrack. Expect a bistro lunch to segue effortlessly into early evening.

Pojoda, Don Cvjetka Marasovića 8, Kut, **t** (021) 711 575 (€€). Zoran Brajčić continues to win plaudits for his seafood plus excellent *peka* dishes or fillers like *pojorski bronzinić*, a broth of lentils and squid thickened with barley. All served on a small terrace shaded by orange and lemon trees.

Komiža

Bak, Gundulićeva 1, **t** (021) 713 742 (€€€–€€). Terrace tables inches from the sea look over the bay into the harbour – one of the most idyllic views on the island. First-class food: catch of the day is on the menu, and for a starter there's octopus cooked in Vis red wine.

★ **Jastožera >>**

Jastožera, Gundulićeva 6, **t** (021) 713 859 (€€€–€€). Bags of character in an old lobster house, now a legendary restaurant where tables are on platforms above the holding pen. Lobster specialities, naturally.

South from Split: Omiš and the Cetina Gorge

The Magistrala coast-road which plunges ever south showcases the best and worst of the Croatian coast. Far ahead ripples Mount Biokovo, the highest, craggiest, most dramatic bit of coastline in the country, but first there's a tawdry straggle of pizza-grills and apartments to service slivers of beach.

You'll find them either side of **Omiš**, whose cobbled medieval kernel spilling over with cafés and postcard racks seems far too sweet to have emerged from a nest of pirates. For two centuries Omiš seafarers levied 'navigation taxes' on any passing galleons, apologetically raiding nearby monasteries whenever passing trade dried up. The plunder of a Crusader ship was the final straw for Pope Honorius III. In 1221, he sailed on Omiš himself and, like every attacker before him, was thwarted as his quarry snuck away out of reach up the Cetina gorge – more on that later.

Mirabela watchtower
open June–mid-Sept daily 9am–10pm; adm

Venice put an end to such buccaneering in 1444 and erected the **Mirabela watchtower** to look out for Ottoman Turk corsairs.

Clinging to a ridge, the 16th-century ruin behind the centre still offers the 'good view' of its name. Even more impressive is that from a Venetian **fortress** which hunkers down on a crag above; with a car, drive up rough road off Put Borka southwest of the centre to suburb-hamlet Baučići, from where it's a stiff 20-minute walk. Tourist authorities are also proud of the church of **St Petar** (Crkva sv. Petra) in north bank suburb Priko, a much-restored pre-Romanesque matchbox that's nearly always shut.

Fortress
Fortica; maps available from the tourist office

Just as it did in its youth, Omiš hopes the splendid **Cetina gorge** will be its salvation – only now, all are welcome. The best bits of the valley carved by the river Cetina on its home straight after bubbling up near Knin are at the beginning and end – a pair of top-notch restaurants fill in the gap between. You can hop aboard a **tourist train**, but the cliffs which guard the river mouth are better seen on **boat trips**. Both go 6km upstream to the Radmanove Milnice restaurant (*see* p.305). If driving, take a road which tracks the river then hairpins away up the south bank to **Zadvarje**, 20km from Omiš. The views are sublime, topped only by those of a **waterfall** that falls in mare's-tail plumes as the gorge performs a U-turn – the valley at its most dramatic. An even better way to experience the upper stretches of the river is on a rafting, canoeing or canyoning trip (*see* below). Unless heavy rain has swollen the river, expect a gentle drift past banks of silver willow, perhaps a minor rapid or two, rather than the white-water ride depicted on advertising hoardings of the tourist agencies beside the quay. A lovely way to lose a morning.

Tourist train
from river quay, summer only, every 2hrs; 20Kn

Boat trips
from river quay; c. 40Kn or boat hire 250–300Kn

Waterfall
Vopod Gubavica; track beside fire station

Festivals in Omiš

On July weekend evenings, Omiš rings to the sound of traditional *klapa* choirs, a sort of Dalmatian barber-shop quartet of close-harmony male-voice choirs, during the **Festival of Dalmatian Klapa**. The grand finale of Croatia's premier *klapa* event is on the last Sat of the month.

Sports and Activities in the Cetina Gorge

Rafting and canoeing trips, plus canyoning excursions down the Cetina gorge, are booked through Omiš tourist agencies on Poljički trg near the river quay. The trips, which start a few kilometres downstream from Zadvarje and finish at the Radmanove Milnice restaurant, last 3–5hrs and cost 200–250Kn per person, including transport.

Try the following:

Nestos, Poljički trg bb, **t** (021) 861 006.
Slap, Poljički trg bb, **t** (021) 757 336.
Active Holidays, just off the square on main street Knezova Kačića, **t** (021) 861 829.

ⓘ Omiš >>
*Trg kneza Miroslava bb (opposite side of Magistrala to Old Town), **t** (021) 861 350, www.tz-omis.hr; open summer Mon–Sat 8–8; winter Mon–Sat 8–2*

Where to Stay and Eat in Omiš and the Cetina Gorge

Omiš

Villa Dvor, Mosorska 13, **t** (021) 863 444, *www.hotel-villadvor.hr* (€€). New in 2005 and with the best location in town by the river mouth; the 23 rooms of this plush family hotel have three-star mod cons and gadgets such as plasma screen TVs. Book a balcony for astounding views of the plummeting gorge or out to sea.

Tourist agencies on Poljički trg offer private **rooms**; *see* 'Sports and Activities in the Cetina Gorge', p.304.

Konoba u našeg Marina, Knezova Kačića 4, mobile **t** 091 577 9999 (€). Go for a *brodet* house special or fishy snacks – grilled sardines, *leso inčuni* (boiled anchovies), or salty fried *girice* (whitebait) – in this gem of a *konoba* that's a credit to its breed; snug and bursting with character, where patrons prop up the bar with house *rogač* brandy.

Cetina Gorge

Radmanove Milnice, 6km up gorge from Omiš, **t** (021) 862 073 (€€). A rustic riverside mill of 18th-century vintage, often swamped by rafters and Omiš day-trippers, but lovely for an alfresco lunch nevertheless. Trout is fresh from the tank, or try regional specials *žabe na žaru sa pršutom* (grilled frogs with *pršut* ham) or grilled crayfish (*rakovi na žaru*).

Kaštil Slanica, 4km up gorge from Omiš, **t** (021) 861 783 (€€). Quieter than its upstream sister, with formal service by waiters in black-and-whites and an excellent menu: alongside freshwater fish are strange eel (*jegulje*) dishes and frog's legs (*žabe*) with mushrooms and olives. The homemade bread baked under a *peka* is superb.

The Makarska Riviera

Half a century of tourism has redrawn this 45km stretch of coast. An earthquake in 1962 proved the last straw for many villagers, persuading them to abandon ancient stock-breeding villages beneath Mount Biokovo for new settlements on the coast. No surprise, then, that this is package holiday territory, knockabout and cheerful, with no pretensions to cultural greatness and, in places, all the crowds of fully fledged holiday mills. What keeps 'em coming are the longest, whitest pebble beaches in the region – quiet crescents as well as sizzling fleshpots.

The Northern Makarska Riviera

First on the riviera, first in style, **Brela** is careful to preserve an air of quiet exclusivity. Occasional snatches of opera drift through the evening air as hotels stage classical concerts alongside the usual Dalmatian *klapa*, and window boxes are watered daily in this resort with a wallful of Golden Flower and National Tourism awards, among pines and sub-tropical vegetation. A string of Blue Flag-quality beaches west of the central harbour adds to its appeal, the finest being pine-cloaked **Punta Rata** beyond the package hotels, a lovely shingle peninsula that in 2004 *Forbes* magazine was moved to rank the finest beach in Europe.

Just 3km south, **Baška Voda** receives more visitors than any other resort on the riviera, and it could not be more different. Pizza-grills and gift shops jostle for attention on the seafront. What the small unpretentious resort has is beds – and by the thousand. Just don't expect space to swing a bikini on its beach from mid-July. Ignored by all in the village centre, an **Archaeological Collection** of Bronze Age and Roman objects unearthed on the hillock of Gradina just west of the centre.

Archaeological Collection
Arheološka zbirka; t (021) 620 244; open summer Mon–Sat 9.30–12 and 6–9.30, adm

Getting to and around the Makarska Riviera

All north–south Dalmatia **buses** stop at northern villages on request (bus stops are above the villages, approx a 15min walk downhill; a coastal path also links the villages), then stop at Makarska (approx every 45mins from Split), and finally pass south through Makarska resorts. From Makarska, 5 buses a day go long-haul to Zagreb. Local bus connections to riviera resorts are approx hourly. The bus station is on the main road, 5mins' walk from the centre along Stjepana Radića.

A **ferry** shuttles from Sumartin, Brač, to Makarska 5 times a day in peak season (otherwise 3 per day). Ferries from Drvenik ply routes to Sućuraj, east Hvar (approx every 90mins in summer) and Dominče, east Korčula (3 per day).

ⓘ **Krvavica** › *on left at village entrance,* **t** *(021) 621 605; open summer daily 9–1*

Although no stranger to tourism, **Promajna**, 2km beyond, isn't quite as commercial and has a mite more space on its sliver of shingle beach. **Krvavica** another 2km further is better still for a quiet bake, its beach developed only by a snack bar and backed by shady pines where you can indulge in a gentle game of *boules*. And then there's **Bratuš**, a quick cut north again beyond Krvavica's harbour. Low-key and charming, this is a well-kept secret on the Makarska riviera, a villagey huddle with a couple of restaurants among palms, a crescent of shingle and nothing else, which is just how its 50 residents like it, thank you. You'll pinch yourself when you realize that Baška Voda is only a 40-minute walk away on the seashore promenade.

Although only 2km inland of Baška Voda, charmingly dilapidated villages **Bast** and **Topići** are different worlds, shaded in the mottled greys of ancient stone rather than the crisp sea-blues and villa-whites of the coast.

Makarska

Beneath the heights of Mount Biokovo that rise almost within touching distance, Makarska leads a double life as a regional centre and a fizzy resort. On a strip of shallow 20th-century newcomers it boasts deep roots, too. A safe protected anchorage encouraged the Romans to establish a port here, and the Ottoman Turks nurtured it as an *entrepôt* for fine goods from Dubrovnik and Venice after their flag fluttered over Makarska from 1499. The Makarska town crest remembers the strong arm and scimitar that evicted them by force nearly two centuries later. The Habsburgs pioneered tourism, which took off in 1923 thanks to the splendidly serious Society for the Beautification of the City. The main drag is **Obala kralja Tomislava**, a characterful harbourfront of Habsburg-era hotels and Venetian stone mansions. Up close, modernity – pizzerias and restaurants, banks and tourist agencies – returns with a jolt.

Central square **Kačićev trg** behind has its share of gift shops too, but stands up to closer scrutiny as a Venetian period piece, boxed in by green-shuttered houses and the parish church of **St Mark** (Crkva sv. Marka), which takes Baroque to its logical conclusion on a façade stripped of all adornment. The friar who stands, quill in hand, is 18th-century author Andrija Kačić Miošić (1704–60). Despite the plodding verse of his *Razgovor ugodni narodna slovinskoga* ('A Pleasant Conversation of the Slavic People'), a Croatian history spiced with Slavic folk tales, the author became the most widely read in Croatia after the Bible as as National Revival fervour swept the nation in the late 19th century. And so Makarska, the first town in Dalmatia to use their mother tongue for official business, engaged the most prominent Croat sculptor of the day, Ivan Rendić, in 1890, to depict the hero.

Town museum
Gradski muzej; **t** *(021) 612 302; open summer daily 9–1 and 5–9; winter 9–1*

Seashell Museum
Malakološki muzej; **t** *(021) 611 256; open June–Sept Mon–Sat 10–12 and 5–7; adm*

Bar a tired **town museum** with local and art exhibitions on Obala kralja Tomislava, Makarska's only cultural sight, such as it is, is east of the square in a lovely 1670s **Franciscan monastery**. Off its cloister, a **Seashell Museum** displays 3,000 shells.

The beaches that make Makarska popular with Croat families lie five minutes west of the centre beyond a park, on the far side of the **Sv. Petar headland**, reached via promenade **Šetalište dr Franje Tuđmana** that arcs off the corner of the harbourfront.

Mount Biokovo

Biokovo Natural Park
Park prirode Biokovo; information centre at Mala obala 16, **t** *(021) 616 924, www.biokovo.com; open Mon–Fri 7–3*

Activity can be found on the limestone flanks of Mount Biokovo behind Makarska, a parched habitat of Mediterranean scrub and sub-alpine flowers trimmed by *mouflon* and wild goats, which gives way to a moonscape plateau pocked by karst sinkholes. A path from Makarska clambers 3km northeast, across a *massif* protected as the **Biokovo Natural Park**, to the hamlet of **Kotišina** and the **Biokovo Botanical Garden** (Biokovski botanički vrt), a bit of a misnomer for a 16.5-hectare rockery gone to seed. Horticulturists may be disappointed, but the views are splendid.

With good footwear you can tackle **Mount Biokovo** itself and its peak of **Sveti Jure**, crowned with a tiny chapel and, disappointingly, a TV transmitter. A lane behind Makarska ascends to the hamlet of **Makar**, from where a well-marked path grunts up to the peak of **Vošac** (1,422m) before the final push to the summit at 1,762m. Jaw-dropping views – across to Italy on clear days and east to the peaks of Bosnia – reward your five hours' effort; a map is a must (from bookshops or tourist information), as is a hiker's weather sense, proper footwear and a high level of fitness. If you laugh in the face of vertigo, you can drive up instead of walking: a road (summer only) hairpins 7km to the summit from a turning 2km south of Makarska.

The Southern Makarska Riviera

The coastal Magistrala south will take you 5km to **Tučepi**, a cheerful Croatian *costa* with a strip of pebble beach shaded by pine boughs after noon. Its concrete quays appeared on the coast in the 1960s after villagers ventured down from tumbledown hamlets **Podpeć** and **Gornji Tučepi** (turn left 2km after Makarska if driving). The stone shells vanishing into *maquis* scrub in the latter are the remnants of 17th-century castles built when the villages were on the front line of the Croatian–Turkish border.

ⓘ Podgora
Branimirova 87 (mall off seafront), **t** *(021) 625 560, www.podgora.hr; open June–Oct Mon–Sat 7.30–8.30, Sun 8–2; Nov–May Mon–Sat 7–2*

Amiable family resort **Podgora**, 3km beyond Tučepi, is lighter on the hard sell and refuses to develop its beach to death. It even has some charm, a pleasant lunch-spot around an old-fashioned stone harbour where fishermen sort the night's catch watched by tourists in restaurants. **Igrane** 7km further on has a kernel village somewhere behind its beachfront of white concrete boxes, while another 11km leads you to **Drvenik**, a minor ferry port for Hvar and Korčula, with its own beach resort.

Museum
open summer daily 4–7; adm

Church
open for Mass

ⓘ Gradac
Stjepana Radica 1, **t** *(021) 697 511, www.gradac.hr; open June–Oct Mon–Sat 8–12 and 5–7, Sun 8–12; Nov–May Mon–Sat 8–2*

Unlike its neighbours, **Zaostrog**, 5km from Drvenik, has heritage. The village developed at the skirts of a **monastery** of Bosnian Franciscans, a 16th-century edifice screened from the beach by its garden. A **museum** displays ethnological items trawled from local houses, and in its **church** there's a marble bust of its most famous friar, author Andrija Kačić Miošić, by Ivan Rendić. Free of large hotels and commercialization, Zaostrog has the charm of half-forgotten childhood summers – there are far worse places to lose a day. It also has one of the last good beaches on the riviera. The finest of a trio in **Podača**, 2km south of Zaostrog, is north beyond a straggle of villas, and strips of white pebbles fringe the coast either side of the peninsula resort **Gradac**. And then the riviera – and the beaches – end abruptly.

ⓘ Baška Voda >>
Obala sv. Nikole 31, **t** *(021) 620 713, www.baskavoda.hr; open June–Sept daily 8–9; Oct–May Mon–Fri 8–12*

ⓘ Brela >
Trg Alojzija Stepinca bb (behind Konzum supermarket near harbour), **t** *(021) 618 337/455, www.brela.hr; open summer Mon–Sat 7–9, Sun 8–9; winter Mon–Fri 8–3, Sat 8–12*

Tourist Information on the Makarska Riviera

Tourist offices will book private rooms: Gradac co-ordinates rooms in Zaostrog and Podača.

Sports and Activities

Biokovo Active Holidays, Gundulićeva 4, **t** (021) 679 655, *www.biokovo.net*. Runs trekking tours on Mount Biokovo, from half-day strolls to five-day hikes, plus horse-riding, canyoning and kayaking trips in the surrounding area.

Where to Stay on the Makarska Riviera

Brela

Soline, **t** (021) 603 207, *www.bluesunhotels.com* (€€). Don't be put off by the stack of Yugo concrete boxes; this was recently refurbished to create a modern quietly stylish resort with a wellness centre.

Tourist agencies **Bonavia**, Obala kneza Domagoja 18 (harbour front), **t** (021) 619 019, and **Adria Service**, by Hotel Soline, **t** (021) 618 393, can book private **rooms**.

Baška Voda

Horizont, **t** (021) 604 555, *www.hoteli-baskavoda.hr* (€€€). A plush Russian-owned four-star with thick, springy carpets and tasteful décor. Renowned for its spa/wellness centre.

Slavija, **t** (021) 604 890, *www.hoteli-baskavoda.hr* (€€). The 1932 hotel that kickstarted the resort, as super-central as ever but now showing its age as a tired two-star. An upgrade to a boutique five-star has been promised for many years – watch this space.

Tourist information and travel agencies **Bonavia**, Obala Sv. Nikole 87, **t** (021) 620 400, *www.bonavia-agency.hr*, and **Mariva**, Obala Sv. Nikole 29,

ⓘ Makarska >
Obala kralja Tomislava bb (near ferry dock), **t** *(021) 612 002, www.makarska-info.hr; open June–Sept Mon–Sat 8–9, Sun 8–12 and 6–9; Nov–May Mon–Fri 7–2*

ⓘ Tučepi >>
Kraj 103 (behind seafront), **t** *(021) 623 100, www.tucepi.com, open June–Sept daily 8–9; Oct–May Mon–Fri 9–1*

t (021) 620 463, *www.marivaturist.hr*, book **private rooms** in Baška Voda and neighbouring villages.

Makarska

Meteor, Kralja Petra Krešimira IV 16, **t** (021) 615 344 *www.hoteli-makarska.hr* (€€€–€€). Makarska's only four-star resort – all 9 storeys of it. Behind the beach, but roadside rooms are small.

Biokovo, Kralja Tomislava bb, **t** (021) 615 244, *www.hotelbiokovo.hr* (€€). While not as stylish as public areas suggest, a pleasant enough harbour hotel with ongoing renovation to modernize rooms.

Porin, Marineta 2, **t** (021) 613 744, *www.hotel-porin.hr* (€€). A friendly little two-star fashioned from a Habsburg-vintage manor (and later the town library) on the harbour. Modern(ish) and comfortable.

Harbour-front agencies **SB Tours**, Kralja Tomislava 15a, **t** (021) 611 005, *www.sb-tours.hr*, and **Turist Biro**, Kralja Tomislava 2, **t** (021) 611 888, *www.turistbiro-makarska.com*, book **private rooms**.

Eating Out on the Makarska Riviera

Brela

Feral, Obala kneza Domagoja bb, **t** (021) 618 909 (€€). Sepia shots of bygone Brela hang on the walls of a harbour-front address where Brela's first tourists bedded down in 1932, now the finest central *konoba* which prepares fresh Adriatic seafood.

Ivandića Dvori, Banje 1, no tel (€€). Locals' choice for slap-up of Dalmatian cuisine in a stone dining room. Find it above Brela, off the main road (signs to Brela-Sćit). *Eves only*.

Baška Voda

King, Ulica Iza Palaca bb, **t** (021) 620 640 (€€€–€€). A semi-smart restaurant behind the Mariva agency.

Biston, Bast 76, **t** (021) 621 517 (€€). House special of this rustic *konoba* in a hillside village 4km from Baška Voda is a mixed meat feast of beef, veal and potatoes slow-baked under a *peka*. Start with delicious slivers of *pršut* ham and homemade bread. The antidote to every plastic pizzeria.

Makarska

Jež, Kralja Petra Krešimira IV 90, **t** (021) 611 741 (€€€). Seafood is consistently excellent in a stylish restaurant behind the Meteor hotel, not just the premier address in Makarska, but a regular in Croatia's top 100.

Peškera, Šetalište dr Franje Tuđmana bb, **t** (021) 613 028 (€€). The best of the restaurants on the promenade west, this prepares the full Dalmatian menu and has the finest terrace in town.

Stari miln, Prvosvibanjska 43, **t** (021) 611 509 (€€). Adriatic seafood plus a sideline in Thai in the cosy 'old mill', with a funked-up stone dining room. The term 'service' can be a misnomer when it's busy.

Susvid, Kačićev trg 9, **t** (021) 612 732 (€€). An ever-popular eaterie on the showpiece centre square, with steaks sizzled over charcoal and the usual grilled fish.

Vrata Biokova, 15km from Makarska, **t** (021) 098 925 5051 (€€). Agrotourism at its finest in a rustic *konoba* en route up Mount Biokovo. Meats slow-cooked under a *peka*, homemade bread and a *rakija* of 48 herbs accompany views at 897m. Ask about horse-riding trips on Biokovo.

Entertainment and Nightlife on the Makarska Riviera

Tučepi

Balatura. Spacious open-plan bar smack on the beach; lazy by day, it picks up the pace when DJs play on summer evenings.

Makarska

Buba Beach Bar, Šetalište dr Franje Tudjmana. Ibiza comes to Makarska at the start of the beach strip; party house tunes for a young party crowd.

Deep, Peninsula Osejava. Another cave nightclub, on the opposite headland, this with a playlist of commercial house tunes.

Grotta, Šetalište Sv. Petra bb. Rock, blues and funk plus occasional jazz gigs in a cave on the Svetog Petar headland west of the harbour.

South to the Border

Rocky shores accompany the drive which slaloms around headlands to industrial **Ploče**. Its official superlative is as the newest city on the Croatian coast, born in 1937 as a rail-maritime node for Bosnia. It is also the ugliest. Stop only for a short cut by ferry to Trpanj on the Pelješac peninsula (*see* p.342).

After hugging the coast since Split, the Magistrala loops inland across the **estuary** of the river **Neretva**, which comes to a rather messy end after flowing down so majestically from the highlands of Bosnia-Hercegovina. In the Middle Ages, Slavic pirates would materialize suddenly from its marshes to plunder merchant caravels in Mediterranean sea lanes, then vanish just as swiftly back into a watery labyrinth of reed beds. Tamed and channelled into a fertile chequerboard of watermelons and tangerine trees, this is now the 'Croatian California', as famous for the fruit hawked at road-side stalls as its waterbirds. **Villa Neretva**, 2km beyond Opuzen on the road to Metković runs bird-spotting safaris by shallow-draught *ladja* boats, usually threading through channels in time for lunch in a restaurant with eel and river-crab specials. Tourist agencies in Makarska and Dubrovnik also organize trips and provide coach transport.

Villa Neretva
t (020) 672 200/201, www.restaurant-villa-neretva.hr

Long before the pirates, the Romans were here in their colony of Narona. It is said that Roman coins are occasionally found by visitors who stroll among the Roman walls being excavated in fields 1km north of Metković. Statutory, mosaics, glassware and jewellery from the site are presented in the under-rated **Archaeological Museum of Narona** on the central square of **Vid**, 2km north.

Archaeological Museum of Narona
Arheološki muzej Narona; t (020) 691 596, www.a-m-narona.hr; open summer Tues–Sat 9–8, Sun 9–1; winter Tues–Sat 9–5, Sun 9–1

Plunging ever-south, the Magistrala climbs uphill to rejoin the coast, then pulls up in **Klek**, the northern border town of an 8km strip of coast ceded to Bosnia-Hercegovina in 1945 as a sop of Adriatic access. No visas are required; passports might be. Much to the Bosnian government's chagrin, a bridge onto the Pelješac Peninsula that will bypass the border is proposed.

Dubrovnik and South Dalmatia

Historically, the narrow tail of Croatia has always been ruled by Dubrovnik. Napoleon Bonaparte ripped up the title deeds two centuries ago, but the queen of the east Adriatic still holds court over the southern sliver from Ploče to the Montenegro border. There are no other urban centres for miles around except charming Korčula Town – and that was nurtured by Venice. So is there really anything else to tempt you from Dubrovnik's luminous beauty? Well, the flip side of stagnation is preservation. Pressed tight by the spectacular Dinaric Alps, this is a coastline of living poetry, where the Mediterranean light is stronger, the sea bluer, and the subtropical vegetation that bit more luxurious. There are sleepy idylls such as the Elafiti islands, and a wild and romantic canvas of coast and country on the Pelješac peninsula, painted in Fauvist colours as rich and earthy as its famous red wines. Then there's Lastovo, a pristine island where the clocks have stopped, self-contained and isolated far out to sea.

12

Don't miss

See map overleaf

pp.228–9

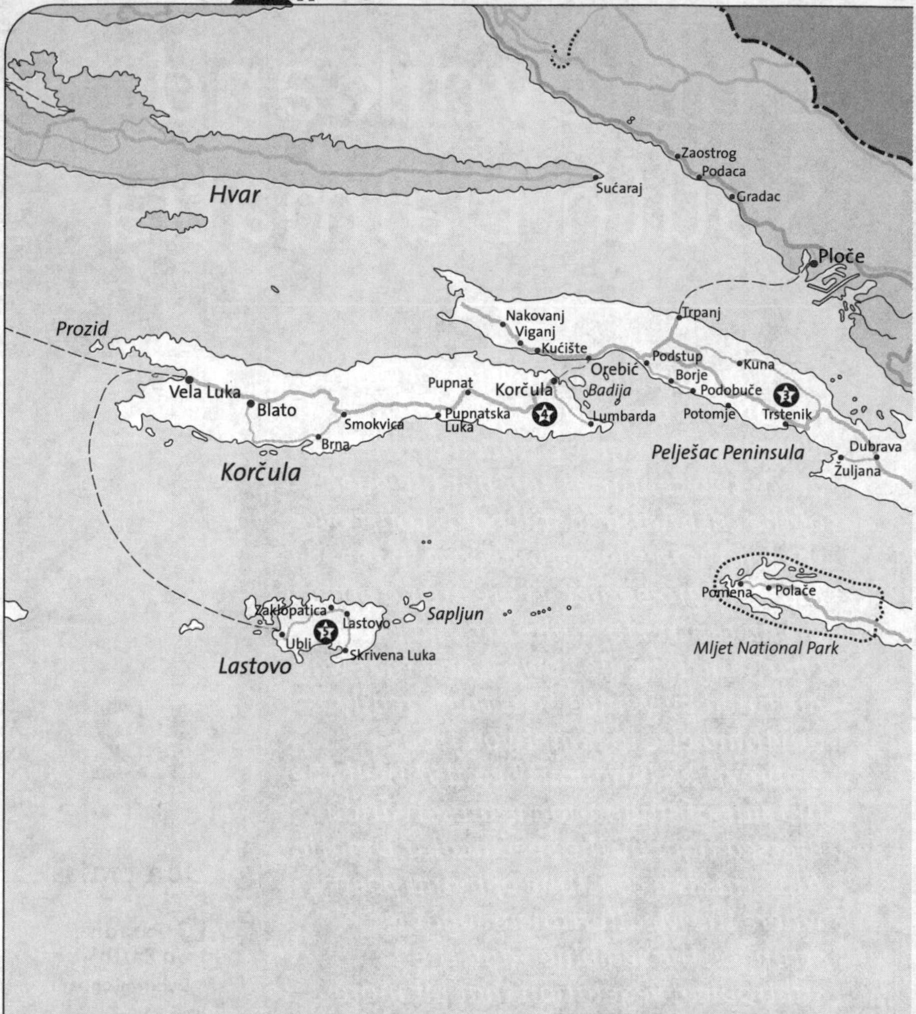

Hvar
Sućaraj
Zaostrog
Podaca
Gradac
Ploče
8
Trpanj
Nakovanj
Viganj
Kućište
Orebić
Podstup
Kuna
Borje
Podobuče
Potomje
Trstenik
Badija
Lumbarda
Korčula
Pupnat
Pupnatska Luka
Prozid
Vela Luka
Blato
Smokvica
Brna
Korčula
Pelješac Peninsula
Dubrava
Žuljana
Pomena
Polače
Mljet National Park
Zaklopatica
Lastovo
Ubli
Skrivena Luka
Sapljun
Lastovo

HUNGARY
SLOVENIA
BOSNIA-HERCEGOVINA
ITALY

Don't miss

- ① Dubrovnik p.313
- ② Elafiti Islands p.334
- ③ The Pelješac peninsula p.339
- ④ Korčula p.346
- ⑤ Lastovo p.353

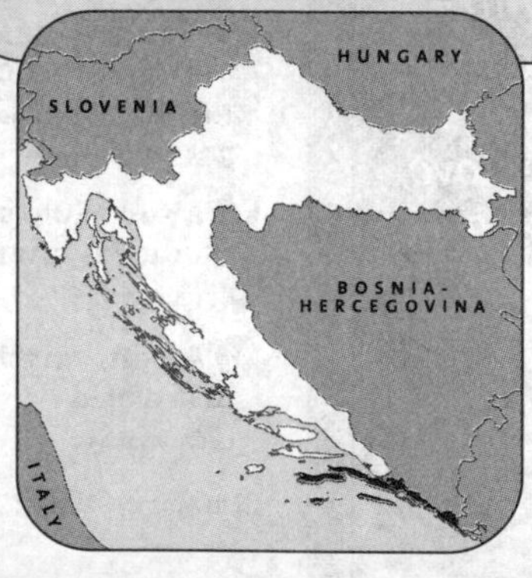

Around Dubrovnik: The Southern Dalmatian Coast

Dubrovnik

1 Dubrovnik Byron acclaimed it the 'Pearl of the Adriatic', and George Bernard Shaw believed that 'those who seek paradise on Earth should come to Dubrovnik'. The August crush can make it more purgatory than paradise. And in recent years, the cruise ships have arrived, bringing with them more day-trippers than the old town can take in comfort. As in its traditional rival Venice, the historic core has

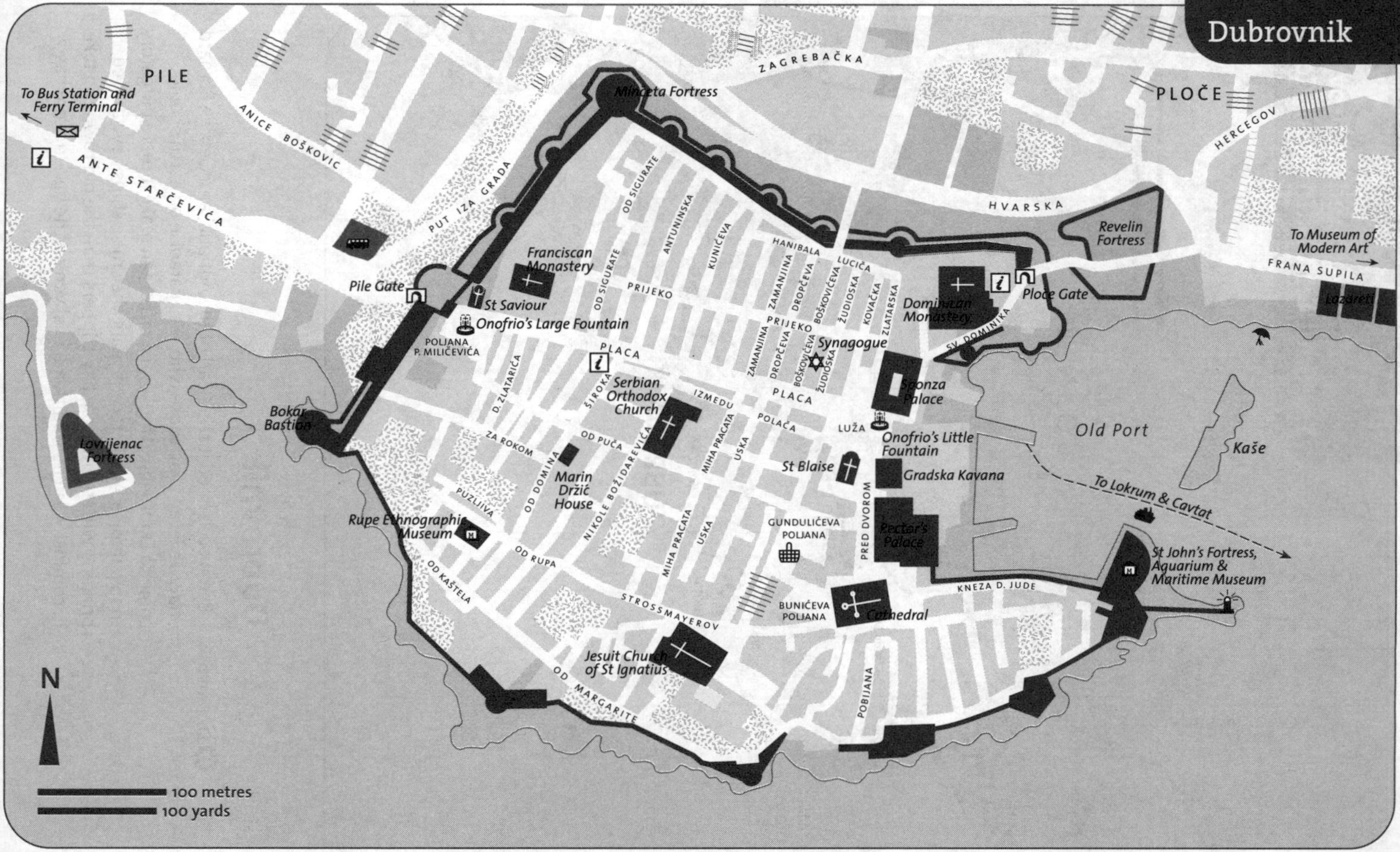

Dubrovnik

PILE
To Bus Station and Ferry Terminal
ANTE STARČEVIĆA
ANICE BOŠKOVIC
PUT IZA GRADA
ZAGREBAČKA
Minčeta Fortress
PLOČE
HERCEGOV
HVARSKA
Revelin Fortress
To Museum of Modern Art
FRANA SUPILA
Lazareti
Pile Gate
Franciscan Monastery
St Saviour
Onofrio's Large Fountain
POLJANA P. MILIČEVIĆA
OD SIGURATE
ANTUNINSKA
KUNIČEVA
HANIBALA
LUČIĆA
PRIJEKO
ZAMANJINA
DROPČEVA
BOŠKOVIĆEVA
ŽUDIOSKA
KOVAČKA
ZLATARSKA
Dominican Monastery
Ploče Gate
SV. DOMINIKA
PLACA
Synagogue
Sponza Palace
Serbian Orthodox Church
IZMEĐU
POLAČA
LUŽA
Onofrio's Little Fountain
Old Port
Kaše
ŠIROKA
D. ZLATARIĆA
ZA ROKOM
OD PUČA
OD DOMINA
Marin Držić House
NIKOLE BOŽIDAREVIĆA
MIHA PRACATA
USKA
St Blaise
Gradska Kavana
To Lokrum & Cavtat
Bokar Bastion
Lovrijenac Fortress
PUZLJIVA
Rupe Ethnographic Museum
OD RUPA
GUNDULIĆEVA POLJANA
PRED DVOROM
Rector's Palace
St John's Fortress, Aquarium & Maritime Museum
KNEZA D. JUDE
OD KAŠTELA
STROSSMAYEROV
BUNIĆEVA POLJANA
Cathedral
Jesuit Church of St Ignatius
OD MARGARITE
POBIJANA
N
100 metres
100 yards

Getting to and around Dubrovnik

By Air

Croatia Airlines operates flights from Zagreb (3 per day in summer). Dubrovnik airport is 17km south, between Cavtat and Ćilipi. Croatia Airlines transfer buses (35Kn), scheduled around its flights, drop off passengers at the Pile Gate, and pick them up 2hrs before flight departure from the main bus station. Expect to pay 200Kn for a taxi.

By Sea

Year-round, ferries cross the Adriatic from Bari (5 a week in summer). Dubrovnik is terminus of the Jadrolinija Rijeka–Dubrovnik coastal service (*see* p.61). Local ferries go to Polače via the Elafiti islands (daily), Sobra and Mljet (1 or 2 a day), and a service calls at all ports on the Elafiti islands (4 a day).

By Bus

Buses connect daily to: Ljubljana; Međugorje, Mostar and Sarajevo; and Trieste. Long-haul bus services connect to: Osijek (daily); Rijeka (4 a day); Rovinj (daily); Split via Makarska (approx hourly); Šibenik (10 a day); Varaždin and Vukovar (daily); Zadar (8 per day); and Zagreb (8 per day). Local routes operate to: Cavtat (hourly); Korčula and Orebić via Pelješac peninsula (daily); Ston (3 per day).

The bus station is located on Put Republik, in the suburb of Gruž, between the Old Town (2km walk east) and the main port, approximately 500m west. The hotel peninsulas of **Lapad** and **Babin kuk** are southwest of the bus station. Public transport provider Libertas (*www.libertasdubrovnik.hr*) operates buses: Nos 4, 5, 6 and 7 operate circuits from the bus station via Pile Gate to hotels on the western peninsulas between 6am and 2am at a fixed price of 10kn from the driver – note that no change is given – or 8kn with a ticket bought from a Libertas counter at the Pile Gate, newsagents or hotels. A day ticket costs 25Kn. Buses 5 and 8 go east to hotels in Ploče, east of the Old Town. Buses 1a, 3 and 7 shuttle between the ferry terminal and the Pile Gate via the principal bus station at Put Republike 7, northwest of the Old Town.

By Car

Forget driving to the old town: parking is near impossible. For car hire (international players are also at the airport): **Hertz**, Frana Supila 9, **t** (020) 425 000, *www.hertz.co*; **Europcar**, Kardinala Stepinca 32, **t** (020) 430 031, *www.europcar.com*; **Avis**, Obala Pape Ivana Pavla II 1, **t** (0)20 417 947 *www.avis.com.hr*; and **Mack**, Frana Supila 3, **t** (020) 423 747, *www.rentacar-croatia.com*.

By Taxi

Taxis wait night and day at a rank outside the Pile Gate or can be called on **t** (020) 970.

---

ceased being a functioning town in any real sense. Yet still Dubrovnik is a stunner – a Baroque cityscape of mansions and churches painted in cool stone and clear light as if caught in a back-eddy of modernity's riptide. For all the praise lavished on the city included on UNESCO's World Heritage list way back in 1978, the sentiment Croatia's *belle* truly prizes is written on her buses – *Libertas*. It's no accident that St Blaise, city icon of independence, salutes citizens in every niche, nor that the Dubrovnik Summer Festival arts extravaganza is inaugurated with the Renaissance poetry of local son Ivan Gundulić: 'O you beautiful, o you dear, o you sweet freedom... All the silver, all the gold, all human lives, cannot pay for your pure beauty.' How fitting, then, that it was the bombardment of this free-thinking city in 1991 that first made the outside world sit up and take notice of Croatia's struggle for independence.

History

Like its great Adriatic rivals Venice and Split, Dubrovnik was founded by refugees. The Greco-Roman citizens of Epidaurum (today's Cavtat) fled before tribes of Avars and Slavs and didn't stop until they came across a rocky islet which they named 'Laus', either for Greek rock (*lave*) or Latin chasm (*labes*) – no one is really sure. The name was chewed further into 'Rausa' as a municipal settlement emerged, and by the 9th century a walled mercant town now called 'Ragusa' busied itself with local trade. It came under the protectorate of Byzantine authority, whose fleet sailed to its aid when Saracen pirates sprang nasty surprises. Meanwhile, a Croatian settlement had emerged among the holm oaks (*dubrava*) which coated the mainland, and, emboldened by centuries of good relations and a now-intermingled Latin–Croat population, some time around the 11th century the two communities filled in the silted channel which divided them, a union confirmed in stone a century later when the settlements were bound within defence walls.

United as the 'Communitas Ragusina', Dubrovnik set up its stall as a trader on Balkan and Mediterranean land and sea routes. Writing in 1153, Arabian scribe Al-Idrisi recorded it as a city whose ships sailed on long journeys, capitalizing on trade deals with Adriatic cities such as Pisa, Bari and Ancona and its status as principal *entrepôt* for landlocked Balkan neighbours Serbia and Bosnia. This was too much for the Queen of the Adriatic, Venice. Never a Republic to smile at a rival, La Serenissima ordered its war fleet east and seized control of the upstart in 1205. Business suffered, of course, but the Venetian rector never gained full control of the city, which continued to strike deals ever further, its horizons now expanded as far as Syria and north Africa. The 1358 peace treaty that ceded Zadar from Venice to Croat-Hungarian king Louis I[er] of Anjou won freedom for Dubrovnik, which in *quid pro quo* acknowledged the authority of the Croat–Hungarian line. But so long as the tributes arrived each year, the monarchs never meddled in administrative and commercial matters. Free of the Venetian yoke, merchants looked at their bank balances with renewed interest.

The Golden Age of Trade

So it was that the 'Communitas Ragusina' became the 'Respublica Ragusina', a semantic tweak for a seismic change. Twitchy about a single authority after nearly 150 years of Venetian dictates, Dubrovnik set up an oligarchy of its richest patricians, the Grand Council, whose members elected the Senate. A puppet rector (*knez*) stood for the sake of appearances, but this élite of the élite lorded it over a society as stratified as Hindu castes. Yes, its rules betrayed an authoritarian bent – Dubrovnik sailors were forbidden from signing aboard foreign ships, and lowly workers certainly had no electoral or democratic clout – but the Senate's iron fist was clad in a velvet glove. Citizens were free to pursue their fortunes, a medieval American Dream on the Adriatic which seemed to suit everyone, since Dubrovnik avoided the peasant rebellions which racked other cities ruled by nobility.

From the late 1300s the good times rolled. Cut-price grain, cotton, leather, wool, salt and spice were sourced throughout the Balkans, Black Sea and Mediterranean, then re-exported for juicy profits. What really gave Dubrovnik the edge over other regional traders was its access to the silver and lead from Bosnian and Serbian mines inland, marked up and re-exported at high profit to Florence and Venice, Spain and France. Some merchants even secured the title deeds to mines to guarantee supplies.

Alongside good sea legs, Dubrovnik cultivated a sweet tongue. While most of Europe wrestled over supremacy, the Senate pursued a policy of neutrality, a wise move for a miniature republic without an army, and one which illustrates a merchant's savvy to avoid international conflicts for the sake of trade. Yet even neutrality has its price. After the Ottoman Turks routed the Hungarian–Croat kings at the battle of Mohács, the Ragusan Republic altered its standing order in 1526. Now the new rising power, the Ottoman Turks, received an annual payment in return for the right to free trade throughout the Turkish empire, and a reduced customs duty of two per cent. When other Christian states let cannonballs do the talking, Dubrovnik dispatched two envoys to Constantinople each year, their beards specially groomed, their wagons attended by a retinue of secretaries, guards and priests, to buy peace with a casket of gold ducats. A fortnight on the well-established caravan route was probably less arduous than the prospect of the next 12 months as an obsequious unofficial hostage of the Sultan until relieved by next year's envoys. This was Dubrovnik's golden age, with no worries about income or rivals. Stable through peace and prosperity, the Renaissance Ragusan Republic was free to indulge in luxuries. The arts and sciences blossomed as the queen of the east Adriatic held court to the region's brightest stars. Luminaries of architecture such as Michelozzo di Bartolomeo Michelozzi or Onofrio della Cava produced monnuments like the defence walls and Rector's Palace, painters such as Nikola Božidarević turned out the most exquisite canvases on the east Adriatic, both Dubrovnik's prizes to this day.

Disaster and Recovery

Then disaster. On 6 April 1667, an earthquake shook Dubrovnik to its foundations, killing around 5,000 people and reducing an unrivalled Gothic and Renaissance city to rubble. They say the sea tilted out of the harbour four times, then roared back in as a flood wave, lifting ships grounded on the dock and smashing them into the harbour wall. With the city weak, dazed and shattered, Kara Mustafa, the alcoholic Pasha of Bosnia, demanded vastly inflated protection money to secure Dubrovnik from wolfish peasants that swooped from the mountains to loot the ruins, and incarcerated every envoy who came to seek clemency.

His execution, after the ill-fated siege of Vienna in 1683, at last gave the Grand Council breathing space to rebuild its city in strict Baroque. But in truth the republic's days were already numbered. The New World had already leached away wealth from the Mediterranean, and now Dubrovnik's trade secret, Bosnia, was sluggish under Ottoman rule. One by one, the republic's 80 foreign consulates began to close. Just as much of a crisis was the fact that centuries of in-breeding and detachment had left the ruling nobility feckless and self-interested. It split into factions – the Francophile Sorbonnesi, offering new blood to replace nobles wiped out by the quake, and old guard Salamanchesi – which refused to talk to each other except in the council chamber. The lower classes turned away from both in disgust.

So when a French general of Napoleon Bonaparte at the head of 800 troops asked politely in 1806, the gates were opened with only a mumbled protest from representatives of the Senate. The republic was dissolved and delivered to erudite Dalmatian governor Marshal Marmont, who fell in love instantly with a 'little country... an oasis of civilization in the midst of barbarians'. Dubrovnik briefly hoisted its flag of *Libertas* again in 1815 after Napoleon's imperial ambitions came to an icy end in Russia, before it was snapped up by Austria through the Congress of Vienna. Demoted to a mere provincial town in the wilds of the Habsburg empire, it mouldered, its self-belief only restored in the late 19th century when it was set upon the altar of Slavic nationalism as a cradle of Croat culture, a resistor of the Turks. The dramas of its 16th-century playwright Marin Držić were staged in every bourgeois parlour in Zagreb.

But even economic stagnation has its benefits. Without building funds, Dubrovnik had to make do with what it had in its Old Town. Foreign tourists marvelled. George Bernard Shaw sighed about paradise on Earth and in 1936 Edward VIII, on an Adriatic cruise with Wallis Simpson, entertained holiday daydreams about renovating that little mansion by the sea and settling down. Only the ever-contrary Rebecca West was unmoved, deriding Dubrovnik's swagger as unbecoming for a small town, smug even. 'I do not like it,' she huffed, in reply to her husband's comment about 'exquisite' looks. 'It reminds me of the worst of England.'

The Homeland War, and Beyond

Like its great demoted rival Venice, Dubrovnik embraced tourism from the 1950s, sprawling ever westward in the late 1970s to reach the Lapad and Babin kuk peninsulas, which it infested with package hotels. So it was a shock for a city with no real economic significance when mortar shells rocked its centre in October 1991, fired from surrounding hilltops by Montenegrin troops of the Yugoslav People's Army (JNA). National leaders and military top brass rationalized the aggression as a war for peace waged to prevent potential ethnic conflict (and never mind that Dubrovnik had no significant Serb community) and protect the territorial integrity of Montenegro (nor that it held little strategic value). Belgrade also accused Zagreb of diverting paramilitaries and mercenaries to the city as a base for guerrilla raids on Hercegovina. The Yugoslav Army would make efforts to save the historic town, it pledged, before 2,000 mortars and rockets smashed into the Old Town. In truth, this was less strategy than statement, intended to snatch a symbol of Croat pride and sap national morale. But as the international community howled in protest, the military realized it was scoring an own-goal and called a ceasefire in July 1992 – not before 88 civilians had been killed, including a squad of firemen targeted as they tackled a blaze in the new town.

While shrapnel scars still pock-mark Placa's paving slabs and some façades, repair using stone from Brač and carefully sourced terracotta tiles has been so meticulous that you'd never know that, when the black smoke cleared, 70 per cent of the Old Town lay damaged. In summer 2005, the Hotel Imperial where Rebecca West and our bearded Irish scribbler bedded down reopened its doors after postwar renovation as a flagship five-star of the Hilton chain. Indeed, Dubrovnik is more popular than ever. It is the flag-bearer for Croatian tourism, marching steadily upmarket as yet another high-end hotel opens. Yet there are constants besides the Old Town that is the reason to visit. If nothing else, Dubrovnik remains as wily as ever. Fiercely protective of its looks, it is rosy with optimism for its future in tourism, the southern belle of Croatia, doing what it has always done best – making money.

The Pile Gate, City Walls and Lovrijenac Fortress

Enter Dubrovnik's compact Old Town like most visitors throughout its history, through the western **Pile Gate** (Gradska vrata Pile). The republic's principal gateway, it is fronted by an outer bastion completed in 1537, where, framed in a niche, **St Blaise** (*see* box, p.321) cradles a model of the Renaissance city. During the republican era, the wooden drawbridge to the Pile Gate was hoisted each night with much pomp in a ceremony that delivered the city keys to the Ragusan rector. Today it spans a dry moat whose garden offers a modicum of respite from the crowds.

Pass through the Pile Gate's original Gothic inner gateway – this St Blaise is by Croat 20th-century giant Ivan Meštrović – and you reach one of a trio of access points to the **city walls** which offer the finest introduction to Dubrovnik there is. Although sections of Dubrovnik's defining feature date back to the 10th century, today's mighty girdle bound the city four centuries later, then was bolstered at lightning pace after panic rippled north from the shock fall of Constantinople to Ottoman Turks in 1453.

City walls
Gradske zidine; open summer daily 8–7; winter 9–3; adm; access also in Svetog Dominika near the Ploče Gate, and by the Aquarium

Florentine architect Michelozzo di Bartolomeo Michelozzi received the commission and took no chances. Sections of the fortifications rise 25m high and are 6m thick on the inland flanks that were most vulnerable to Turkish cannons. A front-guard of a deep moat and scarp wall was added to be safe. The seaward walls are a modest 3m thick. Michelozzi also erected or strengthened the fortresses at each corner of the city. Clockwise from the Pile Gate entry, they are: the mighty **Minčeta Tower**, its crenellated battlements and central tower embraced as a symbol of unconquerable Dubrovnik; the **Revelin Fortress** adjacent to the southeast Ploče Gate; **St John's Fortress**, a massive gun emplacement which has guarded the port since the 1350s; and the **Bokar Bastion**, which watches over sea approaches.

Whatever the defences' warlike conception, the reason to march their 2km circuit is for views over spires and a terracotta roofscape like patchwork. Partly because of its UNESCO status, partly due to pride, Dubrovnik was so precious about repairs to a historic kernel two-thirds destroyed by Serbian shells – maps at the city gates pinpoint hits – that it scoured Europe to match the *kupe kanalice* tiles which were originally shaped over medieval thighs. Those sourced from French and Slovenian factories are a shock of orange beside the weathered originals, but there's magic in the air when late-afternoon sunshine rakes low and ripens the palette of orange and saffron, ochre and cream, especially when seen from the Minčeta Tower. That said, the rampart walkway is at its quietest first thing in the morning.

For a sublime perspective of the city like a model you can almost reach out and pick up, go uphill to main road Jadranska cesta – shame about the traffic, mind. Better still is that from Mount Srđ, the hill (412m) from which Montenegrin forces launched their bombardment. It is reached off the main road on a zigzagging path – bring a hat and lots of water. With a head for hairpin bends, you can drive via the village of Boskana.

Closer to hand is the raking panorama from the **Lovrijenac Fortress** (Tvrđava Lovrijenac; *same times and ticket as city walls*), which hunkers down on a knuckle of rock outside the Pile gate,

St Blaise, Patron Saint

Four centuries after his AD 316 martyrdom under the Christian purges instigated by Roman emperor Diocletian, the Armenian bishop-saint Blaise tipped off a priest in a dream that Venetian galleons anchored off Lokrum (*see* p.329) under the pretence of replenishing water supplies was actually poised to attack. Or so goes the tale to explain the saint's 10th-century adoption as Dubrovnik patron (more prosaically explained by the arrival of his relics). A republic never slow to trumpet its freedom after 150 years' rule by arch-rival Venice (until 1358) hailed its hero in sculpture and painting throughout the city.

Nor is such votive salute simply ancient history. In 1991, despairing of half-hearted peace negotiations in The Hague, a band of Dubrovnik refugees invoked the saint as humanitarian aid mission the 'St Blaise Foundation' and attempted to brazen their way through a Yugoslav naval siege of their city on a passenger ferry. Among their number was Croatian president Stipe Mesic, who warmed to heroics under the protection of global publicity and declaimed, 'You can shoot if you want to, but remember Europe is listening.' It was, too; the Montenegrin army and Yugoslav navy slunk off, embarrassed by the PR disaster of shells lobbed into one of the world's most perfectly preserved citadels.

opposite the Bokar bastion. The Senate demanded walls 12m thick for this castle to guard their western sea approaches. Or did on the seaward side. But a high council with an autocratic streak dictated that those facing inland should be merely 60cm, no protection for any garrison commander who nurtured plans of mutiny. Once inside the shell of a late 1400s fortress you can understand why its fame today is not as the scourge of sea galleons but as a stage set for Elsinore during productions of *Hamlet* in the Summer Festival. Before you enter, look for script on the lintel which drummed into guards that 'Freedom is not sold for all the goods in the world' ('*Non bene pro toto libertas vendit vravo*').

Along Placa

And so to **Placa** (aka Stradun), just inside the Pile Gate. So handsome is Dubrovnik's central street that you'd never guess its origins as the swampy channel filled in the 11th century to unite islet Laus – where the city made its 7th-century debut – with the mainland Slavic settlement christened after holm oak woods (*dubrava*). The devastating 1667 earthquake that allowed city fathers to rethink their map also allowed them to take in hand Placa's jumble of Gothic palaces and impose a regimented Baroque dress parade. For all the authoritarian bent of its conception, there's no denying Placa's good looks; a handsome strip of green-shuttered mansions in shades of honey and clotted cream, an occasional blush of pink, on a street whose limestone cobbles have been buffed shiny by millions of feet. A 19th-century visitor probably had its width in mind when he noted, 'Dubrovnik is not built in such a way to be admired from a coach. This is a place which leaves a great deal of space for pedestrians.' Don't you believe it in high summer.

The earthquake which rethought Placa also did for **Onofrio's Large Fountain** (Velika Onofrijeva fontana) just inside the Pile Gate;

the 16 masks that spout water on a bare dome today barely hint at the heavily ornamented Renaissance original, designed in 1438 by architect Onofrio della Cava. The Neopolitan builder's glorified washbasin for new arrivals was one element in a no-expenses-spared waterworks that piped fresh water by aqueduct from the river Dubrovačka 12km away – no rainwater cistern like other Dalmatian cities for wealthy Dubrovnik. More recent destruction is visible as shrapnel scars which pock the Renaissance façade of **St Saviour's Church** (Crkva sv. Spasa) opposite, a rum deal for a tiny church which survived the 1667 quake in better shape than its neighbours and had itself been erected as a thank-you for the city's survival of an earlier earthquake in 1520. The bare Gothic interior now serves as a temporary exhibition space and concert venue.

The earthquake also destroyed a **Franciscan Monastery** (Franjevački samostan) that was more ritzy than the present bare hulk if the surviving late Gothic portal is proof; local sons the Petrović brothers carved its late-Gothic *Pietà* flanked by St Jerome (in a penitent's hairshirt) and St John. The barn-like interior with so-so Baroque altars is nothing special. Devote your time instead to the late Romanesque **cloister**; locate it from a passageway adjacent to tourists trying out a traditional test of balance atop a moustachioed head beside the west portal – not nearly as easy as it looks. Craftsmen in 1360 gave free rein to their imaginations on capitals of the cloister's double colonnade of pillars, with a menagerie of dragons, dogs and griffins; look too for a balloon-cheeked self-portrait by a sculptor with toothache. It's best appreciated around midday, when the tour groups bustle off for lunch and the garden of oranges and palms returns to serenity, which is when you can explore at leisure the curate's egg of ecclesiastica in the **treasury** (*same ticket and hours*). More charming than its Byzantine icons, votive jewellery and bizarre gold and silver reliquaries of saints' feet and St Ursula's head are the china jars and painted shelves which once graced Europe's oldest apothecary, still doling out medicines beside the cloister as it has done since 1317.

Cloister
t *(020) 321 410; open daily 9–6; adm*

North of Placa, steep staircases crammed with pot plants clamber uphill; the residential alleys beyond **Prijeko** allow a glimpse behind the scenes of Dubrovnik's stage-set. At the east end of Placa's shimmering river of cobbles, **Žudioska** (Jews' Street) was named after the medieval ghetto established by Spanish and Italian Jews in the 16th century. With the self-confidence of wealth, the republic presented the community with a medieval town house, which explains why Europe's second-oldest **synagogue**, a lovely Baroque nook at No.5, where brass lamps and candelabras are suspended from a ceiling framed by Stars of David, is on the second floor rather than in the basement. Not that Dubrovnik

Synagogue
Sinagoga; ***t*** *(020) 321 423; open summer daily 10–8; winter Mon–Fri 10–1; adm*

embraced the Jewish community entirely without reservation – the council demanded they wash in a separate fountain rather than share those of Christians. A small **museum** chronicles the Jewish community, today 30-strong, in facsimiles of official documents and religious artefacts, including a 13th-century Torah treasured by the first exiles.

Luža Square

If there is a centre stage of Dubrovnik it is Luža Square. This was the heart of the merchant council, and here the 3 February procession of the Feast of St Blaise climaxes with the full authority of Catholic pomp, and poetry is recited to inaugurate the Summer Festival (*see* 'Festivals', p.330). The piazza's centrepiece is **Orlando's Column** (Orlandov stup). The lectern for public declarations and shaming post for felons flew the white banner of *Libertas* from its flagpole until Napoleon, never a dictator to recognize such limiting concepts, lowered it after his troops stomped into a weak city, rotten to the core with internal strife. The city council restored the flag as a morale-booster as Yugoslavia imploded in 1990. The column is named after its Gothic effigy of Orlando (aka Roland). A tale claims the chivalric knight slew a 9th-century Saracen pirate named Spucente near Lokrum to lift a 15-month siege of Dubrovnik – casually overlooking that the real-life nephew of Frankish king Charlemagne, hero of medieval French epic *Chanson de Roland*, died in AD 778. It is more probable that the favourite of North European cities was imported by Sigismund, a 15th-century Hungarian–Croat monarch. Whatever the truth, respect was hardly uppermost in the minds of the market traders, who measured out 51.2cm standard lengths of cloth on their hero's forearm.

Sponza Palace
Sponza-Povijesni arhiv, open summer daily 10–10; adm

Archives
open summer Sat 8–3

He stands opposite the **Sponza Palace**, whose Renaissance colonnade and Venetian–Gothic windows, frothily ornamented by Korčula sculptor-brothers the Andrijićs, offer a glimpse of Dubrovnik before the 1667 destruction; florid and graceful without showing off. The city **archives** are stored on upper floors where the republic minted its own currency. Its galleried courtyard once rang to the babble of merchants in the customs house, remembered by a reference to municipal scales above the central arch: 'Our weights do not permit cheating or being cheated: when I measure goods, God measures me.' One room at the rear is devoted permanently to a moving 'Memorial Room of Dubrovnik Defenders', a simple but heartfelt requiem to citizens who lost their lives through the JNA's aggression in the Homeland War. The exhibition directly inspired the opening of **War Photo Limited** off Stradun at Antuninska 6. This modern gallery hangs often shocking photojournalism exhibitons of global conflict, past and present.

War Photo Limited
t (020) 322 166, www.warphotoltd.com; open June–Sept daily 9–9; May and Oct Tues–Sat 10–4, Sun 10–2; adm

'Green men' Maro and Baro strike the hour in the 30m **bell tower** (Gradski zvonik) at the palace's left shoulder, rebuilt to the medieval plans after its tilt became too woozy to ignore. From here you can sidetrack through an arch to the Dominican Monastery (*see* pp.327–8) or pass the mustachioed guard on the massive Baroque portal of the **House of the Main Guard** – renovated to create a restaurant and cinema – to reach **Onofrio's Little Fountain** (Mala Onofrijeva fontana) the little sister to the larger water feature at the other end of Placa.

The backdrop to Luža is **St Blaise's Church** (Crkva svetog Vlaha) elevated on a platform. At the peak of its Baroque bulk, the city's patron (*see* box, p.321) salutes between Faith and Hope. The choice of those Virtues was deliberate. The church rose over the square as a replacement for a Gothic number that was badly shaken in 1667, then delivered a *coup de grâce* by fire in 1706. Inside, upstaged by angels and *putti*, a silver statue of the saint clutches the inevitable city model on the high altar, removed only when it is paraded on St Blaise's Day; that it survived that 18th-century blaze was hailed a miracle by a city desperate for some good news. It is unclear whether Dubrovnik intends to revive the custom of freeing minor prisoners for the high day of its religious calendar.

The Rector's Palace

Diagonally opposite the church is the **Rector's Palace** (Knežev dvor), the state headquarters of the Ragusan Republic and temporary home of the local son who was elevated to preside over council meetings for a month. For all the high talk of republican egalitarianism, the aristocracy kept a tight grip on power and the incumbent was little more than a ceremonial puppet; a more charitable interpretation is that this was a safeguard to prevent a dominant personality upsetting the status quo. The symbol of sovereignty, aged 50-plus, lived apart from his family and was only permitted to leave his glorified prison on state business, when he was preceded by a retinue of musicians and 20 court guards.

But what a prison. The city's most celebrated architectural monument was rebuilt twice due to explosions, fire and earthquake. First was Naples's Onofrio, he of the fountains, who introduced the palace's Venetian Gothic with the help of Korčula's Petar Andrijić. Next came Michelozzi, who put fortifications work on hold to add the Renaissance **loggia**, whose froth must have delighted city fathers even if they decreed the rest of his plans were too racy, sending the architect back to Florence in a huff. Among his capitals is Aesculapius in his pharmacy – a vainglorious attempt to appropriate a Greek demigod physician who was linked with Epidaurum (today's Cavtat, *see* pp.356–7). The Renaissance **courtyard** is pure elegance, a premier venue for classical music concerts. The bust at the rear is Miho Pracat, a shipping magnate from the Elafiti island of Lopud (*see* p.335) who, for want of an heir, bequeathed his fortune to the city. It must have been some fortune – he was the only commoner so honoured in the republic's history.

City museum
Gradski muzej; **t** *(020) 341 422; open summer daily 9–6; winter daily 9–2; adm*

Most of the palace holds a **city museum**. The former courtroom and prison cells on the ground-floor are taken up by musty displays of coins, official seals, documents and weaponry. Things perk up marginally in first-floor state rooms, reached via a Baroque staircase that sweeps up to the assembly hall – the portal lintel exhorts councillors to 'Forget private concerns, focus on public affairs'. There are oils of nobles on the walls of period rooms which fast-forward through decorative style in *objets d'art* and costume – look for the rector's red damask toga, a stole of black velvet over its left shoulder – and hint at the decadence and glory of the Ragusan Republic snuffed out by Napoleonic dissolution. Informative the rooms are not, however; a museum guide is a must if you want to do anything but skim.

The Cathedral and St John's Fortress

The full-stop to **Pred Dvorom** is the **cathedral** (Katedrala). Enthused by the churches of the Eternal City, a Dubrovnik expat recommended Andrea Buffalini of Urbino to design its Roman Baroque hulk crowned by a dainty cupola. It rose over the ruins of a church destroyed in 1667. Local legend claims that the Romanesque original was funded by Richard the Lionheart in thanks for his life after shipwreck near Lokrum on the way home from Crusade in 1192. Fact – or at least early foundations – retorts that a church has existed at the location on the former islet of Laus since the 7th century.

Treasury
Riznica; **t** *(020) 323 496; open Mon–Sat 8–5, Sun 11–5; adm*

The star artwork in a bleached interior is a murky *Assumption of the Virgin* polyptych above the altar, attributed to Venetian master Titian. Inevitably, St Blaise and his model put in an appearance on the left-hand panel, although this time with good reason, because bits of the saint are venerated in the **treasury**, a wonder of the Adriatic before the 1667 earthquake, they say, so valuable that it was safeguarded by entrusting different keys to the archbishop, cathedral rector and state secretary. In this old curiosity shop of body parts crammed into Byzantine gold reliquaries and displayed on shelves are: the saint's right and left hands, the latter reputedly picked up by a Dubrovnik merchant who was trading in the East in 1346; his throat, in a bizarre 11th-century monstrance, shaped like a foot; and, the treasury's prize, his head, encased in a jewel-encrusted Byzantine crown whose *cloisonné* enamel depicts saints in an overgrown garden of gold and enamel. Overlooked among such star pieces is a modest 16th-century silver casket, crafted to hold baby Jesus's nappies, apparently.

Narrow **Kneza Damjana Jude** opposite the cathedral's main portal burrows past side streets stuffed with tatty nobles' port mansions towards the **St John's Fortress** (Tvrđava sv. Ivana). Its refurbished ground floor houses an **Aquarium** where there are small sharks and rays to pet alongside Adriatic sea life such as octopus. Former cannon rooms above host the **Maritime Museum**, a half-hearted salute to the maritime prowess which elevated Dubrovnik to European power-player. Ragusan fleets sailed throughout Europe, the Balkans, the Black Sea, even as far afield as India, and coined the English word 'argosy'. By the late 1700s, 255 large ships sailed in foreign waters under the Dubrovnik ensign, and 230 more plied the oceans. Models of some of those tubby traders plus a snapshot of everyday life afforded by cargo salvaged from a 17th-century trader are the highlights.

Aquarium
Akvarij; **t** *(020) 323 978; open summer daily 9–7; winter Mon–Sat 9–1; adm*

Maritime Museum
Pomorski muzej; **t** *(020) 323 904; open summer daily 9–6; winter Tues–Sun 9–1; adm*

Around Gundulićeva Poljana

For all the architectural ballgowns, Dubrovnik is as charming in her everyday dress, worn in Gundulićeva poljana. It's home to a marvellous morning **market** whose stallholders also hawk Hvar lavender, fat cheeses and, decanted into old water bottles, homemade wines and homemade *rakija* laced with herbs which locals swear does wonders for high blood pressure. The figure on the plinth is Ivan Gundulić (1589–1638). Such is the acclaim for the Ragusan poet's epic *Osman* – a eulogy to the Polish routs of the Turks, pictured in bas-relief beneath the statue by 19th-century sculptor Ivan Rendić – that he is awarded a place on the 50Kn note. Veneration came late, however. Gundulić's *magnum opus* didn't even make it into print until 1826, and even then thanks only to the Croatian Illyrian movement, which hailed his work as exemplary stuff during a campaign to reassert Croatian over German as the official language and which saw Dubrovnik eulogized as the Croatian Athens.

Market
Mon–Sat

Up a staircase (1738) that alludes to Rome's Spanish Steps is the **Jesuit Church of St Ignatius** (Jezuitska crkva i samostan), modelled on Rome's famous Il Gesù church. As if to compensate for the restraint elsewhere, Dubrovnik's finest Baroque church (1729) lets rip in a rich interior. In the frescoed sanctuary, Jesuit founder St Ignatius proffers his religious credo before a quartet of comely *belles*, the four continents on which the Order spread the word. Less cultural but as enjoyable is a Lourdes grotto by the entrance, a dollop of kitsch added in 1885.

In surrounding streets away from public spaces, Dubrovnik relaxes into easygoing mode. West of the church is a residential district whose tangled alleys and staircases knot into small squares or tease with a dead end. A lovely spot for a happy-go-lucky amble with two of the city's most enigmatic bars to discover (*see* p.332).

Od Puča and Around

Halfway along Od Puča, the street parallel to Placa, the **Serbian Orthodox Church** (Srpska pravoslavna crkva) is spacious and dignified with a painted panelled ceiling. A few doors away at Od puča 8 is the **Orthodox Church Museum** of religious icons. The treasures among a four-century *œuvre* of oval-faced Madonnas, mostly from nearby Kotor in Montenegro, Crete and Greece, are a sumptuous 16th-century image of resurrected Christ appearing to Mary Magdalene (in Room One) and an 18th-century Russian calendar crowded with the saints of each religious day.

Orthodox Church Museum
Muzej pravoslavne crkve; open Mon–Sat 9–2; adm

More culture is five minutes' walk away at Široka 7, former home of the Croatian Shakespeare, Marin Držić (1508–67). Gutted as **Marin Držic House**, the multimedia museum displays a few everyday relics from Držić's era and a mock-up of his cell-like bedroom, plus a 40-minute audiovisual presentation (available in English) that explores the Ragusan society he lampooned in comedies such as Croat favourite *Dundo Maroje* (*Uncle Maroje*). Nearby, on Od Rupe, the **Rupe Ethnographic Museum** houses three floors of tradition – folk costumes, from simple smocks to embroidered Sunday best, and rural handicrafts – let down by dull displays and a lack of labels; ask friendly staff to explain quirks such as horses' skulls placed on beehives to scare off evil spirits who soured honey. As much of an exhibit is the museum's Renaissance building itself – ground-floor storage bins (*rupe*) dug from the rock bed reveal its origins as the granary of a city twitchy about sieges and reliant on imported grain – and the views of the town.

Marin Držic House
Kuća Marina Držića; open summer Tues–Sun 10–6; adm

Rupe Ethnographic Museum
t *(020) 323 013; Etnografski muzej Rupe; open Wed–Mon 9–4; adm*

The Old Port and Dominican Monastery

Suddenly intimate after Placa, **Sv. Dominika** east of the Sponza Palace twists past the **old port**, where fishing boats not traders' barques nod at moorings, ferries thrum to Lokrum (*see* p.329) and Cavtat (*see* pp.356–7), and tourist boat captains tout sprees to admire the city walls. A restaurant now occupies the three arches through which galleons were hauled to be refitted in the city arsenal; not a city to take chances, Dubrovnik bricked them up while new ships were in build.

Beyond on Sv. Dominika, the **Dominican Monastery** (Dominikanski samostan, open as a museum, *see* p.328) presses hard against the city walls following its conception as a fortress to protect a chink in Dubrovnik's armour. Chipping in funds, the Ragusan government exhorted citizens to put other projects on hold until the 14th-century edifice stood for 'the preservation, protection and safety of the city of Dubrovnik'. Pope Benedict XI also issued a 1304 papal bull 'inviting' church members to dig deep into their coffers to safeguard a city on the ramparts of Christendom. Ascend a **staircase** whose balustrade is marred by concrete filler – vandalism by monks to spare brothers the temptation of a shapely ankle as ladies ascended to church – to reach the loveliest **cloister** in Dubrovnik, where restrained Gothic and Renaissance arches frame a garden of palms and orange trees. Its hushed haven, a world away from Dubrovnik's summer hubbub, comes from the drawing board of Rector's Palace architect Michelozzi and is an overture to the art treasures stored in the city's richest **museum**. Renaissance works of the Dubrovnik school steal the show, especially the exquisite trio by Nikola Božidarević, the master artist of the republic's golden age: his humanist *Virgin and Child* altarpiece seems wafted from the other side of the Adriatic; a lower panel of an *Annunciation* played out to a rapt audience of cherubs features the anchored vessel of the Lopud captain who commissioned it; and, in a lovely *Madonna and Child* steeped in the incense and candlelight of Byzantine mystery, St Blaise proffers a model of pre-quake Dubrovnik. In the same room is a polyptych by Lovro Dobričević; Dominican Order martyr St Peter suffers the cutlass and sword of pirates and St Stephen wears the stone of his martyrdom like a skull cap to witness the baptism of Christ. (If you fall for the works by these Dubrovnik school superstars, there are more altar pieces in the **Church of St Mary in Danče** (Crkva sv. Marije na Dančana) south of Pile; ask tourist information about who holds the key.) Star piece among works by Baroque foreigners is a Titian altarpiece, *Mary Magdalene and St Blaise*, in an adjacent room.

Museum
open daily summer 9–6, winter 9–3; adm

The **church** itself is a let-down after such magnificence, worth a look only for a *Miracle of St Dominic* altarpiece by late 19th-century Cavtat artist Vlaho Bukovac.

Through the Ploče Gate

The east counterpart to the Pile Gate, the 15th-century **Ploče Gate** signs off the Old Town with its own drawbridge and the statuette of the city's ubiquitous patron, and beyond is the 1540s **Revelin Fortress**; all building work paused while Dubrovnik beefed up a century-old fortress at the vulnerable landward gate because of Venetian sabre-rattling. Beyond the walls, modernity returns with a jolt, broken only by the **Lazareti** 200m away – artists' studios and the performance space of folk group Linđo now occupy the 16th-century brick sheds on the Turkey trade route where all foreign travellers sat out 40 days' quarantine. Beyond these is shingle beach **Banje**. In a restored Thirties villa further uphill there's the excellent **Museum of Modern Art**. Vlaho Bukovac's formal

Museum of Modern Art
Umjetnička galerija; **t** *(020) 426 590, www.ugdubrovnik.hr; open Tues–Sun 10–8; adm*

portraiture, which dabbles with Impressionism, wins plaudits among the gallery of 20th-century Croatian artists. More enjoyable are the colourful landscapes by Marko Rešica or *Lapad*, a dainty work by Antun Masle. The ground floor hosts temporary exhibitions, the terraces on the three above provide broad panoramas across to Lokrum island.

Lokrum

Lokrum
ferries every 30mins from old port, summer daily 9–6; journey 15mins; 40Kn return

Lokrum is the escape from Dubrovnik's summer crowds par excellence. Even in peak season, the islet that lies just offshore from the old port swallows however many visitors disappear into its thick fuzz of pine and macqui. 'Only the imagination of a skilled writer could have placed an island like Lokrum off a city like Dubrovnik,' 20th-century dramatist, author and local son Luka Paljetak said. 'When you set foot upon Lokrum, you encroach upon a mystery... it is under a spell that you cannot hope to undo.'

Believe the local tales, and spells are the *leitmotif* of a 72-hectare idyll unofficially dubbed 'Magic Island'. It may have been the sense of the otherworldly that led Benedictine monks to found an abbey and monastery here in 1023, and legend claims they would have got a church too had Richard the Lionheart fulfilled a pledge to erect one where he staggered ashore after being wrecked en route home from a Crusade in 1192. Their Order dissolved on Napoleon's instructions, the monks allegedly said a final Mass then circled their island at night holding inverted candles and laying a curse on anyone who claimed their sanctuary for themselves. Superstitious locals swear it did for Habsburg archduke Maximilian Ferdinand. He purchased Lokrum as an idyllic retreat in 1859, only to be executed as luckless emperor of Mexico by soldiers in 1867. The battalion of sorrows – bankruptcy, drownings, suicide pacts by thwarted lovers – which befell future owners have only helped sustain the legend.

In the three halcyon years before Maximilian travelled to Mexico to accept his poisoned chalice, he rethought the monastery as a holiday home, imported peacocks and dug a **botanic garden** in which he studied verses of poet Heinrich Heine while his wife Charlotte pored over her silk embroidery. Only his garden remains open to the public, somewhat neglected at the side of his mansion; Australian and South American species spread leafy canopies alongside the archduke's cacti. More enticing is the monks' semi-ruined **cloister**, going nicely to seed with agave, palms and cacti. You'll probably have it to yourself, as most visitors head straight for the excellent swimming off flat rocks a short stroll southwest of the monastery, or wallow in the warmer shallows of an adjacent saltwater lake enclosed by low cliffs; more secluded coves, including a nudist 'beach', are on the island's south tip.

Explore Maximilian's paths, which idle around a drowsy island cocooned in hush, and you'll discover **Fort Royal**. Built by the French as an 1806 stronghold, the star-shaped gun battery broods among the pines at Lokrum's highest point.

ⓘ **Dubrovnik Old Town >**
Ante Starčevića 7, **t** *(020) 427 591/426 253, www.tzdubrovnik.hr, near the Pile Gate bus station; Široka 7,* **t** *(020) 323 587, off Placa, near the Franciscan monastery; and Od sv Dominika 7,* **t** *(020) 312 011; all open summer daily 8–9 (till 10 July–Aug); winter Mon–Fri 8–8, Sat–Sun 9–4*

ⓘ **Dubrovnik New Town >**
Obala S Radića 27, Gruž, **t** *(020) 417 983; Šetalište kralj Zvonimara, Lapad peninsula,* **t** *(020) 437 460; opening times same as above*

Tourist Information in Dubrovnik

All the **offices** stock city maps, bus maps, timetables for Jadrolinija ferries and *The Best in Dubrovnik*, an excellent free booklet that's a mine of information and what's-on listings.

Festivals

3 Feb: St Blaise's Day fills the Old Town with religious pomp and is closely followed by three days of **Carnival**, whose good-humoured lunacy of costumed parades and merriment ends on Whit Sunday.

Early July–Aug: Highlight of the Dubrovnik calendar is the internationally acclaimed **Summer Festival**, *www.dubrovnik-festival.hr*, a feast of classical music and theatre which takes full advantage of Dubrovnik's stage-set squares, courtyards and castles.

Shopping

Placa's mansions are stuffed with touristy shops, boutiques, bookshops and smart jewellers. Algoritam at No.8 has English-language media, books and guidebooks. Parallel **Od Puča** offers a more interesting mish-mash of leather work, jewellers and galleries. For quirky souvenirs, **Art studio Trabakul**, Zlatarska 1, produces clay 'trabakul' fishing boats; it also has a stall at the old port by Lokanda Peskarija restaurant. Several galleries are on Ulica Sv Dominika. Foodies can try the olive oils, wines and good things sold in **Franja**, Od Puča 9.

Sports and Activities

Adriatic Kayak Tours, Zrinsko-frankopanska 6, **t** (020) 312 770, *www.adriatickayaktours.com*. Kayaking trips around the city walls, a sunset paddle with wine and cheese and peddle-and-paddle trips to the Elafiti islands.

Adventure Dalamatia (cove beneath the Lovrijenac Fortress), mobile **t** 091 566 5942, *www.adventuredalmatia.com*. Half-day kayak tours around the walls to Lokrum.

Mediterranean Experience, **t** (020) 436 846, *www.dubrovnik-walking-tours.com*. Themed walking tours go from Big Onofrio's Fountain daily – no reservations required; visit the website for times or pick up a flyer from the tourist office.

Where to Stay in Dubrovnik

Bar two exceptions in the Old Town and the Hilton, most hotels are either a 10mins' walk east of the Ploče Gate (the luxury set) or 2–4km west on the Lapad and Babin kuk peninsulas, where most of the mid-range package jobs are near the beaches. Be warned: Dubrovnik doesn't do cheap. Budget accommodation comes largely from private rooms (*see* below) or the campsite, **Camping Solitudo**, **t** (020) 448 686, on the Babin kuk peninsula, near Copacabana beach.

Villa Dubrovnik, Vlaha Bukovca 6, Ploče, **t** (020) 422 933, *www.villa-dubrovnik.hr*, formerly an exclusive retreat, may open after protracted renovation in 2010.

Bellevue, Pera Čingrije 7, 1km from Pile Gate, **t** (020) 330 000, *www.hotel-bellevue.hr* (€€€). Design-led retro-modern-styled luxury hotel that's funkier than sisters the Dubrovnik Palace and Excelsior. Clifftop views along the coast, deluxe spa facilities and a private beach beneath.

Dubrovnik Palace, Masarykov put 2, Lapad, **t** (020) 430 000, *www.dubrovnikpalace.hr* (€€€). Boutique luxury on a resort-hotel scale in a five-star on the Lapad peninsula with superb views to the Elafiti islands. Tasteful throughout, and sea views from every balcony, plus all sorts of spas, pools, bars and restaurants; terrace *konoba* **Maslina** is hugely atmospheric.

Excelsior, Frana Supila 12, Ploče, **t** (020) 353 353, *www.hotel-excelsior.hr* (€€€). A luxury glass-skinned design hotel reopened in 2008 that oozes celebrity glamour. West-facing rooms have best views of old town around, suites are staggering. Splendid spa.

Grand Villa Argentina and **Villa Orsula**, Frana Supila 14, Ploče, **t** (020) 440 555, *www.gva.hr* (€€€). The traditional luxury five-star, 5mins' walk east of the Ploče Gate; former guests include HRH Queen Elizabeth, Roger Moore and John Malkovich. Standard hotel rooms are plush if fairly ordinary, those in attached Villa Argentina are old-world glamour for just €30 extra. Incorporated 1930s **Villa Orsula** is slated for a refurb for 2010. All share a concrete 'beach' and outdoor pool; its Victoria garden restaurant is recommended for a romantic meal.

Hilton Imperial Dubrovnik, Marijana Blažića 2, Old Town, **t** (020) 416 553, *www.hilton.com* (€€€). A £14m renovation has buffed up two 19th-century palaces to create this 2005 newcomer to Dubrovnik's luxury hotel scene, moments from the Pile Gate.

More, Kardinala Stepinca 33, Lapad **t** (020) 494 000, *www.hotel-more.hr* (€€€). The new kid on the block, an elegant small hotel that hangs over the bay, most rooms with a private balcony. A terrace Jacuzzi and a spa complete the deal as a grown-up retreat.

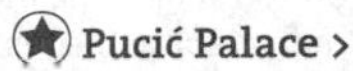

Pucić Palace, Od Puča 1, Old Town, **t** (020) 326 200, *www.thepucicpalace.com* (€€€). Effortlessly elegant five-star boutique hotel fashioned from a stone mansion in the heart of the old town. Baroque-style furnishings meet classy Italian mosaic bathrooms with Bulgari toiletries; a décor tweak will up the glamour for 2009. Its terrace restaurant, **Defne** (€€€), is one of *the* dining experiences.

Stari Grad, Od Sigurate 4, Old Town, **t** (020) 321 373, *www.hotelstarigrad.com* (€€€). A little pricey considering the modest décor in the eight three-star rooms, but you'll be outside anyway, feasting on views and breakfast on the roof terrace, and the location is second only to the Pucić Palace.

Importanne Resort, Kardinala Stepinca 31, Babin kuk, **t** (020) 440 100, *www.importanneresort.hr* (€€€–€€). Four-hotel resort complex: overhauled family hotel Neptun, smarter Ariston, a suite-only hotel and a villa. Uninterrupted views and a location above the Copacabana beach. Rather isolated without your own transport.

Kompas, Šetalište kralja Zvonimira 56, Lapad, **t** (020) 352 000, *www.hotel-kompas.hr* (€€). Former bland three-star revamped by the Adriatic Luxury Hotels group. Still modest but great location on Sumratin beach.

Zagreb, Šetalište kralja Zvonimira 27, Lapad, **t** (020) 438 930, *www.hotels-sumratin.com* (€€). Habsburg-vintage small hotel behind Sumratin beach. Modest yet spacious and affordable. Adjacent sister hotel **Sumratin**, **t** (020) 436 333 (€€), offers more of the same.

Orhan, Od Tabakarije 1, nr Old Town, **t** (020) 414 183 (€). The 11 rooms (although spotless and en suite) are basic, but the location, in a cove beneath the Lovrijenac Fortress, is great. A bargain, with a good restaurant to boot.

Youth Hostel, Bana Josipa Jelačića 15–17, nr Old Town, **t** (020) 423 241, *www.hfhs.hr* (€). Dormitory beds in a basic hostel 10mins' walk from the Pile Gate.

Private Rooms

Any number of tourist agencies will book rooms (€) in private houses.

Atlas, Brsalje 17, near the Pile Gate, **t** (020) 442 574/565, *www.atlas-croatia.com*.

Generalturist, Obala Stjepana Radića 24, **t** (020) 432 974, *www.generalturist.com*.

Globtour, Prijeko 12, Old Town, **t** (020) 321 599.

Gulliver Travel, Obala Stjepana Radića 32, **t** (020) 313 313, *www.gulliver.hr*.

Eating Out in Dubrovnik

Restaurant alley is Prijeko, although it's largely bland tourist tat bar two exceptions. For eats on the go, try 24hr bakery **Tanti gusti** (Između

Polača 11). **Buffet Škola** (Antuninska bb) rustles up delicious sandwiches prepared with homemade bread.

Atlas Club Nautica, Braslje 3, **t** (020) 442 526 (€€€). The formal address for visiting dignitaries and evening blow-outs: views of the city walls and Lovrijenac to accompany exquisite seafood. House special is lobster.

★ Lokanda Peskarija >>

Proto, Široka 1, **t** (020) 323 234 (€€€). Semi-smart and just off Placa, with consistently high-quality seafood specialities, always with a few unusual dishes on the menu. Worth the wait for the first-floor terrace.

Ohran, Od Tabakarije 1, nr Old Town, **t** (020) 414 183 (€€€–€€). Not just about the location on a cove beneath the Lovrijenac Fortress – steaks are a cut above, fish is reliable – but highly atmospheric on the terrace.

Wanda, Prijeko 8 (€€€–€€). A 2008 sensation which brought delicate international-quality Mediterranean cuisine that leans towards Italy to the Prijeko strip. Pricey *à la carte*, good-value *prix-fixe* menus.

Domino, Od Domina 6, **t** (020) 323 103 (€€). The tastiest steaks in Dubrovnik, say some locals, all charcoal-grilled. Carnivore heaven.

Levanat, Nika i Meda Pucića 15, Babin kuk (on road to Hotel Neptun), **t** (020) 435 352 (€€). A gem wedged on a cliff with magic views across the bay. An inventive menu ranges from traditionals like ink-blackened cuttlefish salad from Šipan, to modern inventions: fish carpaccio and rocket leaves fried with mozzarella.

Marco Polo, Lučarica 6, **t** (020) 323 719 (€€). A 10-table charmer squirrelled away down a side alley behind St Blaise's church.

Rozarij, Prijeko 2 (€€). A little pricey, but the most atmospheric restaurant of the glut on Prijeko, with candlelit tables snuggled against the tiny Church of St Nicholas.

Dubrovački kantun, Boškovićeva 5, **t** (020) 331 911 (€). Marvellous bistro-café with chunky sandwiches and Dalmatian *tapas*, much of it vegetarian and all made from the freshest local ingredients: anchovies, sheep's cheese from Pag soused in olive oil and *pršut* ham. *Pašticada* is rich and luxurious.

Kamenice, Gundulićeva poljana 8; **t** (020) 323 682 (€). A favourite of locals and tourists for decades in the lovely square. Fat mussels, *mala riba pržena* (whitebait) and octopus salad make a tasty light bite.

Lokanda Peskarija, Ribarnica bb (beside old port), **t** (020) 324 750 (€). No longer a locals' secret but still unbeatable for mussels or risottos of seafood or cuttlefish, served in saucepans and washed down with plonk. Excellent and unpretentious – expect to wait for a seat.

Mea Culpa, Za Rokom 3; **t** (020) 323 430 (€). Large, tasty thin-crust pizzas alfresco near the Ethnographic Museum.

Cafés and Bars in Dubrovnik

Abakus, Excelsior hotel (*see* p.331). Glamorous glass-walled cocktail bar that looks across to the old town.

Arsenal, Pred Dvorom 1. Wine bar and restaurant in the cavernous old-town shipyard.

Buža I, end of Ulica Ilije Sarake. More random, more secret sister bar to Buža II (*see* below); really just a few tables scattered over rocks with ladders to swim. No sign – go through the door marked '8–20'.

Buža II, Od Margarite. Fabulous palm-shaded bar that hangs above the sea outside the walls; follow signs for 'Cold drinks' from the Jesuit church. Just add cocktail at sunset.

EastWest, Banje beach, Ploče. Bar-club on the beach for a showy clientele dressed to impress.

Gill's Pop Lounge, Sv Dominika. Staggering location for a flamboyant lounge bar, part of a hip retro-styled fusion restaurant on battlements above the old port.

GraDskavana, Luža 2. The *grande dame* of Dubrovnik cafés revamped to lose the yesteryear clutter. Grandstand views over the square.

Jazz Café Troubador, Bunićeva poljana. Rather spoiled by T-Mobile's neon sign, but still a landmark bar in a square full of them – rattan chairs, a stylish clientele and evening live jazz.

Libertina, Zlatarska. A locals' favourite, cluttered with junky mementoes and where the service is refreshingly gruff; an antidote to high-season posing.

Sunset Lounge, Dubrovnik Palace hotel, Lapad (*see* above). Just what the name says, with superb panoramas to the Elafitis to boot.

Talir, Antuninska. Great little theatre and artists' bar covered with photos that spills out onto the steps during the evening.

Entertainment in Dubrovnik

Monthly booklet *The Best in Dubrovnik* (free from tourist office) is a what's-on bible. **Classical concerts** are staged in churches, the Dominican Monastery cloisters and the atrium of the Rector's Palace. **Traditional song and dance** is staged by folk group Lindo in the Lazareti (*see* p.328; Mon and Fri at 9.30pm; summer only). The complex also hosts the excellent Lazareti venue, with a bar, gigs and clubnights.

North of Dubrovnik

Trsteno

With a hop and a skip out of the suburbs, then a jump over the Rijeka Dubrovačka inlet on a futuristic suspension bridge, the Magistrala coast road is free of Dubrovnik and bowling north. It's a lovely, slaloming coast-hugger of a drive, a world lit by crisp Mediterranean light and as vivid as the third day of Creation: on one side are scraggy mountains of mottled limestone, on the other subtropical vegetation and the Elafiti islands like treasure islands in sparkling seas.

The view inspired Dubrovnik's Ivan Marinov Gučetić-Gozze in 1494. He realized the potential for a summer retreat, then *de rigueur* for nobles, and seeded one of the finest landscaped parks in Croatia, the **Trsteno Arboretum**, 15km north of Dubrovnik. Visit in spring and his relic of Renaissance sophistication, lovingly tended and expanded by future Gučetić-Gozze until it was seized by Communists in 1948, explodes with colour and promise. Dawdle in summer among its 63 aromatic acres and you'll wonder how holidaying humanist Nikola Vitov Gučetić ever roused himself sufficiently to jot down his philosophical musings in the 1500s.

Trsteno Arboretum
t (020) 751 019, www.hazu.hr; open daily May–Oct 7–7, Nov–April 8–3; adm

At the heart of the complex, reached by a path beyond two enormous plane trees on the main road, is a **summer villa** rebuilt after the 1667 earthquake which shook Dubrovnik, today a missed opportunity, empty and closed to the public. Fortunately you are free to explore Gučetić's gardens before it, structured in Dubrovnik fashion with an axial walkway and pergola which once supported vines, dividing stone walls and, as a nod to the Age of Reason, orderly triangles of box hedge planted with rosemary, lavender and cyclamen. Sweet jasmine and passion flowers picked up by Dubrovnik merchants complement the indigenous species, a

Getting to and around Trsteno and the Elafiti Islands

All buses travelling north of Dubrovnik stop at **Trsteno** on request.

From Dubrovnik port, Jadrolinija ferries skip along the **Elafiti Islands** calling at Koločep (Donje Čelo), Lopud, then Suđurađ and Šipanska luka on Šipan. G&V line catamarans operate a faster service en route to Mljet. There are also limited services from Dubrovnik old port in summer. If you're in a rush, any number of 'fish picnic' tours (*c.* 250Kn) will give you an hour or so at each over a day, but a rushed visit is not really the point of a visit. On Šipan, buses are co-ordinated with ferry times to link the two villages.

horticultural world tour which in the 19th century brought in exotica: Chinese bamboos, Japanese pines and Mexican palms. A clifftop **pavilion** offers idyllic views over the Elafitis, and hidden in the gloom of nearby outbuildings is an ancient olive press.

Past a family chapel behind the villa, the gardens live up to their name in a **woodland** of specimen trees, dappled by gold coins of sunlight. Deep into its centre, beyond a clearing where Dubrovnik's Ragusan Grand Council occasionally deliberated matters of state, lies a **Baroque grotto** (1736) fed by a 70m aqueduct which loops off into the trees. Neptune strikes a pose with his trident either side of nymphs, and dolphins spout water into a pond stocked with goldfish.

An adjacent garden of southern Adriatic cypresses and pines is somewhat shabby, its ruined sundial and grasses the design of 19th-century neo-Romantics rather than the Yugoslav Army, whose shells set much of the arboretum ablaze in 1991; some trees still bear the scars. Stone steps descend to the sea, where there's a cove for a dip; a footpath on the other side of the arboretum leads to a toy-sized **harbour** with more steps down to the water.

The Elafiti Islands

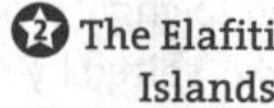

The Elafiti Islands

'Those islets lovelier than gardens,' said 16th-century Dubrovnik bishop Lodovico Beccadelli of the enchanting Elafiti islands, off the coast of Dubrovnik. His comment echoes through the centuries, because the three inhabited 'deer islands' – a corruption of the Greek *elafos* – are minor paradises where tourism is acknowledged only with a shrug and cars are outlawed on all but one. Wander through interiors of pine and aromatic shrubs and you understand why Dubrovnik Renaissance aristocrats chose them for a summer retreat; many of their mansions remain, bolstered with defence towers after raids by Ottoman Turks in the mid-16th century. But the enchanting Elafitis are not about historic sights *per se*. Instead, with no cultural must-sees to nag the conscience, no crowds to infuriate, they are better seen as little haikus of holidaymaking, so simple yet so clear; a return to a gentler age of tourism when lunches were long and nightlife meant perfecting the gentle art of *rakija*-sipping by the harbour. Magic.

Koločep

Just 3km from Dubrovnik, cave-riddled Koločep is a speck just 2.35km square that gathers its 150 residents in the drowsy hamlets of **Donje Čelo**, the port on the northwest coast, and **Gornje Čelo** in the southeast. Little more than clusters of stone houses and a parish church huddled in verdant bays (the best beach is at Donje Čelo), the pair are linked by a footpath which idles through pines. Not that a trip between them is ever direct – paths entice you to wander through olive groves to ruined Romanesque churches, some carved with the plait motifs of Croatia's early medieval stylebooks.

Lopud

Home to 76 families, middle island Lopud is the most developed of the trio for tourism, but then it was always the most outgoing. During days of the Ragusan Republic, this 2km by 4.5km island was renowned for breeding prosperous merchants and future admirals. An 80-strong local fleet also swelled the coffers of island ship-owners, who erected the mansions which crumble on the bay of its village-port.

As you enter the bay of **Lopud Town**, keep an eye open for a trio of **Gothic windows** which recall the Rector's Palace of Lopud's golden age, then start your tour at the 15th-century parish **church of the Franciscan monastery**; the guardian of the harbour's northern entrance was fortified into a refuge from Turks a century after it was built in 1483. Despite decades of talk about renovation into a hotel, the monastery remains a shell, but the church (*if open; consult tourist office for times*) contains some fine Renaissance altars. Crests on the lintels of harbourfront mansions salute the merchant owners, none more successful than Miho Pracat (1522–1607). A nook-like **chapel** just beyond the tourist office is that of the shipping magnate whose bronze is in Dubrovnik's Rector's Palace (*see* pp.324–5); the jury is still out on whether the adjacent derelict mansion, now used as a barn, is his.

Museum of history and ethnograpy
adm

Past a small **museum of history and ethnograpy**, which opens according to whim on the central square, a signposted path ascends inland to the ruins of **Fort Kaštio** (Trvđava Kaštio). Its battlements command the sweeping view over neighbouring islands and sea approaches which made this a prize fortification during Lopud's heyday.

With energy you could continue on a 12km circuit of the island via a signposted **Pješačka staza** ('trekking way'). Otherwise wind downhill past the tiny Romanesque chapel of **St Nicholas the Greek** (Sv. Nikola Grčki), almost lost among olive groves, to **Šunj**, a pine-fringed notch in the coast whose sand beach backed by a beach restaurant and snack bar is the stuff escapist dreams are made of.

Šipan

The largest of the Elafitis, Šipan is the only one with cars, but don't let that put you off. The island remains barely developed – though a couple of classy small hotels mean it is quietly developing into a destination for high-end escapism. Ferries thrum into principal settlement **Šipanska luka**, a pretty palm-fringed bay at the end of a deep inlet where the occasional summer manor of a Renaissance family hints at former glories. The grandest is that of a Dubrovnik ship-building dynasty, who gazed across the bay from a leonine balcony, while at the brow of the hill above is a walled fortress-residence (Knežez dvor). A scrap of sandy **beach** is a short walk from the centre.

Smaller Renaissance villas huddle in **Suđurađ**, an enjoyably tatty fishing village at the opposite end of Šipan. At its back, a pair of 16th-century towers and a ring of walls remain from the palace of a weathy ship-builder who supplied much of the Dubrovnik fleet. Further back uphill is the slab-sided **Church-fort of the Holy Spirit** (Crkva svetog Duh), village refuge during Turkish raids.

Between the two villages is the **Šipansko polje**, literally the luxuriously overgrown 'Šipan field' of olives, figs, melons and vineyards where the eulogy of Beccadelli, who knew Šipan well, rings true. Maps point out the pair are just 5km apart, but you could lose a happy day on paths to discover Baroque chapels and summer palaces.

ⓘ **Lopud >** *harbour, **t** (020) 759 086; open June–Sept Mon–Fri 8–1 and 5–7, Sat–Sun 9–12*

ⓘ **Šipan >** *Šipanska luka, **t** (020) 758 084; open June–Sept Mon–Fri 8–1 and 6–8, Sat 9–12*

Tourist Information on the Elafiti Islands

There are **tourist information offices** on Lopud and Šipan.

Where to Stay on the Elafiti Islands

Villa Vilina, Obala Ivana Kuljevana bb (by monastery), Lopud, **t** (020) 759 333, *www.villa-vilina.hr* (€€€). Boutiquey touches abound in this four-star hotel (2002) created from the 18th-century manor of Vilina nobility. Breakfast on the terrace is a treat, and the décor in the high-ceilinged rooms is styled classical-modern.

Božica, Suđurađ 13, Suđurađ, **t** (020) 325 400 *www.hotel-bozica.hr* (€€). Above the sea at the harbour mouth, a rather smart little four-star hotel created in 2005, where views come with every room. Gorgeous terrace with a pool, and classy restaurant.

La Villa, harbourfront, Lopud, **t** (020) 322 123, *www.lavilla.com.hr* (€€). A good-value newcomer run by a friendly young couple with a taste for streamlined décor and colour in six simple rooms: standards open onto the garden, superiors have French windows on the sea.

Šipan, Šipanska luka bb, Šipan, **t** (020) 758 000, *www.hotel-sipan.hr* (€€). An address to indulge in sybaritic escapism, fashioned from an olive oil factory at the head of the harbour. Renovated in 2007 into minimalist style warmed up with natural colours and jute flooring. Also has a classy Med' restaurant, **Pjut**, and cocktail bar.

Private **rooms** can be sourced through tourist information or through Dubrovnik tourist agencies.

Eating Out on the Elafiti Islands

On all islands but Lopud, eating options are limited to basic bar-grills: two in Koločep, one in Šipan.

★ **Kod Marko** >

Kod Marko, Šipanska luka bb, Šipan, **t** (020) 758 007 (€€€–€€). Understated, pure, excellent – the freshest fish dishes here have a gourmet reputation that belies what appears a tiny family restaurant on the harbour. Only six tables inside and four on the terrace. All in all, as good as it gets. *Booking essential.*

Barbara, Od Šunja 2, Lopud, **t** (020) 759 087 (€€). On the footpath to Šunj, with a vine-covered terrace and light snacks.

Obala, Obala I. Kuljevana 18, Lopud, **t** (020) 759 108 (€€). Rather stylish dining on the seafront, with waiters in black-and-whites and jazzy Muzak to a catch of the day.

Stara Milnica, Sudjuradj harbour, no tel (€). Fish and meat snacks in the old mill on the harbour.

Mljet

Ferry timetables swear the island of Mljet is just 1½hrs from Dubrovnik, but the distance in atmosphere to the Adriatic's greenest island is centuries. This 32km sliver of island clad in Aleppo pines and vineyards is a Mediterranean idyll where tourism is a sideshow to traditional obsessions of fishing, wine and olive oil. Get truly off the beaten track among eastern villages and it doesn't stretch the imagination too far to believe this is indeed Homer's Ogyia, the 'wave-washed island' of 'wood in abundant growth – alder and aspen and fragrant cypress' where the love-sick Calypso held Odysseus captive for seven years. Hotel Odisej in the resort village of **Pomena** organizes trips in summer to the south coast cove **Uvala Jama**, supposedly the 'arching caverns' where she whispered sweet nothings to the Greek hero to seduce him into marriage. You can't fault the nymph's savvy – few Croatian islands are more romantic for those who let Mljet's yesteryear pace get under the skin.

Homer probably knew the island as storm refuge and freshwater source Melita (derived from the Greek *melite*, honey), peopled by Illyrians until they plundered one galleon too many and felt the wrath of Emperor Augustus. He founded **Polače** in 35 BC, named after the 4th-century palace (*palača*) at the back of the village, with a road through its centre – locals saw no sense in diverting inland for the sake of a few old walls. Overlooked nearby is the shell of a century-older Christian **basilica** inspired perhaps by St Paul, who is said to have preached in Mljet after a shipwreck enforced a three-month pause in his Adriatic voyage.

Mljet National Park
t (020) 744 041; www.np-mljet.hr; tickets from kiosks at Pomena and Polače; adm summer 90Kn, winter 60Kn

Officially, the hamlet strung out along a perfect natural harbour is within the **Mljet National Park** but the main draws of the protected area on Mljet's western third are little and large lakes **Malo jezero** and **Veliko jezero**, reached via a well-signed path

Getting to and around Mljet

Jadrolinija **car ferries** go to Mljet's port of Sobra, where a connecting **bus** travels to Polače and Pomena. Be aware that the ferry's afternoon departure necessitates an overnight stay on the island. Car ferries operate 4 or 5 times a day between Prapatno (by Ston on the Pelješac peninsula) to Soba. A high-speed morning **catamaran** operated by G&V goes to Polače (*May–Sept daily*) via the Elafiti islands.

(about an hour's walk). Even summer tour groups cannot mar the tidal lakes fringed by aromatic pines and knitted together by the **Mali most** (Little Bridge), where you can hire bicycles, canoes and rowing boats or laze on a scrap of 'beach'.

Pristanište
included in park ticket

Most tourists, however, are happy just to hop aboard hourly ferries from Mali most and hamlet **Pristanište** for a whistle-stop tour of **St Mary's Islet** (Otočić svete Marije) in the Veliko jezero. Gifted the tiny island in 1151, an Italian Benedictine Order erected a monastery on the islet. Napoleon, never one for religion and exasperated at the Croatian church's resentment of French occupation, dissolved the order in 1809, and the final indignity for a now-neglected monastery was its reinvention as a hotel under Tito (now closed). With the right eyes you can make out the 12th-century core of the Renaissance **monastery** on a circuit, then peer into the gloom of its **church**; turquoise pillars and ruby scrolls of Renaissance and Baroque altars give the shabby interior an unexpected shot of pizzazz.

To escape the worst of the crowds, you can take a forest path which loops around the lakes (a channel which links Veliko jezero to the sea prevents a full circuit) or you can truly escape the hordes by climbing island peak **Montokuc** southeast of Veliko jezero, worth puffing up the steep path for lovely views to Korčula and over the Mljetski kanal to the Pelješac peninsula.

ⓘ Polače ›
opposite ferry dock, **t** *(020) 744 086; open mid-June–mid-Sept Mon–Sat 8–12 and 4–7; mid-Sept–mid-June Mon–Fri 8–1*

ⓘ Babino polje ›
t *(020) 745 125; opening times same as above*

Tourist Information on Mljet

There are **tourist information offices** in Polače and Babino polje.

Where to Stay and Eat on Mljet

The pick of the **private rooms** (*sobe*) are those in sleepy lakeside hamlet Babine kuće. Alternatively, restaurants in Pomena offer accommodation and the tourist offices hold lists of private accommodation.

Hotel Odisej, Pomena, **t** (020) 744 062, *www.hotelodisej.hr* (€€). Mljet's only hotel has 156 adequate three-star rooms spread over three blocks which make up for bland décor with air-con; sea views cost extra. *Closed Nov–Mar.*

Pension Pomena, Pomena 14, **t** (020) 744 075 €). If that's full, a cheap and cheerful restaurant-*pension* next-door, with 10 rooms and a couple of apartments.

Galija, Pomena bb, **t** (020) 744 029 (€€€–€€). Smartest of the harbour-front *pension*-restaurants opposite Hotel Odisej. Seafood is reliable or try a beautifully presented cold platter of *pršut* ham, octopus salad and olives; listed as a starter, the chef's special is a meal in itself. Also offers a handful of en-suite **rooms** (€).

Mali raj, Babine kuće 3, **t** (020) 744 067 (€€). House special lobster comes super-fresh from the tank, and kid goat cooked in a *peka* is washed down with local wines and brandy in this laid-back lakeside *konoba* – a 'little paradise' indeed.

Melita, St Mary's Islet, **t** (020) 744 145 (€€). Often over-run restaurant amid the Benedictine monastery. Nice terrace, though.

The Pelješac Peninsula

The Pelješac peninsula

The fate of the Pelješac peninsula is to be in between. The senators of the Dubrovnik republic paid for it twice in 1333 to appease Serbian and Bosnian rulers squabbling over ownership, then ignored everything except Ston and Orebić. Fast-forward nearly seven centuries and most visitors see it only in air-conditioned detachment as a two-hour transit between Dubrovnik and Korčula Town. But being bypassed isn't always a bad thing. Spared the rough-and-tumble of history, the 60km stretch between the Pelješac's bookend settlements is a self-contained country as wild and vivid as its Fauvist colours. There are rustic villages above chessboards of tiny fields and sleepy resorts like Žuljana, where nightlife means a nightcap by the beach. There are bumpy dirt tracks to idyllic beaches and cliffhanger roads in the truest sense. There are also red wines and sensational shellfish in Potomje and Mali Ston, and gutsy good stuff in *konobe* everywhere. A proposed diversion of the Magistrala coast road from the mainland onto the peninsula may bring change. Yet for now the peninsula conceals the sort of discoveries everyone wants to brag about back at home. Two hours? Slow down and you could lose two days.

Ston and Mali Ston

Set at the neck of the peninsula, Ston and Mali Ston have an open-armed approach to their visitors nowadays. Their car parks are coach-sized and places are set in their many restaurants whatever the hour. Before they were prettified, however, the sister settlements glowered at outsiders from behind the longest defence walls in Europe (5.5km) built over two centuries from 1333 to protect Ston, Dubrovnik's key second city on its northern frontier.

The reason was salt, skimmed here ever since the Romans established a fortified town, named Stagnum because of its swampy pans. The Dubrovnik republic knew salt as the 'white gold' which not only guaranteed its own supply – a strategic imperative for a merchant state – but also coined in the real stuff through a monopoly on production that extended over the Balkan hinterland, from the Neretva estuary to the river Drin in Macedonia. In a good

Getting to and around the Pelješac Peninsula

Ferries in summer go hourly between Korčula (Domince) and **Orebić**, and up to 7 per day ply between Ploče and **Trpanj**. Car ferries operate 4–5 times a day from Prapatno (by Ston) to **Sobra**, Mljet. High-season passenger-only ferries also go 3 times a day from Korčula to **Kučište** and **Viganj**.

All passing mainland coast buses stop on request at **Zaton Doli** at the peninsula neck, 4km from **Mali Ston**. Long-haul routes to Orebić go daily from Dubrovnik, and daily from Zagreb (Sun, Tues, Thurs, Fri via Zadar; otherwise via Knin). To Ston, 3 buses a day go from Dubrovnik.

To get around, this is a region best seen with your own transport. However, 3 buses a day link Ston and Orebić, and Orebić is connected to Trpanj (4 per day, weekends 2 per day) and Viganj via Kućište (3 per day).

---

year, Ston salt accounted for two-thirds of the republic's profits, safeguarded behind those 14th-century fortifications with a fortress guard at each corner, none more solid than the **Veliki Kaštio** fortress on the vulnerable seaward flank. Dubrovnik republic protector St Blaise (*see* box, p.321) watches from a niche, just to be on the safe side.

Restoration of the walls has reopened the pentangle which wraps around Ston, so you can clamber up to a **bastion** at the apex for views over a town that is still tatty in places after a 1996 earthquake that shook 70 per cent of Ston to the ground. You can also look out to the salt-pan chequerboard, the oldest (200 BC) and largest in the Mediterranean that is worked today by Solana Ston. From this vantage point you'll also see, off to the right, the Franciscan **monastery of St Nicholas** (Samostan sv. Nikole) whose church has a gold crucifix from medieval master Blaž Jurjev of Trogir. It's matched only by the pre-Romanesque frescoes in **St Michael's Church** (Crkva sv. Mihovila), a medieval matchbox built near the all-important salt pans for local kings, one of whom proffers his little church to Christ inside. Neither is open except through the tourist office, however. Never mind, because Ston's tidy little grid is a charmer, a little shaken from 1996, perhaps, but genetrifying fast and with lanes full of late medieval houses and blooming bougainvillaea. Only the **Bishop's** and **Governor's Palaces** on the main square testify to its former political clout.

Like a trial run for the Great Wall of China, the walls march relentlessly over the hill behind Ston to little sister **Mali Ston** – Ston is sometimes prefixed 'Veliki' ('big'). By summer 2009 renovation of the walls should be complete to allow you to walk the 1km between the two. Mali Ston's lanes are sleepier still, their rough cobbles hemmed by weeds, with fig trees sprouting in spare corners. A grizzled fortress stands over the heights above and offers good views for anyone with the nerve to clamber onto its parapet. But everyone comes for the seafood from Mali Ston bay, a still inlet of natural stock – water seasoned with a generous pinch of sea salt and interesting minerals washed out of the limestone hills by rainwater. Gourmets say its oysters are the finest in Croatia, which perhaps explains all the couples in its quayside restaurants.

Steps descend from the quay for a dip, or drive west of Ston to **Prapatno bay**, sheltered to a millpond in all but southern *sirocco* winds, and backed by a shingle beach.

Ston to Orebić

This is the bit most visitors only see through glass windows. But with your own transport the centre of the Pelješac peninsula is ripe for exploration, a siren call to deliciously indolent hedonism; languid, luxurious and full of secrets to uncover. There's the sublime landscape, a canvas splashed by rust-red soils and green vines, where aqua bays wink behind hills, woods of dark pine and Mediterranean oak are shot through with the silver of olive leaves, and country villages cling to hillsides beneath limestone bluffs. And then there are the famous Pelješac red wines, as rich as velvet, not nearly so expensive.

ⓘ Žuljana
square behind beach, t (020) 756 227; open (in theory) summer daily 8–8, usually with a lunch pause

After Ston, the road ascends 20km northwest through scraggy hills scratched here and there by stamp-sized fields to **Dubrava**. Turn left and you descend to **Žuljana**, the sort of gentle resort half-remembered from childhood summer holidays, beautifully sited where a lush valley pours down to the sea. Before the village, a strip of shingle beach wraps around the bay, set on fire daily by the most spectacular sunset of the Pelješac. Views of Korčula and Vis hunkered down as blue-grey humps in the dusky Adriatic are best savoured over a sundowner from the handful of simple harbourfront restaurants. The bays in the vicinity are gorgeous, private pieces of paradise only reached on **boat trips** offered by local fishermen. More sweeping sea views are seen back on the main road as you approach **Trstenik**, a sheltered harbour gathered in the crook of a bay behind limestone hills. At the time of writing a ferry service to Polace had been suspended. Instead, all is peace in its cosy stone centre drunk with the perfume of bougainvillaea, just right for relaxing on a strip of sheltered beach.

Boat trips
signs by the beach or consult tourist office

ⓘ Trstenik
harbour, t (020) 748 108; open summer Mon–Sat 9–1

And so to the centre, the **Župa plain** cradled in hills 5km west of Trstenik. This is the Pelješac's rustic heartland, full of rich variegated colours and vineyards, framed by Mount Ilija, ripped out of the bones of the earth. Its rich palette inspired early 20th-century painter Mato Celestin Medović to toy with lighter shades on his brush and dabble in soft-focus Impressionism, blazing a trail for Croatian landscape painting after he returned from Zagreb to his birthplace, **Kuna**. The village on the north of the plain hails its hero in a bronze by Ivan Meštrović; the town's **Franciscan monastery** has a small memorial gallery of his works. Views of the real thing are on available via a suspension-testing track which

Franciscan monastery
opening times vary; adm

Pelješac Wines

No one is sure whether it was the Greeks or Romans who introduced plavac mali vines to the Pelješac, but the autochthonic grape which thrives in the sun-soaked shelter on the steep south coast produces the finest reds in Croatia's cellar.

The best of the best is dingač. Ruby in colour, it can be on the robust side in poor years, but is always rich and complex, with a hint of sweetness that lingers on the palate. It pairs well with *pršut*, dark meats and the finest fish. The 60ha of slopes around its eponymous village west of Trstenik (reached via Potomje tunnel) produce only 2,000–3,000 hectolitres each year, although wags quip that 10 times as much is sold in shops around the nation – as good an excuse as any to taste it at source.

A close second to dingač, postup is also produced from Plavac mali grapes, these grown on the slopes around its village, 5km east of Orebić. Another full-bodied red, well balanced and usually with a slight tartness, it goes well with more robust fare, dark meats such as game, or to wash down oily grilled fish and squid.

In summer you can roll in for tastings and sales of wines in wine village Potomje. Matuško, t (020) 742 393 (*open daily in summer; call in winter*), on the eastern edge of the village produces the full cellar, its dingač flavoured *en barrique* (matured in oak barrels) for several years before bottling, and dabbles in *prošek* dessert wines and herbal *rakijas* said to do wonders for the blood pressure. Also here is a large outlet of Vinarija Dingač, t (020) 742 010 (*open daily in summer; call in winter*), a highly rated producer whose donkey logo is seen throughout Croatia. At the other end of the village, family wine-maker Bartulović, t (020) 742 346, *www.vinarijabartulovic.hr*, offers tastings of its wines – principally a strong Bartul red pressed from plavac mali, one flavoured *en barrique*, indigenous Rukatac whites and a sweet *prošek* – in a stone *konoba*, often accompanied by cheese or *pršut* and sardines. Call ahead to be led through the tipples in English by son Mario. Or you can always take pot luck at the roadside tables laid with homemade plonks decanted into old water bottles.

Tourist agencies in Dubrovnik offer wine tours by coach for those without their own transport (*see* Dubrovnik for contacts), usually stopping in Ston, home to the only *vinoteka* on the peninsula. TIRS at the back of the main square sells Pelješac (and Korčula) wines and *rakijas*.

ascends east of the centre – you have to park before the top and walk the rest of the way.

Anonymous in looks, the village of **Potomje** on the south side of the plain is actually the holy of holies of Croatian wine-making, much of it nurtured in the vineyards on southern slopes reached by a tunnel off the main road. Find it near the centre on the left (driving east–west) and you emerge, blinking, into strong light and sun-drenched terraces planted with plavac mali vines, on a bumpy road which traverses above a coastline scalloped with pocket-sized coves; *see* box above for details of wine-tasting.

After the Župa's flats, the drive to **Trpanj** is almost claustrophobic. Terraced here and there with tiny fields of vineyards, a narrow gorge presses tight and forces the road to slalom the last few kilometres towards the amiable little port-resort on the north coast; named, they say, because its curved harbour reminded the ancient Greeks of a sickle (*drepanon*). There's a smattering of restaurants and cafés, and refreshingly little to do except drink in views of the rugged mountains on the mainland – from either a pebble beach near the centre or concrete platforms beyond the harbour which offer better swimming if you can ignore aesthetics

– and wait until the handful of disco-bars swing into action in the evening. The best beach hereabouts is **Divna-Trpanj**, a strip of shingle hemmed by green-black pines and turquoise waters whose beach bar makes a fair stab at the Caribbean. You'll find it 8km west of the resort via a road that cuts off the gorge.

The drive west of the Trpanj turn-off slaloms on east around the cliffs. Going above third gear is folly, but why go hurry when you can linger over an epic panorama that sweeps over east Korčula and the islets scattered in the Pelješac channel? Just after the descent, you'll find a sharp left turn onto a minor road above the south coast; through wine hamlet **Postup** and tiny **Borje**, to **Podobuče**. The end of the road, this hamlet has a perfect crescent beach, a few fishing boats in its bay and no idea how impossibly sweet it is. Long may it remain so.

Orebić

Orebić is the Pelješac's only holiday mill, small though it is. It wasn't always so. The reputation of the small town near the peninsula's far tip is based on its sea captains – indeed, it took the surname of a local seafaring family of the early 16th century. They were never more prosperous than in the 19th century when, free of the uninterested rule of Dubrovnik from 1806, the industry came into its own. A decade after it was founded in 1863, the Pelješac Shipping Society listed a fleet of 33 4,500-tonne barques, some sailing as far afield as North America. Clippers were jigsawed together in its shipyard and 2,000 sailors, 250 of them captains, were on its books. Not bad for a town of only 500 people. And then, just when the company celebrated a record valuation of two million Austrian gold florins in 1877, along came steamers to take the wind from Orebić's sails, and all it is left with are grand villas in semi-tropical gardens on **Obala pomoraca**, the seafront address every retired seadog aspired to. By the tourist office, a musty **Maritime Museum** that commemorates the fleet's glory days with models and oils won't detain you for long, but press on east and you reach **Plaža Trstenica**, a lovely long swoop of shingle almost as fine as sand.

Maritime Museum
Pomorski muzej; open summer Mon–Sat 8–12 and 6–9; winter Mon–Fri 7–2; adm

The town's other sight is the **Franciscan monastery** on a ridge veiled by cypress spears 2km west of the centre. Although the arch-rivals performed a polite dance of diplomacy, tensions between the Dubrovnik and Venetian republics ran high, and La Serenissima's presence in Korčula Town was far too close for comfort. True, the Gothic monastery emerged on its perch in the 1480s to venerate a miraculous icon. But this was border country, where a fortress would have been deemed provocation. How convenient that its Baroque loggia commanded spectacular watchtower views over the Pelješac sea lane. How coincidental that a friar saddled his

Franciscan monastery
Franjevački samostan; open Mon–Sat 8–12 and 5–8, Sun 5–8

donkey whenever the Venetian war fleet dropped anchor in Korčula Town opposite...

Inside the **church**, embedded in a frame of gold angels and cotton-wool clouds, the Byzantine-styled Lady of the Angels icon protects passing seamen, even if three hoots of a ship's siren no longer sends the friars scurrying inside to reply with a peal of church bells. There's also a creamy relief of the Virgin and Child by Nikola Firentinac, a pupil of Donatello who expresses all the ambition of the Renaissance that so elevated humanity, while a **museum** hangs votive pictures of Pelješac barques tossed by storms or beset by pirates – no wonder they needed protection. More seafaring stuff is in the **graveyard**, its headstones carved with sextants and anchors and barques under billowing sail. The eyecatcher is an onion-domed mausoleum carved by Ivan Rendić for a Russian shipping magnate, Anton Mimbelli. They say son Baldo ordered his father's lead coffin be inched up over three days and three nights to reach its tomb.

Museum
adm

About five millennia ago, the ancient Greeks sailed to these shores and left behind a little lexical memento, the name Pelješac, derived from the *pelios* (blue-grey) of the peninsula's limestone hills. Highest of these is **Sv. Ilija**, which rises above a skirt of pine scrub behind the monastery. Now and then, the skies bruise and there's a deep rumble as St Ilija rides above the clouds in a chariot drawn by two horned goats. Apparently, on one whip-cracking gallop, sparks crackled at the axles and zapped the **chapel** at its summit (961m), and all that's left if you make the stiff ascent on a marked path near the monastery – wear strong shoes and a hat, take plenty of water and put aside a whole day – is a heap of stones and a crucifix. If you're starting from Orebić, you'll find the path signposted off the seafront.

West of Orebić

In long-forgotten days, three local blacksmith brothers fell out. One harrumphed into the wilds with the anvil (Nakovanj), another went west with the bellows (Viganj). The third remained in the family house (*kuća*) to name **Kućište**, a mellow village strung out along the seashore 7km west of Orebić (turn left at the bypass roundabout west of centre). Folklore aside, it has its own tang of sea salt, too. Recognizable by twin-paned dormer windows, the age-stained houses of sea captains line a quay which once secured ships to the most protected anchorage in the region. The nine stone bollards are still there, if not the clippers.

ⓘ **Kucište**
seafront, ***t*** *(020) 719 123; open July–Aug daily 8–12 and 5–8*

Viganj has a few rusty old houses of its own, but nowadays it's surf bums not sea-dogs who gaze at the waves. Flat seas and the steady winds funnelled down the Pelješac channel support a windsurfing scene on the peninsula beach; foam vapour-trails streak the channel throughout summer and early autumn.

The coast road hairpins back on itself at the end of the village, dithers, then ascends northwest, through **Nakovanj** and towards the mysterious limestone anvil which juts suddenly above thick scrub. From as early as 6000 BC, this miniature *massif* attracted residents. Neolithic Man left bits of bone in a **cave** on the opposite side of the road, where prehistoric tribes performed cult rituals around a single white stalagmite. The Illyrians were here too, keeping watch for the Roman galleys which Queen Teuta had decreed were fair game after she ascended to the throne in 231 BC. Piracy was lawful trade and the government had no right to interfere with private enterprise, she suggested to Rome's ambassadors. Incensed at her cheek, the Senate ordered the imperial army across the Adriatic for the first time in 229 BC and Teuta learned a thing or two about Roman law as she was forced to sue for peace after two years. The Illyrian empire ended with a whimper 40 years later, when Gentius, a king of pathetic memory, was brought to Rome in chains.

Cave
currently closed; consult Orebić tourist information

Sports and Activities on the Pelješac Peninsula

Blessed by sheltered seas and steady winds, **Viganj**, host of the Croatian Windsurfing Championships, provides the finest windsurfing and kitesurfing in Croatia. Equipment hire by the hour and courses are available at beach campsites **Perna Centar**, mobile **t** 098 395 807, *www.pernasurf.com*, 4km west of Orebić, and **Camping Liberan, t** (020) 719 330, in Viganj. Novices should leave the afternoons, when the winds pick up considerably, to the experts.

Where to Stay and Eat on the Pelješac Peninsula

Tourist offices book **private rooms**, your only option in smaller resorts.

Ston

Bakus, t (020) 754 270 (€€). A good-value *konoba* with tables in Ston's lovely lanes and a fish menu. Adjacent Maestral is another good choice if that's full, its interior décor a mite more characterful.

Mali Ston

Ostrea, t (020) 754 556, *www.ostrea.hr* (€€), A quietly elegant address on the quayside from the family of **Kapetnova kuća**, its nine rooms tastefully furnished with stone walls, cream and *café au lait* tones and occasional antiques. Book a beautiful apartment (€€€) for a romantic splurge.

Vila Koruna, t (020) 754 359, *www.vila-koruna.hr* (€). Functional rooms plus apartments (€€€) above a restaurant.

Kapetnova kuća, t (020) 754 264 (€€€–€€). Probably the most famous restaurant north of Dubrovnik, celebrated for a menu of fish and seafood – the famous oysters, live or lightly fried in olive oil, or Grandpa's octopus salad. Good Pelješac wine list.

Trpanj

Faraon, Trg kralja Tomislava 16, **t** (020) 743 408, *www.hoteli-jadran.hr* (€€). Functional rooms in a package three-star hotel, saved by balconies and its proximity to the beach.

Orebić

Indijan, Škvar 2, **t** (020) 714 555, *www.hotelindijan.hr* (€€). By far the nicest address in town, a lovely small four-star opened in 2007 that's stylish

ⓘ **Trpanj >>**
harbourfront, **t** *(020) 743 433; open summer Mon–Sat 8–2 and 5–8, Sun 8–2*

ⓘ **Ston >**
Peljeska cesta 2 (main road by car park), **t** *(020) 754 452, www.tzo-ston.hr; open summer daily 8–8, winter Mon–Sat 8–1*

ⓘ **Orebić >>**
Trg Mimbeli bb, **t** *(020) 713 718, www.tz-orebic.com; open summer daily 8–9; winter daily 8–1 (Dec–Jan Mon–Fri only)*

without trying hard. Every room – tasteful in teak furnishings and olive walls – has a sea view. Trendy glass-walled lounge bar and good *à la carte* restaurant, **Korta**.

Milnica, Trg Mimbeli bb, **t** (020) 713 886 (€€€–€€). Once the mill of Orebić, now a garden restaurant in which you dine among the millwheels. House specials are lamb, octopus and veal cooked under a *peka* and served with roast potatoes.

Karako, Šetalište kneza Domagoja 32, mobile **t** 091 513 7489 (€€). All the usuals, charcoal-grilled in a lazy-paced terrace restaurant spread among palms behind Trstenica beach.

Viganj

Villa Mediterane, **t** (020) 719 096 (€€). Where Viganj and Kućište merge, a family hotel has 14 doubles plus three apartments.

ⓘ **Viganj >>**
seafront, ***t*** *(020) 719 295; open July–Aug daily 8–1 and 6–9*

Korčula

Having either made the best of a bad job or betrayed Troy, depending on whose books you read, Priam's counsellor Antenor paused en route to Italy to found Korčula. Ancient yarns and a 16th-century tablet in Korčula Town's western gate aside, the oldest written document in Croatia, a 4th-century BC tile found near Lumbarda, names the ancient Greeks as the first in recorded history to settle Korčula. Even if it wasn't the Argonauts named in another Hellenic shaggy dog story, other members of their tribe were sufficiently reminded of home to name their colony Black Corfu (*Kerkyra Melaine*), inspired by the deep green coat of Aleppo pine and cypress it wears to this day; it was a title the ever-thorough Pliny the Elder jotted down in his *Historia Naturalis* when the Romans arrived some time in the 1st century. Centuries of Croatians have continued to cultivate the Romans' white wine Grk in Lumbarda (and chewed Kerkyra into Korčula). But everyone comes for Korčula Town, a pocket-sized Dubrovnik you can circle in 20 minutes but which is still revealing fresh layers of detail days later – surely the best sort of small town there is.

Korčula Town

Korčula Town

On an island with antique roots, Korčula Town is a latecomer. Slavic pirates from the Neretva estuary (*see* p.310) were the first to settle its peninsula as a base from which to swoop on merchant ships taking a short cut through the Pelješki kanal. They did so with impunity for four centuries, until they plundered one Venetian caravel too many and were quashed in AD 1000, ushering in 800 years of on-and-off rule by Venice.

Korčula Town has always been married to the sea; for better – shipbuilding and stone masonry filled its coffers during a 15th- and 16th-century golden age – or worse – the warships of Algiers viceroy Uluz Ali were so nearly its undoing in 1571 that divine intervention was required. For richer – a casual litter of Venetian-styled sculpture in alleys attests to the wealth of 16th-century

Getting to and around Korčula

Ferries come from Ancona in Italy (via Split and Stari Grad). Ferries go approx hourly from Orebić on Pelješac to Dominče, 3km southeast of Korčula Town. Korčula Town is served by 3 ferries a day from mainland port Drvenik (*summer only*), and daily services on the Rijeka–Dubrovnik route from Stari Grad (Hvar) and Dubrovnik, some via Sobra (Mljet). Vela Luka is on the Split–Ubli (Lastovo) route (2 per day).

Catamarans link Korčula Town to Split via Hvar Town (2 per day summer), and Vela Luka is on the Split–Ubli route; note that the Split–Ubli ferry to Vela Luka also picks up foot passengers at Hvar Town (*except Sat*). A foot-passenger-only Korčula Town–Orebić ferry service docks at the central wharf opposite the tourist office.

Buses for Korčula Town meet Split–Vela Luka ferries. Long-haul bus services link to Dubrovnik and Zagreb daily (via Makarska, Zadar and Split). From Korčula Town there are buses to Lumbarda (hourly). Buses to Vela Luka (6 per day) call at all the villages which line the main road.

---

aristocrats – or poorer – sea routes to the New World finally leached away its wealth alongside that of Venice. Korčula Town looks its best from the sea, too. The finest introduction there is to one of Dalmatia's most bewitching Italianate towns is on the ferry from Orebić – a picture book fantasy of roofs which rise above medieval walls and castellated bastions, as romantic as any desert palace.

With feet on dry land, you enter the compact Old Town via a Baroque staircase that sweeps up to the **Land Gate**, Korčula Town's front door since 1391 bearing a Venetian Republic plaque of the winged Lion of St Mark. Its castellated **Revelin tower**, an afterthought added three centuries later, which salutes the Venetian doge and assorted Korčula military governors in coats of arms, houses a lacklustre **museum** of Korčula sword dance the Moreška (*see* box, p.348) but is better visited for its views.

Museum
open June–Sept daily 9.30–1.30 and 4–8; adm

For all their protection against gunpowder, limestone fortifications were no defence against the scourge of the 13th century. Plague had laid low many a strong medieval city, and Korčula Town's urban planners advocated fresh air to maintain hygiene, a typically advanced insight from a settlement which had drawn up a statute of human rights and legislature by 1214. Their fish-skeleton street plan places residential ribs east–west, open to the summer *maestral* but closed to winter north wind the *bura*. They radiate off spine street **Korčulanskog statuta**. It tracks north beyond the Land Gate, past the foyered **town hall** (1520) and Renaissance **St Michael's Church** (Crkva sv. Mihovila), whose monks passed from friary to devotion on the raised bridge, to elongated central square **Trg sv. Marka**, the heart of town at its highest point.

Around Trg Sv. Marka

You could spend days hunting out the finely turned balustrades or cherubs that ennoble patricians' mansions in side streets. But no building better expresses Korčula Town's skill with stone during its heyday than the façade of **St Mark's Cathedral** (Katedrala svetog Marka), full of the joy of the Renaissance. Lions, dragons, mermen

The Moreška

Korčula Town's celebrated sword dance is actually a 17th-century import of the Venetian *moresca*, common throughout the medieval Mediterranean. A tradition with roots in the Christian expulsion of the Moors from Spain must have struck a chord with an island which repulsed a Turkish raid, then two months later aided the 1571 triumph over the Ottoman navy in the Battle of Lepanto. Like all good tales, it is essentially a story of love and derring-do: bad Black King Moro kidnaps Bula, veiled fiancée of good White King Osman (dressed in red); White King confronts Black King with an army; they clash within a circle of sword-dancers; Bula begs for peace; White King conquers and frees Bula from chains; our sweethearts kiss. And, like any good tub-thumper, the dialogue is wonderfully hammy:

'If it were not that I disdain
To darken my sword with your blood
And stoop from my might
I should destroy you'

'Oh, knights!
Do something to stop your wars
Which wound my heart and draw tears
Of blood from my eyes'

'Stop wailing, my lady,
I have had enough!'

...are typical lines, spoken since the 1930s to a brass band soundtrack rather than the traditional drum. Once reserved for honouring town protector St Theodore (29 July), the two-hour Moreška is précised for tourists in 30 minutes on a stage by the Revelin tower (*currently Mon and Thurs eves; 60Kn; tickets from tourist agencies*).

Not that Korčula Town holds the monopoly on chivalric sword dances. The dances Kumpanija (Blato, 28 April; Smokvica, 14 Aug; Pupnat, 5 Aug; Čara, 25 July; Vela Luka, 19 Mar) and the Moštra (Žrnovo-Postrana, 16 Aug) retain closer ties to tradition and are performed in full to the whine of nasal *mišnice* skin bagpipes and a drum tattoo. In 1999 Pupnat also revived the tradition of beheading an ox but after suffering the newspaper headlines, learned that some customs are best left in the past. Vela Luka, ever-eager to woo tourism, also stages a Kumpanjija for tourists (*currently Tues eves; 25Kn*), and Korčula Town hosts an extravaganza of Croatian and European folk companies for the late July–August Festival of Sword Dances.

with two tails, even a smiling elephant cavort in the cornice that trims a cathedral funded (possibly) by the woman who stares from the apex and who might (or might not) be a regal Hungarian benefactor saluted in local tales. Local boy Marko Andrijić, the finest sculptor Korčula Town ever produced, who contributed to Dubrovnik's Sponza Palace, steadies his creation with a beautiful rose window then crowns the belfry with one of the loveliest lantern cupolas you'll see. A Milanese sculptor's *Adam and Eve*, who prop a pair of lions on the main portal (1412), appear rather staid by comparison.

Andrijić also chiselled the *ciborium*, perfect for a Chinese tea party, inside central Dalmatia's most intriguing cathedral, a mishmash of Gothic and Renaissance propped by capitals on which figures emerge from tangled thickets of vine leaves. An *Annunciation* duo stands guard above Andrijić's creation of 1486, which shelters a recently restored early Tintoretto of St Mark flanked by Sts Jerome and Bartholomew. The late Renaissance Venetian artist also painted the *Annunciation* in the south aisle, its Mary a Renaissance noblewoman interrupted in her studies of the scriptures. You'll find it near a display of pikes included to remember the divine intervention which saved Korčula Town on 15 August 1571. En route to Ottoman–Christian showdown the Battle of Lepanto, Uluz Ali, the Algiers viceroy or corsair according to whose side you're on, led a diversionary strike on Korčula Town. As the town walls began to crumble, 'a north wind started to blow with a ferocity hardly ever seen even during winter,' Archdeacon Rožanović recalled, the *de facto* defence commander after the Venetians had turned tail. Much to the misfortune of neighbouring island Hvar, not all the Turkish warships were smashed on the rocks, which is probably why Korčula Town, unlike Hvar, puts Turkish cannonballs on display.

In the same aisle you'll also find a fine Renaissance bishop's tomb and an age-blackened work by Jacopo Bassano. All very fine, of course, but not a patch on the diocese star pieces on show in an adjacent **treasury** in the Korčula bishops' palace, fronted by the most ostentatious balustrade in town. Whether narcissistic or simply authoritative, the bishops had impeccable taste. There's an exquisite 15th-century polyptych of the Madonna by Blaž Jurjev Trogiranin, the master who imported Italian ideals to the east Adriatic and maintained a workshop in Korčula; plus a masterclass of Italian Old Masters: lovely studies of hands by Tiepolo, works by Carpaccio and Raphael and a Leonardo da Vinci sketch of a soldier who Korčula Town would love to believe is dressed in garb of a Moreška dancer (*see* box opposite). As good a reason to visit is for the curios: a necklace Mother Theresa gifted to Korčula Town, or a bizarre ivory miniature of Mary Queen of Scots, a worshipper hidden among her skirts.

Treasury
Riznica; open June–Sept daily 9–2 and 5–7; adm

Opposite the cathedral, a **town museum** plods through early history with the inevitable amphorae and a copy of that 4th-century BC tablet which set down Greek goals for a new colony, before it perks up above. Model ships salute the trade which filled local coffers until the Second World War, and there are *objets d'art* and 19th-century china. The adjacent **Church of Our Lady** is worth a peek for a mosaic of the Virgin and Child inspired by the pop art of its era, and a floor of aristocrats' tomb-slabs, some of whom lived in the galleried courtyard residences that line the alleys descending west off the square.

Town museum
Gradski muzej; open summer Mon–Sat 9.30–2 and 7–9; winter Mon–Sat 9.30–2; adm

Church of Our Lady
Crkva Naša Gospojina; open summer daily 10–12.30 and 7–11

No Korčula citizen is more famous than **Marco Polo**. Possibly. The list of Depolos in parish records adds weight to a claim that the great adventurer was a Korčula Town son born in 1254. Whatever the truth, contemporary chronicles report that the sea captain was captured by the Genoese in 1298 during a battle off Lumbarda, not such a bad thing as it transpired, because a fellow prisoner, Rusticello of Pisa, compiled the tales Polo told during his year behind bars and published them as medieval blockbuster *The Travels of Marco Polo*. It is unclear whether it was the adventurer or the romance writer who dreamed up the one about the monstrous birds that smashed elephants on rocks. Although the Depolo family didn't actually move in until 1400 (76 years after Marco's death), and despite its Renaissance appearance, a tower residence on alley Depolo north of the main square is claimed as Polo's birthplace. A museum of medieval Korčula Town has been planned for it for at least five years to no avail. Instead the **House of Marco Polo** is best visited for views east down the channel Polo navigated.

House of Marco Polo
Kuća Marca Pola; open June–Sept daily 10–7; adm

The Rest of Korčula Town and its Beaches

Turn right from Trg sv. Marka then right again above the walls, or simply turn right on entering the Land Gate and you'll find the **Icon Museum** hangs Byzantine icons that a Korčula captain removed from Cretan churches rather than see fall into Turkish hands during the Canadia Wars (1645–69). Across from their monastery via an adjoining bridge is more artwork in the **All Saints' Church** (Crkva Svih Svetih; *same times*), an 18th-century *pietà* by Austrian sculptor Rafael Donner and, to the right of the altar, a lovely polyptych by the ever-enchanting Blaž Jurjev Trogiranin. Tiny brothers clad in the white habits the Order still favours kneel before Christ resurrected from the grave.

Icon Museum
Galerija ikona; open July–Aug daily 10–12 and 5–7; June and Sept daily 9–2; other months via tourist information; adm

More art is to be seen in a seafront **villa** where Zagreb-born artist Maksimilijan Vanka (1889–1963) took his holidays. You'll find this retrospective of canvases of Croatia's finest portrait painter of the 1920s and 1930s a 10-minute walk west of the Old Town, along the seafront.

Villa
open July–Aug daily 5–9pm; June and Sept through tourist information; adm

Beaches await those who go the same distance east, although space on the shingle which fronts resort hotel Marco Polo is limited. A quieter beach fringes the north shore of islet **Badija**, home to a 15th-century Franciscan monastery and friendly deer. Crowd numbers and swimming costumes lower the further you go from the shingle by the dock. Other options for a dip nearby are Orebić (*see* p.343) across the channel, or Lumbarda (*see* below).

Badija
water taxi from harbour; 40Kn return

Around the Island

The Greeks were the first to plant vineyards in **Lumbarda**, 7km southeast of Korčula Town. Roman patricians in *villae rusticae* also tended vines in the sheltered bay, mirrored in more recent centuries by Korčula Town aristocrats who had summer castle residences here. Thanks to sandy soils, Lumbarda continues to produce Grk, a unique autochthonic dry white wine the colour of sunshine, its hint of tartness like an apple on a summer's day. There's no finer place to sample it and a fine red than a lovely stone farm building of **Franjo Bire**; it's on a hillside above the village, signposted at the first bay as you enter. Family producer **Cebalo** also provides tastings of a gold medal-winning Branimirov Grk, plus tours of cellars and vineyards, on request. Lumbarda's other claim to fame is the finest sand beach on Korčula. Head 2km east of the village through the green vines and rusty bauxite-rich soil and you reach **Plaža Pržina**, a strip of fine sand backed by a café-*konoba*. Turn left at the chapel on the way and you reach the smooth rock shores of quieter **Bilin žal**.

Franjo Bire
mobile **t** *098 344 712, open summer daily 10–12 and 3–6; call out of season*

Cebalo
t *(020) 712 044, mobile* **t** *098 188 2539; or via tourist office*

There are more wines to taste, more beaches to find elsewhere on Korčula, whose age-worn hamlets and stone terraces offer just enough to while away a day's exploration. Prehistoric Illyrian tribes were first to settle **Pupnat**, 9km west of Korčula Town, from where a rough road detours to **Pupnatska luka**. Locals would probably prefer to keep secret the most idyllic bay on the island, a crowd-free crescent of pebbles with a summer *konoba* to make a day of it. Beyond Pupnat, the road ascends through a dark fuzz of pine scrub to **Smokvica**, which spills downhill into a valley planted with vines of pošip, another excellent Croatian wine that is served at every state function. You can taste and buy this strong dry white with a twang of acidity, plus olive oils, in the barn of family producer **Vinarija Toreta**. There's also a small display of bygone rustic objects.

Vinarija Toreta
t *(020) 832 100; open June–Sept daily 8–8; otherwise call ahead*

Blato, cupped in hills and dissected by an avenue of lime trees 10km west of Smokvica, is the capital of wine-growing Korčula, but it has fallen on hard times after phylloxera hit local vines. A trickle of early 20th-century emigration became a flood that halved the population in the 1960s, and today it is reduced to a mere 4,000 inhabitants; according to estimates, three times as many Australians name Blato as their birthplace. It's worth a coffee-break for a Venetian altarpiece of the Virgin with Saints (1540) in the 17th-century **church**, at the back of a raised piazza where Kumpanjija sword dancers clash on 28 April (*see* box, p.348). For the Korčula faithful, Blato is a pilgrimage site due to Marija Petković, a local nun beatified in 2002 for a life of good deeds and whose sarcophagus is carved of local limestone.

And so on 7km to the end of the road, **Vela Luka**, as workaday as any town which has to work for its living as a port, which is all most tourists see of it while waiting for their ferry. But Vela Luka has diversions other than pizzerias and cafés. A modest **museum** in a culture centre by the tourist office displays model ships and, bizarrely, two Henry Moore sculptures alongside prize finds unearthed in '**Big Cave**'. Signposts direct you to this 40m by 17m cavern where Neolithic Man camped out, but double-check the

Museum
open summer Mon–Fri 9–12 and 7–8, Sat 9–12

Big Cave
Vela špilja; open (in theory) 15 June–mid-Aug daily 5–9; adm

erratic opening times with the tourist office before you make the 3km hike northwest.

Islanders know Vela Luka for its villagers' wit and fine voices. You'll hear the former if you ask about streets named by number – 'Just like New York,' locals quip. The latter are raised in ***klapa* quartet** (*see* p.70) on summer evenings.

Concrete platforms outside hotel Adrija opposite the ferry terminal will do to cool off while waiting for your connection. With more time to kill, you can hunt out a bay at the end of paths on a north headland, or laze on the smooth white pebbles of islet **Prozid**.

***Klapa* quartet**
times vary; check with the tourist office in Korčula Town

Prozid
taxi-ferry from harbour; 40Kn return

ⓘ **Lumbarda >>**
t *(020) 712 005; open July–Aug Mon–Sat 8–9, Sun 9–1 and 5–9; June and Sept Mon–Sat 8–7; May and Oct Mon–Sat 8–2; Nov–April times erratic*

ⓘ **Korčula Town >**
Obala dr Franje Tuđmana 1 (loggia on west waterfront), **t** *(020) 715 701, www.korcula.net; open June–Sept Mon–Sat 8–3 and 4–10, Sun 9–1; Oct–May Mon–Sat 8–2 and 5–9, Sun 8–2*

ⓘ **Vela Luka >>**
Ulica 3 br 19, **t** *(020) 813 619, www.tzvelaluka.hr; open July–Aug Mon–Sat 8–9, Sun 9–12; Sept and June Mon–Fri 8–2*

Activities on Korčula

Active holidays specialist **Kantun Tours**, Plokata bb (opposite Land Gate), **t** (020) 715 622, *www.kantun-tours.com*, organizes sea kayaking, hiking and mountain-bike excursions around the island, plus donkey safaris.

Where to Stay on Korčula

Korčula Town

Most hotels in Korčula Town are managed by a state monopoly and pricey for their dated facilities. Bar the Korčula, all are located behind the town beach 1–2km east of the centre.

Lešic Dimitri, Ulica don Pavla Poše br 1–6, **t** 01 4817 596 (€€€). At last, a five-star boutique residence in the old town opened in a renovated bishops' palace off the main square in summer 2009. Six residences – one- to four-bed – and ornate and sumptuous maximalist glamour throughout.

Korčula, Obala dr Franje Tuđmana, **t** (020) 711 078, *www.korcula-hotels.com* (€€€). Habsburg vintage hotel that's crying out for renovation. Décor is dated, beds tend to sag and there's no air-conditioning, but the location is superb, on the Old Town esplanade. First-floor rooms are marginally better.

Marko Polo, Obala hrvatskih mornara, **t** (020) 726 100, *www.korcula-hotels.com* (€€€). Fully renovated in 2007 to achieve its four stars and introduce classic modern décor. It's still very much a resort hotel, though. Offers views of the Old Town and two pools.

Liburna, Obala hrvatskih mornara, **t** (020) 726 006, *www.korcula-hotels.com* (€€). Heart-sinking resort hotel of mid-1980s vintage, 1km east of the centre. Adequate but frumpy inside – and is best seen as a fallback only.

Source **private accommodation** and holiday apartments from agencies **Kantun Tours** (*see* above) and **Atlas**, Plokata 19, **t** (020) 711 060.

Lumbarda

Pansion Marinka, **t** (020) 712 007, mobile 098 344 712 (€). Quite possibly the finest retreat in the Korčula area is this *pension* uphill opposite the bay cloaked in mandarin trees. That they are served for breakfast (*extra*) sums up a homely place of simple pleasures; clean tidy rooms, some with kitchenettes. Full-board deals are worthwhile for home cooking washed down with the local wines of owner Franjo Bire.

Brna

Feral, Smokvica-Brna, **t** (020) 832 002, *www.hotel-feral.hr* (€€€). Escapism with four-star facilities in a plush, rather glitzy resort hotel that was renovated in 2005 and is located above a quiet bay on the isolated south coast.

Vela Luka

Dalmacija, Obala 4, br 20, **t** (020) 812 042 (€€). Priced just the wrong side of inexpensive, the only year-round hotel in Vela Luka has 14 simple though spotless rooms. A decent overnighter conveniently just moments from the ferry terminal.

Eating Out on Korčula

Korčula Town

Kanavelić, Šetalište Petra Kanavelića, **t** (020) 711 800 (€€€–€€). Long the finest restaurant in town, with old-school charm in spades in its lofty beamed dining room, ruled by waiters who nod at your choice – fish, naturally – and with a romantic courtyard. It's just around the corner from the northern bastion. Eve only.

Morski konjić, Šetalište Petra Kanavelića, no tel (€€€–€€). The best of the restaurants atop the eastern city walls, the stylish 'Sea Horse' is always busy for atmospheric alfresco dining at dusk. Quality fish and seafood.

Adio Mare, Svetog Roka, **t** (020) 711 253 (€€). Touristy yet always popular for its atmospheric medieval house. Food-wise it has a reputation for a traditional menu.

Marinero, Marka Andrijića 13, **t** (020) 711 170 (€€). 'Korčula-style' lobster in a rich tomato sauce and fishy stew *brodet*, plus catch of the day expertly grilled in a nautically themed *konoba* of a fishing family.

Morski konjić, Šetalište Petra Kanavelića, **t** (020) 711 642 (€€). No relation to the grander 'Sea Horse', this the north tip of town with a small menu of meat and fish. A snug interior is hung with fishing nets.

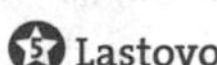

Maslina 2, Plokata bb, mobile **t** 091 51 77 420 (€). The best Dalamatian home-cooking in town, prepared by the charming owner of a celebrated summer-only *konoba* near Lumbarda. Always ask about daily specials for seasonal dishes such as *giriće* (small fish) stewed with ripe grapes or kid goat with vegetables. As seasonal, authentic and tasty as it gets at absurdly low prices. Find it down a passage beside a hairdresser's.

Planjak, Plokata 19. travnja 1914 bb, **t** (020) 711 015 (€). Behind the market, a no-nonsense choice for Balkan snacks – grilled meats and excellent *ćevapčići* and *ražnjići*.

Cafés and Bars

Massimo Cocktail Bar, Šetalište Petra Kanavelića. Drinking atop – or inside – a castellated medieval tower accessed up a ladder at the tip of the town. Magic at dusk if there's space.

Tramonto, Ismaelli bb. Less a bar than a raised terrace above the western harbour advertised by a cardboard sign. There's a decent drinks menu and mellow music – just add the sunset.

Lumbarda

More, west edge of bay, **t** (020) 712 068 (€€€–€€). A marvellous spot for lunch, whose terrace is toe-dipping distance from the sea. House special on a fish menu is lobster; the wine list features local Grks and Pošips. Tailor-made for lazy lunches.

Vela Luka

Pod Bore, Obala 2, III, **t** (020) 812 123 (€€). Dated but decent place on the harbour which is rated for a proper sit-down dinner. The largest local fleet in Korčula means fish is always fresh.

Lastovo

5 Lastovo

Illyrian Ladesta, the '*Augusta Insula*' of Roman emperors, inspiration for Homer and Lord Byron alike, Lastovo is an island for adventurers. Despite the daily car ferries, Croatia's second most distant satellite after Vis (*see* pp.299–302) has the mystery of isolation; a forgotten corner of Europe whose citizens are as proud of their self-sufficiency in fish, fruit and vegetables as they are of the nation's most bizarre carnival rite, the Poklad (*see* 'Festivals', p.355), which expresses the island's sense of self better than any words. Recent history as a Yugoslav naval base until 1989 immured Lastovo from foreigners and development, a move confirmed

Getting to and around Lastovo

Lastovo's port, Ubli, is linked to Split (via Hvar Town and Vela Luka, Korčula) by one **ferry** and one passenger-only **catamaran** a day. Note, cars cannot disembark at Hvar Town. Connecting **buses** go to Lastovo Town.

Car and **scooter hire** is in Ubli (**Brum**, mobile **t** 091 724 9018) and Pasadur (**Ivago**, **t** (020) 805 027; **Merlo**, mobile **t** 091 723 6451) or contact tourist information or Solitudo hotel. Lastovo Town café **Mamilo** also rents out a few scooters, and a prominent thumb yields results.

when the entire island was designated a national park in 2006. This remains frontier country for tourists: an island unconcerned that the capital's church clock stopped longer ago than anyone can remember, whose villages of crusty terracotta tiles and rampant bougainvillaea are just as timeless. Visit to enter life in the slow lane, with little to do but explore a habitat the World Wide Fund for Nature dubbed a last paradise of the Mediterranean.

Although suffering severe depopulation, **Lastovo Town** clings on as capital, a semi-ruin of age-stained stone and rust spread like an amphitheatre with its back to the sea. Why is a something of a mystery, like Lastovo itself. One theory speculates that islanders forswore seafaring for agriculture after they received a harsh lesson about piracy from the Venetian Republic in AD 1000. The town has never really recovered – they say locals only dared to allow roofs above the hill line once Turkish pirates had stopped springing surprises in the 1730s. Another tale explains the anonymous bust on the parish church of **SS Cosmas and Damian** (Crkva sv. Kuzme i Damjana) as an attempt to placate a Slavic king who declared war on former owner Dubrovnik (1254–1806). Local historians scoff, and make woolly suggestions about islanders wanting to aggrandize their most important building. The Gothic-Renaissance church conceals Venetian altarpieces and an icon of the Virgin and Jesus in red dungarees in its Baroqueified interior, as much of a surprise as a pretty 15th-century **loggia** opposite, which gazes over Lastovo's roofscape punctuated by unique *fumari* chimneys like mini-minarets. It's hard to imagine today, but in 1943 Yugoslav Partisans fought street battles here, to liberate the island from 23 years' annexation by Italian Fascists under the Treaty of Rapallo. Time-faded graffiti behind the loggia raises three cheers for the USSR, England and America. However, Italian rule wasn't all bad news for Lastovo. Although Il Duce held no truck with expressions of local culture, Italian occupation introduced the first blip of prosperity in centuries, and many islanders speak good Italian.

After the Venetians came the French, who crowned the hill behind the church with its dumpy **fortress** (*kaštel*, 1810), now a weather station. The old cliché about breathtaking views is all too true, but it's worth your puff for a panorama which sweeps along south Korčula, across the heights of the Pelješac peninsula on the mainland, then east to the blue-grey silhouette of Mljet. Other interesting destinations for a stroll include the 15th-century cemetery chapel **St Mary in the Field** (Kapela sv. Marije u polju), the locals' favourite just free of the centre on the Skrivena Luka road. With a map from the tourist office there are other discoveries to be made on dusty paths which lead through vineyards and aromatic fields.

If you fancy a dip, pop over the hill from Lastovo Town to **Lučica**, a harbour with a huddle of fishermen's houses restored as holiday homes, a splendid spot to stay if you can find a room. Quieter **Sv. Mihovil**, 500m further west, has a quay that shelters waters to swimming-pool calm in all but west winds, while 3km west of Lastovo Town **Zaklopatica** attracts a small fleet of yachties to dine in a first-class *konoba*.

South of Lastovo (7km), isolated bay **Skrivena luka** boasts its own idyllic restaurant and good swimming in mirror-like waters. The best place for a dip, though, is the sand beach of islet **Sapljun**, reached on occasional jaunts around the archipelago northeast of Lastovo Town (*consult tourist information*).

Lastovo Town > *central square (opposite bus stop),* **t** *(020) 801 018, www.lastovo-tz.net; open summer Mon–Sat 8–2 and 5.30–9.30; winter Mon–Sat 8–2*

Tourist Information on Lastovo

The **tourist office** in Lastovo Town co-ordinates private rooms and also hands out useful island maps.

Festivals

Long ago, it is said, a hapless messenger of Catalan pirates was paraded through Lastovo Town for public ridicule, slid down a rope then burned at the stake. The event is re-enacted on Shrove Tuesday as the climax to Croatia's strangest carnival, soundtracked by the hee-haw of bowed lyres and fireworks and with a sword dance to precede the stripping, impaling and incineration of the unfortunate '*poklad*'. Thankfully, his body is made of straw and grain husks nowadays, his feet of cemetery sand.

Where to Stay on Lastovo

All Lastovo's beds are in **private houses or apartments**, booked through tourist information or via the tourist office website. Consider carefully any offers of full board: all bar one of the island's ***konobe*** are in bays, which is fine for yachtsmen, but might be problematic for an evening meal if your room is in Lastovo Town and you haven't got your own transport. Also, most *konobe* are open summer only, so if you visit off-season accept any offer of home cooking, whichis usually washed down with the owner's own wines.

Eating Out on Lastovo

Lastovo Town

Bačvara, Lastovo Town, **t** (020) 801 057 (€€). Unpretentious and honest, Lastovo Town's only *konoba* is beneath the church. Catch of the day or meaty homemade sausages are served beneath a canopy of fishing nets in a cosy stone dining room.

Around the Island

Triton, Zaklopatica, **t** (020) 801 161 (€€€–€€). By popular acclaim the island's finest *konoba*. What is grilled depends on the luck of last night's fishermen, which means super-fresh and simply but expertly prepared. The lobster is highly rated. *Open from 5pm.*

Augusta Insula, Zaklopatica, **t** (020) 801 122 (€€). Another good bet, this is open for lunches of fish or Lastovo lamb. Try an award-winning house red.

Porto Rosso, Skrivena Luka, **t** (020) 801 261 (€€). A favourite with yachtsmen in 'Hidden Bay', this rustic *konoba* in a fisherman's house is an idyllic spot for a lazy lunch: salted anchovies drizzled with olive oil and lemon for a snack or *matar*, chargrilled sea bream and lobster.

South of Dubrovnik

Cavtat

After days as medieval sidekick to the Dubrovnik republic, Cavtat spends her dotage as a lady of leisure; cultured, certainly, but one who always has time for a long lunch. There's culture in its galleries and a touh of class on a lovely harbour of Baroque mansions. But the seduction of this peninsula village deep in pines is as the lazy resort which attracted in-the-know Austrians in the early 1900s. So whether you decide Cavtat is christened for high culture (*civitas*) or the blooms (*cavtiti*, 'to flower') in its alleys may depend on how you spend your time.

Ironically, it's Dubrovnik which owes Cavtat a debt. Slavic and Avar tribes ripped through 7th-century **Epidaurum**, founded by Greeks from Vis (*see* pp.299–302) then Romanized in 228 BC, and the evacuees fled north to start afresh on the town that became Dubrovnik. Only the sunken ruins in the bay – diving centre **Epidaurum** provides trips – and foundation walls on the tip of a peninsula recall that progenitor settlement and, after Dubrovnik looked inward during a collective tightening of belts in the 1700s, Cavtat shrugged and turned to fishing instead.

Epidaurum
*Šetalište Zal; mobile **t** 098 427 550, www.epidaurum-diving-cavtat.hr*

During its halcyon years, a Dubrovnik-appointed governor lorded it over Cavtat from the Renaissance **Rector's Palace**, a grand opening statement to the Old Town and host to its finest museum, the **Baltazar Bogišić Collection**. Treasured books and early European prints of the Cavtat-born promoter of Slavic culture claim most space, although the 19th-century lawyer reveals his cultured mind and jackdaw enthusiasms in collections of Ragusan Republic coins, folksy embroidery and *objets d'art* cherry-picked from France and Italy. His personal treasures are upstaged by the vivacious *Carnival in Cavtat*, whose depiction of the town's finest – Bogišić included – kicking up their heels in fancy dress is by local son Vlaho Bukovac. Three more Bukovacs plus a gallery of glitzy Italian devotional works hang in the **Pinakoteka-Galerija** of parish church **St Nicholas**, at the shoulder of the Rector's Palace, but far better is the career-spanning *œuvre* of the 19th-century father of Croatian art on show in his restored **birthplace** located in side street Bukovčeva. Student works to impress Paris Academy

Baltazar Bogišić Collection
*Zbirka Baltazara Bogišića; **t** (020) 478 556; open Mon–Sat 9.30–1; adm*

Pinakoteka-Galerija
***t** (020) 478 646; open May–Oct Tues–Sat 9–1 and 4–8, Sun 4–8; Nov–Apr Tues–Sun 9–1 and 2–5, Sun 2–5; adm*

Birthplace
Kuca Bukovac; open May–Nov Tues–Sat 9–1 and 4–8, Sun 4–8; Dec–April Tues–Sun 10–5; adm

Getting to and around Cavtat

Bus No.10 from Dubrovnik goes hourly to **Cavtat**. Alternatively, private companies operate summer-only ferries from Dubrovnik's old port (*c*. 80Kn return).

From Dubrovnik, buses shuttle 3 times a day to **Čilipi** and **Molunat**. Dubrovnik agencies also run coach trips to Čilipi's Sunday jamboree.

examiners are an exercise in stuffy realism compared with later dabbles in Art Nouveau and the Impressionism of Cavtat crowd scene *Procession in Tiha* (1902) or a dark, angst-racked vision of Dante's *Inferno*. Look, too, for *Street in Cavtat*, a scene not too changed since 1900. The house is worth a visit in its own right, its rooms richly coloured and frescoed by the 16-year-old Bukovac. Father Bukovac's reaction to the exotic birds and animals his son painted on the walls during convalescence is unrecorded.

Bukovac also painted the Cavtat harbour scene that spans the chancel in the Franciscan monastery church of **Our Lady of the Snow** (Samostan Snježne Gospe) which signs off the seafront promenade. It has a pair of sumptuous Renaissance altarpieces – applauded by sinners and admired by SS Nicholas and John, archangel St Michael smites a demon in a rear chapel, and a tender *Madonna and Child* is lost in the gloom as a main altar. A path from here goes around the peninsula past concrete platforms for a dip to the remains of those Roman foundations at the tip. Busy pebble **beaches** are a 10min stroll around the bay by package hotels.

Račic mausoleum
open daily 10–12, summer also Mon–Sat 5–7; adm

Crowning glory of the town **cemetery** at the peak of the hill above is the **Račić mausoleum**, built of creamy white stone from Brač (*see* p.286) and beautifully sited over the coastline. Croatia's finest modern sculptor, Ivan Meštrović, designed the Cavtat shipowner's tomb in 1912 to honour a parting request of rumoured sweetheart Marija Račić. Not that he succumbed to lyricism in its historicist synthesis of Byzantine, Assyrian and ancient Greek imagery, drawn with his eye for pure lines and softened by a suggestion of Art Nouveau. Or at least not outside. Inside, above allegories of birth, life and death, hidden amid fluttering angels on the cupola, Meštrović engraved the bell with a heartfelt adieu to Marija: 'Understand the secret of love and you will solve the secret of death and believe life is eternal.'

South to the Border

Beyond Cavtat stretches the **Konavle**, the green tip of Croatia's tail watered by the canals of its name and which made this the wheatfield of the Ragusan Republic. The Grand Council valued the region's agricultural workers so highly that it forbade them from signing aboard ships. The Konavle's second claim to fame is its rich spectrum of folk costume. Unwed girls donned cropped waistcoats and round skullcaps, and married women wore white headscarves starched up into sculptural folds, like nuns caught by a sudden gust. Nowadays, both are dusted down only for village high days and for tourists on Sunday morning on the village square in **Čilipi** 6km south of Cavtat near the airport, with a market of embroidery souvenirs. On other days, waitresses at restaurant Konavoski dvori, signposted north of **Gruda** (8km south of Čilipi) do their duty for coach tours and pull on folk costume.

Čilipi
folk costumes and market, April–mid-Oct (in theory) Sun am

From Ćilipi, take a secondary road parallel to the arterial route, away from impatient international lorrydrivers, and you can dawdle in scenery where shells of retired Ragusan Republic fortresses crumble among pasture and vineyards to reach **Molunat**. Low-key and sleepy, it nowadays lures visitors with a clutch of sandy crowd-free beaches rather than the republic harbour sheltered behind a peninsula. The main road rolls on, then 4km further south, Croatia ends and Montenegro begins.

ⓘ Cavtat >
Tiha 3 (marked No.3 but at No.7 by house order; 200yds from the bus station), **t** *(020) 479 025, www.tzcavtat-konavle.hr; open April–Aug daily 8–8; Sept–Nov Mon–Sat 8–4, Sun 8–12; Dec–Mar Mon–Fri 8–3*

Where to Stay and Eat in and around Cavtat

Cavtat

Croatia, Frankopanska 10, **t** (020) 475 555, *www.hoteli-croatia.hr* (€€€). Although not as glam as you'd expect of a five-star and far too vast to be personal, this is comfortable and has all the tennis courts, massages and pools you could want. Located above a beach, too.

Villa Kvaternik, Kvaternik 3, **t** (020) 479 800, *www.hotelvillakvaternik.com* (€€€–€€). Stylish boutique address in a renovated house secluded uphill from the harbour en route to the mausoleum. Unfussy and modern without sacrificing character and harbour views from some rooms – breakfast in the garden is a joy. Also has a tennis court.

Supetar, Obala dr A. Starčevića 27, **t** (020) 479 833, *www.hoteli-croatia.hr/supetar* (€€). No room to swing a suitcase, but a marvellous location on the harbourfront.

Source **private rooms** through **Adriatica**, Trumbićev put 3 (near the bus station), **t** (020) 478 713.

Galija, Vuličevićeva 1, **t** (020) 478 566 (€€). At the other end of the harbourfront near the monastery church, this small place serves consistently excellent fresh fish, either perfectly grilled or in olive sauces, plus more exotic dishes such as sea urchin caviar for adventures *à la carte*. Great terrace, too.

Leut, Trumbićev put 11, **t** (020) 479 050 (€€). An excellent family fish-speciality restaurant that's over 30 years young, whose shady terrace beneath pine trees has hosted the likes of Gerard Depardieu and Roman Abramovic.

Gruda

Konavoski dvori, 3km north of Gruda, **t** (020) 791 039 (*moderate*). A taste of Konavle tradition where coast meets country: water wheels creak, a river chuckles and tourists come by the busload for waitresses in folk costume and traditional dishes from granny's cookbook.

Language

Even for confident linguists *au fait* with Indo–European languages rooted in Latin, Greek or Germanic, Slavonic-based Croatian is fiendishly complex. As if three genders (masculine, feminine and neuter), perplexing plural forms and slippery grammar rules which alter noun endings according to context were not sufficiently baffling, a polyglot of regional dialects will lead the inexperienced astray.

Perhaps for this reason, most Croatians speak another language – hotel staff and young Croats speak excellent English, the older generation prefers German, especially inland, and Italian is widely spoken on the Adriatic coast and in Istria – and locals will not huff if you baulk at wrestling with their national tongue. However, they appreciate the effort made by those who learn the basics – and all the rolled Rs are delicious. Food vocabulary is on pp.49–50.

Pronunciation

Although occasional parades of consonants strike fear, Croatian is not nearly as terrifying as it looks. Every letter is pronounced, and most are spoken as English except for those explained below. As a rule of thumb, the stress falls on the first syllable, and never on the last. Pre-trip tuition, with clear audio files (MP3 and RealPlayer), can be found online at *www.visit-croatia.co.uk/croatianfortravellers*.

C is pronounced as 'ts' as in 'cats', **č** is spoken as 'ch' as in 'church' and **ć** is softer, like the 'ch' of 'cheese'. **Đ/đ** is spoken as the 'j' of 'jam'.

G is always hard, as in 'get'. **J** is spoken as 'y' as in 'yacht' and looks a tongue-twister when combined with other consonants but is straightforward: **nj** is said as 'ny' as in 'canyon', like the Spanish ñ; **lj** as the 'li' of 'million'.

Rs are marvellous, rolled luxuriantly on the tongue and functioning as a vowel when placed between two consonants such as in 'Hrvatska' (Croatia).

Š is pronounced as the 'sh' of 'sheet', similar to **ž**, spoken as the 's' of 'leisure'.

Vowel sounds are short: **a** as in 'cat'; **e** as in 'met'; **i** as in the 'ee' of 'feet'; **o** as in 'dog'; and **u** as in 'oo' of 'hoot'.

Useful Vocabulary

Greetings and Courtesies

hello *dobar dan* (literally 'good day')*/zdravo*
goodbye *doviđenja*
hi/bye! *bog!*
good morning *dobro jutro*
good evening *dobra večer*
goodnight *laku noć*
please *molim* (also used as 'You're welcome')
thank you (very much/for your help) *hvala (lijepo/na pomoći)*
how are you? (formal) *kako ste?* (informal) *kako si?*
fine, thanks *dobro, hvala*
I am from England/Scotland/Wales/Ireland/USA/Canada *ja sam iz Engleske/Škotske/Velsa/Irske/Amerike/Kanade*
pleased to meet you *drago mi je*
sorry (apology) *pardon/oprostite*
excuse me *oprostite*

Basic Words and Phrases

yes/no/maybe *da/ne/možda*
do you speak English? *govorite li engleski?*
I (don't) understand *(ne) razumijem*
I don't speak Croatian *ne govorim hrvatski*
can I have... *mogu li dobiti...*
do you have... *imate li...*
how much is it? *koliko košta?*
that's cheap/too expensive *to je jeftino/preskupo*
keep the change! *zadržite sitan novac!*
do you take credit cards? *primate li kreditne kartice?*

large *veliko*
small *malo*
hot *toplo*
cold *hladno*
why? *zašto?*
when? *kada?*
where? *gdje?*

Accommodation

rooms *sobe*
Can I reserve a room? *Mogu li rezervirat sobu?*
Do you have a single/double room? *Imate li jednokrevetnu/dvokrevetnu sobu?*
no vacancies *nema slobodne sobe*
key *ključ*
shower *tuš*
sheets *plahte*
toilet paper *toaletni papir*

Medical

I am feeling ill (m/f) *Osjećam se bolesnim/bolesnom*
ache/pain *bol*
I've a headache/earache/stomach ache *Boli me glava/uho/želudac*
toothache *zubobolja*
diarrhoea *proljev*
doctor *liječnik/doktor*
dentist *zubar*
hospital *bolnica*
pharmacy *ljekarna*

Around Town

open *otvoreno*
closed *zatvoreno*
entrance *ulaz*
exit *izlaz*
toilet *zahodi/ WC (pronounced 'vay-tsay')*
ladies *ženski*
gents *muški*
bank *banka*
bureau de change *mjenjačnica*
to change *promijenti*
police/police station *policija/policijska stanica*
embassy *ambasada/veleposlanstro*
post office *pošta*
airport *zračna luka/aerodrom*
(main) railway/bus station *(glavni) željeznički/autobusni kolodvor*
(ferry) port *(trajektna) luka*
market *tržnica*
tourist office *turistički ured, turistički informativni centar*
travel agent *putnička agencija*
museum *muzej*
gallery *galerija*
cinema *kino*
church/cathedral *crkva/katedrala*
monastery *samostan*
old town *stari grad*
street *ulica*
square *trg*
beach *plaža*

Getting Around and Driving

when is the next train/bus/boat for... *kada polazi sljedeći vlak/autobus/trajekt za...*
when does it arrive? *u koliko sati stiže?*
arrivals/departures *dolazak/odlazak*
platform *peron*
single/return ticket *karta u jednom smjeru/ povratna karta*
where is (the nearest)... *gdje je (najbliža)...*
how far is it? *koliko je daleko?*
far *daleko*
near *blizu*
left *lijevo*
right *desno*
straight on *ravno*
I am lost (m/f) *izgubio/izgubila sam se*
filling station *benzinska stanica*
petrol/diesel *benzin/diesel*
I want some petrol oil/water (m/f) *Želio/željela bih gorivo/ulje/vodu*
accident *nesreca*
car mechanic *automehaničar*
insurance *osiguranje*
Where can I park the car? *Gdje mogu parkirati auto?*

Days, Months and Time

Monday *ponedjeljak*
Tuesday *utorak*
Wednesday *srijeda*
Thursday *četvrtak*
Friday *petak*
Saturday *subota*
Sunday *nedjelja*
what day is it today? *koli je danas dan?*
January *siječanj*
February *veljača*
March *ožujak*

April *travanj*
May *svibanj*
June *lipanj*
July *srpanj*
August *kolovoz*
September *rujan*
October *listopad*
November *studeni*
December *prosinac*
what time is it? *koliko je sati?*
early/late *rano/kasno*
in the morning *ujutro*
in the afternoon *popodne*
day/week/month *dan/tjedan/mjesec*
today/yesterday/tomorrow *danas/jučer/sutra*

Numbers

1 *jedan*	16 *šesnaest*
2 *dva*	17 *sedamnaest*
3 *tri*	18 *osamnaest*
4 *četiri*	19 *devetnaest*
5 *pet*	20 *dvadeset*
6 *šest*	21 *dvadeset i jedan*
7 *sedam*	22 *dvadeset i dva*
8 *osam*	30 *trideset*
9 *devet*	40 *četrdeset*
10 *deset*	50 *petdeset*
11 *jedanaest*	100 *sto*
12 *dvanaest*	101 *sto i jedan*
13 *trinaest*	200 *dvjesto*
14 *četrnaest*	500 *petsto*
15 *petnaest*	1,000 *tisuća*

Glossary of Terms

General History and Croatian Terms

Austro-Hungary empire of Habsburgs after power-sharing deal with Hungary of 1867

ban foreign-appointed ruler, in practice the stooge of whatever country owned Croatia

Glagolitic old script of Croatian church (*see* pp.40–1)

Illyria Roman name for east-Adriatic/Balkan tribal nations, hence Illyrian

Habsburg dynastic German family that ruled a mighty empire over north and east Europe

Partisan anti-Fascist fighters during Second World War, led by later-president Tito.

sabor Croatian parliament

Uskok originally all refugees of the Turkish incursions in 1500s, later pirates based in Senj

Architectural Terms

apse semicircular or polygonal projection behind the altar

atrium open courtyard to an early church

basilica rectangular church with three naves, first designed by Roman Christians

blind arcades row of decorative arches mounted on to a wall

campanile bell tower (separate)

cardo transverse street of a Roman *castrum*-style settlement, perpendicular to *decumanus* (*see* below)

castrum Roman military camp, usually rectangular with grid of streets, later developed as full-blown settlements

ciborium tabernacle, stone canopy over main altar supported on columns

Cyclopean wall ancient fortification (Greek or Illyrian) built of massive irregular stone blocks

decumanus Roman east–west arterial street to *cardo*'s north–south (*see* above)

forum main square of Roman city, with the major temples and civic buildings

fresco wall paintings, painted with water-based paints on to fresh plaster, so the design is absorbed into the plaster as it dries

loggia gallery, open on one or more sides, often with an arcade; in Venetian Croatia, served as public forum for council and court

putti winged cherubs who flocked into Baroque churches, often perching on altars

sanctuary area around main altar in a church

trifora/trefoil decorative form of three lobes, popular for flashy Venetian Gothic windows

triptych/polytypch painting, usually religious, in three/many sections

trompe l'œil 'fool the eye' art that employs perpective tricks in order to appear three-dimensional

tympanum semicircular panel, often decorated, above church portal; also called lunette

Further Reading

Travellers' Tales

Fortis, Alberto, *Travels in Dalmatia* (out of print, 1774). The first travelogue to these parts, written by a lapsed Paduan priest, whose romanticized impressions of the highland Vlachs wowed the Enlightenment.

Kaplan, Robert, *Balkan Ghosts* (Vintage, 1994) A tendency to tar all politics as anarchic, but a vivid tale of people and place pre-conflict.

Murphy, Dervla, *Through the Embers of Chaos: Balkan Journeys* (John Murray, 2002). The ever-intrepid Murphy takes her bike into war-ravaged states struggling to establish identities. Empathetic and perceptive.

Paton, A. A., *Highlands and Islands of the Adriatic* (Chapman and Hall, 1849). Vintage travelogue through Dalmatia which spices up po-faced history with local colour.

West, Rebecca, *Black Lamb and Grey Falcon* (Canongate, 1993). Reprint of a travel classic of the 1930s, about a sixth of it on Croatia. Full of character studies, self-indulgent historical sidetracks and dubious details, it is a love-it-or-loathe-it idiosyncratic work.

White, Tony, *Another Fool in the Balkans* (Cadogan, 2006). On the trail of Rebecca West; post-war history, politics and culture, told with wit and colour. The title is a self-mocking nod to Western writers' tendency to oversimplify the Balkans.

History

Bracewell, Catherine Wendy, *Uskoks of Senj: Piracy, Banditry and Holy War in the 16th-Century Adriatic* (Cornell University Press, 1992). Engrossing account of the free-wheeling Uskoks, academic not racy. Also good on contemporary political wheeler-dealing, religion and merchant trade.

Dedijer, Vladimir, *Tito Speaks: His Self-Portrait and Struggle with Stalin* (Weidenfeld and Nicolson, 1953). The life of the marshal in his own words, told to a comrade-in-arms.

Đilas, Milovan, *Wartime* (Harvest/HBJ Books 1980). Honest, often brutal, eyewitness account of the Partisan struggle by Tito's right-hand man, later a Yugoslav dissident, hence his bitter *Tito: The Story from Inside* (Phoenix Press, 2001), much of it written in prison, which mixes bile at Tito's pretensions and betrayals with admiration for his brilliance as a leader who defied the Soviets.

Glenny, Misha, *The Balkans: Nationalism, War and the Great Powers, 1804–1999* (Penguin 2001). Provocative background read to his account of the war, which blames the Great Powers, not ethnic hatred, for future conflict.

Tanner, Marcus, *Croatia: A Nation Forged in War* (Yale, 1997). Thoroughly readable and rigorous history of the nation by a journalist who witnessed the 1990s war first-hand.

The Collapse of Yugoslavia

Glenny, Misha, *The Fall of Yugoslavia: The Third Balkan War* (Penguin, 1996). Vivid, subtle and well informed, this is journalism at its best: presenting the political manoeuvring and human texture from the front line.

Hall, Brian, *The Impossible Country* (Penguin, 1995). Subtle, knowledgeable and witty portrait of Yugoslavia on the brink of chaos, written with a perceptive ear for local dialogue.

Silber, Laura and Allan Little, *Yugoslavia*, Death of a Nation (Penguin, 1997). A little one-sided – Silber is firmly decided the war is a Serbian war of aggression, not civil strife – but explodes from the page and full of detail.

Thompson, Mark, *A Paper House* (Pantheon, 1992). An impressionistic travelogue of history and anecdote in pre-war Yugoslavia.

Food and Drink

Pavicic, Liliana, *The Best of Croatian Cooking* (Hippocrene Books, 2003) A taste of the nation: recipes, culinary tradition and wines.

Index

Main page references are in **bold**. Page references to maps are in *italics*.

First American edition published in 2009 by

CADOGAN GUIDES USA
An imprint of Interlink Publishing Group, Inc.
46 Crosby Street, Northampton, Massachusetts 01060
www.interlinkbooks.com
www.cadoganguidesusa.com

Cover photographs: front cover © Jean-Pierre Lescourret/Corbis; back cover © William Manning/Corbis
Photo essay photographs: © Tim Mitchell, except p.9, top: © iStockphoto.com/Jacques Croizer; p.14: © ANDREJ CRCEK/Alamy; p.15, bottom: © Stuart Westmorland/Corbis; p.16, top: © Jeremy Horner/Corbis; p.16, bottom: © iStockphoto.com/Tom Delme.
Maps © Cadogan Guides, drawn by Maidenhead Cartographic Services Ltd
Cover design: Jason Hopper
Photo essay design: Sarah Gardner
Editor: Alison Copland
Proofreading: Susannah Wight
Indexing: Isobel McLean

Printed and bound in Italy by Legoprint
Library of Congress Cataloging-in-Publication Data available

ISBN: 978-1-56656-766-4

Please help us to keep this guide up to date. We have done our best to ensure that the information in this guide is correct at the time of going to press. But laws and regulations are constantly changing, and standards and prices fluctuate. We would be delighted to receive any comments.

Croatia touring atlas

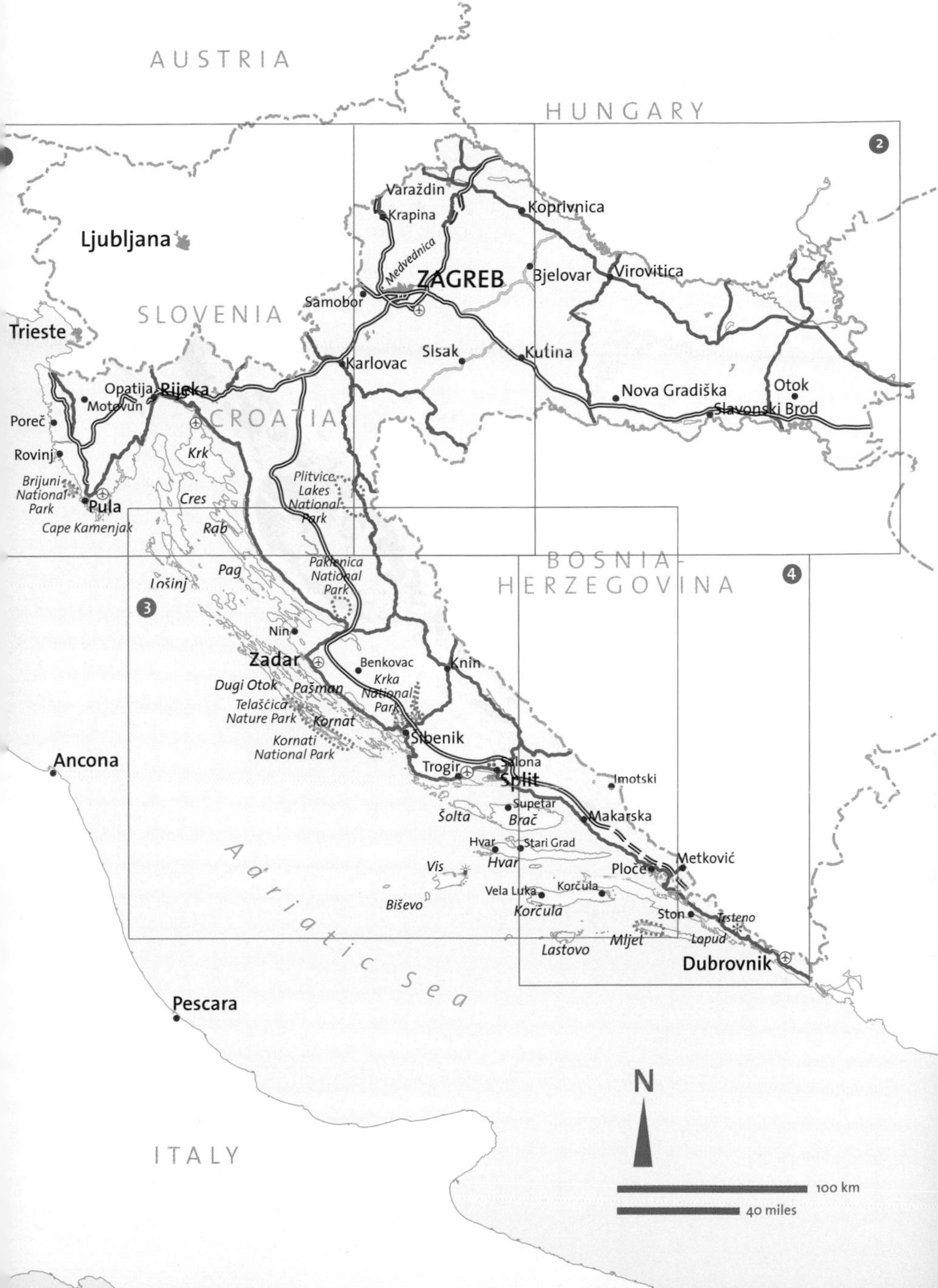

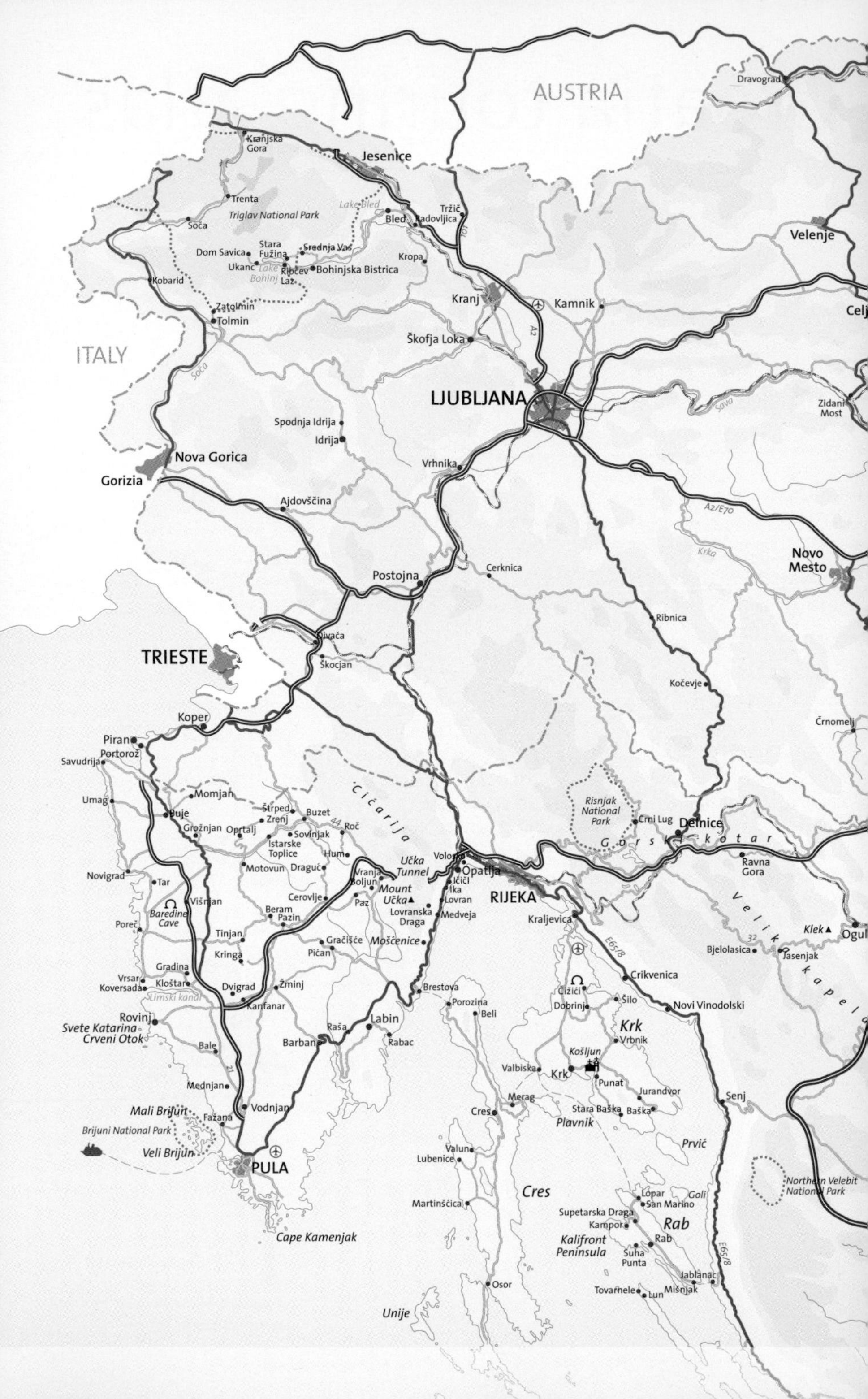

AUSTRIA
Dravograd
Kranjska Gora
Jesenice
Trenta
Triglav National Park
Lake Bled
Bled
Radovljica
Tržič
Soča
Velenje
Dom Savica
Stara Fužina
Srednja Vas
Ukanc
Lake Bohinj
Ribčev Laz
Bohinjska Bistrica
Kropa
Kobarid
Kranj
Kamnik
Celj
Zatolmin
Tolmin
A2
Škofja Loka
ITALY
Soča
LJUBLJANA
Sava
Zidani Most
Spodnja Idrija
Idrija
Nova Gorica
Gorizia
Vrhnika
A2/E70
Ajdovščina
Krka
Novo Mesto
Postojna
Cerknica
Ribnica
Divača
TRIESTE
Škocjan
Kočevje
Koper
Črnomelj
Piran
Portorož
Savudrija
Ćićarija
Risnjak National Park
Umag
Momjan
Buje
Štrped
Buzet
Zrenj
Crni Lug
Delnice
Grožnjan
Oprtalj
Sovinjak
Roč
Gorski kotar
Istarske Toplice
Hum
Volosko
Novigrad
Motovun
Dragué
Vranja
Boljun
Učka Tunnel
Opatija
Ičići
Ika
Lovran
Ravna Gora
Tar
Mount Učka
RIJEKA
Višnjan
Baredine Cave
Cerovlje
Paz
Poreč
Beram
Pazin
Lovranska Draga
Medveja
Kraljevica
Velika kapela
Klek
Ogul
Tinjan
Gračišće
Mošćenice
Bjelolasica
Jasenjak
Kringa
Pićan
E65/8
Gradina
Vrsar
Koversada
Kloštar
Limski kanal
Dvigrad
Žminj
Brestova
Crikvenica
Čižići
Šilo
Kanfanar
Porozina
Beli
Dobrinj
Novi Vinodolski
Rovinj
Svete Katarina
Crveni Otok
Labin
Krk
Raša
Barban
Rabac
Vrbnik
Bale
Košljun
Valbiska
Krk
Punat
Mednjan
Jurandvor
Merag
Senj
Mali Brijun
Cres
Stara Baška
Baška
Fažana
Vodnjan
Plavnik
Brijuni National Park
Prvić
Veli Brijun
Valun
PULA
Lubenice
Northern Velebit National Park
Cres
Lopar
Goli
Martinšćica
San Marino
Supetarska Draga
Kampor
Rab
Cape Kamenjak
Rab
Kalifront Peninsula
Suha Punta
Jablanac
Osor
Tovarnele
Lun
Mišnjak
Unije

1
HUNGARY
Murska Sobota
Mura
Lendava
Drava
Maribor
horje
Štrigova
Ptuj
Ormož
Čakovc
Arboretum
Opeka
Vinica
Varaždin
Trakošćan
Ludbreg
Đurmanec
Lepoglava
Varaždinske Toplice
Krapina
Pregrada
Vinagora
Podčertrek
Veliki Tabor
Desinić
Bežanec
Radobor
Koprivnica
Hlebine
Belec
Kalnik
Zlatar
Krapinske Toplice
Kumrovec
Tuheljske Toplice
Klanjec
Sevnica
Gusakovec
Marija Bistrica
Stubličke Toplice
Gornja Stubica
Donja Stubica
Medvednica
Sljeme (1036m)
E59/A1
E65/E71/A3
Brežice
Bjelovar
2
Popovec
E70/A4
Samobor
ZAGREB
Kupa
Krašic
Ozalj
E70/A4
Karlovac
Sisak
Kutina
Petrinja
Čigoc
Lonjsko Polje National Park
Mužilovčica
E71
6
Novska
Krapje
Sava
Jasenovac
Drenov Bok
Slunj
42
N
BOSNIA-
HERZEGOVINA
25 km
10 miles
Plitvice Lakes National Park
3

HUNGARY
BOSNIA-HERZEGOVINA
Murska Sobota
Mura
Lendava
Štrigova
Ptuj
Ormož
Čakovc
Arboretum
Vinica
Opeka
Varaždin
Trakošćan
Ludbreg
Đurmanec
Lepoglava
Varaždinske Toplice
Pregrada
Krapina
Radobor
Koprivnica
Hlebine
Beženac
Belec
Kalnik
Krapinske Toplice
Tuheljske Toplice
Zlatar
Klanjec
Gusakovec
Marija Bistrica
Stubličke Toplice
Gornja Stubica
Donja Stubica
E59/A1
E65/E71/A3
Medvednica
Sljeme (1036m)
Bjelovar
Popovec
Virovitica
E70/A4
Samobor
ZAGREB
1
E70/A4
Daruvar
Kutina
Sisak
Lonjsko Polje National Park
Petrinja
Pakrac
Čigoc
Mužilovčica
Novska
6
Krapje
Sava
Jasenovac
Drenov Bok
Nova Gradiška
6

2

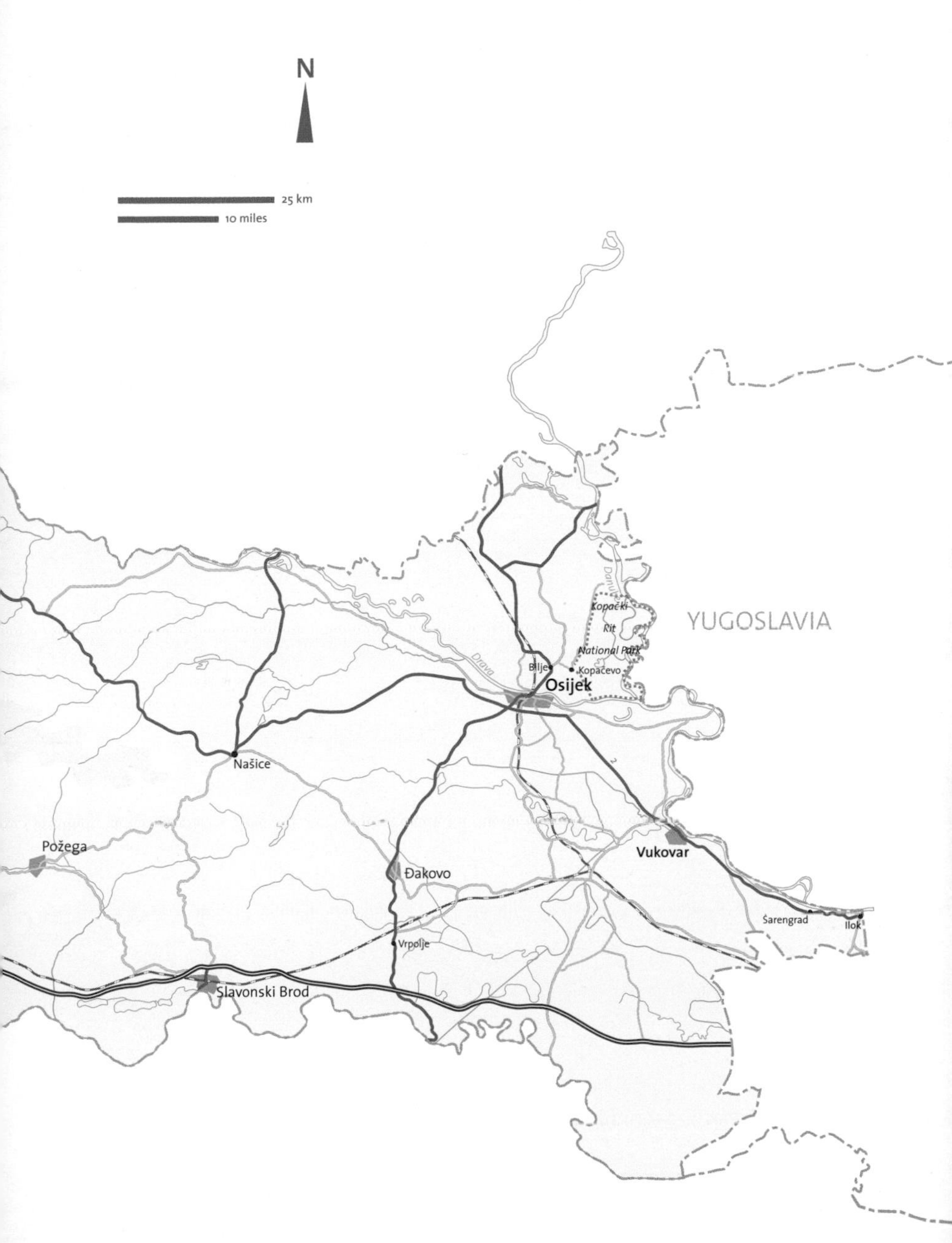

N
25 km
10 miles
YUGOSLAVIA
Kopački
Rit
National Park
Bilje
Kopačevo
Osijek
Drava
Našice
Vukovar
Požega
Đakovo
Vrpolje
Šarengrad
Ilok
Slavonski Brod

1

Osor
Unije
Jablanac
Tovarnele
Lun
Mišnjak
E65/8
Prizna
Žigljen
Novalja
Časka
Karlobag
Gospić
Čikat
Lošinj
Mali Lošinj
Veli Lošinj
Pag
Stražko
Susak
Kolan
Metajna
Sv. Petar
Šimuni
Pag
Ilovik
Silba
Silba
E65/8
Paklenica National Park
Vir
Starigrad-Paklenica
Seline
Vrsi
Molat
Nin
Novigrad
Posedarje
Poličnik
Novigradsko more
ZADAR
Veli Rat
Božava
Dragove
Ugljan
Preko
Galovac
Zaglav
Kali
Brbinj
Veli Iž
Rutnjak
Iž
Kukljica
Mali Iž
Ždrelac
Benkovac
Dugi Otok
Pašman
Babac
Sv. Filip i Jakov
Pašman
Kraj
Sali
Tkon
Biograd-na-Moru
Telašćica National Park
Žut
Murter Town
Kornat
Murter
Jadra
Tribunj
Kaprije
Kornati National Park
Žirje

3
N
25 km
10 miles
BOSNIA-
HERZEGOVINA
Knin
Manojlovački
slapovi
Krka
National
Park
Roški slap
Visovac
Drniš
Otavice
Skradin
Skradinksi buk
Lozovac
Šibenik
Brodarica
Krapanj
Primošten
Kaštel-
Gomilica
Kaštel-
Sučurac
Kaštel-Luksic
Kaštel-Stari
Kaštel-Novi
Kozjak
Trogir
Kaštel-
Štafilic
Čiovo
SPLIT
Salona
Klis
Sinj
Cetina
Vopad
Gubavica
Imotski
Duće
Dugi Rat
Omiš
E65/8
Zadvarje
Sutivan
Supetar
Splitska
Škrip
Brač
Šolta
Milna
Blaca
Vidova gora
Sumartin
Murvica
Bol
Zlatni rat
Brela
Topići
Baška Voda
Sv.
Jure
Bast
Promajna
Krvavica
Biokovo Nature Park
Makarska
Makar
Kotišina
Tučepi
Podgora
Igrane
Drvenik
Zaostrog
Podaca
Gradac
Sućaraj
Stari Grad
Vboska
Jelsa
Hvar
Milna
Zaraće
Dubovica
Sv. Nedjelja
Sv. Nikola
Zavala
Humac
Komiža
Vis
Kut
Biševo
Proizd
Vela Luka
Blato
Brna
Smokvica
Pupnat
Korčula
Pupnatska
Luka
Lumbarda
Badija
Nakovanj
Viganj
Kućište
Orebić
Trpanj
Podstup
Borje
Kuna
Podobuče
Potomje
Trstenik
Žuljana
Dubrava
Pelješac Peninsula
Ploče
Opuzen
Klek
Neretva
4
Zaklopatica
Lastovo
Sapljun
Ubli
Skrivena Luka
Lastovo
Pomena
Polače
Mljet
Mljet National Park
Sobra
Babino
Polje

4

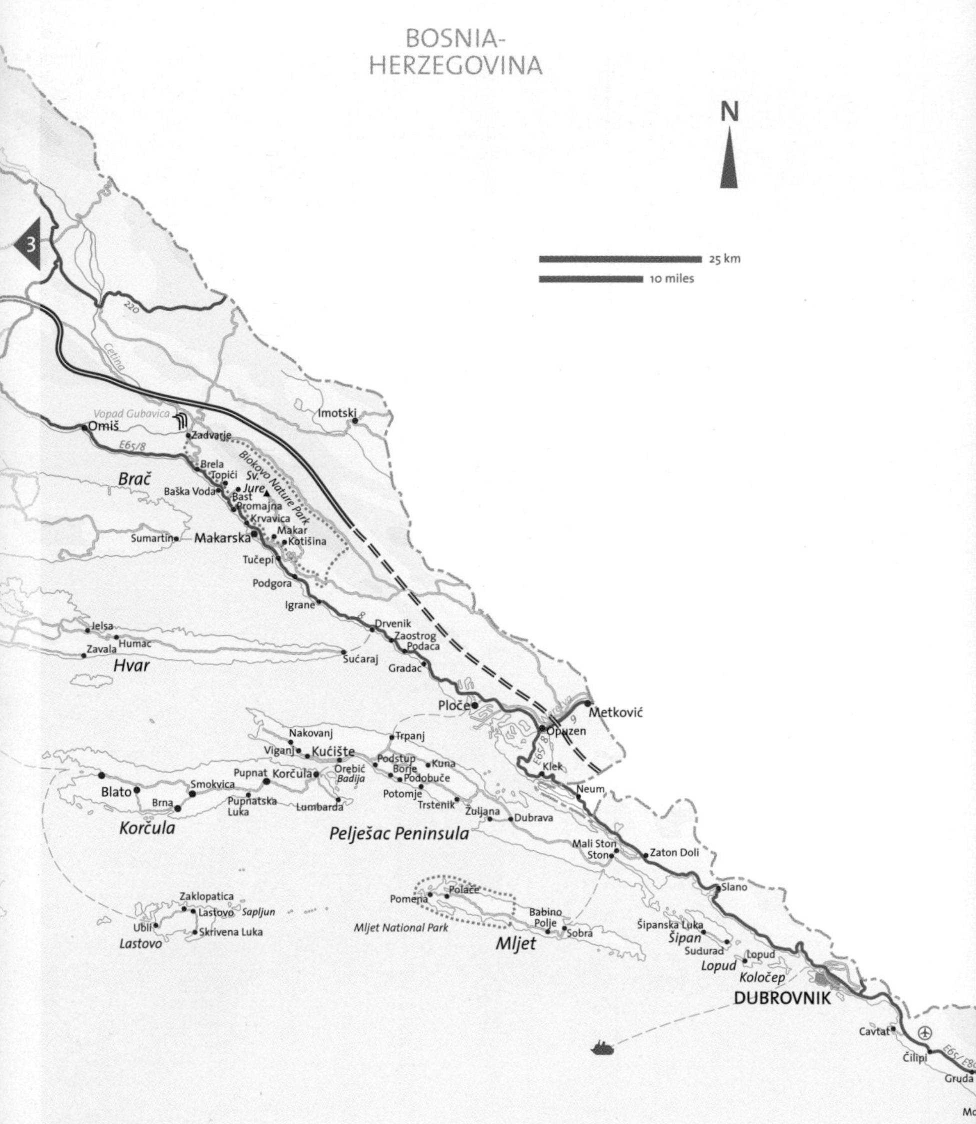
BOSNIA-
HERZEGOVINA
N
25 km
10 miles
3
220
Cetina
Vopad Gubavica
Omiš
Zadvarje
Imotski
E65/8
Brela
Topići
Brač
Baška Voda
Sv.
Jure
Bast
Promajna
Krvavica
Biokovo Nature Park
Makar
Sumartin
Makarska
Kotišina
Tučepi
Podgora
Igrane
Drvenik
Jelsa
Humac
Zavala
Zaostrog
Podaca
Sućaraj
Hvar
Gradac
Ploče
Metković
Opuzen
Nakovanj
Trpanj
Viganj
Kućište
Podstup
Kuna
Borje
Orebić
Badija
Podobuče
Pupnat
Korčula
Blato
Smokvica
Potomje
Klek
Neum
Brna
Pupnatska
Luka
Lumbarda
Trstenik
Žuljana
Dubrava
Korčula
Pelješac Peninsula
Mali Ston
Ston
Zaton Doli
Slano
Zaklopatica
Lastovo
Sapljun
Pomena
Polače
Ubli
Skrivena Luka
Lastovo
Mljet National Park
Babino
Polje
Sobra
Mljet
Šipanska Luka
Šipan
Sudurad
Lopud
Lopud
Koločep
DUBROVNIK
Cavtat
Čilipi
Gruda
E65/E80